PATRIARCH

ALSO BY
RICHARD NORTON SMITH

⚜

Thomas E. Dewey and His Times

An Uncommon Man:
The Triumph of Herbert Hoover

The Harvard Century

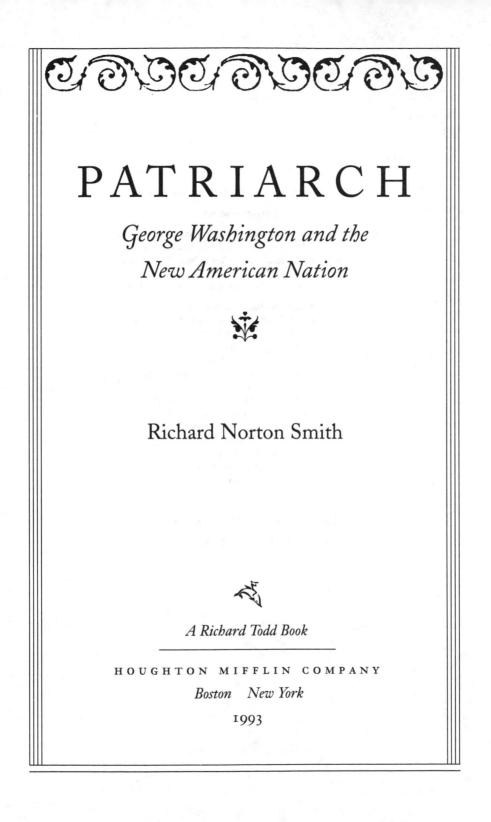

PATRIARCH

George Washington and the
New American Nation

Richard Norton Smith

A Richard Todd Book

HOUGHTON MIFFLIN COMPANY

Boston   New York

1993

Copyright © 1993 by Richard Norton Smith

Library of Congress Cataloging-in-Publication Data

Smith, Richard Norton, date.
Patriarch: George Washington and the new American nation /
Richard Norton Smith.
p.   cm.
"A Richard Todd book."
Includes bibliographical references and index.
ISBN 0-395-52442-3
1. Washington, George, 1732–1799.   2. Presidents —
United States — Biography.   3. United States —
Politics and government — 1789–1797.
I. Title.
E312.29.S65   1993
973.4′1′092 — dc20
[B]   92-21732
CIP

Printed in the United States of America

MP   10   9   8   7   6   5   4   3   2   1

FOR JOHN FAWCETT
AND MY COLLEAGUES AT THE
HERBERT HOOVER PRESIDENTIAL LIBRARY

"The approbation of my country is what I wish and, as far as my abilities and opportunities will permit, I hope I shall endeavor to deserve it. It is the highest reward to a feeling mind; and happy are they, who so conduct themselves as to merit it."

George Washington

"Many a private man might make a great President; but will there ever be a President who will make so great a man as WASHINGTON?"

Connecticut Courant, June 20, 1791

"If ever a nation was debauched by a man, the American nation has been debauched by WASHINGTON. If ever a nation was deceived by a man, the American nation has been deceived by WASHINGTON. Let his conduct then be an example to future ages. Let it serve to be a warning that no man may be an idol, and that a people may confide in themselves rather than in an individual. Let the history of the federal government instruct mankind, that the masque of patriotism may be worn to conceal the foulest designs against the liberties of the people."

Philadelphia Aurora, December 23, 1796

CONTENTS

Author's Note • xi

Prologue: The Man in the Macomb House • xiii

I • NEW YORK 1790

1. "Summoned by My Country" • 3
2. Washingtonopolis, D.C. • 27
3. Caunotaucarius and His Cabinet • 44

II • PHILADELPHIA 1790–1797

4. Town and Country • 63
5. To See and Be Seen • 87
6. Rough Waters • 108
7. The Curse of Duty • 130
8. A Highly Favored Age • 154
9. Philadelphia Fevers • 178
10. "Dash to the Mountains, Jersey Blue" • 203
11. Down from Olympus • 227
12. "The Good Citizen" • 250
13. An Honorable Discharge • 273

III • FARMER WASHINGTON 1797–1799

14. At the Bottom of the Hill • 301
15. Potomac Twilight • 326
Epilogue: "Our Washington" • 356
Notes • 365
Index • 401

AUTHOR'S NOTE

This is the story of George Washington under political, not military, siege. It begins in the spring of 1790, with the aging hero of the Revolution at the height of his fame if no longer, perhaps, at the peak of his form. It covers Washington's presidency, an office that he practically invented, as well as a troubled retirement lasting from March 1797 until his death two and a half years later.

Henry Knox did not exaggerate when he said that it was Washington's character and not the new Constitution that held the infant Union together. Throughout this period, Washington's most potent enemies were the ravages of time and the growth of faction that not even the most celebrated warrior could suppress forever. To modern eyes the first president appears most human because most vulnerable.

In the interests of clarity I have modernized spelling and punctuation. In all other respects I have tried to remain faithful to the spirit of the eighteenth century, to show Washington in his own times, on his own terms, and, wherever possible, through his own words and those of his contemporaries.

THE MAN IN
THE MACOMB HOUSE

GEORGE WASHINGTON was dying. The rumor spread quickly through Manhattan neighborhoods ravaged by influenza, the "contagious distemper" first diagnosed on Roman streets half a century earlier. Impartial to class, color, or politics, the disease was more democratic than the young American republic whose ruling elite it threatened. At a boardinghouse on Maiden Lane, Congressman James Madison took to his bed, too sick to argue with Alexander Hamilton over the secretary of the treasury's audacious plan to consolidate federal power by having the government in New York assume the debts and revenue sources formerly reserved for individual states.

Madison heard increasingly alarming reports of the president's illness from his fellow Virginian Thomas Jefferson, himself confined by an attack of crippling migraine to his $7-a-week quarters at Broadway's sprawling City Tavern. A mile away, in the rural village of Greenwich, Abigail Adams lay ill as her son Charles tossed feverishly and the rest of the household complained variously of bilious attack and Saint Anthony's fire, a painful skin inflammation. Only her husband, the vice president, had escaped the city's prevailing malady, wrote Abigail, before adding with mordant humor, "I compounded to have a double share myself rather than he should have it at all."

Thus New York, the temporary capital of the infant United States, became a crowded infirmary during the first days of May 1790. On Sunday, the ninth, President Washington remained inside his residence at 39 Broadway, nursing a cold and tending to private correspondence. The next day's weakening led his doctors to diagnose a potentially fatal combination of influenza and pneumonia. As a young man, Washington had boasted a constitution hardy enough to withstand the most severe trials. Ague and fever, smallpox, dysentery, violent headaches, aching teeth, and rheumatism: each had surrendered to his massive will and his lighthearted contempt for medical men, with their pills and purges. "Let it go as it came," he habitually told attending physicians.

But as he advanced in years, such ailments were progressively harder to shake off. By Monday, the fifty-eight-year-old president was fighting for his life, and straw was laid on the Broadway pavement to dull the sound of passing carriages. If Washington's illness caused alarm within his official family, it created something close to panic among the few to whom the secret was revealed. So great was the president's hold on the popular imagination that the previous autumn he had even given his name to a disease, the so-called Washington influenza contracted by hero-worshiping Bostonians who braved chill, northeast winds for a glimpse of the most famous man on earth. Now Washington himself was sick.

Notwithstanding official attempts to conceal the news, inevitably word leaked out, bringing knots of anxious New Yorkers to the door of 39 Broadway. The house had a colorful, if brief, history. Built three years earlier for a wealthy merchant, Alexander Macomb, until recently it had been the home of Eleonor François Elie, the comte de Moustier, France's flamboyant ambassador to the United States. Instantly recognizable in his earrings and red-heeled shoes, Moustier had been matched in eccentricity by his sister-in-law, Madame de Brehan, who allegedly shared his bed. The ambassador further scandalized New Yorkers by bringing his personal chef to a dinner at the vice president's. While the other guests dined on Long Island lobster and thick roast beef, King Louis's envoy enjoyed a rich pie of truffles and game. Not long after, he sailed for home, scattering complaints about New York's damp climate and abominable wines.

Washington had seized the opportunity to abandon the modest Cherry Street residence originally provided for him by Congress. In February 1790, he moved into Macomb's house of honey-colored stone, four stories high and fifty-six feet wide, with glass doors at the rear leading to a balcony overlooking the swift Hudson River and Jersey shore beyond. For $1,000 a year, Washington occupied New York's grandest address, pleasantly situated on the west side of Broadway, just below Trinity Church and a short coach ride from Federal Hall. Some $10,000 was spent on refurbishing the house — at a time when the entire federal budget amounted to around $2 million. Washington himself paid for the construction of a new washhouse and stables to accommodate six Virginia grays and as many milk-white horses to pull the presidential chariot on occasions of state. He dipped further into his pocket, spending £665 on some mirrors, a desk, and additional furnishings left behind by Moustier.

In preparation for moving, Washington recast his family silver in more elegant form. He ordered scenic wallpaper then in vogue to embellish a pair of ground-floor rooms suitable for entertaining and fine Turkish carpets to dull the tread of gentlemen's boots. From European admirers came pictures, vases, and other ornaments. Lafayette presented the key to the Bastille, that demolished symbol of Bourbon absolutism, "a tribute which I owe as a son to my adoptive father, as an aide-de-camp to my general, as a missionary of liberty to its patriarch." Washington turned to Gouverneur Morris, his urbane special envoy in London, for help in locating table ornaments "more fashionable but not more expensive than plated ware" and fourteen of the new Argand lamps, which gave off more light than candles while consuming their own smoke.

When he was through, Washington had a residence that reflected him like one of Morris's ten-foot mirrored plateaux: refined, harmonious, plain yet innovative, created with a close watch on expenditure, dependent for its crowning touches on more sophisticated men, and never finished.

For all its charms, the Macomb House was a modern doctor's night-mare, the last place a patient would be sent for restful convalescence. From outside his window, urban sounds hammered on Washington's brain. Maddening cowbells announced the daily trek north by herds penned on Wall Street. Mingled with the shuffling sounds of the cattle were the sharp cries of vendors peddling straw, hickory wood, and steam-ing yellow corn. Chimney sweeps out at daybreak left their verbal calling card: "Sweep ho! from the bottom to the top, with a ladder or a rope, sweep ho!" Congressmen complained of being unable to hear their own oratory for the street traffic outside Federal Hall, at the intersection of Wall and Broad streets, while the bleating of animals interrupted sessions of the Supreme Court, meeting over a farmers' market in the Royal Ex-change building.

With her husband prostrate in a second-floor bedroom, Mrs. Wash-ington took command, leaving the five-man presidential staff to ponder medical and political contingencies. Senior rank in the group was held by Tobias Lear, a sea captain's son from New Hampshire. First employed in the summer of 1786 to tutor Martha's two grandchildren, he was long since regarded as a member of the family. As a newcomer to the general's august presence, Lear had found it difficult to penetrate Washington's hard crust of formality. In time, however, the distance between them vanished. Washington, Lear concluded on reflection, was "almost the only man of an exalted character who does not lose some part of his respect-ability by an intimate acquaintance." The children he found amusing and Mrs. Washington, "everything that is benevolent and good — I honor her as a second mother."

For $800 a year, the congenial Lear oversaw family finances, sensitive correspondence, social invitations, and the distribution of gifts to the poor. Sunday evenings, the senior secretary often read aloud to the Washington family from a book of sermons or other devotional tracts. During the week he accompanied Mrs. Washington on shopping excursions, took her granddaughter, young Nelly Custis, to the theater, and went with the whole family to Bowen's Wax Works to see the effigy of Washington in full military dress being crowned with a wreath of laurel by Fame, suspended overhead. Discreet and methodical, Lear would know how to handle the sudden crisis of Washington's illness. But he was absent in the first days of May, honeymooning with his bride in Portsmouth, New Hampshire.

Second in rank was David Humphreys, self-appointed chamberlain to the republican court of New York. Following wartime service as an aide to Washington, the aspiring poet had been invited to sample Mount Vernon's hospitality amid the fruits of peace.

> 'T was mine, return'd from Europe's courts,
> To share his thoughts, partake his sports.

Having enjoyed a rare glimpse of Cincinnatus behind his plow, Humphreys hoped to write a biography of the president with Washington as willing collaborator. Conscious of his paltry formal education, Washington refused all requests to set down his own commentaries on the Revolution and its aftermath. "I had rather glide gently down the stream of life," he explained, "leaving it to posterity to think and say what they please of me, than by any act of mine to have vanity or ostentation imputed to me."

Using the faithful Humphreys as his amanuensis, Washington left other nuggets for posterity. In June 1789, barely two months after his inauguration, the president had undergone excruciating surgery for a large tumor on his thigh. Almost flamboyantly heedless of death, he had remarked to Humphreys on that occasion, "I know it is very doubtful whether I ever shall rise from this bed, and God knows it is perfectly indifferent to me whether I do or not." Now, less than a year later, with Washington again gravely ill, his countrymen did not share this indifference. Despite strenuous efforts to downplay the president's condition, anxious reports sped north to New England, where one correspondent noted "a universal gloom" at the news. Lacking a national church, royal family or aristocratic traditions to bond them, Americans had but one point of common reference — the man in the Macomb House.

No one seemed more aware of the risks should Washington die than the politically astute wife of the vice president. "Greatly distressed" at the burden that might at any moment descend on her husband and herself,

Mrs. Adams's chief fears were for her country. "It appears to me that the union of the states depends under Providence upon his life," she wrote in anxious solicitude. "At this early day when neither our finances are arranged nor our government sufficiently cemented to promise duration, his death would I fear have . . . the most disastrous consequences."

This was no exaggeration. For months, a fractious Congress had argued conflicting claims and sectional interests: what title, if any, to bestow on the popularly elected leader of a republic; what levies to assess on which products to pay the nation's debts and secure the public credit; how to treat New England molasses, Carolina indigo, and Georgia hemp; what level of protection to accord Pennsylvania shipowners, and what degree of relief for Southerners dependent on foreign shipping. Angered by northern agitation against slavery, South Carolina's William Loughton Smith reminded his colleagues of the fragile bargain struck less than three years before in the Constitutional Convention. "We took each other, with our mutual bad habits and respective evils, for better, for worse," drawled Smith. "The northern states adopted us with our slaves, and we adopted them with their Quakers."

❦ 2 ❧

On May 12, 1790, frightened members of the presidential household took drastic action. Major William Jackson, Washington's unofficial bodyguard, who as secretary to the convention had won the confidence of its presiding officer (if little gratitude from historians, forced to rely on James Madison's much fuller notes), sent in secret for John Jones of Philadelphia. The nation's foremost surgeon, Jones had recently attended Dr. Franklin in his final illness. Jones's own death would occur within the year, when the doctor incautiously dosed himself with seven grains of opium to induce sleep after a high fever. Exactly what course of treatment he prescribed for Washington is unknown. One favorite remedy for congestion of the lungs at that time was turnip broth. Jam was widely used for throat ailments.

Even as the feverish president struggled for breath in his Broadway mansion, by macabre coincidence a bulletin announced the death of his pregnant niece by marriage, "taken with Fits," according to Betty Washington Lewis, "and died in twelve hours without being delivered." Coming just eight months after the death of Washington's aged mother, this second blow emphasized the fragility of eighteenth-century existence, the shroud in every closet.

For the woman sharing his bedroom at 39 Broadway, the sound of

Washington's labored breathing revived terrible memories. Often before the angel of death had darkened Martha Washington's doorway. It had snatched away two infants born to Martha and her first husband, a wealthy planter named Daniel Parke Custis. In 1757 it returned for Custis himself, abruptly ending a deeply affectionate union and leaving the young widow to care for two surviving youngsters and one of Virginia's largest plantations.

Within a year Mrs. Custis was being courted by a strapping colonel of the Virginia Regiment. Neither partner entertained illusions. For him, the plump, amiable widow was a sensible alternative to Sally Fairfax, the worldly, alluring wife of Washington's best friend and Potomac neighbor. For her, the dashing veteran of British campaigns in the Ohio River valley promised to be a good manager of her estate and an attentive guardian to her children. On a snowy January afternoon in 1759, George and Martha stood beneath four white candles and said their vows. They formed a study in contrasts: the groom six feet, three inches tall, reddish-haired, graceful in his movements despite hands too large for any but custom-made gloves, a natural athlete and enthusiastic dancer; and the diminutive bride, barely reaching to her lover's shoulder, round where he was angular, with hazel eyes the shape of almonds, a self-described "old-fashioned housekeeper, steady as a clock, busy as a bee, and cheerful as a cricket."

Martha's confidence grew with the years, yet she was always a nervous, indulgent mother, dreading separation from her children and interpreting every stray dog's bark as a distant cry for help. Flush with the £20,000 his marriage brought him, Colonel Washington sent to England for tea sets, gingerbread, Prussian dragoons sculpted from tin, and "a neat dressed wax baby" to amuse his wife's children. Young Martha Custis, affectionately known as Patsy, learned to play the spinet, while Jack, otherwise preoccupied with "dogs, horses and guns," took violin lessons.

But the black angel hovered menacingly near. At the age of twelve, Patsy was "seized with fits," ushering in a sad adolescence of dance lessons and epileptic convulsions. A doctor believing in the curative powers of iron fitted the girl with a metal ring. His successors prescribed ether, musk capsules, nervous drops. Then, one day in June 1773, while the family was seated around the table in Mount Vernon's verdigris dining room, Patsy collapsed in frozen anguish. As Washington looked on helplessly, Martha's seventeen-year-old daughter expired in less than two minutes, "without uttering a word, a groan, or scarce a sigh." In his diary, a deliberately impersonal accounting of crops, temperatures, and the incessant traffic of visitors, Washington penned a bleak inscription: "At home all day. About five o'clock poor Patsy Custis died suddenly."

A similar restraint characterized the Washingtons' marriage, which over the years developed into what might best be described as love without passion. Visitors calling at the Macomb House and hoping to be admitted to the sickroom were gently turned away by the first lady, knitting hour after hour by her husband's bedside. To friends Mrs. Washington remarked that the president appeared less concerned than anyone about his latest brush with death. Fatalism vied with ambition in Dr. Jones's illustrious patient, who took for his favorite epigraph the sentiment voiced in Joseph Addison's popular play *Cato*: " 'Tis not in mortals to command success."

It seemed a curious motto coming from one who had spent a lifetime battling inner conflicts and external enemies. But Washington was a man of unsuspected depths. Like nearly everyone who encountered the president in person, Dr. Jones was no doubt impressed by his patient's noble carriage and regal gravitas. Not even a sickbed could diminish the aura of force and energy surrounding Washington, whose two hundred pounds were evenly distributed over a bony, muscular frame hardened by a lifetime of outdoor exercise and physical adversity. The symmetry of Washington's long, pale face, lightly scarred by smallpox and easily sunburnt, was ruined by a Roman nose and cavernous sockets in which rested eyes variously described as bluish or gray, dull or flashing.

In the second year of his presidency Washington's chestnut hair was turning white; contrary to popular imagery, he never wore a wig. His peculiarly low, indistinct voice may have stemmed from natural reticence or those badly fitted dentures. His hands and joints were natural wonders, according to Lafayette the largest he had ever seen. A youthful bout with pulmonary illness had left the otherwise imposing chief executive with a sunken chest, verified on a hot Virginia day when the president's adopted grandson found him shirtless in the library at Mount Vernon.

If Dr. Jones was like most of those who came into contact with the president, he found it easier to describe Washington than to explain him. Abigail Adams made a good start at both when she wrote, "He has a dignity which forbids familiarity mixed with an easy affability which creates love and reverence." Yet the love was bound to be somewhat impersonal, for the hero who towered half a foot above his contemporaries and who would give his name to one American state, a capital city, thirty-three counties, at least seven mountains, nine colleges, and one hundred twenty-one post offices was unable to pass it on to another human being. Washington accepted his childlessness with the same unbending discipline that governed his whole life and that isolated him from all but a handful of people. To a young colonel in the Continental Army he had written, "Be easy and condescending in your deportment to your officers, but not too familiar, lest you subject yourself to a want of that respect which is necessary to support a proper command." Similar advice was meted out to the president's favorite nephew, Bushrod. Be courteous to all, intimate with few, counseled the elder Washington, for "true friendship is a plant of slow growth and must undergo and withstand the shocks of adversity before it is entitled to the appellation."

And so he had become a figure deliberately set apart, wrapping himself in a paternal mystique until it became a psychological straitjacket. Losing his father when he was eleven and harboring ambivalent feelings toward his mother, George Washington grew into an emotionally inaccessible man who channeled his considerable passions into, first, self-advancement, and second, building a nation.

True to form, Washington revealed little to the doctors monitoring his temperature and waiting, more or less helplessly, for his fever to break. But then, not even Martha knew all there was to know about the shrewd giant who preferred farming to politics and lost money on both; an expansive host who spent every penny of his $25,000 salary and complained that servants were drinking his Madeira; an iron-willed leader holding to intractable notions of personal honor and justice; a wryly satirical observer with a cordial, not always concealed, dislike of tiresome preachers, financial deadbeats, and virtually anyone with the effrontery to question his motives or challenge his dignity; a painfully sensitive public figure who writhed under the criticism of newspaper editors he held guilty "of stuffing their papers with scurrility and nonsensical declamation"; a Spartan eater favoring pineapples, Brazil nuts, and Saturday dinners of salt cod; and a true stoic who endured near constant toothache caused by ill-fitting dentures that caused his mouth to bulge and his lips to clamp shut in unsmiling repose.

For four anxious days and nights John Jones and a group of consulting physicians alternated between cautious hope and blank resignation. No medical probe could reveal how much of their patient's character, not excluding his ingrained distaste for organized medicine, had been inherited from Mary Ball Washington. According to her Fredericksburg neighbors, Washington's mother had feared lightning, and little else. Certainly the cancer that finally killed her in the fall of 1789 had held no terror for the indomitable old woman.

Her son appeared equally unimpressed with pneumonia. By May 15, less than a week after his first symptoms were reported, Washington was *in extremis*. William Maclay, a cranky provincial sent by the farmers of western Pennsylvania to represent them for $6 a day in the Senate, called at 39 Broadway that grim Saturday and found a household in tears. One of the attending physicians told Maclay bluntly that death was imminent.

Hearing the ominous news for himself, Thomas Jefferson hurried to the Macomb House as the president's quickened, shallow respiration grew fainter.

Suddenly, about four o'clock, the secretary of state reported in a clinical fashion to his daughter, Martha, "a copious sweat came on, his expectoration, which had been thin and ichorous, began to assume a well-digested form, his articulation became distinct, and in the course of two hours it was evident he had gone thro' a favorable crisis."

"Total despair" gave way overnight to cautious hopes for the president's recovery, Jefferson noted the next day. "Indeed, he is thought quite safe." By the twenty-fourth, Jefferson could inform his son-in-law that the man in the Macomb House was "perfectly well, except weak." But it had been a perilously close call. "You cannot conceive the public alarm on this occasion," said Jefferson. "It proves how much depends on his life." That same afternoon, consistent with his doctors' urgings of more exercise and less application to business, Washington rode out in his carriage for the first time in nearly three weeks.

News of his recovery buoyed the nation. "From all let grateful incense rise," proclaimed John Fenno's adulatory *Gazette of the United States*. Washington's reaction was more somber, and for good reason. Neither his father nor grandfather had survived to fifty; his own memory was unreliable, his hearing beginning to falter. "I have already had within less than a year two severe attacks; the last worse than the first," he reminded his friend in Alexandria, David Stuart, on June 15. "A third more than probable, will put me to sleep with my fathers."

PART ONE

New York

1790

❊ I ❊

"SUMMONED
BY MY COUNTRY"

"I have no lust for power."

George Washington,
to the president of Congress,
December 1776

NEW YORKERS UP WITH THE SUN in the first days of June 1790 saw their convalescing chief executive astride a white steed, attended only by a groom as he made his way north on today's Lexington Avenue before turning west into what is now Central Park, crossing the island to Morningside Heights and returning south by way of the Bloomingdale Road and Broadway. Some days he made the island's fourteen-mile circuit in a carriage, accompanied by Martha and her grandchildren. Washington also visited a circus, bought tickets to see a dancing bear, and paid three shillings, nine pence, to hear the silvery sounds of Dr. Franklin's Armonica. Long walks supplied another welcome diversion for a man accustomed to life out of doors.

One June weekend, Washington collected Hamilton and Jefferson, neither yet sufficiently acquainted with the other to regard him as an enemy, and went fishing off Sandy Hook. If they discussed the assumption of state debts or where to locate the nation's capital permanently, it went unrecorded. Instead, the president returned with a large haul of sea bass and warm praise for his "able coadjutors, who harmonize extremely well together."

Washington's rigorous program of exercise gave him time to look back on a fabulous life, vastly more interesting than petrified legend, in which he had disproved the limitations of heredity and mapped out a highly distinctive path to greatness. While most Americans think of Washington as a born aristocrat, he was in fact the eldest son of a second marriage whose prospects had been far from encouraging. The president retained

· 3 ·

few memories of his father, Augustine, an enterprising planter and businessman whose name appears but twice in his son's nineteen thousand surviving letters. By contrast, Washington harbored all too vivid recollections of Augustine's second wife, Mary, rescued from spinsterhood at twenty-seven.

Eighteenth-century writers sanctified Mary Ball Washington. Modern ones have depicted her as Medea in a mob cap, grasping, possessive, envious to a fault. Whatever the truth, Washington owed more to his mother than he suspected or would acknowledge. Said a playmate from his youth, "Of the mother I was ten times more afraid than I ever was of my own parents . . . whoever has seen the awe-inspiring air and manner so characteristic of the Father of His Country will remember the mother as she appeared when the presiding genius of her well-ordered household, commanding and being obeyed."

Mary Washington was known throughout the Fredericksburg area for her self-possession. When, late in the Revolution, a messenger galloped into her yard clutching an important letter from General Washington, the old woman went on working in her garden, conspicuously ignoring the document that so interested her neighbors. Finally she opened the dispatch to learn of a Continental triumph at arms. "George generally carries through anything he undertakes," she remarked with a thin smile. Her son's reserve would be equally legendary.

Beyond the accident of birth, Washington's entire life was a struggle, first to establish a sense of self independent of Mary Ball Washington, then to subdue his volatile emotions. "I wish I could say that he governs his temper," wrote Thomas, Lord Fairfax, to Washington's mother in 1748. "He is subject to attacks of anger on provocation, sometimes without just cause." Time would cure his sixteen-year-old friend of the vice, predicted Fairfax, judging George "a man who will go to school all his life." This was prophetic, for while his formal education consisted of a few months' tutoring in geography, composition, the science of numbers, and the arts of deportment, Washington would travel more extensively and meet a wider range of people than any American of his age. From each experience he gained something, and neither time nor the dulling incense of public adulation would dim his curiosity.

Given the "method and exactness" detected by his titled patron, it was only logical that Augustine Washington's son should be drawn to surveying as a career. Additional reasons provide a window on the youth's psyche. The surveyor is an executive of nature and a wanderer by choice, stamping order on chaos by fixing his name on previously uncharted territory. Washington's lifelong need for control would express itself through a mastery of virtually everyone and everything around him.

As an adolescent working for the Fairfaxes, he readily defied the elements. Much later, Washington's surveying skills enabled him to gauge military positions from a great distance. Did they also contribute to the emotional distance he put between himself and less driven men, coolly taking their measure as if observing a misplaced tree or errant boulder?

Young Washington's journals reveal a lively, observant mind, open to new experiences and foreign cultures. He learned early to read the motives of the French scouts sent out to harass an English scouting party or a silent — too silent — Indian guide leading him toward possible ambush. Although the forest was Washington's first classroom, it was hardly his only one. Consistent with Lord Fairfax's prediction, Washington never stopped learning or putting his newfound knowledge to practical use. At an astonishingly early age he could ford a river, clothe a regiment, chart a mountain road, and charm a lawmaker. He was the surveyor of Culpepper County at seventeen and adjutant inspector of the Virginia militia with a major's commission before his twentieth birthday.

American historiography is periodically enlivened by the discovery that among the rights for which General Washington led a rebellion was that of making money. His faith was instilled early. While still a teenager, Washington pocketed 500 acres of Virginia's Frederick County as a surveyor's fee. Over the next few years his land holdings tripled, providing a ticket of admission to the colonial gentry whose esteem he valued at least as much as their hospitable company. Having lost his father and possessing little genuine affection for the mother he dutifully addressed as "Honored Madam," George naturally gravitated in the direction of his half-brother Lawrence, a battle-scarred veteran of British campaigns against the Spanish in Panama and Colombia.*

The youthful Washington emulated Lawrence's stylishness, refusing on one occasion to venture into the woods without nine shirts, six linen waistcoats, seven caps, six collars, and four neckclothes. He longed to be part of the fashionable society that swirled around the older man's Potomac estate, named for the British admiral Edward Vernon. After Lawrence's marriage in 1743 to Anne Fairfax, whose father served as agent for his cousin Lord Thomas Fairfax, the proprietor of 5 million acres in Virginia's Northern Neck, young George could study at first hand the graces of Tidewater Virginia. He excelled on the dance floor, relished card games, and was not above attending cockfights.

Awkward as a gosling, the aspiring dandy can be glimpsed in a portrait

---

*Lawrence and George together could not persuade Mary Washington to enroll her eldest son in King George II's navy, an act of refusal for which both patriots and historians should be grateful.

drawn with his approval by his earliest biographer, David Humphreys: "Though he was rather unsure and reserved in his appearance, he was frequently animated and fluent in conversation and always discreet in conduct, and in the performance of any business committed to him he was active, indefatigable, persevering." If this passage is any indication, Humphreys's paragon was not guilty of false modesty, nor was he the least bit bashful in proclaiming his physical prowess. "I have several times heard him say," wrote Humphreys, "he never met any man who could throw a stone to so great a distance as himself; and that when standing in the valley beneath the Natural Bridge in Virginia, he has thrown one up to that stupendous arch."

Raw strength was matched by an almost pathetic desire for social polish. The adolescent Washington examined Seneca's *Dialogues* and laboriously copied from a London magazine one hundred and ten "rules of civility" intended to buff a rude country boy into at least the first draft of a gentleman. In addition to warnings about spitting in the fire, turning one's back on another in conversation, and playing the peacock in matters of fashion, Washington jotted down two admonitions that presaged his mature self: "Let your countenance be pleasant but in serious matters somewhat grave," and "Labor to keep alive in your breast that little spark of celestial fire called Conscience." Fortified by such maxims, the desire to escape his mother's narrow world, and a gift for impressing powerful elders in a patriarchal society, no American hero was more completely self-made.

Of course, he had help. Lawrence taught his half-brother to value culture equally with property. Additional inspiration came from the Fairfaxes, with their broad acres, handsome women, and classical devotion to public service in the patrician manner. In 1751 George and Lawrence traveled to the Caribbean island of Barbados, where the older man hoped to find relief from tuberculosis. While there, George contracted smallpox and had the far more pleasurable experience of attending his first theatrical performance. Following Lawrence's death, an improbable set of circumstances — a widow's rapid remarriage, her subsequent death, and that of her infant daughter — made George the sole owner of Mount Vernon. His visits to the Fairfaxes' two-story brick house at Belvoir became more frequent than ever.

Based on two letters, one written just before his marriage to Martha Custis and a second drawn up in wintry old age, historians have conjectured an intense love affair between Washington and Sally Fairfax, the wife of George's best friend, the plodding George William Fairfax. According to this theory, Washington's arctic reserve was really a wall thrown up around a broken heart, designed to keep the prying world at a distance. This seems improbable in light of what we know about his austere childhood and the emotional void between the fatherless boy and his undemonstrative mother. Moreover, in the closely knit society of Fairfax County, such an indiscretion could not easily have been concealed, and there is no contemporary evidence to support a sexual liaison.

More likely was Sally Fairfax's role as social tutor, blending virtue with refinement and personifying life as it ought to be lived. Certainly Washington liked comfort, comely women, and well-ordered houses. As a true Stoic, however, he made the early discovery that he must rely on himself for ultimate happiness. If he lusted after anything, it was glory, self-sufficiency, and an acknowledged position among his aristocratic role models. For in addition to the *Rules of Civility*, Washington jotted down a homely piece of self-help entitled *True Happiness:*

> These are the things which once possessed
> Will make a life that's truly blessed;
> A good estate on healthy soil
> Not got by vice, nor yet by toil;
> Round a warm fire, a pleasant joke,
> With chimney ever free from smoke:
> A strength entire, a sparkling bowl,
> A quiet wife, a quiet soul.

In short, everything that was missing from the Washington household at Ferry Farm on the Rappahannock.

Washington's desires soon carried him to the defense of Virginia's frontiers and into the councils of state. His daring reconnaissance of French and Indian territory in 1753 and the crucial intelligence he brought back to Lieutenant Governor Robert Dinwiddie made him a colonial hero. *The Journal of Major George Washington*, published in London in June 1754, won him modest fame in the British capital. It also earned a rebuke from King George II. Informed that the American hotspur had pronounced the sound of flying bullets "charming," the monarch concluded that he could not have heard many.

He heard more than enough in the next four years, marching in the front ranks of Britain's prolonged campaign to dislodge the French from their lightly defended outposts in the Ohio Valley and playing a conspicuous part in the forest humiliation of the British general Edward Braddock by Indians employing guerrilla tactics to devastating effect. Somehow he managed to retain both his military reputation and a sense of humor. As a green soldier of twenty-two, Washington allowed himself and 400 Virginia volunteers to be encircled by French and Indian attackers in a pitiable stockade, which he promptly dubbed Fort Necessity. Following the rout of Braddock's army, Washington as second in command heard reports of his own death and even his deathbed speech. "I take this early opportunity of contradicting the first," he deadpanned, "and of assuring you that I have not as yet composed the latter."

Jests aside, it was in many ways a disillusioning time for Washington, forced to contend with skulking militia, thieving speculators, and lawmakers who fought war with their tongues a safe distance from the front. More galling still, he had to endure the toplofty disdain of Britain's military establishment for the irregular colonials, who refused to dress or fight according to the Old World's time-honored standards. In the process, his insights into human perversity deepened.

Besides driving the French from British North America, Washington craved a secure place in the colony's ruling caste. This objective led him on a political campaign trail as treacherous as any forest path through Indian country. At the age of twenty-three, gauging his chances like a colonial ward heeler, Washington contemplated running for Virginia's House of Burgesses. "Sound their pulse, with an air of indifference and unconcern," he instructed a friend on the scene, "without disclosing much of *mine*." On election day Washington suffered a crushing defeat at the hands of voters still angry over the upstart colonel's orders to impress their horses for military service and his brash crusades against local tippling houses. When he next sought office in thirsty Winchester County, Washington made sure the liquor flowed generously. Profiting from defeat would become his hallmark, whatever the field of battle.

He would never sway men with his oratory. When a difficult defense of the colony's frontier in 1758 led the assembly speaker to tender Washington profuse thanks, the object of his tribute stood mute and embarrassed until told by Speaker Robinson, "Sit down, Mr. Washington, your modesty equals your valor, and that surpassed the power of any language that I possess." Much later, following his nephew's election to Virginia's Assembly, Washington cautioned the younger man against becoming so buoyed by praise "as to become a babbler." George Washington was no babbler. "With me it has always been a maxim," he explained late in life, "rather to let my designs appear from my works than by my expressions."

Few discerned stage fright in the frontier warrior, but Washington's insecurities — about his education, his rustic background, his early cultural poverty — ran deep. They were never wholly erased. Twenty-five years later, when the toast of two continents returned to Mount Vernon, one of his first acts was to unearth youthful letter books and correct his misspellings, awkward constructions, and faulty grammar. Only after their intellectual sanitization would Washington permit his writings to be copied for posterity.

George Washington has become so shrouded in legend that it is difficult to retrieve the man behind the marble exterior. Yet it would be a mistake to reject every sugary anecdote as hagiography of the cherry tree school. For example, there is solid evidence to support the tale of a violent encounter between Washington and a diminutive fellow named Payne, whom the much larger soldier-politician apparently insulted during a campaign for the Virginia Assembly. Not without resources of his own, the offended Payne grabbed a hickory branch and knocked Washington to the ground. The next day Washington demanded an interview at a tavern. Expecting to be challenged to a duel, Payne received instead a handsome apology and retraction of the original comment, along with Washington's hand in friendship.

The gesture may have been nothing more than shrewd politics, but it was surprising all the same — although no more so than Washington's contempt for dueling, an unavoidable chapter in the gentleman's code of the day. The same could be said of the innovative approach Washington brought to agriculture, with his invention of a plow to break the crumbly red soil at Mount Vernon, his insistence that Martha be inoculated against smallpox, and his growing dissatisfaction with British commercial and political domination. Washington generally meant what he said, never more so than when he criticized other agrarians content to tread in the well-rutted paths of their fathers. Historians who have characterized him as a reflexive conservative do an injustice to the entrepreneurial side of Washington, whose instincts led him into questionable land deals for which he was still paying at the end of his life.

"Land is the most permanent estate and the most likely to increase in value," he wrote while still in his twenties. Not mentioned were the rank and status that vast acreage bestowed in aristocratic Virginia, enough to compensate for emotions withheld from Mary Washington's son. Together with other speculators, young Washington cooked up a scheme to drain the Dismal Swamp by building a canal to the seaside village of Norfolk (a feat not actually accomplished until 1828). Washington's acquisitive streak, another inheritance from his purse-proud mother, led him over the Appalachians and into the upper Ohio Valley, familiar territory from his soldiering days. At the end of 1758, denied a royal commission in the regular British army and miffed at the second-class treatment accorded provincial officers, Colonel Washington resigned his command of Virginia's forces to devote himself to other conquests.

Following his marriage to Daniel Custis's wealthy widow, he created at Mount Vernon an oasis of domesticity in sharp contrast to his Ferry Farm boyhood. At the same time he cultivated a reserve first perfected in the military, where distance was essential to winning the respect and obedience of unruly militia. An officer was perforce a gentleman; anything less and enlisted men would regard him as "no more than a broomstick, being mixed together as one common herd." Consistent with this stratified view, Washington pulled strings in Williamsburg to get his share and more of a 200,000-acre grant voted to the colony's defenders and, along with his friend Dr. James Craik, staked out thousands of acres of rich bottomland around the confluence of the Ohio and Great Kanawha rivers. A much larger vision of landed wealth went glimmering in 1763 when the British ministry in London, fearful that western migration might upset its delicate mercantile economy and plunge the colonists into costly Indian wars, all but closed the trans-Appalachian region to entrepreneurs of Washington's stripe.

As a tobacco planter dependent on British ships and markets for his livelihood, Washington began to chafe under the restrictions placed on his economic freedom by the Mother Country. In addition to his need for control, the ambitious planter was imbued with the sturdy Saxon belief that the state must not only answer to the individual but also keep its hand out of his pocket. Yet mercantilism drained a planter's resources at every step of a tortuous process by which his crop was monopolized for English use, subject to fluctuations in price beyond his grasp or influence. Washington had no choice but to sell his tobacco to Englishmen, paying along the way English import duties, freight charges, insurance premiums, and storage costs. In return he bought English goods, often of inferior make. Borrowing English money to buy land and slaves, he looked on helplessly as these loans were subsequently converted into mortgages on his property. Then interest payments joined the dismal list of obligations ensnaring Washington to men three thousand miles away, typified by the firm of Robert Cary and Company, which marketed his crop and sold him clothing, household utensils, paper, wine, snuff, and playing cards.

The Potomac squire asked for busts of Alexander the Great and Julius Caesar and was offered Homer and Plato instead. (He canceled the order.) Crooked scythes and unusable lumber arrived from the home country. So did a tax on stamps, imposed by London to pay the costs of a 10,000-man standing army. Washington was warmly sympathetic when nine of the thirteen colonies sent representatives to the Stamp Act Congress in New York in the fall of 1765 to register a strong protest. New England mobs did what less vigorous congresses only talked about; Yankee indignation, pointedly directed at tax collectors and royal officials, helped for the moment to convince Parliament that its American brethren would not submit to taxes in which they had no voice.

Ten years before his countrymen formally separated from Great Britain, Washington declared his own economic independence by abandoning tobacco and embarking on a rigorous campaign of self-sufficiency. Mount Vernon became a crude yet thriving industrial village, producing its own cloth in defiance of British restraints and enabling its proprietor to trade flour and fish with French outposts in the West Indies. In just four years, Washington achieved a twentyfold increase in his wheat crop. For his resourcefulness, he and his fellow colonists were hit with new duties on paper, paint, glass, lead, and tea. The squire's patience grew thin. "At a time when our lordly masters in Great Britain will be satisfied with nothing less than the depreciation of American freedom," Washington wrote to his neighbor George Mason in 1769, "it seems highly necessary that something should be done to avoid the stroke and maintain the liberty which we have derived from our ancestors."

That something turned out to be a voluntary association whose members refused to import British goods. Washington ordered his London agent to withhold any taxed items except paper, an essential commodity that neither Mount Vernon's slave population nor anyone else in America could manufacture. Thus, while other patriots gained notice through their pen or oratory, their organizational or legal abilities, Washington led by example, and his conversion from loyal British subject to revolutionary advocate was all the more telling, given his place in the Tidewater aristocracy and his known aversion to hasty or thoughtless action.

Washington's correspondence is notably silent on the subject of the so-called massacre of five Bostonians by British soldiers in March 1770. Not so three years later, when another band of Boston rebels held their tea party in the harbor, which Parliament summarily closed through punitive legislation known throughout the colonies as the Intolerable Acts. Washington joined in a sternly worded rebuff by the Virginia Assembly and in the rump session that followed Lord Dunmore's dissolution of that body. He had more personal reasons to regret the Quebec Act, which attached most of the American continent west of Pennsylvania and north of the Ohio to Britain's frozen northern outpost. Even before Dunmore canceled Washington's latest claims in the valley of the Great Kanawha, now hotly disputed by the Shawnee Indian tribe, the land had little value as long as savages were free to stage hit-and-run attacks and the British government tried to divert reliable tenants to fringe areas like Florida and the Canadian Maritimes.

But if economic resentment caused the first stirrings of Washington's separatist ardor, he was much more than a pocketbook patriot: he called for a provincial congress to discuss a general ban on British imports and American exports. On July 17, 1774, he and George Mason, working in the study at Mount Vernon, drew up a list of two dozen resolutions that became famous as the Fairfax Resolves. Sweeping from Williamsburg to Philadelphia, they infuriated the London ministry for reasons that were obvious. Unlike the earlier voluntary agreement, this nonimportation pact had teeth in the form of local committees charged with reporting violations and publishing the names of miscreants. Where publicity alone failed to enforce the blockade, patriots were urged to resort to boycotts or even the forcible seizure of British wares.

By now the tongue-tied Colonel Washington had found his voice. One South Carolinian at the Virginia convention, overlooking the delegates' characterization of slavery as a "wicked, cruel and unnatural trade," remembered the towering soldier in his regimental uniform. " 'I will raise one thousand men, subsist them at my own expense, and march myself at their head for the relief of Boston,' " he quoted Washington as saying. This was eloquence of a kind universally understood, and it brought Washington to the attention of northern agitators like John and Samuel Adams. At the First Continental Congress, held in Philadelphia's Carpenters' Hall in the fall of 1774, the lanky Virginian impressed others as well. Patrick Henry praised South Carolina's John Rutledge for his oratory while insisting that "if you speak of solid information and sound judgment, Colonel Washington is by far the greatest man on the floor."

Already a myth was forming around the shy soldier in his blue and buff regimental uniform. Washington's was the charisma of competence; this and an almost painfully sincere commitment to his country's cause turned more heads than any flight of silvery words or parliamentary legerdemain. Out of the Congress emerged a Continental Association, designed to accomplish across a thousand miles of British America the same economic self-denial that Virginians had applied to themselves through the Fairfax Resolves. Americans were beginning to think of themselves as citizens, not subjects.

Virginia that autumn authorized the establishment of military companies at the county level; by the spring of 1775 Washington had been chosen to command the forces of seven separate counties. The *Virginia Gazette* sang his military praises:

> In spite of Gage's flaming sword
> And Carlton's Canadian troop
> Brave Washington shall give the word
> And we'll make them *howl and whoop*.

Washington's domestic life during this period was the uncomplicated round of sociable visits and neighborly obligations expected from one of his station. He became a vestryman of Truro Parish and justice of the peace for Fairfax County. His happy marriage was marred only by the absence of bawling infants to augment Martha's two surviving children from her first marriage. Following Patsy's death in 1773, Mrs. Washington's religious feelings, always strong, became more pronounced than ever. Each morning after breakfast she retreated to her room for an hour of prayer and devotional reading. Ensuing events tested her equanimity if not her faith. Deteriorating relations with England led the Fairfaxes to leave Virginia for good. Soon after, Martha's husband rode off to Philadelphia for the Second Continental Congress.

On June 15, 1775, Washington bolted from the meeting room when the delegates unanimously chose him to lead a Continental Army that existed mostly in their imaginations. He responded in character, dolefully telling Patrick Henry, "From the day I enter upon the command of the American armies, I date my fall and the ruin of my reputation." Five days later, having been raised to the rank of brigadier general, he informed his brother John Augustine, "I am embarked on a wide ocean, boundless in its prospect and from whence perhaps no safe harbor is to be found." He made out a will. Hiding personal ambition in lofty references to honor, he sought to reassure Martha that none of his newfound prominence could take the place of his "agreeable consort."

"I should enjoy more real happiness in one month with you at home," he wrote to her, "than I have the most distant prospect of finding abroad, if my stay were to be seven times seven years." His most ardent desire, he concluded, was that she pursue "any plan that is most likely to produce content and a tolerable degree of tranquility." The war years were anything but tranquil for "Lady Washington," as she came to be known. By then her marriage of convenience had ripened into something much greater. Washington acknowledged as much after the war, when he wrote that "more permanent and genuine happiness is to be found in the sequestered walks of connubial life than in the giddy rounds of promiscuous pleasure, or the more tumultuous and imposing scenes of successful ambition."

Before that, however, George sent for Martha, who became "a kind of perambulator" trailing the Continental Army as it eluded the clutches of superior British generalship. Cambridge, Massachusetts, where Washington took formal command in July 1775, pronounced a baptism of fire, courtesy of Bunker Hill's defenders. "I shudder every time I hear the sound of a gun," Martha confessed, "but I endeavor to keep my fears to myself as well as I can." Early the next year her brother, William Dandridge, was reported drowned; 1777 brought the death of Martha's sister Nancy Bassett, "my favorite in all the world." At Valley Forge the commander's lady dined in a drafty log cabin and nursed soldiers back to health. Her industry as a seamstress became legendary as she recruited other women to sew garments for half-naked men and make blankets and bandages for a shivering army. Supplying a warm, maternal touch, she was everything that Mary Ball Washington was not.

❦ 3 ❧

"Unhappy it is to reflect that a brother's sword has been sheathed in a brother's breast," Washington wrote to his quondam neighbor George William Fairfax at the end of May 1775, "and that the once happy and peaceful plains of America are either to be drenched with blood or inhabited by slaves. Sad alternative! But can a virtuous man hesitate in his choice?"

Second only to Washington's dominant personality was a lifelong quest for the impersonal love celebrated by the ancients. From his earliest years Washington had rationalized his pursuit of fame by wedding it to a genuine concern for his country's welfare. With eyes turned toward the distant future, he rejected a salary as commanding general (accepting only his expenses), all the while hoping that the current age and posterity to come would accord him the secular immortality reserved for that noblest of Roman attributes, disinterested virtue.

"I have made a pretty good slam among such kind of officers as the Massachusetts government abound in," he enthused shortly after arriving in Cambridge. With the help of fifty-nine British cannon dragged hundreds of miles across a wintry New England landscape from Fort Ticonderoga, Washington was able to fashion a noose around Boston. The city fell to rebel forces in March 1776, after an initial bold stroke gave way to prolonged siege. It would be that kind of war, with Washington forced to defeat his own temper and impetuosity before he ever met a British redcoat on the field of battle. Early on, the commanding general was forever devising brash tactics that worked better on paper than in practice. As he grew in confidence, he held fewer councils of war, stifling the urge for assaults beyond his meager resources. He came to understand the conflict as a test of political endurance, and while he might lament missed opportunities, he played the fox more often than the lion.

"Perseverance and spirit have done wonders in all ages," he wrote in

August 1775. They would have to perform miracles now against the world's best-trained and best-equipped soldiery, for the Continentals had little else in their arsenal. Lacking men and materiel with which to conduct an aggressive war, Washington and his army posed more nuisance than danger to the king's splendidly arrayed forces. Worse, the support of Washington's countrymen was something less than wholehearted. "Nothing but disunion can hurt our cause," he argued in the spring of 1776; here can be found the seeds of the belief in a strong central government that came to dominate Washington's political thinking for the rest of his life. Yet for all his mounting frustrations with the slow pace of Congress and its refusal to provide long-term enlistments or adequate pay for his troops, Washington never for a moment questioned the supremacy of civilian rule, nor did he take the slightest advantage of his status as America's uncrowned king. The army must serve the country, not rule it, he admonished his men.

Unable to move decisively against the enemy, for eight and a half years Washington endured a raffish assortment of jealous state governments, corrupt suppliers, long-winded congressmen, mutinous subordinates, sunshine patriots, and presumptuous foreigners, not to mention British bullets. "And he did it all," in the words of the historian Edmund S. Morgan, "with that aloof dignity which earned the awesome respect of those he commanded and earned him in victory the honor of the nation that had come into existence almost in spite of itself."

A visitor to Washington's camp in 1779 discovered a near universal veneration for the commanding general. "He is feared even when silent and beloved even while we are unconscious of the motive . . . In conversation, his Excellency's expressive countenance is peculiarly interesting and pleasing; a placid smile is frequently observed on his lips, but a loud laugh . . . seldom if ever escapes him. He is polite and attentive to each individual at table and retires after the compliment of a few glasses."

Military life was not unrelievedly grim. Surely it was better, Washington had written, to go laughing than crying through the rough journey of life. A Virginia colonel's wife wrote to her sister-in-law in 1778 of "our noble and agreeable commander" who at riding parties "throws off the hero and takes on the chatty, agreeable companion. He can be downright impudent sometimes — such impudence, Fanny, as you and I like." He could also dance for hours at wartime balls subsidized with his personal funds. And no one who took part in the British rout at Princeton would ever forget the sight of their commanding officer on horseback pursuing the fleeing redcoats and shouting, "It's a fine fox chase, boys."

When entertaining the president of Congress after the Battle of Princeton, General Washington served wine in cups, the maker of which, someone observed, had become a Quaker preacher. Washington said that it was too bad he had not turned preacher before making the cups. On hearing congressional leaders explain sorrowfully that Robert Morris, the Revolution's financier, had his hands full, Washington retorted, "I wish he had his pockets full." One evening as he sat at dinner, the fire behind him flared up. The American commander moved to a cooler spot in the room, prompting an onlooker to remark that it behooved a general to stand fire. It looked worse for a general to receive it from behind, flashed Washington.

One struggle Washington seems never to have fought was the ancient one between ambition and integrity. His wartime aide Tench Tilghman declared the general "the honestest man that I believe ever adorned human nature." Washington implied much the same thing in different words when he vowed, "I never say anything *of* a man that I have the smallest scruple of saying *to* him." Certainly he was candid in telling the president of Congress the three things that moved soldiers to discharge their duty: "natural bravery, hope of reward, and fear of punishment."

After a near disastrous string of defeats in and around New York, surprise victories at Trenton and Princeton, and the humiliating evacuation of Philadelphia in the fall of 1777, Washington was mired in gloom. "I do not think any officer since the Creation ever had such a variety of difficulties and perplexities to encounter as I have," he moaned. Failing to halt the panicky retreat of some Connecticut troops on Long Island, an observer noted that Washington "laid his cane over many of the officers who showed their men the example of running."

With no outlet for his natural aggression, the commander turned to violent language. He denounced "cowardly rascals" in his ranks, damned Tories as "execrable parricides," and "swore like an angel" at General Charles Lee after that vainglorious popinjay squandered American advantages at the Battle of Monmouth Courthouse in June 1778. Once he threw his hat on the ground and demanded, "Are these the men with whom I am to defend America?" More reflectively, Washington came to see the human race in all its imperfections. "Men may speculate as they will," he wrote a few weeks before the Monmouth disaster; "they may talk of patriotism; they may draw a few examples from current story . . . but whoever builds upon it as a sufficient basis for conducting a long and bloody war will find themselves deceived in the end . . . For a time it may of itself push men to action, to bear much, to encounter difficulties, but it will not endure unassisted by Interest."

Washington's interest in victory led him down some unfamiliar paths. Within months of taking command, the Virginia slaveowner agreed to let free Negroes remain in his army on the grounds that to expel them would only spur British recruitment. Throughout the Revolution he fought just nine major engagements (and won but three), but he locked horns with the enemy in a constant struggle for public opinion. He wrote thousands of letters appealing for fresh men, supplies, and money worth more than the paper on which it was printed. Early in the war the vagabond Congress offered him a dictator's powers — just as after York-town a republican crown was his for the taking. In both instances Washington promised to put away his sword the moment American liberties were firmly established.

In spare moments cadged from strategy sessions and endless correspondence, the commanding general wrote to his distant kinsman Lund Washington, who was managing Mount Vernon in his absence. "I see the impossibility of serving with reputation or doing any essential service to the cause by continuing in command," he confided at a moment of despair, "and yet I am told that if I quit the command, inevitable ruin will follow from the distraction that will ensue. I tell you that I never was in such an unhappy, divided state since I was born." When a British man-of-war anchored in the Potomac off Mount Vernon and demanded provisions, Lund complied, leading to a rebuke from his cousin, who said that he would have preferred a stout refusal, even if it had led the British to burn his house and plunder his estate.

Other American generals, most notably Horatio Gates, won impressive victories while Washington and his ragtag force seemed always retreating or in danger of melting away entirely. Late in 1777, a few in Congress, unhappy over the course of the war and fearing incipient military dictatorship, pondered a change of command. Thomas Conway, a hotheaded Irishman who had accompanied Lafayette from France, flattered Gates by insulting Washington. When Conway's indiscretions were revealed to the commanding general, he frostily demanded an explanation. One of his young aides, Colonel John Laurens, demanded even more: satisfaction on a dueling field, where he seriously wounded the scheming Conway. Not long after, the foreigner left for home.

Others came in his place as the Franco-American alliance took hold in 1778 and Washington's patient husbanding of the limited colonial forces paid off. As the fighting shifted south, America's cause experienced fresh reverses at Savannah and Charleston. Washington continued his war of attrition, hoping to exhaust an enemy he could not defeat in frontal battle. The winter of 1779–80, spent at Morristown, New Jersey, was even worse than the fabled hardship of Valley Forge. France was proving a temperamental ally. Still Washington refused to admit that all might be lost.

"We must not despair," he wrote in June 1781, almost six years after assuming command on Cambridge Common. "The game is yet in our own hands; to play it well is all we have to do, and I trust the experience of error will enable us to act better in future. A cloud may yet pass over us, individuals may be ruined, and the country at large, or particular states, undergo temporary distress, but certain I am that it is in our power to bring the war to a happy conclusion."

Perhaps no soldier in history learned so much from his mistakes. To the end, however, Washington's strategic visions were flawed. That summer he hoped to join forces with a French fleet and drive the British from New York. The French admiral, the comte de Grasse, acting on advice from his counterpart in the army, the comte de Rochambeau, had a different idea. Instead of attacking New York, he sailed his fleet past the Virginia capes, an essential first step toward what Rochambeau would call "the miracle of Yorktown." Washington hurriedly switched course, racing south to trap the British general Charles Cornwallis in Yorktown, a village lapped by the waters of Chesapeake Bay. De Grasse's fleet supplied the stopper in the bottle, and after a short siege Cornwallis (actually his second-in-command, the general pronouncing himself "indisposed") offered up his sword on October 21, 1781.

In his greatest moment of triumph, Washington advised his soldiers against unseemly crowing over their defeated foe. "Posterity will huzza for us," he said, truthfully enough. On October 26 he entertained Cornwallis over dinner. After an exchange of pleasantries, the British commander predicted even greater fame for his victorious rival "on the banks of the Delaware rather than those of the Chesapeake." Philadelphia, the seat of colonial government, was on the Delaware River.

❦ 4 ❧

Yorktown brought the Washingtons public triumph and private disaster. Days after witnessing Cornwallis's surrender to his stepfather, Jack Custis died of a fever, leaving four children and a devastated mother. Martha became more protective than ever of "my pretty little Dear Boy," George Washington Parke Custis, who, along with his sister Eleanor, or Nelly, was adopted by the Washingtons and later installed in the Macomb House. Wrote Martha to her niece Fanny Bassett, "It makes me miserable if ever he complains, let the cause be ever so trifling. I hope the Almighty will spare him to me."

Her husband, meanwhile, struggled to hold his victorious political and military coalition together. No one present at the army's postwar headquarters at Newburgh, New York, in March 1783 would ever forget his emotionally charged appearance before a rump caucus of dissatisfied officers. Elements upset at Congress's failure to provide back pay or future pensions had demanded a mass meeting to air their grievances and consider radical action against the government in Philadelphia. Washington denounced the proceedings as "irregular and disorderly" before convening his own gathering, at which he tried to flatter his sullen audience with visions of a grateful posterity.

None of this had much effect until the general retrieved from his pocket a congressional message promising early redress of legitimate complaints. He fumbled with the paper for a few seconds, then reached again into his coat to fetch a pair of eyeglasses. Begging the indulgence of his men, he explained to a stunned audience, "I have already grown gray in the service of my country. I am now going blind." Instantly, rebellion melted into tears.

It was a galvanizing moment, a brilliant piece of theater and a narrow escape for republican government. Never mind that Washington had used reading glasses for years. Who, offered magic, insists on logic?

Washington was rarely bashful about manipulating the emotions of an audience where the good of his country was concerned. He said as much in yielding back to Congress, a few months after the attempted coup at Newburgh, the absolute power invested in him eight years before: "Nothing now remains but for the actors of this mighty scene to preserve a perfect, unvarying constancy of character through the very last act, to close the drama with applause, and to retire from the military theater with the same approbation of angels and men which have crowned all their former virtuous actions."

Long before assuming the presidency, then, Washington was adept at putting himself in settings designed to exploit his unique standing, displaying a personal magnetism that projected to the second balcony. He soon discovered that it was easier to defeat tyranny than establish popular government. "We now stand an independent people and have yet to learn political tactics," he wrote to Lafayette in April 1783. "We are placed among the nations of the earth and have a character to establish . . . the probability, at least I fear it is, that local or state politics will interfere too much with that more liberal and extensive plan of government which wisdom and foresight, freed from the mist of prejudice, would dictate."

During the war Washington had compared America's political system to a clock, vulnerable to sudden breakdown if the smaller wheels were maintained at the expense of the larger ones. In a similar vein, in retirement at Mount Vernon he railed against the unreasonable demands of individual states and the impotence of the central government. "This is as clear to me as the A, B, C; and I think we have opposed Great Britain . . . to very little purpose if we cannot conquer our own prejudices," he contended.

Not all of Washington's thoughts were so apprehensive. David Humphreys captured his old commander in a postwar mood of relaxed conviviality. "He perfectly relishes a pleasant story, an unaffected sally of wit, or a burlesque description which surprises by its suddenness and incongruity," said Humphreys. James Madison and Thomas Jefferson agreed, Madison adding that his friend laughed more often at the jokes of others than he made jests of his own. Those he did make had a sardonic air to them, mingled with a healthy sense of the ridiculous. For example, in 1787 Washington drew up a contract with a hard-drinking gardener, solemnly binding him to perform his duties sober for a year "if allowed four dollars at Christmas, with which to be drunk four days and four nights; two dollars at Easter, to effect the same purpose; two dollars at Whitsuntide, to be drunk for two days, a dram in the morning, and a drink of grog at dinner and at noon."

Left childless by nature, Washington was paternal by instinct. In preparing his first inaugural address, the president-elect sought to allay fears of a constitutionally sanctioned dynasty by reminding his countrymen that "the Divine Providence hath not seen fit that my blood should be transmitted or my name perpetuated by the endearing, though sometimes seducing, channel of immediate offspring." Although the painfully revealing passage was dropped from the final draft, its very existence hinted at Washington's sense of deprivation. If George Washington had a surrogate son, it was a red-haired Frenchman of noble birth and liberal politics named Marie Joseph Paul Yves Roch Gilbert du Motier, the marquis de Lafayette.

At the end of a visit by Lafayette to Mount Vernon after the Revolution, Washington accompanied his friend as far as the outskirts of Annapolis. When finally their carriages parted, the general wondered plaintively if it was the last he would see of his beloved protégé: "And though I wished to say no, my fears answered yes. I called to mind the days of my youth and found they had long since fled to return no more; that I was now descending the hill I had been fifty-two years in climbing, and that though I was blessed with a good constitution, I was of a short-lived family and might soon expect to be entombed in the dreary mansions of my fathers. These things darkened the shades and gave a gloom to the future . . . but I will not repine, I have had my day."

Although Washington could hardly guess it at the time, his greatest day lay ahead, on the unlikely field of civilian administration. We tend to forget it now, but the Father of His Country was not so coincidentally the sworn enemy of his Confederation, the weak vessel tolerated by states unwilling to part with their sovereignty. "Influence is no government," Washington wrote to Henry Lee in October 1786. Like-minded delegates assembling in steamy Philadelphia the following May to replace the inadequate Articles of Confederation knew their ancient history, especially Rome's cautionary tale of impotent senators and petty tyrants masquerading as gods. So they lodged ultimate sovereignty in the people, even as they hedged the mercurial, easily swayed masses with a series of organizational safeguards — much as Washington himself explained the elite Senate to Jefferson as a coffee saucer in which to cool legislative emotions.

He had but one wish, Washington insisted throughout the period before his inevitable election as the nation's first president, "which is to live and die on my own plantation. It is said that every man has his portion of ambition," he remarked to David Humphreys. "I may have mine, I suppose, as well as the rest, but if I know my own heart, my ambition would not lead me into public life; my only ambition is to do my duty in this world as well as I am capable of performing it, and to merit the good opinion of all good men."

Humphreys offered reassurance that the American people entertained a higher opinion of his friend's talents than did Washington himself. History records Washington's earliest biographer as a better psychologist than poet. Being rowed across New York Harbor toward his inauguration in April 1789, Washington wrote later, he was "filled with sensations as painful as they were pleasing." He took the oath of office before a crowd of 10,000 cheering New Yorkers, telling them, "I was summoned by my country, whose voice I can never hear but with veneration and love."

And so the Virginia planter turned soldier turned chief executive forsook his rural seat for the crowded streets and tangled intrigues of Manhattan. Among the captive, drowsy audience for midnight recitations in the room Humphreys shared with two other presidential aides was Robert Lewis, the son of Washington's sister, Betty. Bob Lewis copied letters for his uncle and served as a social aide to the first lady. At Martha's Friday night levees he retrieved gloves and fans, fetched orange drink and plum cake, and escorted ladies to their carriages — a privilege the president himself accorded the widows of Generals Nathanael Greene and Richard Montgomery.

Washington's junior secretary was Thomas Nelson, a son of Virginia's wartime governor. In hiring him, Washington had outlined the qualities necessary to join his official family: "a good address, abilities above mediocrity — secrecy and prudence — attention and industry — good temper — and a capacity and disposition to write correctly and well, and to do it obligingly." In contrast to Nelson's brief career at 39 Broadway, the president's old friend Major William Jackson possessed all these credentials and more. He could often be seen striding along the Battery beside the familiar figure in brown or gray garb, varied by nankeen the color of butter in summer. At one presidential reception, the intrepid South Carolinian came to the rescue of a young lady whose headdress of ostrich feathers had caught fire from a chandelier.

Washington asked Jackson to put out other fires as well. Even more contentious than Hamilton's scheme to have the federal government take the fiscal reins into its hands by assuming a consolidated debt, yet rapidly becoming entwined with it, was a fierce contest among a dozen candidates vying to become the nation's permanent capital. Jackson took soundings and weighed alternatives as obvious as New York itself and unlikely as Wright's Ferry, Pennsylvania. Although it was widely assumed that Washington preferred a site near the Great Falls of the Potomac, a morning's canter from Mount Vernon, he said nothing for the record. He didn't have to; his silences were more eloquent than most men's words.

❮ 5 ❯

Washington's first year in office was surprisingly uneventful, in keeping with the new president's wishes. Prodded by James Madison, who labeled it a "nauseous project" marked by incessant posturing and verbal warfare, Congress adopted twelve amendments to the Constitution, of which ten were subsequently ratified by the states to form the Bill of Rights. The president kept his distance from this debate and all others. More popular than the federal system over which he presided, Washington knew that much of his strength was symbolic. Once identified with contentious men or measures, even his standing might suffer — all the more so for a feeling of betrayal by voters for whom the Revolutionary hero was above reproach.

Hamilton's plan to assume state debts posed just such a danger. By defining an overriding national interest — shoring up the country's wobbly European credit — to the exclusion of purely local ones, Hamiltonian nationalism had the unintended effect of weakening national unity. By rewarding sharp-witted speculators over old soldiers, many of whom had been forced in hard times to part with government securities at a fraction of their face value, the secretary of the treasury stood accused of redeeming the nation's credit while mortgaging its honor. Finally, by making no distinction between states like Virginia that had repaid much of its war debt and others awash in red ink, Hamilton reinforced suspicions that he was a high-handed agent of national consolidation, indifferent if not hostile to state pride and authority.

The new government was as vulnerable to outside infections as internal strains. Writing to the marquis de la Luzerne, France's wartime ambassador, shortly before taking to his sickbed, Washington had enthused, "A spirit for political improvements seems to be rapidly and extensively spreading through the European countries." Yet in his next breath he cautioned against political innovators in King Louis's combustible capital who were "making *more haste than good* . . . So much prudence, so much perseverance, so much disinterestedness, and so much patriotism are necessary among the leaders of a nation that sometimes my fears nearly preponderate over my expectations," he confessed.

Dealing with the revolutionaries' French allies in the recent war had honed Washington's diplomatic skills. It had also confirmed the president's unblinking assessment of human nature. Grateful as Washington was for military assistance from King Louis, he said at the time, "It is a maxim founded in the universal experience of mankind, that no nation is to be trusted farther than it is bound by its interest." For proof, he need only visit the stable at Mount Vernon housing Royal Gift, an enormous jackass presented by an admiring Spanish monarch for breeding to American mares. Disdaining thirty-three fillies prepared as a harem, Royal Gift appeared to his owner too aristocratic to sample such "republican enjoyments" as the New World offered. Even as Washington, desperate for cash to support his official household, advertised the jack's services in Virginia gazettes at $10 per mare, he wrote humorously that the creature was "too full of royalty to have anything to do with a plebeian race."

His Most Catholic Majesty in Madrid was less generous in granting Washington's countrymen use of the broad, vital Mississippi River, and the president was understandably concerned. Let imperial Spain choke off access to the arterial waterway and more than American commerce would suffer. American unity would be affected as well, especially among Westerners of fluctuating loyalties, for whom the government in New York held credibility in direct proportion to its sanction of their territorial ambitions. "Unless we can connect the new states which are rising to our view in these regions, with those in the Atlantic by *interest* (the only bonding cement)," Washington had written, "they will be quite a different people and ultimately may be very troublesome neighbors to us."

Other foreign powers also encroached on his national vision. As a young man, Washington had taken to cracking walnuts between his powerful jaws. Neither the subsequent loss of all but one tooth nor the swelling inflammation caused by replacements carved from hippopotamus tusk, for which he dosed himself with laudanum, could exceed his discomfort when he looked at a map in the spring of 1789. The United States, with four million inhabitants and 865,000 square miles, resembled one of his walnuts, precariously wedged between Spanish holdings in Florida and Louisiana, excitable Creeks in Georgia, and an arrogant Britain clinging to seven northwestern forts despite the 1783 treaty ending the war.

The task before Washington, then, was one of infinite delicacy, requiring the prowess of a born diplomat. Unhappily, America lost its most experienced legate, Benjamin Franklin, during the first year of the administration. As one of his last acts, Dr. Franklin had bequeathed a crabtree walking stick topped by a golden cap of liberty to "my friend, and the friend of mankind, General Washington . . . If it were a scepter, he had merited it and would become it."

Balding, hook-nosed John Jay, the secretary of foreign affairs under the expired confederation, was also unavailable, having had accepted Washington's offer to become the nation's first chief justice. Irascible John Adams, an expatriate out of touch with the people he represented, had returned from St. James's to serve as Washington's vice presidential understudy. A thankless job for any man, the second office was torture for the proud, prickly New Englander cast as occasional confidant and frequent lightning rod to the vastly more popular chief executive, whom Adams, in moments of pique, called Old Muttonhead.

All of which left Thomas Jefferson as a most reluctant contender for the position of secretary of state. Summoned home from France, where he had brilliantly filled Dr. Franklin's outsize shoes, the Virginian's natural optimism, combined with faith in Washington and favorable news out of New York, persuaded him that the federal experiment might yet succeed. Still, he qualified his hopes with a significant caveat. "If the President can be preserved for a few more years, till habits of authority and obedience can be established," wrote Jefferson, "we have nothing to fear."

Long before Jefferson reluctantly yielded to his friend's entreaties, Washington conveyed his own misgivings in a letter to an English admirer. "Nothing short of an absolute conviction of duty could ever have brought me upon the scenes of public life again," he wrote early in 1790. "The establishment of our new government seemed to be the last great experiment for promoting happiness by reasonable compact in civil society . . . a government of accommodation as well as a government of laws. Much was to be done by *prudence*, much by *conciliation*, and much by *firmness*. Few who are not philosophical spectators can realize the difficult and delicate part which a man in my situation had to act . . . if I may use the expression, I walk on untrodden ground."

Washington underestimated the weapons at his command. They included a vast reserve of public affection, international prestige, and political finesse developed over forty years on the popular stage. When Louis-Guillaume Otto, France's chargé d'affaires in New York, wrote to his government that same month, he marveled at the seeming unanimity of Washington's support. "Never has the citizen of a free country enjoyed among his compatriots a confidence as pure and as universal. In more than one hundred gazettes, often very licentious, published daily in the United States, his name has constantly been respected; in an assembly composed of so many heterogeneous individuals as is that of Congress, he has always been spoken of with veneration."

Sensitive as a tuning fork, Washington regularly inquired into what others said and thought of him. His uneasiness grew in the weeks after his return to New York's social whirl, thanks to whispered complaints about the royalist trappings of 39 Broadway. Democrats like William Maclay objected to the president's Tuesday afternoon levees, rigidly choreographed functions where bows substituted for handshakes and Washington did a convincing imitation of himself, dressed in black velvet ordered from Europe at $5 a yard, along with yellow gloves, silver knee buckles, and glistening dress sword in a white leather scabbard.

When the presidential bow came in for criticism, Washington was hurt. His greetings were bestowed indiscriminately, he protested to friends, "the best I was master of; would it not have been better to throw the veil of charity over them, ascribing their stiffness to the effects of age or to the unskillfulness of my teacher, than to pride and dignity of office, which God knows has no charms for me?" Besides, he insisted, he would rather be at Mount Vernon with a friend or two than surrounded by the officers of state and all of Europe's grandees.

This was true; Washington submitted to the weekly audiences at the behest of advisers who warned against familiarity (for the same reason he refused to attend funerals or private dinners) as inconsistent with the new government's republican dignity. But in doing so he paid a heavy emotional price. Washington's adopted granddaughter recalled a man imprisoned by his own celebrity. "He liked to see us gay and happy," Nelly Custis wrote of the seemingly austere chief executive. "I have often made him laugh heartily at the relation of my frolics and difficulties." Even so, "his presence generally chilled my young companions, and his own near relatives feared to speak or laugh before him. This was occasioned by the awe and respect he inspired and not from his severity. When he entered a room where we were all mirth and in high conversation, all were instantly mute. He would sit a short time and then retire, quite provoked and disappointed, but they could not repress their feelings."

For Washington there was no escaping the consequences of fame. Having carved the statue of his own reputation, he could not easily climb down from the pedestal. Perhaps this as much as anything accounted for the comment made in the spring of 1790 by a visitor to the Macomb House, who said that the president wore a look of habitual gravity, "sobriety that stopped short of sadness."

⁑ 2 ⁕

WASHINGTONOPOLIS, D.C.

"While I am shut up here in this pigsty, smelling per-
fumes from wharves and the rakings of gutters, I long
for the air and company of Springfield."

Congressman Fisher Ames,
on the charms of Manhattan

DISLIKING OFFICIAL LIFE, Martha Washington was at best ambivalent toward America's capital. In a letter of October 1789 she had confided, only half in jest, "I live a very dull life and know nothing that passes in the town. I never go to any public place. Indeed, I think I am more like a state prisoner than anything else; there are certain bounds set for me which I must not depart from, and as I cannot do as I like, I am obstinate and stay at home a great deal."

There was plenty to occupy Martha at home, however. Each morning she had her gray hair dressed. She maintained a lively interest in Mount Vernon, relying on the plantation for Virginia hams, Potomac shad, and vegetables unobtainable in New York. The household staff at 39 Broadway numbered fourteen, including a steward, cook, house and kitchen maids, washers, and a valet de chambre for her husband. With his faithful man-servant Will Lee disabled by drink, Washington employed Julian L'Hoste to keep his hair powder and the black silk bags that held the presidential queue, secured by narrow black ribbons called solitaires. Seven slaves brought from Mount Vernon supplemented the white servants, who earned an average monthly wage of $7. In the scarlet and white livery of the Washingtons, serving the "rich oily wine" favored by the president, they danced to the tune of Samuel Fraunces, "Black Sam" thanks to his West Indian ancestry, whose profligate ways finally got him in trouble after the morning he presented Washington with an out-of-season shad costing $2. Black Sam left the household not long after.

But the bills piled up anyway: $165 a month, not counting the heavy tab for wines, spirits, cider, Madeira, and hickory wood with which to heat the large house. More went for the first lady's clothing, displayed to good effect at her Friday night levees, portrayed by Abigail Adams as "usually very full of the well born and well bred. Sometimes . . . as full as her Brittanick Majesties Room, and with quite as handsome ladies, and as polite courtiers . . . they chat with each other, swish about, fine ladies show themselves, and as candlelight is a great improver of beauty, they appear to great advantage."

Washington unwound at his wife's receptions, laying aside his sword and cocked hat to mingle with the ladies, "which he does with a grace, dignity and ease," according to Mrs. Adams, "that leaves Royal George far behind him." Women occupied the limited seating while gentlemen were content to stand. The center of attention was Lady Washington, her dark gown set off by a coral and gold brooch, earrings, and a locket containing strands of her husband's hair. In Abigail's estimation, Martha was "plain in her dress, but that plainness is the best of every article. Her hair is white, her teeth beautiful, her person rather short than otherwise . . . Her manners are modest and unassuming, dignified and feminine, nor the tincture of hauteur about her."

As the hall clock sounded nine strokes, Mrs. Washington stood beside her husband in the spacious reception room at 39 Broadway. "The General always retires at nine," she announced mildly, "and I usually precede him." With that, they took their leave, an aging couple of dwindling vitality doing their best to play the part assigned them by circumstance.

The same mix of precision and bemused tolerance for human frailty was displayed at the president's weekly state dinners, resumed after his recovery and held each Thursday afternoon at four o'clock. The chief executive waited five minutes for tardy guests to arrive before entering the dining room. "Sir, we are too punctual for you," latecomers were told crisply. "I have a cook who never asks whether the company has come, but whether the hour has come." The misanthropic William Maclay left descriptions, more vivid than perceptive, of mirthless meals at which a distracted president drummed his fork on the table. But Maclay did not take into account the fact that most of Washington's guests were virtual strangers. Under the circumstances, when so much as an arched eyebrow could start rumors, it was better to bore one's guests than provoke them.

A gracious host in the Virginia tradition, the president encouraged diners to help themselves to a profusion of uncovered dishes. He thereby risked the misunderstanding of Maclay, who detected in Washington's singling him out for a generous portion of pudding lobbying for the

Hamiltonian program. As a rule, Washington limited himself to a single dinner course, washed down by a glass of wine and beer drunk from a silver pint cup. Rich confections were turned aside as "too good for me." After the ladies withdrew, the president had a second glass of Madeira and pronounced his customary toast — "All our friends" — before rejoining the women for coffee and light conversation. Women liked Washington, often more than men did, for reasons that went beyond his unfailing chivalry. Perhaps they sensed his enjoyment of their company and more than ornamental talents.

For a taste of New York parlor society, Washington dropped in on Chief Justice Jay, a high-toned Federalist with whom he also hitched a carriage ride to church one Sunday. Alternatively, he could drink tea at the Queen Street residence of Governor and Mrs. George Clinton. The governor was an old friend and amateur botanist who had supplied linden trees for Mount Vernon. He was also a wartime ally from whom Washington was determined to let nothing alienate him, least of all Clinton's anti-Federalist leanings. Men's opinions were as variant as their faces, wrote Washington, and where their motives were pure, no more to be questioned than nature itself.

Striving to remain above partisan politics, Washington was careful to label the new regime "national" rather than "federalist." Little more than a year into his term, the outlook was bright enough to justify a decidedly optimistic prospectus. "Our government is now happily carried into operation," he reported to Lafayette early in June 1790. "Although some thorny questions still remain, it is to be hoped that the wisdom of those concerned in the national legislature will dispose of them prudently." Tiny Rhode Island had recently joined the Union, ending the last holdout among the original thirteen colonies, and Vermont might soon add its name to the federal roster; while in the Northwest Territory, General Arthur St. Clair presided over additional states in the making.

Conceding public anxiety over Hamilton's fiscal program, Washington was quick to add that national revenues were far outstripping forecasts. So long as the East Indies trade flourished, federal coffers would never run dry: a single ship dropping anchor in New York Harbor paid $30,000 in import duties to the Treasury's customs agents. Meanwhile, American commerce was reaching the far corners of the globe. A fur vessel fitted out for $7,000 had managed to dock in Canton, half a world away, depositing $100,000 in earnings from the voyage. "I mention this to show the spirit of enterprise that prevails," said Washington with undisguised pride.

Stung by criticism from "irritable, sour and discontented" Virginians, the president assured a friend in Alexandria that abolitionist agitation was at an end and that restive Southerners could expect justice from a government increasingly friendly to commercial speculation. Then he lodged a complaint repeated by each of his successors, asserting, "The misfortune is the enemies of the government. If they tell the truth, it is not the whole truth."

At length, he came to the most divisive issue of the day.

"The question of Assumption has occupied a great deal of time, and no wonder, for it is certainly a very important one; and, under *proper* restrictions, and scrutiny into accounts will be found, I conceive, to be just. The cause in which the expenses of the war was incurred was a common cause. The states (in Congress) declared it so at the beginning and pledged themselves to stand by each other. If, then, some states were harder pressed than others, or from particular or local circumstances contracted heavier debts, it is but reasonable when this fact is ascertained (though it is a sentiment I have not made known here) that an allowance ought to be made them when due credit is given to others."

❦ 2 ❧

The president's caution explains itself when one understands the extraordinarily diverse society he led. Assumption presumed a uniformity that did not exist in Washington's United States, a sparsely inhabited archipelago stretching fifteen hundred miles from the Bay of Fundy to Spanish Florida. Less than a third of the domain claimed by the government in New York was actually settled, an area roughly the size of modern Texas. "The entire country is one vast wood," concluded a French traveler, C. F. Volney. As befitting a coastal people sandwiched between the Atlantic and the Alleghenies, the 1790 census fixed the country's population center at Chestertown, Maryland, twenty-three miles east of Baltimore.

More than once Washington had cause to complain of roads that were "infamous." How bad they were depended on one's place of residence. Northern stagecoach passengers considered themselves fortunate to make the journey from Boston to New York in less than a week. Far worse was the South. With almost one fifth of the nation's population, Virginia was a nearly impassable backwater; its largest city, Richmond, claimed fewer than four thousand people. Of eight streams athwart his path from Monticello to Washington, Thomas Jefferson once complained, five had neither bridge nor ferry. Except for a lone stage running between Charleston and Savannah, not a single public conveyance served the lower South.

Seventy-seven post offices connected Americans in 1790, but only just. South of Petersburg, Virginia, the mail went on horseback, so obstructed were the roads, and it took three weeks or more for a letter postmarked in Maine to reach Georgia. Slicing across so vast and rugged a landscape, rivers and their manmade equivalents sparked feverish dreams among visionaries like Washington, who long before assuming the presidency had held a similar position in the Potomac Navigation Company. Washington the nationalist hoped to harness the James and Potomac rivers to the mighty Ohio, "la belle rivière," thus defying the Appalachians he had scaled as a callow colonel and stitching together the distinct societies perched on either side of the nation's mountainous spine.

West of the Blue Ridge and north of the Ohio, where "grubbers" cleared land in return for three shillings a day and whiskey for breakfast and dinner, it was said that an enterprising squirrel could travel a thousand miles across a highway of treetops without ever touching the ground. South of the Ohio settlement proceeded more rapidly, with villages like Boonesboro and Nashville providing the seed around which a rougher, more elemental civilization crystallized.

Like ancient Gaul, the United States in 1790 was divided into three parts (exclusive of the unorganized West), each with its own climate, social system, and economic requirements. The previous fall, Washington had renewed his long-standing acquaintance with "the Eastern states" of New England, an uncompromising region of stony fields and stony men. Yet even here pluralism was the rule, as Washington adroitly demonstrated one Sabbath in New Haven, Connecticut, by attending morning Episcopal services and Congregational rites in the afternoon. Elsewhere he sampled the fruits of Yankee industry by ordering Hartford breeches for his servants, examining silkworms in nearby Wallingford, and marveling over 175,000 pairs of shoes produced annually in the North Shore village of Lynn, Massachusetts.

With the Atlantic for their front yard, New Englanders pursued commercial wealth like a Nantucket harpooner chasing the whale's spout over the horizon. Wrote J. Hector St. John Crèvecoeur, "Those who live near the sea feed more on fish than on flesh and often encounter that boisterous element. This renders them more bold and enterprising." Unfortunately, in visiting the port of Marblehead, Washington also found confirming evidence of Crèvecoeur's belief that seagoing men "neglect the confined occupations of the land." The little town's streets were dirty, he said. Worse, "the common people are not very clean."

The Middle States from New York to Maryland served as the nation's breadbasket and its most conspicuous melting pot. Here the schoolhouses of New England yielded to urban countinghouses and a materialistic culture whose polyglot elements shared little but the taste for prosperity. John Adams assessed the difference between Boston, where learning was sacred, and New York, where money was king. "With all the opulence and splendor of this city, there is little good breeding to be found," said Adams. "At their entertainments, there is no conversation that is agreeable; there is no modesty, no attention to one another. They talk very loud, very fast and all together."

Robert Morris, one of Washington's closest associates, talked as much as anyone, mostly of profits to be made. Born in England, he immigrated to Philadelphia as a teenager and by the age of twenty was a full partner in a mercantile house. Initially opposed to separation from Britain, Morris went on to win fame as the Financier of the Revolution, at one critical juncture raising $1.4 million on his personal word to pay Washington's long-suffering troops. After the war, the aspiring tycoon organized the Bank of North America and obtained a monopoly on American tobacco exports to France. Rumor named him Washington's first choice for secretary of the treasury, but the ambitious speculator instead took a seat in the Senate and commenced building a marble palace in Philadelphia.

"The country is rushing into wealth and importance faster than ever was expected by the most sanguine," Morris assured foreign investors. He himself was rushing pellmell toward bankruptcy and a debtor's cell in the Prune Street Prison. At the moment, however, he envisioned his millions of acres in New York State, most beyond the white man's grasp, as a source of incalculable riches. He dreamed of even greater returns should Congress locate the permanent capital on land he owned near the Falls of the Delaware, with a temporary encampment at Germantown, in the Philadelphia suburbs. Not surprisingly, Morris favored Hamilton's assumption plan, since it promised immediate and lavish dividends on his investment. Where the two men did not see eye to eye was on where to build a capital — or whether to build one at all.

Most Pennsylvanians regarded Philadelphia as a natural home for the federal government conceived there in the summer of 1787. Laid out in neat red brick squares, William Penn's city looked and felt English. A French visitor found stark contrasts with his native Paris: "The men are grave, the women serious; no financial airs, no libertine wives . . . no agreeable walks." After sailing a hundred miles up the Delaware River, a European would find Penn's "greene countrie towne" a dull place, "because he could not strut upon a boulevard, babble in a coffeehouse, or seduce a pretty woman by his important airs and fine curls."

As a delegate to the Constitutional Convention, Washington had frequented William Bartram's famous Botanical Garden, America's first, finding the seven-acre plot indifferently laid out and too small for his taste. More to his liking was Gray's Ferry, a popular garden spot three miles southwest of the steamy State House chamber reserved for convention sessions. The shadow of Franklin loomed large over the American Philosophical Society as well as Philadelphia's Library Company, with its twelve thousand volumes. Franklin's radical spirit also informed the most egalitarian politics in America, especially among the frugal German farmers who populated the eastern part of the state and frontiersmen striking out for Pittsburgh and points west.

"Too thoroughly democratic to fear democracy," wrote John Adams's great-grandson Henry, "and too much nationalized to dread nationality, Pennsylvania became the ideal American state, easy, tolerant, and contented. If its soil bred little genius, it bred still less treason. With twenty different religious creeds, its practice could not be narrow, and a strong Quaker element made it humane."

Adams's ideal was anything but for southern advocates of states' rights, fearful of losing their identity in a union authorized to levy stiff taxes and carry a large, continuing debt. Hamilton's assumption plan would transfer both power and money to the central government. This was anathema to democrats like William Maclay and the emerging critics of Hamiltonian finance, led by the secretary's erstwhile friend and literary collaborator, James Madison. Both men found fertile ground in the South, otherwise planted in tobacco, rice, and indigo. In 1790, three years before Whitney patented his cotton gin, Southerners exported just four hundred bales of the snowy white plant. Long before cotton was crowned king, however, the South was already a place apart, dominated socially and politically by aristocrats hoping to reproduce, with the essential aid of African slaves, English country life.

Virginia gentlemen expected to reach heaven as Anglicans or not at all, assuming they wished to forsake God's Country in the first place. Even Washington, for all the breadth of his outlook, was an unabashed booster of the Shenandoah Valley, "the Garden of America" in which he had extensive land holdings. Yet there was a darker side to the haughty Old Dominion, attested to by a French traveler who observed there the first wretchedly poor people he had seen since leaving his native land. The country houses might be sumptuous and the dinner fare plentiful, but summer visitors crowded three or four to a room were nearly devoured by seed ticks and bedbugs.

Clannish and proud, Virginians looked askance at their rustic neighbors in North Carolina, a forested wilderness valued chiefly for its lumber and naval stores. Caste also held sway in South Carolina, where pleasure-loving Charlestonians lorded it over their Tidewater cousins. Everyone, it seemed, felt superior to Georgians forced to subsist on salt pork and hominy while battling Creek warriors and a federal regime hard-pressed to contain the state's greed for Indian lands.

When describing conditions south of the Potomac, the president could not tell a lie. "Toward the seaboard of all the southern states (and farther South the more so)," he contended, "the country is low, sandy and unhealthy, for which reason I shall say little concerning them, for as I shall not choose to be an inhabitant of them myself, I ought not to say anything that would induce others to be so."

❦ 3 ❦

"That there is a diversity of interests in the Union no one has denied," Washington told a friend in the summer of 1790, warning of regional animosities. "That this is the case also in every state is equally certain . . . but I ask again which is most blameworthy, those who see and will steadily pursue their interest, or those who cannot see, or seeing will not act wisely?"

Here was a coded endorsement of the Federalist program, combining a strong central government with a unified financial structure, topped by a presidential cult of personality bordering on adulation. Although there was as yet no formally organized opposition party, neither was there any shortage of anti-Federalists, whose earlier suspicions of the Constitution were daily confirmed by Hamilton's seeming disregard for states' rights, agrarian interests, and the classical republican aptipathy toward concentrated power. For the moment, the president hoped somehow to bridge the widening chasm of partisan politics.

Washington moved aggressively, if stealthily, to knit the sections together, organizing in effect a coalition government around a Cabinet made up of men from Massachusetts, New York, and Virginia. For the first Supreme Court he again chose from the Big Three, diversifying its ranks by reaching out to Pennsylvania, Maryland, and South Carolina as well. The justices' accents differed more than their politics; Washington made certain that each was a warmhearted friend to the new government.

Next to geography and philosophy, personal ability governed Washington's appointments. Old soldiers received little special consideration, the president's kin none at all. Pointedly excluded from office was his favorite nephew, Bushrod. "My political conduct in nominations, even if I were uninfluenced by principle, must be exceedingly circumspect and proof against just criticism," said Washington, "for the eyes of Argus are upon me, and no step will pass unnoticed that can be improved into a supposed partiality for friends or relatives."

Except for his private declaration that assumption of state debts "under proper restrictions . . . I conceive to be just" and a finely shaded critique of Madison's efforts to discriminate between the original holders of government debt and speculators who later bought up postwar bounties earned in blood, Washington was understandably hesitant about entering the legislative arena. Not only was the mythical Argus scrutinizing his conduct; so were authentic, hypercritical anti-Federalists like William Maclay. Through eyes narrowed in suspicion or blazing with mistrust, the junior senator from Pennsylvania seized upon each telltale sign of administration influence behind the Hamiltonian program as proof of the president's partiality toward monied interests.

Maclay was disgusted but not surprised to hear his Senate colleague Robert Morris insist on the passage of assumption. "By God it must be done!" thundered Morris, who had compelling if ethically questionable reasons for believing so. Next came "a florid harangue" from Major Jackson, the president's personal secretary, extolling the virtues of Philadelphia as a permanent capital and the wisdom of bartering Pennsylvania votes to secure both assumption and residence. Worse yet was the comment of Maclay's ally, Speaker of the House Frederick Muhlenberg. Coming straight from a presidential levee, he declared, "The state debts must be adopted." A bitter Maclay concluded, "This, I suppose, is the language of the court."

The court perhaps, but not the king. Unknown to Maclay, the president regularly asked for reports on men and measures "and of none more than myself; not so much of what may be thought commendable parts, if any, of my conduct as of those which are conceived to be of a different complexion." What he heard early in 1790 confirmed his reluctance to advocate assumption openly or designate a personal favorite in the residency sweepstakes. His views on the nation's credit were already on the record. During the Revolution, an irate General Washington had written despairingly that "party disputes and personal quarrels are the great business of the day, while the momentous concerns of an empire — a great and accumulated debt, ruined finances, depreciated money, and the want of credit . . . are but secondary considerations and postponed from day to day, from week to week."

Now, some fifteen years later, with assumption tottering on the brink of defeat, Washington held back. Why? Perhaps because Hamilton's plans had become mired in the toils of private speculation and he hated these "pests of society" almost as much as he desired sound credit. "I would to God that one of the most atrocious of each state was hung in gibbets upon a gallows five times as high as the one prepared for Haman," he had declared angrily during the war. "No punishment in my opinion is too great for the man who can build his greatness upon his country's ruin."

There was more than one way to secure assumption of state debts, however, and Washington had a strong hand to play. The new nation required a capital, and New Yorkers were eager to oblige, but by committing themselves early to Hamilton's schemes, they had unintentionally bargained away their hopes. Even had they played the game more shrewdly, they would still have had to recognize that most Americans in 1790 believed New York almost laughably unrepresentative of the nation it presumed to govern.

Among the city's harshest critics was Thomas Jefferson. Throughout the day, carts carrying water from the Tea Water Pump on Chatham Street creaked down Broadway. One of their stops was City Tavern, which, like the rest of George Washington's capital, had no running water. Inside the rambling wooden structure, Jefferson worked on a report to Congress proposing a national mint and a uniform currency to replace the bewildering array of Spanish pistoles, doubloons, half guineas, pounds, and carolines then circulating from Maine to Georgia. Periodically he dosed his continuing "Head-Ack" with Peruvian bark, a forerunner of quinine.

Jefferson's pain was only partly physical. In becoming secretary of state, the worldly Virginian had traded the civilized joys of *la vie parisienne* for a shabby, provisional capital, the home of 33,000 people, 22 churches, 6 markets, a post office, a bank, and 330 groghouses. Worst of all, New York was teeming with financial speculators unsympathetic to the secretary's agrarian outlook. In Paris, Jefferson boasted, a man might go a lifetime without encountering a single rudeness. New York was a raucous reproach to French *politesse*, reeking of mud, horses, and "corporation pudding," human wastes carried off in the night by Negro slaves bearing tubs, then dumped in gutters to tempt roving schools of pigs and wild dogs.

According to one congressman, John Page of Virginia, "The town is not half so large as Philadelphia, nor in any way to be compared to it for beauty and elegance . . . The streets are badly paved, dirty and narrow, as well as crooked." Page was premature; New York's first sidewalks were being laid out that spring. Just wide enough for two persons to walk abreast, they hugged the west side of Broadway from Vesey to Murray. No shade trees lent dignity to the ramshackle wooden houses set back from the street. (Most of them had recently been cut down, by municipal order, for reasons never fully explained.) Privately dug wells pitted Broadway every four blocks. Many streets lay ankle deep in dust except when it rained, when they became mud baths for the unsuspecting. Hogs on the prowl for garbage sometimes impeded the Father of His Country as he made his way down Broadway in a canary yellow coach, pulled by four white horses. The contingent grew to six if Washington's destination was Federal Hall, a structure described with hometown hyperbole by the *New York Morning Post and Daily Advertiser* as "an edifice that would grace any metropolis in Europe" and scorned by enemies of the new government as "a fool's trap."

Actually, Federal Hall was a hasty improvisation, having served as New York's crumbling City Hall until its $65,000 reconstruction in 1788–89 by Pierre Charles L'Enfant. The president had mixed feelings about the place. At the time of his inaugural, Wall and Broad streets had resounded to cheers from twenty thousand onlookers. In their formal response to his address, senators bent the knee. "In you all parties confide, in you all interests unite," they gushed. Yet just four months later, Washington met his match in William Maclay, as suspicious of an energetic national government as Washington was supportive.

Regarding the recently adopted Constitution as "the vilest of all traps that was ever set to ensnare the freedom of an unsuspecting people," the populist tribune from Harrisburg opposed the creation of a 5,000-man standing army — or a War Department, for that matter. Maclay spoke out against a $40,000 appropriation with which to establish a diplomatic presence for the United States overseas. He took violent exception to Hamilton's plan to consolidate $75 million in outstanding debt, thereby spinning a golden web linking monied interests to a government strong enough to protect their investments. As he saw it, Hamilton and his stock-jobbing allies hardly bothered to conceal their true object, "to create a mass of debt, which will justify them in seizing state legislatures and erecting an empire on the basis of consolidation."

On August 22, 1789, taking literally his constitutional charge to advise and consent with lawmakers over a proposed treaty involving southern Indian tribes, Washington had appeared in Federal Hall. Senator Maclay moved to refer the whole business to an appropriate committee of Congress. For a moment, Washington lost his legendary poise. "This defeats every purpose of my coming here," he exploded. Soon after he withdrew, vowing he would be damned rather than face such public humiliation again. In a single exchange Maclay and his colleagues had asserted their independence, undone the executive's plan to treat them as a kind of privy council, and laid the groundwork for a very different set of presidential advisers, the Cabinet.

It is an enduring irony that most of what we know about the first Congress, its ninety-five members and the ninety-four bills they enacted into law, comes from the splenetic pen of William Maclay. What makes his diary so irresistibly quotable is its author's lively gift for personal invective leavened by rough wit and a lightning streak of paranoia. Five-foot, four-inch James Madison was not the legislative genius behind the

Bill of Rights but a diminutive pedant, "His Littleness." Maclay dismissed Gouverneur Morris, Washington's rakish personal representative to the Court of St. James's, as "half envoy, half pimp." A special target of the diarist's wrath was John Adams, already in bad odor for trying to bestow a grandiloquent title on the president. Maclay glanced at the presiding officer under his canopy of crimson damask one afternoon and was reminded of a "monkey just put into breeches."

Most of all, Maclay loathed New York. Its men were fops, he concluded, its women overpadded slaves to fashion. New Yorkers strolled Broadway "bent forward at the middle . . . as if some disagreeable disorder prevented them from standing erect." Working in primary colors, Maclay missed the shadings of a city still struggling to its feet. Fourteen years after a devastating fire destroyed much of its housing, seven years since the end of British occupation, scarcely less demoralizing than the flames, the town was feverishly rebuilding. Land was almost absurdly plentiful; a Lutheran church spurned the gift of six acres at Canal and Broadway as not worth fencing in.

George Washington's New York was a horizontal city. At two hundred feet, the spire of Trinity Church was Manhattan's tallest. An hour's ramble encompassed official New York, from Bowling Green to distant Greenwich, where Vice President Adams and his saucy, outspoken wife, Abigail, lived in a manor house called Richmond Hill. The serenading partridge and woodcock of Richmond Hill held little allure for old-line barons like the Livingstons — eighteen of whom petitioned Washington for jobs in the new government — or the Beekmans, Osgoods, Courtlandts, and Van Rensselaers holding court in stone mansions downtown outlined by streetlamps on moonless nights.

The Washingtons were frequent visitors at the tiny John Street Theater, where a stage box was set aside for the couple and the president's attendance was heralded by playbills inscribed *Vivat Republica*. Yet even here Washington could not fully relax, for he knew that the audience had assembled to see him as much as any cast on the stage. The president was on hand for *Darby's Return*, a farce revolving around an old soldier's return home to America. Vowed the male lead:

> There too I saw some mighty pretty shows;
> A revolution, without blood or blows,
> For, as I understand, the cunning elves,
> The people all revolted from themselves.

Washington stiffened visibly as Darby was asked to describe "a man who fought to free the land from woe." Surely, if past practice were any guide, this portended a fulsome tribute. Much to the president's surprise and amusement, however, Darby said that he could not comply with the request, having mistaken for the chief magistrate another figure, "all lace and glitter, botherum and shine." Delighted by the gentle satire, Washington indulged in hearty laughter.

Grumbling about the cost of living in Washington's capital was endemic. A saddle horse earned more in an hour than a skilled laborer could in a day. One French visitor noted that "the fees of lawyers are out of all proportion." Others complained of paying 20 shillings a month for hairdressers and $4 for a cord of wood. One adult male in seven languished in debtors' prison, some in attic apartments from which they solicited passing strangers by hanging out old shoes as secular collection plates, or the almshouse, where paupers were maintained for ten cents a day.

Then as now, New York was a babble of tongues. German, French, Portuguese, Italian, Polish, Hebrew, the brogue of Ireland, and the Scot's burr competed with the Dutch of New Amsterdam's original settlers. One in ten residents was black, one in fourteen the property of a white master. Many of the city's four thousand houses had Dutch gables, but the prevailing style was English: in brick homes with tile roofs, in drawing room fashions, and in a busy port where more than a thousand ships, nearly all of British registry, docked each year to swap gold snuffboxes, Canton china, Siberian wolfskins, blue satin gowns, chairs carved from West Indian mahogany, vegetable face powder, and bananas for Yankee wheat, flour, lumber, and hides.

Both its diversity and its tolerance made New York an easy target for outlanders like Maclay, to whom it appeared a modern Babylon. An army of prostitutes patrolled the city's red-light district, the Holy Ground. Another offensive local habit involved smoking tobacco leaves rolled into six-inch tubes. "It must be disagreeable to the women," judged Jean Pierre Brissot-Warville, the son of a French innkeeper, "by destroying the purity of breath." At City Tavern, Jefferson found a boisterous taproom crowded with government clerks and New England lobbyists quaffing huge amounts of rum, mimbo, rack punch, and pumpkin flip. Few New Yorkers sampled milk, and for good reason: it tasted of garlic, thanks to heavy concentrations of the plant among Long Island dairy herds. Admiring French moderation second only to French cooking, Jefferson was left to shake his aching head.

According to the *Boston Gazette*, "Our beloved President Washington stands unmoved in the vortex of folly and dissipation which New York presents." Abigail Adams registered a familiar complaint. "It is next to impossible to get a servant from the highest to the lowest grade that does not drink, male or female. I have at last found a footman who appears sober," she wrote to her sister, "but he was born in Boston."

{ 4 }

To advocates of limited government like James Madison, worried that an energetic government might actually implement the preamble of the Constitution — operating directly upon individuals ("We, the People") rather than through the states — money-mad New York was the enemy and Alexander Hamilton a serpent in the agrarian Eden of America. On June 13, 1790, Madison wrote to his father that "the business of the seat of government is become a labyrinth, for which the votes furnish no clues and which it is impossible in a letter to explain." Two hundred years later, it is scarcely easier to make sense of the opéra bouffe played out in Manhattan's streets, taverns, and parlors that June. New York was loath to concede its unsuitability as a national capital. Philadelphia nourished hopes, but the wearisome agitation of Quaker abolitionists undermined its claims to southern support.

Virginia, on the other hand, was impossible to overlook, a republican linchpin whose population, translated into modern terms, would exceed that of Texas and California combined. The home of Patrick Henry and George Mason as well as Washington, Jefferson, and Madison, the Old Dominion's distinguished contributions to the Revolution were equaled by its stubborn adherence to anti-Federalist dogma. It was close to the West of manifest destiny and a Potomac River judged by Jefferson "the only point of union which can cement us to our western friends when they shall be formed into separate states."

Thus Washington's preference and Jeffersonian logic together dictated that the capital be located between Virginia and Maryland. It was not logic, however, but local pride, individual greed, and sectional advantage that staked their claims to congressional preference. A confused series of votes awarded the prize variously to New York, Philadelphia, and Baltimore. Philadelphia regained a shaky advantage after a sickly North Carolina lawmaker was brought into the chamber in his bed and nightcap to support the Quaker City, but no one in the middle of June 1790 could predict the final outcome with confidence. Congress, it appeared, was hopelessly lost in Madison's labyrinth.

It was at this juncture that Hamilton arranged to meet Robert Morris for an early morning stroll along the Battery, a popular destination for New York tourists and congressmen engaged in open-air debate. A few weeks earlier, the bluff, broad-shouldered Morris had jested that "we must remove [Washington] to Philadelphia, where he will have room enough to ride as far as he pleased" without resort to Long Island. More seriously, the Financier of the Revolution offered $100,000 on Pennsylvania's behalf, promising to advance the money himself if the state were so short-sighted as to refuse a down payment on residence. Here was language that Hamilton understood, and on the Battery that day, the secretary offered Morris a deal: the capital in exchange for one vote in the Senate and five in the House to pass assumption. Morris lunged at the idea like a cat before a canary, but Hamilton's allies in Massachusetts and South Carolina would not hear of it, so the nimble New Yorker turned to an unlikely place for his margin of victory.

On June 18, Thomas Jefferson had his own encounter with Hamilton outside 39 Broadway. Jefferson's report of the meeting, colored by time and partisan animosity, portrayed an agitated Hamilton walking him up and down the street for half an hour, pleading for help in averting a total collapse of the national experiment. "He observed that the members of the administration ought to act in consort," Jefferson long after recalled, "that the President was the center on which all administrative questions ultimately rested, and that all of us should rally around him and support with joint efforts measures approved by him."

Implicit in Hamilton's appeal was the knowledge shared by Washington's colleagues of the president's support for a modified assumption plan. This set the table for the famous candlelight bargain, when Jefferson prodded Madison to switch just enough votes from Virginia and Maryland to ensure the passage of assumption in the House. In return, after a ten-year interim during which Philadelphia would serve as the nation's capital, the seat of government would remove permanently to a new city to be created on the banks of the Potomac (sometimes confused with its western tributary, the Conococheague).

Senators narrowly approved the Potomac site on July 1. The House concurred a few days later, and before the month was out assumption, recast to meet Washington's objections, sailed through both houses of Congress. One congressman, returning from a tour of the future city, urged that it be named Washingtonopolis. More immediately, lawmakers authorized the president to name three commissioners to assist him in creating the Grand Columbian Federal City, for which they provided neither money nor a reasonable plan to obtain any. Washington was personally entrusted with the capital's final location, somewhere along an eighty-mile line from the Eastern Branch of the Potomac to the distant, much-maligned Conococheague.

All this was enough to make a grown New Yorker cry, as Rufus King demonstrated on the Senate floor once news of the deal leaked out. His constituents expressed less delicate feelings of abandonment. Some predicted that grass would grow in their streets and wolves appear on Wall Street. The poet and satirist Philip Freneau gave voice to this anger in his ode "The New York House Maid to Her Friend in Philadelphia."

> This Congress unsettled is, sure a sad thing,
> Seven years, my dear Nancy, they've been on the wing,
> My master would rather saw timber, or dig
> Then see them removing to Conococheague —
> Where the homes and the kitchens are yet to be framed,
> The trees to be felled and the streets to be named.

Not a few among Freneau's bitterly disappointed readers pointed accusing fingers at 39 Broadway. When the mayor and council commissioned John Trumbull to celebrate Washington's "well-known virtues" by painting his portrait, Thomas Greenleaf's *New York Journal* demanded justification: "It is asked, which are the virtues that render him so respectable . . . that inflexible justice, that distinguished gratitude to the city of New York, in giving his sanction to the unconstitutional residence bill?" Greenleaf denounced the move in colorful language, assailing the prostitute "Miss Assumption" and her bastard twins "Potowmac" and "Philadelphia." An irreverent letter writer managed the unlikely feat of denigrating and deifying Washington in the same sentence, describing the proposed transfer as "a political trap set for the integrity of the executive . . . tempting our Savior into sin."

But the last and harshest word was left, typically, to William Maclay. "The President of the United States has (in my opinion) had great influence in this business," he alleged on July 15. "The game was played by him and his adherents of Virginia and Maryland . . . But I did not then see so clearly that the abomination of the funding system and the Assumption were so intimately connected with it. Alas! That the affection, nay almost adoration, of the people should meet so unworthy a return . . . the President has become in the hands of Hamilton the dishclout of every dirty speculation, as his name goes to wipe away blame and silence all murmuring."

Washington's exact role may never be known. Certainly he left nothing on paper to justify Maclay's intemperate charges. Neither did Hamilton write a line, then or ever, to buttress Jefferson's version of the celebrated swap of assumption for residence. On August 10, Washington analyzed recent events in a blandly informative letter to his French admirer, the marquis de la Luzerne. "Nothing very remarkable" had occurred since May, said the president, before contradicting himself in the next paragraph.

"The two great questions of funding the debt and fixing the seat of government have been agitated, as was natural, with a good deal of warmth as well as ability. These were always considered by me as questions of the most delicate and interesting nature . . . They were more in danger of having convulsed the government itself than any other perils. I hope they are now stilled in as satisfactory a manner as could have been expected, and that we have a prospect of enjoying peace abroad, with tranquility at home."

Washington said more than he perhaps intended when he explained, "In a government which depends so much on its first stages on public opinion, much circumspection is still necessary for those who are engaged in its administration." Almost as an afterthought he added, "Congress is just on the point of adjourning, after which I propose to pass some time at Mount Vernon."

✦ 3 ✦

CAUNOTAUCARIUS AND
HIS CABINET

"That the government, though not absolutely perfect,
is one of the best in the world, I have little doubt."

George Washington,
January 9, 1790

IN THE SUMMER OF 1790 the North American continent resembled a gigantic chessboard, with Great Britain as black bishop to Spain's white knight. Four nations disputed sovereignty over the Mississippi Valley, each player with its own strategy. The British hoped to incite northern tribes and thereby slow the vanguard of American expansion; the Indians sought protection from the hated Yankees, even at the risk of becoming a cat's paw to continental statesmen. Spanish diplomats summoned bluster where they lacked major settlements or a potent fleet to enforce their country's claims. Brooding in the wings sat France, professing loyalty to its Bourbon allies in Madrid while secretly coveting the return of its former North American empire. Too proud to accept a British presence in the waters of Nootka Sound, near Vancouver Island, and too weak to contest one, Spain pinned its hopes on French support against John Bull.

The resulting war clouds darkened New York skies three thousand miles to the east. The British were in no mood for concessions, as Gouverneur Morris learned during his frustrating stint at the Court of St. James's. From the duke of Leeds, King George's foreign minister, Morris had received little but drawing room courtesies and silken deceptions. Concerning his country's refusal to evacuate western outposts or reimburse slaveholders for property carried off at the end of the war, as stipulated in the Treaty of Paris, his lordship was evasive. Mention of a possible commercial treaty between the former combatants produced "general professions and assurances" that barely cloaked the minister's unwillingness to commit himself or his government.

After Washington showed Morris's latest dispatch to his vice president, John Adams, no stranger to British intransigence, urged a tilt toward Spain lest the United States risk handing over to King George New Orleans and control of the Mississippi River. Washington, aware of a Spanish intrigue involving a military adventurer with the unlikely name of Carlos Howard, was noncommital. The Irish-born Howard, formerly Spain's deputy governor at St. Augustine, had scurried north to Philadelphia carrying $50,000 with which to purchase the quicksilver loyalties of Alexander McGillivray.

The son of a Scot trader and a Creek girl descended from the aristocratic Wind family, McGillivray was a brilliant exotic, destined for tragedy. Suspicious of whites yet dependent on them for trade, the charismatic sachem harbored dreams to equal his resentments. He envisioned a great Indian confederacy uniting the tribes north of the Ohio and south of the Tennessee. To this end he played a complex game involving England, Spain, and the "distracted republick" whose southern outriders were forever encroaching on Creek hunting grounds.

If hell lay to the west, ran a popular refrain, Americans would cross heaven to reach it. For four years white men and red men had made war on each other in the raw Southwest. Hoping to avoid a full-scale confrontation with the Creeks and their Spanish patrons, Washington hatched a secret plan to lure McGillivray to New York, where he might indulge his reported weaknesses for alcohol, women, and bribes to American advantage. Spain, equally resolved to keep the allegiance of its Indian clients, dispatched Carlos Howard in hot pursuit of the backwoods Machiavelli.

Expecting news of the wagon caravan bearing the "Good Child King" and his court north from Georgia, on July 8 Washington heard instead of an extraordinary back-door approach from the British. Major George Beckwith, an aide to Canada's governor-general, Lord Dorchester, was looking for allies wherever they could be found. This caused him to bypass the Francophile Thomas Jefferson in favor of Alexander Hamilton, who thoughtfully informed Beckwith, "We think in English." Assuming as much, the British agent expressed his government's view that in the event of war with the superannuated Spanish regime, the United States was expected to side with King George.

However Hamilton thought, Washington had his own ideas, and at the moment he was feeling none too charitable toward British diplomats. Beckwith's clumsy explanation of his government's refusal to deal with Morris — the American lacked proper credentials, he claimed — moved the president to a derisive outburst.

"We did not incline to give any satisfactory answer to Mr. Morris,"

Washington imagined the men in London to be saying, "who was officially commissioned to ascertain our intentions with respect to the evacuation of the Western posts . . . and other matters . . . until by this unauthenticated mode we can discover whether you will enter into an alliance with us and make common cause against Spain. In that case, we will enter into a commercial treaty with you and *promise perhaps* to fulfill what they already stand engaged to perform."

Sarcasm aside, Washington turned to his closest advisers before taking action. On July 10 he combined business with sightseeing, traveling up Manhattan to the site of old Fort Washington. Joining the party were three future chief executives: John Adams, his son John Quincy, a lawyer just three years out of Harvard and already a skilled polemicist, and Thomas Jefferson. Also present were the secretaries of war and the treasury, Henry Knox and Alexander Hamilton. For once, Washington's dinner conversation must have crackled.

If nothing else, John Adams could be counted on to keep things lively. Perhaps the only American in the summer of 1790 with a tougher assignment than Washington, the vice president was caught between republican ridicule of his aristocratic leanings and Hamilton's aggressive angling for Federalist leadership. Outspoken as always, he was especially heated on the subject of Hamilton's personal morals. "Debauched . . . as old Franklin," he groused. No one questioned Adams's character, only his judgment — and his position. The First Congress was sharply divided between those who thought the vice president should be paid on a perdiem basis and others, like Madison, who argued for a salary commensurate with the second position in the land.

Yet no amount of money could salve Adams's ego or dispel his confusion. "I am Vice President," he remarked a few weeks after assuming office. "In this I am nothing, but I may be everything. But I am president also of the Senate. When the President comes into the Senate, what shall I be?" For much of his first term, Adams cast himself as a majority leader of sorts, actively participating in debates and making no secret of his Federalist sympathies. As time and resentful senators curbed his tongue, he confessed to a friend, "I have no desire ever to open my mouth again upon any question."

Being an Adams, he could not possibly mean it. But he was no Throttlebottom, content to dwell in comfortable obscurity. During his eight years as Washington's understudy, Adams cast twenty-nine tiebreaking votes, more than any of his successors. Washington reciprocated in his own fashion, hinting to northern friends that Adams might succeed him once the new government was firmly established, asking his opinion of official entertaining, and directing Cabinet members to meet with Adams in the president's absence. Each man was indelibly linked to the cause of liberty and to a government sufficiently energetic to protect liberty from mobs and monarchs alike. Each found joy in his field and conversation in his compost — Washington arguing for Potomac mud, Adams loyal to Quincy seaweed.

Yet for all this, the two giants of the Revolution found it difficult to communicate across a gulf imposed by Washington's status and Adams's envy. Fussy, opinionated, and hypersensitive, honest John Adams wore his heart where he displayed his faults, for all to see. Lacking the gift of popularity, he lived uncomfortably in Washington's penumbra. His wife fumed over attacks from journalists too timid to assail the president. "The vice president ten times to one goes to the Senate in a one-horse chaise," she wrote in frustration, "and levees we have had none. The president has his powdered lackeys waiting at the door . . . How inconsistent, railing at titles and giving those which belong to the Deity. Thus it is to be seated high."

Thus indeed. Much later, Abigail's resentful husband would attribute Washington's success to a fortunate marriage, to his Virginia birthright, "as all Virginian geese are swans," even to a majestic physique, "like the Hebrew sovereign chosen because he was taller by the head than the other Jews." In a postscript etched in acid, Adams declared, "You see I have made out ten talents without saying a word about reading, thinking, or writing."

Jefferson, for one, admired such honesty without always appreciating it. Following Washington's victory at Yorktown, he had been made uneasy by news of Adams's appointment to serve on the peace commission. "He hates Franklin, he hates Jay, he hates the French, he hates the English," admitted Jefferson. "To whom will he adhere?" The answer, of course, was the United States, the only thing Adams loved on a par with his family and his farm.

⟨ 2 ⟩

Jefferson shared the general distrust of political factions stamped upon America in 1790. "If I could not go to heaven but with a party, I would not go there at all," he once wrote. Orthodox Christians thought it unlikely that the secretary, embarrassed by miracles and convinced that Unitarianism was his country's national religion, would ever confront the choice. Conspicuous in his red silk breeches, a costume first popularized by French philosophes, Jefferson had less complaint with New York cuisine — in his skylit blue dining room at Monticello, the gourmand secretary of state was accustomed to serving from eight to thirty-two dishes at a setting — than with its intellectual bill of fare; above all, with those anxious to divorce revolutionary France and consort with the harlot England.

Compounding his unhappiness was a bad case of heartache, quite beyond the recuperative powers of Peruvian bark. "I am born to lose everything I love," the normally unemotional Jefferson had lamented while in Paris to Maria Cosway, the beautiful, artistically accomplished wife of a gnomish society painter seventeen years her senior. Sadly for her middle-age suitor, Mrs. Cosway was Catholic as well as married; indeed, she had once hoped to become a nun. This inspired the famous dialogue between Jefferson's head and his heart wherein reason prevailed over passion, as it generally did whenever the two collided in his darting, speculative mind. Finding activity a better antidote for Cupid's disease than Peruvian bark, Jefferson coolly informed Maria, "No laborious person was ever yet hysterical."

Across the Atlantic, Washington watched as his hopes for a union worthy of wartime sacrifice were undermined by local enmities and a confederation government too weak to impose its will. Daniel Shays's pitchfork rebellion of western Massachusetts farmers had caused sleepless nights at Mount Vernon but not at Paris's Hôtel de Langeac. What seemed to Washington an omen of national dissolution struck Jefferson as a necessary purgative. As the worldly diplomat put it, "What signify a few lives lost in a century or two? The tree of liberty must be refreshed from time to time with the blood of patriots and tyrants. It is its natural manure."

Much more skeptical was his response to the Philadelphia convention. Condemning the new Constitution for leaving out a Bill of Rights, Jefferson reserved his harshest censure for the presidential office tailored to Washington's outsize dimensions, yet easily exploitable by future, less exalted occupants bent on winning perpetual reelection, like a bad Polish king. "I own I am not a friend to a very energetic government," Jefferson explained to Madison. "It is always oppressive." In the first week of October 1789, Jefferson sailed for home, leaving behind a city without bread and a people taking the law into their own hands. He expected to return to Paris after a few weeks in which he might place his two daughters and settle his far more numerous debts.

Waiting for him at the Norfolk pier was a letter in Washington's stately hand, inviting the forty-six-year-old diplomat to join the administration in New York as secretary of state. For three months he weighed the costs of relinquishing his front-row seat on revolutionary France for an ill-defined office in graceless Manhattan. To heed the presidential summons meant exchanging his cherished independence for service in a new regime, built to a plan holding little charm for this splendidly self-taught architect. *"I am born to lose everything I love."* Although his only previous administrative experience, a wartime governorship of Virginia, had ended disastrously in flight from invading redcoats, Jefferson eventually yielded to the older man's entreaties.

Even so, his acceptance betrayed his anxieties. "My chief comfort will be to work under your eye," he told Washington, "my only shelter the authority of your name." It was almost as if, having already severed so many emotional connections, Jefferson would cling all the tighter to the aging lion in New York.

The new secretary arrived to take up his duties on a Sunday in March 1790. Amid personal briefings from Washington and a backlog of official correspondence, Jefferson explored a government in embryo. At the State Department he discovered a toy bureaucracy of five clerks spending $8,000 a year to administer the foreign service, oversee territorial affairs, prepare the census, instruct federal marshals and attorneys in their duties, recommend executive pardons, and correspond with state officials as the government's designated intermediary. At $3,500, Jefferson's salary was less than the vice president's but more than Attorney General Edmund Randolph was paid to head his "mongrel department," whose sole occupant was left free to compete for private legal business with New York's one hundred and twenty-one other lawyers.

Unable to secure lodgings on Broadway, Jefferson rented a small house at 57 Maiden Lane. An urgent appeal went out to Petit, his indispensable majordomo at the Hôtel de Langeac. One reading it might gauge the cultivated Virginian's personal pursuit of happiness. Filling eighty-three crates were an epicure's delight: exotic wines, raisins, and almonds; Marseilles figs; a brace of red-legged partridges; an oval looking glass, eight hair mattresses, and fifty-nine silk damask chairs; portraits of Jefferson's trinity of heroes, Bacon, Newton, and Locke; plus a generous store of French macaroni.

Revolutionary partisans at Le Havre, suspicious of smuggling by émigrés loyal to the discredited Louis XVI, insisted on examining Jefferson's shipment before allowing it to leave France. They needn't have worried; the secretary of state much preferred macaroni to monarchs. Henceforth by day, Jefferson crafted a radically new system of weights and measures for the foundling republic. At night, his throbbing headache in temporary remission, he jotted down calculations of the earth's motion on its axis.

The fruit of his labors was shared with a head-scratching Congress in July 1790. The people's representatives hardly knew what to make of the secretary's proposed decimal system — ten inches to a foot, eight gallons to a firkin, one and one-third tierces to a hogshead — so they tabled the whole fanciful scheme. Jefferson lodged no complaint that has survived, grateful perhaps that scholars, at least, were inclined to praise what politicians ignored. But it could not have been a happy time for the returned exile. Divorced from his second home in France, trapped in jostling, gritty New York, where summer was unreliable and spring nonexistent, Monticello's sun-loving master employed his time in mathematics, interior decorating, and Spanish intrigue.

{ 3 }

Inevitably the first presidential Cabinet became an arena of conflict, its protagonists stock figures — or stick figures — in our history books: Jefferson, the apostle of the yeoman, versus Hamilton, the mercantile prophet; one an aristocrat who lived on a mountaintop and considered himself a friend to man; the other a self-made elitist with a Calvinist belief in original sin. Hamilton's corresponding pessimism about human nature contrasted sharply with his rival's faith in the mass of men from whom he was temperamentally estranged. Like fire and frost, they were opposites whom not even Washington could reconcile.

At the time of Washington's excursion to the old fort bearing his name, a surface unity prevailed between the secretaries of state and the treasury. But the seeds of future conflict were already planted. Alexander Hamilton, like Alexander McGillivray, was a man without a country or the often crippling preconceptions that attend national pride. Born under strange stars on the Caribbean island of Nevis, he spent a lifetime escaping his origins as the illegitimate son of a Scottish merchant and his common-law wife of French Huguenot ancestry. From his precocious boyhood Hamilton intended to go up and to go up high. In this he foreshadowed a host of plucky Horatio Alger heroes, scaling heights of poverty and exclusion to best favored rivals through raw determination.

"My blood was as good as that of those who plume themselves upon their ancestry," Hamilton insisted, more than a bit defensively. It wasn't enough to prevent John Adams from dismissing his upstart challenger as "the bastard brat of a Scots peddler." The truth, as usual, was more complex. Three years after Alex's father abandoned Rachel Lavien, the self-styled Madame Hamilton moved to St. Croix, where her son became a countinghouse clerk. Already he thirsted for the glory won through great deeds. In 1769, the year his mother died, Hamilton wrote to a friend in New York, "I wish there was a war."

Not a war but a hurricane provided the young Hamilton with his escape. His romantic, overwrought description of a howling storm brought him to the notice of an island clergyman and schoolmaster. In 1773 the sixteen-year-old enrolled at King's College (later Columbia University) in New York, where he indulged in combat, verbal and otherwise. Following the Boston Tea Party and Parliament's decision to punish the rebels by closing the port of Boston, Hamilton warned that there was no end to British truculence. One day, he forecast, inventive ministers in London would devise ways to tax every child, perhaps every kiss bestowed by a sweetheart. This satire would come back to haunt him later, when as Washington's fiscal wizard he displayed considerable ingenuity in taxing southern carriages and western whiskey.

On joining Washington's revolutionary family, Hamilton quickly won the commander's affection, prompting the normally undemonstrative Washington to call his youthful aide "my boy." Perhaps, never having had a real father, Hamilton did not know how to respond. Perhaps he feared the emotional consequences of dependence. Or perhaps his combative, quick-to-take-offense nature was bound to lash out at the earliest opportunity. Whatever the reason, Hamilton deliberately provoked an incident by keeping the general waiting, then spurning his apology for the harsh words he had spoken.

"For three years past I have felt no friendship for him and have professed none," Hamilton confided to one for whom he did have such feelings. "The truth is, our dispositions are the opposites of each other, and the pride of my temper would not suffer me to profess what I did not feel."

Like his later disciple Theodore Roosevelt, Hamilton never got over his wartime experiences or his love of a fight. Every day was a drama, lived at a higher pitch than that of his contemporaries. At the Constitutional Convention, the cocky New Yorker stunned delegates by praising Britain's monarchy and demanding that senators be chosen for life. He embraced abolitionism, an impolitic course in a republic already strained by southern fears and northern resentments. On a personal level, Hamilton tactlessly challenged Jefferson's worship of the Enlightenment deities Newton, Bacon, and Locke by declaring to his face that Julius Caesar was the greatest man in all history.

As Jefferson's temperamental and philosophical opposite, Hamilton loved the American union more than the people inhabiting it. He never forgave their refusal to share his vision of a great commercial and military power held together by an elective monarch. Having little affinity for his adopted homeland, Hamilton felt still less of Jefferson's almost mystical attachment to the land he farmed. Rachel Hamilton's son was an aristocrat of brains, not inherited wealth. Offsetting his natural pugnacity was a briskly analytical turn of mind, especially perceptive in boring through to the root of men's motives.

Since a desire for personal reward is universal, he argued, government must find ways to make interest coincide with duty. What would prompt a man to plan and carry out arduous enterprises for the public benefit? According to Hamilton, nothing but "the love of fame, the ruling passion of the noblest minds." However Jefferson might dispute this, it neatly reflected Washington's value system. And it made it easier for the president and his secretary of the treasury to form their historic partnership, with fateful consequences for agrarian democracy.

From the balcony of his home at 57 Wall Street, Hamilton watched as the new president was sworn into office. Two months later, the secretary climbed into the pulpit of St. Paul's Chapel on Broadway to eulogize General Nathanael Greene. He found in Greene's tragically shortened career parallels with his own breathtaking ascent. "Descended from reputable parents" though Greene might be, he had lacked the elevated rank necessary in a monarchy to realize his fullest potential. Indeed, Hamilton continued, Greene might easily "have contented himself with the humble lot of a private citizen, or at most with the contracted sphere of an elective office . . . scarcely conscious of the resources of his own mind, had not the violated rights of his country called him to act a part on a more splendid and ample theater."

There was nothing after September 1789 to suggest that Hamilton's sphere was contracted or that he was unconscious of his resources. Working furiously behind a mahogany and satinwood desk in Federal Hall, he produced a 22,000-word manifesto, the *Report on the Public Credit*, that baffled most of those it did not outrage. Washington typically kept his counsel, yet under the circumstances silence was taken for assent. Said one Virginia representative of Hamilton's report, "I think it well calculated to keep us all in the dark except those . . . who thrive on speculation."

Few of the theories Hamilton espoused were novel. Since Yorktown, he had argued strenuously for a national debt as a powerful cement of union and for increased taxes to enable a consolidated government to assume debts left over from the war. Tax collectors are not noticeably popular, and Hamilton's aggressive self-regard, coupled with a massively untidy personal life, did little to endear him to those taxed. Yet even his harshest critics conceded the personal magnetism of George Clinton's much-hated "little Great Man." A French traveler recorded in 1788, "He looks thirty-eight or forty years old, is not tall, and has a resolute, frank, soldierly appearance." Women found him irresistible, and Hamilton cheerfully reciprocated, confessing to an older beauty at the age of seventeen, "ALL FOR LOVE is my motto."

No doubt Washington caught in the younger man a glimpse of his earlier self, all fearlessness and cold energy. But there was a crucial difference between them. Taking stock of his weaknesses, Washington had transformed himself, creating a modern Galahad that in time all but eclipsed the person within. Hamilton did no such thing. Courting danger and practicing deception, he balanced his wife, Betsey, and their four children against his passion for Betsey's captivating sister, Angelica Church, with whom Jefferson, too, had enjoyed a European dalliance. For twenty years Alex and Angelica engaged in literary flirtation. "I seldom write to a lady without fancying the relation of lover and mistress," he playfully informed his sister-in-law in December 1787. "It has a very inspiring effect."

Eventually such behavior would inspire Hamilton's enemies to blackmail. In the meantime, more public affairs occupied Hamilton the policymaker. Not content to manage the economy, he swaggered into the diplomatic arena. Beckwith's unorthodox approach gave him the opening he sought. So did Washington's view of his Cabinet officers as general advisers, not limited by strict lines of departmental authority. The president's relations with his Cabinet associates were a bit like God's with the archangels: collegiality had its limits. According to Jefferson, files were dispatched daily from 39 Broadway to each of the departments, accompanied by requests for an oral or written response within twenty-four hours.

"If an answer was requisite, the secretary of the department communicated the letter and his proposed answer to the President," said Jefferson, who adopted the system for himself in 1801. "Generally they were simply sent back after perusal, which signified his approbation. Sometimes he returned them with an informal note, suggesting an alteration or a query. If a doubt of any importance arose, he reserved it for conference. By this means he was always in accurate possession of all facts and proceedings in every part of the Union and to whatsoever department they related; he formed a central point for the different branches, preserved a unity of object and action among them, exercised that participation in the suggestion of affairs made incumbent on him, and met himself the due responsibility for whatever was done."

Following the Cabinet's dinner en famille on July 10, the president fashioned explicit instructions for his secretary of the treasury. Hamilton was to treat Beckwith "very civilly" while simultaneously hinting "delicately" that his mission carried no marks "official or authentic." Gouverneur Morris would appreciate that. Besides avenging the envoy, Hamilton "was to extract as much as he could . . . and report it to me, without committing, by any assurances whatever, the Government of the

United States, leaving it entirely free to pursue, unreproached, such a line of conduct in the dispute as her interest (and honor) shall dictate."

Interest and honor were Washington's alpha and omega. They had led the president up a long and winding staircase to supreme power, a summit where the air was thin and loneliness inescapable.

❮ 4 ❯

Whatever the British did and however the Indians gauged their strategic interest, Henry Knox would be affected. During the Revolution, Brigadier General Knox had far outranked Hamilton, a mere captain of artillery. Their roles in the Cabinet reversed their status, leading to Knox's historical underestimation as a vassal of the ardent, intellectually fertile New Yorker. Weighing in at more than three hundred pounds, the forty-year-old shipmaster's son added more than ballast to Washington's circle.

None of the president's advisers so enjoyed his trust as the massive Yankee who had masterminded the transport of heavy guns from Fort Ticonderoga to Boston through a brutal New England winter. At Valley Forge, Washington and Knox endured together the darkest of America's trials, while Knox's bride, Lucy, whose father was the royal secretary of Massachusetts, won Martha through her vitality and infectious laughter. Less endearing were Lucy's gambling debts, which, combined with her husband's prodigal entertaining, pushed Henry into extensive land speculation in Maine.

Peace opened new fields for Knox, blessed, in the words of the historian Geoffrey Perret, with "a thin man's hustle in a fat man's body." Hardly had he removed his uniform than the confederation Congress asked him to don it once more, this time as head of the War Department. That Washington would invite his trusted colleague to join the new regime was a foregone conclusion. That the United States would create an armed force adequate to defend its frontiers was anything but. "Give Knox his army," raged William Maclay, "and he will soon have a war on his hands."

Knox warmed to the challenge. Backed by Washington and a department of three clerks, in April 1790 the secretary doubled the nation's infantry to "one thousand two hundred and sixteen noncommissioned officers, privates and Musicians," their monthly pay ranging from $3.50 for a private to $60 for a lieutenant commander. Each enlisted man was issued one hat, coat, vest, and blanket per year, along with four shirts, two pairs of socks, and four pairs of overalls. Officers supplied their own wardrobe.

Having mustered a single regiment on paper, Knox next turned to the

Indian threat in the Northwest. Still more pressing was the danger posed by McGillivray's Creeks, their Spanish confederates, and Georgia's unilateral session of 25 million acres it did not own to land companies in Virginia, South Carolina, and Tennessee. The rapacious Georgians threatened to plunge the entire Southwest into war. Clearly, they needed humbling, but such a step carried its own risks, repugnant to a president anxious to remain above politics. David Humphreys warned his chief that any negotiations with the Creeks were bound to be difficult. Though weakened from syphilis, McGillivray possessed "the good sense of an American, the shrewdness of a Scotchman, and the cunning of an Indian."

When McGillivray's caravan finally appeared in New York on July 20, 1790, Washington's capital summoned such pomp as consistent with republican virtue to greet the foreign visitors. Secretary Knox and some ersatz warriors from the new Society of St. Tammany escorted the Creek warriors and their "Beloved Man" up Wall Street. Washington himself appeared on the stoop of 39 Broadway to give McGillivray his customary bone-crackling handshake.

"I am glad you have come, Colonel. I have long felt we had much in common."

"I cannot flatter myself that much, Mr. President, but it has long been my ambition to shake your hand in friendship."

Pleasantries exchanged, the Native Americans were taken to their lodgings on the banks of the North River, henceforth known as the Indian Queen. New York society indulged itself in an early version of radical chic, Abigail Adams pronouncing McGillivray and his companions "the very first savages I ever saw" and marveling at their leader's fluency in politics, philosophy, and literature. Only the archconservative Fisher Ames failed to see what all the excitement was about, saying of McGillivray, "He is decent and not very black."

Accustomed to pale-faced condescension and official duplicity, the Beloved Man encountered much of each in New York. First Carlos Howard warned of America's reluctance to vacate the disputed Oconee Strip, between Georgia's Oconee and Ogeechee rivers. Within twenty-four hours, the Spanish minister himself appeared in Henry Knox's parlor to curry favor by offering the Creek leader $2,000 a year and the title of brigadier general. Major Beckwith came in his turn, seeking crumbs from the diplomatic table for his masters in London. McGillivray turned him away coldly.

His talks with the Americans proved almost as contentious, for Washington was used to giving orders, not haggling over details. (To the end of his life, Washington gloried in the title of Caunotaucarius, or the

Towntaker, bestowed upon him in his youth by an Iroquois chieftain named the Half King.) After failing to break the Creeks' trading monopoly with Spain, he did secure, for $10,000 in booty and an annual subsidy of $2,000, clear title to the Oconee Strip. A secret proviso opened the door to $50,000 in U.S.-Creek trade should McGillivray's usual sources be threatened by a European war. McGillivray also received the title promised him by the Spanish, sweetened by an annual retainer of $1,800. Other chiefs won smaller annuities.

The Senate wasted no time in approving the Treaty of New York over the strident objections of Georgia's lawmakers. Infuriated by the government's concession of 3 million acres, Georgia Senator James Jackson was livid over Washington's treatment of a Creek "savage" as his diplomatic equal. The newspapers in his state picked up on the racist theme, one of them asking if it were not ludicrous "that a power who would not think herself too much honored by the alliance of the greatest monarch on earth should condescend to enter into a formal treaty with a *half-breed Spanish colonel?*"

On August 17, Washington, acting for the government and people of the United States, did exactly that. At noon he appeared in the chamber of the House of Representatives, where he addressed an assembly numbering Knox, McGillivray, and two dozen Creek kings, chiefs, and warriors among its members. After scratching his signature on parchment, Washington gave McGillivray books and an epaulette from his wartime uniform. To the other chiefs he presented strings of beads, representing perpetual peace, and a paper filled with tobacco to smoke in remembrance of the great occasion. (Washington personally disdained the aromatic leaf on which his state's economy depended; tobacco made his head swim.) McGillivray and the other Creeks passed, one by one, in front of Washington, each giving him the shake of peace. A native song concluded the ceremony, ringing down the curtain on the administration's first diplomatic triumph.

❊ 5 ❊

Before seeing his visitors off, Washington played a practical joke on McGillivray's party. As fate would have it, John Trumbull's heroic portrait of the president had just been completed and was awaiting its final home in New York's City Hall. Washington was curious to see what reaction it would spark from men who had never glimpsed such formal art. To heighten the effect, he donned a uniform identical to the one pictured on Trumbull's canvas.

The artist was present when Washington threw open the door to the room in which his likeness was displayed. One warrior approached the picture slowly, stretching his hand out to feel the living Washington, only to touch a flat, inanimate surface. He grunted in confusion. A second repeated the gesture, venturing to place one hand on the canvas and the other behind. He was astonished to find that his hands nearly met.

Which Washington was genuine, which the invention of his admirers? The Creeks were not alone in wondering. In a letter to Lafayette on August 11, the president hailed the Treaty of New York, insisting that "the *basis* of our proceedings with the Indian nations has been and shall be *justice*." Yet even as he composed this boastful message, Washington and Knox were outfitting a military expedition against the tribes in the Northwest. Lafayette's correspondent significantly qualified his prediction of general peace by mentioning the presence of "small refugee banditti of Cherokees and Shawanese, who can be easily chastised or even extirpated if necessary."

Washington was still less hopeful about his other continental neighbors, Spain and England. From France alone he anticipated great things, leading him to reject out of hand the exaggerated claims of revolutionary violence made in British journals. "For had we credited all the evil stories we have seen in them," Washington told the comte de Rochambeau, "we should almost have set it down for granted that the race of Frenchmen were . . . becoming extinct and their country a desert . . . Happily for you, we remembered how our own armies, after having been all slain to a man in the English newspapers, came to life again and even performed prodigies of valor against that very nation." Meanwhile, Washington added mischievously, "Mr. Jefferson, Mr. Trumbull and some others have taught us to believe more cautiously and more correctly on these points."

Washington's government prepared to vacate New York, "and if we live so long," wrote Oliver Wolcott of the Treasury Department, move "to the Indian place with the long name on the Potomac." On August 26, Tobias Lear advised Philadelphia of Washington's impending departure and repeated an earlier request for as little ceremony along the route as possible. "The President wishes to command his own time," said Lear. "He wishes not to exclude himself from the sight or conversation of his fellow citizens; but their eagerness to show their affection frequently imposes a heavy tax on him."

It was a tax he could not escape. The Washingtons rose early on Monday, August 30, hoping to slip away without public demonstration. Outside 39 Broadway they discovered Governor Clinton, the mayor, richly robed clergymen, and a large body of ordinary New Yorkers, willing for the moment to forgive their government its hasty departure. "Well," said the president, "they must have their way." As the impressive procession moved smartly down Broadway toward a waiting barge, thirteen guns fired their salute from the Battery and ships in the harbor bobbed respectfully at the distinguished group. Thirteen sailors wearing white jackets and black caps rowed the presidential party across the open water to Powles Hook ferry (later Jersey City), where carriages sat poised to continue the journey south. Mrs. Washington seemed much affected by the parting. Some thought they saw the president wipe away tears.

Ordinarily Washington frowned on such displays. That very morning, he had entrusted a pair of errands to Lear. One called upon any person having bills outstanding against the president of the United States or his household to make them known at 39 Broadway no later than September 15. The other presented twenty guineas to the Reverend John Rodgers for the relief of distressed debtors confined to New York jail cells. The first was advertised in local newspapers, the second kept secret on orders of the president.

❄ 6 ❄

Washington's diaries for the second half of 1790 have been lost, but it is possible to reconstruct both his hands-on management style and the formidable negotiating skills he brought to his dealings with a McGillivray or Beckwith. One need simply read the volley of instructions fired at Tobias Lear during the government's interregnum from August to December. At issue was the house of Robert Morris, the finest in Philadelphia, though too small for "the *commodious* accommodation of my family," as Washington phrased it. So he suggested a long list of alterations — among them bow windows in a pair of front rooms, the construction of a new servants hall, and conversion of a "cow-house" into additional stables. Although facing southern disaffection and possible war on the northwestern frontier, the president was not too busy to dictate green or yellow curtains in an upstairs hall, the precise placement of table ornaments on a dining room sideboard, and the swap of a glass lamp belonging to the Morrises for one of his own.

Domestic problems added to Lear's woes. John Hyde, Sam Fraunces's profligate successor as steward, was unhappy at leaving New York. Washington was perfectly willing to let him go, the sooner the better. After all, wrote the president on September 10, "there can be no propriety in saddling me with the cost of his transportation, and that of his baggage, if he has it in contemplation to leave me at or soon after his arrival."

Washington returned to the subject a week later, mentioning the heavy consumption of Pintard's wine at Hyde's table and repeating, in case Lear may have missed his earlier inference, "If he has . . . it in contemplation to *talk* . . . of increased wages, it would be best to separate at once."

Three days passed: Washington was still gnawing the bone. "I strongly suspect that nothing is brought to my table of *liquors, fruit,* or *other things* that is not used as *profusely* as his." Blaming Hyde for his own spacious style of living, the president added sourly that he could not understand how other families were able to entertain more liberally than he on one tenth his salary.

But if he would not be taken advantage of, neither would Washington take advantage of others. He praised Lear's action in selling an old chariot for £45 pounds, "for although the price is small, it will be so much saved for the public." Offered an exchange of Mrs. Morris's ironing mangle for a similar device in his own laundry, the president voiced no objection, "provided mine is equally good and convenient, but if I should obtain any advantage besides that of its being up and ready for use, I am not inclined to receive it."

Costs must be kept down in the Washington household, appearances kept up. A pair of kitchen workers should be strongly discouraged from accompanying the first family to Philadelphia, said Washington tartly, "because the dirty fingers of Mrs. Lewis and her daughter will not be a pleasant sight." Although an old friend of Robert Morris's, the president had his patience tried by his prospective landlord's continuing refusal to spell out terms. So he resorted to bluff, reiterating the many inadequacies of the house at 190 High (later Market) Street, one block north of the Pennsylvania State House and the smart brick additions designed for Congress and the Supreme Court.

Morris's home was smaller than Alexander Macomb's, Washington pointed out. Since it lacked an office on the ground floor, visitors would be forced to climb two flights of stairs, passing public rooms on their way. Then, too, fire would be a constant hazard, as unreliable servants disobeyed orders against carrying lamps into stable lofts. Despite these and other shortcomings, Washington allowed as how he would pay as much for Morris's property as he had for 39 Broadway. Nor would he complain if asked to pay more, within reason.

On the other hand, "Extortion, if it should be intended by delay . . . to see to what heights rents will rise, I should be unwilling to [submit to]." Still more emphatically he added, "To take it at the expense of *any* public body I will *not*."

Lear had his marching orders.

The president concluded another letter with a brisk comment about his refitted carriage. "I had rather have heard that my repaired coach was plain and elegant than 'rich and elegant.' " Spoken like the homeowner forever reminding overseers and anyone else who would listen, "Many mickles make a muckle." At his most imperious, Washington disproved the sentimental tale of a youth hurling a silver dollar across the wide Rappahannock River, for no man was less inclined to throw money away.

PART TWO

Philadelphia

1790-1797

❈ 4 ❈

TOWN AND COUNTRY

"The more I am acquainted with agricultural affairs
the more I am pleased with them . . . I am led to
reflect how much more delightful to an undebauched
mind is the task of making improvements on the earth,
than all to vain glory which can be acquired from
ravaging it, by the most uninterrupted career of conquests."

George Washington,
December 4, 1788

SEPTEMBER 12, 1790, was a softly beguiling Sunday with hints of
autumnal flamboyance to come. On that date Washington pulled up at
his lodge gate, from which an unbroken vista stretched three quarters of
a mile to a plain white house of two and a half stories, sheathed in pine
boards painted and sanded to imitate stone. The squire was accustomed
to setting his watch by the sundial on the lawn, but a pewter-colored sky
on this day of homecoming overcame force of habit. Once inside, he
crossed the great central passage, which in another architectural deceit
he had grained to resemble mahogany paneling. A few loping strides
carried him under a pair of black plaster lions to a soaring piazza designed
for life outdoors.

Like a queen enthroned, Mount Vernon commanded a view of the
loitering Potomac and Maryland's heavily wooded shore. On inclement
days, Washington worked off nervous energy by pacing the ninety-six-
foot veranda paved in English fieldstone, halting occasionally to peer
through a spyglass at boats plying the river nearly two hundred feet
below. In the capital, protocol forced him to walk a narrow line between
aloofness and accessibility. At Mount Vernon he could relax his guard
without lowering his standards. Formal levee dress gave way to buckskin

· 63 ·

breeches and tall boots, if only because here Washington felt less keenly the weight of responsibility as a republican monarch competing with Europe's real thing.

"My manner of living is plain," he had written soon after the Revolution, when the house became "a well-resorted tavern," in the sardonic words of its owner, "and I do not mean to be put out of it. A glass of wine and a bit of mutton are always ready, and such as will be content to partake of them are always welcome. Those who expect more will be disappointed."

Of the countless strangers who took the invitation at face value, few went away disappointed. Within days of returning from New York that September, the president welcomed a distant relative by marriage, Thomas Lee Shippen. "Hospitality indeed seems to have spread over the whole its happiest, kindest influence," wrote Shippen afterward. "The president exercises it in a superlative degree, from the greatest of its duties to the most trifling minutiae."

In this he was matched by Mrs. Washington, whose happiness, Shippen concluded, "is in exact proportion to the number of objects upon which she can dispense her benefits." It was the first lady's unvarying habit every morning after breakfast to visit her kitchen and check on the bread risen overnight before moving on to the larder and scullery. Martha personally oversaw the preparation of the salt cod loved by the president, alternating the homely dish with mutton, veal, pigeon, or hare. She frequently consulted the Fannie Farmer of her day, *The Art of Cooking Made Plain and Easy, Which far exceeds anything of the Kind yet published . . . by a Lady,* which wasn't published by a lady at all but by a physician in London named John Hall.

Twice rebuilt to reflect the maturing tastes of its owner, through its conscious pursuit of symmetry Mount Vernon was a metaphor of George Washington. By adding a full story to the house, encasing the river facade behind tall pillars, and surmounting it with a graceful cupola, Washington concealed the irregularity of doors and windows disfiguring the original structure, a conventional eight-room dwelling dating from 1735. In a final, paradoxical touch, the victorious general added a weather vane shaped like a dove of peace.

Observant visitors to Mansion House Farm saw everywhere reflected Washington's love of order, his balance of the practical and the ornamental, his blending of classical tradition with scientific experiment. When a smoky fireplace ruined his office walls, the president had them repainted the color of stone. He treated woodwork to approximate English walnut and brightened gloomy chambers through the use of verdigris, Prussian blue, and similarly vibrant colors. On the north side of the house, Washington raised his Adam-style New Room, adorned by a Palladian window copied from Batty Langley's *City and Country Builder's and Workman's Treasury of Design*, published in London in 1756. When an English admirer sent him a hand-carved marble mantel, the recipient protested that the gift, packed in ten shipping cases, was "too elegant and costly, by far, for my room and my republican style of living."

Republican or not, Samuel Vaughan's mantel was installed in conformity with Washington's preference for things "neat and fashionable." Lit by the newest whale oil lamps and heated by a coal fireplace, the New Room was a dining room without a table. So unpredictable was the number of guests who might appear at any moment, curiosity their only reference, that the family substituted trestles and sawhorses, a device first employed at Washington's army headquarters.

To escape such demands, Washington built a second wing to accommodate his private pursuits. Upstairs, he and Martha shared a bed that, at six feet, six inches, was scarcely adequate for his frame. A narrow staircase led directly to Washington's study below, where the resourceful plantation owner indulged his love of gadgetry through a washstand that doubled as a card table and a letterpress invaluable to the businessman and amateur archivist. On hot days Washington sat in a fan chair purchased in Philadelphia during the stifling summer of 1787. By pumping treadles with his feet he could ward off flies and mosquitoes, the latter chronic to Virginia's tidal marshes, giving rise to malarial chills during the steamiest months of the year.

Whatever the season, Mount Vernon acted on its master like a tonic. Rising each day long before the first olive light bathed his silent house and its stirring dependencies, the president lit his own fire, washed, and shaved alone. The hours before breakfast were spent in his study, working on correspondence. His first meal of the day set the pattern for those to follow. In contrast to the usual country repast of fish, fowl, ham, or game, biscuits, and eggs, the squire settled for three Indian cakes smothered in honey and as many cups of tea. Breakfast consumed, he left for his daily survey of five farms covering 8,000 acres.

More people labored at Mount Vernon than in the executive department of Washington's government, and its proprietor knew his workers as intimately as the red clay soil and gullied fields that regularly defeated their efforts. As a self-contained community Mount Vernon typified the economic independence Washington hoped to implement on a national scale. Long before the Revolution, he had replaced his tobacco crop, which depleted the soil, with tawny wheat and corn. The president used no cheese or porter but what he found in America. From the teeming Potomac he harvested shad, perch, bass, and carp, some for his personal table, the rest salted down to vary the cornbread and buttermilk diet of his slaves.

To balance the deficiencies of climate and location, Washington fell back on long hours and a protean attention to detail. He missed nothing on his twenty-mile inspection tours, poking his head into the icehouse, checking a millrace, and performing a tender ritual by feeding a handful of clover or grain to Nelson, his aging Yorktown mount, now retired to a life of ease. Washington's judgment of horseflesh was impeccable; by Jefferson's not uncritical standards he was the finest horseman of the age.

He had nevertheless been forced to abandon fox hunting, for the passage of time had thinned the ranks of his fellow riders. Lord Fairfax lay under a chancel stone in a church in Westchester; his nephew George William had gone to ground for the last time in 1787. Whenever Washington gazed south from his portico across Dogue Creek, the charred remains of Belvoir taunted him with its memories. Sally Fairfax, his former flame and social instructor, was in England, but she may as well have been on the moon. George Mason, Washington's collaborator on the Fairfax Resolves, still resided at nearby Gunston Hall, but political differences only slightly narrower than the Atlantic stood between the neighbors.

Routine provided its consolations. By midafternoon, Washington usually returned to Mansion House Farm to change clothes and powder his hair before dinner, a substantial meal recalled by one visitor as "a small roasted pig, boiled leg of lamb, roasted fowls, beef, peas, lettuce, cucumbers, artichokes, etc., puddings, tarts, etc., etc." Later he would escort guests through his botanical garden, where the tulip tree's cloying fragrance mingled with spicy kitchen aromas and the pungent smell of freshly cut hay. Boxwood and catalpas perfumed the air, along with the scent of lilacs, mock oranges, and magnolias rustled by a gentle wind off the Potomac.

From a distance it all sounds idyllic, but Washington knew better. The neglect of his farms during the Revolution he estimated to have cost him at least £10,000, while wartime inflation had sharply eroded the value of Martha's estate. Mount Vernon's soil was poor, its absentee management worse. With a hundred cows in his fields, Washington was forced to purchase butter for his family. Yet for all the demands it made upon his pocket and peace of mind, Mount Vernon occupied a special place in his heart. His land holdings were three times the size of Lawrence Washington's 1754 bequest; for its proprietor, in need of cash, even this was not enough. "I shall begrudge no reasonable expense that will contribute to the improvement and neatness of my farms," Washington asserted, "for nothing pleases me better than to see them in good order, and thriving."

With such thoughts to contradict economy and with tea and toast to nourish his evening labors, the president would return to his study, using the hours until bedtime to squeeze profit out of a wasteful system and his thin, unproductive soil. For help he turned to volumes like *Tull's Horse-Hoeing Husbandry*, ordered as "a new system of Agriculture, or a speedy way to grow rich." He also subscribed to Arthur Young's *Annals of Agriculture*, to which George III contributed under the pseudonym Ralph Robinson and in whose pages William Pitt discoursed on turnips and deep plowing.

Failing to find a panacea in books, with a candle in his hand Washington wearily climbed the stairs to Martha's room. The rest of the house fairly bulged with visitors. "I rarely miss seeing strange faces," he confided, "come, as they say, out of respect for me. Pray, would not the word curiosity answer as well?" In the moments before sleep overtook him, Washington may have employed his mathematical skills in figuring the price of fame, that young man's grail worn as the hair shirt of old age. No visible escape lightened his future, only the treadmill of forced hospitality and official demands.

❧ 2 ❧

Mount Vernon was no island. With every courier and mail packet came news of a world in ferment in 1790. Wielding his anger at French extremism like a sharp weapon, Edmund Burke published his conservative cri de coeur, *Reflections on the Revolution in France*. Elsewhere in Europe, Austria crushed Belgium's claims to nationhood and Czar Alexander rejected pleas for the emancipation of Russian serfs. Far to the east, the ubiquitous British consolidated their toehold on the Indian subcontinent by concluding an alliance with the nizam of Hyderabad. Americans took shelter behind the vast moat of the Atlantic, at least until the Nootka Sound affair erupted in their back yard in the tense summer, threatening to crush Washington's government between the millstones of archrivals Spain and England.

One of the president's last acts before leaving New York had been to poll his closest advisers. "The consequences of having so formidable and enterprising a people as the British on both our flanks and rear, with their navy in front . . . are too obvious to need enumeration," Washington wrote, then posed two questions determining whether the young nation could remain out of the fighting. Should the United States permit King George's troops to use its territory as a staging ground from which to assault New Orleans? Could it deny an ultimatum from the greatest power on earth, especially when a brushfire war was already raging between American frontiersmen and Indian tribes in the Northwest loosely aligned with the British throne?

By the middle of September, Washington at Mount Vernon was pondering the counsel of a divided Cabinet. Vice President Adams opposed British audacity with New England pluck. If Lord Dorchester asked permission to march his forces south from Detroit, he should be refused "in terms clear and decided, but guarded and dignified, in a manner which no power has more at command than the President of the United States." Did Adams smile to himself as he penned the backhanded compliment? It is tempting to think so.

Jefferson's response contained no such trace of irony. Discarding his muzzy idealism where territorial expansion was concerned, the secretary of state hoped to use the crisis to coerce Spain's peaceful surrender of New Orleans and the barren Floridas. Jefferson envisioned a grand alliance uniting Madrid, Paris, and Philadelphia. To obtain it he urged delay, during which Lafayette and other friends of the United States at the French court might pressure Spain into acquiescence. Washington signaled his agreement with this approach by sending David Humphreys to Lisbon as a first step toward better relations with Spain and American access to the Mississippi.

Eastern isolationists worried less about Spain than the growing power of their trans-Appalachian countrymen. Many Easterners thought the United States should remain what it had been for a century and a half, a coastal society dependent on Atlantic commerce and culture. Their spokesman in the Cabinet was Hamilton, who on September 15 dispatched to Mount Vernon a dense, erudite document laced with references to such giants of international jurisprudence as Grotius and Vattel. Boiled down to its essentials, however, it was little more than a weak endorsement of peace over war.

Better than either in Hamilton's mind was the good opinion of Great Britain. True enough, Spain had played a friendly part in the Revolution. But in the canon of Hamiltonian realpolitik, "Gratitude is a duty or sentiment which between nations can rarely have any solid foundation." Convinced that America's destiny lay with Britain's, Hamilton continued his back-alley meetings with George Beckwith, conveying American military secrets to King George's agent in the bargain.

There was no shortage of sensitive information to impart. Between 1783 and 1790, raiders from the Wabash and Miami tribes were thought to have killed 1,500 settlers in Kentucky and made off with 20,000 horses in the rich bluegrass country. Washington responded late in August 1790 by ordering an invasion under the command of Josiah Harmar, the hard-drinking commander of the United States' shadow army. Entrusted with 300 regular soldiers and 1,000 militia from Pennsylvania and Kentucky, Harmar was to punish the harassing Indians north of the Ohio River. By informing Beckwith of the pending assault, Hamilton threw the campaign into jeopardy before it even started. As a result, the redcoats could relax in their Detroit fortifications — maintained in open violation of the 1783 peace treaty — while forwarding news of the planned movement to their Indian confederates.

Hamilton cared little for the Ohio Valley or the ragged entrepreneurs pouring over the Appalachians to lay claim to the old Northwest Territory. But he didn't dare voice his objections openly to Washington, the eastern man of western outlook, the canal builder and frontier soldier, for whom the Ohio was a river of gold. In the end, the president's policy of cultivating France and Spain was overtaken by events as a distracted regime in Paris buckled under pressure from the English, abandoning Spain and making its position at Nootka Sound untenable. The British never marched south from Detroit. Hamilton's visits to Major Beckwith continued anyway, the British diplomat immortalizing his caller as "Number Seven" in the rudimentary code he used to cloak his intrigues.

Whatever Hamilton said, he failed to convey Washington's abiding distrust of London's ruling circles. He may not have understood the president's feelings; more likely, he did not share them. On September 30, Hamilton made a bold attempt to discredit Gouverneur Morris and replace him with a more pliable agent. According to the secretary of the treasury, Morris's ineffectiveness in the British capital could be traced to his open intimacy with the French ambassador and his indiscreet friendship with members of His Majesty's Loyal Opposition. While the insinuating pen belonged to Hamilton, the hand that pushed it was Beckwith's. Suspecting as much, Washington waited for ten days before sending a frosty reply.

The motives of the secretary's informant "may have been pure and . . . praiseworthy," said the president, who clearly thought them anything but. On the other hand, such a blatant intrusion in domestic affairs might "admit of a different interpretation and by an easy and pretty clue." Washington signed his letter "With sincere regard." At this same time he was concluding his correspondence with Jefferson at Monticello "Yours affectionately." A small but revealing gesture, it was a fair gauge of presidential trust and intimacy during Jefferson's first months in office.

❦ 3 ❧

Like foxhounds and the civilized pleasures of Belvoir, surveying was a thing of Washington's past. The president's tripod gathered dust in a corner of his study. But that did not mean his land hunger was sated. From the beginning Washington took an active role in creating a capital for his young nation, drawing on his vast experience and $200,000 earmarked by bordering states for the construction of public buildings in the ten-square-mile district authorized by Congress. His first assignment was to fix the borders of the new city, with Jefferson serving as architectural and aesthetic consultant.

The two men did not always agree. For example, when the secretary of state imagined 1,500 acres to be sufficient for the capital of the United States, his superior rebuked him gently. If Philadelphia, the seat of government for a single state, could sprawl over several square miles, said Washington with his usual capacious thinking, why should the capital of an entire nation not be larger yet? The Grand Columbian Federal City would live up to its name.

October in Virginia was a season of hushed contradictions, of forests tinted scarlet and river landscapes bracing for bitter months to come. On the fifteenth, heeding Madison's advice, Washington left Mount Vernon to inspect possible building sites. The residents of Georgetown, fifteen miles to the north, were waiting for the president. So were other delegations of prospective sellers, each eager for the profits and prestige sure to flow from his favor.

Wherever he appeared, promoters made joyful noises about their climate, soil, transport, and scenery. At Elizabethtown, close to the confluence of the Potomac and the Conococheague, Washington took dinner at Beltzhoover's Tavern, concluding with a fervently noncommittal toast: "To the River Patowmac. May the residence law be perpetuated and Patowmac view the Federal City." No one could disagree with that, least of all the people of Elizabethtown, who petitioned Washington "to be included within your more especial command and jurisdiction . . . the grand center of virtues."

His head unturned, the grand center of virtue pushed on upriver to Williamsport, where he boarded a vessel that returned him to Mount Vernon on October 26. His twelve-day romp illustrated both the glories of the American countryside and the cunning of its inhabitants. Not that Washington lacked guile himself. Pondering his options in secret, the president waited until January 1791 to draw the district lines even farther east than originally proposed. With Congress's permission, he would build his capital from Georgetown to the Potomac's Eastern Branch, taking in the city of Alexandria on Mount Vernon's doorstep for good measure.

Washington's recommendation was "the most imprudent of all acts," raged William Maclay, since "the general sense of Congress certainly was that the commissioners should fix on the spot." Instead, they were reduced to "mere surveyors," running four lines determined solely by the chief executive. "I really think it not improbable," he predicted, owing to the president's highhandedness, "that opposition may find a nest to lay its eggs in."

But Maclay misread his colleagues. If anyone detected a potential conflict of interest between the president's long-standing financial relationship with the Potomac Navigation Company, chartered to connect the Potomac and inland rivers with the Eastern Branch site, they kept silent about it; Congress ratified the plan without dissent. Washington further consolidated his position by choosing three old friends to serve as commissioners. One had nominated him to be commander in chief of the American forces in June 1775. Another was his relative by marriage David Stuart. Although more than "mere surveyors," none of the commissioners was likely to oppose Washington in the greatest real estate deal of his speculative life.

❦ 4 ❧

Like many an executive facing the end of his vacation, Washington turned irritable during his final weeks at Mount Vernon. His anxiety over Josiah Harmar's improvised foray into Indian country grew daily. Five weeks after setting out from Fort Washington, near present-day Cincinnati, with his untrained, untried column, Harmar was as silent as the forests into which he had plunged. Taking note of rumors, Washington could not decide which was Harmar's greater enemy, whiskey or the Wabash Indians. Adding to his concerns, Arthur St. Clair, whose Northwest Territory was about to become a battlefield, had blithely repeated Hamilton's furtive warning to the British at Detroit.

Fearing the worst, Washington instructed Henry Knox on November 2 to prepare a full justification of Harmar's campaign in time for the opening of Congress one month later. He reasoned that should disaster befall the expedition, lawmakers were bound to ask questions; better to have the answers in advance. Meanwhile, with no news from the front to dissuade him, the president was already blaming the hapless American commander for an imagined rout. "I expected *little* from the moment I heard he was a *drunkard*," he wrote on November 19. "I expected *less* as soon as I heard that on *this account* no confidence was reposed in him by the western country. And I gave up *all hope* of success, as soon as I heard that there were disputes with *him* about command."

The storm passed like a summer thunderclap, and three days later Washington departed for Philadelphia, still ignorant as to Harmar's whereabouts. The journey was anything but pleasant. Roads made more than usually impassable by heavy rain contributed to the president's depression. So did an inebriated coachman, who, evicted from his customary seat and placed in charge of a baggage wagon, turned it over twice.

Washington arrived in the new capital on the morning of November 27 to find the Morris house unfinished. At that he was lucky compared with other members of his official family. Lucy Knox, to name one, was as alarmed about her missing furniture as Washington was about his missing army, since the vessel carrying her family's belongings had not been heard from since leaving New York two weeks earlier. Abigail Adams's ship *had* come in, although carrying so much water in its hold that a trunk full of cherished dresses was thoroughly soaked. A ruined black satin gown symbolized for Mrs. Adams "the blessed effects of tumbling around the world." The vice president's lady was disappointed in her new home, Bush Hill, which had no bushes and only a few inadequate storerooms and closets. Uprooted from New York, Mrs. Adams missed the soothing sweep of the Jersey wheatfields and the majestic river at her door, saying, "The Schuylkill is no more like the Hudson than I to Hercules." Finding no firewood provided on her arrival, Abigail turned around and went to City Tavern for the night. In the morning she returned to tackle damp rooms and the overpowering smell of fresh paint.

Congressmen straggling into the city voiced their displeasure over a scarcity of affordable housing as labor shortages slowed the remodeling work on public buildings and private homes. Washington's tirade against extortionate landlords and shopkeepers was taken up by James Monroe, a former law student of Jefferson's who, at thirty-three, had been chosen to represent Virginia in the Senate. "The city seems at present to be mostly inhabited by sharpers," he said, a sentiment echoed by New Hampshire's Jeremiah Smith. It was not uncommon to hear of a man or woman losing $400 at the gaming table. "The Philadelphians are, from the highest to the lowest, from the parson in his black gown to the fille de joie, or girl of pleasure, a set of beggars," wrote Smith. "You cannot turn around without paying a dollar."

Washington, as was his custom, gave generously to both the parson and the beggars. He became a reassuringly familiar sight, walking on the sunny side of the street in good weather accompanied by Jackson or Lear and setting his watch each noon by Clark's standard at the southeastern corner of Front and High streets, where porters removed their hats in tribute and the tall officer of state returned their gesture, with a courtly bow in parting. On December 7, the president held his first levee at 190 Market Street. Jefferson was on hand to formally present Ignatius Palyrat, the consul general from Portugal, with the precise enunciation Washington demanded to offset his encroaching deafness.

The next day, the chief executive climbed a steep flight of stairs to the Senate chamber in the county courthouse, renamed Congress Hall. In his annual message to the lawmakers, he mingled optimistic reports of general prosperity — confirmed by a recent loan of three million Dutch florins — with stern admonitions to reduce the national debt "as far and as fast as the growing resources of the country will permit." He renewed earlier calls for a uniform militia, national mint, post office, and highway improvements as well as a standardized system of weights and measures. He alluded to the conflict in Europe and the potential dangers to American commerce unless the republic broke free of its reliance on foreign vessels for transport.

But his strongest words were reserved for the seething West and the "aggravated provocations" of savages determined to block American expansion north and west of Kentucky. Having heard nothing from Harmar, the president could not hazard a guess at the success of his Indian policy. But he could define and implicitly defend that policy for the first time in public. It was designed, said Washington, to teach renegade tribesmen that "the government of the Union is not less capable of punishing their crimes than it is disposed to respect their rights and reward their attachments."

This had a high-minded sound, but in fact, neither Washington nor his countrymen were prepared to confront the hard choices that went with assimilation. Washington's personally humane instincts toward the Native Americans on his borders conflicted with his soaring vision of a continental United States. It had been much simpler during the Revolution, when a beleaguered General Washington had warned Congress that only a sustained apprehension of danger could dispose Indians to peace. Then he had advised his troops to make rather than receive wilderness attacks and to do so "with as much impetuosity, shouting and noise as possible . . . to rush on with the war whoop and fixed bayonet. Nothing will disconcert and terrify the Indians more than this."

After the war, Washington wished to ameliorate the red man, not exterminate him. Foreshadowing Lincoln's quixotic scheme to colonize former slaves outside the United States, the first president anticipated the reservation system by urging that large tracts be set aside for former savages converted to Christianity, who would in turn exchange their knives and arrows for axes and plows. Washington was more generous than the intrusive, often murderous, frontiersmen who believed that the only good Indian was a dead Indian. But in the end, both sought to domesticate wild creatures for whom captivity meant cultural and spiritual death.

The president reminded his Indian representative, Timothy Pickering, that winning the attachment of the red men required a rare selflessness. "Whoever undertakes this business must be activated by more enlarged views than his individual interest," wrote Washington, whose current interest coincided with the political necessity of subduing the Northwest tribes. This prompted an appeal to Chief Cornplanter of the Senecas for help against "those bad people" the Miamis, who were guilty of heinous crimes against white settlers in the Ohio Valley. Considering the weakness of his position, Washington played his hand with breathtaking boldness, expressing the hope that Harmar's conquerors would listen to reason "and not require to be further chastised. The United States desire to be the friends of the Indians upon terms of justice and humanity," he told Cornplanter. "But they will not suffer the depredations of the bad Indians to go unpunished."

The reaction from Congress was predictable. While pronouncing the president's address "tolerably" delivered, William Maclay condemned any war undertaken without congressional approval. Washington moved quickly to disarm his critics. Within twenty-four hours, he had Knox's carefully edited report on Harmar's expedition delivered to Congress Hall. It glossed over St. Clair's indiscretion and barely mentioned the inadequate provisions made for Harmar's pitifully small army. But it served its purpose, forestalling censure as the nation rallied around its chief executive and what remained of Harmar's ravaged force.

On December 13 Washington's premonitions were confirmed when news arrived of a forest rout two months earlier near today's Vincennes, Indiana. Harmar had been dealt a pair of devastating defeats by the Shawnee warrior Little Turtle, whose volleys cut through American ranks like a scythe, killing nearly 200 men and sending the panicky survivors dashing pellmell for the relative safety of Kentucky. Harmar's reputation was destroyed along with his army.

Once again, frontier families huddled in their log houses for protection against emboldened Miamis, Maumees, and Shawnees. But the government was in no position to make guarantees. On the heels of Little Turtle's triumph, secessionist talk, fanned by Spanish agents and native opportunists, flared deep into the Northwest Territory. Only the president's foresight in keeping Congress informed — and the inexplicable delay in word from the battlefield — had prevented Harmar's fiasco from touching off a political witch-hunt. Stung by defeat, Congress soon authorized preparations for a second expedition against the Northwest tribes, with a larger force to be commanded by Arthur St. Clair.

The president, too, resolved that next time would be different. In his annual address he had spoken of punishing crimes and rewarding attachments. But his words were bound to ring hollow as long as wilderness errands were entrusted to undisciplined militia led by second-rate generals.

Jefferson drew his own conclusions from the loss. In his view, the government had yet to discover "what experience has long ago taught us in Virginia, that rank and file fighting will not do against Indians." The fact that Washington had learned this painfully for himself as a frontier colonel, at a time when Jefferson was studying schoolboy Greek at William and Mary, only made the president's humiliation all the more personal.

❦ 5 ❧

At the end of the year, frontier combat was replaced by a war of words as Washington increasingly came to be identified with Hamilton's emerging economic program. Since January the treasury's payroll had nearly doubled, to seventy officers and clerks. The secretary was a bureaucratic dervish, commissioning ship captains, christening an armada of revenue cutters, acting as purchasing agent for Knox's little army, and supervising the construction of lighthouses and the placement of offshore buoys.

So much power and patronage raised fears of parliamentary corruption among the likes of William Maclay. "What a set of vipers I have to deal with," he groaned early in the congressional session. He dutifully if inconsistently attended Washington's levee on December 14, as did other Republicans seemingly "borne down by fashion and a fear of being charged with a want of respect to Genl. Washington." The Pennsylvanian had no such fears. "If there is treason in the wish, I retract it. But would to God this same Genl. Washington were in Heaven. We would not then have him brought forward as the constant cover to every unconstitutional and irrepublican act."

True to form, Washington pretended not to hear such mutterings; encroaching deafness had its uses. In a letter to Gouverneur Morris on December 17 he chose instead to emphasize favorable tidings. Congress had resumed its work and the outlook was bright. "Public credit is high, and stocks have risen amazingly." Except for a few hostile Indians on the western frontier, "instigated . . . I am persuaded by the British traders . . . the wheels of government move without interruption and gather strength as they move." Washington expected that when the final numbers were in, the 1790 census would show a population of five million or more. "Whilst this will on the one hand astonish Europe, it may on the other add consequence to the union of these states."

Not every American accepted this view of union. That same week Patrick Henry and the Virginia Assembly lodged a sharp protest against funding and assumption and the administration's alleged bias toward monied rather than landed interests. Picking up the gauntlet, Hamilton warned that Virginia's action was the first symptom of a spirit that must be destroyed "or it will kill the Constitution of the United States."

A missionary impulse in Hamilton's character had led him while still in college to write hymns as zealously as he refuted the Tory arguments of New York's Anglican bishop, Samuel Seabury. Hamilton's climb from the humblest of origins confirmed the parable of the ten talents: for those blessed with ability, burying it in the ground was sinful. With similar fervor, the secretary now leapfrogged Washington's call for a uniform currency, better roads, and improved postal service. Let others create agencies of national consolidation, he reasoned. He would diversify and democratize the American economy by expanding federal power and the opportunities it afforded to the venturesome.

Hamilton's overarching goal was nothing less than the unsentimental meritocracy first outlined in *The Federalist*, Number 72: "There are strong minds in every walk of life that will rise superior to the disadvantages of situation and will command the tribute due to their merit, not only from the classes to which they particularly belong, but from society in general."

For Hamilton, capitalism was high and holy work, and the future belonged to him. America's industrial revolution was born on December 21, 1790, in a Pawtucket, Rhode Island, cotton mill. But its genesis lay in stolen British technology, Richard Arkwright's cording and spindle machinery to be precise, whose parts were reconstructed from memory by Arkwright's former apprentice Samuel Slater. A Scottish immigrant named Duncan Phyfe opened a chair shop in New York in 1790, the same year Washington's dentist, John Greenwood, invented a crude drill and the American publishing industry came of age with *Dobson's Encyclopedia*, to which the president, in his capacity as a patron of letters, duly subscribed.

Washington was almost drawn into industrial espionage himself when Governor Beverly Randolph of Virginia asked his help in establishing a woolen manufactory. Washington begged off, explaining, "It certainly would not carry an aspect very favorable to the dignity of the United States for the President in a clandestine manner to entice the subjects of another nation to violate its laws." Moreover, "I am told that it is a felony to export the machine."

Few of Hamilton's entrepreneurs had Slater's memory or Washington's scruples. Fewer still commanded the necessary resources to turn an idea into a process or a blueprint into a factory. Lacking working capital, Washington's economy was a mill without grist. At the time of his inauguration, the president had been forced to borrow $600, at ruinous rates, just to get to New York. Investment funds were universally scarce and chronically so in the South, whose wealth was routinely siphoned off into land and slaves to the neglect of machinery and roads.

Hamilton, typically, had a solution in mind. On December 14, as congressmen reacted to the first official word of Josiah Harmar's drubbing, he delivered to the House of Representatives a long-awaited sequel to his *Report on the Public Credit*. To pay off the debts assumed earlier that year, Hamilton urged nearly $900,000 to be raised in excise taxes on domestically distilled spirits. Short of a direct tax or increased tariffs, neither of which was politically feasible, Hamilton had little alternative. This didn't make the idea any more popular in the South and West, whose grain farmers, lacking access to eastern markets, converted their crops into a truly liquid currency. Three thousand back-yard distilleries dotted the hills and hollows of western Pennsylvania alone, as vital to the agrarian economy as bonds and brokers to eastern manufacturers.

Class distinctions rubbed salt into the farmers' wounds. Medical men in Philadelphia petitioned Congress for duties burdensome enough to restrain the intemperate use of spirits, much as their latter-day counterparts would demand strong federal action to discourage cigarette smoking. In response, Georgia's James Jackson vehemently defended the constitutional right to imbibe and branded the doctors hypocrites and elitists for enjoying the product of local breweries and cider presses while poor Georgians, lacking either apples or barley, "cannot drink a bowl of grog or toddy without paying such a nefarious d-ble excise, as will oblige them to go to bed sober almost every night of the week." Start down this road, said Jackson, and in time the College of Physicians would demand the abolition of catsup, "because some ignorant persons had been poisoned eating mushrooms."

Georgia's thirst notwithstanding, the House easily passed the excise plan at the end of January 1791. The Senate followed suit a few days later. While there was never any doubt of Washington's assent to the new taxes, the second half of Hamilton's plan was a very different story. Assumption and the excise tax were the yin and yang of Hamilton's undeclared war on state sovereignty. But as long as the American economy was starved for working capital, the Constitution would remain an economic dead letter. It was Hamilton's audacious vision to believe that the government must take a leading role in creating wealth, not least of all to cement the loyalty of commercial and mercantile interests to the new regime. Taking the Bank of England for his model, Hamilton wanted Congress to charter a National Bank — the name was deliberately, even provocatively, chosen — that could serve the government's convenience and act as a motor of commercial development. The secretary would have the federal government contribute $2 million of the bank's $10 million initial capital, entitling it to five of the institution's twenty-five directors. The Bank of the United States would then issue banknotes supported by government bonds (only a fraction of the bank's assets could be redeemed in gold or silver). These notes would serve the cashless republic as a circulating medium, drawing out additional bonds that might otherwise be hoarded.

As if by waving a magic wand, Hamilton hoped to create a substantial new capital reserve at attractive rates of interest. Businessmen reassured by the bank's twenty-year charter would respond by making long-range plans of their own. For the government, a safe place to store its funds was no more welcome than the establishment of branch offices, allowing Washington's administration to shift accounts on paper, paying its bills and receiving tax revenue without moving so much as an ounce of precious metal. To angry agrarians, for whom the only good debt was one honorably (and tangibly) extinguished through the sale of land or a cash crop, this was prosperity by bookkeeping, the most odious kind of social engineering.

William Maclay spoke for many rural Americans when he denounced banks as aristocratic structures imposing taxes on the poor. Yet not even he questioned Congress's right to incorporate a bank. Neither did his fellow senators, who approved Hamilton's plan by voice vote on January 20.

Traditional accounts of what happened next have Madison, after a careful review of Virginia's election returns, reversing his earlier nationalism and opposing the bank with the tortuous argument that Congress had no expressly delegated power to charter such an institution. Jefferson advanced similar claims within the president's official family, swaying an executive whose scrupulous regard for constitutional niceties exceeded his economic sophistication. Disaster in the form of strict constructionism was narrowly averted only at the last minute, when Hamilton hastily crafted one of the great papers of American statecraft, brilliantly contending for the theory of implied powers and permanently freeing the Constitution from a Jeffersonian straitjacket.

To Hamilton's visionary genius, goes the theory, and not Washington's robust simplicities, we owe the vitality of our organic charter. The problem with this interpretation is that it minimizes Washington's adroitness in dealing with Congress *and* his knowledge that a single misstep could prove fatal to the republican cause. At the height of the debate, for example, the president took Arthur St. Clair to task for unilaterally governing in a Northwest Territory devoid of federal judges. The governor must be more circumspect, said Washington, "for there are not wanting persons who would rejoice to find the slightest ground of clamor against public characters." For a man in Washington's position, where every action established a precedent as it breathed life into the constitutional parchment, prudence was an essential element of leadership.

Actually, the president paid little attention to the bank bill that winter. He was busy formulating plans for the Federal City, reassuring the Chickasaw Nation that the United States had no designs on its rich farmlands along the Tennessee River and seeking fresh expedients with which to pacify an inflamed frontier. Family obligations also competed with public duties. Having taken upon himself the education of his dead brother Samuel's two sons, neither of whom showed much inclination to scholarship, Washington enrolled both at the College of Philadelphia early in January 1791. In an instance where sparing the rod may have spoiled the child, George Steptoe Washington eventually eloped with Dolley Madison's fifteen-year-old sister, Lucy. George's brother, Lawrence, pursued a more conventional path, applying himself to the study of law.

Tobias Lear was deputized to write to Joseph Cook of Philadelphia and dissuade him from placing the Washington family arms over his shop door in the style of British craftsmen patronized by royalty. Billing himself as "Silversmith to the President" would be "very disagreeable" to his employer, said Lear. Surprising as this may have seemed to William Maclay, it could no more perplex him than Washington's deferential behavior at a valedictory dinner for the curmudgeon from Harrisburg, about to be retired against his will.

"He knows the weight of political odium under which I labor," wrote Maclay in his diary for January 21, 1791. "He knows . . . my uniform opposition to funding systems . . . assumptions, high compensations and expensive arrangements."

Given his sensitive political antennae, Washington would also have known of Maclay's impending defeat at the unclean hands of "all the Speculators, Public Creditors, Expectants of Office and Courtiers" in Federalist Pennsylvania. Yet here he was, the arch-Federalist, Hamilton's dupe, paying court to his most vocal tormentor, inviting him to share a sofa and a friendly glass of wine. An unconverted Maclay threw up his hands over the contradiction.

"To the score of his good nature must I place these extra attentions," he finally concluded. "Be it so: it is at least one amiable trait in his character."

Misjudging Washington's kindness for weakness was a mistake repeated by more charitable associates than Maclay. Jefferson knew better. The president's desk was piled high with the output of his versatile pen that winter. Between December 11 and the end of January, the secretary of state all but monopolized Washington's attention with half a dozen major reports covering foreign trade, American navigation rights, the plight of United States citizens held captive by Algerian pirates, and the state of New England's fishing industry.

In his annual message to Congress, drafted with help from Jefferson and Madison, the president had urged Congress to consider how it might "render . . . commerce and agriculture less dependent on foreign bottoms." He shared with Jefferson a deep-seated mistrust of the British ministry and its virtual stranglehold on international shipping. This attitude was by no means unanimous, even around the Cabinet table.

Thanks to the inspired deductions of Julian Boyd, the editor of Princeton University's Jefferson Papers Project, it is possible today to reconstruct a shadowy debate within the Washington administration that complemented the more public controversy surrounding Hamilton's excise and bank proposals. At issue was Jefferson's preference for "reciprocal advantage" in America's foreign relations and the violent interference with free trade caused by Great Britain's maritime dominance.

American trade with China, to cite but one expanding market for U.S. goods, accounted for one seventh of all U.S. imports. But unlike the kettle-bottomed ships of the British East India Company, which weighed up to fifteen hundred tons, American carriers rarely exceeded two hundred tons. Some were so small as to masquerade as tenders for larger ships. Only daring seamanship and fast sailing could enable Yankee captains to compete with Britain's monopoly. Far worse was the Atlantic, a virtual British lake where discriminatory duties placed on American ships by a greedy ministry in London finally provoked calls for economic retaliation.

Enter Thomas Jefferson. When, early in 1791, the French lodged a protest against American laws that treated their ships on an identical footing with those belonging to King George, Jefferson found himself torn between sympathy for a wartime ally and hard-headed nationalism. Unlike Britain, France was a reliable consumer of American tobacco, livestock, whale oil, and wheat. The government in Paris did not discriminate against U.S. shipping. Yet no sooner did Jefferson urge the exemption of French vessels from American tonnage laws than Hamilton registered a strong dissent. Hamilton's congressional allies, meanwhile, dragged their heels on the president's proposed navigation law.

To break the impasse, Washington supplied his secretary of state with the complete record of Gouverneur Morris's ill-fated mission. For two months it lay like a coiled serpent under the diplomatic table, ready to strike at Britain's friends should their delaying tactics destroy chances for the navigation bill favored by the administration. On February 8, Hamilton's supporters in the House overwhelmed Madison's crusade against the bank. "Congress may go home," growled William Maclay the next day. "Mr. Hamilton is all-powerful and fails in nothing he attempts." Equally chagrined by his rival's domination, Jefferson was less certain of his ultimate triumph. "There are certainly persons in all the departments who are going too fast," he notified a friend from Virginia before adding, "The prudence of the President is an anchor of safety to us."

Prudence gave way to daring when a House committee on trade and navigation issues adjourned without acting on American complaints about the preference given to foreign — that is, English — vessels. Dramatic action was called for, and on February 14 Washington took it, publicly revealing for the first time the indignities suffered by his personal representative at the hands of insolent British officials. Not content to let the diplomatic record speak for him, Washington offered the most unflattering interpretation of which Jefferson's pen was capable. The sum of the actions taken by King George's ministers was clear enough: "They declare without scruple they do not mean to fulfill what remains of the Treaty of Peace," including the evacuation of northwestern forts and payment for runaway American slaves.

On the subject of a commercial treaty the British had been at best evasive, holding out for a formal military alliance. As for sending a minister of the first rank in place of Beckwith, Hamilton's confidant, "They made excuses in the first conference, seemed disposed to it in the second, and in the last express an intention of so doing. Their views being thus sufficiently ascertained, I have directed Mr. Morris to discontinue his communications with them." Hamilton put the best possible face on the disclosure, assuring Beckwith with a confidence he could hardly feel that the president held no animosity toward Britain, "yet I do not pretend to say that such views may not have struck the minds of certain persons who have recommended this measure." The Hamilton-Jefferson feud was on.

On February 17, an unusually animated Washington dined with his official family. "He asked very affectionately after you and the children," wrote Abigail Adams to her daughter-in-law, "and at table picked the sugar plums from a cake and requested me to take them for Master John."

Five days later the president observed his fifty-ninth birthday by receiving members of Congress, Cabinet officers, foreign representatives, clergymen, and "Strangers and Citizens of distinction," as classified by the *Gazette of the United States*. Washington also marked the occasion by asking Congress for $40,000 with which to ransom American seamen held captive in Algiers for up to four years. It was among Jefferson's top priorities.

❦ 6 ❧

Offstage, a greater drama was nearing its climax. For almost a week Washington had held in his hands negative opinions from Jefferson and Attorney General Randolph concerning the proposed Bank of the United States. The Virginians based their opposition on a narrow reading of Article I, Section 8, of the Constitution, which authorized Congress to "make all laws which shall be necessary and proper for carrying into execution the foregoing powers." Few imagined it at the time, but the future course of American union pivoted on those delphic adjectives, necessary and proper. For Jefferson, convenience should not be confused with necessity. He buttressed his claim by citing the unratified Tenth Amendment, reserving to the states any power not clearly enumerated in the Constitution.

Shaken by the force of opposition, Washington dashed off a bluntly worded invitation for Hamilton to refute his detractors. Although willing to loan him papers with the reasonings of Jefferson and Randolph, Washington made it plain that he wanted them back as soon as possible. He added the humiliating condition "that no copies of them be taken, as it is for my own satisfaction they have been called for." Could Washington have had Major Beckwith in mind when he wrote this harsh, almost insulting, directive to his secretary of the treasury? Adding to the suspense, the president signified his continuing trust in Madison by asking the congressman to draft a short veto message.

Rumors that the bank might be stillborn touched off savage criticism in financial circles. Some of Hamilton's supporters talked confidently of overriding a veto by Washington. Hamilton saved them the trouble, using ridicule where logic did not suffice to point out the inconsistencies of strict constructionism. A government empowered to build lighthouses to promote commerce could hardly balk at chartering a bank to collect its taxes, pay its salaries, and service its debt. "Every power vested in a government is in its nature sovereign," he wrote, "and includes by force of the term a right to employ all the means requisite . . . to the attainment of the ends of such power . . . If the end be clearly comprehended within any of the specified powers, and if the measures have an obvious relation to that end, and is not forbidden by any particular provision of the Constitution, it may safely be deemed to come within the compass of the national authority."

Here was consolidation writ large. But the question remains: did Hamilton's brief for a central authority supply the rationale Washington required to approve the bank bill? Many historians have tended to view Washington as an Eisenhower-like chairman of the board, uneasily presiding over an opinionated squad of advisers whose intellectual firepower matched their talent for recrimination. In truth, the president did his own thinking, displaying the same firmness and energy in running a government as in commanding an army or managing a plantation. The bank bill should be seen in this light. Hamilton knew that his old commander was already convinced from his brushes with disaster during the war that a strong central government was the price of American survival.

"It is only in our united character, as an empire, that our independence is acknowledged, that our power can be regarded, or our credit supported among foreign nations," Washington had insisted in an impassioned appeal to the states in June 1783. Dissolve the union, and "we shall be left nearly in a state of nature, or we may find by our unhappy experience that there is a natural and necessary progression from the extreme of anarchy to the extreme of tyranny, that arbitrary power is most easily established on the ruins of liberty abused to licentiousness."

Thus Hamilton's plea for the bank, powerful as it was, played perfectly to Washington's muscular nationalism. It did not convert the president so much as it reinforced his natural inclinations. Indeed, shortly before his inauguration, he had written of the need to place the nation's credit on a firmer footing, going so far as to reveal, "I think I see a path, as clear and direct as a ray of light, which if pursued will ensure permanent felicity to the Commonwealth."

Pro-bank forces in Congress, unwilling to trust their case to intellectual arguments alone, exerted pressure on the president by withholding formal approval of the Federal City's boundaries. Washington had but forty-eight hours in which to digest Hamilton's arguments and make up his mind. Jefferson made his job easier by urging approval *if* the executive found the arguments for and against the bank to be evenly divided. The secretary did so out of genuine respect for the legislative function and from a certain ambivalence about personal responsibility that often led him to work through other men to achieve his objectives.

Washington signed the bank bill on February 25. Three days later Jefferson offered a clerk's position in the State Department to Philip Freneau, a classmate of Madison's at Princeton. Destined to become

Washington's least favorite journalist, Freneau had a burning hatred of Britain that colored his life and literature. During the war, he had been imprisoned in a floating British jail, and long after gaining his freedom "the Poet of the American Revolution" remained uncompromisingly hostile to King George, "the Caligula of Great Britain." Asked Freneau:

> Can we ever be thought to have learning or grace,
> Unless it be sent from that damnable place?

It was as a poet turned sea captain that Freneau found his voice in the idiom of popular speech, producing much-loved works like "The Pilot of Hatteras" and "The Jug of Rum." Back in New York, he began yet another career as an anti-Federalist journalist under the tutelage of Francis Childs, whose *New York Daily Advertiser* was the nemesis of royalists, "monocrats," and stockjobbers everywhere. For American independence to be complete, Freneau told his friends, their country must produce a Milton or Addison. His own inclinations, as Madison could attest from personal acquaintance, ran to Swiftian satire. These alone made Freneau a natural counterweight to John Fenno's "paper of pure Toryism" (Jefferson's words), the *Gazette of the United States*.

The modest salary Jefferson could offer his prospective champion was the least of his blandishments, since the position of language clerk — Freneau knew French only — "gives so little to do as not to interfere with any other calling the person may choose." In case the person in question failed to get the hint, the secretary promised to bestow on Freneau a better-paying sinecure as soon as one turned up.

Either their signals were crossed or the poet-polemicist was waiting for a better deal, for in the spring of 1791 Freneau disappointed Jefferson and Madison by rejecting their invitation. When Washington sat down to write to his old friend David Humphreys that March, no scribbling controversialists disturbed his peace. Before adjourning, Washington informed Humphreys, Congress had granted statehood to both Vermont and Kentucky. It had also devised ways to pay the interest on the national debt, established Hamilton's bank, and taken steps toward the long-delayed mint, significant achievements made in a spirit of great cordiality. Granted, in the matter of higher excise taxes and the bank, "the line between the southern and eastern interests appeared more strongly marked than could have been wished . . . but the debates were conducted with temper and candor."

Omens from abroad looked equally auspicious. Spain and England had backed away from war. No one greeted the news more warmly than the pacific republic still licking its wounds from Harmar's catastrophic defeat in the heart of nowhere. "Of the state of things in France we can form no just idea," wrote Washington, "so various and contradictory are our accounts . . . but we most devoutly wish a speedy and happy termination of the struggle, which has for some time past convulsed that kingdom."

Closer to home, peace along the northwestern frontier remained elusive. "The Indians still continue their hostilities, and measures are now taking to convince them (if they do not see the folly of their ways before they can be carried into effect) that the enmity of the United States is as much to be dreaded as their friendship is to be desired."

Overall, Washington had good reason to praise the First Congress, and by implication his associates in the executive branch. Less than two years after vowing to protect a Constitution enacted largely through his personal influence, the president could report, "Our public credit is restored, our resources are increasing, and the general appearance of things at least equals the most sanguine expectation that was formed of the effects of the present government."

Washington was about to embark upon a strenuous journey through the southern states, risking his horses on atrocious roads in hopes of conserving his health before the summer's heat made travel dangerous as well as disagreeable. Preparations for the trip had already consumed two weeks, he told Humphreys, and pressing departmental affairs occupied the rest of his days. "If I have not said everything in this letter that I intended or that you might expect, it must be imputed to the hurry of the moment," Washington scrawled in haste. "But at any rate there is one thing I must not omit, which is to tell you that I am very sincerely your affectionate friend."

A still warmer message went out on March 19 to Lafayette. "My health is now quite restored," Washington reassured his French protégé, "and I flatter myself with the hope of a long exemption from sickness. On Monday next I shall enter on the practice of your friendly prescription of exercise." Underlining his anxiety over affairs in France, Washington broke his rule against offering transatlantic counsel to the rebels of Paris. He was well aware, he said, "that it is impossible to judge with precision of measures the motives of which are sometimes unknown and the necessity of them not always understood."

But there was one matter of surpassing concern, for the president was apprehensive lest "the present National Assembly may not protract their existence so long as to beget any uneasiness on that score." Even this mild expression of alarm was offset by apologetic explanation: "My affection for the French nation, my sincere wish that their government may be respectable and their people happy, will excuse the disclosure of this sentiment, the only one, I believe, that I have ventured to offer on the subject of the revolution."

Halfway through his term, resigned to three months of southern parades, toasts, and public gawking, Washington concluded his first letter to Lafayette in almost a year with a strangely mournful comparison. "Like you, my dear Sir, I sighed for retirement," he wrote. "Like me, I am afraid, you must continue the sacrifice."

❊ 5 ❊

TO SEE AND BE SEEN

"On Monday the second at 2 o'clock P.M. the beloved and excellent GEORGE WASHINGTON, Esq. President of the United States of America, arrived in this city, with his suite, to the inexpressible satisfaction as well of the citizens as of strangers. Never, it may be truly said, was joy, love, affection, and esteem more universal upon any one occasion — and never did these amiable passions of the human heart animate or more brilliantly display themselves than upon this occasion — an occasion so worthy of their indulgence and their operation."

Virginia Herald,
May 26, 1791

POLITICS IS THEATER, and George Washington was America's first actor-president. The Constitution made Washington head of state as well as head of the government, and no man had a better grasp of ceremonial leadership than George III's American usurper. The Washington presidency was nothing if not theatrical. Why else the elaborate rituals of levee and drawing room, of triumphal progress to occasions of state and deferential responses from lawmakers for whom the president was both symbol of continuity and instrument of change? As the embodiment of revolutionary virtue, Washington knew that wherever he appeared, partisan murmurs would be lost in a chorus of hero worship. This alone was enough to make him the young republic's greatest asset and only glue.

It also helps to explain much of the man's formality and reserve. Kings might have been in bad odor after 1789, but familiarity still subverted prestige, and republican institutions no less than royal ones had their dignity and legitimacy to maintain.

Beyond this, much of Washington's public life had been calculated for effect, his skills perfected on a military stage. In the spring of 1789, thousands cheered the president-elect as he made his way through the Middle States from Mount Vernon to New York. A few months later, New Englanders accorded him as great a triumph as ever befell a Roman Caesar, one versifier in the *Keene* (New Hampshire) *Recorder* calling the eminent visitor "next unto the Trinity," at the very least a worthy rival to any known object in the universe:

> Behold the matchless Washington —
> His glory has eclip'd the sun;
> The lustre of his rays so bright,
> 'Tis always day, there's no more night.

Now, in the spring of 1791, Washington began planning a third swing around the circle. Several factors influenced his decision to undertake this grueling journey over nineteen hundred miles of primitive southern roads, putting up with blistering heat, unreliable ferries, indifferent accommodations, tedious public dinners, and the heave and pull of local factions, each vying to outdo the other in welcoming matchless Washington to the neighborhood. While the trip might be arduous enough to keep Martha at home, it promised plenty of the rugged outdoor life that the president needed to stay healthy.

Washington welcomed a touch of adventure at the same time that he hoped to gain direct knowledge of southern agriculture and commerce and, like the aging actress who hates publicity but adores attention, not a little ego gratification. In addition, he wished to see with his own eyes the condition and disposition of his fellow Southerners, many of whom were said to be unhappy over Hamilton's excise taxes and national bank. So, at least, Tobias Lear confided to David Humphreys. Proving he could be as lachrymose as any Yankee editor, Lear expected the president to submerge sectional feelings through "the vivifying influence of a vernal Sun."

The real thing was barely above the horizon on the morning of March 21, when Washington climbed into a magnificent white coach recently rebuilt for $950 by the Clark brothers of Philadelphia and ordered his coachman, a tall, muscular Hessian named John Fagan, to crack the whip. For lucky bystanders, a presidential visit combined the more picturesque aspects of a royal progress, Fourth of July rally, and society ball. The mere sight of Washington and his traveling retinue was enough to last a lifetime in the memory of rural Americans starved for pageantry. Besides Major Jackson and Hessian John on his leopard-skin-covered coachman's box, the president was accompanied by a valet, two footmen, and a postilion escorting the Washington chariot. Bringing up the rear were a light baggage wagon and five saddle horses, most prominent among them Prescott, a pure white charger of sixteen hands accustomed from many campaigns to the crash of artillery and the bugle's shriek.

The trip nearly ended before it began. On the stormy night of March 24, both Prescott and his rider risked drowning when a ferry grounded in the mouth of the Severn River outside Annapolis, Maryland. The president's discomfort increased as he lay for hours in a cramped berth, unable to remove his drenched greatcoat and boots, while lightning bolts flashed and sheets of rain battered the frail craft. A second near-disaster occurred the next morning when Washington's coachman almost drowned as he transferred the chariot and horses to a smaller ship.

Readers of the *Maryland Journal and Baltimore Advertiser* were treated to reverential prose describing "the chief treasure of America" as he made the hazardous crossing of the Severn. Striking a sandbar near shore, the wayward vessel had been cut off from rescuers by rising waters. "It was impossible, before daylight, to go to her relief," reported the newspaper. Fortunately, "the guardian-angel of America was still watchful, and we are happy in assuring our countrymen that the health of their dearest friend has not been at all affected by an accident far more distressing to those who were apprised or rather apprehensive of his situation than to himself." Washington used much harsher language to describe the ineptitude that had grounded him not once but twice within a mile of Maryland's capital. "I was in imminent danger from the unskillfulness of the hands and the dullness of her sailing," he wrote.

Shaking off the effects of both, he walked around the little city on the morning of the twenty-fifth, at one point stopping to revisit the room in which he had given up command of the Continental Army. Washington made no reference to the earlier scene in his diary, observing merely that the State House "seems much out of repair." He mistakenly called the wife of Governor John Edgar Howard "Mrs. Howell," praised the faculty of St. John's College, and sat down to a marathon dinner at Munn's Tavern, where fifteen toasts reflected the political priorities and physical endurance of a ceremonial age:

1. The People of the United State of America.
2. The Congress.
3. The dearest Friend of his Country.
4. The State of Maryland.

5. Wisdom, Justice, and Harmony, in all our Public Councils.
6. Agriculture, Manufactures, Commerce, and Learning, may they all flourish with virtue and true Religion.
7. The king of the French.
8. The National Assembly of France.
9. The Sieur la Fayette, and generous Friends to America in the Day of her Distress.
10. The memory of all those who have fallen in the Cause of America.
11. The Patriots of all nations and Ages.
12. The powers of Europe friendly to America.
13. May all Inhabitants of the Earth be taught to consider each other as Fellow Citizens.
14. The virtuous Daughters of America.
15. The perpetual Union of distinct Sovereign States under an efficient Federal head.

Amid the hilarious comradeship of the banquet hall, few stopped to consider how sovereign states could remain distinct within perpetual union, especially under a head as efficient as the guest of honor.

{ 2 }

From Bladensburg, Maryland, Lear's "sincere and affectionate friend" tended to a personal matter. "Furnish Mrs. Washington with what money she may want — and from time to time ask if she does want, as she is not fond of applying." System was the soul of business, Washington liked to say, and by the time he reached Mount Vernon this most methodical of men was able to supply his Cabinet officers with a detailed itinerary of his journey that would prove astonishingly accurate. He also left instructions for the departmental heads to coordinate government business while he was absent and how, in the event of sudden need, they could summon him back to Philadelphia.

Had he achieved nothing else, by the first week of April the tour could already be considered a success, thanks to a compromise he negotiated between landholders in Georgetown and Carrollsburgh, the proposed federal district. At a meeting in Suter's Tavern in Georgetown, Washington convinced the rival camps "whilst they were contending for the shadow they might lose the substance" of a real estate boom sure to enrich both communities. The upshot of his appeal — and his implied threat — was a series of concessions that included large donations of land for public buildings. The way was cleared for Pierre Charles L'Enfant, the

Continental Army officer who had rebuilt New York's Federal Hall, to fashion a plan for the Federal City.

Thinking small was never L'Enfant's way. The precocious architect envisioned a metropolis of 800,000 people (Washington, D.C., in 1993 houses just over 600,000), bisected by eighty-foot avenues and crowned by a vast park surrounding the "Presidential Palace." Subsequent events would prove the audacious L'Enfant better at planning cities than dealing with their inhabitants.

On the heels of his triumph in Georgetown, on April 4 Washington replied to Hamilton's deliberately provocative news that New York State might pursue its own, separate negotiations with Cornplanter and the Senecas. What would the Indians think of such irregularity? the president asked with rising temper. "Why, that we pursue no system," for Washington a nearly sacrilegious offense, "and that our declarations are not to be regarded. To sum the whole up in a few words, the interferences of states and the speculations of individuals will be the bane of all our public measures."

A second communication, from Hamilton's rival, awaited the president at Mount Vernon. Avoiding contentious public affairs, Jefferson offered the much-traveled chief executive commiseration and some counsel. "I shall be happy to hear that no accident has happened to you on the bad roads you have passed," wrote the secretary of state, who knew at first hand the jolting agony of riding through the Virginia countryside, "and that you are . . . prepared for those to come by lowering the hang of your carriage and exchanging the coachman for two postilions."

Washington thanked his subordinate without taking his advice. He may have entertained second thoughts on April 7, when one of his horses, "hitched to the chariot by the neglect of the person who stood before them," panicked at a river crossing north of Fredericksburg, nearly dragging the other animals and Washington's coach into the Ocquoquam Creek. In Fredericksburg the president renewed acquaintances with his sister, Betty, and her thirteen children. There was the obligatory public dinner and more toasts, Washington's ("The town we are in, prosperity to its inhabitants") proving most popular. So popular, in fact, that it became his standard exit line throughout his tour, a fragrant, bipartisan rose tossed at local sensibilities.

Few men are at their best at six o'clock in the morning, and Washington was no exception. He found it hard to maintain his majesty when a band of Fredericksburg's brightest social lights insisted on attending the presidential coach at that hour for several miles, oblivious of the clouds of red dust kicked up by their horses. Things went more smoothly on Tuesday, the twelfth, when Washington, together with Virginia's governor and the directors of the James River Navigation Company, went to view the canal and locks above Richmond. Each of the locks, designed to raise vessels six feet, had cost £3,000, an extravagance Washington found appalling. "I could see nothing in them to require such a sum," he snorted.

Reports of his adopted grandson's poor performance in the classroom led to fresh grumbling. "Boys of his age are better pleased with relaxed discipline — and the inattention of their tutors," Washington wrote to Lear from Richmond. Before deciding young Wash's future, the president wanted Lear to consult with the attorney general and secretary of the treasury, each of whom had sons in college. As Patrick Henry's fiefdom and an anti-Federalist bastion, Richmond might fairly be considered enemy territory. To help him assess the local temper, Washington talked politics with Edward Carrington, John Marshall's brother-in-law and a staunch Federalist who had recently been appointed U.S. marshal for Virginia. Carrington was inclined to tell Washington what he wanted to hear, minimizing restiveness over the administration's fiscal policies and dismissing as alarmist talk of organized resistance to the excise tax.

A more authentic source was readily available in Richmond's formal address of greeting, exquisitely worded to avoid offense while reminding the president that the voice of the people was the Almighty's trumpet. Virginians understood that to a mind such as Washington's, "fraught with benevolence and affection for all mankind . . . nothing could be more painful than the servility which would convert the sentiment of love into the language of adulation." Anything but servile, the Richmonders nevertheless invoked divine protection for the American empire and the successful completion of Washington's tour. His hosts added a typically morbid petition, that when providence saw fit to summon the president home, "you may be wafted to the regions of eternal happiness, lamented by men and welcomed by angels."

Washington's more immediate concern was avoiding the dust storms that pursued him as he made careful note of the region's crops, attended a ball in the company of "between 60 and 70 ladies," and viewed the tobacco port of Petersburg from the heights overlooking the town of 3,000. On April 15 the president neatly executed his retreat from the area. "Having suffered very much by the dust yesterday," he wrote, not feeling in the least guilty over his falsehood, "and finding that parties of Horse and a number of other gentlemen were intending to attend me part of the way today, I caused their enquiries respecting the time of my setting out to be answered that I should endeavor to do it before eight o'clock; but I did it a little after five, by which means I avoided the inconveniences above mentioned."

Only by practicing the arts of deception could Washington enjoy a few hours to himself, riding bleak southern roads instead of inhaling them. Four hundred mostly desolate miles separated Petersburg from Charleston. As his chariot bumped its way through the "level piney country" of southern Virginia, his horses rapidly lost flesh, and traveler's amenities grew less appealing with every mile. "The only inn short of Halifax having no stables in which the horses could be comfortable," he confessed near the state line, "and no rooms or beds which appeared tolerable, and everything else having a dirty appearance," Washington resigned himself to the makeshift hospitality of North Carolina and points south.

❧ 3 ❧

The tour developed its own rhythm as it rolled across Tarheel country. Up before dawn, Washington and his party often rode twenty miles or more before breakfasting at a roadside inn or tavern; fifty miles a day was not an unusual distance for the tightly scheduled group to cover. To mask his distaste for extemporaneous oratory, Washington's appearances were structured to cut down on spontaneity, much as today's candidates ration events with television in mind. Welcoming remarks from his hosts, even the most cloying or innocuous, were submitted to the president's staff in advance and only later answered in formal, stilted language drafted by Major Jackson with Washington's approval.

On the road, Washington spent most of his time in the Clark brothers' splendid coach of state, with its silver-plated harnesses and engraved copper plates fashioned by an Italian artist who had done similar work for George III. When approaching a settlement, Washington left the coach to mount Prescott for his carefully choreographed entrance into town.

Washington's horses seem to have enjoyed better treatment than any human members of the official party. Every night the handsome white chargers were covered with paste and swathed in body cloths before being put to bed on clean straw. In the morning, they were rubbed vigorously and brushed until their glossy coats shone like satin. Hooves blackened and polished, mouths washed, teeth picked and rinsed, the stately beasts drew admiring stares wherever they pranced.

So did their owner, although even Washington had his off days. April 17, 1791, was one. The residents of Halifax, North Carolina, twenty miles south of the Virginia line, seemed unusually restrained in their enthusiasm. The county seat on the Roanoake River was the home of Willie Jones, the spearhead of North Carolina's original opposition to the Constitution. The state had since reversed its position, but not Jones, who refused to greet Washington in his capacity as president of a United States that he, Willie Jones, wished to treat as a foreign power.

Washington put Halifax behind him on April 18, journeying thirty-six miles to Tarborough, there to be greeted by "as good a salute as could be given by one piece of artillery." Despite its ceremonial shortcomings, the village appeared to Washington "more lively and thriving" than Halifax, its economy buttressed by "Corn, Porke and some Tar." Twenty-five miles beyond lay Greensville and a second-rate inn lacking stables. Washington's horses were forced to spend a night in the open for the first time in a month. No such indignity marred the president's schedule, but accommodations were haphazard as he turned toward New Berne on the twentieth.

That morning Washington appeared in the yard of Colonel John Allen and his family, whose home he mistook for a public house. As Colonel Allen bade his unexpected guests welcome, Mrs. Allen summoned help and within an hour produced an enormous spread of ham, turkey, fried chicken, sausages, waffles, several kinds of eggs, and hot soda biscuits. Washington contented himself with a single hard-boiled egg and some coffee flavored with rum. Only in asking Allen for a bill did the president discover his error, but by then it was too late to do anything but yield gracefully to his host's wishes.

Of course, even southern hospitality could be carried to extremes. "Another small party of horse under one Simpson met us at Greensville," Washington wrote with unconcealed annoyance, "and in spite of every endeavor which could comport with decent civility to excuse myself from it, they would attend me to Newbern." He may have thought longingly of the Allens' groaning board during his two-day visit in New Berne: privately, he lamented the absence of griddle cakes from his table. The strain of the journey was beginning to show on the fifty-nine-year-old traveler, who passed up an evening illumination to spend rare hours alone in some "exceedingly good lodgings."

Washington was more than sufficiently rested the next night to attend a ball at the rambling brick folly built by the royal governor William Tyron. Stabling his horses in Tyron's former office and dancing a minuet under the marble gaze of George III, the guest of honor stayed on the dance floor until eleven o'clock, the presence of seventy ladies softening his usual reserve to the point where he was observed shaking hands. Before setting out for Wilmington on April 22, the president wrote to Tobias Lear that he had come through the journey thus far "tolerably well," which was more than could be said for some of his horses. The country between New Berne and Wilmington was the most barren Washington had ever seen, in some stretches little more than vast, white sandbeds.

A party of light horses and some leading citizens were outside Wilmington to greet the president and guide him to the elegant downtown dwelling of the widow Quince. In describing the city Washington noted, "It has some good houses pretty compactly built." A mudbank several miles below the town did not prevent vessels of 250 tons from carrying away substantial cargos of tobacco, corn, rice, lumber, and flax seed. At a public ceremony on Monday, the twenty-fifth, Washington was visibly pleased to receive from his hosts one of the most explicit endorsements yet of the Constitution, "that admirable political fabric." Not to be outdone, he issued a sweeping forecast of continued prosperity based upon the rapid improvements everywhere noticeable in the youthful republic and "a well-founded expectation that every aid which a wise and virtuous legislation can render to individual industry will be afforded."

Was this a veiled pledge of support for Hamiltonian economics? Or merely one more bromide issued for the benefit of Wilmington's industrious burghers? Whatever the president's motive, republican journals stirred uneasily as Washington made his way toward aristocratic, hedonistic Charleston. On April 30, Philadelphia's *Independent Gazette* warned of incipient monarchist tendencies:

"We find by the southern papers that the President, on his journey, is still perfumed with the incense of *addresses*. However highly we may consider the character of the chief Magistrate of the Union" (one ponders the journalistic fate of "America's chief treasure"), "yet we cannot but think the fashionable mode of expressing our attachment to the defender of the liberty of his country savors too much of monarchy to be used by Republicans or to be received with pleasure by a President of a Commonwealth."

The plainspoken editor would have been still more shocked by the harbor full of gaily dressed Charlestonians who watched as Washington was rowed to a wharf at the foot of Queen Street. Throughout the short passage he stood in a twelve-oared barge built for the occasion and manned by captains uniformly clad in jackets of blue silk and round black hats decorated with the arms of South Carolina. Forty ships joined in the tribute, led by the waterborne choir of St. Philip's Church:

> He comes! he comes! the hero comes.
> Sound, sound your trumpets, beat your drums,
> From port to port let cannons roar,
> His welcome to our friendly shore.

So began a week of superlatives, the most exciting in Charleston's history. In preparation for Washington's visit, the Common Council had voted to purchase black varnished wands six feet long for the intendant (mayor) and his twelve wardens (city councilors) to carry in public processions. The bells of St. Michael's Church had been repaired and the residence of Thomas Hayward on Church Street leased for £60 to serve as a presidential guest house. Hayward was away from the city, like many in the planter oligarchy who devoted themselves to society each winter and during warmer months to the rice culture on which much of the city's prosperity depended.

Whatever the season, Charlestonians were a festive lot. A visiting Frenchman said that no one thought of anything but pleasure after four in the afternoon. This was not Washington's style, but the president won the city's heart anyway, and some precious freedom for himself, the moment he set foot on Prioleau's Wharf to be greeted by Governor Charles Pinckney, Senators Ralph Izard and Pierce Butler, and strutting members from the Society of the Cincinnati. When an artillery battalion offered to stand guard throughout his visit the president declined, explaining that no harm could come to him "in the affection and amicable attachment of the people."

A cheering throng escorted Washington to the red brick Exchange on Broad Street, from whose steps he reviewed a procession of civic and military officials, professionals, and craftsmen. The parade neatly reflected the makeup of Charleston, a rigidly stratified town of 16,000 equally divided between whites and black slaves. The populace struck Washington as "wealthy, gay, and hospitable." They also appeared to support their new government, but as with Edward Carrington in Richmond, it cannot be said that the president spent much time seeking the opinions of day laborers or the stevedores who loaded rice onto ships in the harbor.

Their opinion didn't count in a state where voting was a privilege, restricted to white males owning at least 50 acres of land, and officeholding a right determined by wealth and breeding. Washington would remove his hat and bow gracefully to the man on the street, but he dined and danced with the elite, beginning with fifteen or eighteen nabobs invited by Governor Pinckney to entertain "in a family way" on the day of the president's arrival.

No tourist could have been more tireless in exploring the colorful city. Not for Charlestonians the brick monotony of Philadelphia or Boston's sober wooden mazes. Riding through streets filled with sand, Washington saw a sprinkling of pink and blue stucco houses, built to replace wooden structures destroyed in the war, shaded by palmetto trees and washed by warm harbor breezes. On Tuesday, May 3, he breakfasted with Elizabeth Rutledge, whose husband, John, was out riding the circuit as the state's chief justice. That afternoon at two, the president wrote in his diary, he was visited "by a great number of the most respectable ladies of Charleston — the first honor of the kind I had ever experienced and . . . flattering as it was singular." Two addresses were received and answered before a public dinner at the Exchange, where Washington sat under a triumphal arch engrossed in conversation with a prominent wit, Miss Claudia Smith, and the legendary beauty Mrs. Richard Shubrick.

Fifteen toasts notwithstanding, a clearheaded chief executive was up early the next day to examine what remained of the city's defenses and to refight the controversial, failed battle of Charleston conducted by General Benjamin Lincoln in the spring of 1780. To a journalist, Washington praised Lincoln and the city's gallant defenders, reserving for the privacy of his diary criticism of a campaign "undertaken upon wrong principles and impolitic." It is a safe bet that he said nothing of the kind at dinner that day with the Cincinnati or at the evening's "very elegant dancing assembly" graced by "256 elegantly dressed and handsome ladies."

May 5 brought more visits to ruined forts, another dinner at Governor Pinckney's house, and, best of all, an evening concert by St. Cecilia's Society "at which there were at least 400 ladies — the number and appearances of which exceeded anything of the kind I had ever seen." Contributing to their appeal were bandeaux worn around the forehead inscribed in gold with such patriotic sentiments as "Health to Columbia's noblest son, her light and shield — great Washington." The sixth was relatively quiet, allowing the president to see the town on horseback before yet another ball "where there was a select company of ladies." Over the weekend, he visited an orphanage, admired Charleston's gardens, and climbed the steeple of St. Michael's, to which he returned for the first of two Sunday services, not neglecting its crosstown rival, St. Philip's.

The city fathers wished to commission a presidential portrait; Washington, hiding the distaste he felt whenever he was asked to pose for an artist, gave his consent. Affecting good-natured resignation to his lot, he went so far as to mock his own vanity, writing, "I am so hackneyed to the touches of the painter's pencil that I am now altogether at their beck and sit like patience on a monument . . . At first I was as impatient at the request, and as restive under the operation, as a colt is of the saddle. The next time I submitted very reluctantly, but with less flouncing. Now, no dray moves more readily to the thill than I do to the painter's chair."

It wasn't true, of course. Already by 1791 Washington was limiting portrait sittings to official bodies and municipal requests. In time, even those would be denied. At six o'clock on the morning of May 9, Washington took leave of Charleston's "principal Gentleman" at the Ashley River Bridge. The intendant delivered a short farewell address, for which the president tendered thanks, and as a final volley of musket fire crackled in the soft spring air, Washington climbed into his coach, passed under a triumphal arch, and disappeared from view.

❈ 4 ❧

Washington was not the only statesman on the road that May. As his chariot clattered toward Savannah, Thomas Jefferson made final preparations for a month-long circuit of New England and the Hudson River valley. Leaving Philadelphia on May 17, he stopped in New York City to pick up James Madison. Together, they hooked speckled trout from Lake George, visited a thriving nailery, and took copious notes about northern firs, junipers, and azaleas. This was ostensibly a scientific expedition, one of whose purposes was to learn more about the noxious Hessian fly. But since Jefferson and Madison's route included Governor George Clinton's Albany and allowed time for visits with Hamilton's downstate enemies Aaron Burr and Chancellor Robert Livingston (not to mention renewed lobbying with Philip Freneau in New York City), historians ever since have speculated that the travelers were thinking of pests other than the Hessian fly.

Adding to the air of intrigue was a seemingly minor personnel dispute arising from the death of Comptroller of the Treasury Nicholas Everleigh on April 16. Within twenty-four hours, Jefferson wrote to the president in Charleston, urging him to fill the vacancy with Tench Coxe, an assistant to the secretary of the treasury but in fact a loyal Jeffersonian. With equal speed, Hamilton contacted the president on behalf of his dependable Federalist auditor, Oliver Wolcott. "I am influenced by information that other characters will be brought to your view by weighty advocates," wrote Hamilton in justifying his haste. But Coxe's advocate had less weight than he imagined. Washington selected Wolcott, who went on to a distinguished, if partisan, career at the Treasury.

No sooner had he recommended Coxe than Jefferson again made himself unpopular by endorsing Thomas Paine's *Rights of Man*, a recent publication. Fresh from his triumph carrying an American flag in Paris's Festival of the Federations, celebrating the first anniversary of the Bastille's fall, Paine had dashed off a fiery rebuttal to Edmund Burke's indictment of a French revolution veering toward anarchy.

King Louis retained his head, but little else, in the spring of 1791. He was a prisoner of the National Assembly, which was a prisoner of the streets. Lafayette, "le Vassington français," was a prisoner of his own insatiable appetite for popularity and of boyish enthusiasms that swung him like a weathercock from mesmerism to the colonization of emancipated slaves in the distant colony of Cayenne. The shortcomings of individual revolutionaries mattered less to Jefferson than the "beautiful" revolution itself, inseparably linked to his own country's liberation. For an arch-Tory like Burke to denounce it only confirmed the "rottenness" of his mind.

Recommending Paine's counterblast to an American publisher was fairly innocent in itself. But it bordered on absurdity to believe, as Jefferson later claimed, that Paine's words would not be widely circulated or contrasted for political effect with the aristocratic social philosophy put forward in John Adams's recent book, *Discourses on Davila*. In thirty-two provocative installments appearing in John Fenno's pro-administration paper, the vice president expounded his theories of human vanity and their implication for republican governments. Adams's fellow creatures cared more for public praise than personal duty, and it was foolish to believe that this most basic human instinct could be legislated away. Knowledge might be disseminated more widely, but greed for reputation lived on, stubbornly resistant to Utopian reformers. Government, said Adams, was established "to set bounds to passions which nature has not limited." To succeed, civil institutions must themselves strike a balance.

The vice president broke ranks with his old friend over France's gathering tumult. Anticipating as much, on May 8 Jefferson wrote again to the president, insisting that his endorsement of Paine should not be taken as a criticism of Adams. Jefferson distinguished between the vice president's erstwhile republicanism and his current "apostasy" in favor of hereditary rule by an imagined governing class. As for himself, "I certainly never made a secret of my being anti-monarchical and anti-aristocratical, but I am sincerely mortified to be thus brought forward on the public stage, where to remain . . . will be equally against my love of silence and quiet and my abhorrence of dispute."

However genuine Jefferson's desire for silence, he rarely shied away from speaking through others, whether the voice employed was that of Freneau's newspaper, Madison's speeches on the House floor, or the slowly organizing mass of opposition to the Hamiltonian program that in Washington's second term would coalesce into the nation's first Republican party.

❦ 5 ❧

Jefferson's letters were an unpleasant foretaste of what the president could expect to encounter in the next state on his itinerary. For if he had fences anywhere that required mending, surely Georgia was the place.

Yet when Washington arrived in Savannah on May 13, his reception proved every bit as tumultuous as that in Charleston. Although it was a Friday, there was nothing unlucky in Washington's deft handling of the Georgians still resentful over the Treaty of New York and his administration's generous treatment of McGillivray and the Creeks. A welcoming committee presented the first of six addresses, recalling their deprivation during the war at the hands of red men and redcoats alike. The president, in turn, lavished praise upon a state "no less distinguished by its services than by its sufferings." A second communication, from the religious community at Midway and Newport, thanked him for making it possible to bury the hatchet with the Creek Nation.

For once, real emotion could be heard as Washington rebuked the Georgians for ascribing their country's many blessings to his exertions. "From the gallantry and fortitude of her citizens, under the auspices of Heaven, America has derived her independence. To their industry and the natural advantages of the country, she is indebted for her prosperous situation . . . Continue, my fellow citizens, to cultivate the peace and harmony which now subsist between you and your Indian neighbors . . . A knowledge of your happiness will lighten the cares of my station and be among the most pleasing of their rewards."

That evening, Washington went to dinner at Brown's Coffee House, where he delivered one of his patented toasts to local prosperity. Another kind of presidential gallantry was displayed at the Filature, a former silkmaking establishment dating from the 1750s, when the colony passed a law denying office to anyone failing to plant one hundred mulberry trees for every 50-acre tract in his possession. Here Washington was introduced to ninety-six ladies, after which he joined in a few minuets and a country dance before retiring around eleven o'clock. While he slept, the people of Savannah celebrated his presence, one alderman illuminating the front of his house with three hundred candles forming a giant W.

Savoring the warmth of his reception, Washington lingered in the coastal town. The feeling was mutual, as the *Georgia Gazette* made plain. Washington's admirable qualities had spread his fame "to the utmost limits of civilization," asserted the *Gazette*, "but it is only by personal interviews that a just idea can be acquired of the amiableness of his temper and his engaging manners." Another side of the great man emerged in his correspondence. Before leaving the coast, he wrote to Tobias Lear with unconcealed frustration that "the ceremonial hurry into which I was thrown by entertainments — visits — and ceremonies of one kind or another scarcely allowed me a moment that I could call my own." (Not so much, however, as to prevent him from advertising the stud services of his Spanish jack, Royal Gift.) Even Prescott was much worn down, his owner confided, "and I have yet 150 or 200 miles of heavy sand to pass before I fairly get into the upper and firmer roads."

A few miles outside Savannah the president dined at the Mulberry Grove plantation of Nathanael Greene's widow, Catherine, a once bewitching creature with whom he had danced for hours in spite of wartime sorrows. Time had not been kind to the Greenes, for Catherine's husband had died from sunstroke in 1786, and his heirs were now sliding toward genteel impoverishment. By the time of Washington's visit, the gracious life of Mulberry Grove was visibly fraying, but if the president felt any trace of melancholy he kept it to himself, reserving the pages of his diary for a terse, farmer's accounting of rice tillage and indigo exports.

Governor Edward Telfair and the Augusta Volunteer Light Horse met Washington outside Georgia's capital on May 18, but the fatigued tourist appeared only briefly at a ball that evening, just long enough to meet a group of ladies invited by the governor's wife. In more businesslike surroundings, the president and Telfair met again the next day. Southerners seeking federal help in reclaiming slaves who had crossed into East Florida, since 1783 a Spanish possession, presented Washington with a quandary. The Spaniards had lately agreed to deny sanction to runaways without making any provision for losses suffered in previous years. Jefferson was understandably fearful that aggressive diplomacy on the issue might jeopardize whatever chance the United States had of obtaining free use of the Mississippi. The best he could promise the unhappy Georgians was a fair hearing.

It fell to Washington to honor this pledge, and he nodded sympathetically as Governor Telfair recited the slaveholders' plight. But when the president sat down to write instructions to James Seagrove, the port collector at St. Mary's, Georgia, on the Florida border, he subordinated past claims to the presently improving relations with the Spanish king. While Seagrove was to do all he could to ensure strict enforcement of the new policy prohibiting runaways, he was also free to use his own judgment when it came to old claims. Washington reminded him that any such attempt would "require peculiar delicacy and must be entered on with caution and circumspection, or not . . . be taken up at all."

{ 6 }

More than two months had passed since Washington left Philadelphia. Weary of ceremony and eager to spend at least a few days at Mount Vernon, he expressed growing irritation at delays caused by nature and circumstance. The road from Augusta to Columbia, South Carolina, he complained on May 22, "is a pine barren of the worst sort, being hilly as well as poor." Slowing things still further, one of his horses had foundered, requiring an extra day in Columbia and an especially early start on May 25. It was two hours before sunrise when the presidential party left for "Cambden," with Washington's lame horse being led every step of the thirty-six-mile route.

Practically the entire population of Camden was on hand to greet the president at two that afternoon. His spirits revived, he paused for a few moments at the grave of Baron de Kalb, the French army officer killed at the Battle of Camden in August 1780. So impressed was Washington with his local host that on returning to Mount Vernon, he dispatched to Colonel John Chestnut a barrel drill plow, his own invention and a source of much pride, for use in planting indigo.

On Friday, the twenty-seventh, Washington again took to the road. Near the North Carolina line he met a delegation of Catawba Indians, concerned about the designs of white Carolinians on 144,000 acres that had been guaranteed to the natives by a 1763 treaty. Neither Congress nor the president wished to handle this particular hot potato, and six years later Washington was still being lobbied by the fearful Catawbas. Charlotte, North Carolina, reached on the twenty-eighth, seemed "a very trifling place." When the captain of a light dragoon company was struck speechless in Washington's presence, the president took the initiative, asking for particulars of the countryside and its part in the war for independence. Informed that, when passing through Charlotte, Lord Cornwallis swore that he had never been in such a damned nest of Whigs, Washington seemed delighted.

The sightseer's diary entries grew shorter as he quickened his homeward pace, with four in the morning a routine time of departure. Dismissing a party of horsemen assigned to escort him to Salisbury, North Carolina, Washington turned around and pronounced a group of forty uniformed youths drawn up to greet him there "the nicest thing he had seen," their very rusticity a welcome contrast to the pompous, preening regulars. Tired or not, the president appeared in good spirits, drinking tea with twenty ladies at Hughes's Hotel and, according to local tradition, declaring himself more pleased with Salisbury's earnest welcome than the far gaudier reception accorded him in Charleston.

Thirty-five miles away lay Salem, a well-ordered Moravian community whose inhabitants worked and worshiped with equal fervor. It was Washington's kind of town, "a small but neat village," as described in his diary, "and like all the rest of the Moravian settlements . . . governed by an excellent police." A band played for his arrival, and the church organ wheezed most of the night. Alighting from his carriage, Washington greeted onlookers warmly, making a special effort to befriend some children gathered to see him. He flattered the residents by requesting music with his evening meal and inviting six of the Moravian brethren to join him.

Washington spent the next day investigating the shops of Salem's industrious craftsmen. He saw tanners and shoemakers, brewers, tinners, and saddlers. While he visited the single-sex housing provided for unmarried members of the community, Major Jackson made inquiries about the congregation's beliefs and social customs. Afterward the president and Governor Alexander Martin went to a musical service; the day concluded with an impromptu concert of wind instruments outside Washington's tavern. Accompanied by Governor Martin, on June 2 Washington visited the bloody field at Guilford Court House where Lord Cornwallis had won a costly victory over Nathanael Greene, attributable to cowardly North Carolina militia who fled after firing a single volley. The president examined the terrain and came away confirmed in his low opinion of amateur soldiers. He registered similarly acerbic disapproval on encountering a large crowd in the area "who had received notice of my intention to be there today and came to satisfy their curiosity."

Before crossing into Virginia on June 4, Washington satisfied his own curiosity in conversations with North Carolina's governor. Opposition to the excise tax was nowhere stronger than among the Tarheel State's congressional delegation, yet Martin believed popular discontent with "the General Government" to be on the wane. Thus reassured, the president summed up his impressions in a lengthy diary entry. He catalogued the region's soil, its topography, forests, and crops, and compared land prices along the coast and in the Tidewater. He also dismissed the South's famed hospitality in terms sure to offend any chamber of commerce: "Excepting the towns (and some gentlemen's seats along the road from Charleston to Savannah), there is not, within view of the whole road I traveled from Petersburg to this place, a single house which has anything of an elegant appearance." Southern accommodations were judged barely adequate for man or beast. "It is not easy to say on which road — the one I went or the one I came — the entertainment is most indifferent — but with truth, it may be added that both are bad."

To the region's credit, its people were orderly, and political contentment seemed the rule. "Where the case was otherwise, it was not difficult to trace the cause to some demagogue or speculating character," Washington wrote, attesting to his conservative outlook, adding that Georgians disgruntled over the treaty with the Creeks were nothing more nor less than "Land Jobbers, who maugre every principle of justice to the Indians." As for the much-vaunted opposition to Hamilton's excise tax, it subsided as soon as the law was explained. Washington heard little of the bank controversy, which was hardly surprising since few of the invariably "respectable" characters who greeted him were about to interrupt the royal progress with unseemly arguments.

On Sunday, June 5, Washington forded the Staunton River. Safely across, he was met by Colonel Isaac Coles, a former congressman from southwestern Virginia, who insisted that the president halt at his house. Washington gratefully accepted, first quartering his servants and horses at a nearby tavern "that they might give no trouble or be inconvenient to a private family." He tarried an extra day to allow the animals the run of Coles's pasture. Leaving at daybreak on the seventh, he covered fifteen miles before stopping to have the horses reshod. Another delay ensued on the ninth, when, thanks to a ferry on the James River being out of commission, the presidential party was forced to wait while smaller vessels made the crossing, carrying one carriage at a time. That night Washington again broke his rule against accepting private entertainment, lodging at a Mrs. Jordan's after riding more than forty miles in sultry weather and taking a wrong road in the bargain.

Turning his face toward Mount Vernon, the president paused to visit his sister in Fredericksburg before reaching Mansion House Farm in time for Sunday dinner on June 13. During the next two weeks he applied to his farms the acute powers of observation employed on his recent journey. Mount Vernon was in the throes of a severe drought, its grass crop scarcely worth cutting, its oats and corn hanging in the balance. In addition, Washington confronted the old bugaboo of domestic problems.

"I am glad to hear that the affairs of our own family are going on well," he told Tobias Lear on June 15, "and it might not be improper to hint to the servants who are with you (before they are joined by those with me) that it will be very idle and foolish in them to enter into any combinations for the purpose of supplanting those who are now in authority . . . these characters are indispensably necessary to take the trouble off the hands of Mrs. Washington and myself and will be supported; any attempts therefore to counteract them in the line of their duty, whilst they act agreeably to established rules and their conduct is marked with propriety, will be considered as the strongest evidence . . . of their own unworthiness, and dispositions to be lazy if not dishonest. A good and faithful servant is never afraid or unwilling to have his conduct looked into," Washington remarked complacently, "but the reverse, because the more it is inspected, the brighter it shines."

Four days later, another letter was on its way to Lear, requesting a copy of "Mr. Payne's answer to Mr. Burke's Pamphlet." The secretary was told to scout out possible replacements for a shiftless stableboy and an incapacitated postilion. From newspaper accounts Washington concluded that it might be possible to obtain, for little more than the cost of their food and clothing, the services of German immigrants. Assuming this was so, he stressed the desirability of "low and squat (well-made) boys."

Before leaving Mount Vernon on June 27, Washington entrusted a formidable program of building repairs to his ailing nephew, George Augustine, and his overseer Anthony Whiting. High on the list were the leaky huts of Washington's people at Dogue Run. River Farm needed a cornhouse, and a Necessary, with two seats, must be erected in the New Quarter. An overseer's house required shingling, the Muddy Hole barn was to be renovated, gravel walks should be laid out in the upper garden. New posts were to be set in the ground bordering Washington's 5-acre bowling green.

An even larger building project awaited the president at Georgetown, where the agreement he had brokered earlier now threatened to unravel in the face of complaints by major landholders that the proposed Federal City was too large. L'Enfant's grandiose schemes, coupled with his dictatorial manners, made the Frenchman a lightning rod for greedy or provincial interests. Faced with rebellion, Washington resorted to a little economic blackmail, reminding his speculative audience that there were many gentlemen in Philadelphia anxious to retain the capital for themselves after 1800 and that delay along the Potomac could only feed northern fantasies of rescinding the great compromise of 1790.

On the twenty-eighth, he toured possible sites for the Capitol and executive mansion, agreeing with L'Enfant's assessment of Jenkins Hill as a pedestal awaiting its monument but exercising his prerogative to move the president's house to take advantage of higher ground. That evening yet another compromise was reached with landowners, and for the moment at least, the Federal City appeared back on track. Well satisfied, Washington indulged himself on June 30 by exploring the heavily timbered country north of Georgetown. His progress was slowed by a rainstorm and the need to compose a reply to an address from the inhabitants of Frederick, Maryland. The rich, rolling fields of western Maryland he thought "remarkably fine," enhanced by solid stone barns and owners to match.

On Sunday, July 3, there being no Episcopal minister in York, Pennsylvania, Washington attended morning services at the Dutch Reformed Church, "which, being in the language not a word of which I understood, I was in no danger of becoming a proselyte to its religion by the eloquence of the Preacher." Following this seriocomic scene, the president steered for Lancaster. The national banner flew from the courthouse cupola and the town's bells delivered a full-throated greeting when he entered town at six-thirty that evening. Since the next day was the anniversary of America's independence, the chief executive consented to remain and participate in the local celebration. On the Fourth he tramped village streets in the forenoon, received and answered yet one more address, chatted with clergymen of varying denominations, and drank tea with the wife of General Edward Hand, one of the "principal characters of Lancaster" and recently appointed the federal inspector of revenue by the president.

Bells pealed again on July 6 when Washington returned to Philadelphia after the longest, most crowded trip of his life. He was welcomed by a fulsome verse in John Fenno's *Gazette of the United States.*

> Not heroes in triumphant cars,
> Victorious in their country's wars,
> With captives, spoils and glory crown'd,
> Whose paeans make the skies resound;
> Experience half the joys they know
> Who live to lessen human woe;
> The progress of whose godlike mind,
> Is but a TOUR to bless mankind.

Godlike or not, Washington was pleased with most of what he had seen. "The country appears to be in a very improving state," he wrote to David Humphreys two weeks after his return. Regarding the South, "industry and frugality are becoming much more fashionable than . . . hitherto. Tranquility reigns among the people, with that disposition toward the general government which is likely to preserve it. They begin to feel the good effects of equal laws and equal protection."

Dire forecasts of regional resistance to the duty on homemade spirits, scheduled to take effect on August 1, did not overly trouble the president. From what he had gathered at first hand, "and I took some pains to obtain information on this point," compliance with the law was all but assured. At the same time Washington hedged his bets, informing Humphreys that it was possible "and perhaps not improbable that some demagogue may start up and produce and get signed some resolutions declaratory of their disapprobation." He sounded less equivocal in writing to Gouverneur Morris on July 28. "Two or three years of good crops, and a ready market for the produce of their lands, has put everyone in good humor," he explained, hastening to add in words suggesting his own priorities that "in some instances they even impute to the government what is due only to the goodness of Providence."

Washington did not assign Providence a role in establishing the young nation's credit, an event that took place with breathtaking speed on the morning of July 4, 1791, when would-be investors oversubscribed Hamilton's bank to the tune of four thousand shares. As a pragmatist, Washington could only be impressed by the bank's stunning success. As a nationalist, he was apt to confuse southern cheers for himself with wholehearted support for the policies of his administration. Having spent most of his life seeking applause from one audience or another, he returned to Philadelphia sated with popular approval, more than ever convinced that the country's fortunes depended on the strong government imagined in the Constitution and realized in the Bank of the United States. He had seen and been seen by tens of thousands, in the process winning mass allegiance for a regime his presence made real. Only time would reveal what, if anything, Washington had heard over the din of popular adulation.

⁕ 6 ⁎

ROUGH WATERS

"The great Ruler of events will not permit the happiness of so many millions to be destroyed; and to his keeping I resign you."

George Washington
to Lafayette,
September 10, 1791

NO SOONER HAD WASHINGTON resumed his schedule in the middle of July 1791 than he was again taken ill. For the second time in as many years, Jefferson mailed medical bulletins to friends in Virginia, alerting Edmund Pendleton, Washington's colleague from the First Continental Congress, "The president is indisposed with a tumor like that he had in New York the year before last. It does not as yet seem as if it would come to a head." Washington himself described his "slight indisposition" as a mild form of the life-threatening carbuncle that had been surgically removed in the spring of 1789. No complications ensued, and by the first week of August he was fully recovered.

Less easily treated were some longstanding sores on the body politic. "You will have seen the rapidity with which the subscriptions to the bank were filled," Jefferson remarked. "As yet, the delirium of speculation is too strong to admit sober reflection. It remains to be seen whether in a country whose capital is too small to carry its own commerce, to establish manufactures, erect buildings, etc., such sums should have been withdrawn from these useful pursuits to be employed in gambling."

Madison reported a similar rise in New York bank shares. Rumors of ships and expresses headed south to purchase every scrap of paper that might be traded prompted men of every station to wager borrowed money in a mad plundering scramble. "My imagination will not attempt to set bounds to the daring depravity of the times," wrote the prim, bookish congressman to the secretary of state. "The stockjobbers will become the praetorian band of the government, at once its tool and its tyrant."

However harsh his language, however parochial his mistrust of Hamilton's financial alchemy — which conjured up liquid wealth in place of the military warrants, oxen, whiskey, and even cowbells that served rural districts as currency — Madison did not exaggerate the speculative fever sweeping urban America. Within a week of the opening of the Bank of the United States, its shares had grown by 50 percent in value. A similar scene was played out in New York, where coffeehouses were packed by get-rich-quick artists, some of them lawmakers hoping to take advantage of the market their votes had created. With mordant superiority, republicans like Benjamin Rush, a doctor, teacher, abolitionist, and temperance crusader, Thomas Paine's friend as well as Washington's wartime critic, captured both the euphoria and the despair attending the hunt for fool's gold. "The city of Philadelphia for several days has exhibited the marks of a great gaming house," he wrote on August 10. "At every corner you hear citizens talking of nothing but script, 6 percent, 3 percent, deferred debt, etc. A young broker (Mr. Seber) from New York, who had made 10,000 dollars, lost his reason . . . Genl. Stewart, who had just begun to deal in script, said he could not sleep at nights. Never did I see so universal a frenzy. Nothing else was spoken of but script in all companies, even by those who were not interested in it."

The next day Rush reported the spreading of "scriptomania" as "merchants, growers, shopkeepers, clerks, prentice boys, and even a sea captain" forsook their honest endeavors to play the market. Rush himself sold two shares at eight o'clock one morning; by nightfall they had gained $200 in paper value. The day of reckoning came on August 12, Black Friday, when shares plummeted below $150 and long faces were seen on every street. From New York came word of a similar panic. Sleepless General Stewart went to see Hamilton in tears, it was said, predicting imminent ruin unless dramatic steps were taken to reverse the freefall.

As the secretary pondered his options, Rush began treating rich Philadelphians for symptoms of sudden impoverishment — no appetite, pains in the breast, insomnia, and agitation. The good doctor heard an old Negro woman in the marketplace crying out, "Hot corn, hot corn, hot corn for krip." On August 18, the pathetic Seber refused to take his medicine without first asking "on what terms." When finally he swallowed Rush's prescription, the broken speculator pronounced it "a good bargain." He died that afternoon. Hamilton, wrenched from his complacency by the gathering alarm, moved decisively to halt the slide. "A bubble connected with my operations is of all the enemies I have to fear . . . the most formidable," he wrote to Senator Rufus King of New

York. To keep the bubble afloat and his enemies at bay, the secretary channeled $200,000 from the Bank of New York to support the price of government bonds.

It is inconceivable that such a step could have been taken without Washington's approval, yet it is equally difficult to reconcile scriptomania with the president's ingrained hostility toward speculators as a class. As recently as January 1, 1788, Washington had told Jefferson that "an extensive speculation . . . or the introduction of anything which will divert our attention from agriculture must be extremely prejudicial if not ruinous to us." Now, less than four years later, Washington's government looked on passively as a rabid financial dog chased its tail.

The truth of it was that Washington believed such temporary dislocation a cheap price for establishing the public credit of the United States. Having approved the assumption of state debts, the creation of a banking system, the levying of taxes, and the doctrine of implied powers; having given his blessing to a *financial* union at least as binding as the political one enshrined in the Constitution, the president had become his administration's premier Hamiltonian.

{ 2 }

The panic quickly subsided, which was just as well for an executive preoccupied by household illness and foreign contagion. Washington's consumptive nephew, George Augustine, was leaving to take the waters at Berkeley Springs, Virginia, but before going over the mountains he informed his uncle that crops at Mansion House Farm looked as if they had been devoured by fire. Prospects for a decent corn harvest were poor, and until rains fell, the sowing of wheat was out of the question. Worse, his chest pains had returned and he was spitting blood. According to James Craik, the president's personal physician and perhaps his closest friend, the prognosis appeared grim as young Washington overtaxed his strength in conscientiously promoting his uncle's interests.

That was just the beginning of Craik's bad news. The overseer Anthony Whiting, although to all appearances a stout, well-made man, showed alarming symptoms of the same disease. In the same letter Craik announced that the president's cousin Lund had gone blind and the wife of his nephew William Augustine Washington had died within twenty-four hours of giving birth. Closer to home, young Wash was in bed with the measles. Bob Lewis was leaving the presidential household to pick up the reins at Mount Vernon from George Augustine. And Major Jackson intended to marry in the fall, before entering business in Philadelphia.

Faced with such a wholesale turnover in his official family and fully expecting to leave office in the spring of 1793, Washington resolved to hire none but clerks to attend him in the closing scenes of his presidency. Among the additional burdens this imposed on Tobias Lear and Washington himself, the fate of France and a much-loved Frenchman ranked high. On July 28 Washington wrote to Lafayette, "I have often contemplated with great anxiety the danger to which you are personally exposed by your peculiar and delicate situation in the tumult of the times . . . But to one who engages in hazardous enterprises for the good of his country and who is guided by pure and upright views (as I am sure is the case with you), life is but a secondary consideration."

The happiness of twenty-four million people was no small concern, said Washington, particularly to Americans who had been liberally aided in their hour of greatest distress by Louis's disintegrating regime. With characteristic fatalism (or faith?), the president looked to "the Providence who rules great events, trusting that out of confusion he will produce order." In a passage that might as easily have flowed from Jefferson's pen, he pointed an accusing finger at the mobs of Paris. "The tumultuous populace of large cities are ever to be dreaded," claimed Washington. "Their indiscriminate violence prostrates for the time all public authority, and its consequences are sometimes extensive and terrible. In Paris we may suppose these tumults are peculiarly disastrous at this time, when the public mind is in a ferment, and when (as is always the case on such occasions) there are not wanting wicked and designing men, whose element is confusion and who will not hesitate in destroying the public tranquility to gain a favorite point."

Washington's uncanny forecast of the Terror about to commence was based on an acceptance of human nature gleaned from a lifetime of close observation. "Until your Constitution is fixed, your government organized, and your representative body renovated, much tranquility cannot be expected," he reminded Lafayette, "for until these things are done, those who are unfriendly to the revolution will not quit the hope of bringing matters back to their former state."

Here we might pause to examine Washington's seeming ambivalence toward revolutionary France and look for clues to the political thinking of a man often considered ideologically neutral. Yet just because Washington lacked the literary gifts of a Jefferson or the oratorical skills of a Patrick Henry does not confirm the slightly condescending picture of a leader known more for his spotless character than his originality of thought. As a youthful surveyor, Washington had imposed at least a mathematical order on nature's untamed wildness. As a public man, he had grown accustomed to imposing his will on others. What he now sought, for France as for his own country, was not the tyrant's strangle-hold but the popular self-restraint and moderation essential to accommodate differing views.

Even at this stage of his career, then, Washington remained a revolutionary. But it was a revolution of character, not of politics, to which he committed himself. By asserting individual claims against the state, he staked his presidency — and his place in history — on a belief that men could be wise enough to restrain their passions and reasonable enough to keep government in check.

A few weeks after his cautionary message to Lafayette, the president outlined his credo for an unlikely audience. Writing to his niece Harriot, yet another wayward child left by Samuel Washington's death, the president said, "You are just entering into the state of womanhood, without the watchful eye of a Mother to admonish or the protecting aid of a Father to advise and defend you; you may not be sensible that you are at this moment about to be stamped with that character which will adhere to you through life. Think, then, to what dangers a giddy girl of 15 or 16 must be exposed in circumstances like these. *To be under but little or no control may be pleasing to a mind that does not reflect, but this pleasure cannot be of long duration.*" (Italics added.)

Read as autobiography, Washington's words convey hard-won wisdom and an almost obsessive belief in personal accountability. Did France in the spiraling chaos of 1791 appear to Washington like the giddy girl tempted by evil companions? Was chaos the inevitable price of democracy? The contrast between youthful America and the Old World from which it had sprung was too striking to overlook, Washington wrote to Lafayette. On reflection, Europe's turmoil might even have beneficial aspects if it caused his countrymen to give a more complete allegiance to the constitutional order responsible for their prosperous state. "But we do not wish to be the only people who may taste the sweets of an equal and good government," said Washington. "We look with an anxious eye to the time when happiness and tranquility shall prevail in your country and when all Europe shall be freed from commotions, tumults and alarms."

The moment seemed pregnant with great events, Washington told Gouverneur Morris, and Americans of every persuasion were united in desiring a victory for the rights of man on French soil. "But I trust we shall never so far lose sight of our own interest and happiness as to become, necessarily, a party in their political disputes . . . it is among nations as with individuals, the party taking advantage of the distresses of another will lose infinitely more in the opinion of mankind and in subsequent events than he will gain by the stroke of the moment."

Washington's objectivity stood him well on August 10, when, in a ceremony whose simplicity astonished King Louis's latest and last ambassador, the president welcomed Jean Baptiste de Ternant to his republican court. "You and I are old friends, and it is a great pleasure to me and Mrs. Washington to see you again among us," he remarked to the forty-year-old Ternant, a volunteer in America's war for independence who had risen to second place under Baron von Steuben as army inspector. So relaxed was the ensuing visit that France's representative did not (or could not) raise the unpleasant subject of his government's recent actions against American fishermen and producers of whale oil.

Ternant found a noticeably cooler atmosphere two days later, when the president greeted him in a strictly official capacity. After receiving the envoy's credentials in all his thorny grandeur, Washington unbent a little, inviting Ternant to sit beside him for another lengthy conversation. Again the trade reprisals went unmentioned, the diplomat being thrown off balance by the president's unpredictable mix of formality and charm. He encountered a Washington both shrewd and amiable, who was all but missing from William Maclay's jaundiced diaries. The same was true of Jacob Hiltzheimer, who boarded some of the president's horses at his stalls on Minor Street. Following a dinner at 190 Market Street on September 5 with members of Pennsylvania's legislature, Hiltzheimer wrote, "I cannot help remarking that President Washington is an unassuming, easy and sociable man, beloved by every person."

Washington believed that relations between nations were dictated by self-interest, not table manners. Yet he valued the personal element, making certain to praise Ternant's "abilities, discretion and proper views." He displayed a more tangible loyalty in the third week of September, when France asked for a $40,000 advance on the United States' war debt to help crush a slave uprising on the island of Hispaniola. Washington wasted no time in directing Henry Knox to withdraw a substantial store of muskets, flints, gunpowder, and shot from the arsenal at West Point. He cut his order from Mount Vernon, which he had reached on September 20, only to find himself drawn into a new controversy involving Philadelphia's pretensions.

Before leaving the capital, Washington had read in the newspapers remarks attributed to him implying unhappiness over Morris's house. These came as manna from heaven to a group of legislators hoping to keep the government permanently in Pennsylvania. The cabal was led by Samuel Powel, a former mayor who, along with his wife, Eliza, a highly intelligent and independent woman, was counted among the president's intimates. In seizing on Washington's purported complaints to advance their agenda, however, Powel and his circle ran up against a stonewall of presidential opposition. Washington, extraordinarily sensitive where his personal motives were concerned, found it easy to override friendship if he believed his honor at stake.

It may be argued that the president's appetite for applause and his need to appear his country's disinterested friend provided emotional recompense for the denial of more conventional forms of love. Forty years in the public eye had failed to thicken Washington's skin or make him less susceptible to hurt, as he now demonstrated to the faithful Tobias Lear. How did Lear interpret the inquiries made by Powel and others regarding the president's true wishes? Washington demanded of his secretary on September 26. Did these involve misrepresentation on the part of Albert Gallatin, the state representative Lear used as a conduit to make Washington's preferences known to the legislators?

Or was Washington himself being faulted for meddling in legislative business? "If the latter, I have no scruple in declaring . . . that no one has a right to publish sentiments *as mine* that were never uttered, or conceived, *by me.*" Regaining his composure, Washington thanked Lear for conveying his thoughts to Powel in writing, as "sentiments and communications expressed in that manner cannot be misconceived or misrepresented from the want of recollection." A week later the president, his annoyance still fresh, authorized Lear to publish the correspondence with Powel, "since the matter has been introduced into the legislature of the state and so unfairly stated . . . by *both* parties."

In itself a trifling affair, Washington's tetchy response to the Pennsylvania legislature has larger implications when considering his later actions steering a neutral course between warring European powers. One can see a formidable will exerting itself in Washington's italicized protest; woe to any man *but* the president who presumed to speak *for* the president. Could anyone so quick to take offense at slights, real or imagined, be likely to endure affronts to his nation passively?

{ 3 }

Washington's stay at Mount Vernon was unexpectedly cut short in a way that could only reinforce the president's fears about his failing memory. Responding to a notice from Lear on October 14, Washington expressed astonishment that Congress would reconvene on the twenty-fourth instead of a week later, as he had believed. "I had no more idea of this than I had of its being doomsday." Any hope of a leisurely journey was quickly discarded; even with the aid of Lear and the members of his Cabinet, Washington would have barely enough time to prepare his annual message to Congress. Moreover, thanks to his "strange mistake," he was able to pause for less than a day in Georgetown, where October 17 had been designated for the first public auction of building lots in the proposed capital (named the City of Washington a month earlier).

The president's personal interest in the capital was greater than ever. Writing to Jefferson that summer, the amateur architect of Mount Vernon looked askance at wooden houses and urged a ban on stoops and other projections that might intrude on urban thoroughfares. He debated the right kind of paving stone for the city's streets. He made no attempt to hide his anxiety over the prospects of his namesake, which L'Enfant proposed to finance with a million-dollar government loan, an impossible burden for a nation already in hock to foreign bankers. Merely floating such a request would gladden the hearts of Philadelphians, as Washington from his recent experience knew all too well.

In a note hurriedly scrawled at dawn on the eighteenth from Bladensburg, Maryland, the president asked his friend David Stuart, one of the three commissioners selling lots in the Federal City, for news of the previous day's auction before the sun went down. "I am now writing by candlelight," Washington added by way of explanation, "and this is the only piece of paper the landlord is able to procure for me." Stuart's report was less than encouraging. Only thirty-five lots were sold, generating less than $2,000 in cash. And all the while L'Enfant smoldered on the sidelines, his artistic temperament offended by the brisk, commercial minds of the commissioners.

⟨ 4 ⟩

On Tuesday, October 25, Washington appeared in the House to congratulate his countrymen on the success of the republican experiment to date. He singled out for special praise the "striking and pleasing" rise in the nation's credit evidenced by the instant success of the Bank of the United States. August's brief panic was a distant memory now, lost amid the portents of a rapidly expanding economy. Crude as they were, all yardsticks of growth pointed to a major upswing beginning around the time of Washington's first inauguration. Wholesale prices in Charleston rose 28 percent between March 1789 and mid-1790; a survey in Philadelphia showed virtually identical results. Even as Washington read his message in the flat, unemotional voice he reserved for such occasions, entrepreneurs were validating his faith in market capitalism by planning new toll bridges and turnpikes, chartering additional banks, and organizing insurance companies. To Hamilton's enemies, multiplying as fast as the opportunities for investment, the strong endorsement left no doubt as to who ruled the policymaking roost.

The bulk of the president's message was reserved for the troubled frontier. Here Washington adopted a carrot and stick approach, reflecting his somewhat muddled feelings of nationalist expansion coupled with resentment toward exploitative speculators in the western lands. In one hand he brandished provisional treaties of friendship with the Cherokees and Six Nations, in the other such a club as Arthur St. Clair and his slowly advancing army might wield against "deluded tribes in the Ohio Valley." Washington did promise to conduct offensive operations "as consistently as possible with the dictates of humanity." In hopes of avoiding armed confrontation altogether, he unveiled plans to win over the Indians peaceably, promising the natives impartial justice, redress of "the mode of alienating their lands, the main source of discontent and war," a more equitable distribution of commerce, and the strict punishment of anyone caught violating Indian rights and thereby endangering the peace of the Union.

Confronting other domestic issues, Washington employed lessons learned on his recent travels. He sounded a conciliatory note on the excise taxes passed to fund Hamilton's assumption program. While conceding the novelty of such levies and the discontent they bred in some parts of the country, he took heart — prematurely, as it turned out — that opposition to a tax on distilled spirits melted away in the face of "proper explanations" of the law's true nature. Washington held out the prospect of minor modifications to the law, consistent with his desire "to consult the wishes of every part of the community and to lay the foundations of the public administration in the affections of the people."

He delivered an optimistic report on the Potomac building project, the first census (recently completed at a cost of $44,000), and additional loans negotiated at favorable rates of interest in the Dutch money market. He also renewed earlier calls for a mint to redress a scarcity of currency that was most harmful to "the poorer classes." He plumped for a strengthened militia and a comprehensive program of post offices and post roads, the latter vital in diffusing knowledge of the laws and proceedings of government, thus furthering the people's security by guarding them "against the effects of misrepresentation and misconception."

Elsewhere in Philadelphia, Jefferson welcomed his younger daughter, Maria, from Virginia and happy in the company of Mrs. Washington and her granddaughter Nelly Custis. "Congress met today," he added near the end of a letter to his son-in-law. "The President's speech ran on the following subjects. The Indians — a land law. Militia law. Post office. Weights and measures. Navigation and commerce — the English minister, Mr. Hammond, is arrived. Affairs in France are going on well. Their new legislature is probably now sitting. I imagine a general peace has taken place throughout Europe."

❊ 5 ❋

Two days after what was, in effect, his State of the Union address, Washington repeated to Madison his customary request for help in drafting a response to the House's formal rejoinder. The versatile congressman from Orange County was thereby placed in the unique position of having contributed to the president's annual message, the response from the House, *and* his reply. Madison said later that if his tastes alone had prevailed, "the cooking would not have been precisely what it was." On October 31, it was the Senate's turn to answer the president. Led by stocky John Adams, the upper body trooped to 190 Market Street to pledge loyalty to the executive and promise quick action on his agenda.

A less deferential voice was raised on the streets of the capital that day when Philip Freneau, won over at last by Jefferson and Madison, entered the journalistic arena with his long-awaited *National Gazette.* Freneau's first issue proclaimed fidelity to "the great principles upon which the American Revolution was founded and which alone can preserve the blessings of liberty." Over time, a chorus of critics would take their tune from Freneau's semiweekly paper, some going so far as to accuse Washington of betraying the Revolution and selling his country out to England. For now, however, Freneau's chief concern was the *Gazette of the United States,* a slavishly pro-administration sheet edited by John Fenno, formerly an editorial assistant on the *Massachusetts Centinel.* Having failed in his early campaign to win for Washington the title "Your Supremacy," Fenno settled for fulsome praise of "the Supreme Executive" and uncritical descriptions of his court. In Fenno's view, the Constitution was above amending, and if anything threatened domestic peace, it was narrow-minded state governments that opposed the far-sighted program of national consolidation developed by his favorite Cabinet officer, Alexander Hamilton.

It would be simplistic to say that Fenno's support of the treasury's policies was purchased with personal loans extended by the secretary — Hamilton with his overstretched resources was in no position to buy anybody — yet if Fenno's paper was less obviously indebted to official sponsors than Freneau's was to Jefferson, it was hardly a model of disinterested journalism. When the government pulled up stakes in the autumn of 1790, Fenno predictably moved his operation to Philadelphia. A change of scene produced changes of in style. No longer did the Federalist stalwart serve exclusively what Douglas Southall Freeman called "the overrich wine of adulation." To be sure, Hamilton and Vice President Adams continued to receive favorable treatment and the president remained beyond criticism, but Fenno's editorial menu was broadened to include occasional barbed pieces aimed at the Hamiltonian program.

Time revealed Fenno's shift to be more tactical than real, a shrewd attempt at boosting his credibility rather than a fundamental change in attitude. To readers of the *Gazette of the United States*, Hamilton was "a star of the first magnitude in our political hemisphere." Other stars, some of them languishing in the New Yorker's penumbra, burned brighter after the appearance of Philip Freneau. Beginning on November 21, 1791, and running through April 1792, Madison published a series of unsigned articles laying the groundwork for Republican opposition to the administration's policies. Avoiding overt partisanship or personal attacks, he drew upon his vast reserve of book knowledge to advance the whiggish fear of executive power and argue for the Union as a compact of sovereign states.

Continuing his long retreat from the national doctrines contained in *The Federalist*, the president's trusted adviser celebrated public opinion as the supreme law of a free republic. He insisted that war, should it come, could only be declared by the people themselves, and he saluted Jeffersonian agriculture, not Hamiltonian commerce, as the bulwark of national prosperity. Emboldened by these articles, others took the field to wage the republic's first campaign of class warfare. By March of 1792 "Brutus" was declaiming powerfully in Freneau's pages against Hamilton's program. Striking the theme of Us versus Them that has been a staple of American politics and journalism ever since, Brutus drew a stark contrast between "an impoverished peasantry on the one hand and a privileged aristocracy on the other," each the inevitable product of political consolidation and economic discrimination.

If Hamilton smarted under Freneau's lash, it was not apparent in the confident way he carried himself. Later, he cited October 1791 as the moment he first discerned an organized movement to discredit him, but at the time, Freneau's "First Lord of the Treasury" seemed firmly in control. On his own initiative, Hamilton tested the diplomatic waters with France's new ambassador, winning the president over to his none-too-generous version of a commercial treaty between the allied nations and deepening Jefferson's suspicion that what his rival really sought was a pretext to dissolve the French alliance and turn to Great Britain.

It was a disheartening time for the secretary of state, forced to play cat and mouse with King George's latest envoy, George Hammond. On

November 11, Jefferson ushered him in to meet the president. Hammond reported to his London superiors that he had been received "with the utmost politeness and respect." Courtesy was not conversion, however, and there was nothing to indicate any lessening of Washington's deeply rooted skepticism toward Hammond's government. Adding to Jefferson's frustration, the mercurial Gouverneur Morris was about to be sent to Paris as the United States' representative.

When Morris's nomination squeaked through the Senate, Washington issued some unvarnished advice to his friend. No one questioned Morris's abilities; his discretion and a personal hauteur "disgusting to those who happen to differ from you in sentiment" were something else. The president next defined *for* Morris the case *against* Morris: "that the promptitude with which your lively and brilliant imagination is displayed allows too little time for deliberation and correction and is the primary cause of those sallies which too often offend and of that ridicule of characters which begets enmity not easily to be forgotten, but which might easily be avoided if it was under the control of more caution and prudence." The minister must be especially careful to mask his feelings among the French, "a people who study civility and politeness more than any other." In short, Morris must mind his tongue, a sharp instrument frequently wagged in opposition to France's revolution. This remarkable set of diplomatic instructions was delivered by Washington personally in the solemn belief "that a mind conscious of its own rectitude fears not what is said of it, but will bid defiance to and despise shafts that are not barbed with accusations against honor or integrity."

By the time he wrote to Morris late in January 1792, Washington had reasons aplenty to despise journalistic accusers of his administration, including some on its payroll. Not being in the habit of giving advice without accepting it himself, the president rigorously observed the counsel of caution he gave to Morris, three thousand miles away. He was less successful at enforcing it among his contentious subordinates, who met with increasing frequency in the drawing room of 190 Market Street.

⟨ 6 ⟩

The fruits of victory can often hold the seeds of later defeat. By December 1791, Alexander Hamilton was at the height of his power and influence. These were days, wrote James Thomas Flexner, "when Hamilton's youthful fantasies came almost altogether into being. Powerful men were his sycophants; women adored him; and if he made a flood of enemies, that was, as long as he could overcome, an integral part of his triumphant dream." So entrenched was the secretary in the Washington administration that no one could possibly defeat him — except himself.

Fittingly, this godfather to American entrepreneurism was a born risk-taker. On December 5 he sent Congress his *Report on Manufactures*, the most daring argument yet for a federal government that served as an intervening agent and not merely a restraining influence. Hamilton would employ its fostering hand through protective tariffs, direct bounties, and extensive internal improvements to bolster an American manufacturing sector then in its infancy. Was investment capital at a premium? Hamilton had a solution. "The public purse must supplant the deficiency in private resource," he argued.

Unwilling to settle for mere theory where any chance for practical implementation existed, Hamilton included for Congress's perusal a prospectus from the Society for Useful Manufactures (SUM), still another product of his restless brain. On thirty-six square miles of pastureland near today's Paterson, New Jersey, Hamilton imagined a modern corporate state, its buildings designed by the ubiquitous L'Enfant, its funding channeled through public as well as private sources. SUM would build and maintain transportation and other facilities, conduct its own lotteries, charge its own tolls. Tax incentives and exemptions from military service would lure skilled workmen from all over the world. With turbines and waterwheels fueled by the Great Falls of the Passaic River, SUM's artisans would produce paper, shoes, carpets, sailcloth, and beer, among other staples. Even for Hamilton, it was a visionary scheme.

There is no evidence that he consulted his chief before releasing this economic bombshell, but neither was there reason for him to doubt Washington's broadly sympathetic reaction. After all, the president's father had been a principal force in colonial Virginia's iron industry, and Washington himself had led the fight in the state's House of Burgesses for a nonimportation act, leading to a more self-sufficient America. Left to his own devices, Farmer Washington might well have endorsed Hamilton's call for economic diversification, for no one more than the proud chief executive was aware of his country's deficiencies in skilled managers, artisans, and modern machinery.

The United States in 1791 was not without pockets of industrial promise. Reading, Pennsylvania, was famous for its wool hats. Pittsburgh's glassware was much admired, and Americans looked to Waterbury, Connecticut, for their timepieces. Most industrial leaders, however, found greater profit in exporting raw materials than manufacturing products for domestic consumption. To a nation builder like Hamilton, this lingering residue of colonialism provided abundant justification for a government strong enough to reward manufacturers at home and enlarge foreign markets. That he could not carry the president with him says less about Hamilton's persuasiveness than it does about Washington's political acuity.

To tell the truth, the president had little choice. Coming as it did in the wake of assumption, the bank, and excise taxes, Hamilton's futuristic blueprint exposed as never before the fault lines of sectional and economic rivalry. Commercial interests drew back in horror at the prospect of sharply higher import duties and a subsequent loss of traffic. Agriculture feared the bad example of federal bounties, higher prices caused by tariff barriers, and the siphoning off of scarce labor to urban factories and millyards. However Washington the businessman and industrialist might feel personally, Washington the president and symbol of national unity could hardly lend his name to so divisive a scheme.

In the end, Hamilton's manifesto rallied his critics, for whom the essence of republicanism lay in strict limits on government's mandate, to a pivotal sequel. On February 28, 1792, Jefferson interrupted a conversation with Washington about the new post office to lash out at Hamilton's treasury as a malignant influence poised to "swallow up the whole executive powers." Then, having drawn a line in the sand, Jefferson pointedly declared himself above such turf wars since he fully intended to retire from office at the same time as the president. At breakfast the next morning, a plainly worried executive tried "in an affectionate tone" (the words are from Jefferson's personal account) to dissuade his fellow Virginian from any rash action.

As for himself, said Washington, the reasons for leaving at the end of his term were many. Every day brought home the accumulating effects of age and a weakening memory. Now, when he looked into a mirror, an old man stared back at him. Less physically active than in the past, Washington found the cares of office more irksome. He longed for nothing so much as rural tranquility; retirement, he asserted with a touch of desperation, was his "irresistible passion." By staying on after March 1793, he fretted, he might sacrifice his cherished reputation for selflessness, fostering a public view that "having tasted the sweets of office, he could not do without them."

Washington's retrospective distaste for office was matched by his secretary of state's. Although eager to forsake power himself, Jefferson expected his bitterest enemy to remain in office until he succeeded in implementing his entire consolidationist program. Resentments long dammed up burst forth as Jefferson slashed away at paper money, unhealthy speculation, and legislative corruption, the whole Hamiltonian agenda calling into question "whether we live under a limited or an unlimited government."

Washington asked to what, specifically, Jefferson alluded, and was heatedly informed of the secretary's objections to the *Report on Manufactures*, "which, under color of giving *bounties* for the encouragement of particular manufactures, meant to establish the doctrine that the power given by the Constitution to collect taxes to provide for the *general welfare* of the United States permitted Congress to take everything under their management which *they* should deem for the *public welfare* and which is susceptible of the application of money."

Not for the first time Jefferson saw windmills and imagined giants. Washington knew, as Jefferson should have known from his earlier experience in drafting a radically new system of weights and measures, that the *Report on Manufactures* was politically dead on arrival. Since Hamilton's program had not a ghost of a chance of adoption, Washington was only too willing to treat it as a political orphan. Meanwhile, if the secretary of state intended to use it as a club with which to beat his rival, he failed. Jefferson did not even secure control of the post office, his ostensible object, although the president did award oversight of the proposed mint to the State Department.

By balancing such favors, Washington hoped to retain both men in his orbit, where he could keep an eye on each and coopt or at least delay partisan political activity. What some detractors, then and later, faulted as executive weakness seems more nearly the self-effacement of a born leader sufficiently comfortable with himself to permit dissension among his subordinates.

Hamilton failed to press his case for central economic planning for personal reasons. A few days before Christmas, he confronted demands of blackmail from the shadowy job seeker James Reynolds, whose wife, Maria, a woman of high spirits and few scruples, had been conducting an intense affair with Hamilton for at least six months. The secretary was a summer bachelor in 1791, his wife having gone to visit her family in Albany. One day Maria Reynolds presented herself at his home as the impoverished victim of a faithless marriage. Maria was a complete stranger but a beguiling one. As Hamilton recalled long afterward, "It took a harder heart than mine to refuse . . . a pretty woman in distress." His suspicions were not aroused, but other emotions were, as that evening he went to Maria's residence on Vine Street (substantial enough for a destitute woman, with or without an abusive husband) with lust in his thoughts and a $30 bill in his pocket.

It is unnecessary to dwell on the tawdry details of Hamilton's infatuation, still less to credit the theory of one biographer that Hamilton was in fact set up by Aaron Burr, doing the dirty work of Jefferson and Madison. The passionate, impetuous Hamilton needed no outside guidance to stray from the path of marital fidelity. Done in by his own vanity, believing Maria's passion for him to be real, Hamilton carried on the affair for at least a year and a half, thereby delivering himself into the hands of his enemies. In time, it would cost him far more than the thousand dollars he handed over to the cuckolded husband in lieu of a treasury clerkship.

❦ 7 ❧

According to Tobias Lear, an authoritative source, few sounds on earth were so blood-curdling as that of George Washington swearing a blue streak. For evidence, Lear could point to an interrupted dinner party on the night of December 9, 1791. Almost a year after receiving Josiah Harmar's tidings of military disaster in the forests of Ohio, the president waited nervously for word of a climactic battle reportedly fought between Arthur St. Clair and the same Wabash tribes guilty of Harmar's humiliation. From the start, Washington had entertained doubts about St. Clair, a fifty-seven-year-old political general who, before his appointment as governor of the Northwest Territory, had occupied the presiding officer's chair in the Continental Congress. Throughout the spring and early summer of 1791, Washington had urged St. Clair "by every principle that is sacred" to move with greater dispatch against the Delawares, Shawnees, and other warlike tribes shadowing the white man's foothold north of the Ohio.

He may as well have saved his breath, for among St. Clair's virtues, decisiveness was notably lacking. At the time he was supposed to be chasing Little Turtle and his allies, Major General St. Clair was suffering from gout so severe that it took four aides to lift him onto his horse. His daily teaspoonful of brimstone failed to combat either his bilious fever or inspire confidence among his men. Disregarding the president's counsel, St. Clair's force did not get away from its camp at Fort Washington until mid-August. Dense growth and improperly tempered axes slowed its progress north to six miles a day; it was further hobbled by the lack of reliable maps and experienced Indian scouts. Torn by dissension at the top and dysentery in the ranks, starved for provisions and weakened by desertions, the invading force showed little grasp of Indian tactics or skill in countering them.

The result was the worst defeat for American arms since the bloody afternoon in July 1755 when Edward Braddock's redcoats, accompanied by a vainglorious colonel from Virginia named Washington, had fallen to a foe whose lust for plunder supplied the only restraining influence on its annihilation of Braddock's tattered army. For thirty-five years, memories of that harrowing day haunted Washington. They flared anew on December 9, when he was called from his dinner by a flushed and agitated Henry Knox, who brought a communiqué from Fort Washington, the starting and ending point for the ill-fated expedition.

St. Clair's opening words were enough to ruin anyone's meal: "Yesterday afternoon, the remains of my army got back to this place, and I now have the painful task to give you an account of as warm and as unfortunate an action as almost any that has been fought." In the few minutes available before the host must rejoin his guests, Washington was able to learn the deadly magnitude of St. Clair's rout. Two thirds of an army numbering 1,400 men lay dead or wounded, among them 35 commissioned officers. St. Clair's second in command, General Richard Butler, much admired by the attacking tribes for his valor on the field, fell while trying to organize a last, desperate resistance; the victorious Shawnees cut open his corpse and devoured his heart. St. Clair himself took eight bullets through his clothing; had he worn his customary uniform of rank, he, too, would have presented an irresistible target for the Indians.

Washington scanned the dispatch in silence, then returned to dinner and his wife's weekly levee. He would not keep his guests waiting, but neither could he restrain his emotions once the drawing room formalities were over. As Lear described it more than twenty years later, the president gave full vent to his anger, empurpling the air with oaths. Had not St. Clair brazenly disregarded Knox's instructions and Washington's explicit warning to heed the lessons of Braddock's rout? "Beware of a surprise," Washington had drilled into him. "You know how the Indians fight." St. Clair had engaged in butchery, not battle. As far as the president was concerned, the white-haired veteran of Trenton and Brandywine was a murderer whose callousness was matched only by his stupidity.

Then, as suddenly as he had given way, Washington throttled his emotions. He went a step further, promising nothing less than full justice for the defeated St. Clair. Let him come to Philadelphia — the president would receive him with an open mind. And so Washington did, accepting the general's resignation and ordering Knox to provide Congress with a complete accounting of the steps that had been taken to secure peace north of the Ohio. Months later, when St. Clair was largely exonerated by his former colleagues in the legislature, Knox protested the implied failure on *his* part. At that, the secretary of war got off easier than the greedy contractors who had gouged St. Clair's army on everything from blankets to pack horses and whose thievery soon found its way into the nation's press.

Especially vulnerable was William Duer, at one time Hamilton's assistant at the Treasury Department, who was already in jail on an unrelated charge when Congress discovered he had received an unsecured requisition of $85,000 from his friend and patron. Besides criticizing the fraudulent contractors, a surprising number of Americans asked what right their western countrymen had to invade and occupy Indian territory in the first place. Washington, however, entertained no such doubts. On December 12, he formally transmitted news of the inglorious setback to Congress, asserting that the nation's loss might yet be repaired "without great difficulty." Only the coming of winter saved the western frontier from renewed atrocities, as the Indians, with good reason, feared the elements more than Washington's military.

Although Washington never wavered in his determination to subdue the Northwest tribes, many members of Congress resisted the radical measures necessary to avenge Harmar and St. Clair. Acting in March 1792, Congress did authorize the formation of a 5,000-man standing army, grandly christened the Legion of the United States. But when it came to establishing a national militia, neither house was buying what the president wished to sell. Instead, a spirit of localism prevailed, fanned by republican fears that a ready reserve could one day threaten recalcitrant states incurring the displeasure of the central government.

Creating an army was easier than finding a leader to replace St. Clair. Washington cast a fishy eye over the list of available talent and was disheartened. Old Benjamin Lincoln was "sober, honest, brave . . . but infirm." Baron von Steuben knew his tactics better than his place. "High in his ideas of subordination," Washington concluded, "impetuous in his temper, ambitious, and a foreigner." Moultrie of South Carolina had the advantage of having actually fought the Cherokees but was otherwise a stranger to Washington. George Weedon was all too well known, hence his dismissal as "rather addicted to ease and pleasure, and no enemy it is said to the bottle." Pennsylvania's Edward Hand was sensible but unimaginative, James Wilkinson "lively . . . pompous and ambitious." Daniel Morgan, taken prisoner in Benedict Arnold's disastrous invasion of Canada, had long since redeemed himself and his riflemen at Saratoga. Even so, Gentleman Johnny Burgoyne's nemesis inspired conflicting views among those acquainted with his exploits in battle. Washington questioned his sobriety; nearly as bad, wrote the president, "it is not denied that he is illiterate."

At first glance, Anthony Wayne — whose terse advice to General Washington before the Battle of Monmouth had been "Fight, sir!" and who had demanded a trial by court martial following his nighttime surprise by a British force in September 1777 — seemed no more prepossessing than his indolent, rash, alcoholic, or decrepit comrades. Washington's unsparing appraisal of Wayne is worth quoting in full, if only because of the president's subsequent willingness to entrust the nation's military fortunes to such a man: "More active and enterprising than judicious and cautious. No economist it is feared. Open to flattery, vain, easily imposed upon, and liable to be drawn into scrapes. Too indulgent (the effect perhaps of some of the causes just mentioned) to his officers and men. Whether sober, or a little addicted to the bottle, I know not."

It was hardly a glowing recommendation. Left on his own, Washington would have catapulted Governor Henry Lee of Virginia into the top spot, but such blatant disregard for Lee's elders might have sparked mass resignations. Unenthusiastic about "Mad" Anthony Wayne, wistfully imagining a reorganized army under Lighthorse Harry Lee, Washington had few options other than to name the Pennsylvanian. This alone says volumes about the limits on presidential power and Washington's willingness to observe those limits.

❈ 8 ❈

That Washington could be astringent in his judgment of subordinates was made clear through the process of elimination leading to Wayne's appointment. That he had a volcanic temper, restrained only with difficulty, was the worst-kept secret in Philadelphia. But the anger subsided quickly, and the president's exacting standards were balanced by his rigid insistence that no man be done an injustice knowingly.

The case of Pierre Charles L'Enfant shows just how far Washington would go to accommodate even the prickliest of characters. Late in November 1791, he confessed astonishment over L'Enfant's refusal to supply the commissioners of the Federal City with a map of the proposed settlement, without which the sale of building lots, already sluggish, would grind to a halt. It was regrettable, Washington confided to a member of the commission, that the most able men often mortgaged their talents to an "untoward disposition or are sottish idle or possessed of some other disqualification by which they plague all those with whom they are concerned."

Washington had not expected such perversity from Major L'Enfant. Yet he was prepared to overlook repeated provocations, if only because no obvious replacement was at hand. Patience came naturally to Washington, but so did positive action. The latter inspired a fruitless attempt to restore harmony between the agitated commissioners and an architect reluctant to take orders from anyone but the president (and none too eager to take them from him). Unfortunately for Washington, this task alone was enough to occupy completely an executive already busy putting out frontier fires, courting representatives of the Iroquois and Cherokees, overseeing the formation of a new army, refereeing the growing dispute between Hamilton and Jefferson, and coming under the first, tentative pressures to accept a second term.

Confronted with a painful choice between his appointed commissioners and a gifted but unmanageable architect, Washington relied heavily on Jefferson and Madison for assistance. To L'Enfant, whose architectural gifts were the equal of his political deficiencies, this guaranteed fresh obstacles, since neither man shared his soaring vision of a city comparable in scale and elegance to Europe's ancient capitals. When L'Enfant repeatedly failed to produce the map, Washington turned the job over to surveyor Andrew Ellicott. L'Enfant reacted to Ellicott's work as if it were a desecration, and the president hastily backtracked, instructing Jefferson to remove Ellicott's name from the grid. Much more serious was L'Enfant's inability to produce plans for the Capitol and President's House. Another building season was about to commence, Washington reminded anyone who would listen.

L'Enfant moved boldly, all right, but not in putting up walls. Quite the opposite: the brash Frenchman inflamed feelings by pulling down the unfinished house of one of the commissioners' nephews because the offending structure stood in the middle of what would be New Jersey Avenue. Again Washington tried to broker a compromise, urging restraint on the unhappy homeowner while expressing "real mortification" to the commissioners. As gently as possible he tried to teach the impulsive L'Enfant some rudiments of politics and diplomacy. "It will always be found sound policy to conciliate the goodwill rather than provoke the enmity of any man," admonished the president, "where it can be accomplished without much difficulty, inconvenience or loss."

But even Washington had his limits. Early in January 1792, without telling the commissioners, the architect sent his chief assistant, Isaac Roberdeau, to quarry stone downriver at Aquia, where he was in fact trespassing. Roberdeau was fined and eventually jailed. While he languished behind bars, on January 17 L'Enfant submitted a five-year, $1.2 million plan of operations to the president. Since Virginia and Maryland could together supply but one sixth of this enormous sum, L'Enfant resurrected his old nostrum of a foreign loan with which to complete America's capital. Washington's reaction must have been withering, for the next few days brought fresh reports of professional insubordination and redoubled attacks on the commissioners' integrity. Washington found

L'Enfant's continued refusal to put his ideas into writing astonishing beyond measure.

As the Frenchman dug in his heels, the president invited Jefferson and Madison to confer with him on February 16 in an effort to save the project before it collapsed in a sea of mutual recrimination and red ink. Five days later, after approving Ellicott's version of L'Enfant's plan, Washington dispatched Jefferson on a final attempt at reconciliation. The secretary reminded L'Enfant that it was the commissioners' job to receive his proposals, decide which plans to pursue, and submit them to the president for final action.

L'Enfant, failing his assigned task of building bridges, now seemed intent only on burning them. It was easy for a man verging on paranoia to rebuff Washington's secretary when Lear reinforced the president's firm yet friendly overture. But by deliberately insulting the president of the United States (or, more precisely, the presidency), L'Enfant sealed his fate. Just as bad was a long screed categorically rejecting the commissioners' authority. Faced with no alternative, on February 27 Washington commanded Jefferson to terminate L'Enfant's services. The president proposed giving the planner 500 guineas and a lot in the city that other men would build. An angry L'Enfant spurned both, starting on the downhill trajectory that landed him in a pauper's grave forty years later.

Lear came as close as anyone to defining the "unlucky misunderstanding" between the artist and the commissioners. "The President did everything that he could with propriety to retain L'Enfant's service," he said in a letter to David Humphreys, and two centuries later it is hard to challenge this assessment. However preoccupied Washington may have been with internecine quarrels involving the city that bore his name, the attention of his secretary was focused elsewhere. According to Lear, the dangerous state of western affairs had revived speculation about Washington's plans. "I fear more from the election of another President, whenever our present great and good one quits his political or natural career, than from any other event." Lear prayed to God that Washington might live many more years "and incline his heart" (Washington's, not God's) "to retain his present station."

Washington observed his sixtieth birthday on the evening of February 21, when Philadelphians paid homage at a ball given by the City Dancing Assembly, attended, in the words of *Dunlop's Daily Advertiser*, by "one of the most brilliant displays of beauty ever exhibited in this city." Not to be outdone, the rival New City Dancing Assembly staged a birthday tribute of its own the following day. Eliza Powel celebrated her friend's milestone by sending him some amateurish verses, to which Washington responded with his famous tact.

Not even the semiroyal birthday observances, however, could effect a truce in Philadelphia's escalating newspaper wars. Washington awoke on the morning of the twenty-second to find John Fenno aiming a salvo at Freneau and his Republican sponsors, declaring in the *Gazette of the United States* that sedition had a thousand tongues, all of them brass. Washington's birthday came and went with no lessening of the president's desire to be released from the servitude of office. Nearing the end of his term, Washington looked forward to nothing so much as handing the baton to a successor and resuming the life of a Virginia husbandman.

❧ 7 ❧

THE CURSE OF DUTY

"Not George himself escapes the spleen,
of canker'd malice and chagrin."

Gazette of the United States,
March 17, 1792

THE PRESIDENCY CHANGED George Washington. By his third spring in office, the reluctant politician was more assertive of his prerogatives, less forgiving of congressional intrusion into foreign policy and other fields reserved, or so he thought, to the executive. On April 5, 1792, heeding advice from Jefferson, Madison, and Attorney General Randolph, Washington issued the first presidential veto, rejecting as overly favorable to northern states a congressional reapportionment plan based on the census of 1790.

A more acceptable map was quickly drawn, yet wherever he looked that spring, a weary president confronted growing suspicion and disunity. In February, Congress narrowly defeated attempts by Jefferson's admirers to place the secretary of state next in line to the president and vice president should both die, resign, or be disabled. Federalist joy was cut short, however, when Madison introduced a resolution in the House directing Hamilton to produce a supply plan for Anthony Wayne's impending western expedition. Given the recent scandalous conduct of William Duer, the secretary's former assistant, this could only be intended to embarrass Jefferson's bête noire.

Hamilton narrowly averted humiliation on a House roll call, but in confronting Duer's demands for continued help, the secretary could give his friend only advice. "Do not plunge deeper," he told the doomed speculator, whose financial shenanigans threatened to take the Society for Useful Manufactures down with him. "Have the courage to make a full stop . . . I have experienced all the bitterness of soul on your account which a warm attachment can inspire."

At the State Department Jefferson had troubles of his own, dramatized by a private meeting on March 12 at which the president expressed doubt at the confused state of French affairs. Jefferson detected the influence of Gouverneur Morris, "a high-flying monarchy man" who kept Washington's mind "constantly poisoned" with forebodings of disaster. Especially disturbing was Washington's casual remark about a proposed treaty with the outlaw regime in Algiers. Assuming senators approved $40,000 with which to ransom captive American seamen, Washington inquired whether the House, too, must give its assent before the money became available. Of this Jefferson had no doubt, and his forcefully expressed conviction touched off fresh complaints about unwanted partners in the making of foreign policy.

Just as Washington, strictly interpreting the Constitution on presidential prerogatives, distanced himself from most legislative business, so he expected similar deference from Congress. Should the people's representatives fail to observe appropriate limitations, he warned, "the government would be at an end, and must *then assume another form*" (italics added by Jefferson). Washington did not go nearly so far in predicting radical change as the wife of the vice president. Writing to her sister late in April 1792, Abigail Adams forecast a division of North and South within ten years "unless more candor and less intrigue, of which I have no hopes, should prevail."

One did not have to share Mrs. Adams's Federalist politics to echo her pessimism. Election-year Philadelphia was a town of marble and mud, a hornet's nest of partisan newspaper editors who stung their victims with every edition. The proposed Federal City was but one object of scorn; so, increasingly, was the man for whom it was to be named. By no means did all the malice originate in hostile party sheets. As secretary to Britain's new ambassador, George Hammond, Edward Thornton was well placed to observe Washington and his court.

"His person is tall and sufficiently graceful," he reported to a friend across the ocean, "his face well formed, his complexion rather pale, with a mild philosophic gravity in the expression of it. In his air and manner he displays much natural dignity; in his address he is cold, reserved, and even phlegmatic, though without the least appearance of haughtiness or ill nature." According to Thornton, caution was stamped on Washington's face, "for his eyes retire inward (do you understand me?) and have nothing of fire or animation or openness in their expression. If this circumspection is accompanied by discernment and penetration, as I am informed it is, and as I should be inclined to believe from the judicious choice he has generally made of persons to fill public stations, he possesses the two great requisites of a statesman, the faculty of concealing his own sentiments and of discovering those of other men."

Harsh personal criticism offset the diplomat's praise of Washington as a gifted manipulator. "He is a man of great but secret ambition, indefatigable in business, and extremely clear and systematic in his arrangement of it . . . Of his private character I can say but little positive. I have never heard of any truly noble, generous, or disinterested action of his; he has very few who are on terms of intimate and unreserved friendship, and what is worse, he is less beloved in his own state than in any part of the United States." Should Washington be judged among the great men of history, Thornton concluded sourly, it could only be due to force of circumstance. "I cannot help thinking that the misconduct of our commanders has given him a principal part of that greatness."

Even allowing for national bias, this was an ungenerous estimate. It is hard to imagine how any official representative of King George could glimpse nobility in Washington's wartime conduct or sacrifice in his reluctant donning of the presidential harness. Yet for millions of Americans, the vast majority outside their president's small circle of unreserved friendships, these were home truths, uncritically accepted. In a second letter a few weeks later, the British guest revealed more of himself than of his host by dismissing the "dull and unentertaining" rituals of dinner at 190 Market Street.

Forgetting the shrewd, deliberate concealment he had earlier perceived, Hammond's assistant now chose to attribute Washington's lack of conviviality reserve to personal pride and "constitutional diffidence." As a matter of fact, the evening had been rescued from utter boredom only by Jefferson's verbal jousting against European thrones and his prophecy of coming revolution upon the death of Sweden's aged king Gustavus III.

Jefferson's supporters in the press echoed Thornton's portrayal of a wooden autocrat. Philip Freneau and Benjamin Franklin Bache, the sage's radical grandson who edited Philadelphia's *Aurora*, castigated Washington as yesterday's man, "the American Caesar" out of his depth in grappling with revolutionary currents at home and overseas. When Hamilton proposed stamping the president's profile on new currency, Freneau rushed into print, breathlessly demanding, "Shall Washington, my fav'rite child, be ranked 'mongst haughty kings?" From his friend and confidante Eliza Powel the president received an outspokenly critical tract then appearing on the streets of Philadelphia. Washington responded blandly, claiming that the broadside's accusations "have not given me a moment's painful sensation." He did express regret that the author, "if his object was to convey accurate information to the public mind, had not devoted a little of the time and pains he appears to have employed in writing this pamphlet in the investigation of facts." By doing so, Washington added stiffly, he might have discovered his charges to be without foundation.

Freneau and Bache, take heed.

The very awkwardness of Washington's reply counters Thornton's picture of a frosty, calculating careerist. Indeed, it is one of the crowning paradoxes of Washington's intricate character, attributable to the self-sacrificing traits invisible to the British observer, that he could sputter endlessly over the imagined sins of light-fingered domestics yet lapse into silence in the face of rank insubordination within his official family. Long after most men would have tolerated the public bickering of Hamilton and Jefferson (not to mention their journalistic mouthpieces), Washington pretended obliviousness. By treating the feud as strictly a clash of principles, he hoped to preserve at least a semblance of official dignity — essential to the new republic's credibility — even as the combatants themselves sank to the level of street brawlers.

Yet in soothing their ruffled feathers Washington paid a terrible price, for it was only by forsaking the prospect of retirement that he could persuade his fractious ministers to remain on the job. In the ultimate irony and against his wishes and better judgment, Washington found himself dragooned into accepting a second term by lieutenants quick to abandon the administration at the earliest opportunity. Under the circumstances, honeyed assurances of his personal indispensability must have carried a hollow ring when mouthed by men less wedded to duty.

❦ 2 ❧

For weeks, speculation over Washington's plans had gripped political Philadelphia. By the time the president summoned James Madison to a conference on the morning of May 5, his mind was made up. The two men formed an incongruous sight as they greeted each other in the president's small, second-floor study: the graying executive looming nearly a foot above the slight, balding scholar from Orange County, dressed in his customary black coat, short black breeches, and silk stockings of the same drab shade. Pleasantries exchanged, the pair quickly got down to business. The president had a decision to confide and a favor to ask. He wanted Madison's thoughts on how and when to inform the public of his impending departure from office.

Madison answered with an argument, insisting that retirement, however pleasing it might be to Washington personally, would be calamitous for the young nation. The real calamity, Washington responded, would be for him to overstay his welcome. He felt stale, vexed by official demands, and heartsick over the spread of factional dispute. Stoical disclaimers to the contrary, he took offense at attacks made upon him and his administration through vulnerable underlings. Madison rejected out of hand the executive's harsh self-criticisms, claiming that without his continued presence the growth of party spirit might easily swamp the fragile constitutional bark. The congressman dismissed prospective successors like Adams, Jefferson, Jay, and himself as unacceptable for reasons of geography or political shading. Half an hour after it began, the meeting ended inconclusively.

Soon after, the president left for Mount Vernon, an unavoidable journey given the rapidly declining health of his nephew George Augustine. Intimations of mortality must have mingled with practical fears for the future of his beloved plantation should Washington yield to the politicians of Philadelphia and condemn himself to four more years in official purgatory. Nothing he saw that sunwashed spring weakened his determination to return for good before another wheat crop was planted. On May 20, unwilling to forgo dreams of life behind the plow, Washington wrote plaintively to Madison. "I have again and again resolved them with thoughtful anxiety," he said of his friend's impassioned arguments. Yet however he viewed the situation, Washington could not be reconciled to a second term. "I therefore still look forward to the fulfillment of my fondest and most ardent wishes to spend the remainder of my days (which I can not expect will be many) in ease and tranquility," he told Madison. Nothing short of a national convulsion over choosing a successor would dissuade him, and "my vanity, I am sure, is not of that cast as to allow me to view the subject in this light."

Washington now renewed his earlier request for Madison's assistance in preparing a "plain and modest" valedictory to which he might bring his own great gift for self-presentation. Hoping to impress the American people with their historical responsibilities, Washington would remind them "that we are *all* the children of the same country, a country great and rich in itself, capable, and promising to be as prosperous and as happy as any the annals of history have ever brought to our view. That our interest, however diversified in local and smaller matters, is the same in all the great and essential concerns of the nation . . . That the established government being the work of our own hands, with the seeds of amendment engrafted in the Constitution, may by wisdom, good dispositions, and mutual allowances . . . bring it as near to perfection as any human institution ever approximated."

Washington's sensitivity to criticism made him warn his political descendants "that however necessary it may be to keep a watchful eye over public servants and public measures, yet there ought to be limits to it; for suspicions unfounded and jealousies too lively are irritating to honest feelings and oftentimes are productive of more evil than good."

At the start of June, Washington returned to Philadelphia. Henry Lee invited him to sit for a portrait, to grace the meeting room of a Masonic lodge in Alexandria. Much as he would like to gratify his friend, said the president, "I am so heartily tired of the attendance . . . given to these people that it is now more than two years since I have resolved to sit no more for any of them." Eventually he relented, only to have his criticism of the itinerant artist confirmed. The resulting work was more caricature than likeness.

Writing from Virginia, Washington's niece Harriot beseeched her uncle for a guitar, preferably with keys and strings, "but if one with keys is dearer than without, I shall be much obliged to you for one with strings." For $17 Harriot got her guitar. Before long the girl was sent to Fredericksburg to live with Washington's sister Betty Lewis. She came well provided with everything proper for a young lady in her situation, explained Uncle George. "This much I know, that she costs me enough to place her in it." Should the young lady want for any necessity, he promised to advance a banknote within ten days of the request. "I do not mean by this to launch into expensiveness," he added as if by reflex. "She has no pretensions to it, nor would the state of my finances enable me to indulge her in that if she had." Meanwhile, he had no intention of neglecting his niece's social instruction, and Betty Lewis was just the woman to cure Harriot's idleness and careless disregard for appearances.

Harriot Washington was easily packed off to acquire such graces as a river town and a vinegary aunt might supply. The secretary of state was another matter. Greeting the president on his return from Mount Vernon was a fresh appeal for him to accept a second term, which on closer examination turned out to be nothing more nor less than a political platform for Jefferson's nascent party. Washington's continuation in office would answer every argument used to lead citizens toward violence or secession. As Jefferson put it, "North and South will hang together if they have you to hang on."

Historians unable to resist this gracefully turned phrase have paid less attention to its long, rancorous prologue, wherein Jefferson echoed many of the arguments being made by his Republican brethren. Excessive debt, a "corrupt squadron" of legislators feathering their nests, Hamilton's barely concealed desire to subvert popular government in favor of a monarchy: all were lined up before the firing squad of Jeffersonian rhetoric. Sectional differences reared their ugly head as well. "When northern and southern prejudices have come into conflict," Jefferson maintained, "the latter have been sacrificed and the former soothed."

Jefferson placed his trust in a vastly enlarged House of Representatives — and the president. "I am perfectly aware of the oppression under which your present office lays your mind and of the ardor with which you pant for retirement to domestic life." But there were uniquely eminent characters on whom society had "peculiar claims . . . This seems to be your condition." Jefferson's condition was different. Thanks to lavish spending on scientific equipment and five hundred bottles of Bordeaux's finest *vin rouge*, "such as is drunk at the best tables there," the secretary of state was sinking deep into debt. His expenses in Philadelphia dwarfed his salary of $3,000, not to mention the costs of Monticello's latest reconstruction.

"Multitudes can fill the office in which you have been pleased to place me," Jefferson told Washington. "*I*, therefore, have no motive to consult but my own inclination, which is bent irresistibly on the tranquil enjoyment of my family, my farm, and my books."

The only hope for the survival of constitutional government, it seemed, lay in an honestly republican party arrayed against the "monarchial and paper interest." "I can scarcely contemplate a more incalculable evil than the breaking of the union into two or more parts," said Jefferson. Yet so long as "monarchial federalists" ignored southern objections, then "republican federalists" were helpless to prevent the subversion of American liberty. With this remarkable letter — a campaign speech, really — the secretary all but formally proclaimed the birth of a party opposed to the administration he served, confidently predicted victory for this new force in the approaching congressional elections, and dangled the tantalizing possibility of Washington's retirement halfway through his second term *if* this forecast provided accurate. Nowhere in Jefferson's text was there the slightest recognition that Washington might differ from his secretary's prescription for national contentment. If Jefferson believed what he said, then he knew Washington little and understood him less.

Jefferson's agitated state can be better understood in the context of Hamilton's continued diplomatic meddling. Intimate exchanges between the secretary of the treasury and George Hammond undermined regular negotiations aimed at forcing British compliance with the peace treaty of 1783. Yet even here, Jefferson discounted the president's support in ways that baffle the modern observer. For instance, on June 2 Washington confided doubts about an impending meeting with Hammond to his secretary of state: "I wish more favorable explanations than I expect from your interview with the British minister."

Washington went further still in a message to Gouverneur Morris, of all people, angrily dismissing rumors in Paris that the United States sought British mediation to hasten peace with the northwestern Indians. There would be no such feeler as long as he held office, the irate president said. Instead, he would continue meeting personally with visiting chiefs, the latest among them the legendary Mohawk leader Joseph Brant. Additional emissaries from Philadelphia would be dispatched to the disputed territory north of the Ohio in hopes of convincing hostile natives of the administration's peaceful intentions.

Had the secretary of state been more open to Washington's signals, he might have used them to political advantage. At the least, the two men could have enjoyed the unspoken camaraderie that comes from shared enmities. But Jefferson's hostility toward King George was mild compared with his feelings about the Caribbean upstart who sat across from him at the Cabinet table. Jefferson readily believed a secondhand report that his antagonist was preparing a place of asylum in Britain as a retreat from the pending triumph of republicanism at home. Hamilton, no less inclined to credit the worst about his nemesis and fearing that enemies were on to the scent of his affair with Maria Reynolds, threatened to expose Jefferson's youthful attempt to throw himself upon the wife of his best friend, until recently a United States senator from Virginia.

❦ 3 ❧

"The President has fixed on the 12th to leave this place for Mount Vernon," Martha Washington told her niece Fanny at the start of July. To prepare for his arrival and the ensuing social obligations, Mrs. Washington wanted Mansion House scoured "from the garret to the cellars." Every bed should be aired and mended, bedclothes checked, headboards prepared for quick assembly, for "I have not a doubt but we shall have company all the time we are at home." With instincts honed by a quarter century as George Washington's wife, Martha directed the house staff to examine each piece of china but to delay stuffing old "chares," since their canvas coverings would likely last a while longer. The gardener must be able to supply items required for a sociable table, most critically fresh vegetables, "the best part of our living in the country."

The president had instructions of his own for Anthony Whiting, on whose capable shoulders most of the estate's management fell now that Fanny's husband, George Augustine, was practically incapacitated. Much as Washington looked forward to spending the summer at Mount Vernon, he was unsparing in his assessment of the state of agriculture in Virginia. On the eve of his departure for home, he drew a caustic portrait of

American farming practices for the famous English agronomist Arthur Young.

"A piece of land is cut down and kept under constant cultivation, first in tobacco and then in Indian corn (two very exhausting plants), until it will yield scarcely anything," Washington explained. "A second piece is cleared and treated in the same manner; then a third, and so on until probably there is but little more to clear." The impoverished landowner had only unpalatable choices: "either to recover the land which he has ruined, to accomplish which he has perhaps neither the skill, the industry, nor the means; or to retire beyond the mountains; or to substitute quantity for quality, in order to raise something."

The master of Mount Vernon spoke as an authority on wasteful practices, one with firsthand knowledge of life's allure beyond the mountains, where an elastic frontier promised second and third chances for anyone defeated by crowded cities or barren farmland. At the age of sixty, with 58,000 acres to his name, Washington was possessed by his possessions and anxious to liquidate much of his inland empire for cash. His constant pennypinching assumes a different aspect when his benefactions are taken into account. Besides the demands of official entertaining and his elaborate establishment, the president provided financial support for nine of his relatives' children. It cost him $500 just to apprentice his nephews George Steptoe and Lawrence to Attorney General Randolph. Among the lesser charges these two dandies ran up to Washington's account were beer tabs, music lessons, and fashionable black silk ribbon in place of shoe buckles.

One expense Washington never begrudged was Mount Vernon. By personal definition he was a farmer, not a planter, and a scientific farmer at that. Nearly half his lands were tilled under a complex rotation plan, enabling him to test sixty different crops. When his efforts to grow grapes failed, the erstwhile vineyard became a laboratory for horse chestnuts and treebox. Since seeds were difficult and costly to obtain in the United States, Washington's gardener used the old "vineyard inclusure" to nurture rare grasses, pumpkins, and lemon carrots. Exotic varieties of apples, pears, plums, peaches, and cherries also took root there.

Farmer Washington marinated seed wheat in brine and alum to ward off rust. He planted oats and English peas to increase the fertility of his soil and saluted the lowly potato, despite its poisonous reputation, as "an improving and ameliorating crop." After coating his lawns with plaster of Paris, Washington sprinkled the residue on his least fertile clover lot. He purchased lightning rods, commonly called Franklin's rods, to protect his buildings, not hesitating to gild their iron points in hopes of improving upon Dr. Franklin's device.

Washington's passion for soil and seed provided a safe topic for conversation with Jefferson. Yet even as the president's thoughts turned to the design and construction of a sixteen sided brick barn, visions of plantation life were rudely interrupted. On July 10, the secretary of state appeared at 190 Market Street to renew his war on imaginary royalists. That there were zealots desiring an American throne, Washington readily conceded; but almost no one, he maintained, was so foolish as to believe one might actually be established. With equal candor, he criticized Freneau's paper for stirring up opposition to government policies and inciting farmers in western Pennsylvania to forcibly resist the excise law. Unchecked, such tendencies would lead to the dissolution of the Union, "the most dreadful of all calamities" and an inevitable precursor to the absolutism most feared by Jefferson and his followers.

Up to this point, Washington had said nothing unfamiliar to Jefferson from previous encounters. Yet in his next breath he shattered the convenient fiction that somehow he stood above and apart from the legislative and financial measures undertaken by his administration. He entertained no illusions about the motives of journals such as the *National Gazette*, Washington said, adding tartly that "he must be a fool indeed to swallow the little sugar plums here and there thrown out to him." By condemning policies pursued under his name, opposition editors condemned him as well. Anyone believing to the contrary must regard the president as "too careless to attend to them or too stupid to understand them." Either way, Washington felt mightily insulted.

Undaunted, Jefferson pressed his indictment of Hamilton's policies and methods. A claim of legislative corruption at the hands of treasury agents met with stony silence. On the question of assumption, presumably long since settled, Washington said that he viewed it as an honorable way of extinguishing a common debt. Let the North have its excise, Jefferson cut in, as long as Southerners could impose upon themselves a direct levy. Here the discussion came to an abrupt halt, for they had reached a philosophical impasse, Washington hewing to the Federalist view of a national government operating directly on individuals, Jefferson dispersing sovereignty among state and local authorities.

Within forty-eight hours of this aggravating scene, the president was making his way home. At the end of a hard journey through parched countryside ravaged by the Hessian fly, Washington found Virginia's Tidewater beset by the flux and malarial fevers. George Augustine's condition was "unpromising and precarious"; his wife appeared likely to follow him to an early grave. With Lear pursuing business connections in New Hampshire and both the president's nephew Howell Lewis and Martha's nephew Bartholomew Dandridge visiting friends, Washington shouldered a heavy load of correspondence on top of managing his estate.

One letter especially threatened his peace of mind. On July 30, Hamilton sat down to craft an appeal that might succeed where Madison and Jefferson had thus far failed. Washington's departure would constitute the greatest evil yet to befall the United States, said Hamilton, who added craftily that such a step would be seen as a blow "critically hazardous to your own reputation." His letter crossed in the mails with one from Washington containing a thinly disguised rehash of Jefferson's allegations, designed to bring about at least an indirect confrontation between accuser and accused. En route to Mount Vernon and since his arrival, said Washington, he had sought the views of "sensible and moderate men." Their responses confirmed his optimism about the country's prosperity and general contentment.

Yet they did not quiet his doubts. Hiding behind the specter of his disaffected neighbor George Mason, with whom he had last communicated in 1788, Washington told Hamilton that he sensed latent opposition bobbing to the surface. Twenty-one specific complaints followed, among them familiar strictures against a debt beyond the nation's productive capacity to pay, the greasing of legislative palms, and the dire effect of excise taxes in transferring America's indebtedness abroad. Other objections of more recent vintage included paper money, accused of chasing coinage out of rural sections, and speculative capital, the handmaiden of vice and idleness. Brusquely, Washington flung the whole lot in Hamilton's face.

Through a frantic outburst of literary energy, Hamilton sent a fourteen-thousand-word reply to Mount Vernon on August 18, pounding to bits the arguments of rivals and reaffirming his personal devotion to republican principles. The accusation that he aimed at monarchy "from its absurdity refutes itself." As for the national debt, it was nothing new, Hamilton reminded his chief, but an unsought inheritance that could only be repudiated at grave cost to American honor — a point Washington himself had made in his conference with Jefferson on July 10. Compared to the tax burden laid upon honest Englishmen, Hamilton contended, Yankees were fortunate indeed. Far from driving capital overseas, the treasury's policies had lured European wealth to America's shores, increasing domestic purchasing power and the store of circulating capital. The charge of legislative corruption was a hateful falsehood, the product of "narrow and depraved ideas" maligning those public-minded souls who girded the nation's credit.

Hamilton argued persuasively that he was guilty of nothing more heinous than conspicuous success, in politics a crime worse than failure. Few students of Hamiltonian finance, then or since, would characterize the secretary as a flaming democrat. Yet that is exactly what he was, for in challenging the stifling conventions of agrarian rule, in disputing the hereditary privilege of large landowners to whom he was an arriviste of shameful origins, in exalting money rather than bloodlines and factories before farms, Hamilton freed his countrymen from many of their past denials and Old World restraints. Jefferson opened doors for average Americans; Hamilton raised the ceiling on exceptional ones.

If, over the course of two centuries, the yeasty American way of doing things has dispersed wealth and determined the modern world's material way of life, then the greatest debt of all may be owed to Rachel Hamilton's son, who saw the interdependence of men and machines as he proclaimed the mutual reliance of rural yeoman and urban mechanic.

‹ 4 ›

Commencing the final week of July 1792, Hamilton became a one-man battery raking Jefferson's flanks, with John Fenno and his *Gazette of the United States* passing the ammunition. On the twenty-fifth Hamilton pitched a firebrand into the enemy camp, disguising himself as "T.L." to ask whether Philip Freneau's government salary was paid for his translations or his polemics. Jefferson's editor, reacting like a man whose hand had been called, hit back with an attack in doggerel:

> Since the day we attempted the Nation's Gazette
> Pomposo's dull printer does nothing but fret;
> Now preaching and screeching, then nibbling and scribbling,
> Remarking and barking, repining and whining
> And still in a pet
> From morning till night with the Nation's Gazette.

The wit might sting, but Freneau had been bloodied at last, and Hamilton moved quickly to exploit his advantage. Early in August he singled out an unnamed Cabinet member for launching a somewhat novel experiment in the annals of government, "a newspaper instituted by a public officer . . . the editor of it regularly pensioned with the public money in the disposal of that officer." Freneau responded by swearing out an affidavit declaring the secretary of state to be innocent of any part in hiring him or influencing what he wrote. This might be true in a technical sense, said Hamilton, using one of many aliases, names like Amicus, Metellus, and A Plain Honest Man. But didn't "a particular friend of that officer" have a hand in Freneau's original employment, not to mention a regular place in his editorial columns? (In later years Freneau recanted, claiming that Jefferson had indeed contributed to his journal.)

As sulfurous clouds of invective spread over Philadelphia, Hamilton kept changing his literary identities and Freneau stepped up his efforts to unmask the secretary of the treasury as the evil genius behind dull Pomposo's coruscating slanders. On August 11, two separate articles denouncing Jefferson by name appeared in the *Gazette of the United States*. Traveling the high and low roads simultaneously, Hamilton scoffed at the enlightened Jefferson and Madison as "pretenders to profound knowledge yet ignorant of the most useful of all sciences — the science of human nature."

Thrusting savagely at Jefferson's supposed duality, Hamilton forecast a time "when the visor of stoicism is plucked from the brow of the epicurean; when the plain garb of Quaker simplicity is stripped from the concealed voluptuary; when Caesar, coyly refusing the proffered diadem, is seen to be Caesar rejecting the trappings by grasping the substance of imperial domination." One day, Hamilton predicted, "the great, modest, retiring philosopher" would be revealed as "the intriguing incendiary, the aspiring turbulent competitor."

Madison and Monroe rushed to their friend's defense, refuting insinuations that Jefferson had been lukewarm in support of the new Constitution. Madison called Hamilton's latest charges "as impotent as they are malicious." By the middle of September, as it became clear that Hamilton had overshot the mark, Freneau unlumbered his heavy artillery for a go at Hamilton's insubordination during the Revolution. "The devil rageth while his time is short," jabbed the editor, prefacing the recycled tale of Hamilton's youthful resignation from Washington's staff. Freneau wondered aloud how any public character could be so ungrateful "as to erect his little crest against the magnanimous chief" who at present directed the American government.

This was posturing, pure and simple, from a man who had made a name for himself by singing Jefferson's virtues and detailing the wickedness of his opponents. But Freneau's strategy was sound. On balance, Hamilton's vituperative campaign did him no good, as it did Jefferson no harm. Sledgehammer attacks on the secretary of state had the unintended consequence of making Jefferson, not the congressional stalwart Madison, the unquestioned leader of Republicans throughout the country. Hamilton's newspaper war was no more successful in tipping the scales of the president's affections. Thanks to Tobias Lear, Washington received two helpings of journalistic vitriol each week, paying $3 a year for the privilege of seeing his administration vilified in Freneau's columns.

Caught in the escalating crossfire, late in August Washington sent virtually identical peace feelers to each combatant. He opened his letter to Jefferson with an ominous account of the dangers in foreign policy. Alexander McGillivray, purchased with American dollars, was refusing to stay bought, and in league with his old Spanish allies he was threatening to annul the Treaty of New York. Rumors of Spanish troops landing at New Orleans vied with the brutal murder of two presidential emissaries sent to talk peace with disaffected western tribes. If, as appeared likely, Spain was intriguing with restless Creeks and Cherokees, Washington felt it could only be with London's connivance.

How regrettable, he told Jefferson, "whilst we are encompassed on all sides with avowed enemies and insidious friends that internal dissensions should be harrowing and tearing our vitals." Washington's most earnest wish was that instead of "wounding suspicions and irritable charges, there may be liberal allowances, mutual forbearances, and temporizing yield-ings on *all sides.*"

Three days later, Washington put pen to paper a second time, ostensibly to thank Hamilton for his exhaustive vindication of his treasury stew-ardship. Although political differences were unavoidable, said the pres-ident, they should not be allowed to damage public administration or poison personal relations. He found it appalling that "men of abilities, zealous patriots, having the same *general* objects in view and the same upright intentions to prosecute them," should imagine the worst of their fellow officials. "How unfortunate it would be if a fabric so goodly, erected under so many providential circumstances . . . should from diversity of sentiments . . . (for I cannot prevail on myself to believe that these meas-ures are as yet the deliberate acts of a determined party)" be wracked by controversy and brought to the edge of collapse. "Melancholy thought!"

On the subject of political parties, Washington refused to acknowledge what he must have known in his heart. He was just as stubborn in deflecting campaign overtures. Attorney General Randolph joined the movement to draft Washington with a bald-faced appeal to his vanity, writing, "It is the fixed opinion of the world that you surrender nothing incomplete." Although Washington's delphic reply avoided the "inter-esting subject" raised in the letter, his gloom was palpable. Watching his nephew die with agonizing slowness and measuring the shadows of his own approaching dissolution, "the subject never recurs to my mind but with additional poignancy . . . But as the all-wise disposer of events has hitherto watched over my steps, I trust that in the important one I may soon be called upon to take, he will mark the course so plainly as that I cannot mistake the way."

Washington could implore, but neither of the Cabinet's warring parties was inclined to yield, even to his entreaties. True enough, Hamilton manfully affirmed his part in the newspaper row, but he also justified such conduct as a necessary defense against partisans out to overthrow his financial system and besmirch his reputation. Should Washington be forced to replace all his contentious associates, the secretary of the treasury would comply most cheerfully. On the other hand, were his chief able to reunite the Cabinet upon "some steady plan of cooperation," then Hamilton would faithfully adhere to it while in office. Gestures like this came easily to one who had started the fight and who reliably counted Washington in his corner on most substantive matters, U.S.-British relations excepted. For the quarrelsome secretary, the best way out of a difficult situation was to sound a dignified note of forbearance while assuming that Jefferson would dig in his heels and refuse to play along.

Hamilton's psychological sixth sense did not betray him. On September 9 the secretary of state composed an elaborate if less than wholly convincing apologia. With a combination of dovelike innocence and wounded pride, he asserted that he had been "duped" upon his arrival in New York two years earlier "and made a tool for forwarding Hamilton's schemes, not then sufficiently understood by me." Following this apparent reference to his part in the bargain by candlelight whereby Hamilton secured assumption and Virginia, the capital city, Jefferson savaged the *Report on Manufactures* and his rival's repeated intrusions on foreign policy.

He was less forthright in denying paternity of Freneau's paper. "I cannot recollect whether it was at the same time" he had learned of a prospective rival to Fenno's gazette that he had promised a clerkship to the fiercely republican poet, but knowing of Freneau's political sympathies, said Jefferson, "it is likely enough I may have expressed it in conversation with others."

Loftily, Jefferson disclaimed interest in the Fenno-Freneau duel for public favor: "The one courts them by flattery, the other by censure: and I believe it will be admitted that the one has been as servile as the other severe." Jefferson reiterated his earlier promise to leave the administration in the near future: "I look to that period with the longing of a wave-worn mariner who has at length the land in view." Once safely onshore, he would reserve the right to enlist popular support against Hamilton and his aristocratic nostrums.

A final thunderbolt warned of future campaigns: "I will not suffer my retirement to be clouded by the slanders of a man whose history, from the moment at which history can stoop to notice him, is a tissue of machinations against the liberty of the country which has not only received and given him bread, but heaped its honors on his head." Jefferson signed his letter "with great and sincere affection and respect, dear Sir, your most obedient and most humble servant." But in the contemptuous vigor of his language, the master of Monticello, born to privilege, revealed volumes about his feelings for the parvenu from Nevis.

❦ 5 ❧

From a fractious official family Washington turned his attention to another kind of disorder, potentially fatal to his dream of a continental, constitutional republic. Several western Pennsylvania counties were up in arms about Hamilton's excise tax on whiskey, expressing their anger through violence against federal agents as well as more peaceful routes. Delegates to a convention in Pittsburgh late in August vowed to obstruct collection of the tax through every legal device possible or until Congress backed down and wiped the levy off the statute books. Until then, anyone found cooperating with the tax collector would face ostracism from the community. Reports of similar discontent filtered in from southern New York, distant Kentucky, the Carolinas, and parts of Washington's Virginia.

Hamilton wanted to punish the frontier rebels, the sooner and sterner the better, but the president favored delay, persuasion — anything but a repeat of the forest humiliations inflicted upon Harmar and St. Clair. Concurring in this strategy were Chief Justice Jay and Attorney General Randolph, neither exactly friendly to sedition. Facing a solid phalanx of opposition, Hamilton shifted his focus from southern hotbeds to the overexcited countryside around Pittsburgh. His motives were not hard to fathom. Pennsylvania was home to the nation's capital, and the very proximity of discontent, matched by an increasingly open disregard for legal authority, made Washington more receptive to federal intervention.

Resistance to the law, he said, was "exceedingly reprehensible" under any circumstances, but particularly so when those resisting were the prime beneficiaries of government protection against ferocious Indians. Hamilton pressed for indictments of the Pittsburgh ringleaders, and Washington, well acquainted with the area's rebellious nature from years spent dunning Appalachian squatters, was inclined to go along. Edmund Randolph contested the putative man on horseback, insisting that while the actions taken at Pittsburgh might be offensive, they were in no way illegal. When Hamilton urged a presidential proclamation asserting federal supremacy in the dispute and warning of stronger action should the rebels persist, the attorney general edited the text to remove inflammatory language or explicit threats of military reprisal.

Washington affixed his name to the document on September 15 before sending it on to Jefferson for comments. "I have no doubt but that the measure I am about to take will be severely criticized," the president acknowledged. But he must disregard public censure, however painful, whenever called upon to discharge the duties of his office, of which none was "more important than to carry the laws of the United States into effect." Warmly sympathetic to the protesters, Jefferson might have been expected to oppose the proclamation as the act of a government becoming more authoritarian as it lost authority. In his loyalty to a besieged chief, however, the great republican's behavior was impeccable. Of course rural dissatisfaction would do nothing to harm the prospects of Jefferson's supporters in the fall elections. So he returned the draft with no significant changes, only the stated wish that events might yet make possible its retirement to the national archives.

With his political flanks thus secured, Washington moved to rein in his swashbuckling secretary of the treasury, telling the overeager Hamilton that while the Constitution and laws must be obeyed, no American could relish the prospect of enforcing them at the point of a bayonet. Indeed, military action should be a last resort. "Otherwise there would be a cry at once, 'The cat is let out, we now see for what purpose an army was raised.' "

Were it not for "the peculiar circumstances of my family," Washington said, he would return to the capital and take personal charge of the crisis. As it was, his nephew's illness and the attendant press of business kept him at Mount Vernon through the first week of October. Congressional elections were fast approaching, and he angrily rebuked an office seeker in Maryland for implying a presidential endorsement. "Conceiving that the exercise of an influence (if I really possessed any), however remote, would be highly improper," the president protested the tactic as an in-fringement on the people's right to choose whomever they pleased to speak for them.

Washington professed indifference to reports that the offending can-didate had spoken disrespectfully of him. "If nothing impeaching my honor or honesty is said, I care little for the rest. I have pursued one uniform course for threescore years and am happy in *believing* that the world have thought it a right one; of its being so I am so well satisfied myself that I shall not depart from it by turning either to the right or to the left until I arrive at the end of my pilgrimage."

❦ 6 ❦

Revolt in the west had sputtered out by the time Jefferson stopped at Mount Vernon on October 1. At this meeting Washington claimed ig-norance of the personal enmity tearing at the vitals of his Cabinet. His assertion was not as disingenuous as it sounds. After a lifetime of sepa-rating his politics from his friendships, Washington was honestly bewil-dered by the shrill intolerance poisoning his inner circle. Still, it strains credibility to believe that the man at the center of the storm was wholly unaware of the tempest before October 1792. As early as Jefferson's appeal cum campaign manifesto of May 23, he had received firsthand evidence of the bitter divisions around him. It was in his interest — and his country's — that he delay the outbreak of partisan warfare as long as possible. Better than anyone else, Washington knew that lurking behind his calls for national unity were objectives whose pursuit could endanger the Union's survival, not the least of them an economic independence to match its political sovereignty.

Washington told Jefferson that practice alone would determine the validity of Hamilton's funding system. Speaking from a personal standpoint, the president volunteered that he had seen the country's affairs desperate and its credit lost, only to have both rescued and the latter raised to the highest pitch. "All that was ever necessary to establish our credit," countered Jefferson, "was an efficient government and an honest one." Washington, though empathetic, was immovable: the secretary's fears were misplaced. Further attempts at persuasion came to an abrupt end when both men were summoned to breakfast. Jefferson evidently left feeling less secure of his position, for soon after he mailed portions of his Parisian correspondence to the president in an obvious attempt to disprove Hamilton's charge of disloyalty to the nation's organic charter.

Back in Philadelphia, Washington sought to ease his friend's mind. He required no documentation to prove Jefferson's attachment to the Constitution or his country's general welfare, he said, adopting his most paternal tone. He again lamented the row estranging the chief author of the *Federalist* papers from the father of the Declaration of Independence. Their mutual accommodation would strengthen the foundling government; failure would inevitably lead to confusion and mischief, "and for what? because mankind cannot think alike, but would adopt different means to attain the same end . . . I have a great, a sincere esteem and regard for you both and ardently wish that some line could be marked out by which both of you could walk."

From the acrimonious tone of certain newspapers, Washington disclosed to Gouverneur Morris on October 20, Europeans might believe the republic to be unraveling. The truth was very different, for most Americans were both aware of and grateful for the benefits accruing from what Washington persisted in calling "the general government." These included the unavoidable evil of journalistic excess, to be placed "in opposition to the infinite benefits resulting from a free press . . . I am sure you need not be told that in this country a personal difference in political sentiments is often made to take the garb of general dissensions."

On November 4, Washington delivered his fourth annual address to

Congress, dealing largely with the unsettled frontier and including a forthright defense of his recent proclamation. But it was what he left out of the thirty-minute speech that drew far more notice than anything he said. Those hoping to divine his political intentions went away disappointed. Instead, as if to compensate for his continuing exile from plantation life, Washington threw himself into exhaustively detailed instructions to Anthony Whiting at Mount Vernon.

These missives were generally composed on Sunday afternoons, after services at Christ Church. Washington, for many years a vestryman of his parish, failed to take communion, for which he was duly taken to task by the presiding bishop of Philadelphia. Some historians have interpreted this abstention as evidence that Washington's faith was largely formal, a social obligation like the alms he regularly provided for the poor. But if he never knelt in prayer at Valley Forge as portrayed in legend and only rarely used the word God in describing the author of the universe, Washington was no Franklinesque deist.

As a deeply private man who guarded his heart, it would have been out of character for him to advance a public religious agenda or even confide reverence to the prosaic pages of his diary. As he grew older, however, Washington became noticeably more dependent on religious support to carry out his crushing responsibilities. Perhaps because he had listened to more bad sermons than anyone of his age, he had little stomach for the finer points of theological disputation. But no one privy to his correspondence or accounts of his intimates can doubt Washington's essential belief or fail to trace his genuine if poorly articulated relationship with his maker.

An element of Christian philanthropy found its way into Washington's directives to Whiting concerning his human property. Amid explicit orders to plant willows and lombardy poplars around Mansion House, gather in corn before the first frost, dig up potatoes at Dogue Run, and coat the smokehouse roof in red paint, Washington did not forget the black men and women whose enforced presence hung heavy on his conscience.

"Although it is last mentioned," he told Whiting in a typical communication, "it is foremost in my thoughts, to desire you will be particularly attentive to my Negroes in their sickness, and to order every Overseer *positively* to be so likewise; for I am sorry to observe that the generality of them view these poor creatures in scarcely any other light than they do a draft horse or ox, neglecting them as much when they are unable to work instead of comforting and nursing them when they lie on a sickbed."

Tobias Lear observed that Washington's slaves, spared the lash, were fed and clothed as well as any paid laborer. ("But still they are slaves," added Lear, an avowed abolitionist.) When Mrs. Washington's personal attendant, Oney, deserted her mistress in search of freedom, the president refused to advertise for her return. More than sentiment lay behind his actions. In conveying his views to Whiting, the squire mentioned that sickness had cost him more Negroes the previous winter than in all the twelve to fifteen prior years combined. Should his people fall ill and their disorders exceed ordinary complaints, Dr. Craik should be sent for. In the event that no cure was possible, the good doctor needn't be disturbed, as "it is incurring an expense for nothing."

❦ 7 ❧

As a shrewd student of the human race in all its fallibility, John Adams liked to tell of an impoverished old gent whose only companion was a dog who fed on scraps from his meager table. Sensible neighbors advised the man to destroy the animal or risk starvation himself. This was out of the question, replied the dog's owner, for if his canine friend were eliminated — even to assure his own survival — "who will love me then?"

Few were convinced by Adams's protestations that he was immune to mankind's pathetic need to be needed. Conspicuously absent from Philadelphia during the closing stretch of the fall campaign, the vice president affected indifference toward Republican plots aimed at replacing him with New York's governor George Clinton, narrowly reelected following a disputed race with John Jay. It was one thing for Clinton and his henchmen to steal enough votes to retain power in Albany, but could such an anti-Federalist warhorse really hope to eliminate a patriot of John Adams's caliber? Perhaps — *if* the emerging coalition between New York and Virginia, based on Jeffersonian ideals, snagged Pennsylvania and its rich harvest of electoral votes.

To prevent such a catastrophe, Hamilton tried for weeks to lure the emotionally bruised vice president from his Quincy farm, where he had retreated to nurse a sick wife and a prodigious list of personal grievances. Depressed about the recent arrest of King Louis and dismayed by popular enthusiasm for the violent acts of "that light, airy and transported people" the French, the grizzled revolutionary expressed doubts to his son John Quincy whether the French republic would last any longer than Cromwell's English one a century before. Adams's discontent was physical as well as political. His hands betrayed the palsy of old age. Aching eyes curtailed his daily helpings of Cicero, Tacitus, and Thucydides. A disease of the gums caused his teeth to fall out, and a lisp made the vice president reluctant to preside over the Senate.

Hard work supplied therapy of sorts. Defying his popular image as a slave to ceremony, Adams left off his wig as he toiled in the broiling heat of a New England summer. At least building stone walls was preferable to seeing himself excoriated in the press. Feeding his self-pity were Republican attacks led by John Hancock and his own cousin Sam. Unable to extract any clarification of Washington's plans and unwilling to launch a frontal assault on the popular president, critics of the administration did what their successors ever since have done: they went after the vice president.

Adams, a familiar object of abuse, maintained a brave front. "I am of the cat kind and fall upon my feet, throw me as they will," he vowed with a sangfroid Hamilton feared might enable Clinton or, far worse, the slippery Aaron Burr to back into the nation's second office. The secretary of the treasury, sensing in the thirty-six-year-old Burr a mortal enemy athwart his path, warned Washington in writing of the dangers Burr posed. The president prudently held his tongue. Privately he denounced the whispered reports of Adams's disloyalty. Yet a public endorsement was unthinkable from a man who had yet to reveal his own thoughts regarding a second term.

So while the vice president brooded in rustic seclusion and Hamilton maneuvered on behalf of a reluctant ticket, it fell to an old yet unlikely friend to smoke out Washington's intentions. The forceful Eliza Powel, identified by one writer as "a saucy, interesting, attractive, intelligent, flirtatious woman . . . the epitome of confidence, determination, and class," was all that and a good deal more. As the wife of Philadelphia's leading merchant prince and former mayor, she was fluent in the language of politics and, as a friend whose association with the president went back to 1776, was in a special position to influence his thinking. Now she took it upon herself to remonstrate with Washington, declaring it improper and impractical for him even to contemplate "quitting a trust, upon the proper execution of which the repose of millions might be eventually depending."

Few had ever used such unvarnished language in addressing Great Washington, but Mrs. Powel was rarely shy about deploying her strongest weapons, beginning with Washington's famous sensitivity to public opinion. "Be assured that a great deal of the well-earned popularity that you are now in possession of will be torn from you by the envious and malignant should you follow the bent of your inclinations," she alerted him.

To leave office in the spring of 1793 would cause rejoicing among the Constitution's bitterest foes. Eliza envisioned the reaction of evil or envious minds, who were sure to conclude "that ambition had been the moving spring of all your actions . . . that as nature had not closed the scene while your career was glorious, you had with profound address withdrawn yourself from a station that promised nothing to your ambition and that might eventually involve your popularity." Appearances aside, Eliza wondered how the president could abandon the struggle for constitutional government "or what is still worse, behold the monster licentiousness, with all his horrid attendants, exalted on its ruins?"

Washington, his friend insisted, was "the only man in America that dares to do right on all public occasions . . . You have shown that you are not to be intoxicated by power or misled by flattery. You have a feeling heart and the long necessity of behaving with circumspection must have tempered that native benevolence which otherwise might make you too compliant . . . the soundness of your judgment has been enriched on many and trying occasions, and you have frequently demonstrated that you possess an empire over yourself. For God's sake, do not yield that empire to a love of ease . . . You love philosophic retirement; convince the world, then, that you are a practical philosopher and that your native philanthropy has induced you to relinquish an object so essential to your happiness."

None of his contemporaries ever drew a better word portrait of the proud, emotionally repressed patriot, but George Washington and Eliza Powel, after all, were kindred spirits. Subject to fits of depression — she once excused herself from the dinner table at Mount Vernon in hopes of lightening the mood — Eliza saw beneath an unrevealing surface the torment of a divided soul, suspended between a lifelong hankering after fame and the disillusionment bred by its consequences. It was only natural that Washington, aware of his infirmities, sick of the political cockpit, and angered by truculent journalists, should wish to resume the interrupted life of a Potomac squire.

Eliza Powel understood and sympathized with this longing. More than womanly intuition shaped her conviction that the president was guilty of self-deception in believing that he could be happy far removed from great events. Perhaps because she thought like Washington, Eliza could bluntly inquire whether retirement would really produce contentment. "Have you not often experienced that your judgment was fallible with respect to the means of happiness?" she asked. "Have you not, on some occasions, found the consummation of your wishes the source of the keenest of your sufferings?"

We can only guess at Washington's response. Unable to bridge the gulf between his distaste for office and an honest groundswell demanding a second term, the president said nothing. The country took his silence for consent. When 132 members of the electoral college met across a staggered calendar, not a dissenting voice was heard. Declared Congressman David Cobb of Massachusetts, "Our electors are unanimous for the old King and his second." In fact, John Adams was far from universally popular. Only 77 votes went to him, with 50 cast for Clinton and a handful scattered between Jefferson and Burr. Envisioning four thankless years in "the most insignificant office that ever the invention of man contrived," Adams's joy was understandably muted.

But perhaps Washington had other plans for his embattled vice president. Denied the immediate release he longed for, Washington found succor in fantasizing an early retirement. On December 13 he sought advice from his secretary of state regarding some new table china. The president said he had discussed his requirements with a Mr. Shaw, who promised a suitable set of Germanware the next time he visited the East Indies. Unfortunately, Shaw would not return for at least two years, by which time Washington would no longer need the service. To make certain Jefferson got the point, Washington repeated his observation. In two years, he seemed to be saying, a different man would sit in his place.

Washington waited for six weeks before confessing to Henry Lee that anything less than "a pretty respectable vote" in the recent contest would have caused him chagrin. "But to say that I feel pleasure from the prospect of *commencing* another tour of duty would be a departure from the truth . . . it being my fixed determination to return to the walks of private life at the end of my term." With the habitual reserve that Mrs. Powel called his empire over himself, the president expressed regret at the recent death of his friend Colonel Burwell Bassett, whose daughter Fanny was married to George Augustine Washington. "We shall all follow, some sooner and some later," said Washington, "and, from accounts, my poor nephew is likely to be among the first."

Writing from his diplomatic listening post in Lisbon, David Humphreys thanked the president for bowing to the inevitable. "The certain knowledge you have, that no human character ever enjoyed so much untarnished fame in his lifetime, should more than compensate for any little perplexities, troubles and vexations you may encounter," Humphreys assured his friend. Ranking high on the list of vexations was Philip Freneau. No sooner was Washington's reelection confirmed than Freneau turned his heaviest guns on the previously sacrosanct chief executive. The editor who dined on controversy gorged himself mocking the qualifications needed to succeed in Washington's court. He chortled, "A certain *monarchial prettiness* must be highly extolled, such as *levees, drawing rooms, stately nods instead of shaking hands*, titles of office, seclusion from the people."

"The President has been openly abused in the *National Gazette*," wrote Abigail Adams, stunned if not entirely displeased to find someone other than her husband a target of editorial venom. Although Washington grew accustomed to seeing himself compared to Cromwell, he never grew to like it. Taking the only course consistent with self-respect, he canceled his subscription to Freneau's paper. Not to be put off so easily, the offending journalist ordered three copies of each day's run personally delivered to 190 Market Street.

❋ 8 ❋

A HIGHLY FAVORED AGE

"Rather than it should have failed, I would have seen
half the earth desolated. Were there but an Adam and
an Eve left in every country, and left free, it would
be better than as it now is."

Thomas Jefferson,
on the French Revolution

THE DULL CRASH OF CANNON FIRE roused Philadelphians at daybreak
on January 9, 1793. Soon thousands were converging on the Walnut Street
Prison yard, across from the State House, where a dashing Frenchman
named Jean Pierre Blanchard hoped to take his place among the birds
overhead in a yellow silk balloon. Present to send off the Lindbergh of
his age was George Washington, for once a spectator and not a spectacle.
After handing Blanchard a passport recommending "the BOLD AERO-
NAUT" to anyone he might encounter in his travels, the president gaped
as the airship rose on a jet of flame and began drifting toward the wheatfields of New Jersey at twenty miles an hour. Crossing the Schuylkill
River, Blanchard hoisted the French Tricolor and the Stars and Stripes
in deference to the fraternal republics led by grave Washington and the
giddy cutthroats of Paris.

"How dear is the name of Washington to these people," said Blanchard
of the people on the Jersey shore who greeted him at the end of his forty-
five-minute flight. As for the president, tethered to responsibilities from
which there was no escape, he probably envied the balloonist his freedom.
Topping the new year's concerns was Blanchard's homeland, where 1793
was dawning in a blaze of republican zeal, aristocratic horror, and political
tumult.

Americans drank fewer toasts to King Louis after his botched escape
attempt in the direction of Hapsburg Austria, and it was easy for some,

forgetting that they owed their republic to France's wartime assistance, to feel smugly virtuous. On November 19, 1792, a revolutionary decree had converted France's inner turmoil into a worldwide crusade for the rights of man against aristocratic or priestly oppression. Royalist Europe trembled while many Americans saw the transformation of France as a vindication of their own political doctrines. In the third week of January, Louis XVI was guillotined by radical reformers, followed by word that a new French minister, Edmond Charles Genêt, would soon be arriving in Philadelphia. Across the Atlantic, Republicans of all persuasions seized upon the news to confirm their hopes or justify their dread. By a strange kind of reasoning, wrote Oliver Wolcott, Hamilton's assistant secretary and a Federalist stalwart, "our Jacobins . . . suppose the liberties of America depend on the right of cutting throats in France."

Washington never thought that, but ten days before Monsieur Blanchard invaded the skies over Philadelphia the president did surprise Jefferson by proposing "to effect a stricter connection" with the French republic. The secretary immediately took steps to revive payments on the French war debt, briefly suspended amid the turmoil of the previous autumn. After Thomas Pinckney, the American envoy in London, sought guidance on how to treat a kingless France, his diplomatic superior reminded him of "the catholic principle of republicanism, to wit, that every people may establish what form of government they please and change it as they please, the will of the nation being the only thing essential."

By mid-February, Washington found himself steering a dangerous course between Scylla and Charybdis. With France exporting revolution, England warily eyed its former colonies for signs of republican solidarity. The Cabinet remained deeply divided. Indians menaced the Southwest and Ohio Valley as if there had been no Treaty of New York and in spite of two disastrous military expeditions. The troubled Federal City was not yet out of the woods, figuratively or literally. A southern newspaper intoned:

> O FEDERAL TOWN! Proud men prepare,
> Vast schemes within your ten mile square:
> There, high-born dames shall make abode
> And poets squeak the birthday ode.

L'Enfant's successor, Andrew Ellicott, threatened to carry his feud with the city's commissioners into the press, forcing Washington to rein in yet another temperamental artist. On January 27 the president composed a brief farewell to his nephew, awkwardly explaining that he did not write to the dying man more often because he thought it unnecessary "to repeat the assurances of sincere regard and friendship I have always professed . . . I conceive the more undisturbed you are, the better it is for you." In the face of death, Washington offered a stoic's consolation. "The will of Heaven is not to be controverted or scrutinized by the children of this world," he reminded his namesake. "It therefore becomes the creatures of it to submit with patience and resignation to the will of the Creator, whether it be to prolong or to shorten the number of our days. To bless them with health or afflict them with pain."

Two weeks after receiving this wintry benediction George Augustine Washington died. Consoling words came hard to the grieving uncle. Not for six weeks did his mask slip even a little, and only then in a letter to his intimate friend David Humphreys. Although George Augustine's death had long been expected, the president confessed, "yet I have felt it very keenly." He invited Fanny Washington and her three small children to make their home at Mount Vernon, where a young widow might live more cheaply than if she attempted independent housekeeping. Fanny thanked her illustrious relative but elected to remain in Alexandria, where Washington made a town house available for her use.

Adding to his sorrow, the president learned that Lafayette, denounced by the Jacobins for trying to save the king's life, had fallen into Austrian hands. His first thought was to assist the unfortunate man's family, yet amid the prevailing chaos no one in America could say with precision where Madame de Lafayette might be hiding. Based on sketchy information, Washington deposited 200 guineas with an agent in Amsterdam, informing the wife of his surrogate son that this represented the least of his unaccounted debt to the gallant soldier. "I could add much," said Washington, obviously moved, "but it is best perhaps that I should say little on this subject. Your goodness will supply my deficiency."

Not all the intelligence reaching 190 Market Street was so gloomy. The president heaped praise on the architectural drawings of William Thornton, a West Indian renaissance man whose plans for a Capitol appeared far superior to Stephen Hallett's original concept. Mindful of his earlier contretemps with L'Enfant, however, the president advised the city's commissioners to move cautiously, pacifying Hallett while embracing the "grandeur, simplicity and beauty" of Thornton's vision. Early in February, delegations from the Wabash and Illinois tribes set their seal of approval on a treaty of friendship negotiated by General Rufus Putnam. Hoping to repeat this achievement on a far greater scale, Washington chose Benjamin Lincoln, Beverly Randolph, and Timothy Pickering to represent his government at a peace conference in April set for Sandusky, a village on the shores of Lake Erie. The president simultaneously registered a vigorous protest with South Carolina's governor over the murder of some visiting Cherokees: "In vain may we expect peace with the Indians on our frontiers so long as a lawless set of unprincipled wretches can violate the rights of hospitality, or infringe the most solemn treaties, without receiving the punishment they so justly merit." Evidently the author of these lines entertained doubts over the identity of the real "savages" inhabiting the American wilds.

Conflicting rumors out of Paris competed for the president's attention with backstairs intrigue closer to home. Barely a month after Washington startled Jefferson by embracing the French republic, it was Jefferson's turn to surprise by revealing his willingness to remain in office a while longer. On February 7, the president brought up the perennially worrisome subject of discontent in Virginia. Jefferson confirmed southern unhappiness and resisted Washington's recommendation that he and Hamilton "coalesce" for the good of the country. It mattered little what coalitions he might join, said Jefferson, for he had steadfastly "kept myself aloof from all cabal and correspondence on the subject of the government."

While providing these reassurances, however, Jefferson was masterminding the most serious campaign yet to drive Hamilton from office. Taking advantage of the congressional calendar, the secretary of state's fiery protégé William Branch Giles rose on the floor of the House to demand an official probe into allegations of treasury mismanagement and corruption. Through superhuman exertions, Hamilton succeeded in burying his accusers in a mass of unassailable fiscal detail. There was no time to gloat, however, for on February 27, with only days remaining in the session, Giles struck again, this time with a set of nine resolutions bearing Jefferson's stamp.

Like Hamilton with his overreaching newspaper attacks, Jefferson had walked squarely into a trap set for his enemy. Not only was he misrepresenting his activities to Washington, but his congressional followers were assaulting the vanguard of Hamilton's strength. Hamilton's defenders, supplied with copious facts and figures by their hero, made quick work of the indictment. The secretary of state initially refused to admit his part in the proceedings. Later he ascribed the defeat to partisan Federalists, insufficiently partisan Republicans, and venal lawmakers battening on the state.

Freneau took the occasion to send a shaft of wit into the Federalist hide, taunting ministerial favorites whose support of the administration had proven so lucrative:

> On coaches, now, gay coats of arms are bore
> By some who had hardly a coat before —
> Silk gowns instead of homespun, now are seen,

> Instead of native *straws*, the bighorn hat:
> And Sir, 'tis true
> (Twixt me and you)
> That some have grown prodigious fat
> That were — prodigious lean!

With Hamilton more entrenched than ever, frustrated Jeffersonians cast about for fresh targets. They did not have far to look. "The hell hounds are now in full cry . . . against the President," recorded John Adams, self-proclaimed Libel-lee General of the administration. The vice president worried about the impact of such attacks upon his chief, since "he has not been used to such threshing and his skin is thinner than mine." Washington's sixty-first birthday on February 22 inspired public demonstrations of joy. Ships in the Delaware River hoisted their colors, the bells of Christ Church rang out every half hour, and light infantry and artillery companies marched past 190 Market Street, cheering its occupant and firing volleys in his honor.

Only the *National Gazette* spit into the wind, grumbling, "Were he virtue's self, the strains of panegyric could not have been louder in order to complete the shame and disgrace of republican dogmas." To this discordant music Washington rode three short blocks to his second inauguration on March 4, passing Potts's brewery and a Baptist cemetery en route. Ushers with white wands preceded the executive, outfitted in a black coat purchased at the time of his mother's death as he walked to the chair customarily occupied by Vice President Adams. Among those spilling out of the Senate chamber was Edward Thornton, whose sharp eye alighted on portraits, now curtained from view, of France's recently deposed king and queen. "Alas! poor Louis," Thornton exclaimed with a flood of crocodile tears.

> Deserted at his utmost need
> By those his former bounty fed!

Before Justice Cushing of the Supreme Court administered the oath, Washington stepped forward to deliver the shortest, oddest inaugural address in American history, two self-conscious paragraphs written with Freneau and other journalistic detractors looking over the presidential shoulder. One day, said Washington, he would more fully express the appreciation he felt for the confidence reposed in him "by the people of United America." Until then, he would content himself with taking the constitutionally required oath. "If it shall be found during my administration of the government I have in any instance violated willingly, or knowingly, the injunction thereof, I may (besides incurring constitutional punishment) be subject to the upbraiding of all who are now witnesses of the present solemn ceremony."

Washington withdrew as quietly as he had come. Later in the day, he subscribed $150 for distribution among the city's poor. But his real gift was beyond measuring. Writing to David Humphreys after taking his oath, the president indulged in self-justification tinged with self-pity. "Perhaps in no instance of my life have I been more sensible of the sacrifice than in the present," he said, "for at my age the love of retirement grows every day more and more powerful." Yet he would willingly relinquish "those personal enjoyments to which I am peculiarly attached in order to sink the roots of constitutional government in the virgin soil of America."

Washington unintentionally betrayed another reason for staying on, one at least as telling as his country's unanimous voice, when he wrote, "If it can be deemed a happiness to live in an age productive of great and interesting events, we of the present age are very highly favored. The rapidity of national revolutions appear no less astonishing than their magnitude. In what they will terminate is known only to the great ruler of events; and confiding in his wisdom and goodness, we may safely trust the issue to him, without perplexing ourselves to seek for that which is beyond human ken; only taking care to perform the parts assigned us in a way that reason and our own consciences approve of."

For all his bows toward rural contentment, then, Washington had not lost his taste for the stage. In his sixties he was still battling youthful ambition, a master of gesture who left nothing to chance, sounding a note of resignation while playing to the galleries.

⊰ 2 ⊱

"A few friends only." So Washington described the little band of mourners who assembled at his invitation on April 11 to stand before Mount Vernon's brick vault and usher his nephew into the next world. Portentous reports from abroad distracted from the simple rites. Louis Capet had lost his caput, snickered the irreverent, and in the wake of his execution, simmering tensions between the French republic and its royalist neighbors reached flashpoint. "Allied kings threaten us," brayed France's newest master, Danton, "and we hurl at their feet as a gage of battle the head of a king." From Philadelphia came word of France's declaration of war against the martial coalition of perverse Albion, Austria, Prussia, Sardinia, and the Netherlands.

The outbreak of hostilities prompted the most fateful decision of Washington's presidency, taken in an instant. As the president later explained to Henry Lee, "I foresaw in the moment information of that event came to me the necessity for announcing the disposition of this country toward the belligerent powers and the propriety of restraining, as far as a Proclamation would do it, our citizens from taking part in the contest." Washington was packing his bags before the funeral dinner could be cleared away. Already, reports had reached him of American ships being outfitted as privateers to wage war against the mighty British navy. Lacking a corresponding force, he concluded that the only practical course for his vulnerable country was adherence to "a strict neutrality."

His decisiveness was far from universally acclaimed. To the large majority who felt emotionally tied to the French republic, official neutrality was a fig leaf masking aid and comfort for imperialist England. By defying pro-French sentiments, the president hazarded the loss of his carefully nurtured image of nonpartisanship. Jefferson's claim that ninety-nine out of every hundred Americans shared his enthusiasm for King Louis's self-appointed successors may have been an exaggeration. But a sudden flowering of tricolor cockades and streetcorner renditions of the revolutionary anthem "Ca Ira" testified to widespread support for a sister republic. John Adams imagined more cannon fired in celebration of French military triumphs than the French themselves had employed to sweep their enemies from the field.

Ironically, there had been nothing in Washington's conduct during the weeks leading up to war to suggest that the president was out of step with popular feelings. Quite the contrary: he willingly obliged a request from France's departing ambassador for a payment of 3 million livres against the United States' outstanding war debt. He accepted Jefferson's view that the hopelessly compromised Gouverneur Morris must be replaced, even trying at one point to persuade Jefferson himself to return to the French capital. The secretary of state quickly scotched the idea, arguing that with the impending arrival of Citizen Genêt, Philadelphia and not Paris would be the main scene of diplomatic activity.

With the president back in the capital, the Cabinet met on April 19 to consider a suitable response to Europe's convulsions. Spirited debate produced unanimous agreement that Americans should be discouraged from joining the fight on the seas or aiding combatants by carrying contraband. Principles were easier to decide than personalities, however, and mention of Genêt shattered the group's surface unity. Before going to Mount Vernon, the president had agreed with Jefferson that France's envoy should "unquestionably" be received in his absence. But Genêt had been delayed in his ocean crossing. Now the secretary of state listened as Hamilton questioned the legitimacy, not only of Genêt's appointment, but of the 1778 treaty binding rebellious America to Bourbon France.

To Hamilton, the mobs of Paris had themselves torn up the treaty when they sliced off their monarch's head and consigned Louis's government to the flames. He used an unintentionally revealing metaphor to bolster his argument for strict neutrality. "A dispassionate and virtuous citizen of the U States," he wrote, "will regard his own country as a wife, to whom he is bound to be exclusively faithful and affectionate, and he will watch with a jealous attention every propensity of the heart to wander toward a foreign country, which he will regard as a mistress that may pervert his fidelity and mar his happiness."

Having invited written opinions from his councilors, Washington confided to Jefferson his personal belief in the treaty's continuing validity. That settled it: Genêt would be welcomed as the authentic representative of a duly constituted regime. On April 22 Washington's proclamation went out to the world, provoking anger or applause depending on the loyalties of its readers. The word *neutrality* was never used in the text drafted by Edmund Randolph. Instead, American citizens were enjoined to pursue "a conduct friendly and impartial towards the belligerent powers."

On the same day the president reassured the earl of Buchan of "the sincere wish of United America to have nothing to do with the political intrigues or the squabbles of European nations; but on the contrary, to exchange commodities and live in peace and amity with all the inhabitants of the Earth . . . To administer justice to and receive it from every power with whom they are connected will, I hope, be always found the most prominent feature in the administration of this country."

By establishing the principle that nations recognized each other and not governments subject to change, Washington set a critical precedent in American foreign policy. It would stand, more or less unchallenged, until Woodrow Wilson pronounced an anathema on Lenin's Soviet regime in 1917, when another autocrat was snuffed out and revolutions were judged acceptable or not according to their ideological content.

❴ 3 ❵

The neutrality proclamation divided Americans and isolated their president. James Monroe called it "both unconstitutional and impolitick" for the executive to arrogate the nation's foreign policy to himself. "A most unfortunate error," concluded James Madison, adding that if revolutionary France prevailed, "the ill-fated proclamation will be a millstone which would sink any other character except Washington and will force a struggle even in his."

The *Gazette of the United States* argued just the opposite: "There is a difference between the French and American Revolution. In America no barbarities were perpetuated — no men's heads were stuck upon poles — no ladies' bodies mangled . . . the Americans did not, at discretion, harass, murder, or plunder the clergy — not roast their generals unjustly alive . . . whatever blood was shed, flowed gallantly in the field."

France's revolving-door governments had a special poignancy for Washington, who now pressed Gouverneur Morris to make discreet inquiries into Lafayette's whereabouts and condition. The president asked Jefferson to what extent "consistent with my public character and the national policy" he might aid Madame de Lafayette. The verbal support he offered, meager as it was, surpassed the reception accorded Lafayette's brother-in-law, the viscount de Noailles, when he appeared in Philadelphia during the first week of May. Few friends had stronger claims on Washington's time than Noailles, who had helped arrange the details of Cornwallis's surrender at Yorktown before enlisting in liberal reform movements at home. As with his hapless relation by marriage, however, events had outpaced the advocate of constitutional monarchy. Stranded in the backwash of escalating violence, Noailles fled France for his life.

His arrival in Philadelphia forced Washington to take evasive action. Through Hamilton, the president apologized for avoiding his onetime comrade in arms, explaining that the delicacy of his official position prohibited familiarity. He did not mean by this, Washington was careful to add, to withhold "such civilities as are *common* to others. Those *more marked*, notwithstanding our former acquaintance, would excite speculations which had better be avoided." Never was the Janus face of power more bitterly apparent. During Noailles's first days in the capital, he got no closer to the president than Martha's weekly reception.

The bypassed revolutionary took up residence in a third-floor chamber overlooking the extensive gardens of William Bingham, Robert Morris's business partner and the richest man in Philadelphia. No friend to royal assassins, Bingham welcomed the aristocratic visitor and other émigrés who sat on Noailles's bed while a dinner table was set in the same room. Drawing upon Morris's inexhaustible ardor for promotion, Noailles envisioned a new town called Asylum. Others were less enthused. The cynical Charles Maurice de Talleyrand-Périgord, who celebrated his first and last mass at his ordination as bishop of Autun, was then a decade away from diplomatic immortality as Napoleon's chief apologist. In due course Voltaire's favorite clergyman took his place at Noailles's table, where he heard of a proposed émigré colony in the fertile valley of the

Susquehanna. Chattering endlessly with his mouth full, Talleyrand expressed a droll wish that Asylum's inmates might one day escape and resume their former status in a stable France.

With the Bourbon throne forcibly overturned, Philadelphia assumed a Gallic character. The duc de la Rochefoucauld took up residence there after the confiscation of his princely estates, and a future king named Louis Philippe lived in a single room over a barber's shop. According to legend, the pretender to Louis's discarded crown was turned down flat when he appealed for the hand of Bingham's daughter in marriage. If the sallow Frenchman were ever restored to his hereditary rank, said the nabob, "you will be too great a match for her; if not, she is too great a match for you."

Nearly as trying as Frenchmen fleeing to America were Americans wishing to take up foreign arms. Impetuous as ever, Henry Lee informed the president that he planned to resign Virginia's governorship and win glory as a major general in France's revolutionary armies. Washington reacted with more than his usual caution: "As a public character, I can say *nothing* on the subject. As a private man, I am unwilling to say much." What he did say was that his friend should think twice before abandoning his position, with all the resulting speculation and no foreseeable result. "It would appear a boundless ocean I was about to embark on from whence no land is to be seen." Measuring his words carefully, he described France as being "in the highest paroxysm of disorder; not so much from the pressure of foreign enemies . . . but because those in whose hands the government is entrusted are ready to tear each other to pieces."

Washington begged Lee to burn the unsigned letter as soon as he read it. Three weeks later the president revealed more of his thinking to Jefferson when they met to review parting notes with Jean Baptiste de Ternant, a man of the old regime displaced by the new. The president thought the phrase "our republic" in Jefferson's draft gratuitous. Insisting that a royalist coup posed far less threat to America's future than the prospect of anarchy, he lashed out at Freneau's paper for censuring his person and his policies in unmerited ways. "He was evidently sore and warm," concluded Jefferson, not without reason. The secretary of state assumed that Washington's rare outburst was staged to bring pressure on the offending journalist, perhaps even terminate his State Department sinecure. "But I will not do it," he asserted in his diary. "His paper has saved our constitution."

Writing to Madison soon after, the secretary displayed little sympathy for his hypersensitive chief: "Naked he would have been sanctimoniously reverenced, but enveloped in the rags of royalty, they can hardly be torn off without laceration."

❬ 4 ❭

May 16 was a typical Wednesday at 190 Market Street. Washington signed 176 passports, received from Hamilton the latest installment of antitax discontent in western Pennsylvania, approved a contract for Moses Hayes of Boston to furnish fourteen thousand gallons of oil for the nation's lighthouses, and vetoed "a person rather careless and inattentive to his affairs" who aspired to the post of assayer in the fledgling mint. Amid this routine, Washington pondered the behavior of Citizen Genêt. Since arriving in Charleston some five weeks earlier, Genêt had busied himself fomenting sentiment against the British and commissioning American ships as privateers to seize British vessels — a flagrant violation of international law.

Just after noon, Philadelphia's calm was shattered by three artillery charges from the French frigate *L'Ambuscade*. In no time a large crowd assembled at Gray's Ferry, several miles upriver, to greet the ship and its celebrated passenger. Genêt uncharacteristically chose to elude his admirers and slip into town by democratic stagecoach. The short, heavyset Frenchman who had traveled five thousand miles to fan the spark of world revolution seemed at first glance an unlikely firebrand. At the age of thirty, Edmond Charles Genêt was a red-haired dumpling with coarse features and a high forehead. His magnetism was almost entirely verbal, for when he opened his broad mouth, out came a silver torrent infecting his listeners with contagious enthusiasm for the rights of man.

Genêt set fire to any language he spoke. As a toddler, this son of an established court family (his sister had served as a lady-in-waiting to Marie Antoinette) had astonished onlookers with his linguistic abilities. The king of Sweden presented the boy with a gold medal for his translation of *The History of Eric XIV*. The adolescent Genêt spoke seven languages and counted the celebrated Dr. Franklin among his friends. So precocious and well connected a youth seemed fated to join the diplomatic corps, and Genêt dutifully made the rounds of Europe's gilded ballrooms and audience chambers. Along the way he received a pair of diamond knee buckles from Catherine the Great. He also earned a reputation for hot-tempered insubordination.

By the time Genêt returned home in the fall of 1791, the Bourbons were gone. Lafayette's supporters in the National Assembly were thoroughly cowed and the marquis himself implicated in a desperate plot to snatch Louis from the executioner's block. Taken into custody by an Austrian officer, le Vassington français claimed the status of an American citizen. But instead of a warm bed in the American legation of The Hague, Lafayette was thrown into a dungeon cell at Magdeburg. The new French proconsul was Danton, darling of the Parisian mobs who constituted authority in a nation that had chopped off its crowned head. A decree from the Legislative Assembly abolished war, and the Girondins, arrayed in benches at the extreme left of the hall, pressed for total victory against enemies of the people wherever they lurked. Riding the crest of history, confident Girondists reached out to make common cause with their republican brethren across the Atlantic. Thus Citizen Genêt was packed off to Charleston with orders to exploit American sympathies, ignite uprisings against Spanish and British rule in the New World, and repair whatever damage Louis's violent end may have done to Franco-American unity.

Charleston was a good place to sample Francophile opinion and nearly as good a base from which to harass Spanish interests in Louisiana and the Floridas. Southerners huzzahed themselves hoarse in greeting France's latest export. "The example of France has struck terror into the heart of governments," proclaimed an exultant Freneau, implying that Washington's administration was no exception. Lost in the ovations accorded Genêt was a warning from Gouverneur Morris that the young envoy was notoriously reckless. More predictable still, George Hammond on behalf of King George's government filed the first of many protests against the newcomer, who brought with him three hundred letters of marque commissioning theoretically neutral vessels to act as privateers for profit and glory.

Hammond had a point — and a formidable navy to enforce it. On May 15 Washington and his Cabinet agreed to restore the British vessel *Grange*, seized in U.S. waters, and to liberate its crew. In a direct slap at Genêt, the president assured Hammond that the American government would take strong action against anyone commissioning privateers in U.S. ports. None of this diminished Genêt's reception in Philadelphia. Ecstatic supporters gathered outside City Tavern to hail his arrival. Red caps of liberty filled the air, and cheer after cheer washed over the zealous representative of the Republic of Virtue.

Freneau printed an open letter critical of Washington's almost painfully evenhanded policy. "I doubt much whether it is the disposition of the United States to preserve the condition you enjoin," he lectured the president. "The cause of liberty is the cause of mankind, and neutrality is desertion." As if to confirm this view, the banquet hall of Oeller's Tavern on Chestnut Street resounded to democratic toasts and the throbbing baritone of Citizen Genêt himself, singing passages from the latest revolutionary opera:

Should France from her lofty station,
From the throne of fair Freedom, be hurl'd,
'Tis done with every other nation,
And Liberty's lost to the world.

"I live in the midst of perpetual feasts," Genêt enthused. Jefferson, scanning the nation's press, was hardly less rhapsodic. "All the old spirit of 1776 is rekindled," he wrote, contrasting the fervent people of America with "the cold caution of their government." Faster than Monsieur Blanchard's blue-spangled flying boat, however, Genêt returned to earth on the afternoon of May 18 when he accompanied Jefferson in calling on the president. Expressions of personal attachment to Washington, "the only person on earth who can love us sincerely and merit to be so loved," gushed from the voluble diplomat, pretending not to notice a portrait of the late king in Washington's drawing room.

All smiles, Genêt promised increased access to French markets and the termination of existing treaty obligations binding the United States to help defend endangered French possessions in the West Indies. A jubilant secretary of state told Madison that France's delegate offered everything and asked for nothing in return. Washington was more skeptical. Courteous but reserved, he reminded his visitor of the United States' wish to live peaceably with all nations, France most of all. Of the war then raging and the fierce debate splitting the Cabinet over the illegal seizure of British vessels, among them a merchantman called the *Little Sarah* that had been snared by a French warship in Delaware Bay, Washington said nothing. Confident of his standing with the cheering masses, Genêt shrugged off Washington's diplomatic balancing act.

On May 24 the French envoy tipped his hand with a proposal opening the West Indies to American shipping in exchange for immediate liquidation of the outstanding $2.3 million war debt. The money thus raised would supply revolutionary armies fighting Europe's royal houses and also bankroll North American adventures aimed at Louisiana, Florida, and British Canada. Pointedly left out of Genêt's package was any reference to privateering, something specifically banned under the Franco-American treaty of 1778. Washington invited Hamilton to consider the financial implications of such a deal, and Hamilton asked what might happen if today's republic reverted to a monarchy in the future. Could the United States be held liable twice for the war debt? Cabinet meetings grew warmer than ever.

Along the tender southwestern frontier a new danger vied with the impetuous Genêt for Washington's attention. Spain had joined the coalition against the French and with England's encouragement was up to its old tricks inflaming the Creeks, whose leader, McGillivray, had died a dissolute death. Only this time the men in Madrid were backing up their threats with 1,500 regulars, a force dwarfing anything Washington could muster. Terrified Georgians beseeched Washington's help in fending off the Indians' savagery, but the government had none to provide. A thousand miles to the north, Anthony Wayne's Legion of the United States, facing possible combat should the Sandusky conference end in failure, was unprepared for action against the Creeks or anyone else.

A high fever during the first week of June prevented the president from participating in Cabinet discussions of Genêt's latest provocations. Speaking for him, Jefferson on June 5 told this most undiplomatic of diplomats that by granting military commissions on American soil and convening admiralty courts to judge prizes taken by privateers, he had infringed upon United States sovereignty. For good measure Washington ordered the arrest of two American sailors on board a French warship named — what else? — the *Citizen Genêt*, only to have one of them set free by a Republican judge.

An unrepentant Genêt gloried in his popular triumphs: "Everything has succeeded beyond my hopes . . . but old Washington, *le vieux Washington*, a man very different from the character emblazoned in history, cannot forgive me for my successes and the eagerness with which the whole city rushed to my house, while a mere handful of English merchants went to congratulate him on his proclamation. He puts thousands of obstacles in my way and makes it necessary for me to urge secretly a convocation of Congress a majority of which, led by the best brains of the American Union, will be decidedly on our side."

In one respect, at least, Genêt did not exaggerate. Washington did feel old and more than ever rueful about having agreed to a second term. Rising from a sickbed, his attention shifted abruptly to Mount Vernon, where Anthony Whiting had fallen victim to the same wasting illness responsible for George Augustine's death. A solicitous employer urged the overseer to wear flannel next to his skin and adopt a vegetable and milk diet for his lung complaint. Washington shortened the usual insistent list of demands, concluding with sincere wishes that Whiting "may be perfectly restored to health, being your well-wisher and friend."

Perhaps the only member of the Cabinet who actually practiced the neutrality Washington preached was the president himself. On June 6 Washington rejected, as likely to give offense, Hamilton's draft reply to Genêt's debt proposal. He questioned the secretary closely about a proposed Dutch loan of three million florins. And he shared Jefferson's anger over seemingly coordinated demands coming from Britain and Spain, the one protesting administration treatment of privateers, the other seeking advantage in a long-standing rivalry between the Chickasaw and Creek. It appeared neither country would be satisfied with America's actions, Washington told Jefferson, until they pushed matters to the extreme. Meanwhile, preparations were set in motion for yet another high-level mission to Madrid. Washington could only hope that Spain's rulers were more reasonable than their New World representatives.

Yet none of these insults, however irritating, could begin to match Genêt's undeclared war on British shipping waged from American soil. Resorting to his most patronizing tone, Genêt offered voluntarily to restrict his activities until Congress was convened and the people "whose fraternal voice has resounded from every quarter around me!" could judge Washington's neutrality. His gesture was received with studied contempt. The pot continued to boil. Threatening to blow the lid off was a vessel berthed at Philadelphia's shipyard. There the former *Little Sarah*, rechristened *La Petite Democrate* by her French captors, was being outfitted with fourteen cannon for a new life of preying upon the commerce and pride of its country of origin.

For the moment the president was forced to follow events at a distance. Since tuberculosis had claimed Anthony Whiting on June 21, Washington described his plantation as a body without a head. No better solution being available, he asked Howell Lewis, his twenty-two-year-old nephew, to take Whiting's place. Hurrying south to take the reins of management into his own hands, the president paused at Georgetown to referee a dispute between William Thornton, the amateur architect entrusted with construction of the Capitol, and Stephen Hallet, still another French émigré whose original vision had been shunted aside for Thornton's low-domed structure. Hallet was joined in his complaint by James Hoban, an Irish-born professional responsible for the President's Palace, both men faulting Thornton's design as impractical and ruinously expensive. Washington urged all three to come to Philadelphia for thorough discussions with Jefferson, for an early start on the Capitol was imperative; if only to defeat "the demon Jealousy . . . a plan must be adopted; and good or bad, it must be entered into."

An even greater loss than Whiting's death was Tobias Lear's departure to launch a business career in the Federal City. His leavetaking was bound to be a wrench, for Lear enjoyed the president's confidence as did few men. In addition, Mrs. Washington had grown deeply attached to Polly Lear and to the couple's young son, Benjamin. No one could replace Lear, but Bartholomew Dandridge, Martha Washington's fatherless nephew, moved up a notch and into a room with young Wash. Bart proved conscientious, but he was no match for the president's original team of five assistants.

The end of June 1793 found Washington anxiously pacing the long veranda at Mount Vernon overlooking his English-style deer park. The gentle creatures had long since slipped their bonds and now ran unimpeded across the fields. Their owner, by contrast, remained in the grip of events beyond his control. Informed by Governor Clinton of renewed activity by French privateers in and around New York Harbor, Washington asked his Cabinet to consider a possible response. In the event, all too likely, that they were unable to reach unanimity, his advisers were to send him their opinions for his review. "I know the urgency and delicacy of our public affairs at present will not permit me to be longer absent," the president concluded resentfully. "I must therefore submit with the best grace I can to the loss and inconvenience which my private affairs will sustain from the want of my personal attention."

Before returning to the capital, however, Washington insisted on keeping one appointment. On the afternoon of July Fourth, he sat down with more than a hundred of his neighbors in Alexandria for a celebratory dinner in the long room of Wise's Tavern. Cloying devotion to Washington was as essential a part of the national birthday as militia lineups and spreadeagled patriotism, and this Fourth was no exception. "Words cannot express the happiness of the company, which was increased by beholding the pleasure that beamed on the countenance of their illustrious and revered neighbor," said the correspondent from *Dunlap's Daily Advertiser*. "His extraordinary talents and virtues had contributed, in a single manner, to the attainment of that blessing which they were now assembled to commemorate."

When the time came, Washington delivered his customary toast to local prosperity. But he also plunged waist deep into the swirling debate over his government's foreign policies. The Cabinet had agreed on neutrality without being able to agree on what it meant. Now the president defined it for them, for his countrymen, and for posterity. "To complete the American character," he told the people of Alexandria, "it remains for the citizens of the United States to show to the world that the reproach heretofore cast on republican governments for their want of stability is without foundation, when that government is the deliberate choice of an enlightened people." He was fully persuaded, said Washington, that every patriot would demonstrate through his conduct in the coming trial "that we live under a government of laws; and that, while we preserve inviolate our national faith, we are desirous to live in amity with all mankind."

❦ 5 ❧

One hundred and fifty miles to the north, residents of the nation's capital observed the Fourth in a highly charged atmosphere. French sympathizers belonging to the newly chartered Democratic Society of Pennsylvania — a name proposed by Citizen Genêt — met to elect officers and polish a statement of principles. Disdaining honorary titles and decrying court pomp, Hamilton's excise tax, and the influence of England, this popular descendant of the revolutionary Sons of Liberty summoned Americans to "erect the temple of LIBERTY on the ruins of *palaces and thrones.*"

The appeal did not fall on deaf ears. Philip Freneau's office at 209 Market Street was converted into a recruiting station for the Patriotic French Society and Pennsylvania's Democrats gave birth to over thirty like-minded offspring during the next eighteen months. Critics like Oliver Wolcott found them uniformly populated by "hot-headed, ignorant or wicked men devoted entirely to the views of France." Organizers, not surprisingly, saw their motives and membership in a quite different light. Imagining a world divested of crowns and castes (slavery excepted), wherein education, the rich man's luxury and the poor man's necessity, would be open to all, the printers, shopkeepers, laborers, and scholars pledged to the democratic cause wanted nothing so much as to realize the promises made on revolutionary battlefields and signed with the blood of patriots.

Washington and Jefferson shared a vision of the United States as a haven for the oppressed of many lands. But they parted company when treating with foreign powers or even in defining oppression. On July 5, Jefferson listened calmly as Genêt related plans to enlist American officers in risings against the Spanish in Louisiana. He had already provided an introductory letter to Kentucky's governor for a French botanist named André Michaud, for whom plants were secondary to political agitation. On discovering Michaud's intent to recruit Kentuckians for an assault on New Orleans, Jefferson made no attempt to retrieve his endorsement. Instead, he wrote a second letter, this one to the state's staunchly Republican senator, John Brown. In what a later generation would call a nondenial denial, Jefferson informed Genêt that by commissioning American officers to link up with southwestern Indians against the Spanish, he was condemning them to the hangman's noose.

Neutrality or no neutrality, Jefferson seemed willing to overlook Genêt's insurrectionary activities, even if they led to the establishment of an independent power controlling the lower Mississippi. At least that is how Genêt, cheered by the prospect of new troubled waters in which to fish, interpreted his latest subversion of "old Washington." "I excite the Canadians to break the British yoke," he boasted to his superiors in Paris. "I arm the Kentukois and propose a naval expedition which will facilitate their descent upon New Orleans."

As the president sped back toward Philadelphia, events were unfolding that would burst Genêt's balloon. On the same day Jefferson heard from the French envoy of his ambitious plans in the West, the secretary learned that the captured *Little Sarah*, heavily armed and equipped with a 120-man crew, was preparing to violate American neutrality by slipping out to sea. Pennsylvania's Republican governor, Thomas Mifflin, confirmed that several American citizens were on the ship's roster. On the night of July 6, Mifflin called out the state's militia to prevent Genêt's refitted war vessel from leaving U.S. waters. An urgent message brought the secretary of the state back from his country house the next morning.

What he heard was far from encouraging. Genêt had rebuffed the governor's emissary, Alexander Dallas, himself a mainstay of Pennsylvania's Democratic Society, reportedly going so far as to threaten "an appeal from the President to the people" if Washington and his administration continued to frustrate French recruitment. Anxious to defuse the situation, Jefferson asked Genêt for assurances that the *Little Sarah* would be detained, at least until Washington's return. The ambassador was evasive, claiming that the ship was merely being moved downriver to a new anchorage. When the Cabinet met the next morning, without Washington and Attorney General Randolph, Hamilton and Knox demanded that a battery of guns be set up on Mud Island to thwart any attempt to escape by the renamed *Petite Democrate*.

Jefferson resisted, fearing that military action would ensure retaliation by a vastly larger French fleet, which was momentarily expected from the West Indies. Hearing this, Governor Mifflin dismissed his militia, thereby enabling *La Petite Democrate* to embark upon a new and potentially devastating career against the enemies of the National Convention. Within twenty-four hours, Genêt coolly informed the secretary of state that the fleet raider was on its way. The sole possibility of detaining the ship was a highly risky boarding party, which Genêt firmly discouraged. "When treaties speak, the agents of nations have but to obey," he pronounced complacently.

What had tasted sweet in Jefferson's mouth only a few weeks before proved sour in his belly. The secretary of state began a dance of disengagement, "quitting a wreck which could not but sink all who should cling to it." "Never in my opinion, was so calamitous an appointment made," he told Madison. "Hot-headed, all imagination, no judgment, passionate, disrespectful and even indecent towards the President . . . He renders my position immensely difficult." The old migraine returned; Jefferson took to his sickbed at Gray's Ferry. He was still there on July 11, when Washington returned to find an official packet of documents marked for his immediate attention.

The president's reaction was unpredictable. Anger directed at an insolent French envoy spilled over onto his warmest defender when, in the midst of the greatest crisis of Washington's presidency, the secretary of state was nowhere to be found in Philadelphia. A scalding message went off to Gray's Ferry. "Is the minister of the French republic to set the acts of this government at defiance, *with impunity*, and then threaten the executive with an appeal to the people? What must the world think of such conduct, and of the government of the United States for submitting to it?"

The next morning Washington presided over a feuding Cabinet in search of expedients. Members voted to refer Genêt's offense to the Supreme Court and to instruct both warring powers that foreign ships should remain in port pending the court's review. On Saturday night, the thirteenth, Washington attended a benefit performance at Ricketts' Circus to raise a fund for firewood for Philadelphia's poor. Midway through the program, the proprietor raised a toast to "The Man of the People." "This operated like electricity in producing a general clap of applause, accompanied by a huzza from every part of the Circus," reported *Dunlap's American Daily Advertiser*. The cheers faded quickly from Washington's ears, replaced by irritation and wounded pride. In a letter to Henry Lee, he fulminated against Europe's "petulant representatives . . . the trouble they give is hardly to be described."

As Democratic Societies multiplied and deflating editors hosed a torrent of abuse his way, the president tried to make sense of public attitudes. "That there are in this, as well as in all other countries, discontented characters, I well know," he remarked to Lee. At the same time, he acknowledged a variety of motives for such unhappiness: "Some good, from an opinion that the measures of the general government are impure: some bad, and (if I might be allowed to use so harsh an expression) diabolical." Under the circumstances, Washington told Lee that he felt less the public's servant than its slave.

"In what will this abuse terminate?" he inquired angrily. "The result, as it respects myself, I care not; for I have a consolation within that no earthly efforts can deprive me of . . . that neither ambitious nor interested motives have influenced my conduct. The arrows of malevolence, therefore, however barbed and well pointed, never can reach the most vulnerable part of me; though whilst I am *up* as a *mark*, they will be continually armed." Washington's only solace was that men "of cool and dispassionate minds" would see through such "outrages on common decency." Near the end of his diatribe, the president acknowledged Lee's censure of Citizen Genêt, "but mum on this head. Time may unfold more than prudence ought to disclose at present." Washington did manage a humorous sendoff to his recently married friend, congratulating him on having "exchanged the rugged and dangerous field of Mars for the soft and pleasurable bed of Venus."

On July 23, at a Cabinet meeting the president proposed showing Genêt's offending correspondence to Paris with a hope that the troublesome diplomat might soon follow. Complications arose when Chief Justice Jay and his black-robed brethren, declaring foreign policy the responsibility of elected officials, bucked the neutrality issue back to the executive branch. A renewed journalistic war broke out as Hamilton defended Washington's proclamation in print and Madison raised the specter of executive domination. So powerfully did Hamilton contend for the president's foreign policy franchise that he provoked a desperate appeal from Jefferson to his political consort. "For God's sake, my dear sir," he told Madison, "take up your pen, select the most striking heresies, and cut him to pieces in the face of the public. There is nobody who can and will enter the lists with him."

Still another hope went glimmering as the Sandusky peace conference collapsed, Washington's commissioners never even reaching the settlement. In a humiliating turn of events they were compelled to accept British protection at Fort Niagara, one of the garrisons held in violation of the ten-year-old treaty that promised their return to the United States.

❖ 6 ❖

Frantically trying to avoid conflict in Europe, Washington's administration was at war with itself. Hamilton decried Jefferson's "womanish" attachment to France and supplied Cabinet secrets on a regular basis to George Hammond. Jefferson thought Henry Knox "a fool" and Attorney General Edmund Randolph, the legal Hamlet on whom Washington increasingly relied, "the poorest chameleon I ever saw, having no color of his own and reflecting that nearest him. When he is with me, he is a whig. When with Hamilton he is a tory. When with the President, he is that [which] he thinks will please him."

On July 30, hours before a critical Cabinet discussion of Genêt's recall, Jefferson tendered his resignation, effective in December. During the ensuing marathon debate over the first three days of August, he more than held his own. At issue was whether to make public documents justifying Genêt's involuntary departure, an action sure to rouse American opinion and shatter what remained of Washington's apolitical standing. Did the president wish to appear as head of a party rather than a nation? asked Jefferson, sure of the answer before he put the question. No doubt Genêt would respond with a public appeal of his own, guaranteeing an unseemly contest between the executive and a foreign representative. In such an atmosphere, anonymous writers would flourish. Congress would boil over in acrimony. And all this to discredit the Pennsylvania Democratic Society, an election-year contrivance certain to fade away unless singled out for criticism by the government.

At the moment, attacks by the government mattered less to Washington than attacks upon it. Knowing this, Henry Knox, the simple soldier with the face of an overfed child, introduced on August 2 Freneau's latest satire, "The Funeral of George Washington and James Wilson, King and Judge," depicting a tyrannical executive laid low on the guillotine. Jefferson's description of the ensuing scene is unforgettable:

"The President was much inflamed; got into one of those passions when he cannot command himself; ran on much on the personal abuse which had been bestowed on him; defied any man on earth to produce one single act of his since he had been in the government which was not done on the purest motives; that he had never repented but once having slipped the moment of resigning his office, and that was every moment since; that *by God* he had rather be in his grave than in his present situation; that he had rather be on his farm than to be made *Emperor of the World;* and yet that they were charging him with wanting to be a King. That that *rascal Freneau* sent him three of his papers every day, as if he thought he would become the distributor of his papers; that he could see in this nothing but an impudent design to insult him."

The heads around the Cabinet table jerked up like bloodhounds on a scent. There was an awkward silence. Seconds crawled by with eyes downcast or averted. Finally, after what seemed an eternity, some brave soul, not identified by Jefferson, cleared his throat and a halting discussion resumed. Washington, exhausted and no doubt embarrassed by his outburst, agreed that no immediate decision need be taken. Steps already agreed upon could be implemented, leaving a public airing of Genêt's insolence to wait for events.

On August 3 came news of a pitched sea battle between *L'Ambuscade* and a British frigate, the *Boston*, in the waters off Sandy Hook, New York. For once, British and not French bravado was responsible, the *Boston*'s captain rashly challenging his Gallic counterpart to a duel before a fleet of spectator boats and 10,000 French supporters onshore. They had much to cheer about, as the *Boston* lost her main topmast and her captain lost his life. Spurred on by the engagement, Washington's Cabinet announced a set of eight rules designed to implement the April proclamation of neutrality by clarifying provisions in the 1778 Franco-American treaty and serving notice that privateering and foreign recruitment would not be tolerated.

But how to enforce the new code? Thomas Mifflin's highly partisan reaction to the *Little Sarah* imbroglio dashed the president's original hope of relying on state governors. Jefferson wanted enforcement turned over to grand juries; Hamilton, to customs collectors. Randolph split the difference, and Washington approved his idea of having collectors report infractions to local district attorneys for transmission to the attorney general. On August 6, Washington visited Gray's Ferry in yet another attempt to dissuade Jefferson from retirement. The president stunned the secretary by revealing that Hamilton, too, intended to leave office before the end of the next congressional session. Would his old friend consent to remain for even a few months?

Jefferson's answer was a passionate denunciation of the aristocratic circles in which he found himself, social parasites attached to England and their instant paper wealth, dandies who fabricated and misconstrued his words before they were out of his mouth. As far as Genêt was concerned, Jefferson insisted that Republicans would abandon the bumbling Frenchman the moment his true conduct was known. Washington might have asked why, then, did his secretary of state oppose a public airing of the ambassador's communications. Instead, he conceded Jefferson's point about Republican purity, adding only that it was difficult, once a machine was put in motion, to know where it might stop.

Washington reiterated his earlier opposition to those desirous of placing a crown on America's president. Jefferson was unimpressed. "No rational man in the United States suspects you of any other disposition," he remarked, "but there does not pass a week in which we cannot prove declarations dropping from the monarchial party that our government is good for nothing, is a milk and water thing which cannot support itself; we must knock it down, and set up something of more energy."

If that were true, the president answered, it only proved their insanity, for no one in his right mind would attempt to subvert the republican spirit pervading the United States. Here Washington, the alleged monocrat, displayed greater faith in the people than did their accustomed champion, but neither man paused long enough to consider the ironies of the situation. The discussion turned to possible successors, Washington floating the names of Madison, Jay, Rufus King, and Oliver Wolcott.

Asked for his opinion of Randolph, Jefferson responded delicately that his colleague's tangled private affairs might compromise his independence.

On August 12, Chief Justice Jay and Senator King, probably egged on by Hamilton, splashed across the Federalist press Genêt's alleged threat to go over the president's head. Their evidence, based on Alexander Dallas's hearsay recollections, would not have stood up in Jay's court or any other. Washington, forgetting his earlier attempts to defer the neutrality issue to the Supreme Court, was furious over the judiciary's wanton plunge into partisan politics. Wounded by this apparent ingratitude, Jay and King failed to reckon with the majestic detachment that had served the president so well throughout the crisis. Amid all the shifting currents of public opinion and diplomatic intrigue, Washington alone had clung to a principled neutrality. But he had not turned his back or his coat on America's first ally. As late as August 20 he endorsed Jefferson's argument that for the United States and France to separate would present a spectacle of liberty warring on itself. Unabashedly, Washington declared that France was pursuing liberty, however imperfect some of its methods, that he had never doubted its ultimate success, and that contradictory accounts made it impossible to judge the current turmoil.

But this was in private; all the public saw was a row between Washington and the French ambassador. A scornful Freneau demanded, "Is the President a consecrated character, that an appeal from his decisions must be considered criminal?" For most of Freneau's countrymen, however, the revelation that Washington had been insulted by a foreign representative outweighed any emotional attachments to French égalité. By the start of September, Edward Thornton could report that French influence in Philadelphia was fast declining. A tide of favorable addresses inundated 190 Market Street, and huge rallies in support of the administration filled the streets of Newark and New York.

Genêt by his blundering egotism and Washington through his coolheaded judgment had given Americans a frightening taste of Europe's ordeal by fire. Many were glad to reconsider their enthusiasm for the French cause and rally around the president, whose "strict neutrality" looked shrewder than ever. Yet the calm was deceptive, for Citizen Genêt had hastened the political divisions most dreaded by Washington. As a result of the envoy's machinations, Anglomen fought Gallomen, factions became parties, and the Cabinet came unglued. Now as never before, the president was the fulcrum of American security and nationhood, something Gouverneur Morris recognized in a June missive. "It is time enough for you to have a successor when it shall please God to call you from this world's theater," he told Washington. "Do not imagine, my dear sir, that you can retire."

Almost overlooked as the drama built to its climax was the little man who had condemned himself the moment he ordered the *Little Sarah* into open waters, thus enraging the president. A shift of power in Paris, where the Girondins were shoved aside by the more radical Jacobins, transformed Philadelphia's hero into a hunted man. To return home would mean ignominious death on the guillotine. So in a final, ironic twist, Genêt was spared that fate by "old man Washington," who permitted his sworn enemy to become a naturalized American citizen. Genêt married Governor Clinton's daughter and moved to upstate New York, where he outlived the revolution, Talleyrand's Directory, Napoleon's empire, and the pale pageantry of Louis XVIII and Charles X. When at last he died in 1834, France's throne was occupied by Louis Philippe, William Bingham's attic tenant and would-be son-in-law.

❋ 9 ❋

PHILADELPHIA FEVERS

"Deaths are now about 30 a day. It is in every square
of the city. All flying who can. Most of the offices are
shut or shutting. The banks shut up this day. All my
clerks have left me but one: so that I cannot go on
with business."

Thomas Jefferson
to James Madison,
September 12, 1793

AS WASHINGTON SEARCHED for a way out of the diplomatic thicket,
his family sustained a brutal and unexpected loss. On August 4, 1793,
the first lady reported the death of Tobias Lear's twenty-three-year-old
wife, Polly, "a pretty spritely woman" who in the course of her short
marriage had endeared herself to all the Washingtons. Polly's son, Benjamin Lincoln Lear, had been born at 190 Market Street, and despite the
demands of motherhood, the vivacious Mrs. Lear had eased Martha's
burden in planning official entertainments. Now she was gone. The president broke his rule against attending funerals to stand beside the sor-
rowing husband at Christ Church. Hamilton, Jefferson, and Knox helped
carry Lear's bride to her final resting place, and for one afternoon, at
least, partisanship was swallowed up in grief.

In the days that followed, Polly's symptoms were repeated in countless
Philadelphia dwellings. Some victims, feverish and incontinent, died
within twelve hours of the onset of a ghastly yellow pallor. Others lingered
for days with lifeless eyes and deranged brains, only to choke horribly
on their own blackened vomit. "I am truly sorry to hear of so many
deaths," Mrs. Washington wrote to her niece. "The wet rainy season has
made it sickly everywhere — I shall be glad when the frost comes to
clear the air."

Benjamin Rush dismissed the rainy season as a cause of Philadelphia's deadly invasion or frost as a cure. Instead, he diagnosed "bilious remitting yellow fever," resulting from noxious effluvia released into the air by a cargo of spoiled coffee dumped on an Arch Street wharf. Few dissenting voices challenged the most famous medical man in America, who held the first chair of chemistry at the University of Pennsylvania and was a shining light in the American Philosophical Society. Fewer still questioned his plan of attack. Prodded by Rush, the College of Physicians proposed marking every house visited by the plague. Gunpowder should be burned to clear the air. Pedestrians were advised to carry bottles of camphor or sponges soaked in vinegar. Those who could afford to leave town ought to do so; on second thought, they should remain and consult "mercurial" physicians who shared Rush's faith in purging and bleeding lethal fluids from the patient's system.

In medicine as in politics, Rush was not the sort to entertain doubts. He began by feeding weakened victims massive doses of calomel and jalap. Bleeding ensued, up to 80 percent of the blood supply being drained off. Since Rush overestimated the actual amount of blood in the human body by a factor of two, the results of such heroic measures can be easily, if painfully, imagined. When French doctors, more familiar than Rush with West Indian tropical fevers, urged alternative treatments emphasizing rest, cool liquids, and cool baths, Philadelphia's medical community divided along partisan lines, some doctors prescribing Federalist remedies, others advocating Republican cures.

While yellow fever and organized medicine ravaged his neighbors, Washington picked his way through the European minefield. On the western frontier, Genêt's filibustering expedition against Louisiana was slowed for lack of funds, but rumors of an impending attack led to protests from Spanish authorities — this at a time when the Washington administration hoped to negotiate free navigation of the vital Mississippi. His anxiety plain to see, the president demanded the removal of William Carmichael as America's representative at the bargaining table, "for from him we should never hear a tittle of what is going forward at the Court of Madrid."

Late August brought ominous news from another quarter. Hoping to starve its continental enemy into submission, the government of William Pitt the Younger threw a blockade around French ports. Pitt's Order in Council, commonly known as the provision order, declared corn, flour, and meal as contraband subject to forcible seizure. By undermining the traditional view that free ships make free goods (another way of saying that neutral vessels were immune to capture), Britain's escalation of commercial tensions endangered American shipping and brought war between the two nations measurably nearer.

Adding to the tense atmosphere, Republican journals carried lurid accounts of British insolence, the impressment of U.S. sailors, and the intimate search of female passengers by coarse tars. "Are our sailors to be maltreated, our ships plundered and our flag defied with impunity?" thundered the *American Daily Advertiser.* In a second, unrelated provocation, King George's Portuguese allies concluded a treaty with the piratical dey of Algiers, opening the Atlantic to seagoing predators just as David Humphreys embarked on a special mission to purchase the freedom of American hostages held by the Algerians.

"We are all well at present but the city is very sickly, and numbers dying daily," Washington informed Howell Lewis on August 25. Refusing to abandon the stricken capital, the president busied himself responding to addresses favorably contrasting his firm neutrality with the clumsy meddling of Citizen Genêt in domestic American politics. Even at this critical juncture, however, Washington's thoughts drifted south to his rudderless estate. For 100 guineas a year, he secured the managerial services of a widower from Maryland named William Pearce, whose salary was supplemented by twelve hundred pounds of pork and five hundred of beef, plus bread, butter, and milk for his young family, hay and fodder for his horses, the cooking and washing talents of a Negro woman, and two slave children to attend to his house and garden. The steep price was tolerable to a plantation owner saddled with shiftless overseers.

During the first week of September, Washington learned that Alexander and Betsey Hamilton were among the fever's latest victims. The president invited them to dinner anyway, and Martha sent her prayers, fortified by three bottles of medicinal wine. From the rural safety of Gray's Ferry, Jefferson mocked his rival's imaginary illness. "A man as timid as he is on the water, as timid on horseback, as timid in sickness, would be a phenomenon if courage of which he has the reputation in military occasions were genuine." Courageous enough to spurn Rush's nostrums, Hamilton turned to a boyhood friend from the West Indies, Dr. Edward Stephens, whose mild regimen and light medication hastened the recovery of both Hamiltons.

"Colonel Hamilton's remedies are now as unpopular in our city," claimed Dr. Rush, "as his funding system is in Virginia and North Carolina." No amount of suffering shook Rush's confidence in his debilitating treatments. A tragic case involved six-year-old Edward Pickering, the youngest son of Postmaster General Timothy Pickering, by early September one of the highest-ranking officials left in the city. Outspoken in his support of Rush's theories, the elder Pickering had already taken ten ounces of blood from a fevcrish maid and unhesitatingly opened his own vein when feeling ill. Then his son fell sick. Subjected to the inevitable bleeding and purging, the child refused all nourishment, leading his anxious father to seek Rush's opinion of force feeding. Soon after, Edward Pickering went to his grave, the latest in an unending series, many of them trenches hastily dug to receive the remains of people who died alone, abandoned, and unmourned.

On the cusp of autumn, Philadelphia resembled a ghost town. "The streets are lonely to a melancholy degree," said Henry Knox. "Hundreds are dying and the merchants have fled." Getting out was no simple task, as Knox discovered for himself when fearful New Yorkers forced him to spend two weeks in quarantine before letting him pass through their city en route to Boston. The Hamiltons faced similar obstacles attempting to reach the safety of Albany. Turned away from a New Jersey tavern, the convalescing couple was halted a second time at the gates of Manhattan by wild-eyed vigilantes.

Bad as the disease was, fear was nearly as deadly a contagion. Refugees left behind a city whose social contract was fast unraveling. Confirmed Republicans stopped shaking hands lest they contract the lethal virus. Theaters went dark. Banks closed their doors. Newspapers suspended publication. Freneau alone continued to distribute his journal, insisting it was safe to read because it was produced on the "uncommonly healthy" upper end of Market Street. The editor kept up a brave face, supporting Citizen Genêt long after he had become an acute embarrassment to Republican leaders and resorting to gallows humor to jolly his terror-stricken readers:

> Blame not Orlando if he fled
> So little's gained by being dead.

Members of the Supreme Court and Pennsylvania Assembly took Freneau at his word; both bodies adjourned pending the all-clear. A port visited by a thousand ships a year went into drydock as goods from the tainted capital were shunned in other markets. Said Oliver Wolcott on September 12, "The apprehensions of the citizens cannot be increased . . . the true character of man is disclosed, and he shows himself a weak, timid, desponding and selfish being." Wolcott's indictment was based on more than High Federalist disdain for the masses. All around him, families were dissolving and marriages coming apart. For long weeks the city's only reliable providers of care were members of the Free Africa Relief Society led by Richard Allen, the founding bishop of the African Methodist

Church, and Absolom Jones, who would go on to organize the country's first Negro Episcopal church.

Both men and their followers were kept busy nursing the sick and hauling corpses from the streets. The chronic shortage of doctors was equaled by the lack of clergymen to preside over the monotonous rites of death. A vigorously anticlerical Philip Freneau had fun at the expense of some cowards in ministerial robes:

> Priests retreating from their pulpits —
> Some in hot and some in cold fits
> In bad temper
> Off they scamper
> Leaving us — unhappy culprits.

❊ 2 ❊

Martha Washington refused to leave her husband, and he would not expose her or her grandchildren to the spreading menace. So early in September the first family pulled up stakes and moved south to Virginia. Before departing, Washington asked Henry Knox to supply him with weekly reports from the capital as long as it was safe to do so. The presidential household barely got out in time, for the citizens of Baltimore voted on September 13 to deny passage to any Philadelphian without a certificate from a health officer. To enforce the measure, militia were posted two miles north of the city.

Washington turned his attention from a dying city to one struggling to be born. On September 18 the former Worshipful Master of Alexandria's Masonic Lodge 22 took his place at the head of an unlikely procession marching east from Georgetown along a narrow dirt road grandly designated Pennsylvania Avenue. The little parade passed excavations for the President's Palace — reduced for reasons of economy from three stories to two — before halting at Tiber Creek, a pestilential stream whose periodic flooding gave the neighborhood of Marsh Market its name. Drums fell silent and flags were lowered long enough to permit Washington and other celebrants to scramble over logs and rocks sticking out of the shallow water. Safely across the Tiber, they ascended Jenkins Hill, future site of the United States Capitol. The sharp crack of artillery rounds escorted the president and a quartet of Masonic dignitaries to a shallow pit dug into the hillside, above which a ceremonial block of sandstone hung by a winch.

After the intoning of prayers, the blessing of ritual corn, wine, and oil, and an oration heard "with brotherly love and commendation," according to the *Alexandria Gazette*, Washington led the way to a nearby booth, where a five-hundred-pound ox was served to the crowd. The *Gazette*'s reporter noted that before darkness fell, "the entire company departed with joyful hopes of the production of their labor." Well they might, for after countless reverses and false starts, and notwithstanding temperamental architects and repeated brushes with financial disaster, the City of Washington was at last rising from the marshes.

The president became a welcome sight around town, driving himself in a handsome phaeton with a silver W on its side or holding court in his accustomed rooms at Suter's Tavern. Another hotel was then being planned, courtesy of Samuel Blodgett, the supervisor of public buildings, who envisioned a $50,000 edifice designed by James Hoban and financed through a gigantic lottery. Washington bought a ticket to present to "our little favorite," Benjamin Lincoln Lear, age two and a half. "If it should be his fortune to draw the Hotel," said the president, "it will add to the pleasure I feel in giving it." He added a touching postscript for the boy's father: "In whatever place you may be, or in whatever walk of life you may move, my best wishes will attend you, for I am and always shall be — Your sincere friend and Affectionate Servant."*

A few days later the president picked up the strands of another friendship interrupted by politics. He expressed delight at hearing, for the first time in four years, from his associate in the Continental Congress Edmund Pendleton. Pendleton's bitter strictures against the secretary of the treasury failed to ruffle Washington, earning instead the suave reply that Hamilton himself desired a congressional inquiry to clear his name. As deftly as possible, the president tried to change the subject. "I wish you had more to do on the great theatre," he told Pendleton, who had cited his ignorance of current affairs as an excuse to avoid political activity in the new regime. Washington added the familiar lament that "some infamous Papers" were intentionally disturbing the peace of the community. With unusual warmth he asked Pendleton to write more often, not omitting candid criticism of the president's personal conduct in office. "I only wish whilst I am a servant of the public, to know the will of my master, that I may govern myself accordingly," Washington explained.

He granted that on some occasions he had given his assent to legislation

---

*Tobias Lear's infant son did not draw the hotel, nor did any guest ever stay there. Instead, the lottery winner sued Blodgett over the unfinished structure, forcing the developer into bankruptcy. Unfazed, he announced a second lottery, promising a $30,000 mansion to the lucky ticketholder.

not altogether to his liking: "From the nature of the Constitution, I must approve all the parts of a bill, or reject it in toto. To do the latter can only be justified upon the clear and obvious ground of propriety; and I never had such confidence in my own faculty of judging as to be over tenacious of the opinions I may have imbibed in doubtful cases." Here was Washington at his most disarming, refuting critics with becoming modesty, distancing himself from unpopular subordinates, subtly shifting blame onto Congress for actions that had more of his approval than he cared to admit, and forever proclaiming his aversion to grubby politics.

The approaching session of Congress would supply the president's latest "doubtful case." With the fever continuing to rage out of control and no signs of recovery at hand, Washington asked Edmund Randolph to explore the possibility of renting temporary quarters for the executive department in the suburb of Germantown: "To prevent any misunderstanding of my meaning, I declare explicitly that it is hired lodgings *only* I will go into, for unless such can be had, I would repair to one of the most decent inns."

Washington showed less decisiveness in confronting a second issue. Congress was scheduled to reconvene at the start of December. What if Philadelphia remained under a death sentence? Could a president convene the legislature anywhere but the designated seat of government? Jefferson thought not. Madison agreed that the Constitution provided for no such contingency. A different response came from Speaker of the House John Trumbull, if only because Washington's failure to move the session might expose Congress — and its Speaker — to unnecessary risk. Days stretched into weeks as Washington, at Mount Vernon, pondered his options. What if the plague spread to Germantown? he wondered. Wilmington? Trenton? Annapolis was worth considering as a meeting place, but then again, "it might be thought I had interested and local views in naming this place." Reading, Pennsylvania, could hardly offend sectional advocates; Lancaster, on the other hand, would likely be seen as a sop to disgruntled Southerners.

Washington was not alone in his cautious approach, as Hamilton showed in arguing for the executive's *right* to convene Congress anywhere expediency dictated. After all, the capital might be leveled by an earthquake or captured by invading armies. But the secretary for tactical reasons urged restraint, and Washington, no more anxious than the New Yorker to afford "food for scribblers," renewed his standing request to the attorney general for a constitutionally acceptable solution. He also passed on to Madison the latest "really affecting" reports estimating Philadelphia's death toll at 3,500. Among the casualties was Eliza Powel's husband, Samuel, who had returned to the city out of solicitude for a favorite servant. "My life has been sufficiently embittered to make me now very little anxious about protracting or preserving it," the widow told Washington. "Death has robbed me of many friends, and time has abated the ardor of others."

Not every fatality was cause for mourning. On October 11, Philip Freneau resigned his clerkship in the State Department, tired, he said, of deciphering the Brother of the Sun at Constantinople and China's Very Sublime Majesty, Kien-Long. In fact, the editor had been forced to subcontract his translating labors to more linguistically gifted men. Two weeks later, badly in debt and more isolated than ever over his pro-Genêt politics, he announced that the *National Gazette* was ceasing publication. Others would don his mantle, but none matched Freneau's savage wit or singular ability to get under Washington's skin.

"To write was my sad destiny," concluded the unhappy newspaperman. "The worst of trades, we all agree."

On October 24, Randolph offered a simple, pragmatic solution to the congressional dilemma, telling Washington to do nothing prior to the scheduled convening of a body whose failure to appear would automatically constitute an "extraordinary occasion" warranting executive intervention. The president happily endorsed the tactic. Four days later, as he left Virginia for the capital, in Philadephia Timothy Pickering awoke to find half an inch of frost, providentially timed, in his garden. A cold rain was falling as Washington and Jefferson arrived in Germantown together; the fever, it appeared, was in retreat. From makeshift quarters at the King of Prussia Tavern, Jefferson reported a steady stream of residents returning to their homes.

In desiring an end to the rainy season, Martha Washington had been more prescient than she knew, for rain bred the female mosquito *Aedes aegyptie*, carrier of the plague and scourge of Philadelphia until the first frost put an end to its ravages. Benjamin Rush, meanwhile, clung grimly to his original diagnosis of noxious effluvia as the epidemic's cause. Insistent to the end on heroic measures, Rush blamed the loss of yet another patient on an inexperienced doctor's failure to carry out a prescribed fourth bleeding.

❦ 3 ❧

Autumn 1793 saw two capitals in the grip of terror, each resounding to the dull clatter of wooden wheels rumbling over cobblestones — in one city carrying yellowing corpses to common graves, in the other bearing citizens condemned for political heresy to their execution. One city had given birth to the Declaration of Independence and a successful colonial rebellion against a mother country trampling on traditions of self-government. The other served as midwife to the Declaration of the Rights of Man and a bloody civil war convulsing a land encrusted with royal and priestly tyranny.

Long after Philadelphia emerged from the yellow fever scare (having lost 10 percent of its population), Jacobin Paris remained transfixed by the shifting orthodoxies and savage reprisals of revolution in the name of the people. Between 1792 and 1795, 2,794 Parisians were beheaded by a device promoted as a humane alternative to the rope and the sword. Two months after Louis's queen followed him to the guillotine in October 1793, a twenty-four-year-old artillery officer of Corsican birth recaptured the port of Toulon for the Committee of Public Safety. Mass executions followed, 200 victims being a typical day's toll. Said Napoleon Bonaparte of his first great military triumph, "Considering the alternative, it is better to eat than be eaten."

Before learning of Marie Antoinette's grisly end, Washington reiterated his affection for her subjects. Answering an address from Jefferson's Albemarle County on November 16, he thanked his fellow citizens for their loyalty to the Constitution and the system of government he had tried to shield against the effects of foreign war and domestic turmoil. Washington took the occasion to add that nothing in his neutrality proclamation either "canceled nor weakened our obligation to the French Nation."

A series of Cabinet meetings before the president's annual address to Congress refined the meaning of American neutrality and demonstrated Washington's continued hostility toward Britain. More than a year had passed since Jefferson's request of George Hammond for a status report on the northwestern outposts held illegally. Even Hamilton favored a stiff protest of the provision order leaving U.S. vessels subject to capture on the high seas and their cargoes vulnerable to forced sale in British ports, but he also put up furious resistance to Jefferson's idea of treating both combatants equally. Jefferson held his ground, arguing that if information about Genêt's behavior derogatory to France was to be shared with Congress, then the executive should be no less forthcoming on the subject of King George's undeclared war against American commerce and neutral rights.

A lengthy debate on November 18 resolved nothing. Washington said he had never intended to permanently bind the people's representatives with his proclamation, issued when Congress was not in session, and reasserted his guiding principle — to keep the United States out of a conflict for which it was neither militarily nor psychologically prepared.

At another Cabinct session five days later, Jefferson raised strenuous objections to fortifying the nation's harbors, less for the provocation such a move implied than the expansion of federal authority it represented. Wishing to avoid any subject "which might generate hate and ill humor," the president backtracked. But only partially; believing in the wisdom of creating a national military academy at West Point, Washington said he would let Congress be the judge of its constitutionality.

Jefferson fared better when the discussion turned to Europe. On the critical question of whether and what to publish regarding the antagonists' conduct toward the United States, the secretary of state won a handsome victory. No one was more frustrated with Hammond's footdragging than the president. He now overrode a majority of his advisers, who hoped to keep the provision order secret to afford Hamilton more time to win in private talks with Hammond what Lord Grenville had been unwilling to grant officially credited U.S. diplomats. Writing to his wife in Massachusetts, Vice President Adams registered an equivocal dissent: "How a government can go on, publishing all their negotiations with foreign nations, I know not. To me it appears as dangerous and pernicious as it is novel; but upon this occasion it could not, perhaps, have been avoided." Adams had a point, one that Washington himself would eventually affirm with historic implications for the executive's conduct of foreign policy, but the politically inept vice president failed to grasp the effect of his chief's evenhandedness in restoring credibility among disgruntled Republicans.

Washington used the occasion of his fifth annual message to Congress, on December 3, to justify his neutrality proclamation and explain the motives behind its adoption. He invited the lawmakers to "correct, improve or enforce" his plan. To counter European hostility and strengthen the nation for whatever trials might lie ahead, the president urged a crash program to build several frigates carrying as many as forty-four guns apiece. Preparedness was the unavoidable price of national self-respect. "There is a rank due to the United States among nations," said Washington, "which will be withheld, if not absolutely lost, by the reputation of weakness. If we desire to avoid insult, we must be able to repel it; if we desire to secure peace, one of the most powerful instruments of our rising prosperity, it must be known that we are at all times ready for war."

Much of the rest of the message was given over to the chronic problem of Indian relations. Gifts of corn and clothing had eased tensions with the Creeks, and legal proceedings were under way to compensate the Cherokee victims of American violence. Only by forging permanent ties of interest, however, could a temporary suspension of hostilities be transformed into lasting peace. Next to impartial justice, commercial relations were the surest guarantee of friendship. In Washington's opinion, these "ought to be conducted without fraud, without extortion . . . with a ready market for the commodities of the Indians and a stated price for what they will give in payment, and receive in exchange."

Surprisingly, in view of his stormy relations with some newspapermen, the president recommended repealing taxes on the transport of public journals: "There is no resource so firm for the Government of the United States as the affections of the people guided by an enlightened policy; and to this primary good, nothing can conduce more than a faithful representation of public proceedings diffused, without restraint, throughout the United States."

Two days later Washington sent Congress a special message condemning Genêt for actions tending "to involve us in war abroad and discord and anarchy at home." The president was careful to distinguish between the offending diplomat and the friendly nation responsible for his errant appointment. Going a step further, he evened the score by upbraiding Pitt's ministry for its spoilations on American shipping and its persistent refusal to vacate the northwestern forts. For once, reaction was uniformly positive, Federalist New York agreeing with Republican Virginia that Washington had risen above faction in consulting the people's elected representatives. Even Benjamin Franklin Bache, Freneau's intemperate successor as a Federalist bête noire, pronounced Washington's neutrality rationale "perfectly satisfactory" and his call for strengthened national defenses unexceptionable.

Only days from retirement, Jefferson put the finishing touches to a powerful indictment of British maritime policies that his congressional allies might use to punish King George's plundering navy. He rejected Genêt's insistence that Jay and King be sued for libel in leaking the French envoy's purported threat to appeal over Washington's head. Thoroughly disenchanted with the bumbling Frenchman, Jefferson looked forward to imminent release from his official purgatory. He was fortunate. "Every day, more and more, discovers the intention of agents to perplex this government and to scatter thick and wide the seeds of dissension," Washington told his fellow Virginian late in December.

Private obligations weighed equally heavy on a man just weeks from his sixty-second birthday. Early in December, the president wrote to Arthur Young with a radical proposal. The master of Mount Vernon offered to rent all his farms but one, reserving the acreage immediately around Mansion House for his private residence, occupation, and amusement. He painted a highly flattering picture of his Tidewater estate, the most pleasantly situated in America. Mount Vernon's soil was inclined to be sandy, but the Potomac supplied inexhaustible reserves of natural manure. "A husbandman's wish would not lay the farms more level than they are, and yet some of the fields (but in no great degree) are washed into gullies, from which all of them have not, as yet, been recovered." Moreover, he continued, warming to his subject, the nearby Federal City was likely to become "the emporium of the United States," greatly adding to the value of his downriver property.

Washington used blunter language to instruct his new manager in handling the estate's overseer corps. William Pearce was to admonish them calmly but firmly when occasion called for it. "If this proves ineffectual discharge them, at any season of the year and without scruple or hesitation, and do not pay them a copper . . . To treat them civilly is no more than what all men are entitled to, but my advice to you is to keep them at a proper distance; for they will grow upon familiarity in proportion as you will sink in authority."

Getting to specific cases, Washington assessed the overseer Stuart as "a sober man, and according to his own account a very honest one." Crow was active yet overfond of visiting. "McKoy appears to me to be a sickly, slothful and stupid fellow . . . As to Butler . . . I am persuaded he has no more authority over the Negroes he is placed, than an old woman would." A scorching round of letters addressed to the overseers themselves directed each to correct his shortcomings. "I know full well," Washington informed his head carpenter, "that to speak to you is of no more avail than to speak to a bird that is flying over one's head."

The squire made the effort anyhow, his aspersions softened somewhat by compassion for lesser men's foibles. To one employee he delivered an impassioned lecture on the evils of liquor. "Consider how little a drunken man differs from a beast," he wrote on the eve of Christmas, 1793. "The latter is not endowed with reason, the former deprives himself of it . . . Show yourself more of a man and a Christian than to yield to so intolerable a vice," which must give more pain than pleasure to even the greatest imbiber. "I am your friend," Washington concluded truthfully.

⟨ 4 ⟩

The start of a new year was cause for rejoicing among the battered capital's surviving inhabitants, many of whom paid ceremonial calls on the Washingtons in keeping with January 1 tradition. Two weeks later, the first lady described a city suspended between grief and apprehension. Only those of a "glumay disposition" were anticipating an early return of the fever, she thought; still, "almost every family has lost some of their friends and black seems to be the general dress." Adding to the sober mood, Philadelphia was without theatrical diversion, for no company would appear until the municipal authorities decreed it was safe for crowds to assemble.

The city's mood rose as the mercury fell, for cold weather was safe weather. By mid-February Martha was able to report a lifting of the ban on performances and none too soon, "as a great number of people in this town is (sic) very much at a loss how to spend their time agreeably." Fashionable elements were always fond of something new, "be what it may," at least until the novelty wore off and boredom took its place. The New Theatre opened on Chestnut Street that spring, the motto above its stage — "The Eagle Suffers Little Birds to Sing" — a humorous rebuke of Quakers who had tried to enlist congressional support for suppressing theatrical entertainments. The president and his lady were among the first to experience the New's magnificent galleries, holding nearly 1,200 spectators, and lit by oil lamps that could be raised or lowered depending on the mood onstage. Thomas Wignall, the proprietor, was a former comic actor who greeted the Washingtons with a pair of wax candles in his hands before escorting them to a special box, where cushioned chairs and a military guard awaited.

Among those most impressed by the New Theatre and its itinerant troupes was Joshua Coit, a liberal-minded Federalist from Connecticut. "You can't think what a fine place it is," he told his wife in provincial New London, "all lighted up with candles and lamps so as to look as light as day — and there are fine paintings which they call the scenery. Some look like trees and some like houses — and the music, there are as many as twenty fiddles all playing together."

The president enjoyed *The School for Scandal* at the New as well as Henry Fielding's *Miser*. Between acts, all manner of stunts and acrobatics leavened the drama. There was Monsieur Placide, celebrated for his hornpipe done while balancing a peacock feather on his nose; and his sidekick, a child star billed as the Little Devil, who beat a drum and danced on a tightrope with eggs beneath his feet. At Rickett's Equestrian Circus, a brick building two hundred feet in diameter, the Irish proprietor rode at full gallop around a ring with a small boy perched on his shoulders. Equipped with a portable floor, the Circus could accommodate up to two hundred couples for dancing; the Washingtons went as often as their crowded schedule permitted.

Theatrics aside, Federal Philadelphia offered diversions for every taste. Just across Chestnut Street from the New Theatre the House of Representatives gave daily performances of its own. Self-conscious senators remained cloistered despite James Monroe's campaign to discard their veil of secrecy and enable voters to observe them at work. Visitors could observe for a fee an African lion at the Rising Sun Tavern or stroll through the brick market, stretching half a mile along the street to which it gave a name. Three days a week, the freshest produce, dairy goods, meat, fish, and poultry were available. Some tourists went just for the spectacle of polyglot Philadelphia. In the words of one bystander, "There seemed to be some of every nation under heaven" perusing the stalls.

The city's greatest tourist attraction, next to Washington himself, was Charles Willson Peale's Repository for Natural Curiosities, which had mushroomed from a portrait gallery with a few mastodon bones into the Smithsonian of its day. Housed in Philosophical Hall, Peale's scholarly hodgepodge was as eclectic as its curator. Busts of Revolutionary War heroes sat cheek by jowl with stuffed swans, baboons, and snakes, Indian scalps and tomahawks, fossilized jawbones, geological specimens, and a six-footed cow. Washington made a contribution of his own to the museum, loaning for display an ornate Otaheitian feather dress from Nootka Sound given him by charterers of a northwestern expedition from Boston.

Nearly as exotic was Hypolite Philip, a Parisian hairdresser advertising the latest wigs, scalps, frizettes, and pomade. French expatriates like Philip gave the capital a distinctly Gallic tinge. Neither the death of Marie Antoinette nor the long arm of Robespierre could diminish the American passion for Monsieur de Quesnay's illuminations and Old World terpsichory. Market Street's poplars might be a poor substitute for the Bois de Boulogne, and Jefferson's maître d'hôtel complained that vanilla was unavailable at any price, but visitors of many nationalities admired the French wallpaper and imitation festoons at Oeller's Hotel, otherwise known for its pineapple punch and the most comfortable beds in town.

Yankee claims of a classless society were disputed by Moreau de St. Mercy, the publisher of a French-language newspaper aimed at his fellow émigrés. He was told by the captain of the *Columbia*, a vessel berthed in New York, that he never dined alongside his first mate "because eating together necessitates conversation, and conversation leads to familiarity." Equally memorable was the Philadelphia ball interrupted by fisticuffs between the wife of a jeweler and the wife of a hairdresser. Washington's capital, concluded Moreau, was rife with artificial distinctions and snobbery.

Atop this highly stylized social pyramid stood William and Anne Bingham, the latter a daughter of Thomas Willing, a founder of the Bank of North America. Not yet thirty years old, Anne Willing Bingham was the undisputed queen of Philadelphia's society, her only rival Mrs. Robert Morris, whose close ties to the Washingtons were no match for "the dazzling Mrs. Bingham's" wit, weath, and worldliness. Abigail Adams pronounced Anne "the finest women I ever saw" even while objecting to her slavish imitation of Regency London. "Less money and more years may make her wiser," said the tart New Englander, "but she is so handsome she must be pardoned."

Having already captivated courts in London, Paris, and The Hague, Anne Bingham had no intention of hiding her light under the drab Quaker bonnets of Philadelphia. Nor was she averse to upstaging her competition, appearing on one occasion dressed in "a Rose a la Turke of black Velvet, Rich White Sattin Petticoat, body and sleeves, the whole trimmed with Ermine. A large Bouquet of natural Flowers supported by a knot of Diamond Springs interspers'd with artificial flowers, above all, wav'd a towering plume of snow white feathers." Moving assuredly through the masculine world of political power, Mrs. Bingham welcomed France's homeless aristocrats to the capital's most glittering salon and commissioned Gilbert Stuart to paint the president's portrait for her British admirer, Lord Landsdowne. Jefferson esteemed her charms sufficiently to overlook their ideological differences, venturing into the Bingham mansion at the risk of encountering George Hammond, a frequent visitor. Washington came too, suitably dressed in a blue Spanish cape faced with red velvet and thrown over his left shoulder. After climbing a set of marble stairs to the vestibule, the president was formally announced by servants, who then conducted him to the drawing room with its expensive carpets, lyre-backed chairs imported from Seddon's in London, and continental wallpaper patterned after the Vatican in Rome.

"The profusion and luxury of Philadelphia on great days . . . are extreme," commented the duc de Rochefoucauld Liancourt, then engaged in a study of the city's model prisons. "I have seen balls on the President's birthday where the splendor . . . did not suffer in comparison with Europe; and it must be acknowledged that the beauty of the American ladies has the advantage." Others were beginning to question the part traditionally assigned the so-called weaker sex. Many Philadelphians were reading Mary Wollstonecraft's *Vindication of the Rights of Women* during the winter of 1793-94. Joshua Coit praised the book and its author, who soared above vulgar prejudices to write "in a bold nervous and manly style . . . Minds which are superior to the shackles of fashion will sometimes point out brilliant improvements, their lights may help in forming of individual characters, but the world at large is not so easily mended."

Like Coit, Colonel John Trumbull was a Federalist from the Nutmeg State, but there the similarities ended, for this revolutionary painter, the country's premier visual historian, guardian of its myths and celebrant of its heroes, was a confirmed traditionalist sharply at odds with Coit's mild feminism and deist religion. At a dinner enlivened by the attacks of Jefferson's Republican admirer William Branch Giles on puritanical New Englanders and their dour Calvinist faith, Trumbull clashed with the secretary of state, a friend of twenty years' standing. As Giles made sport of Yankee "delusion and priestcraft," Jefferson nodded in smiling assent. David Franks, the only Jew at the table, came to Trumbull's defense. But it wasn't enough to keep the famed portraitist from storming out of the room or severing a friendship forged in the heat of revolution.

⊰ 5 ⊱

It was amazing how much could be done, Washington told visitors, if one was always doing. Keeping to his rural routine, he made time to visit his stables in Philadelphia each morning and still complete a few hours of paperwork before breakfasting at eight. An English visitor named Henry Wansey, invited to dine with the first family, observed that "the President in his person is tall and thin, but erect, rather of an engaging but dignified presence. He appears very thoughtful, is slow in delivering himself, which occasions some to conclude him reserved, but it is rather, I think, the effect of much thinking and reflection, for there is great appearance to me of affability and accommodation."

Breakfast at 190 Market Street was a Spartan business. Two small platters of sliced tongue sat on the table next to some dry toast, bread and butter, "but no broiled fish, as is the general custom . . . There was but little appearance of form; one servant only attended, who had no livery; a silver urn for hot water was the only article of expense on the table." The president buttered his own corncakes. Mrs. Washington poured tea and coffee. Washington and his guests rose from their meal to examine a model sent by a Virginia canal enthusiast hoping to replace floodgates with water-powered levers. Good or bad, ingenious or harebrained, a constant stream of new inventions flowed Washington's way. Somehow he found time and patience to consider each one, along with the feelings of its promoter.

After breakfast Washington pitched into his steward's account book, reviewing the previous day's household expenditures. On learning that Fanny Bassett Washington had drained fifty-six bottles of wine in entertaining visitors to Mount Vernon, her uncle enjoined a less spacious hospitality, telling his manager that there were but three classes of people deserving of fine Madeira: "first, my particular and intimate acquaintances . . . 2dly some of the most *respectable* foreigners . . . or, thirdly, to persons of some distinction (such as members of Congress, etc.) who may be traveling through the country." He had no objection, he added, to gratifying the desire of any sober or orderly sightseer to view his buildings and gardens, "but it is only to such persons as I have described, that I ought to be run to any expense . . . beyond common civility and hospitality."

His accounts in order, Washington called in Bart Dandridge for a look at overnight correspondence. Early in 1794 a wave of official vacancies competed for attention with British sea captains and Republican editors. This required finding able, geographically dispersed candidates willing to assume the responsibilities of office for the pittance authorized by Congress. Henry Knox gave notice of his intention to leave the War Department, forcing Washington to scramble for a replacement at the height of the crisis in Anglo-American affairs. Both David Stuart and Thomas Johnson planned to resign from the commission overseeing construction of the Federal City. And with Genêt facing involuntary retirement, it was only a matter of time before the Jacobin regime demanded the head, so to speak, of Gouverneur Morris.

To find temporary relief from such pressures, Washington often rode out to Belmont, the country estate of his wartime friend Judge Richard Peters. There, on the banks of the Schuylkill, he found seclusion and refreshment among towering firs, hemlocks, and pine trees. On fine summer days the president, usually accompanied by friends, walked into the countryside around Philadelphia. Mechanical curiosity drew him to Pearce's Cotton Manufactory, where a single workman could simultaneously weave two pieces of cloth, each forty-two inches wide. On another occasion Washington looked on proudly as a ship launching took place at Emmanuel Eyre's yard, afterward leaving behind two crowns for workmen. The dinner table afforded no respite from official labors, especially after Cabinet officers began dining together as part of conferences that took the entire day. "He is generally sedate and serious," recalled one of Washington's dinner guests, "and only after having two or three glasses of wine and when roused by the conversation around him, does his face assume an expression of liveliness." With sufficient champagne the president became positively merry.

Washington's private life, though not without its trials, provided a satisfying counterpoint to the presidency's splendid misery. Although content to live in her husband's shadow, Martha commanded respect from all but the most frivolous elements of Philadelphia society. Resolutely unfashionable, in her familiar mulberry velvet gowns she offered scant competition to the Binghams or Morrises. "She appears something older than the President," said Henry Wansey, "short in stature, rather robust; very plain in her dress, wearing a very plain cap, with her gray hair closely turned up under it." The only thing remotely stylish about the president's wife was the carved ivory fans of Chinese workmanship with French mounts that complemented her muslin handkerchiefs and garnet earrings.

The first lady received visitors each morning at eleven, passing around the room to shake hands before seating herself for more relaxed conversation than what passed for social intercourse at the president's levees. Emulating her husband's punctuality, Mrs. Washington rose as the clock struck twelve, bid her guests a good morning, and went to her room, where, aided by servants, she mixed lemons, sugar, spices, and rum to make a potent punch to be served before dinner. Two or three afternoons a week she presided over a tea party at which Betsey Hamilton and Mrs. Robert Morris were usually to be found. So was Lucy Knox, whose ample girth and foot-high hair arrangement gave her an appearance both comic and formidable.

Accustomed as an army wife to living in other people's houses, Martha accepted life in Philadelphia without complaint but also without enthusiasm. "I am only fond of what comes from the heart," she explained in the most revealing letter she ever wrote. "I little thought, when the war was finished, that any circumstances could possibly have happened which would call the general into public life again . . . I will not, however, contemplate with too much regret disappointments that were inevitable. Though the General's feelings and my own were perfectly in unison with respect to our predilection for public life, yet I cannot blame him for having acted according to his duties in obeying the voice of his country . . . With respect to myself, I sometimes think the arrangement is not quite as it ought to have been; that I, who had much rather be at home, should occupy a place with which a great many younger and gayer women would be prodigiously pleased . . . I know too much of the vanity of human affairs to expect felicity from the splendid scenes of public life. I am still determined to be cheerful and to be happy, in whatever situation I may be; for I have also learned from experience that the greater part of our happiness or misery depends upon our dispositions, and not upon our circumstances. We carry the seeds of the one or the other about with us, in our minds, wherever we go."

Repressing her distaste for public life, she objected to self-indulgence in others. When the children of her niece Fanny complained of stomach problems, Martha said it came as no surprise; "children that eat everything they like and feed heartily as yours do must be full of worms." After spraining a shoulder, Bart Dandridge "has been a good while complaining," his aunt reported disapprovingly. Nelly Custis's toothache and colds were just as easily disposed of, the product of "a pore thoughtless child." Yet for all her emphasis on flinty self-reliance, Martha had no lack of maternal warmth, as discovered by Tobias Lear and every other schoolmaster who despaired of teaching her overly indulged grandson, George Washington Parke Custis.

The president's wife failed dismally to inculcate her stoical creed in "the Child of Mount Vernon," less grandly known to his family as "Tub" or "young Wash." Instead, Martha's "pretty little Dear boy" was all but smothered in grandmotherly affection. At the theater he sat on his grand-father's lap. The cream of Philadelphia society attended his eleventh birthday party, and on July Fourth the boy and his sister joined their elders atop the ell of 190 Market Street to watch showers of sparks above the rooftops. Young Wash remained very much his father's son, every bit as spoiled, charming, and resistant to learning as Jack Custis had been. Lear could do nothing with him, and the president would not try lest it upset the boy's grandmother. Martha blamed everyone for her grandson's shortcomings but the boy himself. Youths of his age were shamefully ignored by instructors, she alleged, adding improbably that young Wash attended to his studies "as constant as the day comes, but he does not learn as much as he might if the master took proper care to make the children attentive to their books."

Outwardly Martha appeared less pleased with her granddaughter, "a little wild creature [who] spends her time at the window looking at car-riages etc. passing by." On the advice of Eliza Powel, Eleanor Parke Custis was fitted with a neck collar that promised, when screwed tightly enough, to improve the girl's posture. A different kind of restraint was imposed by pianoforte lessons and the four or five hours of daily practice enforced by Nelly's grandmother. Although fond of music, Washington was unable to play any instrument himself, which made Nelly's performances on the harpsichord he imported from England all the more enjoyable. Few people behaved naturally in Washington's presence; Nelly, with her pet parrot named Snipe and her cheeky sense of humor, was a prankish exception.

Admirers drawn to Nelly's dark-eyed good looks and obvious delight in being alive forgave her caustic tongue. "I hope when Nelly has a little more gravity she will be a good girl," explained her grandmother. "At present — she is I fear half crazy." The girl's irreverence peeks through a message declining a friend's invitation to a party because "we have a large company of the *Honorable Congress* to dine with us, and I must not be so remiss to go out in the evening as they like *to hear musick*." Nelly added that congressmen as a rule did not know one note from another.

Martha respected Nelly's latent abilities enough to insist upon their realization, in stark contrast to the free rein given her dawdling grandson. In addition to her music, Nelly studied French, Spanish, and Italian. She wore a spangled dress to dance classes taught by one of the city's leading lights, and she accumulated more than a passing knowledge of art. From her grandmother she learned needlework, beaded embroidery, and religious devotion, reading from the Bible or singing hymns as Mrs. Washington prepared for bed. Having no living daughters, the first lady looked the other way as her beloved Nelly grew toward womanhood, dismissing Lear's comments at the fifteen-year-old's maturity by pointing out that she was still able to wear clothing made a year earlier.

Harriot Washington was growing too, but her aunt, the president's nearly destitute sister, could no longer afford to dress her charge. Betty Lewis finally agreed to keep the fatherless adolescent after receiving £100 pounds from her brother toward the girl's upkeep. Early in 1794 Harriot wrote to "the only Friend on earth that I can apply to for anything," requesting funds for a silk jacket and shoes to wear to a ball commemorating Washington's birthday. Her persistence was rewarded. Within weeks she submitted a fresh list of clothing requirements. These included dimity with which to make petticoats and a great coat ("Mine is not entirely worn out," admitted Harriot pathetically, "but it is so much that I can't get it on").

Not all his relations made such demands on Washington's time and budget. To his favorite nephew, Bushrod, the president expressed pride in his budding legal career and cautioned him, "In this, and every transaction of your life, let honor and probity be your polar star." Still more personal counsel was offered to yet another of Martha's granddaughters, Elizabeth Parke Custis, then on the brink of marriage to an Englishman named Thomas Law. Miss Custis should not believe the fine tales told by poets and lovers of old or expect to find earthly paradise in the arms of her beloved. "Love is a mighty pretty thing," declared Washington, "but like all other delicious things, it is cloying; and when the first transports of the passion begin to subside," Elizabeth would find it "too dainty a food to live on *alone*."

Passion was just one of many ingredients necessary to matrimonial happiness, none more important "than that the object on whom it is placed should possess good sense, good dispositions, and the means of supporting you in the way you have been brought up. Such qualifications cannot fail to attract (after marriage) your esteem and regard, into which or into disgust, sooner or later, love naturally revolves itself . . . Without these, whatever may be your first impressions of the man, they will end in disappointment; for be assured, and experience will convince you, that there is no truth more certain than that all our enjoyments fall short of our expectations; and to none does it apply with more force, than to the gratification of the passions."

Thus spoke the veteran of a union of thirty-five years' duration. However bleak Washington's reading of the most basic human emotion may strike modern eyes, his words were intended as a tribute to a woman fully as honest, realistic, and self-reliant as himself.

❖ 6 ❖

The first months of 1794 were notable for British piracy on the high seas and skulking in the forests of the American Northwest. To posts at Mackinaw, Detroit, Fort Erie, Niagara, Oswego, Oswegatchie, and Dutchman's Point, John Bull now added Fort Miami, on the Maumee River, as his latest mockery of American sovereignty. Thirteen years after Yorktown, 1,000 of the king's soldiers remained on U.S. soil. In the same vicinity, General Anthony Wayne and his 3,000 troops were preparing for war with red men and, if need be, redcoats. Coming out of its winter quarters at Greeneville, on the southwestern branch of the Miami River, Wayne's Legion built a string of forts as it pushed on to the confluence of the Maumee and Au Glaize. Recovery, Defiance, Adams: their names bespoke a grim determination to avenge Harmar and St. Clair.

As the British attacks on American shipping increased, so did popular anger at the country's traditional adversary. On January 3, Madison reintroduced his 1791 program of commercial retaliation against Pitt's government, whose latest order in council all but eliminated American trade with the West Indies. Genêt's insolence quickly faded from memory, replaced by news of Yankee vessels caught in King George's Caribbean net: one hundred in Barbados, three times as many in the turquoise waters off Jamaica. Yet a third order in council revoked part of these offending instructions to English captains without releasing any of the hundreds of U.S. sailors confined to the filthy holds of British prison ships. To the Federalist elite, British arrogance was matched by British stupidity. "The English are absolutely madmen," sputtered Fisher Ames, whose Anglophile voting record in the House of Representatives had got him burned in effigy by Republicans in Charleston.

Perhaps because Washington had few illusions to begin with, he was less surprised by the Royal Navy's aggression. He was nevertheless incensed, all the more so when Lord Dorchester, in a speech to Indian emissaries in February, predicted war with the United States at any moment. The governor-general's indiscreet talk confirmed widely held suspicions that the previous year's peace feelers and the aborted Sandusky conference had been ploys calculated to stall Wayne's advance while solidifying the alliance between British Canada and the militant tribes along the American frontier. Washington was moved to examine his nation's long, exposed borders with its northern neighbors and ponder invasion routes "if matters should come to extremities."

As British trophies piled up in tropical harbors and Mad Anthony Wayne drilled his men for the coming fight, Congress debated Madison's comeuppance for those violating American rights or undermining Yankee commerce. Republicans argued that King George should, at the least, pay for American neutrality by lifting unfair trade barriers and opening home and colonial ports to American skippers. Thrown on the defensive by the bullying tactics of George Hammond and his government, Hamilton called on the British minister and gave him a taste of his own medicine by demanding the return of all U.S. vessels and full payment for illegally seized cargoes.

Hammond was astonished. If the secretary of the treasury, "uniformly the most moderate of the American Ministers," was now taking a hard line, Hammond told his superiors in London, what might congressional Republicans or the burgeoning Democratic societies be capable of? Already New Yorkers by the thousands were cheering virulent anti-British rhetoric in their streets and vigorously constructing defenses in their harbor. In Philadelphia, patriots not content to jeer the king's envoy from the sidewalks outside his residence tore a bas-relief of the monarch from the walls of the establishmentarian Christ Church.

Late in January, Republicans in the Senate opened a second front in their assault on the administration by demanding copies of all diplomatic correspondence between the executive branch and Gouverneur Morris in Paris. Washington discussed the request with his Cabinet before supplying thirty-nine of the forty documents sought, confident that nothing in them would embarrass him or his administration. The president's sixty-second birthday coincided with the arrival of Citizen Genêt's replacement, Jean Antoine Fauchet, described by the first lady as "a plain, grave and good-looking man." Washington seemed equally taken with the thirty-three-year-old lawyer, whose "strong and apparently sincere" professions of friendship for the United States contrasted favorably with the meddling ways of his predecessor.

A Federalist congressman from Massachusetts looked on as Washington welcomed a broad cross section of admiring Philadelphians to his home. "He was standing in the middle of the room, and bowed politely to everyone as we entered," George Thacher informed his wife. "After walking socially among the company and inquiring about the health of the individuals, he opened a door leading into another apartment and, smiling, asked us if we were disposed for a little cake and wine." The "little cake" proved to be three feet across and a foot thick. Aided by a highly flavored punch, "we all joined in the conviviality, the President mingling and partaking with the company." When a contingent of Pennsylvania militia trooped past the house, Washington took the initiative of asking them inside, chatting informally without any apparent social distinctions.

Peter Van Gaasbeek, another Federalist representative inclined to see the president in the most flattering light, marveled at a ruler who treated the lowliest of enlisted men with the same unfailing courtesy accorded officers. "I had the pleasure to mortify many who called themselves democrats, but in reality are . . . disappointed-crats, by asking them in what republic but this, the humble peasant had access to the first magistrate," he wrote. Unable to resist a jab at the opposition, the congressman urged "Madisonites" in the crowd to adopt "real Republican principles . . . and quit your Genêtism."

Actually there were role reversals going on in both parties that spring, Republicans capitalizing on British transgressions at sea to rouse maritime New England while Federalists tried to establish anti-British credentials by seizing on the issue of military preparedness. For Federalist kingpins the most vexing problems involved, not their confirmed enemy, France, but their ardently courted yet faithless friends in the British ministry. For a pregnant moment, conventional expectations were turned on their head. The failure of party realignment to occur can be chalked up to Republicans more fearful of Washington's government than of King George's. Instead of aiding their drive for majority status, the crisis touched off by British trespasses exposed the fault lines in Jefferson's party.

Republicans in Congress let themselves be outmaneuvered by the Federalists, whose nationalistic agenda included coastal fortifications, ships of war, and executive authority to oppose possible invasion with an army of 25,000 soldiers. As prisoners of their agrarian ideology, Jefferson's followers refused to employ any but commercial weapons to express their outrage or enforce their demands. Rather than have the United States build its own warships, Madison would hire Portugal's navy. Typical of those wanting to have it both ways was James Monroe, quick to attack what he called the administration's "pusillanimity" in the face of British provocations, yet immovable in his opposition to any enlargement of the nation's military establishment.

The majority was less stingy. By the third week of February, it had approved six frigates as part of a record defense budget totaling nearly $1.5 million. A month later Congress enacted a thirty-day embargo on all foreign trade, buying the administration precious time in which to reclaim the initiative and perhaps remove the explosive issue of Anglo-American relations from the legislative arena altogether. Such was the hope of Federalist leaders, who recognized that an extended ban on trade could spell disaster for a fragile economy dependent on foreign exports. Washington shared this belief, cannily ordering William Pearce at Mount Vernon to stockpile flour in anticipation of rapid price increases after the embargo.

Two days after writing to Pearce, Washington turned down the job application of James McHenry, a Baltimore surgeon and the commanding general's physician during the Revolution, who hoped to free Lafayette from his Austrian jail cell. At the time of his first inauguration, explained the president, "I resolved firmly that no man should ever charge me *justly* with deception." In the years since, he had often been compelled to rethink his original intentions and deny trusted associates for the sake of appearance. It was a self-imposed restraint that Alexander Hamilton was about to experience for himself. "Heartily tired" of post-Cabinet life, of carping congressmen and vicious editors, the dynamic New Yorker longed for a change, for new fields to conquer and new muscles to exercise. Hamilton imagined a life with Angelica Church at his side in the brilliant English capital, where, as Washington's envoy, he would negotiate a permanent commercial and military alliance between his adopted and his spiritual homelands.

Just who conceived the idea of a presidential emissary superior in status to Thomas Pinckney remains obscure, but it was entirely consistent with Washington's outlook and record. During his first weeks in office the president had, in the face of Madison's objections, sent Morris to Britain, hoping to cut a deal on commercial ties and the British evacuation of the northwestern posts. In doing so, he established a commanding precedent for every chief executive since. Now Washington proposed to repeat the trick at a time of far greater tensions. At a caucus of Federalist party elders on March 10, Connecticut's Oliver Ellsworth was chosen to float Hamilton's name before the president. Ellsworth found Washington polite, attentive, sympathetic even, but on the main point unpersuadable. Simply put, Hamilton did not possess the country's confidence. Neither John Jay nor Gouverneur Morris was able to change the president's mind.

Washington rejected for different reasons the unsought counsel of James Monroe, who offered to make his case against Hamilton as a Francophobe intriguer in private. Languid in appearance but keenly partisan, Monroe resented Washington's failure to grant him a wartime command worthy of one of the youngest heroes of the Battle of Trenton. Since coming to the Senate in the fall of 1791, he had established himself as a staunch advocate of Virginia's agrarian, states' rights viewpoint. Washington could barely stand his state's junior senator, and when he replied to Monroe's letter on April 9, inviting him to submit in writing any negative information he possessed, his tone fell somewhere between correct and frigid.

"As I *alone* am responsible for a proper nomination, it certainly behooves me to name such a one as in my judgment confirms the requisites for a mission so peculiarly interesting to the *peace* and happiness of this country," he wrote. This did not prevent other officeholders from trying to forestall what seemed to them a disastrous selection. Madison and Randolph quickly joined the "anyone but Hamilton" camp, the latter confiding his misgivings to Jean Antoine Fauchet, whom time would reveal to be neither as modest nor deferential as originally thought.

On April 14, stymied by his own reputation and a host of enemies whose hatred he cordially reciprocated, Hamilton threw in the towel. By then Washington had already settled on another candidate. At dawn the next day, he composed a hurried note to the chief justice, inviting him to call at the earliest possible hour. "At eight o'clock we breakfast," Washington told John Jay. "Then, or after, as suits you best, I will expect to have the satisfaction of conversing with you on an interesting subject. Yours etc." A second message summoned Edmund Randolph for a detailed review of the draft announcing Jay's appointment.

Washington's sense of urgency was justified, for on April 7 members of the House had enthusiastically embraced a Republican plan slapping a permanent embargo on British trade until that nation vacated the northwestern forts and made restitution for its war on U.S. shipping. Now the same bill was under discussion in the Senate, where its passage appeared certain to touch off a bloody confrontation. Thus Jay's nomination was timed to defuse hard feelings toward the British and recast the vote in the Senate as a test of presidential strength. By the narrowest of margins — Vice President Adams's tiebreaking vote — the ploy worked, sending the harsh Republican package down to defeat.

Relations between the United States and Great Britain hung in the balance, Jay had told his wife after dining at 190 Market Street earlier in the week. "I am rather inclined to think that peace will continue," he went on, with the clinical detachment for which he was famous, "but should not be surprised if war should take place."

❊ 10 ❊

"DASH TO THE MOUNTAINS, JERSEY BLUE"

"As far as my information extends, this insurrection
is viewed with universal indignation and abhorrence,
except by those who have never missed an opportunity
by side blows, or otherwise, to aim their shafts at the
general government."

George Washington
to Henry Lee,
August 26, 1794

WASHINGTON WAS FEELING unusually introspective early in May 1794,
when he wrote Tobias Lear to thank him for several recent communications. The president envied his friend's freedom to sample opinion
outside the gilded cage. "From mixing with people in different walks,"
he said, Lear enjoyed a much more extensive range "than could fall to
the lot of a stationary character, who is always revolving in a particular
circle." The attention of his own circle was taken up with feverish preparations for war and Jay's mission to prevent it, the departure of Jefferson
and his replacement by Randolph, and the selection of William Bradford,
a Pennsylvania supreme court justice, to fill Randolph's shoes as attorney
general.

Washington had business to transact as well as information to impart.
Lear, already in Europe, was ideally placed to promote thousands of acres
of the president's land in western Pennsylvania and Virginia, along the
Ohio and Great Kanawha rivers. By ridding himself of this distant,
unmanageable property, Washington hoped to unburden himself of the
demands that went with absentee ownership, for although in the world's
estimation he possessed a handsome estate, "yet, so unproductive is it,

that I am oftentimes ashamed to refuse aids which I cannot afford unless I was to sell part of it to answer the purpose." In a paragraph marked "(Private)," he confessed another motive for disposing of this land, one "more powerful than all the rest; namely to liberate a certain species of property which I possess, very repugnant to my own feelings, but which imperious necessity compels." To use Jefferson's haunting phrase, Washington the slaveholder had the wolf by the ears.

The president entrusted his letter to John Jay, whose nomination had provoked stiff opposition from Republicans in both houses of Congress, mindful of his recent role in smearing Citizen Genêt and his earlier performance as secretary of foreign affairs under the Confederation. Then, championing eastern interests to the exclusion of western ones, he had failed to press Spain for unfettered access to the Mississippi. Regional animosities aside, Jay's gilt-edged credentials included service in the First and Second Continental Congresses and subsequent stints as wartime diplomat, a negotiator of the 1783 peace treaty, the first chief justice of New York, the leading draftsman of its constitution, and a persuasive contributor to *The Federalist Papers*.

Since 1790 the tall, stooped lawyer had presided over the Supreme Court, where he made an impressive sight as he entered the courtroom wearing a black robe trimmed with salmon-colored facings, his grave self-assurance reflecting not only the majesty of the law but also a personal status as what one writer has called "the scion of a ruling family in the most dynastically ruled of all states." Not least among Jay's social advantages was a dazzlingly beautiful wife, whose arrival at a Parisian opera house had once provoked tumultuous applause from patrons mistaking her for Marie Antoinette.

The forty-eight-year-old Jay was too good a judge to be a diplomat, let alone a politician. Relentlessly legalistic, he readily saw the British viewpoint in their refusal to hand over frontier outposts until the former colonists made good on prewar debts owed to English merchants. Along with this almost religious belief in contractual obligations went a healthy sense of the judiciary's importance, and of John Jay's as well. A confidential report prepared for Lord Grenville qualified praise of the chief justice's abundant good sense by concluding that "almost every man has a weak and assailable quarter, and Mr. Jay's weak side is Mr. Jay." Perhaps it was exaggerated pride, perhaps his reputed presidential ambitions, that kept Jay from agreeing to become Washington's permanent representative to Great Britain, thus releasing Thomas Pinckney to replace Gouverneur Morris across the Channel.

Republicans objected to a sitting chief justice moonlighting as a diplomatic troubleshooter. (Bache's *Aurora* had its own, typically provocative reason for condemning Jay's absence from the bench. According to the editor, there could be no presidential impeachment while Jay was on foreign soil, for the Constitution specified that only the chief justice could preside over such a trial.) In point of fact, Jay had long been an adviser, ex officio, to the Washington administration, sharing his conservative views on the Nootka Sound crisis and urging strong measures against the farmers in western Pennsylvania protesting Hamilton's whiskey tax. In the spring of 1793, the New Yorker submitted a draft of a neutrality proclamation spiced with criticism of troublesome newspaper editors for presidential review, only to see his harsh strictures passed over for the milder wording of Edmund Randolph.

Jay's politics were Federalist to the core. In the early, pivotal case of *Chisholm* v. *Georgia*, the chief justice had spoken good party doctrine by upholding the right of individual citizens of one state to sue another state, thereby diminishing state pretensions while elevating the Court and the central government whose laws it interpreted. Popular anger over the decision led to enactment of the Eleventh Amendment, prohibiting such lawsuits, but even in defeat Jay had opened the door to the muscular nationalism of another Federalist stalwart, John Marshall. His soaring visions of the nation's highest tribunal — a sentiment hardly justified by its skimpy workload and circuit-riding drudgery — had, ironically, narrowed the jurisdiction of Jay's court. For by rejecting Washington's plea to define American neutrality at the time of the *Little Sarah* affair, Jay had not only evaded the immediate crisis caused by Genêt's unorthodox diplomacy; he had kept the Court out of partisan snares.

Though momentarily frustrated, Washington deferred to Jay's chilly integrity and dispassionate legal mind. As an experienced negotiator, the chief justice would presumably command similar respect from King George's foreign ministry. At least, that is what the president hoped. Best of all, Jay carried none of Hamilton's excess baggage, an almost certain obstacle to ratification of any treaty emerging from Washington's initiative. Opponents of the administration, unable to prevent the peace mission, vented their anger at the patrician chief justice. Madison called his appointment the greatest blow yet to Washington's popularity, while Monroe and Aaron Burr spearheaded a brief, intense debate in the Senate that ended in a strict party-line vote approving the nominee.

A thousand New Yorkers turned out to cheer Jay when he set sail on May 12, taking with him deliberately broad instructions and the authority to discuss both the unfulfilled peace treaty of 1783 and the much larger issue of Anglo-American commercial relations. On the subject of a proposed league of neutrals to protect shipping from British predators, he enjoyed an equally generous mandate. Rejecting Hamilton's counsel,

Washington left open the possibility of America's participation in this early attempt at collective security, if only to increase the uncertainty of the British and thereby strengthen Jay's hand at the bargaining table.

For two hundred years, students of Washington's presidency have portrayed Hamilton as its Warwick or Mephistopheles, singlehandedly responsible for the administration's economic policies, constitutional purity, and bias toward England. In Washington's first term, the treasury secretary had failed to win the president over to his blatant Anglophile sympathies, and he had been overruled by the president as often as he had been sustained. Never mind: after Jefferson's departure removed a worthy intellectual rival, runs the argument, Hamilton became the virtual prime minister to a fading, distracted monarch. The facts suggest otherwise. Before 1794 was half over, Washington had effectively foreclosed Hamilton's diplomatic escape route to London and turned aside the secretary's request to welcome the aristocratic refugee Talleyrand into his drawing room. Moreover, the president told Hamilton that his own reading of Jay's mission "differs very widely from your interpretation."

Then Washington delivered a constitutional lecture, sounding not at all like the puppet on a string imagined by Hamilton's warmest admirers and bitterest foes: "The powers of the Executive of the United States are more definite, and better understood perhaps than those of almost any other country; and my aim has been, and will continue to be, neither to stretch nor relax from them in any instance whatever, unless imperious circumstances should render the measure indispensable."

The question of Gouverneur Morris's long-rumored replacement supplied yet another disappointment for the supposedly omnipotent Hamilton. Washington initially leaned toward Madison for the Paris ministry, but the little philosopher, recently married to the bewitching Dolley Todd, had no desire to establish even temporary residence three thousand miles from Philadelphia. Equally reluctant was Robert Livingston, another good Republican whose selection would have grated on Hamilton as much as it pleased his enemies. Washington dismissed Aaron Burr as chronically ambitious and morally unfit. Scarcely less surprising was the man on whom he ultimately settled, James Monroe, in an attempt to balance the Federalist Jay with a staunch Republican, sure to be seen as a kindred spirit by the French. On May 26, Randolph invited Monroe to join the administration of which he had been so critical. After checking with Madison, the senator from Virginia gave his assent. Three weeks later he left Baltimore Harbor with his wife, Elizabeth, and their eight-year-old daughter.

The ambitious Virginian would have subsequent cause to regret the journey and an appointment that all but scuttled his political career. Yet those who attacked Monroe for kowtowing to French Jacobins and for serving the interests of his party over those of his president could not have been privy to his instructions from Randolph. On their face, they were unambiguous orders, even if cloaked in the deliberately flexible language with which professional diplomats keep their options open. "You go, sir, to France, to strengthen our friendship with that country," Randolph told Monroe. "You will show our confidence in the French Republic, without betraying the most remote mark of undue complaisance. *You will let it be seen that in case of war with any nation on earth we shall consider France as our first and natural ally.* You may dwell upon the sense which we entertain of their past services."

Bold words, these, from one revolutionary partisan to another, strengthening Monroe's prior conviction that he, a staunch advocate of Jeffersonian dogma, was being sent abroad to atone for Morris's unconcealed Francophobia. Yet far more important than anything Randolph said was what he withheld from Monroe. Washington's envoy left for Paris entirely ignorant of the instructions governing his counterpart in London, John Jay; his mission was limited, Monroe believed, restricted to infractions of the old peace treaty. That Jay was in fact empowered to do much more was regarded by Washington as a closely guarded secret between him and the chief justice.

Across an ocean no wider than the temperamental and political divisions separating him from his reluctant spokesman, Washington read fragmentary press accounts of Monroe's maiden appearance before the National Convention, trumpeting the American executive's "immutable" wish for revolutionary success, and was not happy. "The affairs of this country *cannot go amiss,*" the president remarked with heavy-handed jocularity to Monroe's predecessor. "There are *so many watchful guardians of them,* and *such infallible,* that one is at no loss for a director at every turn."

It was easy enough for the old man to suspect Monroe, so long a thorn in his side. But by withholding vital information about the nature and extent of Jay's mission, Washington and his erratic secretary of state had inadvertently planted the seeds of future misunderstanding and worse.

❦ 2 ❦

The president gave far more explicit orders to his new household steward, James Germain. After first claiming that his public duties left but little time for domestic oversight, Washington imparted some revealing "general ideas . . . 1st. that my table be handsomely, but not extravagantly, furnished on the days that company are entertained. 2d. that a decent and economical board be spread at other times. And 3d. that my domestics should be plentifully fed at all times with what is wholesome and proper beyond which . . . in quantity nor quality you are not to go; nor suffer them to carry away anything from the house unless they have permission to do so. Whatever remains after these purposes are served, and is not necessary for another day, I would have given to the poor and needy housekeepers in the neighborhood who may want and would not apply for it."

On June 9 Congress finished its work; eight days later Washington made a "flying visit" to Mount Vernon. Slowing his journey was a team of horses grown fat from want of exercise and the inevitable pause to inspect construction sites in the Federal City. On the morning of June 22, while examining the Potomac Navigation Company's canal and locks, Washington and his mount nearly tumbled into the river. Strenuous horsemanship saved the president, but at the cost of a severely wrenched back, which kept him out of the saddle for weeks. Forbidden were the long inspection tours with which he exercised control over his sprawling estate. Suddenly an ailing Washington felt much older. The whole purpose of his trip had been defeated in an instant, he complained.

Back in Philadelphia, the first lady was frantic. "I have been so unhappy about the President that I did not know what to do with myself," she confessed to Fanny Bassett Washington. "He tells me in his letter of Wednesday that he is better. I hope in God that he is so. If I could have come down with any convenience, I should have set out the very hour I got the letter." An agitated Martha begged her niece for an honest report of the president's condition, adding, "it would make me exceedingly unhappy to be told or made to believe that he is getting better if he is not."

That same month, Washington summoned a specialist in Philadelphia to treat a suspicious growth on the right side of his face. Under the mild treatment prescribed by Dr. James Tate, the spot disappeared over the summer months. No such miracles were being worked in Washington's fields. The well-rutted roads between Philadelphia and the Potomac estate carried a heavy traffic of advice, inquiry, exhortation, veiled criticism, and open complaint. The president directed William Pearce to plant timothy and clover in the New Meadows. How was the buckwheat stacked? he demanded, and how did the oats appear? Why were Betty and Doll on the sick list more than half the time? Pearce must watch out for "extremely deceitful" Ruth, who would try anything to get into the main house and out of her assigned tasks, thereby setting a bad example for Hannah and Pegg, "none of whom would work if by pretexts they can avoid it."

Washington suspected an overseer's wife of selling butter from Mount

Vernon in Alexandria, where the merchants were little more than traffickers in stolen goods, eager to get their hands on "every thing that can be filched" from the estate. The absent husbandman bemoaned a sharp decrease in the amount of wool per sheep since his election to the presidency. Lambs were being sold against his orders; worse, "the money for which they were sold never found its way into my pockets." An enthusiastic proponent of mules — once envisioned as replacements for Prescott's majestic stablemates in pulling the presidential coach — Washington cautioned his manager against overworking the creatures when young. A mule was not to be confused with a dray horse; it did not reach its prime until twelve or fifteen years of age. But with proper care, Washington guessed, the offspring of Royal Gift might enjoy a useful life of thirty years or more.

Slavery, his evil inheritance, continued to bedevil the president. He explained his distaste for the institution to a prospective land buyer. "Were it not . . . that I am principled against selling Negroes, as you would do cattle in the market, I would not, in twelve months from this date, be possessed of one as a slave. I shall be happily mistaken if they are not found to be a very troublesome species of property 'ere many years pass over our heads; (but this by the bye)."

To both reduce expenses and clear his conscience, Washington offered thousands of acres of his western lands to Robert Morris and his partner in speculation, James Greenleaf. Greenleaf, a shady character, simultaneously played on the president's anxieties to curry favor with the Federal City's commissioners and achieve his real goal of purchasing six thousand lots in the undeveloped capital at highly favorable terms. He then leveraged this property with nonexistent Dutch loans, creating a financial mirage on which Morris based *his* purchase of 6 million acres stretching from western Pennsylvania to Georgia. In time, the whole fraud would bury both men in dishonor; meanwhile, the usually canny president was bamboozled.

So desperate was Washington to unload his western property that he bent his previously inflexible rule against mixing public and private business to accept the offer of Pennsylvania's senator James Ross to promote 4,000 acres in Washington and Fayette counties. For additional help he turned to Colonel Presley Neville, whose father, John, was entrusted with collection of federal whiskey taxes in that excitable region. "The cream of the country" had been sold once already to a French nobleman unable to produce the asking price of 65,000 crowns, explained Washington. "From the experience of many years, I have found distant property in land more pregnant of perplexities than profit," he confessed to young Neville.

Early in July Washington left Mount Vernon, riding through a driving rain to reach Philadelphia on the seventh. A cold picked up along the way did not prevent him from greeting members of the Chickasaw tribe and their chieftain, Piomingo, four days later. John Quincy Adams, celebrating his twenty-seventh birthday, watched as the president took two or three puffs from a fifteen-foot-long leather pipe before passing it along to Piomingo, seven warriors, four boys, and an interpreter. The head of the Chickasaw delegation pled illness to delay his response to Washington's brief formal remarks. But he was not too sick to make pointed inquiries about a second group of Indian emissaries in town, representing the rival Cherokee Nation.

In between sips of wine and bites of cake, Piomingo and his confederates denounced the Cherokees and tried to gauge their standing with the phlegmatic Great White Father. Adams, no stranger to diplomatic wiles, found the spectacle both amusing and instructive. "The *fides punica*, it seems, is not confined to civilized nations," he concluded.

❊ 3 ❊

By the summer of 1794, the people of western Pennsylvania were out of luck and out of patience. Detesting the taxes on their whiskey, a crushing federal debt, and the Hamiltonian economic system based on trade with high and mighty Britain, many in the hardscrabble counties west of Pittsburgh felt abandoned by the central government bulking over the Appalachians. Far from the elegant drawing rooms of Philadelphia, where the Washington administration dared to hope that Mad Anthony Wayne's current offensive would defeat or at least contain the Indian threat, frontier inhabitants felt as vulnerable to midnight savagery as ever. Washington did not escape criticism, especially among the dispossessed farmers; they considered him but one more grasping speculator who, through none too scrupulous methods, had separated many a colonial soldier from his land bounty. Refusing to sell on any terms but those most favorable to himself, the hero of legend and panegyric had filed suit against the squatters, skipping the county courts for the much friendlier venue of the state's highest tribunal.

Colonel Neville's correspondent was not unaware of the spreading unrest in western Pennsylvania. Two centuries later we may ask whether Washington's response to the so-called Whiskey Rebellion was influenced by personal concerns. One can easily imagine how the modern media would treat similar real estate dealings — the firestorm greeting their disclosure and the crescendo of popular anger leading, perhaps, to calls for impeachment. A different ethic prevailed in 1794, when appearances were less likely to equal reality and journalists did not question the gentleman's code governing such matters.

Yet a lust for land represented only part of Washington's complex love affair with the American West. None of his countrymen thought on so continental a scale. To be sure, Jefferson might talk learnedly with European philosophers about the unique zoological attributes of the trans-Appalachian West (some in the Old World believed that dogs actually lost their bark in the thin American air). But no one could claim, as did Washington, to have actually tramped the forests and taken the measure of this vast trackless empire in the making. Nor could anyone match his strategic and emotional grasp of a region that served simultaneously as granary, marketplace, buffer zone, and battlefield.

Above all, Washington was sensitive to the area's delicate political balance. "The western states," he had written after the war, "stand as it were on a pivot; the touch of a feather would almost incline them any way." What he was referring to, of course, was the complex rivalry of European powers, each seeking to establish its domination over the trans-Appalachian region. England, France, and Spain all nurtured territorial ambitions. So did the native tribes for whom Washington's migrating countrymen posed an imminent threat to their hunting grounds and way of life. This intuitive reading of western hopes and doubts helps to explain the administration's repeated military forays against the frontier tribes, its wooing of Spanish courtiers who might favor more liberal access to the Mississippi, and the president's measured response to the first wave of grass-roots resistance to Hamilton's excise tax back in the summer of 1792.

Since then, Congress had taken steps to pacify agrarian discontent, but they were half measures at best. Paying nine cents' tax on a gallon of distilled rye liquor seemed as onerous to this generation of Americans as a two-cent tax on British stamps had to their fathers. Even those willing to swallow their opposition to the tax in principle gagged on the means by which it was enforced.

On July 15, 1794, a federal marshal named David Lenox unwittingly struck a spark that engulfed the whole region in flames. Attempting to serve writs on more than sixty tax evaders, he succeeded only in panicking the residents into believing that their friends and loved ones were being hauled off to appear in a Philadelphia courthouse. The next day, an angry militia went to Bower Hill and attacked the home of John Neville. As the government's well-fed tax collector, Neville symbolized everything offensive to frontier dwellers trapped in virtual peonage. Shots rang out; one of the insurgents fell mortally wounded. That night a mass meeting heard demands for Neville's head. This was Pennsylvania, however, not Paris, and the tax man was in any event disinclined to gratify his vengeful neighbors.

Neville was powerless, however, to halt a much larger force from setting a torch to his property the next day. After an exchange of gunfire in which two of the attackers were killed, Neville was lucky to escape with his life. Rebels seized the feckless David Lenox and forced him, on penalty of death, to recant his support of the tax. In the ensuing days, liberty poles sprouted throughout Washington, Fayette, Westmoreland, and Allegheny counties. Mock trials condemned local respectables to imaginary guillotines. Talk of secession mingled with threats of violence. The Whiskey Rebellion was on.

Delegates meeting at Mingo Creek on July 23 produced an unlikely Daniel Shays in David Bradford, a thirty-four-year-old deputy attorney general for Washington County and vice president of its Democratic Society, allied with the state organization of the same name. At the time of his election, the only violence Bradford engaged in was rhetorical, but three days later he led a raiding party that held up an eastbound mail coach. Inside were found letters from conservative townspeople, petitioning Philadelphia for help in restoring law and order.

Bradford's call for area militia to assemble at Braddock's Field, outside Pittsburgh, on August 1 caused prosperous residents of the little city, dubbed "Sodom" by the rebels, to hide what valuables they were unable to spirit away. Those remaining behind were easily cowed by a ragged line of 7,000 "white Indians" that snaked two miles through apprehensive neighborhoods. At the head of this improvised army rode Bradford, resplendent in a plumed hat and with a glittering sword at his side. One of his soldiers stuck his own, more modest headgear on a rifle barrel and hoisted it high in the air. "I have a bad hat now, but I expect to have a better one soon," he crowed.

When word of the skirmish at Bower Hill reached Philadelphia on July 25, horrified conservatives reacted predictably. At first glance both the government and the rebels stood on familiar ground: it was 1792 all over again. Closer examination revealed significant differences between this uprising and the earlier, mostly verbal, protest. Two years of bitter charges and countercharges had poisoned the political climate, as European hatreds were reflected among Federalists and Republicans who had come to question their opponents' patriotism. In 1792 there had been no Democratic Societies to alarm Washington and other friends of the Constitution. Citizen Genêt was unheard of, Philip Freneau but a mild irritant.

Congress in that year had enacted legislation defining the conditions under which the executive might be empowered to call up troops. Now, in holding to the law, Washington asked Justice James Wilson of the Supreme Court to certify a state of near anarchy in the alienated region around Pittsburgh. Making judicial sanction even more critical was the refusal of Governor Thomas Mifflin, no friend of the president's, to mobilize his state's forces. A stalemate threatened at the end of July, when a stretch of hot dry weather rekindled memories of the previous summer's epidemic of yellow fever. As a precaution, the first family retreated to the stone house in Germantown that Washington had used during the most lethal months of 1793. After paying Colonel Isaac Franks a rent of $201.60, the president had two wagonloads of furniture hauled out from the city to make the place habitable.

The Washingtons took naturally to the semirural ways of Germantown. The first lady was seen leaning out a window to chat with her neighbor, a blacksmith's wife. Young Wash irregularly attended classes at Germantown Academy while his sister rose before dawn each day to perfect her Italian. So attached did Nelly Custis become to the place that she teasingly refused to return to Philadelphia except on her nag, Rozinante, at the head of a "grand cavalcade." By the first week of August, it looked as if her grandfather might soon be leading a cavalcade of his own. At a pivotal conference on the second, Washington decried the western unrest as an ax aimed at the root of constitutional government. Mifflin was unconvinced. By questioning how many Pennsylvanians would take up arms against their fellow citizens and insisting that nothing would drive wavering moderates into the rebel camp faster than overreaction on the part of federal authorities, the governor planted doubts in Washington's mind.

Conflicting advice snowed the president's desk. On the one hand, Hamilton and Knox insisted that 12,000 men were needed to crush the uprising, reassert federal supremacy, and avoid the specter of national dismemberment. "Government can never be said to be established until some signal display has manifested its power of military coercion," argued Hamilton. Opposing him, Randolph, Mifflin, and Attorney General Bradford were unanimous in counseling delay. As Randolph put it, "The strength of a government is the affection of the people." Why destabilize an already fragile situation, alienating responsible elements who might rally behind the administration given time and a conspicuous display of moderation?

Washington cast his lot with administration doves by appointing Attorney General Bradford, his former colleague on the state's supreme court Jasper Yeates, and Senator James Ross to a peace commission. But the president also kept his powder dry. Should David Bradford and his ragtag army fail to negotiate in good faith, a proclamation on August 7 commanding all the insurgents to disperse peaceably by the first day of September hinted at stronger actions. During the period of watchful waiting that followed, the putative peace commissioners tested attitudes on the other side of the mountains. The alarmist reports they relayed back, based largely on secondhand observations, did little to advance a negotiated solution.

Chafing against his self-imposed limits, Washington privately chastised the troublemakers belonging to Genêt-inspired Democratic Societies who were "spreading mischief far and wide either from *real* ignorance" of the government's intentions or in hopes of discrediting the Federalist system. Painful as it was to contemplate "such violent and outrageous proceedings" as held the deluded Pennsylvanians in their grip, the president expected far worse unless his government operated to remove the canker of sedition. "If the laws are to be trampled upon with impunity, and a minority (a small one too) is to dictate to the majority, there is an end put, at one stroke, to republican government."

Throughout August the administration talked peace while preparing for war. Cabinet officers discussed the mechanics of stockpiling arms and supplying a large force in the field. On August 17 Henry Lee tendered his personal services in suppressing the rebellion, whose representatives were reputed to have contacted the British and Spanish ministers in Philadelphia. Thoughts of western treachery were very much on his mind when Washington told Lee, "I consider this insurrection as the first *formidable* fruit of the Democratic Societies. I early gave it as my opinion to the confidential characters around me that, if these Societies were not counteracted (not by prosecutions, the ready way to make them grow stronger) . . . they would shake the government to its foundation." The president castigated frontier agitators for "the most diabolical attempt to destroy the best fabric of human government and happiness that has ever been presented for the acceptance of mankind."

It is easy today to dismiss the threat to Washington and his government in the summer of 1794. Even its name has given the Whiskey Rebellion a faintly comic tinge among historians who have arraigned the administration for employing military force absurdly disproportionate to the handful of malcontents ranged under David Bradford's banner. More recent scholarship has cast doubt on the traditional depictions of impoverished farmers staging a landlocked version of Boston's Tea Party. Yet almost no one has asked the question essential to understanding Washington's behavior during the crisis, indeed, throughout his presidency. Simply put, how much faith did the first president have in the ability of his countrymen to govern themselves?

Daniel Shays's 1786 uprising in western Massachusetts had occasioned a rare but unmistakable airing of doubt. "We have probably had too good an opinion of human nature in forming our confederation," Washington had written in obvious distress during the gravest crisis of his brief postwar furlough at Mount Vernon. "Experience has taught us that men will not adopt and carry into execution measures the best calculated for their own good, without the intervention of a coercive power." The retired general could be forgiven his wary assessment of humankind. Having sparred with Robert Dinwiddie in his youth, outwitted the revolutionary usurper Charles Lee, and stared down the Newburgh Conspiracy that threatened civilian supremacy in the new republic; having experienced personal betrayal and political chicanery at all levels of government, Washington knew at first hand the levers of power and the petty intrigues that attended their use.

As president, he harbored none of the modern reformer's illusions about human perfectibility. Nor did he ever confuse republicanism with pure democracy. Even indirect democracy assumed a virtuous citizenry as the bulwark of popular liberties. Washington had said as much in his first inaugural address, insisting that "there is no truth more thoroughly established than that there exists . . . an indissoluble union between virtue and happiness; between duty and advantage." His was a highly practical idealism, more Roman than Greek in its antecedents, with little of Rousseau's unquestioning celebration of natural man and much of Tidewater Virginia's noblesse oblige.

Still, if he lived apart from most of his fellows, it was at a distance that lent surprising charity to his judgment. "It is to be regretted, I confess, that democratical states must always *feel* before they can *see*," he told Lafayette a year before Shays's insurgency shook his confidence, adding, "It is that that makes their governments slow, but the people will be right at last."

The people, yes, but hardly *vox populi vox Dei.*

Philosophical abstractions aside, Washington had compelling reasons for fearing the whiskey rebels and the leveling impulse they represented. He was only human. He had spent a lifetime climbing the social ladder of respectability, escaping his modest origins, sacrificing personal serenity and physical comfort to win a brutal war and found a nation. With an aristocrat's sense of entitlement, he expected both gratitude and intellectual deference from the cheering masses. For all his assertions of individual modesty, by 1794 Washington regarded himself as the surest interpreter of the Constitution to which he had given sanction and in whose defense he was now prepared to risk bloodshed.

On the personal level, he took umbrage at democrats who questioned his truthfulness while putting harshly critical words about him in the mouths of others. Jefferson, for example. Washington refused to credit a report from the tattling Henry Lee that the former secretary of state was describing the president to friends as a British tool. Jefferson could not possibly think such a thing, Washington countered, "unless . . . he has set me down as one of the most deceitful and uncandid men living." To demonstrate continued faith in his friend, he proposed sending him to Madrid. Who better to pry open the Mississippi — or quiet secession talk in restive Kentucky — than Jefferson, the West's most ardent champion?

There was only one problem. Having been coopted before to support offensive policies, Jefferson had no intention now of forsaking his little mountain for the squalid arena of politics. Pleading a bad case of rheumatism, the Sage of Monticello ruled out any return to public affairs. "I thought myself perfectly fixed in this determination when I left Philadelphia," he told Randolph, "but every day and hour since has added to its inflexibility." Patrick Henry proved no more willing to cross the ocean and test his oratorical powers on Spanish diplomats. Washington, disappointed, finally moved Thomas Pinckney from London to Madrid. At the end of August, the president gave fresh instructions to Jay, urging him to punish any Canadian agents who had incited Indian attacks on the American frontier and vowing that if King George wished to be at peace and to enjoy the benefits of trade with his former colonies, he must vacate the northwestern posts promptly. Washington was adamant: war would be the inevitable price, he insisted, of Britain's failure to implement the yellowing treaty signed eleven years earlier.

❦ 4 ❧

Judging by the latest reports from western Pennsylvania, the president may have thought himself transported to revolutionary France. At a stormy meeting of western representatives on August 28, Albert Gallatin strongly argued for accepting the terms posed by Washington's peace commissioners: amnesty for all lawbreakers and forgiveness of uncollected taxes. Gallatin ridiculed the idea that western Pennsylvania could exist either as an independent nation or as a vassal state of Britain or Spain. But David Bradford dismissed this cautionary appeal, insisting that watergruel Easterners would prove no match for Appalachian sharpshooters. When the roll was called, Bradford's supporters mustered 23 votes against 34 in favor of Washington's offer, not enough to prevail but more than enough to dash hopes for a peaceful settlement.

Quick to perceive his opportunity, Alexander Hamilton was quicker still to seize it. Hamilton was hungry for glory and feeling even more than usually combative that summer. With Henry Knox away from the capital trying to save his overextended Maine investments from ruin, the secretary of the treasury was free to enact his favorite fantasy, that of the avenging man on horseback. To prepare the public for military adventures, he took to the gazettes to pound the ragged sans culottes of western Pennsylvania, by his jaundiced estimate a tiny fraction of the population. He defined the issue in stark terms: "Shall the majority govern or be governed?"

Hamilton had not been noticeably concerned about majority rule in the past. Washington, on the other hand, paid close attention to public opinion as the guiding light of republican government. Far from being Hamilton's tool, as often alleged, the president through his initial conciliatory response went directly against his secretary's advice. Before confronting the rebels with muskets, Washington would attempt to isolate them with words. If force must be used, it would be only after weeks of patient negotiation had demonstrated to the public's satisfaction that no alternative existed.

By the beginning of September, the Whiskey Rebellion had spread to twenty counties in four states. Sedition flourished at Pigeon Creek, Pennsylvania, Isle of Wight, Virginia, and Hagerstown, Maryland. The authority of Washington's government was openly challenged in Washington County, Ohio, as well as Washington County, Pennsylvania. Ragged men intoxicated with rhetoric and whiskey tarred and feathered treasury agents and obstructed the recruitment of militia. With rebellion metastasizing along the nation's Appalachian spine and his War Department unable to send payment to Wayne's Legion for fear that highwaymen would pick the federal pocket, Washington faced a choice between moving forcefully during the weeks of Indian summer or permitting insurgents to use the coming winter to gain fresh credibility.

On September 11, thousands of Pennsylvanians took a loyal oath, but others refused, stranding moderates who added their voices to the chorus demanding federal intervention. Governor Mifflin, relieved of public responsibility for summoning the Pennsylvania militia by Washington's highly visible leadership, came around with a belated call to arms that produced an enthusiastic response from the same countryside held to be of doubtful loyalty just days earlier. The way was cleared for Washington to issue a final proclamation, lamenting that "the well-disposed . . . are unable by their influence and example to reclaim the wicked from their fury." His anger at the Democratic Societies had not cooled, judging from a letter of September 25 blasting the notion that "self-created bodies, forming themselves into *permanent* censors," could arrogate the right to pick among the laws deserving of obedience.

Having come this far, Washington now chose to lend his personal prestige to the federal army in the making by joining the march to Carlisle; from there he could weigh crossing the mountains and invading the heart of the disaffected region. Shortly after ten o'clock on Tuesday morning, September 30, Washington boarded a carriage outside 190 Market Street, with Hamilton on his left and Bartholomew Dandridge on his right. Off they went, general and generalissimo, until they reached the tiny German settlement of The Trappe, their overnight destination. It was close to midnight when the furious pounding of hooves announced Major John Stagg, Knox's chief clerk. Washington's face brightened and his spirits soared as he read Stagg's news, a graphic account of Anthony Wayne's violent encounter with Little Turtle and his confederates.

On the hot, misty morning of August 20, Wayne's Legion had collided with 2,000 warriors from the Shawnee, Wyandot, and Ottawa tribes supplemented by small contingents of English, French, and Canadian Tories. The Indians occupied a high ridge within sight of the British garrison at Fort Miami, their lines stretching for nearly two miles in the twisted remains of a forest blown down years earlier in a tornado. This natural fortress, made seemingly impregnable by additional breastworks, gave the ensuing battle its name: Fallen Timbers. At first it looked to be a repetition of earlier disasters visited on American armies. A few minutes after ten o'clock, an advance party came hurtling back from its forward position pursued by shrieking tribesmen. This was the signal for Wayne to execute his carefully devised plan of attack, deploying well-drilled troops in a double line, with mounted volunteers taking up positions to the front and on the left while the Miami River protected the American right.

Now it was the red men who were exposed, tied to a fixed line of defense and forced to fight a conventional battle. Wayne ordered a bayonet charge to flush the enemy from behind protective stumps and the tall grass of the prairie. As the American cavalry rounded the Indians' left flank, an Ottawa chief named Turkey Foot climbed on top of a prominent boulder and promised his men that the Great Spirit would give them the courage to prevail. Then he fell, mortally wounded by an American bullet. Less than an hour after it began, the battle degenerated into an uneven contest between the horse's hoof and the moccasin. Brightly painted faces made conspicuous targets. Sharp as the blades that cut down fleeing Indians was the betrayal of the tribes' supposed friends, the British. Warriors retreating to the stout walls of Fort Miami found the outpost shut up like a turtle in its shell. Desperate pleas for admission fell on deaf ears, so the murderous chase continued for seven miles along the banks of the bloodied Miami. It was a race the Indian could not win. Some of the defeated tribesmen kept on running until they reached Canada.

Fallen Timbers was marked by savagery on both sides. Among Wayne's reported forty-four dead was an officer hacked into pound pieces as retaliation for the quartering of a young Shawnee chief. The Indians' losses were far more severe. By the time the firing sputtered to a halt, the myth of the red man's invincibility in forest warfare had been punctured. So had his alliance of convenience with the British. The triumphant general moved quickly to consolidate his gains, wiping out several Indian villages and laying waste to 5,000 acres of corn before moving on to decimate the stores of Britain's agent for the region. No stronger message could be sent to the foreign ministry in London that it had better deal seriously with John Jay.

Before the bloody encounter, Little Turtle had warned his fellow chiefs that Wayne was not to be confused with the pedestrian Harmar or indolent St. Clair. This soldier played for high stakes, all right, but without neglecting the unending drills and the thousand routine but vital details that turn a rabble into an army. Wayne deserved the title given him by a respectful adversary: "General who never sleeps." So did his commander in chief. Tossing on his cot during the early hours of October 1, Washington could hardly envision Wayne's Treaty of Greeneville, signed in the summer of 1795, under which the defeated tribes would cede 25,000 square miles in present Indiana, Michigan, and Ohio for $20,000 outright and the promise of $10,000 annually, conditional on their behavior toward the expansive republic now firmly established on the west bank of the Ohio. But the president quickly grasped the implications of Fallen Timbers on both sides of the Appalachians — and both sides of the Atlantic.

With this triumph, Wayne handed Washington a key capable of unlocking the northwestern frontier to thousands of land-hungry American settlers *and* of imprisoning the rebels in Pennsylvania who were trying to dissolve the ligaments of republican government. If the decisive victory did not render Washington's invasion of rebel country anticlimactic, it dramatically shifted the psychological odds against David Bradford and his supporters. Like Wayne, Washington had won his campaign before ever firing a shot. For months he had restrained his urge to smash the rebels militarily. He had skillfully maneuvered public opinion until it crystallized behind tough action and nerved reluctant warriors like Thomas Mifflin. Merely by appearing in the inflamed region, Washington's peace commissioners had enhanced the administration's credibility and exposed radical elements hoping to contest federal might on the field of battle. The resulting split between moderates of Albert Gallatin's stripe and militants itching for blood was skillfully exploited by Washington's advisers. So were scattered (and grossly exaggerated) reports of rebel atrocities.

As the fog cleared around the chief protagonists, ordinary men and women came to realize with the force of revelation that what they confronted was no longer simply a question of internal taxation, noxious since colonial days. As important as the principles being contended for were the rival personalities who had come to symbolize order versus disorder. By the beginning of October 1794, Americans were being asked to choose between George Washington and David Bradford.

❬ 5 ❭

The first part of Washington's western march took him through the rich agricultural country between Philadelphia and Harrisburg. In this prosperous region, heavily populated by German immigrants, the president admired a profusion of Lutheran churches, neat stone barns, and orderly fields. He observed abundant rockfish in the rivers and "a fish which they call salmon." On the morning of October 4, driving his own coach, he forded the Susquehanna at a point where it stretched three quarters of a mile from shore to shore. The only confrontation that day pitted the militias of Pennsylvania and New Jersey against each other for the honor of welcoming the chief executive to Carlisle. By leaving town two hours before dawn, the Philadelphia Light Horse took the prize.

Word of Washington's arrival filtered quickly through the ranks. "The horse marched down the road about two miles," one who was there remembered, "followed by the Jersey cavalry in great numbers. We were drawn up on the right of the road, when our beloved Washington approached on horseback in a traveling dress, attended by his secretary, etc. As he passed our troop, he pulled off his hat and in the most respectful manner bowed to the officers and men." A swelling train of admirers accompanied him into Carlisle, whose streets were clogged with soldiers struck dumb by his presence. Said an onlooker, "Every heart expands with joy except the whiskey boys." Looking out over 3,000 men and sixteen guns, the president declared it the most respectable army he had ever seen. At dinner that night he offered a confident toast: "A happy issue to the business before us."

His optimism was well placed. At Presbyterian services the next morning, the eminent visitor heard "a Political sermon" against the insurrection. On the subject of drunken army officers and mutinous enlisted men the loyal preacher was less outspoken. Yet the so-called Watermelon Army hastily assembled to put down an even more ragtag force reflected society's divisions as much as its collective will. Aristocratic regulars made no secret of their disdain for impoverished or foreign-born volunteers of questionable sentiments and unappeasable hunger. Green soldiers might uncover in the presence of Great Washington, but an hour later they were likely to be foraging for chickens and chopping up fences for firewood.

Washington planned on accompanying this motley army as far as Bedford, there to choose between continuing with them over the mountains or returning to Philadelphia for the reconvening of Congress. Until then, the War Department was advised to send only such articles as were "absolutely necessary" for the president's table, including beef and bread supplied by army contractors. Since Washington was about to enter whiskey country, Bart Dandridge reported, "he proposes to make use of that liquor for his drink." At sixty-two, the fabled equestrian could no longer spend a full day in the saddle and so covered most of Pennsylvania's roads in his carriage. Undiminished, however, was Washington's hold over his fellow citizens. Thousands of Carlisle's residents cheered a courthouse transparency proclaiming WASHINGTON IS EVER TRIUMPHANT. A second banner conveyed local viewpoints held with equal fervor. THE REIGN OF THE LAWS, it read on one side, WOE TO ANARCHISTS on the other.

No anarchists being present, on the morning of October 7, Washington met with the next best thing when two emissaries from the rebel camp presented themselves. Congressman William Findlay was a Republican originally from Ireland, now living in Westmoreland County; his countryman David Redick was a lawyer in Washington County and the former vice president of Pennsylvania. Washington listened carefully as the men described a mass conversion taking place among their constituents. Civil authority was reestablishing itself throughout the region around Pittsburgh, Findlay insisted, although only after a tense period during which friends of the government had slept with firearms at their side. Just as fever animates a sick man, giving him a false sense of strength, so few among the insurgents had actually believed a federal army would take the field against them. Once Bradford's allies recognized their miscalculation, arrogance gave way to terror.

Fearing that a vengeful army might punish residents inclined to accept the administration's offer of amnesty, Findlay and Reddick requested time for the moderates to regain firm control of the situation. Washington promised to hold those arrayed under the federal banner strictly accountable to the laws they enforced. Any soldier disobeying orders or taking reprisal against civilians would "be discharged with infamy." Toward the rebellion itself, however, the president was firm. Too much money and effort had been invested for anything "short of the most unequivocal *proofs* of absolute submission" to forestall the armed columns from moving west.

Before leaving Carlisle on October 12, Washington entrusted command of the army to Lighthorse Harry Lee. Governor Mifflin received second place, despite his questionable politics and alcoholic buffoonery, while behind him ranked New Jersey's governor Richard Howell, whose musical talents had produced a rousing anthem sung in recruiting offices and in the rain-lashed hollows of western Pennsylvania:

> To arms once more our hero cries
> Sedition lives and order dies,
> To peace and ease then bid adieu,
> And dash to the mountains, Jersey Blue.

One did not have to wear a uniform to pick up the song's infectious spirit. On the night of October 13, lights blazed in every window in Williamsport in honor of the visiting chief executive. Crossing into Virginia the next day, Washington paused at the warm springs to which, nearly forty years earlier, he had taken his dying half-brother Lawrence. The roads deteriorated as the presidential party neared Cumberland, the assembly point for the militia of Virginia and Maryland. Swelling the population were 3,200 men in uniform, among them Major George Lewis, one of five Washington nephews in the federal army. Eight hours away by carriage lay Bradford, the common destination for volunteers from New Jersey and Pennsylvania. Here fresh units of artillery, horse, and infantry were lined up for official review. Following a conference on the morning of the twentieth, Washington gave orders for the entire force, 13,000 strong, to begin a final march within seventy-two hours.

He would not go with them, for political battles in Philadelphia now claimed his attention. In a farewell address, he praised the men for their patriotic zeal and unselfish devotion to constitutional government. But he also reminded them of their ultimate duty "to support the laws." It would be a gross violation of trust, he said, for any soldier to disregard that which he was sworn to protect. "The essential principles of a free government confine the provinces of the military to these two objects: 1st to combat and subdue all who may be found in arms in opposition to the national will and authority; 2nd to aid and support the civil magistrate in bringing offenders to justice. The dispensation of this justice belongs to the civil magistrate and let it ever be our pride and our glory to leave the sacred deposit there unviolated."

Early on the twenty-first, Washington climbed into his carriage, leaving Hamilton behind to tie up loose ends. Ahead stretched a week's journey through the glorious plumage of autumn and long hours in which to ponder the origins and lessons of the rebellion so thoroughly crushed. Washington arrived home on the twenty-eighth, still searching for the right words with which to impress Americans of their narrow escape.

❊ 6 ❉

His recent triumph in the field did not incline the president to magnanimity. To Hamilton, still chasing a phantom army in remote hamlets like Jones's Mill and Budd's Ferry, he expressed a desire to send Bradford and other ringleaders to Philadelphia for the winter "by Hook or by Crook." Although Bradford managed to escape to Louisiana, Hamilton rounded up 150 scruffy prisoners and trotted them across the frozen mud of western Pennsylvania. Falling temperatures, inadequate provisions, and taunts from their captors provided a grim escort, as did a victorious general who vowed to chop off the head of any other rascal attempting escape.

The capital was spared the grisly spectacle so familiar to Parisians, but 20,000 Philadelphians turned out anyway to jeer a wretched handful of insurgents who marched through the city with paper cockades in their hats and chains on their ankles. Official juries proved more lenient than the self-appointed judges of the street, acquitting all but two of the accused men, whom Washington later pardoned as mental defectives. Even so, the president approached his forthcoming speech to Congress in a score-settling mood. The more he brooded, the more he convinced himself that the Democratic Societies had seriously miscalculated in provoking the abortive uprising. While the rebels may have changed their language, he told Jay, "their principles want correction," and he intended to set them straight when he addressed Congress.

More than revenge guided his pen. Washington knew that quite apart from its impact on domestic politics, the rebellion had international repercussions — on Jay's mission and Pinckney's looming talks with the Spaniards over western access to the Mississippi. The slightest hint of American disunity would make the work of these diplomats all the more difficult. Better to tell his own story in his own words, Washington concluded, "than to let it go naked into the world, to be dressed up according to the fancy or inclination of the readers, or the policy of our enemies."

On November 19, Philadelphians expecting a dramatic performance packed the House of Representatives. Washington did not disappoint his audience. After sketching the history of the original excise act, the steps taken to enforce it, and the violent opposition they had aroused, the president lashed out at "certain self-created societies," an obvious reference to the Pennsylvania Democratic Society and its ill-mannered offspring. Most Americans had accepted the tax, however grudgingly. But a few counties in western Pennsylvania had combined to frustrate its collection. Disgruntled agrarians had openly defied the law, detained a federal marshal behind bars, and destroyed the property of a revenue collector. Unwilling to temporize with incipient anarchy, the administration had sought and won judicial sanction to move forcibly against the rioters.

The decision to use force against other Americans had not been an easy one. "On this call, momentous in the extreme, I sought and weighed what might best subdue the crisis," said Washington. "On the one hand, the judiciary was pronounced to be stripped of its capacity to enforce the laws; crimes, which reached the very existence of social order, were perpetrated without control; the friends of government were insulted, abused, and overawed into silence." Yielding to such behavior "would be to violate the fundamental principle of our constitution, which enjoins that the will of the majority shall prevail."

Reluctant to incur the embarrassment of a revolutionary government marching to snuff out a rebellion by its own people, the president had postponed hasty action. Commissioners had been sent into the troubled area offering pardons on no other condition than satisfactory assurances that the laws would be obeyed. But "the vicious and turbulent" had spurned his offer, leaving Washington no choice but to summon an army to protect law-abiding citizens and punish miscreants. The subsequent outpouring of volunteers convinced him beyond doubt "that my fellow citizens understand the true principles of government and liberty; that they feel their inseparable union; that notwithstanding all the devices which have been used to sway them from their interest and duty, they are now as ready to maintain the authority of the laws against licentious invasions, as they were to defend their rights against usurpation."

He would not soon forget, said Washington, the exhilarating sight of Americans from all classes serving side by side in "the army of the constitution," undeterred by jagged mountains, country roads that were little more than icy gashes in the steep terrain, and unceasingly hostile weather. He contrasted the instinctive patriotism of the enlisted man with that of the guileful Westerners, who had set themselves up, like a modern Caesar's Legion, in opposition to the people's elected representatives. "And when in the calm moments of reflection, they shall have retraced the origin and progress of the insurrection," the president said of his countrymen, "let them determine whether it has not been fomented by combinations of men who, careless of consequences and disregarding the unerring truth — that those who rouse, cannot always appease a civil convulsion — have disseminated . . . suspicions, jealousies, and accusations of the whole government."

Washington's audience sat immobilized, the stillness in the crowded chamber broken only by muffled sounds of weeping from the galleries. In weathering the challenge, he had fulfilled his sacred oath to preserve, protect, and defend the Constitution. Now he proclaimed, with undisguised emotion, that "on you, Gentleman, and the people by whom you are deputed, I rely for support."

Among the opposition members in Congress Hall were many who squirmed in embarrassment for the aging hero. Could he really be so out of touch with popular sentiments? Had the sound of cheering crowds dulled his instincts or drowned out the distress cries of peaceably assembled farmers? Madison declared Washington's unbridled attack on the Democratic Societies the greatest political blunder of his life. More perceptively, he reminded lawmakers that "the censorial power is in the people over the government and not in the government over the people."

A fierce debate erupted over the House's official response to the executive. Republicans, half defiant, half apologetic, moved to repudiate the most extreme of Washington's claims by striking out the inflammatory phrase "self-created societies." Tempers flared as Madison's allies identified numerous such organizations flourishing in the United States. There were the Sons of Tammany, they reminded anyone who would listen, and the Society of Friends; even that prideful bastion of old soldiers whose taste for rank mirrored the titled society against which they had fought and won a revolution, the Society of the Cincinnati. Moreover, said William Branch Giles, with a sly dig at the aristocratic Senate meeting upstairs, if the chief offense of the Democratic Societies was that "they began their business after dinner, bolted their doors and voted in the dark . . . is there no other place where people bolt their doors and vote in the dark?"

Washington's speech and its stormy sequel strained old friendships. Thomas Jefferson, for one, was moved to personal condemnation. Already recorded in opposition to the administration's military campaign ("An insurrection was announced and proclaimed and armed against, but could never be found"), the great champion of free speech and free thought apprehended in Washington's strident words confirmation of his worst fears — the monocrats had at last captured the president. What a tragedy, thought Jefferson, that George Washington, the symbol of man's age-old desire to taste the fruits of liberty, should now permit himself to become an instrument in the suppression of basic rights to discuss and dissent and publish.

In this, Jefferson misread his former chief, although no more than Washington himself underestimated the chilling effect of his emotionally charged sentences. As the president saw it, nothing less was at stake than the survival of a central government strong enough to defend the republican system adopted in 1787 and since confirmed by the voting public. While others formed ranks around party standards or economic systems or European alliances, Washington planted his banner where he had always stood, upon a Constitution whose delicate balance was threatened by the ancient enemies of republics, domestic factionalism and foreign influence.

The House was just as resolute in its opposition. Ten days later, Washington listened politely as Speaker Frederick Muhlenberg delivered a mild rebuke in the parlor of 190 Market Street. Pointedly missing from his comments was any mention of "self-created societies," the deleted catchphrase. A far more welcome sound lured Washington from his desk on a frosty December afternoon when the shrill fifes of a company of Jersey Blues led by Major William MacPherson marched into Philadelphia for an impromptu homecoming parade. The president reviewed the column from his doorstep with unconcealed pride. A reporter observing the scene wrote that "the father of his country expressed in his countenance more than can be described." The look on his face was answer enough to Washington's growing body of critics.

❈ II ❈

DOWN FROM OLYMPUS

"One John, surnamed Jay, journeyed into a far country, even until Great Britain. 2. And the word of Satan
came unto him saying, Make thou a covenant with this
people, whereby they may be enabled to bring the
Americans into bondage, as heretofore. 3. And John
answered unto Satan, of a truth . . . let me find grace
in thy sight, that I may secretly betray my country
and the place of my nativity."

"An Emetic for Aristocrats,"
Summer 1795

WASHINGTON ENJOYED playing paterfamilias to the unruly brood of
nieces and nephews, adopted grandchildren, and assorted young men
beginning their careers who constituted his surrogate family. Halfway
through January 1795, he took it upon himself to counsel Nelly Custis
on the snares and satisfactions of intimate love. Echoing the warnings
administered to Nelly's sister, the president saw through his granddaughter's caustic appraisal of would-be suitors, including one unfortunate
gallant dismissed as a "little milk and water monkey."

No revolution could repeal the iron laws that governed human emotions, Washington told the sharp-tongued young woman; "men and
women feel the same inclinations to each other *now* that they have always
done." Neither should Nelly strike quite so disinterested a pose, for the
day would come when she discovered "that the passions of your sex are
easier raised than allayed . . . In the composition of the human frame
there is a good deal of inflammable material, however dormant it may lie
for a time."

As an involuntary emotion, love was held to be irresistible. With this

Washington disagreed, and to clinch his case he conjured up an imaginary woman of ravishing beauty and accomplishment — the principle applied equally to either sex, he hastened to add — who fired men's hearts all around her. Let this stunning creature once plight her troth to another, however, and what was the result? "The madness ceases and all is quiet again." Washington thought he knew why. "Not because there is any diminution of the charms of the lady, but because there is an end of hope."

A corollary to this rule was that love must be guided by reason and self-interest. Said Washington, "When the fire is beginning to kindle, and your heart growing warm, propound these questions to it. Who is this invader? Have I a competent knowledge of him? Is he a man of good character; a man of sense? For, be assured, a sensible woman can never be happy with a fool." Assuming that her prospective life partner was neither gambler, spendthrift, or drunkard, that he could support Nelly in her accustomed manner, and that he inspired among her friends no reasonable objection, the most critical factor of all remained to be weighed: "Have I sufficient ground to conclude that his affections are engaged by me?"

Here Washington the traditionalist insisted that any declaration of the heart "to render it permanent and valuable" must come from masculine lips. Sally Fairfax may have flashed across the old man's mental screen as he cautioned his granddaughter against toying with the emotions of vulnerable Lotharios. Many was the coquette who died celibate as punishment for encouraging looks, words, or actions given "for no other purpose than to draw men on to make overtures that they may be rejected."

Giving advice is a privilege of the elderly, and Washington indulged himself often during the grim winter of 1794–95. Concerned that American scholars pursuing their studies in Europe might become infected with the anti-republican virus, he questioned John Adams's scheme to import the entire faculty of the University of Geneva, believing it much better for the young nation growing into a sense of itself to develop its own men of letters, far removed from the hazards and temptations of European society. So Washington campaigned for a great national university to be established in the Federal City, where it could melt local prejudices and regional attachments in a nationalist solvent. The president would help his academy for patriots by donating fifty shares of stock in the Potomac Company.

Washington's visionary proposal was doomed at a time when apprehensive Republicans, fearing for the survival of state and local jurisdictions, viewed a national university as a federal Trojan horse. These concerns had scarcely diminished thirty years later, when the first president's political heir, John Quincy Adams, earned ridicule for his ambitious attempt to forge a stronger union through social and intellectual assimilation.

Late in January, Washington wrote elegiacally to Edmund Pendleton, congratulating his Virginia friend on completing seventy-three years in tolerable health and with vigorous mental faculties intact. The president could not resist a grim postscript: "A month from this day, if I live to see the completion of it, will place me on the wrong (perhaps it would be better to say, on the advanced) scale of my grand climacteric; and although I have no cause to complain of the want of health, I can religiously aver that no man was ever more tired of public life, or more devoutly wished for retirement, than I do."

Few rays of light penetrated Washington's growing melancholy. Although buoyed by Wayne's triumph at Fallen Timbers, the executive differed with Pendleton and other Virginians bent on eradicating the red man as part of their own racial manifest destiny. He told his friend plainly that Americans were breaking the law when they encroached upon Indian lands protected by treaty. And he sounded a note of authentic, if ineffectual, sympathy for the retreating tribes: "They, poor wretches, have no Press through which their grievances are related; and it is well known, that when one side only of a story is heard, and often repeated, the human mind becomes impressed with it, insensibly."

Washington did take heart from the defeat of the western rebels, convinced that his government's actions in crushing the tax revolt disproved once and for all the sneers of contemptuous British statesmen that the United States was ungovernable. Republicanism was a force to be reckoned with, and even transatlantic skeptics must soon conclude "that under no form of government will laws be better supported, liberty and property better secured, or happiness be more effectually dispensed to mankind." Turning his gaze from the turbulent frontier to the "madness" of Europe, ravaged by war, Washington found in the Old World's boiling cauldron irrefutable evidence for his policy of constructive isolation. Let others succumb to national jealousies, hatreds, and military designs; the United States would vindicate popular government on its own soil without threatening the peace or prosperity of its neighbors (excepting the Indian).

One thing was obvious: America's existence depended on the continuation of peace. Scanty reports from London hinted at progress in Jay's talks with Lord Grenville, but a rigid secrecy imposed by circumstances and the prying eyes of French sympathizers caused maddeningly few details to leak out. In the absence of fact, Philadelphia fed on gossip and rumor. The aristocratic Jay was maligned for a veritable catalogue of crimes, real and imagined, beginning with his deferential manners at the British court. By pressing his lips to the hand of Queen Charlotte, screamed Bache's *Aurora* and like-minded journals, the chief justice was guilty of the greatest betrayal since Judas kissed his Lord in Gethsemene. At the end of January the *Aurora* reported that a treaty had been concluded. Three weeks passed with no confirmation, leading Bache to jibe that perhaps Jay's treaty had frozen in mid-Atlantic.

Washington had other things on his mind, chiefly the impending loss of his most valued adviser. By the start of 1795, his diplomatic ambitions thwarted, his political base eroding, his freedom to set financial policy coming under increasing scrutiny from the House's new Ways and Means Committee, Alexander Hamilton had had enough. The fiscal wizard whose controversial policies had made fortunes for others estimated his personal worth at less than $500. "A rising family hath its claim," he told friends, who did not have to be reminded of Betsey Hamilton's recent miscarriage while her husband was off subduing rebellious farmers.

On January 31, Hamilton sent his resignation to the president, who replied that "in every relation which you have borne to me, I have found that my confidence in your talents, exertions, and integrity has been well placed." The same day Comptroller of the Treasury Oliver Wolcott, an intimate of Hamilton's, was nominated to succeed the retiring secretary. As the Little Great Man made his way north, he was lionized by those of the business and commercial classes most directly aided by Hamiltonian prosperity. Back in New York he plunged into the practice of law, where his brains and connections guaranteed immediate success. For most men this would have been enough, but Hamilton was sui generis. Neither handsome retainers nor verbal fisticuffs in front of sedate judges could compensate for his exile from power.

Angelica Church understood. Like Eliza Powel stripping away Washington's disinterested mask to reveal his voracious appetite for fame, Hamilton's perceptive sister-in-law wondered if "a mind engaged by Glory can taste of peace and ease?"

With Hamilton's departure, only Edmund Randolph remained of Washington's original Cabinet, and he, thoroughly disenchanted with the bombardment of Monroe's demands from Paris, was jockeying for a seat on the Supreme Court. Monroe's discomfort mattered little to the president, who was perfectly willing to let the Virginian stew in the juices he had so rashly stirred through his uncompromising support of France's revolutionary excesses.

Washington counted the days until the adjournment of Congress early in March. On February 19 he attended a service of thanksgiving at Christ Church for the defeat of the western insurgency. He sent Robert Livingston a pamphlet on the cultivation of potatoes, paid his dentist in New York $60 for a new set of dentures, endorsed a process to improve the manufacture of nails, and signed five hundred "Sea letters" required of vessels leaving U.S. territorial waters. For a relative with adolescent sons, Washington analyzed the relative merits of academies at Andover and Hingham, Massachusetts. Without hesitation he urged a northern education for the boys, explaining that "order, regularity and a proper regard for morals" were more prevalent in cooler climes than in torpid Virginia and mentioning the nearby presence of Harvard College, an institution which was, "I am told, in high repute."

Washington warmly greeted the usual throng of well-wishers observing his sixty-third birthday. That evening, nearly 500 admirers squeezed into Rickett's Circus for a ball and supper, whose master of ceremonies was the same Benjamin Franklin Bache renowned for poisoning the fountains of opinion against the man whose birthday celebration he now improbably managed. The object of this lavish tribute would have gladly traded all the flattery in Philadelphia for one authenic copy of Jay's treaty. He could not know that two copies of the precious document had been put aboard the same English packet, only to be hurled into the sea when a French privateer drew alongside. By the time a third copy eluded the French searchers of another vessel and arrived safely in Norfolk, Washington despaired of action being taken during that session of Congress.

On March 3, less than twenty-four hours before the lawmakers were scheduled to adjourn, he sent a cryptic message to the Senate, inviting it to reconvene in June to address "certain matters touching the public good." Three days later, after a harrowing journey of more than three months, the treaty was delivered to Randolph's office by a dusty courier. The secretary hurried to the president's house, where he deposited the sealed copy and a brief letter from Jay dismissing any hope of further concessions from a British ministry still puffed up over recent military triumphs against the French. "If this treaty fails, I despair of another," said the chief justice with depressing candor. "If I entirely escape censure, I shall be agreeably disappointed. Should the treaty prove, as I believe it will, beneficial to our country, justice will *finally* be done. If not, be it so — my mind is at ease."

Jay could afford to take the long view, for he did not have to sell the treaty to a suspicious populace. Neither, it appeared, did he have any intention of defending his diplomatic creation. "It must speak for itself," he told the president. "To do more was not possible."

❊ 2 ❊

Jay's defensive tone was borne out in the treaty he had negotiated. Indeed, a first reading of the twenty-eight articles suggested that Washington's experiment in secret diplomacy had blown up in his face. Instructed to secure American rights and open British markets, the chief justice did neither. Although agreeing to evacuate the northwestern posts no later than June 1, 1796, the British retained a share of the lucrative fur trade on both sides of the U.S.-Canadian boundary. In exchange for this concession, no more than a belated promise to carry out the terms of the old peace treaty, Jay had bargained away his country's wartime rights as a neutral power.

Jettisoning the idea that free ships make free goods, the American envoy accepted Britain's broad definition of contraband, opened U.S. ports to British vessels without obtaining reciprocal concessions, closed the American coastline to any ship or privateer in service to the king's enemies, and awarded most favored trading status to a nation currently waging an undeclared war upon the Yankee fleet. Jay did manage to breach the high wall around India, a concession denied English captains at the mercy of the monopolistic East India Company. But he failed dismally in obtaining damages for British spoilations against Yankee commerce. Instead, the question of illegal maritime seizures was referred to a joint arbitration commission, as was the disputed northeastern boundary and the claims of British creditors for prerevolutionary debts blocked by American legislators.

Deciding not to decide the debt issue was sure to anger Southerners, who owed a disproportionate share of the bill. And by making no mention of U.S. sailors impressed into the British navy, Jay was just as likely to offend northern shipping interests. A committed abolitionist, he exerted little pressure on Pitt's government to return southern slaves carried off by British troops or to reimburse their owners. As a result the document Washington held in his hands early in March 1795 was silent on the slave question.

Another likely target of southern anger was Article 12, which struck at the region's rapidly expanding cotton economy through a clause prohibiting American ships from carrying such staples as cotton, coffee, sugar, cocoa, and molasses to any foreign destination. The same article opened the British West Indies to U.S. carriers of seventy tons or less, but in such humiliating terms as to solidify Yankee subservience to the British lion. Finally, Jay had been instructed to make no commitment violating his country's existing treaties with France. Yet Article 12 would practically eliminate trade, direct or indirect, between the allies.

Washington had every right to be disappointed and every reason to keep the treaty secret as long as possible. The first week of June would bring senators back to Philadelphia for what promised to be a contentious debate. If the document leaked before then, opposition editors would run riot, caricaturing the pliant John Jay tugging his forelock while repealing America's economic independence. Politicians would follow where the press pointed. Fiercely alert to any political opening, Republicans in Congress smelled diplomatic surrender or, worse, treachery.

Those who knew Jay best knew better. The chief justice was a patriot, but also a realist. Had he resorted to threats or even dropped hints that the former colonies contemplated joining an armed league of neutrals in opposition to British raiders on the high seas, the men across the bargaining table would have laughed in his face before handing him his passport. In the end, Lord Grenville settled with the upstart republic on what many in Parliament, if not Congress, viewed as unnecessarily generous terms, not because he feared America's might but because he valued America's neutrality in the much larger contest with Jacobin France. Put bluntly, it was in King George's interest to strengthen Federalist elements against Gallic sympathizers, while British merchants had compelling reasons of their own to cultivate peace with their American cousins, who owed them far too much money to be warred upon.

But this view from London was shared by almost no one in the United States. Jay's Treaty left the president in a quandary. Having invested so much political capital in the mission, Washington could not reject the barren spoils of his diplomacy without increasing the chances of war or yielding the initiative to congressional Republicans, who blithely expected an imminent English defeat at French hands. (Jefferson said he looked forward to drinking tea in London with a republican government.) Yet by 1795, Royal George showed no inclination to disappear in accordance with the Jeffersonian timetable. He retained the world's most formidable naval fighting force, against which the United States could muster but a handful of paper ships and firebreathing journalists.

If no one around the president was happy with Jay's creation, few could plausibly imagine a better pact resulting from a second round of negotiations. What most justified the treaty was American self-interest, pure and simple. Jay had bought peace, the most precious of all commodities and essential if the United States was to survive, much less grow into the continental power envisioned by Washington.

The president was hardly alone in being challenged by Jay's diplomatic conundrum. In many ways Edmund Randolph had the toughest job that spring. Balancing his personal doubts about the treaty against loyalty to the man he venerated more than any other, the secretary of state was also trying to cajole French representatives in high dudgeon over what they perceived to be an Anglo-American stab in the back. Before leaving American shores in August 1795, Joseph Fauchet contemptuously dismissed Randolph's assurances of continued friendship. For good measure, he engaged in a furtive newspaper campaign charging Jay with selling out his country for English gold.

Needing time to think, to calmly review the narrowing options before him, on April 14 the president set out for Virginia. His visit, the first in eight months, was marred by legal wrangling in the Federal City and an attempt by revolutionary forces to replace the Dutch Stadtholder with a French puppet regime. By early May, Washington was back in Philadelphia, expressing sorrow over the death of a plantation slave, a young fellow of considerable promise. "I hope every necessary care and attention was afforded him," he told William Pearce. "I expect little of this from (Overseer) McKoy, or indeed from most of his class, for they seem to consider a Negro much in the same light as they do the brute beasts on the farms, and often treat them as inhumanely."

About this time Hamilton returned to the scene of his earlier triumphs, successfully arguing before the Supreme Court the case for a federal tax on carriages, a measure that upset southern stomachs on fiduciary as well as constitutional grounds. He and the president presumably compared notes on the flawed treaty and on the Federalist campaign to reverse George Clinton's theft of 1793 by installing Jay in the New York governor's office. Electoral victory was in sight on the morning of May 28, when the returning diplomat sailed into New York Harbor after a dreary voyage marked by thirty-two consecutive days of rain. Rheumatic, seasick, his eyes smarting from London's infernal fogs and smoke, the ailing chief justice was escorted to his home by cheering admirers. It is significant that Jay won the governorship before the results of his mission were made public; no future electorate would entrust him with office.

Early in June senators reconvened for the most critical foreign policy debate in the young republic's history. Jay's highly spiced diplomatic stew would be more palatable, Federalists believed, if divested of the hugely unpopular Article 12. On the night of June 8, as Washington and his vice president discussed over dinner the administration's emerging strategy to detach the offensive article in hopes of salvaging the remaining twenty-seven, Fauchet was assuring his government that at least eleven senators, one more than necessary, would stand fast in their opposition.

To guard against undue influence by the voice of the people, Federalists soundly defeated a Republican motion to publish the treaty's contents immediately. Thus stymied, opposition editors opened their batteries on the elitist Senate, with Bache aiming his deadliest fire at "the secret lodge of Philadelphia."

Shutting out the public worked both ways, insulating lawmakers from popular anger but also breeding rumors of impending defeat that caused a wave of panic to sweep New York's financial circles, already reeling from the unexpected sight of a French Tricolor fluttering atop the Tontine Coffee House, citadel of Manhattan's financial establishment. On June 15 Federalist legislators, taking their cue from Hamilton, rewrote the treaty by setting aside the obnoxious Article 12. Aaron Burr leapt up to propose gutting the treaty and authorizing a new mission, closer in spirit to Jay's original instructions. In losing, Burr won a victory of sorts by introducing the explosive issue of compensation for southern slaves emancipated by British redcoats.

Proslavery, antitreaty Republicans looked upon the South's peculiar institution as a test of sectional solidarity, one strong enough to breach party lines. They were very nearly right. Believing the momentum to be with them, Burr and his supporters rolled the dice a second time in hopes of killing the treaty outright. This time, however, with slavery relegated to the sidelines, party discipline reasserted itself. On June 25, the administration prevailed on a 20-10 vote, the minimum required for passage. Sixteen days of heated, often bitter, debate had failed to change any minds. And this was just the beginning. For while the Senate could advise and consent, only the president, through his signature, could formally ratify a diplomatic agreement. And thus far neither Washington nor the average American had been heard from.

❦ 3 ❧

Within twenty-four hours of the Senate's approval, treaty opponents found a new stage for action and a voice for their rage. Bache's *Aurora* hit the streets of Philadelphia with a full-throated assault on "this imp of darkness, illegitimately begotten." At seven o'clock on the morning of July 2, long lines formed outside the *Aurora* office, where copies of the hotly disputed document were on sale at twenty-five cents apiece. Enthused Bache's wife, "It was more like a fair than anything else." She had reason to be pleased as she anticipated a new house made possible with the proceeds from her husband's most profitable publication ever.

Beaten to the punch, administration supporters found themselves limply arguing for a bad treaty as preferable to none at all. Complicating their task was a new Order in Council from Pitt's government resuming the seizure of neutral vessels. Washington struggled to maintain his objectivity. He asked Hamilton to submit a detailed critique of the treaty without hesitating to express his personal resentment of Article 3, which opened U.S. ports to the British while forgoing similar access for Americans. Washington thought it grossly unfair to admit British fur traders south of the Canadian border yet permit the Hudson's Bay Company a royally sanctioned monopoly over much of the frozen north. His rationale was based on much more than fur trappings. By restricting each country's residents to their native territory, he hoped to reduce chances of Indian mischief-making and, with it, the possibility of accidental warfare between the treaty's signatories.

In July's suffocating heat, Washington cast longing eyes toward Mount Vernon. The political temperature was rising faster than the mercury as Bache furnished ammunition to the treaty's foes and crowds celebrated July Fourth by torching an effigy of "Sir John Jay." Henceforth, claimed the opposition, the nation's birthday would be observed as a day of mourning for Liberty, slain at the hands of King George. A satirical toast reflected the popular mood: "A Perpetual Harvest to America, but clipped wings, lame legs, the pip and an empty crop to all Jays." Only the timely arrival of some cavalry troops prevented the demonstrators from burning the despised treaty on Washington's doorstep. Denied that pleasure, the crowd gratified itself by hurling insults at the British minister and a stray brick or two through Anne Bingham's elegant windows.

It was a tense and divided capital that the president left behind him on July 15. Even as he wavered between approval and rejection of Jay's Treaty, the mood of the country was unmistakably hostile. Bostonians, their indignation raised to a fever pitch by the ubiquitous Bache, turned out in massive numbers at a Faneuil Hall rally that denounced the treaty without bothering to have it read. Yankees for whom civil disobedience in the name of liberty was old hat happily burned a British privateer in Boston Harbor. News of the protest reached Washington as he was boarding his carriage in Baltimore. He immediately forwarded the information to Randolph, confiding at the same time his belief that the amended treaty, however imperfect, was preferable to the status quo. Assuming the British called a halt to their illegal seizure of American vessels, Washington would sign the treaty and brave the inevitable storm of public anger.

Anything was better than the rise of party spirit so evident in the Boston proceedings. "This difficulty to one who is of no party, and whose sole wish is to pursue with undeviating steps a path which would lead this country to respectability, wealth and happiness is exceedingly to be lamented," sighed Washington. As a wave of opposition rolled across the land, support for his foreign policy crumbled in the unlikeliest of places. A fistfight broke out in the pews of the Quincy, Massachusetts, meetinghouse attended by Vice President Adams. Merchants in Portsmouth, New Hampshire, assembled outside the State House to shake their fists at "that perfidious corrupting and corrupted nation," England. Charleston's Republicans accused Federalist senators of treason; hotheaded legislators in Virginia whispered of seceding from the Union.

And everywhere, it seemed, Jay was pilloried for his diplomatic sellout. Effigies of the hated New Yorker were pelted with stones, dragged through streets in dung carts, suspended from a hundred branches. The chief justice wryly commented that he could make his way across the continent by the light of his flaming likenesses.

On July 18 it was Hamilton's turn to feel the leveling force of the streets. Thinking he would improve the occasion of a mass rally outside New York's City Hall with some pro-treaty oratory, the advocate was forced off his soapbox by a hail of stones. Hamilton said that he had no choice but to retire in the face of such "knock down arguments." Embittered Federalists accused the mob of trying to reduce the secretary to its level by first dashing his brains out. A rally in Philadelphia two days later drew 1,500 or 5,000 to register a noisy dissent, depending on which partisan editor one chose to believe.

Washington, at Mount Vernon, learned of the fracas in New York on July 27. The next day he sent a formal reply, drafted with Randolph's help, to the selectmen of Boston. "In every act of my administration, I have sought the happiness of my fellow citizens," he began. "My system for the attainment of this object has uniformly been to overlook . . . personal, local and partial considerations . . . and to consult only the substantial and permanent interests of our country." Concerning the treaty, "I have weighed with attention every argument which has at any time been brought into view. But the constitution is the guide which I will never abandon." Under its provisions, the executive and senators were assigned exclusive responsibility for the conduct of foreign relations "without passion and with the best means of information" available, never yielding to mere popular opinion where it clashed with their own deeply held convictions. "While I feel the most lively gratitude for the many instances of approbation from my country," he concluded in a voice both plaintive and proud, "I can no otherwise deserve it than by obeying the dictates of my conscience."

Washington's response would have been more effective, if perhaps less emotionally satisfying to its author, had he taken Randolph's advice and explicitly linked his signature on the controversial treaty to the cancellation of Britain's most recent offensive against neutral shipping. His failure to make this connection suggests that he was preparing public opinion for eventual ratification, whatever the personal consequences. Strengthening this view was a letter the president wrote to Hamilton near the end of July. "At present the cry against the Treaty is like that against a mad dog," Washington remarked in something close to despair. Brightening, he archly complimented a certain New York scribbler who, under the pen name Camillus, was endeavoring to place the treaty before the public in the most favorable light. Washington's only concern was that Camillus's persuasive voice might not reach into enough homes to turn the tide "whilst the opposition pieces will spread their poisons in all directions."

Here Washington paused to define a crucial difference between the dangerously complacent friends of order and those in the enemy camp, complaining that "the latter are always working, like bees, to distill their poison; whilst the former, depending, often times *too much* and *too long* upon the sense . . . of the people to work conviction, neglect the means of effecting it."

Hamilton required no reminder of the people's shortcomings, or of the threat popular sovereignty posed to the Federalist establishment, to motivate his furious output. Armed with private information from Jay and girded by Rufus King's occasional literary assistance, the Little Great Man dashed off thirty-eight installments, vividly portraying every imaginable horror resulting from the treaty's defeat. In his feverish prose western Indians ravaged an unprotected frontier, civil war tore the United States asunder, Americans staggered under the weight of unsecured debt, and republican theories of government were permanently discredited. So powerful were Hamilton's arguments, so provocative his words, that Jefferson beseeched Madison to unsheathe his pen and join the battle. "Without numbers he is a host within himself," Jefferson concluded of his brilliant adversary.

There was much truth in this, but the veteran pamphleteer was not without allies. Also writing pieces in support of the treaty that August was Noah Webster, a fervent nationalist as committed to standardizing America's political culture as its spelling. But the path to ratification was all uphill. Old fears of popular emotionalism flooded in upon Washington, who sounded as if he were trying to persuade himself of a doubtful case when he told Randolph, "In time, when passion shall have yielded to sober reason, the current may possibly turn." Sure enough, chambers of commerce in New York, Boston, Philadelphia, and Charleston bestirred themselves at last. Still, their belated endorsements were all but lost in a wave of negative resolutions swamping Mount Vernon.

Lacking secretarial assistance, Washington had trouble keeping abreast of his correspondence. Not that every petition warranted a civil response. "Tenor indecent. No answer returned," he scrawled on a message from unhappy residents of Petersburg, Virginia. An address from Republicans in New Jersey received the same treatment, filed away as "too rude to merit a reply."

Born of desperation, the strategy of the treaty's supporters was plain. Unable to win a majority on the substance of their case, they fell back on a slogan made familiar by repetition over two centuries: Support the President. Some Republicans were disinclined to give up on the old hero so easily. The Portsmouth *Gazette* was among those believing the president open to persuasion. "Thank heaven we have a Washington left to check the growth of British influence," it declared at the end of July. By then Washington had rejected Randolph's offer to come to Mount Vernon for a personal review of the treaty's tumultuous reception. His Cabinet opposed the president's counterproposal — that he interrupt his vacation for a quick trip to Philadelphia — as likely to only encourage the mobs in the streets.

A summer cloudburst drenched the countryside around Mount Vernon, sweeping away bridges and leaving the president physically as well as politically isolated. Increasing his frustration, a blundering postmaster at Alexandria mixed up correspondence addressed to and from the executive. On August 5, Washington opened two letters, one from the Cabinet advising against a trip to Philadelphia anytime soon; the second, an appeal from Randolph to come back as quickly as possible.

Yet a third missive signed by Timothy Pickering urged the president to make diplomatic hay while the sun shone by cutting short his vacation and taking advantage of George Hammond's imminent departure. Deepening the mystery, an overwrought Pickering expressed "extreme solicitude" on the subject of the treaty, "and for a special reason which can be communicated to you only in person." He further requested that Washington defer any significant decisions until he was back in the capital, concluding this melodramatic appeal by identifying himself as "Yours and my country's friend."

Understandably puzzled by the contradictory signals, Washington decided to return to Philadelphia as soon as the weather permitted. Not until August 6 did his coach rumble out of Mount Vernon's gate and head north. With a moist finger raised in the breeze of public opinion, Washington anxiously sought news en route of mass meetings called in Richmond and Baltimore to discuss the treaty.

❦ 4 ❧

"I am a child of the Revolution," Edmund Randolph once asserted, as if hoping to conceal the politically dubious parentage of a Tory father, who had fled to England early in the rebellion with Virginia's deposed royal governor. Young Edmund's family disgrace had been salved by General Washington, who accepted Randolph into his personal circle as an aide de camp. With no children of his own on which to project future hopes, Washington grew close to the deferential youth. Their intimacy survived publication of letters forged by Randolph's father denigrating the commanding officer's patriotism.

Made legitimate, so to speak, by his brief military career, Randolph went on to twenty years of public service as mayor of Williamsburg, attorney general of his state, a member of Congress, Virginia's postwar governor, and moving force behind the Annapolis Convention of 1786 that led to the Constitutional Convention of the following summer. At Philadelphia, Randolph introduced the Virginia Plan for a federal government resting upon the power and wealth of large states, then backed away from his proposal and refused to sign the convention's final product. A self-proclaimed "recusant" in Virginia's bitter ratification struggle, Randolph was finally goaded by Patrick Henry's harshly personal criticism into leading a successful Federalist drive. After engineering ratification by the narrowest of margins, Randolph zigzagged again, this time endorsing Henry's call for a second convention to address the shortcomings of the first.

Long before joining the Cabinet as attorney general in the summer of 1790, the forty-year-old Virginian had earned a reputation for amiable equivocation. Nothing about his bland face, huge, placid eyes, or mellifluous courtesies diminished the suspicion that Randolph was too emotionally scarred by his traitorous parent, too vulnerable to fears of abandonment to hazard his fragile self-esteem for the sake of conviction. Thomas Jefferson considered his cousin, descended from one of Virginia's most prominent officeholding families, an intellectual weather vane. A more perceptive observer would say of Randolph that, having witnessed at first hand the destructive passions sparked by war and the constitutional ratification process, he instinctively shied away from factional loyalties and their consequences.

Like Washington, Randolph fancied himself a man of the middle, struggling to maintain a precarious foothold as waves of domestic upheaval and foreign intrigue eroded the political center. Both men traveled naturally in paths of conciliation, shunning extremes and disdaining partisan entrapment. But where the president floated serenely above political parties, his less gifted protégé appeared merely to be without one. His stubborn adherence to the middle of the road had won him few friends as attorney general. Federalists resented his support for Jefferson's stance on sixteen of nineteen major disputes referred to the Cabinet, while Republicans emotionally committed to suppressing Hamilton's monocrats did not stop to admire Randolph's plodding judiciousness.

Only in Washington's book was moderation counted no sin. Over time, Randolph became increasingly useful for his independence and his literary skills. The president heeded his attorney general in vetoing a congressional reapportionment plan in the spring of 1792, turning to him again a year later to draft a neutrality proclamation distancing the United States from Europe's murderous quarrels. Washington could not fail to observe how Randolph kept his head during the crisis that followed, showing a devotion bordering on sycophancy. He handled the president's personal legal business without charge, instructed Washington's nephews in the law, and faithfully reported Mrs. Washington's state whenever her husband was away from the capital on official business.

At the end of 1794, when Jefferson finally made good on his long threatened resignation, Randolph had assumed a special place at the heart of Washington's government. Despite his affection for the younger man, Washington did not view Randolph as his first choice to succeed Jefferson, or even his second. Neither, apparently, did Randolph himself, who envisioned at most a short-term appointment to the portfolio of state, followed by elevation to the Supreme Court, where he could indulge his judicial temperament without the costly entertaining demanded of the nation's chief diplomatic officer. Not to put too fine a point on it, Edmund Randolph was broke. Poor management and the demands of a large family to which he — unlike his father before him — set an example of deep devotion had driven the attorney general to cadge money from resentful colleagues.

In his impecuniousness as in his politics Randolph was bipartisan, borrowing a few hundred dollars at a time from Cabinet associates and members of Congress on both sides of the aisle. This fact, widely broadcast, did as much as anything to foster a climate in which his adversaries could blacken his character. What prevented the high-strung Virginian from becoming a political outcast was his constituency of one. Washington tolerated his uncertainties, tortured interpretations, and hypersensitivity, just as he had overlooked Hamilton's bullying and Jefferson's guile.

Others were less generous. Called upon as secretary of state to pacify warring nations instead of soreheaded ministers, Randolph was exposed to withering fire from French and British partisans. The vainglorious

Joseph Fauchet, less intent on winning American friends than on impressing his changeable superiors in Paris, exaggerated his intimacy with Randolph to suggest an insider's knowledge of the turmoil racking the administration. On the other end of the diplomatic spectrum, George Hammond counted the secretary of state as Britain's mortal enemy, so it came as no surprise that King George's representative should joyfully receive into his hands a packet of "peculiarly interesting" documents removed from a French corvette late in March 1795. Suddenly the British were in a position to change the course of Anglo-American relations without firing a shot. All they required was a little help from friends closest to the president.

⟨ 5 ⟩

With his genius for making enemies, Randolph generated as much hostility around the Cabinet table as in Hammond's communications to the British foreign ministry. The least important of his critics was Attorney General William Bradford, a Federalist mediocrity then in the final stages of a lingering illness. Even in the bloom of health, however, he could not begin to match the conspiratorial zeal displayed by two New Englanders, Timothy Pickering and Oliver Wolcott.

Pickering was a native of Salem, Massachusetts, famed for its colonial witchcraft trials; one glance at Knox's successor at the War Department, with his sharp nose, sharp chin, and sharp, dogmatic expression, and it was easy to imagine him dispensing rough justice on Gallows Hill. After turning in a creditable performance as Washington's Indian agent, Pickering had shown himself to be an honest and dutiful if not overly imaginative postmaster general. Thrifty to a fault, he pinched pennies by understaffing his department, for which he paid dearly in misplaced files and neglected business. He regularly declined dinner invitations from foreign representatives and even Anne Bingham, contending that Congress frowned upon department heads who incurred social debts. And then he added, with the proud fanaticism that had inspired earlier citizens of Salem to burn witches, "It is deemed honor enough for executive officers to toil without interruption for their country, and indulgence enough to live on mutton, mush and cold water."

In contrast to the plain-spoken Pickering, Connecticut's Oliver Wolcott was gracious and genial. The secretary of the treasury turned a wry face to the world, but behind the wit lay a penchant for intrigue worthy of his mentor Alexander Hamilton. Wolcott even looks like Hamilton in the admiring portrait by John Trumbull. Wolcott's subservience to his predecessor was only slightly greater than his devotion to Federalist orthodoxy, which by the summer of 1795 made him a staunch supporter of Jay's Treaty. Wolcott, the second-rater, was destined to play second fiddle to Pickering, even when sowing tares between Washington and anyone who stood in the way of early ratification. Randolph, true to form, did not stand so much as he straddled, but on the theory that their enemy's enemy was their friend, Pickering and Wolcott made common cause with Hammond to bring down the Cabinet's only remaining Republican.

Their moment came at the end of July, when Hammond thoughtfully provided the secretaries with Fauchet's intercepted Dispatch #10, composed at the height of the Whiskey Rebellion from a viewpoint decidedly hostile to the administration. Neither Pickering nor Wolcott was fluent in French, but neither was the sort to let linguistic shortcomings interfere with their patriotic duty. With the aid of a grammar and dictionary, Pickering produced a rough translation of the incriminating document. When in doubt, a rare occurrence for the emphatic Yankee, he invariably cast Fauchet's words in the most unflattering light possible, especially when doing so might raise doubts about Randolph's honor and loyalty. Taking advantage of his credulity, the conspirators tricked the secretary into reversing his earlier stand and inviting Washington's early return to Philadelphia.

On the evening of August 11, the president and Randolph were reviewing the latter's draft of a memorial to Hammond conditioning U.S. ratification of Jay's Treaty upon Britain's repeal of the predatory Order in Council when Timothy Pickering, evidently distressed, suddenly interrupted their discussion. Rising from the dinner table, Washington showed him into an adjoining room, where he demanded an explanation for Pickering's histrionic letter. The secretary pointed beyond the door through which they had just come, toward the solitary figure left at the dinner table.

"That man is a traitor!" said Pickering. To back up his charge, he claimed access to sensitive diplomatic papers documenting Randolph's solicitation of French bribes. Washington would be able to read and judge the evidence for himself that very evening, just as soon as Wolcott delivered the incriminating folio. Concealing the shock he must have felt, the president somehow maintained his composure, saying at length that he and Pickering should return to the dining room lest their prolonged absence rouse suspicion. Washington resumed his meal, picking up the conversation with Randolph where it had left off. But as he gazed into the face of his most trusted adviser, the president may for a fleeting moment have imagined the features of another young man whom he had befriended at a critical juncture of the Revolution. The leering ghost of

Benedict Arnold sat at Washington's table that night, an uninvited guest enjoying his long-delayed revenge.

Shortly after dinner, Wolcott handed the president Dispatch #10, all twenty-nine torturously reconstructed pages. Washington was up late that night scrutinizing its ambiguous phrasing and indiscreet political analysis. At one point, Fauchet reported Randolph's "precieuses confessions," a phrase Pickering naturally chose to interpret literally. (A more accurate rendition would have been "valuable disclosures" or "invaluable acknowledgments.") The distinction in wording may appear insignificant until understood in the context of a turbulent era in the Washington presidency. Referring to an earlier dispatch, #6 (of which no copy was supplied to the Cabinet cabal by Hammond), Fauchet described a visit from Randolph only days before Washington's neutrality proclamation of August 7, 1794. It was at this encounter that Randolph had broadly hinted that America's friendship was for sale, causing Fauchet to throw up his hands in virtuous astonishment. Imagine, he told his Parisian superiors, these bumptious Yankees believing that for a few thousand dollars, revolutionary France would weight the scales toward war or peace. "Such, Citizen, is the evident consequence of the system of finances conceived by Mr. Hamilton. He has made of a whole nation a stock-jobbing, speculating, selfish people."

Here Pickering's damning version of Fauchet's report attributed to his Cabinet colleague "an air of great eagerness" — a far more damaging phrase than the alternative translation "a countenance expressive of much anxiety." Pickering and Wolcott knew that these were magic words to purge the Cabinet of France's warmest admirer. Circumstantial evidence could finish what malevolence began. Had not Randolph counseled moderation toward the bloodstained assassins of Louis XVI? Who else but he had urged delay in ratifying Jay's Treaty? Might not Randolph, the political chameleon and odd man out, have stirred the boiling pot of hatred for England and encouraged the mobs to believe that the proper place to make America's foreign policy was in the streets?

Dismayed by the implications of what he was reading, Washington may have been angrier still over Fauchet's belittling of the Whiskey Rebellion and the administration's response. The French envoy quoted Randolph as calling the military incursion a ruse designed "to introduce absolute power, and to mislead the President in paths which will conduct him to unpopularity." If, as some modern historians have argued, the president by the summer of 1795 entertained second thoughts about the insurrection — a claim buttressed by his recent pardoning of convicted traitors — then he might well have felt a special vulnerability to the revisionist interpretation of Dispatch #10. Whatever his attitude toward the rebels, Washington could only take offense at Fauchet's implication that he was merely Hamilton's stooge.

One must remember that this was Washington's first exposure to uncensored extracts from the amateur diplomats in his Cabinet. (One wonders at his reaction had he been privy to Hamilton's furtive correspondence with Hammond.) In any event, it did not take long for the president to conclude that Randolph was two-faced, in the pay of France, or both. On the strength of an intercepted report, supplied by a British minister desperate to clear away the final obstacle to the ratification of Jay's Treaty and doctored by Cabinet partisans whose timing was better than their French, Washington was prepared to condemn a friend of twenty years. It was the low point of his presidency.

In reaching this conclusion, he discounted Fauchet's unreliability, political bias, and recycled facts. And he underestimated the Frenchman's desire to impress a critical government back home through a spurious intimacy with Washington's closest councilor. Since Washington never even saw the earlier dispatches cited as supporting evidence of Randolph's venality, it is hard to view his rush to judgment as based on anything more than wounded pride. Randolph's real crime was the ancient one of hubris. After denouncing policies he had supported as a member of the administration, he boasted to a foreign agent that he controlled the president. Here was an offense that Washington, a notoriously independent man, could neither tolerate nor overlook.

Overnight history was rewritten, as Randolph's resistance to hasty action against the whiskey boys assumed a sinister aspect. Had the secretary of state been merely indiscreet or was he, as the excitable Pickering claimed, a traitor? Did betrayal run in the Randolph blood?

Washington said nothing of Dispatch #10 the next day at the Cabinet meeting. He also passed over the subject of Randolph's memorial, casually approved but twelve hours earlier. Instead, after a cursory debate, he announced his intention to ratify the treaty immediately, not even waiting for the formal repeal of Britain's latest Order in Council. In a matter of minutes, the administration's painstakingly crafted formula for extracting British concessions went out the window. It took a full day for Randolph to get over his shock. Then he hurried to 190 Market Street in a fruitless attempt to dissuade the president.

Washington wore a mask of bland equanimity throughout the ensuing week, never breathing a word of Randolph's suspected treachery to the thoroughly confused secretary of state. Enforcing his silence were the travel plans of George Hammond, due to sail for home on August 15 with the ratified treaty. To accuse Randolph before that date would lead to an open breach. The newspapers would explode in venomous charges and countercharges, and the treaty would almost certainly be lost in the tempest. So Washington held his tongue, pretending an intimacy he no longer felt, all too aware that whatever he finally decided, the British could publish Fauchet's dispatch at any moment, thereby discrediting not only the secretary's patriotism but the president's judgment in harboring such a wretch. Without knowing it, Randolph was about to become the final casualty of the Whiskey Rebellion.

⟨ 6 ⟩

On Tuesday, August 18, Washington signed the Treaty of London. When an unsuspecting Randolph arrived at 190 Market Street the next morning for a meeting, he found Pickering and Wolcott already there. Washington's greeting had none of its usual warmth. "Mr. Randolph," said the president, "here is a letter which I desire you to read, and make such explanations as you choose." He handed him a large, folded document written in French. Randolph, who had a fair reading knowledge of the language, plunged into Fauchet's convoluted account of the politics surrounding the Whiskey Rebellion. He quickly discerned that his own role as a confidant of the French envoy was exaggerated — how typical of Fauchet, Randolph must have thought — but the reference to "confessions" drew a blank. Indeed, without access to the earlier dispatches, #3 and #6, to which Fauchet referred in #10, the secretary could only respond in the most general terms.

Wolcott and Pickering studied Randolph closely as he delivered some brief and necessarily vague comments in his defense. He cited Fauchet's earlier warnings of British "machinations" aimed at destroying him, Governor Clinton of New York, and other Republican leaders. When Randolph offered to put his case in writing, Washington agreed to let him retain the incriminating dispatch. But the secretary's ordeal was just beginning. The president invited Pickering and Wolcott to join the cross examination, and Wolcott, himself a virtual British agent, had the nerve to ask about the alleged plot to discredit American friends of France.

Ransacking his memory, Randolph dredged up year-old stories about a negative campaign by Hammond and his Spanish counterpart in the diplomatic corps. Turning to the president for confirmation, Randolph got the surprise of his life. Deflecting the question angrily, Washington said that no one had accused *him* of concealment. At this point an unexpected caller demanded the president's attention, leaving Randolph alone with his interrogators. Awakening to his danger, the secretary of state asked how Fauchet's dispatch had found its way into Washington's hands. Wolcott replied brusquely that any such explanation was for the president alone to make.

Returning, in a barely civil manner Washington asked Randolph to wait in an adjoining room while the rest of the group reviewed the facts and, in effect, debated his fate. Three quarters of an hour passed, an eternity to the man in the docket. Did he imagine himself already judged and convicted? How else could he explain the humiliating procedure to which he was being subjected? He tried to recall meetings between himself and Fauchet during the emotional weeks when Washington and Hamilton were off pursuing tax resisters in Pennsylvania. Fauchet had mentioned "confessions," but he was unreliable, and the evidentiary trail led to a pair of earlier dispatches, now withheld from him. Had Randolph's accusers seen these for themselves? And if not, didn't that in itself argue the weakness of their case?

It is no less tempting to speculate on what transpired on the other side of Randolph's wall as Washington and his ministers analyzed every nuance of their colleague's reaction. His composure was duly noted; indeed, in Wolcott's notes of this pivotal conclave are tantalizing hints that the president, at least, was not convinced of his old friend's guilt. The whole embarrassing scene might have run its course, with no outcome worse than some wounded feelings, but Randolph's initial bewilderment shaded into anger during his lonely vigil, and his resentment degenerated into open hostility.

It was when the secretary returned to the Cabinet room that the real tragedy unfolded. Tense and peevish, he told Washington that without Fauchet's complete diplomatic record he would be handicapped, perhaps fatally, in trying to disprove complicity in the Whiskey Rebellion. Showing no emotion, Washington asked how long it would take the secretary to compose his defense. "As soon as possible," he snapped, by now close to the breaking point. Under the circumstances, he said that he could not remain in office another second; a letter of resignation would be on Washington's desk that very day. Then he rushed off to his office, which he ordered locked so that no one could tamper with its contents.

Randolph's anger was unmistakable. "Your confidence in me, Sir," he wrote to Washington, "has been unlimited and, I can truly affirm, unabused." He denied soliciting or receiving any bribe. He had asked nothing of Fauchet but the sharing of information about Britain's involvement in the Whiskey Rebellion. (Fauchet disagreed, asserting that the secretary of state had sought funds with which to pay informants knowledgeable about Britain's meddling.) Until he was able to track down Fauchet, on the verge of sailing for home, Randolph asked the president to keep quiet about the train of events leading up to his resignation. He also sought a copy of Fauchet's Dispatch #6, should Washington have one.

The president's reply was correct, if distant. He acknowledged that the intercepted Dispatch #10 had been channeled from Lord Grenville to George Hammond to Oliver Wolcott. He agreed to say nothing about the tumult in the Cabinet "unless something shall appear to render an explanation necessary on the part of the government, of which I will be the judge." Dispatch #10 would be made available to Randolph; as for #6, it had never crossed the president's desk.

By the time Washington could make good on these promises, Randolph was engaged in a desperate chase after Fauchet, temporarily detained by the menacing presence of the British cruiser *Africa* outside Newport Harbor. Seeing the Frenchman, Randolph believed, would clear up the whole misunderstanding, and his good name, if not his office, might be restored. Reaching Newport on the thirty-first, he secured Fauchet's promise of an exculpatory statement within twenty-four hours. The next day a northeast storm raised Fauchet's hopes of eluding the British pursuers. Randolph returned at the appointed hour only to discover that the retiring minister had flown the coop. Frantic, Randolph commandeered the fastest sailing vessel he could find and sent it off in pursuit of Fauchet. But it was a futile exercise; the French ship had escaped into open water.

Then, as suddenly as an offshore breeze springs up, Randolph's fortunes improved. The Yankee pilot who had guided Fauchet's vessel out of the harbor appeared with a note confirming that a defense of Randolph's actions was on its way to the new French envoy, Pierre Adet, and a copy would be sent to the former secretary of state. This would form the basis for Randolph's *Vindication*, 107 intemperate pages that, when published in December, opened a chasm between its author and the president that would never be healed. By reprinting Dispatch #10, with its portrayal of Washington as a tool of his treasury secretary and the decision to ratify Jay's Treaty as the snap judgment of a badly informed and easily manipulated old man, Randolph exposed his former chief to public ridicule.

The publication of what Washington called "the long promised vindication, or rather accusation" sent him into a towering rage. (According to one account, Washington pounded the table and called Randolph "by the eternal God . . . the damnedest liar on the face of the earth!") The president's anger extended beyond the obvious reasons, for the assembled documentation, much of which Washington now read for the first time, made plain his error in condemning his friend and factotum. The very artlessness of Randolph's diatribe both argued for its sincerity and defeated its purpose. With no political base to fall back on the embittered

Virginian quickly faded from the scene, his public life over forever. Having failed to clear his own name (except to later historians, who judged him guilty of nothing worse than indiscretion and credulousness), he succeeded only in spattering mud on the mentor he had once cherished.

His fall from grace, breathtaking as it was, abounded in irony. During the Revolution, Timothy Pickering had been implicated in the military cabal of dissatisfied officers that took its name from Thomas Conway and nearly toppled Washington from his command. Now, eighteen years later, the schemer was still spinning his web, only this time Washington himself was caught up in the partisan snares of lesser men. Each of the chief actors in the drama suffered a devastating emotional loss. For the second time, Edmund Randolph experienced humiliating rejection from a father figure. For Washington, the Randolph affair not only deprived him of a much-loved protégé but also tore the scab off the old wound inflicted by the traitorous Benedict Arnold. One man squandered his patrimony, the other was cruelly reminded that nature had left him childless.

❈ 12 ❈

"THE GOOD CITIZEN"

"In politics, as in religion, my tenets are few and simple: the leading one of which . . . is to be honest and just ourselves, and to exact it from others; meddling as little as possible in their affairs where our own are not involved. If this maxim was generally adopted wars would cease, and our swords would soon be converted into reap-hooks, and our harvests be more abundant, peaceful, and happy . . . But alas! the millennium will not I fear appear in our days. The restless mind of man cannot be at peace; and when there is disorder within, it will appear without, and sooner or later will show itself in arts."

George Washington,
December 24, 1795

LIKE FAUST, forced to pay the price of his ambitions, Washington discovered that the fame and veneration pursued over a lifetime could only be had at enormous cost. Past glory was no defense against current criticism. One month after Randolph's ouster, unable to quell the fury over Jay's Treaty or fill the decimated ranks of his Cabinet, an embattled president poured out his heart to the faithful Henry Knox: "If any power on earth could, or the Great Power above would, erect the standard of infallibility in political opinions, there is no being that inhabits this terrestrial globe that would resort to it with more eagerness than myself . . . But as I have found no better guide hitherto than upright intentions and close investigation, I shall adhere to those maxims while I keep the watch; leaving it to those who will come after me to explore new ways, if they like or think them better."

Beneath an impassive exterior, Washington seethed as British captains in the waters off Newport, Rhode Island, impressed American seamen. Finally, provoked beyond endurance, he sent the British consul in Newport packing and instructed Governor Arthur Fenner to employ the state militia if necessary to prevent His Majesty's Navy from snatching additional American citizens.

The offshore skirmishing distracted Washington from his most pressing task, that of rebuilding a shattered Cabinet. Besides the vacant portfolio of state, he also needed an attorney general. William Bradford's death on August 23, coming just three days after Randolph's angry departure, symbolized the administration's growing decrepitude. Three months and two refusals later, Bradford's place was taken by Lighthorse Harry Lee's lightweight brother, Charles, whose credentials seemed to consist chiefly of his family name.

Choosing a secretary of state was even more of a trial; five candidates, Patrick Henry and Rufus King among them, turned down the job. To Henry, Washington offered assurances that while the administration desired strict compliance with America's foreign and domestic engagements, his most ardent wish was "to keep the United States free from political connections with every other country, to see them independent of all and under the influence of none. In a word, I want an *American* character, that the powers of Europe may be convinced we act for *ourselves* and not for others." But Henry chose to remain in Virginia, forcing Washington in extremis to recruit Timothy Pickering to fill the vacancy he had done so much to create.

Pickering's acceptance created yet another opening, at the War Department, and a fresh round of invitations and rebuffs. Charles Cotesworth Pinckney of South Carolina wanted no part of the office or the accompanying torrent of press abuse. Neither did Washington's Richmond intimate Edward Carrington or Governor John Edgar Howard of Maryland. Not until January 1796 would James McHenry, a second-rater from Baltimore, succeed Pickering at War. An equivocal Hamilton summed up the prevailing attitude when he wrote to the president, "McHenry you know. He would give no strength to the administration, but he would not disgrace the office." It was a far cry from the heroic days of Hamilton, Jefferson, Randolph, and Knox, something Washington himself acknowledged through his increasing reliance on Hamilton's counsel.

A cut-rate Cabinet was not the president's only source of embarrassment. In a bizarre twist, Federalist senators rejected Republican John Rutledge, Washington's nominee for chief justice, on grounds of insanity. Truth be told, the only madness evinced was by the lawmakers, out to avenge Rutledge's harsh criticism of the Anglo-American treaty. After being abandoned by his own troops, Washington named Oliver Ellsworth of Connecticut to Jay's old position. Yet the defeat of the admittedly eccentric Rutledge may not have been a total disappointment, for events since the Whiskey Rebellion had shaken Washington's former insistence upon a politically balanced administration. By the fall of 1795 he had reached the limit of bipartisanship, telling Pickering that it was "a sort of political suicide" to bring anyone not firmly committed to the government's program into the official fold.

In retrospect, the wonder is not that Washington became a covert partisan during the last eighteen months of his presidency, but rather that the opposition's caustic attacks had not driven him into Federalist arms much earlier. Certainly the steady drumbeat of criticism had its effect. In the middle of September 1795, John Beckley, the gossipy Republican clerk of the House, was telling Madison that by accepting Jay's Treaty "old Washington" had gone too far. Others mocked the president as a British toady or royalist usurper. A dinner of New Jersey Republican was enlivened by a toast to "a despot from the South, with Democracy on his lips and tyranny in his heart." Washington was called to account for poor generalship during the Revolution and worse statesmanship since. His meager formal education was held up to ridicule; so was his slavish reliance on ghostwriters. As discerned by his fiercest detractors, Washington had no talent for leadership and no taste not implanted by that West Indian Svengali, Alexander Hamilton.

Citizen Pierre Adet, already in bad odor for conferring with Republican leaders in Congress and for sending French agents across the Appalachians to incite western secessionists, used characteristically undiplomatic language to rail against Washington's alleged servility before George III. Drawing upon information from Beckley and Governor Sam Adams of Massachusetts, the French minister penned a scathing estimate of a clay-footed hero: "Stubborn in his resolutions, athirst for power, eager to keep it, rabidly fond of false praise, responsive to flattery, he has rejected the counsels of men truly interested in his glory and in the good of their country" (read: supporters of Jefferson and American friends to the Republic of Virtue). The day had dawned, claimed the Frenchman, when thinking Americans would see their idol shorn of prestige and exposed as "a wretch whose strength has been exaggerated by a superstitious credulity."

Philip Freneau drew blood in the pages of the *Jersey Chronicle*, pronouncing his old nemesis a republican in name only. "He holds levees like a King," snorted Freneau, "receives congratulations on his birthday like a King, makes treaties like a King, answers petitions like a King, employs his old enemies like a King . . . swallows adulation like a King and vomits offensive truths in your face."

On October 23, Bache's *Aurora* came forward with the most sensational allegation yet. Relying on leaked details probably supplied by John Beckley or the disgraced Randolph, the editor now accused the chief executive of regularly and illegally overdrawing his $25,000 salary. Washington's friends closed ranks around him, but their tortured explanations could not conceal the fact of presidential borrowing against appropriated funds, sometimes in amounts equaling three months' pay. Deeply hurt, Washington withdrew into a great and distant silence, waiting for the frenzy to run its course. Competing for his attention in this dismal autumn was a Federal City once more flirting with bankruptcy. Washington's friend Robert Morris had contracted for several hundred lots without paying a cent to the federal commissioners. As delicately as possible, Washington dunned Morris for at least a token payment, but it was hopeless; the senator was starting down the slope that would deposit him two years later in debtors' prison.

Washington cautioned the commissioners against seeking a loan from Maryland's legislature. Such an appeal, he argued, made in the face of stiff opposition from interests in Baltimore, could only revive doubts about the city's commercial viability. At length, persuaded that without the loan the proposed capital might never be built, the president gave his consent. As it turned out, Maryland's lawmakers proved unwilling to extend credit, forcing commissioners to look elsewhere for funds. On October 4, responding politely to Jefferson's account of the growing season at Monticello, Washington devoted several pages to Indian corn, chicory, buckwheat, winter vetch, the depredations of weevils, and the charms of the Albany pea — everything, in short, but what was really on his mind. After making so much history together, the two men were now political adversaries, a partnership of silence the best they could hope for.

❖ 2 ❖

Reports of Thomas Pinckney's negotiations with Spain over American access to the Mississippi and the disputed southwestern border were few and far between, leading Washington to complain that "a kind of fatality seems to have pursued" the Pinckney mission. In communicating with Philadelphia, Pinckney had used a cipher that no one in the State Department could translate. Yet even without direct information, Washington had seen enough to judge the temper of the Spanish court, and he was not sanguine about the "procrastination and trifling" going on in Madrid.

Forced to suppress his anger at the misrepresentation of editors and his anxiety over the nation's diplomatic prospects, Washington had one obligation of the heart that neither Bache nor Congress could keep him from discharging. Several months had passed since George Washington Lafayette, the only son of the imprisoned marquis, had strode down the gangplank of a vessel moored in Boston Harbor. At fourteen, Lafayette was determined to start a new life under the protection of his namesake, the president of the United States, who conveyed an intention "to be in the place of a father and friend to him."

But how would France react to the thought of America's president sheltering Lafayette's son? For several weeks Washington debated the question with Hamilton in a correspondence shadowed by memories of past services and imagined sufferings in an Austrian prison cell. On November 18, a defiant Washington instructed Hamilton to send the boy and his tutor, Felix Frestal, to Philadelphia immediately. The normally impetuous New Yorker counseled prudence, advising the president to write affectionately to the youth while delaying a personal encounter to avoid giving a handle to the complaint that Washington had betrayed France.

Of all the restrictions imposed by office, this was the hardest for him to accept. "It has . . . like many other things in which I have been involved, two edges, neither of which can be avoided without falling on the other," he told Hamilton. "On one side, I may be charged with countenancing those who have been denounced as the enemies of France; on the other with *not* countenancing the son of a man who is dear to America."

And, he might have added, dear to himself. Washington dispatched a warm greeting to this latest and most poignant of French émigrés. A month went by with no response, prompting him to ask if Hamilton had seen or heard anything of "young Fayette" since their previous exchange of letters. (In fact, the boy and his companion were comfortably ensconced with the Hamiltons in New York. But Washington did not know this, and his conscience was acting up.) "His case gives me pain and I do not know how to get relieved of it. His sensibility, I fear is hurt."

Under the circumstances, Washington's money was a poor anodyne compared to the emotional refuge or paternal guidance that a hospitable Virginia planter would extend without a second thought. As so often before, politics stood athwart his preferences, and though Washington issued an incautious invitation for Fayette to visit Philadelphia early in 1796, it was not until the first days of April that the youth was at last welcomed into the presidential household.

❦ 3 ❧

Aside from his brief outburst over young Lafayette, Washington kept his churning emotions to himself, devising instead a strategy as simple as it was effective. The president was convinced that the tide of public opinion would soon turn his way, a belief strengthened early in December, when the Maryland legislature unanimously adopted a resolution of continued confidence in the old hero. He was especially gratified by the timing of the action, Washington replied, coming as it did at a moment "when the voice of malignancy is so high-toned." While waiting for America's silent majority to make itself heard, the president pretended indifference to attacks on his character and conduct. Certainly no one listening to his annual address to Congress, on December 7, would have guessed at his inner turmoil. Wrote an observer of the scene, "This was the first time he had ever entered the walls of Congress without a full assurance of meeting a welcome from every heart."

Washington had learned a lesson from the previous year, when in defending his actions in the Whiskey Rebellion he had inadvertently stoked the fires of popular anger. Gone was the fervor and bite with which he had fingered the Democratic Societies as culprits in a plot to bring down his government. In their place were soothing assurances and pious expressions of gratitude to the Almighty for the blessings showered on the people of the United States. Overseas, American prospects had never been so bright, claimed the president. Morocco's emperor had recently confirmed a peace treaty with the United States entered into by his late father, and the piratical dey of Algiers appeared willing to free American hostages for a price to be determined. Washington even managed a brave show of confidence in Pinckney's Spanish diplomacy.

Buried halfway through the speech was a single paragraph about Jay's Treaty, sanctioned by the executive only "after full and mature deliberation." Tranquility likewise was the order of the day on the domestic front, dramatically so in contrast to haggard, bleeding Europe. "Faithful to ourselves, we have violated no obligations to others," said Washington, making the closest thing to a debatable statement in the whole address. Peace had settled in along the northwestern frontier and was tantalizingly close in the disputed Southwest, delayed only by a handful of bloodthirsty Georgians preying upon innocent Creeks. Making explicit what had earlier been only implied, he invited congressional protection of the red man from "the lawless part of our frontier inhabitants . . . To enforce upon the Indians the observance of justice, it is indispensable that there shall be competent means of rendering justice to them."

A general prosperity vindicated the administration's economic program, with agriculture, commerce, and manufacturing thriving as never before. Recent self-inflicted wounds were fast healing, as Pennsylvania's rebels laid down their arms and earned presidential forgiveness. "For though I shall always think it a sacred duty to exercise with firmness and energy the constitutional powers with which I am vested," explained Washington, "yet it appears to me no less consistent with the public good, than it is with my personal feelings, to mingle in the operations of government every degree of moderation and tenderness which the national justice, dignity and safety may permit."

Washington did not have to add that moderation and tenderness had been noticeably lacking in the national discourse of late. Fortunately for him, censure by a partisan press carried its own antidote. Just as anticipated, a popular backlash now developed which the president did his best to fan into a full-scale repudiation of his critics. A few days after his conciliatory appearance in Congress Hall, Washington thanked the citizens of Frederick County, Virginia, for their endorsement of his policies and took a swipe at the Republican opposition. Were truth and candor used to gauge the conduct of public men, he said, then public approval would naturally follow the conscientious execution of duty. "But the reverse is so often the case that he who, wishing to serve his country . . . runs the risk of being miserably disappointed." Facing rank ingratitude, "the good citizen will look beyond the applauses and reproaches of men," hoping to gain the approval of Heaven and posterity.

As a keen student of public opinion, Washington was not the sort to wait for either God or the muse of history to render a verdict on his stewardship. Once again his instincts proved right, enabling him to inform Jay of subsiding hostility to the treaty. Britain's repeal of the latest offensive Order in Council had done much to draw the sting of Francophile sentiment. But so had the president, by holding his tongue and offering himself as a punching bag for vituperative editors. In adhering to a strict neutrality, he had brought a storm of criticism upon his head. But he would not be diverted from his chosen path, whatever the cost. "I have nothing to ask and, discharging my duty, I have nothing to fear from invective," he told Gouverneur Morris during the closing days of 1795. "The acts of my administration will appear when I am no more, and the intelligent and candid part of mankind will not condemn my conduct without recurring to them."

For the first time since Europeans went to war two and a half years earlier, Washington seemed at peace with himself. Yet there was still the gauntlet of domestic factionalism for him to traverse. Thinking he would trip up "old Washington" on a point of diplomatic etiquette, Pierre Adet, on behalf of the Committee of Public Safety, chose January 1 to present the richly ornamented colors of revolutionary France to the American people through their president. Washington was more than equal to the challenge, as he showed in his deliberately effusive speech of acceptance ("Wonderful people! Ages to come will read with astonishment the history of your brilliant exploits!"). Four days later, he consigned the gift to the honorable obscurity of the State Department archives; only then did the cunning minister realize how skillfully his thrust had been parried.

Washington had pragmatic reasons to praise the revolutionary experiment in Paris, for he knew that Jay's Treaty was by no means home safe. The House of Representatives, dominated by Republicans, would soon be asked to provide $80,000 to implement the treaty of commerce and amity with the archenemy in London. No one expected the battle to be won easily. Still, by February 1796, Washington had reason to believe the worst behind him. He could even indulge in a rare bit of whimsy at his own expense. Thanking a correspondent for his solicitude about attacks on the administration, Washington concluded, "If the enlightened and virtuous part of the community will make allowances for my involuntary errors, I will promise that they shall have no cause to accuse me of willful ones."

⟨ 4 ⟩

That the House was in no mood to bow to presidential wishes was made clear on February 22, Washington's sixty-fourth birthday, when its members defeated a motion to adjourn for half an hour in order to pay compliments of the day. The holiday passed "with unexpected splendor anyway," Madison told Jefferson, adding, "The crisis explains the policy of this." The crisis was occasioned by that hardy perennial of executive-legislative dispute, Jay's Treaty, which Washington proclaimed in effect at the end of February. House Republicans intended to have their own say in the matter, however. Through skillful use of the appropriations process, administration opponents asserted an equal role in making treaties for the popularly elected chamber.

On the rain-slicked evening of the twenty-ninth, Washington and his vice president went to the New Theatre to see a double bill of *The Rage* and *The Spoiled Child*, a fitting curtain raiser to the furious debate that

Washington's funding request was sure to kick off. Adams detected a strong inclination on the part of his chief to retire from office as soon as possible. Of course, there was always the possibility that outside persuasion might change his mind. "But if it should, it will shorten his days," concluded Adams, not exactly a disinterested spectator in the drama of succession. "His heart is set upon it, and the turpitude of the Jacobins touches him more nearly than he owns in words."

Adams was a perceptive observer, but virtually anyone with the price of a Philadelphia newspaper could gauge the intensity of the president's longing for retirement. On February 1, Washington advertised four of his Mount Vernon farms for rent, at a bushel and a half per arable acre, and put up for sale more than 41,000 acres along the Ohio, Great Kanhawa, Miami, and Green rivers. A few days later he informed his trusted friend David Stuart that he was at last embarked on a campaign to end his dependence on slave labor, starting with the Negroes brought to Mount Vernon as part of Mrs. Washington's dowry. "I have very little expectation of accomplishing the renting part of my plan for next year," Washington wrote Thomas Pinckney on February 20, "nor would I attempt it all with the slovenly farmers of this country, if there was a tolerable . . . hope of getting them from any other where husbandry is better understood and more rationally practiced."

In a second letter the president accepted Pinckney's request to be recalled from Madrid and tried, none too subtly, to confirm rumors of a successful end to the delayed negotiations. When reliable intelligence finally did reach Philadelphia, it heralded a political achievement exceeding the administration's fondest expectations. Tricked into believing that Jay's bargain with the British foreshadowed a formal Anglo-American alliance, the Spanish foreign minister Manuel de Godoy yielded on virtually every one of Pinckney's demands. The Treaty of San Lorenzo, signed on October 27, 1795, opened the entire Mississippi River to American navigation, permitted Yankee goods to be exported out of New Orleans tax free, and confirmed U.S. claims to sovereignty over an area extending as far south as the thirty-first parallel. As frosting on this stunningly rich cake, Godoy also promised to use his government's influence to restrain hostile Indians along the new southwestern border.

By far the greatest victory yet for American diplomacy, Pinckney's Treaty won unanimous Senate approval within days of its announcement. In a second diplomatic achievement, far more costly than the first, Washington was able to secure the liberty of U.S. sailors held by Algerian pirates. The price was steep, $800,000, plus an additional $24,000 a year to guarantee unmolested passage for Yankee ships in the Mediterranean. These twin triumphs could not have been more timely, for on the morning of March 2, as the House debate over Jay's Treaty got under way in earnest, Republican Edward Livingston caused a sensation by demanding from the executive all documentation relating to Jay's mission, including the private instructions fashioned by Washington with Hamilton's explicit involvement.

The president learned of Livingston's resolution by reading about it in Bache's *Aurora*. His first reaction was to call on someone he could trust, so he asked Wolcott to raise the issue with Hamilton, then in Philadelphia. The former secretary might recall a similar request that "was made, or *about* to be made, I do not now recollect which," a few years before. Washington's allegedly faulty memory had not played tricks, for there *had* been an earlier occasion on which the House sought confidential papers from the executive: Arthur St. Clair's humiliating defeat in the autumn of 1791. Then Washington had cooperated with a congressional committee investigating the disaster, but that was a strictly internal affair, a military inquiry, not a treaty with a foreign power.

The House's desperate effort to kill Jay's Treaty baffled the president. "If the people of this country have not abundant cause to rejoice at the happiness they enjoy, I know of no country that has," he told Gouverneur Morris on March 4. "We have settled all our disputes, and are at peace with all nations. We supply their wants with our superfluities, and are well paid for doing so." The earth yielded its fruits generously, and there was hardly a city, town, village, or farm that did not display evidence of increasing wealth, "while taxes are hardly known but in name. Yet by the second sight; extraordinary foresight; or some other sight," Washington jibed, "attainable by a few only, evils afar off are discovered."

In fairness to his opponents in Congress, this was not the first time that the administration had used its exclusive treaty-making power to get around domestic opposition. The year before, following House refusal to enact legislation nullifying Georgia's sale of 50 million acres reserved to the Creeks under the Treaty of New York, Washington had taken the issue out of the domestic realm by appointing federal commissioners to negotiate a new deal with the Indian nation, which he then submitted as a treaty for Senate approval. Then as now, what was at stake was nothing less than the strong presidency, preeminent in the conduct of foreign affairs, to which he had committed himself at the Constitutional Convention.

Although Livingston modified his resolution slightly, permitting the executive to withhold documents whose disclosure might endanger ongoing negotiations, the House would not retreat from its main assertion: the Senate might ratify a treaty, but only the people's chamber could implement one. A parade of speakers marched to the well to defend or refute this claim, led by Albert Gallatin, the Swiss-born financial genius who had tried to calm his angry constituents in Pennsylvania at the time of the Whiskey Rebellion and who now brought to the debate a logic as finely calibrated as the timepieces for which his native land was famous. Gallatin maintained that a treaty was simply another statute whose execution required the consent of both houses of Congress. Much could be said against so radical an interpretation of the nation's organic law; regrettably, nativist editors and not a few of Gallatin's colleagues chose instead to rant about "an itinerant Genevan" setting himself up against "your General in war and your President in peace." Party lines held, however, and on March 24, Gallatin's position was upheld on a strict party line vote.

⟨ 5 ⟩

As a grave constitutional crisis loomed, all eyes turned to 190 Market Street. Would Washington defy the House? And if he did, what would be the consequences of his refusal to turn over the documents? That night the president detained John Adams until nine o'clock for the frankest political discussion the two men had ever enjoyed. Adams went away well satisfied. "I found his opinions and sentiments are more exactly like mine than I ever knew before," he told his wife afterward. "He gave me intimations enough that his reign would be very short." Indeed, three times that evening Washington dismissed pending matters as personally irrelevant, "as he had but a very little while to stay in his present situation."

The next day the president managed a cordial greeting for Gallatin and Livingston, sent by the House to officially notify him of its insistence on seeing all the papers relating to Jay's mission. Washington stalled, promising to consider the request and calling a meeting of the Cabinet for Saturday, March 26. A large part of Washington's genius for leadership consisted of knowing precisely what questions to ask. The president demonstrated this gift anew on the twenty-sixth. Did the House have a constitutional right to call for the papers in question? he inquired of his advisers. If no such right was acknowledged, might there be a political justification for complying with the request anyway? And however the first two queries might be answered, on what terms should he accept or reject the House's demand?

The Cabinet to a man denied Gallatin's breathtaking grab for power. Chief Justice Ellsworth took a similarly hard line, as did Hamilton, who came up with no fewer than thirteen reasons to keep secret the diplomatic correspondence, "a crude mass that will do no credit to the administration." Only Attorney General Lee sounded a conciliatory note, suggesting that for reasons of expediency the president might turn over at least a portion of the contested record. Although Washington was not spoiling for a fight with the House, neither would he shirk from one if that is what it took to maintain his concept of the presidential office. He rejected Hamilton's 4,000-word draft denying the House's claims, saying that it arrived too late; in fact, he preferred the more incisive language of Timothy Pickering.

Before applying the stick, however, Washington would hold out an especially alluring carrot. On March 29 he transmitted to the House Pinckney's triumphant agreement with Manuel de Godoy, already unanimously approved by the Senate and sure to be immensely popular with Westerners — even western Republicans. Twenty-four hours later the ax fell, Washington telling House members that he had considered their request with "the utmost attention . . . I trust that no part of my conduct has ever indicated a disposition to withhold any information which the Constitution has enjoined upon the President as a duty to give, or which could be required of him by either House of Congress as a right."

Score one for Washington.

Yet the conduct of foreign relations by their nature demanded caution, said the president, and success or failure often depended on an atmosphere of secrecy. A full disclosure of private demands or concessions, proposed or contemplated, would be "extremely impolitic." Indeed, "the necessity of such caution and secrecy was one cogent reason for vesting the power of making treaties in the President," subject to the approval of the small and presumably closemouthed Senate. Surrendering to the House's demand would establish a dangerous precedent. Moreover, it was difficult to see what purpose would be served in the present case by the House's review "except that of an impeachment, which the resolution has not expressed."

Score two for Washington, in raising a straw man certain to horrify conservatives and engender popular pressure against the majority in the House.

The president played his trump card next, reminding the lawmakers that as a member of "the General Convention," he was well aware of the principles on which the Constitution was formed. "I have ever entertained but one opinion on this subject . . . that the power of making treaties is exclusively vested in the President, by and with the advice and consent of the Senate . . . and that every treaty so made, and promulgated, thenceforward becomes the law of the land." So foreigners had believed when entering into negotiations with Washington's administration. So had every previous House in readily acceding to the financial provisions required to implement earlier treaties. So had the states, in particular the smaller ones, when deliberating whether to ratify the Constitution and take advantage of the special protections afforded them by equal representation in the upper chamber of the national legislature.

Finally Washington referred congressmen to the Convention journals and a defeated motion "that no treaty shall be binding on the United States which was not ratified by a law." Having thus dismantled to his own satisfaction the rickety structure of Republican logic, Washington concluded his message with the flat statement "A just regard to the Constitution and to the duty of my Office, under all the circumstances of this case, forbids a compliance with your request." He explained himself further in a letter to Hamilton. Insisting that an ultimate refusal had never been in doubt, only the manner of justifying it to the public, the president threw off the restraint of recent months and directed George Washington Motier de Lafayette to come to Philadelphia as soon as convenient to him and his tutor. Hamilton was buoyed by the president's firm stand. "Whatever may happen, it is right, and will elevate the character of the President, and inspire confidence abroad," he enthused. Washington proved sufficiently elevated to become a target for angry Republicans in and out of Congress, who pictured him as a dictator at war with his own citizenry, a tyrant building an empire upon the ruins of popular representation. Bache's *Aurora* compared Washington, somewhat inconsistently, to Cromwell and to France's late, unlamented monarch. Demanded Boston's *Independent Chronicle*, "Shall the *people* or the PRESIDENT be the sovereign of the United States?" Madison thought his fellow Virginian a mere extension of Hamilton and the message of rejection entirely written in New York. Equally dissatisfied with the executive's reasoning, Madison's colleagues in the House voted to refer Washington's response to a Committee of the Whole and scheduled a fresh round of public debate for April 6.

The president took advantage of the brief intermission to attend to more personal matters. Fanny Basset Washington, the widow of his nephew George Augustine and subsequently the third wife of Tobias Lear, died in February 1796, and Lear's old friend beckoned his confidant to rejoin the presidential household. Washington took a wary approach to the marriage plans of his impoverished niece, although readily admitting that "Harriot, having very little fortune herself, has no *right* to expect a great one in the man she marries." But after launching inquiries into the family connections and business prospects of his niece's fiancé, one Andrew Parks of Fredericksburg, Washington threw no obstacles across the path of young love, and Harriot and young Parks were duly wed the following summer.

Vice President Adams was present on the evening of April 11, when Washington at last welcomed Lafayette's son to his household. Adams thought the youth "studious and discreet," qualities essential if he was not to embroil the administration in fresh controversy. Before dinner the president jotted a note to the painter Gilbert Stuart, inquiring about a sitting the next day. Should he come to the State House or to Stuart's studio at the corner of Chestnut and Fifth Streets?

This was not the first time Washington had posed for the temperamental artist favored by European aristocrats more for his lively chatter than his realistic portraiture. The previous autumn, Stuart had depicted the president with a sagging face on which every day of his six and a half years in office was deeply etched. Besides the largest eye sockets he had ever seen, Stuart captured a physical force that he said would have made Washington the fiercest of savages had he lived in a forest instead of Federalist Philadelphia.

With an ego to match his talent, the profligate, alcoholic Stuart had come to regard the Father of His Country as an inexhaustible source of income with which to ward off swarming creditors. In history the two men are inescapably linked. In life they barely spoke to each other. Throughout the many hours of sittings, Stuart tried and failed to draw the president into conversation. Only the topic of agriculture could coax more than a few sentences out of Washington, who refused to let down his guard, much less grant Stuart the kind of instant intimacy the voluble society painter expected as his due.

"Now sir, you must let one forget that you are General Washington and that I am Mr. Stuart," said the artist.

Not so fast, replied the subject. "Mr. Stuart need never feel the need of forgetting who he is or who General Washington is."*

Yet whatever his private thoughts about the saucy genius with his London training and his ragbag mind, Washington submitted a second time to Stuart's fixed stare in order that Ann Bingham might have a gift for her friend Lord Landsdowne. Stuart got his revenge by removing Washington's lower dentures and inserting cotton in their place "to fill

---

*Stuart might have thought better of the president had he been privy to a conversation between Henry Lee and the Washingtons. Lee retailed the artist's remark that Washington had a tremendous temper, which caused Martha to say that Mr. Stuart assumed a great deal. Lee then finished Stuart's statement, to the effect that the president had his temper under "wonderful control." Washington pondered this for a moment before answering, with a smile on his lips, "Mr. Stuart is right."

out the lip." The result was what connoisseurs ever since have called the postage slot mouth, the forerunner of a series of reproductions whose blank eyes and stony expression have entered American folklore, freezing the first president's historical image while filling Stuart's pockets with the proceeds of inferior copies dashed off to pay his mounting bills. For her money Mrs. Bingham received a full-length image of a sham potentate, looking every bit an American George I as he stood amid flowing drapes and the papers of state. This was very much an *official* Washington, less vital and more distant than Stuart's earlier likeness, betraying none of the president's apprehension as the House of Representatives convulsed itself in a final marathon over Jay's Treaty.

Madison led off the argument with familiar reproaches against American concessions to the royal bully in Windsor Castle. Buttressed by a heavy Republican majority, on April 18 the little Virginian boldly forecast victory with twenty votes to spare. But Madison reckoned without Hamilton's audacity in employing grass-roots pressure — that bulwark of republicanism — against the party of the people. "We must seize and carry along with us the public opinion," wrote the former secretary to Rufus King, who obliged with a mass meeting of Philadelphia's merchants. John Marshall organized a similar rally that drew nearly 400 treaty sympathizers in Richmond, and other communities followed suit in a chain reaction that shook Republican confidence throughout the Old Dominion. Hamilton's campaign soon reached national proportions. Congregational clergy in New England mixed Federalist politics with divine instruction. Bostonians, reversing their earlier opposition to the treaty, now perceived its economic benefits as uncertainty over war with England drove up insurance rates and confined most of the local fleet to the docks. In Baltimore, the pinch of hardship was equaled by the pull of old loyalties as citizens rallied around the cry "Washington and Peace."

With the current of opinion clearly flowing their way, some Federalists urged the Senate to withhold approving other treaties that formally acknowledged Spanish, Algerian, and Indian concessions in hopes that Westerners would demand acquiescence in Jay's much less popular covenant. Hamilton disagreed with such an approach, contending that all the upper chamber had to do was remain in session until the House, drowning in pro-treaty petitions, capitulated and approved the funds needed to implement it. Failing that, said Hamilton, "the President [must] be called upon . . . to *keep his post* till another House of Representatives has pronounced." John Jay went still further, making a direct appeal to Washington on April 18. "Remain with us at least while the storm lasts," he said, "and until you can retire like the sun in a calm unclouded evening."

Madison looked on helplessly as his twenty-vote margin evaporated under relentless Federalist hammering. "The people have been everywhere made to believe that the object of the House of Representatives in resisting the treaty was war, and have thence listened to the summons 'to follow where Washington leads,' " he wrote in disgust. On April 26, lawmakers on both sides of the aisle sat spellbound as Fisher Ames, the Federalists' greatest orator, rose from what many believed to be his deathbed to make a soaring argument for the treaty, his eloquence heightened by halting gestures and a gruesome pallor. (In fact, Ames would survive his melodramatic performance by twelve years.) But as glittering as Ames's words were, they could hardly match in practical terms the West's subsiding opposition to a pact that did, after all, yield up the British outposts and promise an end to frontier terrorism.

On April 28, sitting as a Committee of the Whole, the House was deadlocked on whether to bring the treaty to the floor. Unexpectedly, Speaker Frederick Muhlenberg, a Republican stalwart, voted in the affirmative. This set the scene for a second roll call, an up or down vote on the appropriation itself, which passed by a 51–48 vote. A few days later Muhlenberg's brother-in-law registered a violent dissent by plunging a knife into the apostate's chest. The Speaker survived the attack, which was more than could be said of his political career. Like Governor Jay, his hopes for higher office were permanently blasted by association with the controversial treaty.

Muhlenberg's party, having aimed at the king and missed, staggered from the battlefield clutching its own, self-inflicted wound. From Monticello, Jefferson conceded that as long as Washington remained at the helm of state, "Republicanism must lie on its oars, resign the vessel to its pilot, and themselves to the course he thinks best." Publicly silent, Washington loosed his wrath in private correspondence against those who had brought the Constitution to "the brink of a precipice." Representatives not concerned with the merits of the treaty had focused instead on "whether there should be a *treaty at all*" without House concurrence.

Yet "every true friend to this Country must *see* and *feel* that the policy of it is not to embroil ourselves with any nation whatever; but to avoid their disputes and their politics," Washington declared, "and if they will harass one another, to avail ourselves of the neutral conduct we have adopted. Twenty years peace with such an increase of population and resources as we have a right to expect . . . will in all probability enable us in a just cause to bid defiance to any power on earth."

Washington told his friend Edward Carrington that while it would always be his earnest desire to learn and comply with public sentiment, "it is on *great* occasions *only,* and after time has been given for cool and deliberate reflection, that the *real* voice of the people can be known." He carried this argument a step further in writing to Jay on May 8: "I am *sure* the Mass of Citizens in these United States *means well*, whenever they can obtain a right understanding of matters." But this was not easily accomplished in sections of the Union where opposition editors planted doubts about his government's commitment to popular liberties.

"To this source all our discontents may be traced and from it our embarrassments proceed," Washington added, anticipating the resentments voiced at one time or another by each of his successors.

❧ 6 ❧

From its beginning in the Senate chamber of Congress Hall Washington's second term had been a more or less constant exercise in crisis management. The troubles and perplexities occasioned by journalistic misrepresentation "added to the weight of years which have . . . worn away my mind more than my body" now made retirement imperative. Only dire events or such circumstances as would render his retreat dishonorable could prevent Washington from announcing his intention to leave office in March 1797. Compounding his unhappiness were fresh rumors of a French fleet sailing west to enforce the Franco-American alliance ruptured by Jay's Treaty. The president put scant credence in the report; still, he told Hamilton that if faced with a foreign ultimatum, "we will not be dictated to by the politics of any nation under heaven, farther than treaties require of us . . . if we are to be told by a foreign power . . . what we *shall do*, and what we shall *not do*, we have Independence yet to seek, and have contended hitherto for very little."

In mid-May, Hamilton received Washington's proposed farewell address, grafting onto Madison's text of 1792 new language cautioning Americans against domestic factionalism and foreign alliances. Long before, Washington had said of the ideal secretary that he "ought . . . to possess the soul of the General; and, from a single idea given to them, to convey his meaning in the clearest and fullest manner." Building upon many years of intimate association, Hamilton would take full advantage of his friend's invitation to recast his valedictory, starting with Washington's notion that he must justify his decision to retire lest others attribute it wrongly to a decline in popularity and despair over his chances of reelection. Given wide latitude to edit any unseemly passages, Hamilton eliminated the president's tart critique of newspapers teeming "with all the invective that disappointment, ignorance of facts, and malicious falsehoods could invent to misrepresent my politics." After having raised the specter of base ingratitude, Washington professed (less than convincingly) not to notice it. He also strained to dispel rumors of personal enrichment while in office. To the contrary, declared the aging chief executive, he left the presidency "with undefiled hands, an uncorrupted heart," and ardent vows to heaven for his country's welfare and happiness.

As Hamilton scribbled for posterity, Washington turned his attention to other matters, inquiring of Frederick the Great in a carefully worded private letter whether the unfortunate Lafayette might not be released from his jail cell and permitted to immigrate to the United States. Up from the South came a familiar lament: work on the Federal City, infested, in the words of one building contractor's wife, with "dolts, delvers, magicians, soothsayers, quacks, bankrupts, puffs, speculators, monopolizers, extortioners, traitors, petit foggy lawyers, and ham brickmakers," was lagging. The president spurred its builders to pick up the sluggish pace by reminding them, "The year 1800 is approaching by hasty strides."

So was March 1797 and the prospect of imminent emancipation. We are indebted to a pair of British visitors for some unusually candid observations of Washington in the penultimate months of his presidency. Shortly after noon on Friday, May 13, Thomas Twining knocked on the door of 190 Market Street. At the age of twenty, he was a seasoned world traveler, a protégé of the same Lord Cornwallis whose defeat at Yorktown had completed the Washington legend while turning John Bull's world upside down. For Cornwallis, the road out of Yorktown had led to the governor-generalship of India, where he befriended the youthful Rugby graduate from the family whose name was synonymous with exotic coffees and teas. Twining advanced rapidly thereafter, becoming the first clerk in the Honourable East India Company's Bengal Service to be received by the great mogul in Delhi.

In November 1795 he embarked for America to see yet another bashaw, albeit in less baroque surroundings. A Bengal cow and an Afghan mountain sheep called a doombah accompanied him on his fourteen-thousand-mile journey from the Bay of Bengal to the mouth of the Delaware River. In Philadelphia, Twining enjoyed the ample hospitality of William Bingham, who generously offered to house the visiting menagerie while the young Englishman toured the American countryside. The doombah duly took his place among the capital's most popular attractions as its owner set off for the small red brick house, where a servant escorted Twining to a second-floor parlor. In a few minutes Mrs. Washington appeared to receive a letter of introduction from Tobias Lear and a miniature of the president by an artist unknown today. She took these offerings to her husband, leaving the visitor to make a mental picture of the plainly carpeted room, without pictures on the walls or ornaments on the chimneypiece.

After a short interval the door opened to reveal Washington, a sight worth several doombahs. "So completely did he *look* the great and good man he really was," recalled Twining, "that I felt respect rather than awe in his presence, and experienced neither the surprise nor disappointment with which a personal introduction to distinguished individuals is often accompanied." Washington put his caller further at ease by drawing a chair up beside the sofa where Twining sat next to the first lady. The president inquired about the youth's voyage and his own granddaughters in Alexandria, whom Twining had recently met. Washington beamed with pleasure over a report of heavy business activity in the riverfront town. He smiled again when Twining mentioned the high regard Cornwallis felt for his former rival. His Lordship was a gentleman, after all, and it was not in Washington's nature to hold a grudge, least of all against a soldier who, by falling fortuitously into a Franco-American trap, had disproved lingering doubts about Washington's generalship. After an hour of animated conversation Twining rose to go. He left "entirely satisfied" with the interview, convinced that George Washington was an even greater man than portrayed in legend.

Hardly less admiring was a second British visitor, one far more accustomed than Twining to official pretensions. King George had at last decided to replace the haughty and intrusive George Hammond with a Scottish diplomat named Robert Liston. Almost from the moment of his arrival in May 1796, the congenial Liston won the president's trust. An encyclopedic knowledge of agriculture recommended the new man, as did a shrewd and sympathetic wife to whom Washington responded much as he had to the perceptive Eliza Powel.

The couple made several visits to Mount Vernon, where they tramped over every corner of the estate, the men comparing notes on Virginia soil and the obstacles to scientific farming in a nation where land was cheap and labor dear. Henrietta Liston recorded expansive talk of plows and planting seasons while noting that on the subject of politics the president held back from committing himself. Yet the sprightly Highlands beauty soon bridged the moat of formality with which Washington guarded his private thoughts. Deeply moved by his recollections of an emotionally stunted youth and inferior education, she was no less amazed by her friend's "perfect good breeding" and mental detachment. Mrs. Liston disputed the claim of critics who said that Washington could hardly frame a letter without assistance from more polished wordsmiths. Marveling at the finesse with which he drafted official papers as well as private correspondence, the diplomat's wife concluded that "he has always written better than the gentleman to whom the merit of his letters was ascribed."

This should have come as no surprise, for Washington, a rigorous student in the school of self-improvement, was more of a reader than generally supposed. In his personal library at Mount Vernon he had assembled almost nine hundred titles neatly apportioned among husbandry and history, statecraft, travelogues, geographical surveys, and works of imaginative fancy. Besides the speeches of Cicero, Milton's poems, *Aesop's Fables*, and John Locke's *On Human Understanding*, Washington could turn to novels by Henry Fielding and Samuel Butler, Adam Smith's *Wealth of Nations*, and a well-thumbed copy of his favorite play, Addison's *Cato*, which the general had once staged at Valley Forge to raise the morale of a dispirited army.

"Turn up thy eyes to Cato," said royal Juba to the bewitching Marcia:

> There may'st thou see to what a godlike height
> The Roman virtues lift up mortal man.
> While good, and just, and anxious for his friends,
> He's still severely bent against himself . . .
> The pomps and pleasures that his soul can wish,
> His rigid virtue will accept of none.

Washington's inordinate fondness for the play and its hero was revealing. Henrietta Liston, for one, saw enough of the president's rigid Roman virtue to judge him coldblooded. Yet she also caught glimmers of youthful irony — or was it the tragicomedy of old age? — in Washington's rationale for stepping down at the end of a second term, related through the story of Gil Blas's doddering old archbishop, who insisted that a servant inform him when his pulpit powers began to decline, only to sack the honest retainer the moment he complied with the order. Better a graceful exit, the president implied, than the humiliating spectacle of creeping senility.

Mrs. Liston aside, the number of intimates to whom Washington might confess fears of outstaying his welcome remained astonishingly small. On June 12 he wrote to David Humphreys, his putative biographer, of an impending trip to Mount Vernon in hopes of getting "a little relaxation from the unpleasant scenes which . . . are continually presenting themselves to my view." From State Department messages and the public gazettes Humphreys could easily form an estimate of the quickening campaign to choose the next president as well as the related attacks upon the incumbent for steadily opposing every measure tending to disturb the nation's peace and tranquility. No amount of barbed arrows, "unjust and unpleasant as they are," would change Washington's conduct or affect his thinking, other than to increase an already powerful longing for escape from the toils of office.

Congress had adjourned at the beginning of the month, Washington told William Pearce at Mount Vernon, but it would be some time yet before the first family appeared at their front door. "I shall travel slow," he explained, "to avoid what usually happens to me at this season — that is, killing or knocking up a horse." In the meantime, the estate manager should expect heavy traffic "of the most respectable sort," as diplomats from several European powers took a final opportunity to pay their respects at Washington's country seat. Besides the Listons, Farmer Washington welcomed Spain's recently accredited minister Carlos Martinez, the marquis de Casa Yrujo, "a young man, very free and easy in his manners." The president anticipated a visit from Pierre Adet, but the French envoy, still fuming over Jay's Treaty and scheming to conquer Louisiana for the Directory in Paris, had no wish to cross Washington's threshold — much less after a French privateer seized an American merchant ship, ironically named *Mount Vernon*, as a harbinger of stormy relations between the former allies.

Events in Europe were entering a new and dangerous phase in the summer of 1796. On the strength of his latest victories in Italy, Napoleon Bonaparte was the continent's rising man. With Austria cracking under relentless French pressure and the pope held a virtual prisoner in his Vatican apartments, the king of Italy was forced to cede Savoy and Nice to the Gallic invader. Sensing an imminent crisis in Franco-American relations, Washington concluded that James Monroe was the wrong man in the wrong place at the wrong time. Monroe, not surprisingly, held a different view: when the Directory in Paris formally abrogated the Treaty of 1778, the American envoy claimed credit for averting even harsher measures against his government.

This was cold comfort to Washington. It was quite bad enough for Monroe to house the veteran pamphleteer Thomas Paine, the hero of two revolutions and gadfly of two continents, whose bitterness over the president's failure to spring him from a French jail cell would inspire the most scathing attack ever made on the old hero. Even more offensive to the administration was Monroe's refusal to curtail his own Republican politicking, which included sending heavily slanted accounts of French superiority to Bache's *Aurora* under the ill-disguised signature of "a gentleman in Paris [writing] to his friend in Philadelphia." Unfriendly gossips made capital out of an incident at a Parisian dinner party of Americans celebrating the Fourth of July. When a guest critical of Jay's Treaty took issue with a toast to Washington, Monroe countered by raising his glass to "the executive." Only after diners who supported the treaty persisted in drinking to General Washington's personal health did Monroe reluctantly join in.

By the middle of 1796, Yankee commerce was under assault from French captains on the high seas and Monroe's days were clearly numbered. In June the envoy received a sternly worded reprimand from Timothy Pickering, whose tone reminded the Virginia slaveowner of an overseer disciplining his gang. By then, Pickering was openly lobbying for Monroe's replacement by John Quincy Adams, a presidential favorite. But Washington had his own plan to conciliate the sullen French, hoping to repeat the special envoy trick that had already soothed contentious relations with Great Britain, Spain, and Algiers. Although the Senate was out of town, and the executive's authority to dispatch such a mission without congressional approval was clouded at best, on July 8 Washington cut an order dismissing Monroe. That same day he chose as a successor Charles Cotesworth Pinckney, another Southerner broadly sympathetic to France's Revolution, whose brother Thomas had negotiated the hugely popular Treaty of San Lorenzo.

When Benjamin Franklin Bache touched off a fresh uproar by disclosing the earlier Cabinet deliberations on U.S. neutrality, Jefferson hastened to deny responsibility for the leak. The former secretary of state, having recently told political friends that the administration's actions were being carried out "under the sanction of a name which has done too much good not to be sufficient to cover harm also," tried to smooth over the affair with some agricultural chatter. "I put away this disgusting dish of old fragments," he wrote from Monticello, "and talk to you of peas and clover."

But Washington was not to be put off so easily. While absolving Jefferson of blame for the leak — widely attributed to an embittered Edmund Randolph — the president acknowledged that the story had touched a nerve. It would not be "frank, candid, or friendly" to deny that he had heard reports alleging uncomplimentary references by Jefferson. Even so, "My answer invariably has been, that I had never discovered anything in the conduct of Mr. Jefferson to raise suspicions in my mind of his sincerity." Following this less than ringing endorsement Washington asked, in obvious distress, how anyone of Jefferson's perspicacity could really believe him a mere pawn of Hamilton's. If only the Republican leader retraced the president's conduct while they were both in office, he would find abundant proof of executive evenhandedness.

Until the last year or two, Washington told Jefferson, he had no idea to what lengths parties would go to blacken his reputation, even though "I was using my utmost exertions to establish a national character of our own, independent . . . of every nation on earth." What was his reward for keeping the United States out of war? Why, "that I should be accused of being the enemy of one nation, and subject to the influence of another; and to prove it, that every act of my administration would be tortured and the grossest, and most insidious misrepresentations of them be made . . . in such exaggerated and indecent terms as could scarcely be applied to a Nero; a notorious defaulter; or even to a common pickpocket. But enough of this; I have already gone farther in the expression of my feelings than I intended."

Or had he? Washington could have easily torn up the angry passage and started over. But he was in no mood to understate his feelings of betrayal or wink and nod while Jefferson rewrote history for partisan advantage. Henrietta Liston did not exaggerate her friend's ability to say precisely what he wanted in phrases sure to reverberate.

❊ 13 ❊

AN HONORABLE DISCHARGE

"A solemn scene it was indeed, and it was made affecting to me by the presence of the General, whose
countenance was as serene and unclouded as the day.
He seemed to me to enjoy a triumph over me. Me-
thought I heard him say 'Ay! I am fairly out and you
fairly in! See which of us will be happiest!' "

> John Adams,
> describing his inauguration,
> March 5, 1797

WASHINGTON SPENT THE LAST SUMMER of his presidency where he
hoped to pass all his days out of office, at Mount Vernon. Come the
spring of 1797, there would be no shortage of constructive labors to
occupy a statesman turned farmer. The manager of the estate, William
Pearce, was leaving, his rheumatic complaints forcing him to make way
for a younger, more vigorous man. The diligent Pearce would be missed,
yet the evidence of physical decay in Washington's fields and outbuildings,
even in Mansion House itself, showed the limitations of oversight by an
absentee owner.

An engaging description of Farmer Washington comes to us from the
pen of Benjamin Latrobe, an urbane, European-trained architect who fled
the Old World to offer his services to the fledgling republic across the
Atlantic. The thirty-year-old Latrobe was still recovering from a nervous
breakdown following the death of his wife and the collapse of London's
building market when he landed at Norfolk in March 1796. He spent the
next four months exploring the countryside of Virginia, charming its
barons with stories of the immortal Dr. Johnson — with whom his parents were on intimate terms — and being disappointed by its great
houses, so much shabbier than their British counterparts. Armed with

a recommendation from the president's nephew Bushrod, the English artist with French sympathies approached the front gate of Mount Vernon on July 17. He was pleasantly surprised by Washington's "good fences, clean grounds, and extensive cultivation." The main house he judged about the norm for "a plain English country gentleman's house of five hundred or six hundred pounds a year."

Latrobe tethered his horse, sent in his letter of introduction, and strode around to the riverfront, where he gazed admiringly at the broad Potomac. "In about ten minutes the President came to me. He was attired in a plain blue coat, his hair dressed and powdered. He shook me by the hand and desired me to sit down." The two men spent a pleasant hour in a conversational tour of the Old Dominion. Washington spoke freely of rivers and canal-building plans and the Dismal Swamp property he had recently (and unprofitably) unloaded on Henry Lee. Fearful of detaining his host from his correspondence, Latrobe rose to leave, but Washington waved him back to his chair for a second discussion, this time about English architecture and the nascent American economy. Latrobe raised the possibility of finding silver in Virginia; Washington dismissed the idea, expressing a wish that America's soil "might contain no mines but such as the plow could reach, excepting only coal and iron."

In the time before dinner, the foreign visitor toured Mount Vernon's grounds and made sketches of what he surveyed. Back inside, he found Mrs. Washington an agreeable and good-humored hostess. But it was Nelly Custis who fixed Latrobe's attention. At seventeen, Nelly was "everything that the chisel of Phidias aimed at but could not reach," her dark ringlets and hourglass figure flatteringly displayed in a Parisian gown of the latest style. The enchantress said little at dinner, a meal otherwise enlivened by banter between the president and young Lafayette, "whom he treats more as his child than as a guest." The party soon repaired to the portico, there to be joined by Tobias Lear and his sons. Again Latrobe signaled his intention of leaving and again Washington urged him to stay. After coffee was served at six, the president gave a detailed account of the alarming southern progress of the Hessian fly (presumably no worse than the mosquitoes of New Jersey, which in Washington's puckish phrase "bite through the thickest boots").

That the sophisticated European was intellectually engaged by such homely chatter may be doubted. Nor was there any mistaking Latrobe's surprise when Washington turned in for the night around eight o'clock and the rest of the household — sans supper — followed suit. Up at dawn the next day, Latrobe continued his inspection of the landscape around Mansion House. At precisely seven-thirty the squire appeared for a light breakfast and the morning newspapers (he received as many as ten on a regular basis). As Latrobe took his leave, he looked over his shoulder and saw Washington standing in the west doorway, extolling his pet project of a federally chartered university to be located in the future capital.

Recounting the most memorable experience of his American journey, Latrobe wrote, "Washington had something uncommonly majestic and commanding in his walk, his address, his figure, and his countenance." Dozens of observers had said as much over the years, but with an artist's gift for seeing beyond the surface, Latrobe characterized the president's face as marked "more by intensive thought than by quick and fiery conception. There is a mildness about its expression; an air of reserve in his manner lowers its tone still more." Washington's frequent silences produced an awkwardness in everyone present. Moreover, said Latrobe, "he did not speak at any time with remarkable fluency. Perhaps the extreme correctness of his language, which almost seemed studied, prevented that effect." Henrietta Liston had noticed a similar hesitancy, as if every word were being weighed for its possible impact.

Yet the master of Mount Vernon also had a sense of humor, making repeated jests and heartily laughing at the wry comments of others. More than a gracious host, he displayed a gift for friendship. "On the morning of my departure he treated me as if I had lived many years in his house, with ease and attention," Latrobe concluded, "but I thought there was a slight air of moroseness about him, as though something had vexed him." Far better than Gilbert Stuart, Benjamin Latrobe caught the multiple layers of Washington's personality — the smiling innkeeper and agricultural enthusiast; the relaxed paterfamilias and high-strung statesman; the actor, offstage, glad for the chance to remove his paint yet unable to permit genuine spontaneity. Most of all, Latrobe detected in the president an unarticulated resistiveness lurking behind the stern Roman front.

❧ 2 ❧

Washington's skittishness may have hinged on his country's rapidly deteriorating relations with France. In mid-August the president interrupted his vacation to return to Philadelphia for discussions with Pickering and formal meetings with the ministers of Holland and Spain. A new problem presented itself in the form of a five-month-old letter from Monroe revealing that the French Directory, through unspecified means, had intercepted a presidential communication to Gouverneur Morris written in December 1795. According to Monroe, the French were distinctly unhappy with what they read.

Muting his anger over this blatant invasion of his privacy, Washington voiced astonishment that a stated intention to remain at peace with all the world could really offend the rulers of France. In fact, the bulk of Washington's message to Morris had reiterated America's displeasure over British conduct in provoking Indian attacks on western settlers, impressing U.S. seamen, and otherwise menacing neutral shipping in international waters. Having placed his rebuke of Lord Grenville's harassing tactics in context, for Monroe Washington summarized his prevailing attitude toward the prickly French. "I have always wished well to the French revolution," he declared. Nevertheless, as a staunch believer in national self-determination, "I have always given it as my decided opinion that no nation had a right to intermeddle in the internal concerns of another; that everyone had a right to form and adopt whatever government they liked best to live under themselves." Neutrality was the only course open to "a people situated as we are, already deeply in debt, and in a convalescent state from the struggle we have been engaged in ourselves."

Three thousand miles away, undeterred by modesty, still ignorant of his impending recall, Monroe rode an emotional roller-coaster. "Poor Washington!" he sighed patronizingly. "Into what hands he has fallen!" The American envoy despaired at rumors, subsequently disproved, that France was about to replace Pierre Adet with a new representative personally obnoxious to Washington; he was plunged into gloom when the Directory formally suspended relations with its faithless ally. "We must raise up the people and at the same time conceal the lever by which we do so," wrote Charles Delacroix, the minister of foreign relations, to his Directory masters. To achieve their goals, Adet was "to use all means in his power in the United States to bring about a successful revolution and Washington's retirement," this being considered the surest way to abrogate Jay's Treaty and firmly fix the North American republic in France's orbit.

Consistent with such a hard-line policy, France launched attacks on neutral vessels carrying British goods, severed U.S. commercial ties to the West Indies, and publicly snubbed Monroe's successor, Charles Cotesworth Pinckney, when he arrived in Paris that December. Yet if the final months of Washington's term were darkened by the possibility of war, they were alleviated for the president by the knowledge that if ever shots were fired, the responsibility of leading Americans into battle would fall to another man. By the start of September, Washington was examining Hamilton's revision of the Farewell Address and regretting that he had not published his valedictory upon the adjournment of Congress three months earlier. The longer the delay, the greater the credence given his enemies' theory that only the fear of rejection at the polls motivated him to abandon Philadelphia, like a wounded animal creeping back to its lair. Before returning to Virginia at midmonth to gather up his family and bring them back for a final northern social season, Washington thanked Hamilton for eliminating the bitterness in the original text, sheepishly justifying earlier complaints about journalistic abuse as being directed at "the yeomanry of this country . . . in language that was plain and intelligible to their understanding."*

A few days later the president received a delegation from the Cherokee Nation. Addressing them as "Beloved Cherokees," he urged them to walk the path of coexistence with their white neighbors, accepting protection, instruction, and aid in converting from their nomadic status to become established tillers of soil. "What I have recommended to you I am myself going to do," he told the Indians. "After a few moons are passed I shall leave the great town and retire to my farm. There I shall attend to the means of increasing my cattle, sheep and other useful animals; to the growing of corn, wheat, and other grain, and to the employing of women in spinning and weaving."

It would give him great pleasure, said Washington, to hear that the Cherokees had embraced the self-sustaining livelihood he now proposed for their consideration, a program of critical significance, not only for the Cherokees, but for the future of their relations with the white man on the continent both races must share. If successful, "the beloved men of the United States will be encouraged to give the same assistance to all the Indian tribes within their boundaries. But if it should fail, they may think it vain to make any further attempts to better the condition of any Indian tribe; for the richness of the soil and mildness of the air render your country highly favorable for the practice of what I have recommended."

In a second letter to Hamilton, Washington proposed renewing in the Farewell Address his plea for a national university. Such an institution would be indispensable for "those . . . disposed to run a political course" and who, by residing in the Federal City, might observe at first hand the principles and practice of republican government. Seven years of war against Great Britain had done more to dispel sectional attachments than a century of normal intercourse between the states. Would not a national university likewise serve to accelerate the process of social and political integration? Hamilton dissented, arguing that the Farewell Address was intended to be read in distant times, and that the university scheme in

---

*Coming full circle from his first draft, Washington even deleted an apology for involuntary errors "to avoid the imputation of affected modesty."

any event was more suited to the president's annual speech opening Congress. Washington grudgingly yielded the point; his faith in Hamilton's literary and political judgment was by now undisguised.

No small agency in this growing reliance was a Cabinet less talented, if also less quarrelsome, than its celebrated predecessor. As a courtesy, Washington submitted the Farewell Address for review by his nominal advisers on the morning of September 15. Twenty-four hours later he sent for David Claypoole, publisher of the reliably Federalist *American Daily Advertiser*, who had been chosen to carry the president's parting thoughts and summary counsel to a worldwide audience. Suitable precautions were taken to maintain confidentiality prior to publication, set for Monday, September 19. Tobias Lear delivered the text in Washington's hand to be set in type and reviewed by Claypoole himself. By Saturday, the president was examining a proof sheet; he changed little, according to Claypoole, "except in the punctuation, in which he was very minute." Seeing the newspaperman's face fall at the thought of losing the marked copy, Washington handed over the priceless document to Claypoole, with the dry comment that the printer might have what he wished for.

The president was up earlier than usual on the morning of the nineteenth. Before dawn he signed 147 ships' passes for the secretary of state along with half a dozen blank commissions. Washington's old flair for the dramatic had not deserted him: public release of the Farewell Address was carefully timed to coincide with its author's departure for Mount Vernon, his last official journey to the beloved estate soon to be a permanent refuge from the storms of political life. When next he traveled the uncertain roads between Philadelphia and Virginia, it would be as a private citizen whose administrative domain had shrunk to an agricultural village of thirteen square miles.

❦ 3 ❦

At first glance, there was nothing about the issue of the *American Daily Advertiser* on September 19 to set it apart. On the front page was the usual diet of advertisements and commercial notices. Only on turning the page did readers find any hint of the unusual:

> To the PEOPLE of the United States
> Friends and fellow citizens:

What followed confirmed the president's fears of Hamiltonian prolixity, as the final text of this, the most important public message of Washington's life, filled an entire page of Claypoole's gazette and part of another. Vastly more ink has been spilled in the years since trying to settle conflicting claims of authorship. Beyond dispute are the first ten paragraphs, which closely follow Madison's draft of May 1792. Equally certain is that much of the rest of the paper bears Hamilton's unmistakably assertive stamp.

Yet the Farewell Address is justifiably viewed as Washington's political testament. Why? Largely because of the parallels with Washington's famous circular of June 1783, sent to the states loosely affiliated in their postwar confederation. Support for the Union as a guarantor of individual liberty and national greatness; the mutual dependence of separate regions for the economic survival of all; a denunciation of political factions for their destructive effect on public confidence in government; and a stern admonition against American citizens holding foreign allegiances or American leaders locked in permanent alliances abroad — all but the last of these themes were apparent in Washington's appeal after the Revolution, while his private correspondence and public statements as president are replete with calls for national self-sufficiency and a firm neutrality toward every other power on earth.

Perhaps the best way of attributing responsibility is to say that Hamilton coined what Washington had mined during twenty years of public advocacy. Yet this does not begin to resolve all the mysteries surrounding a document that ranks as a statement of American purpose alongside Jefferson's Declaration and Lincoln's new birth of freedom proclaimed at Gettysburg. For example, how could it be that a leader so inherently suspicious of organized factions could have any clearly defined politics of his own? The answer lies in the fact that Washington was less a politician in the modern sense — wheedling support, threatening or cajoling legislators to enact his personal agenda — than a gifted psychologist and manipulator of public symbolism. He was a Federalist before there was a party of that name, if only because federalism offered a restraining influence on men whose innate tendency to abuse liberty threatened the American republic from birth.

His illusions burned away by hard experience in peace and war, Washington never suffered the excessive faith in the goodness of man that is a chronic affliction of most modern reformers. One must accept the natural limitations of his fellow human beings, the general had asserted of his patriot soldiers: "After the first emotions are over, to expect among such people as comprise the bulk of an army, that they are influenced by any other principles than those of Interest, is to look for what never did, and I fear never will happen."

In common with other framers of the Constitution, Washington faced the conundrum: how could a free society harmonize its competing interests? But he was better prepared than most, for with his intuitive understanding of the age-old clash between duty and advantage, he did not fear Interest. Far from it. For what else *but* Interest had led him to amass vast land holdings, not always through the nicest of methods; or pursue youthful fame and adult fortune with an ardor that would put twentieth-century candidates for office to shame; or deny Great Britain's traditional right to tax his property, restrict his commercial dealings, and dismiss his protests?

But there were interests greater than Interest, and causes nobler than personal advancement. Over time, private gain had taken a back seat to Washington's campaign for nationhood, rooted in the radical concept that grasping men could be entrusted to govern themselves without the superintendency of an established church or divinely appointed monarch. He wrote the Farewell Address for the same reason and in the same spirit with which he had sacrificed eight years to the thankless demands of office — hoping to demonstrate by force of example that men could love their country no less than themselves. "The shade of retirement is as necessary to me as it will be welcome," said Washington, an expression that carried multiple meanings. For in renouncing a third term, he gave the lie to those who thought him a dictator in embryo. More important, by establishing an orderly transfer of power, he demonstrated that a strong government was compatible with the most cherished liberties of English-speaking peoples.

The dominant theme of Washington's address was national unity, the underlying mood, one of buoyant optimism about the nation's prospects *if* it could hold in check the centrifugal forces associated with domestic factionalism and foreign intrigue. Hamilton was the president's natural partner, for he, too, envisioned the best government as that which harnessed primitive drives to society's advantage. Thus his fervent support for capitalist institutions designed to transform a weak confederation into a wealthy and powerful nation capable of maintaining its independence against all rivals. And so the Farewell Address became, like the administration it capped, an intellectual alliance between two like-minded nationalists.

Not content merely to reinforce patriotic feelings of pride — any Fourth of July orator, in his day or ours, could do that — Washington invited his readers to look beyond narrow ties of regional and state loyalty to see themselves as an entirely new breed in a young and rapidly evolving land: "The name of AMERICAN, which belongs to you in your national capacity, must always exalt the just pride of patriotism more than any appellation derived from local discriminations." Consistent with this outlook, he fashioned a straightforward appeal to sectional interests, reminding Northerners of their reliance on southern markets and ports and the South of its dependence on Yankee ships and seamen. Eastern merchants required western customers, said the president, but no more than western development needed eastern investment.

Obviously Washington's United States was greater than the sum of its parts. But what if disaster struck and this delicately balanced structure were to fall apart? The president could foresee nothing but misery, bloodshed, and privation as bloated military establishments trampled popular liberties and rump republics fell victim to the same strife defacing the map of Europe. It required little experience of statecraft to envision Old World powers, unable to resist the lure of easy conquest, moving to destabilize from within what remained of republican government. All this was in Washington's mind as he wrote, "Your Union ought to be considered as a main prop of your liberty, the love of the one ought to endear to you the preservation of the other."

Suspicious of extremes, ardent for moderation, Washington threw all his prestige on the scales of constitutional government, "uniting security with energy, and containing within itself a provision for its own amendment." In defining the essence of American liberty as the people's right to make and alter their fundamental charter, Washington captured in a sentence both the fluidity and permanence of true republicanism. Still, no Constitution could begin the world over or make human beings into angels. The best that Washington could realistically hope for was to create political institutions inhibiting the baser side of men while channeling their energies toward subduing the continent and uniting a polyglot America. It was against this background that he warned his countrymen to reject factionalism and the "small but artful and enterprising minority" whose primary allegiance was to a party. In their place, the president demanded "a government of as much vigor as is consistent with the perfect security of liberty."

This was not the seeming contradiction that it may appear to modern eyes, for Washington and his contemporaries labored under the frowning example of imperial Rome, the more recent abuses staining seventeenth- and eighteenth-century Britain, and post-Bourbon France, wherein the intoxicating brew of liberty had produced anarchy and dictatorship. Americans must guard against party strife as the serpent in their constitutional Garden of Eden. "It serves always to distract the public councils and enfeeble the public administration," claimed Washington. "It agitates the community with ill-founded jealousies and false claims, kindles the animosity of one part against another, foments occasionally riot and insurrection." Worst of all, "It opens the door to foreign influence and corruption" (shades of Pierre Adet's western adventuring and James Monroe's love affair with Thermidorean France).

For two hundred years, Washington's critics have accused him at worst of antidemocratic tendencies, at best of a raging case of political naiveté. Yet nowhere in his Farewell Address did he deny the ingrained human tendency to take sides or the ultimate supremacy of public opinion in a free society. Quite the contrary. "A fire not to be quenched," he labeled party politics, but one that "demands a uniform vigilance to prevent its bursting into a flame, lest instead of warming it should consume." The brunt of Washington's attack was aimed at mindless politicking that results in the triumph of petty self-interest over the larger good. This is a position not unattractive to latter-day voters, fed up with the paralysis of democracy in a superficial civic culture of sound bites, Rose Garden ceremonies, greedy special interests, and unresponsive officeholders. Who today would rush to deny that the flame of factionalism threatens to gut our faith in the democratic process, just as Washington feared that the collapse of republican self-restraint would lead inevitably to a man on horseback?

Likewise, Washington's admonition to avoid *both* "permanent, inveterate antipathies against particular nations and passionate attachments for others" has been misrepresented from the moment it was made. Contemporaries who read into his words an apology for England and a thinly veiled rebuke of revolutionary France underestimated Washington's perceptive reading of human nature. "The nation which indulges toward another an habitual hatred, or an habitual fondness, is in some degree a slave," the president contended. "It is a slave to its animosity or to its affection, either of which is sufficient to lead it astray from its duty and its interest."

Duty and Interest: these were the twin imperatives of the good life as defined by Washington. Among nations as well as individuals, judgment could be clouded by excessive partiality. Imagined common interests led to unwise concessions, which in turn bred resentments and reprisals by those less favored. But the greatest danger of domestic factionalism lay in the innumerable avenues it opened for foreign agents seeking to bewitch the republican mind, invading government councils and aligning themselves with political cliques. It was not French schemers alone who confirmed this brutal fact of life, but British officials playing upon the red man's wounded pride and Spanish representatives dangling the prospect of an independent West before turncoats on both sides of the Appalachians.

Washington had struggled too long for personal independence to accept himself or his country as a mere satellite of Europe. While the United States should develop extensive commercial relations with the Old World, he believed that it must avoid formal political allegiances. Europe had its own interests, remote from or incompatible with those of a youthful republic highly vulnerable to internal stresses. Why quit America to stand upon foreign ground? Why entangle America's destiny in the spider's web of European rivalries, animosities, racial hatreds, and territorial lusts?*

" 'Tis our true policy to steer clear of permanent alliances," Washington insisted, even as he opened the door to "temporary alliances for extraordinary emergencies." Thus his parting advice bore little resemblance to the Splendid Isolation or ostrich policy often ascribed to him by later historians. Rather, it was a course dictated by events then transpiring in Europe, a continent tearing itself apart, as well as by political and economic requirements at home, where a fierce rivalry between Federalists and Republicans whipsawed the president and threatened to demolish the fragile house of constitutional government. With the earnestness of a missionary, Washington never tired of pointing out that interest ruled the universe. "There can be no greater error than to expect or calculate upon real favors from nation to nation," declared this unblinking realist. " 'Tis an illusion which experience must cure, which a just pride ought to discard."

Until recently, Washington's Farewell Address was read each February 22 in the halls of Congress. The tradition died out in the 1970s, however, when the House, at least, no longer had time to listen, much less heed, "these counsels of an old and affectionate friend." But among his contemporaries, for whom he was all but synonymous with the nation over which he presided, Washington's political valedictory had very nearly the force of divine writ. No paper that ever came from his hand so thoroughly reflected Washington's personal qualities of balance, restraint, and justice, nor his insights into the folly of emotionalism as a determinant of policy. Today, the Farewell Address is justly famed, not merely as the capstone of Washington's political philosophy, but as a brilliantly drawn road map to national survival and a fully realized independence.

❦ 4 ❧

Not everyone welcomed Washington's advice. One newspaper in South Carolina responded by printing "A Humble Address to George I, Perpetual Dictator of the U.S." Pierre Adet, awaiting the return of western scouts and still hoping to detach the trans-Appalachian region from the American union, denounced the president as a liar and ingrate preoc-

---

*The phrase "entangling alliances" famously attributed to Washington by generations of isolationist politicians was never spoken by him; Jefferson used it in his 1801 inaugural address.

cupied with sordid interest to the exclusion of French *gloire*. A more temperate observer, the duc de la Rochefoucauld-Liancourt, found irony in Washington's professed horror over the party spirit engulfing his country when the president willingly aligned himself with the British sympathizers in Congress. Ever the stylist, Rochefoucauld thought Washington's greatest crime the verbosity with which he bid adieu to his countrymen.

The president's plans caused little sensation among the duke's Boston hosts, ceasing even to dominate conversations once the initial surprise wore off. Was this because the Yankees of Massachusetts possessed minds so "engrossed by interested pursuits . . . as to leave no room for any other object?" One of those Yankees, the always quotable Fisher Ames, had a pithy answer for the Frenchman's query. The Farewell Address, said Ames, was a signal "like dropping a hat, for party racers to start, and I expect a great deal of noise, whipping, and spurring . . . some virtue and more tranquility lost; but I hope public order will be saved." Henrietta Liston concurred, anticipating a "very interesting" political season as Americans focused on Adams and Jefferson and the profound differences that separated these old friends "both in politics and morals."

But perhaps the voters would have a third alternative. Much as he despised the sunny Virginian, Alexander Hamilton had little more fondness for his dour New England rival, whose superior claims to office clashed with a personal popularity that barely registered outside the Northeast. Far worse, from Hamilton's viewpoint, while Adams might or might not be unelectable he was most definitely uncontrollable. With the New Yorker's first choice, Patrick Henry, refusing to enter the lists, Hamilton settled with crudely obvious reasoning on Thomas Pinckney, the forty-six-year-old war hero, governor of South Carolina, and diplomatic wunderkind. As a Southerner lauded for his work on the Treaty of San Lorenzo, Pinckney hoped to break the Republican hammerlock on the South and West much as he had gained access to the Mississippi for northwestern flatboats and fur traders. When word of Hamilton's intrigues leaked out, an indignant Abigail Adams labeled the scheming New Yorker part Julius Caesar, part Cassius. The vice president, not his wife's inferior in hurling insults, took a less classical approach, dismissing Hamilton as a "Creole bastard."

The ensuing campaign did little to encourage the friends of democracy. Character assassination flourished, with Jefferson variously branded a coward, a better philosopher than governor, and an infidel seduced by France and dusky Sally Hemmings. Adams fared no better, his indiscreet writings about "simplemen and gentlemen" being dusted off and placed in the worst possible light. Improbably enough, the pudgy, self-righteous

Yankee also got his own taste of sexual innuendo when gossips claimed that the real reason for Pinckney's French mission was to procure a female quartet to gratify the lascivious desires of Washington and his vice president. Adams responded with laughter, protesting that by keeping the lovely ladies for himself, General Pinckney had "cheated me out of my two."

Far removed from the acrimony of the campaign, Washington, at Mount Vernon, had no desire to poke his hand into the hornets' nest. Before an old friend he modestly disclaimed credit for agricultural trailblazing, explaining wistfully that his public activities had been so demanding and his absences from home so frequent and lengthy as to forestall truly significant investigations. Added Washington, "And now, though I may amuse myself in that way for the short time I may remain on this theatre, it is too late in the day for *me* to commence a scientifical course of experiments."

Late in October, he visited the emerging Federal City, where construction workers earned up to $2 a day amid complaints of lavish spending by the commissioners, who were prepared to let Congress meet in the President's House rather than get on with the Capitol. After selecting departmental office sites and reviewing proposed public squares, he urged the commissioners to set aside ground for his cherished national university and to establish a botanical garden both useful and ornamental. Returning to Philadelphia, the president received a nasty shock. Pierre Adet, hard on the heels of a campaign tour for Jefferson in Massachusetts, threw off the last shreds of political or diplomatic neutrality. On October 31, readers of the pro-Jefferson *Aurora* were treated simultaneously with Secretary of State Pickering to Adet's revelation that henceforth France's Directory would treat all neutral vessels precisely as they allowed themselves to be treated by the British. The result of this policy, if allowed to stand, would be to cripple the vital American trade with the French West Indies.

Yet even now Washington sought to be fair. If Adet was conducting diplomatic relations in the opposition press on orders of the Directory, he was merely executing a duty. On the other hand, should he choose to pursue so offensive a course on his own volition, he was guilty of a gross insult to his host government. Washington sought Hamilton's opinion on how best to receive the Gallic troublemaker in the future and was told to maintain a "dignified reserve, holding an exact medium between an offensive coldness and cordiality." The distinction was admittedly a fine one, said Hamilton, "but no one will know better how to do it than the President." In the event, Adet saved Washington the trouble by absenting himself from official entertainments. But the envoy refused to fade away. During November he published one explosive announcement after another — instructing all true friends of France ("a government terrible to its enemies but generous to its allies") to wear the Tricolor cockade, characterizing Jay's Treaty as a virtual alliance with Great Britain, and finally announcing the suspension of diplomatic relations between Paris and Philadelphia. "Oh, America," he proclaimed with Genêt-like impertinence. "Oh, you who have so often flown to death and to victory with French soldiers . . . Let your government return to itself."

Adet's clumsy attempt to influence the election in Pennsylvania, where Adams and Jefferson were running neck and neck and a large Quaker vote was thought susceptible to war talk, goaded the president into firing back. He directed Pickering to publish a bluntly worded rejoinder despite Hamilton's warning that a debate in the nation's press might fatally tarnish the executive's dignity. Besides, said Hamilton, an open rupture with France must be avoided at nearly any cost. But Washington was in no mood to equivocate. Henrietta Liston attended a dinner party at 190 Market Street when suspense over the balloting in the Keystone State was at its peak. "I was as usual at his right hand," Mrs. Liston recorded of her friend the president, "and we had a great deal of conversation. As the conduct of the French minister during this election has very much disgusted Washington and his ministers he seemed to show even more than usual attention to Mr. Liston and me." Alas, "the spirits of the party I imagine were a little damped in the evening when the proclamation came that Jefferson's ticket had gained the election in this state."

It was true. By 200 votes out of 25,000 cast, the Republican candidate laid claim to all but one of Pennsylvania's fifteen electors, which, added to twenty of Virginia's twenty-one and expected strong showings throughout the South and West, cast a pall over Adams's prospects. While his countrymen hung on the latest returns, Washington quietly attended to the details of governing. On November 14 he issued a tart directive to Attorney General Lee, whose frequent absences from the capital were the cause of much negative comment. After the Bank of the United States turned down a loan request for the Federal City, Washington swallowed his pride and authorized an application to Maryland's legislature, whose members duly provided $150,000 so that the construction project might stagger on.*

Visiting delegations of Indians made the last week of November a fatiguing round of dinners and receptions. Reviewing his formal remarks, Washington crossed out a reference to the white man's God and replaced it with the more sensitive "Great Spirit Above." On December 7, with

---

*The lame duck president found Adet's newspaper attacks "as unjust as they are voluminous" and correctly guessed that they would backfire in the end.

the identity of his successor still in doubt, he delivered his eighth and final address to Congress. Henrietta Liston recorded the scene as the president appeared at noon "in full dress, as he always is on public occasions, black velvet, sword, etc." Flanked by his Cabinet and trailing the sergeant at arms with his ceremonial mace, Washington bowed right and left as he approached the speaker's platform.

What happened next is described by Mrs. Liston: "After composing himself he drew a paper from his pocket. Washington writes better than he reads, there is even a little hesitation in his common speaking, but he possesses so much natural unaffected dignity, and is so noble a figure as to give always a pleasant impression. I happened to sit very near him, and as every person stood up at his entrance and again when he began to read I had an opportunity of seeing the extreme agitation he felt when he mentioned the French. He is, I believe, very much enraged, this is the second French minister who has insulted him and the people."

This was not entirely accurate; outright condemnation of France's behavior was temporarily muted as Washington mingled familiar topics with visionary appeals. He was able at last to report British evacuation of the northwestern forts and the start of negotiations to fix the disputed northeastern boundary between the United States and Canada. Looking to the future, he justified an expanded navy and financial incentives to domestic manufacturing as steps away from America's dependence on unreliable or hostile European powers. He presaged the Department of Agriculture and farm subsidy payments by calling for the establishment of boards that would gather data and distribute money to foster agricultural improvements through the latest scientific advances.

Washington was equally assertive in making the case for his national university, a primary object of which should be the education of American youth in the science of government. He proposed a national military academy as well, contending that "however pacific . . . a nation may be, it ought never to be without an adequate stock of military knowledge for emergencies." He asked the lawmakers to raise government salaries or else risk making personal wealth the chief qualification for public service, a position wholly repugnant to "the vital principles of our Government." On the perilous topic of Franco-American relations, the president prepared the ground for a later, more detailed accounting by restating his wish to maintain cordial ties to the younger republic "consistent with a just and indispensable regard to the rights and honor of our country."

Washington concluded, not without emotion, by recalling the origins of the present government and congratulating both his immediate audience and the much greater one outside Congress Hall on the success of their common endeavor. Many in the room fumbled for their handkerchiefs. Unmoved by the tears of their colleagues, twelve House members — among them Andrew Jackson, an uncompromising Republican freshman from the new state of Tennessee — refused to join in the courtesy of a formal reply to the address or affix their names to a document praising the executive as "firm, wise, and patriotic" and expressing regret over his departure from office.

Sulky reluctance, it seemed, was the order of the day, even among Washington's prospective successors. Shrinking from the obloquy that was a president's daily portion, Jefferson, at Monticello, insisted that "no man will ever bring out of that office the reputation which carries him into it." Moreover, he denied any personal ambition to govern men: "I leave to others the sublime delights of riding in the storm, better pleased with sound sleep and a warm berth below, with the society of neighbors, friends, and fellow laborers of the earth than of spies and sycophants."

Jefferson's Federalist opponent seemed equally resigned to defeat, protesting with even less conviction that his happiness did not depend upon reaching the top of the greasy pole. So what if he lost out to his rival from Virginia? "Then for frugality and independence, poverty and patriotism, love and a carrot bed," John Adams vowed to Abigail. Adams's nightmare was of himself, as presiding officer of the Senate, called upon to formally proclaim the election of Thomas Jefferson as the next president of the United States. It was a test the vice president faced only in his sleepless nights. Still, thanks to Hamilton's wire-pulling, it was astonishingly close. "The difference between sixty-eight and seventy-one votes is little sensible," Jefferson remarked in a rare burst of understatement. Martha Washington dropped all restraint, informing the president-elect that his victory brought joy throughout the Washingtons' household.

As well it might, for release was at hand. When making his gloomy assessment of the nation's highest office and the toll that it must inevitably extract, Jefferson could have had but one man in mind. Sure enough, early in December, the *Aurora* printed a diatribe from the pen of Thomas Paine, still embittered over Washington's failure to make him postmaster general in the new regime or spring him from the French jail cell where he had been tossed by Robespierre. The veteran controversialist was in fine, venomous form as he accused the president of fraud, assassination, and a craving for public adulation. Paine reserved his sharpest invective for Washington's alleged treachery. "The world will be puzzled to decide, whether you are an apostate, or an impostor," he spit out, "whether you have abandoned good principles, or whether you ever had any."

Not to be outdone, other editors ran political obituaries for the dying administration. In the *New York Journal* Washington could see himself labeled "a most horrid swearer and blasphemer," whose education had consisted of gambling, revelry, horse races, and horse whipping. "Would to God you have retired four years ago," thundered a Boston scribbler, "while your public conduct threw a veil of sanctity around you."

On December 23, Washington thanked Maryland's legislature for its friendlier sentiments. He took pains to deflect compliments to his fellow citizens, whose virtue and valor had achieved independence and whose subsequent moderation and humanity had prevented America's Revolution from being sullied with innocent blood. Most gratifying of all was the realization by some, at least, that he had steered a consistent course, directing his actions toward the maintenance of peace even as Europe and its New World dependencies waged their empty, murderous struggle.

❊ 5 ❧

Only a few weeks remained in Washington's presidency, but on the subject of France the executive's mood was anything but elegiac. Early in January 1797 the president and his secretary of state toiled away on a special message to Congress, tracing the long, downhill course of Franco-American relations since King Louis's violent end. Pierre Adet, meanwhile, joined Benjamin Franklin Bache to indict the Washington administration in a widely disseminated pamphlet. The *Aurora* opened a second front by reprinting the forged "Lund Washington Letters," allegedly written by the commanding general during some of the darkest days of the Revolution and throwing doubt on his patriotism. Although every action of his life gave the lie to such brazen falsehoods, Washington grumbled in private, "that is no stumbling block with the editors of these papers and their supporters."

In a startlingly frank letter to his old friend David Stuart, the president rendered his harshest judgment to date of the impetuous Adet and "the restless temper of the French." It was a well-known historical fact that "they attempt openly, or covertly, by threats or soothing professions, to influence the conduct of most governments." Having failed to sway public opinion through exaggerated reports of British atrocities, the representative of this hot-tempered race now turned his batteries upon America's chief magistrate "and although he is soon to become a private citizen, his opinions are to be knocked down, and his character reduced as low as they are capable of sinking it, even by resorting to absolute falsehoods."

It was a good thing that none of this leaked out, as Washington himself demonstrated in his markedly softer communication to Congress on January 16. Fulfilling his promise to open the books on all diplomatic exchanges between Philadelphia and Paris, he took the further, highly unusual step of sharing with the people's representatives his government's detailed instructions to its designated spokesman in the French capital, Charles Cotesworth Pinckney. Personally the president thought France's conduct "outrageous beyond conception," intolerable under existing treaties and the law of nations. With the special accuracy afforded by hindsight, he now claimed to have expected such behavior. "On her professions of friendship and loving kindness I built no hopes," he said of his former ally, "but rather supposed they would last as long, and no longer, than it would accord with their interest to bestow them."

Was the Directory justified in its accusations of an American double standard? As we have seen, there was no shortage of British meddling in Washington's government, some of it quite heavy-handed. Edmund Randolph could attest to that. Moreover, until the summer of 1796, British warships had been guilty of far graver offenses against American commerce and sovereignty than the less powerful fleet based in the French Indies. There lay the rub. For Washington could never forget how war with England would destroy an economy that relied on British imports and the foreign duties they brought to the federal treasury. Whatever resentments he harbored toward George III and his arrogant henchmen were outweighed by simple calculations of national survival.

But there was another reason for President Washington to differentiate between his country's once and future enemies. Smarter, shrewder, more coldblooded, and less emotional than their continental antagonist, the British played a deft game of inside politics. Unable to win the American masses over to their thinking (no doubt questioning whether the masses thought to begin with), they concentrated instead on centers of influence in the ruling elite. The French, by contrast, trumpeted their misgivings over Washington's rule to anyone who would listen and to millions who did not care to. So while the English tried to convince individual policymakers, the French sought to influence the American political process itself. Small wonder, then, that Washington repudiated his wartime allies when the heirs to revolution seemed suddenly bent on world domination, devouring their European neighbors and leapfrogging whole oceans in a forcible attempt to impose the Gallic vision of popular democracy on the American republic.

From international relations, Washington turned to the plight of an intellectually lazy boy who would prove every bit as recalcitrant as Monroe's Parisian idols. In the fall of 1796, George Washington Parke Custis enrolled at Princeton; the early omens were decidedly unfavorable. Always inclined to look the other way where his wife's petted grandson was concerned, Washington sent the boy $10 toward the purchase of an academic gown. With the gift went still more valuable counsel. "Endeavor to conciliate the good will of *all* your fellow students, rendering them every act of kindness in your power," the president wrote his namesake. "Be particularly obliging and attentive to your chamber mate." To this common sense Washington added an admonition that might have been lifted verbatim from his boyhood copy of 101 Rules of Civility: "Never let an indigent person ask, without receiving *something,* if you have the means; always recollecting in what light the widow's mite was received."

Two weeks later Washington interrupted work on a message to Congress to warn the reluctant scholar against idleness and vice, the latter of which "will approach like a thief, working upon your passions; encouraged, perhaps, by bad examples." Admirable as it was to maintain good relations with his fellows, Custis should select for his friends "the most deserving only." In reaching an opinion of his classmates, as in all judgments, he should avoid haste and seek balance. "And even then, where there is no occasion for expressing an opinion, it is best to be silent, for there is nothing more certain than that it is at all times more easy to make enemies than friends," said Washington, concluding with words familiar to students from time immemorial: "If you meet with collegiate fare, it will be unmanly to complain."

Custis did not acknowledge his guardian's gift any more than he followed the advice that had transformed a bumptious Virginian of the mid-eighteenth century, hungry for reputation and contemptuous of his uniformed superiors, into a universally admired patriot. Disinterested gravitas was not the boy's style. For a while, the youth was reasonably diligent in writing to his relations in Philadelphia. His reward was a barrage of high-minded admonition. Yield up his personal preferences to the learned tastes of his professors, Washington told him. Display "affectionate reverence" for the college president while avoiding any taint from contact with less noble characters. Young Wash ought to immerse himself in volumes of lasting significance. "Light reading . . . may amuse for the moment, but leaves nothing behind," said Washington, whose enjoyment of the theater, and in particular Addison and his fictional paragon, Cato, was apparently not to be confused with pulp literature.

But Jack Custis's son, true to his genes, proved to have a short attention span for books of any sort, and by the middle of January 1797 Washington's doubts were multiplying. The president urged the boy to keep a diary and daily account book, the better to record his actions as well as his expenditures. Custis nodded, applied himself for a few weeks, then let his attention wander from the arid charms of arithmetic and geography to the red-blooded society of the university's Whig Society. Elderly finger wagging led to youthful promises of repentance and reform, and the cycle would start afresh. But who are we to judge? If it was difficult being

George Washington, imagine the emotional burdens that went with the name of George Washington Parke Custis. All he wanted was to be his father's son — careless and lovable, glib and sunny-tempered. Yet fate decreed otherwise. Thus the highly touted "Child of Mount Vernon" remained just that for the rest of his days, Martha's "pretty little dear child" unburdened by perfection. Young Wash. Tub.

❧ 6 ❦

"The third of March, which is fast approaching, will put an end to my political career; and I shall have another to commence through mud and mire, to reach more tranquil scenes." So Washington in the first week of February 1797 prefaced a request for two strong draught horses to pull the presidential baggage wagon. "I should prefer cheapness to appearance," he added, noting that mares were preferable to geldings, for he fully intended to resume his mule-breeding experiments at Mount Vernon.

The president was hard-pressed to conduct the necessary business of transition and still fulfill his social obligations. All of Philadelphia, it seemed, wished to have a moment alone with him. He gave dinners for army and naval officers, members of Pennsylvania's House of Representatives, and two of his staunchest Indian allies, Joseph Brant and the Seneca chieftain Cornplanter. (He had already held a dinner party for the diplomatic corps, all but the representative of France, who stayed away in pique.) There were numerous addresses from diverse corners of the Union, each requiring a suitably grateful response. One night he took Martha to an ambitious production of *Columbus, or a World Discovered*, with stage effects simulating an earthquake and a volcanic eruption. Later in the month they attended a "Ladies Concert."

February was a blur of last-minute official directives and housekeeping details. Washington got his two draught horses, returning a third as "too clumsy about the head and legs, and too high in price for a common plough horse." For $1,000 he sold his magnificent coach horses to Eliza Powel. Less successfully, he offered John Adams his pick of furnishings from 190 Market, leaving the frugal Yankee to complain after his inauguration that there was not a chair fit to sit in. (Worse, grumbled Adams, "the beds and bedding are in a woeful pickle," while the Washingtons' servants had devoted themselves during the interregnum to "the most scandalous drunkenness and discord.") On a happier note, he was touched by Washington's solicitude for his diplomat son, John Quincy Adams, a young man whose promotion to higher things should not, said Washington, be postponed for fear of whispered comments about nepotism.

February 22 was the president's sixty-fifth birthday, and a well-dressed mob filled the executive residence between noon and three. That night 1,200 admirers squeezed into Rickett's Circus for a lavish salute to the first couple. The dancing skills of American ladies evoked admiring comments from Henrietta Liston. Indeed, concluded the British ambassador's wife, "it was the only advantage they seemed to have derived from their intercourse with the French." At eleven o'clock the president led the procession into supper to the strains of "Washington's March," a popular standard of which Philadelphia theatergoers could never get enough. Brilliant as the occasion seemed to Justice James Iredell of the Supreme Court, he could not resist observing that several at the party were nearly trampled to death in the mad scramble for supper.

Mrs. Washington was moved to tears as she confided to Iredell both her gratitude for the public display of affection and her relief at the purely domestic life that would soon be hers. As for the president, his normally impassive face betrayed "emotions too powerful to be concealed. He could scarcely speak," offering but a brief pleasantry in response to the evening's single toast. But he was loath to break away, and it was nearly one in the morning before the guests of honor finally took their leave. Back at his desk, the president prepared a final flurry of orders for the commissioners in what he now openly called the City of Washington. He vetoed a bill discharging two companies of dragoons and was sustained by the House. Washington sent Henry Knox condolences on the recent loss of three children to disease. As for himself, he felt akin to "the wearied traveler who sees a resting place, and is bending his body to lean thereon."

He told Knox that he had no wish "to mix again in the great world or to partake in its politics." Yet he could not escape feelings of regret over parting, perhaps forever, from "the few intimates whom I love, among these, be assured you are one." Washington expected his life at Mount Vernon to be a secluded one, filled with rural amusements to the exclusion of "the noisy and bustling crowd." On the subject of politics he was deliberately silent, urging Knox to obtain details of the recent session from members of Congress. "The Gazettes will furnish the rest."

A second invitation to his Potomac retreat went out to John Trumbull, another of Washington's revolutionary intimates whose warnings of impending disaster the president did his best to knock down. The constitutional gyroscope might wobble in the tumult of election season, especially when influenced by "foreign machinations," he acknowledged to the Connecticut pessimist. But it was sure to right itself. Not even the possibility of war with France could shake Washington's faith in the future of republican government. As he put it, "I can never believe that Providence, which has guided us so long, and through such a labyrinth, will withdraw its protection at this crisis."

On March 3, his last full day in office, Washington wrote again to the District commissioners, thanked the clergy of Philadelphia for their prayerful support, and pardoned ten men convicted of treason in the Whiskey Rebellion. He deposited with Secretary of State Pickering, "as a testimony of the truth to the present generation and to posterity," a detailed rebuttal of the notorious Lund Washington Letters, about whose forgery he had been silent for twenty years. That afternoon he stood between the windows in the rear drawing room at 190 Market Street to receive guests led by his close friend Robert Morris. A large and convivial party joined the Washingtons for dinner. The president-elect was there. So were the incoming vice president, several foreign diplomats, the Episcopal bishop of Pennsylvania, and other dignitaries. All tried hard to sustain the mood of determined lightheartedness set by the president.

When the tablecloth was removed, Washington rose with wineglass in hand and a smile on his face, declaring, "Ladies and gentlemen, this is the last time I shall drink your health as a public man. I do it with sincerity, and wishing you all possible happiness!" The finality of his words struck the company hard, shattering their pretended mirth. Bishop White stole a look at Henrietta Liston and saw tears streaming down her face. Identical emotions hung heavy over Mrs. Washington's final levee, held later that evening.

On Saturday morning, March 4, Washington donned his best black velvet suit and walked to Congress Hall. For his final act as president, he dispensed with coaches, prancing horses, and flanking postilions. This was to be a day of conspicuous simplicity, with symbolism, not officeholders, in the saddle. Loud applause greeted him in the first-floor House chamber, where he joined Vice President-elect Jefferson on the dais, their chairs separated by that ordinarily reserved for the Speaker, now awaiting the new president. Just before noon, a cheer went up outside, signaling John Adams's arrival. Adams alighted from his carriage resplendent in a pearl-colored suit of native broadcloth set off by a dress sword and cockaded hat. As foolish as these martial touches looked on the squat Yankee with his lumbering gait, they were unavoidable in a nation too young to have traditions besides those already sanctified by its great military hero turned civilian leader.

After a sleepless night, the president-elect was about to cast off his role as understudy and claim center stage for himself. Yet even in a silent part, his predecessor held the crowd's interest. Wherever Adams looked, he beheld streaming eyes. At one point he covered his own face to disguise a flood of tears. Nelly Custis, unwilling to trust her composure, stood removed from her grandfather, "terribly agitated," according to an observer. Nor was Washington immune to the intense emotions surrounding the historic transfer about to take place. It was probably just as well that he was not called upon to speak during the brief ceremony.

The inaugural address concluded, the new president waddled up the aisle and out of the hall. Ex-President Washington motioned for Jefferson to follow, but the tall Virginian in his blue frock coat held back out of deference. Washington repeated the gesture a bit more forcefully, and the vice president reluctantly preceded him to the door. Outside, a large crowd cheered Washington, slowing his progress down Chestnut Street to the Francis Hotel, where Adams was waiting for him. The door closed behind the former president, but only for a moment. Suddenly it reopened to reveal him framed in the doorway, hatless, silently bowing in appreciation of the public's tribute. Then he vanished, remaining inside long enough to wish his successor a "happy, successful, and honorable" term.

But Philadelphia was unwilling to part with the familiar figure so quickly. That night hundreds of residents attended a dinner where the strains of "Washington's March" again filled the air and a roar of approval greeted the unveiling of Charles Willson Peale's allegorical transparency, showing Washington on horseback beside a female who wore the cap of Liberty and an altar inscribed PUBLIC GRATITUDE. A few rejoiced at his departure. "Every heart . . . ought to beat high with exultation, that the name of Washington from this day ceases to give a currency to political iniquity and to legalize corruption," shouted the *Aurora*. Washington declined to engage his nemesis in public debate. Privately he confided to a friend, "This man has celebrity in a certain way, for his calumnies are to be exceeded only by his impudence, and both stand unrivalled."

On the evening of the sixth, the former president welcomed Adams and Jefferson to dinner at 190 Market Street. The next day Washington rewarded his household steward with 20 guineas (a full year's wages for a common laborer), giving lesser amounts to the rest of the staff. The squire presented gifts to the Cabinet and wrote a generous recommendation for Bart Dandridge, who was about to embark on a diplomatic career at The Hague. As quietly competent as ever, Tobias Lear was on hand to assist in packing ninety-seven boxes, fourteen trunks, forty-three casks, thirteen packages, and three hampers for transport on the sloop *Salem*. Venetian blinds were taken down and a tub shower packed away. Finally all was in readiness. Shortly before seven on the blustery morning of March 9, the Washington family caravan departed. The journey south was marked by public ceremonies in Baltimore, Georgetown, and the

Federal City. Martha caught cold, while her husband used the long hours to give last-minute instructions to those remaining behind in the empty house on Market Street.

He cautioned Lear to stow large looking glasses so that they would not be tossed about in the ship's hold. According to Martha, Nelly's bedstead belonged to the Washingtons after all, so it should be dismantled for shipping. Lear should check on the whereabouts of the servants' livery, let Dandridge have $250 for his travel expenses in Europe, and take out a subscription to *Peter Porcupines's Gazette*, a fervently partisan sheet that gave no quarter and took no prisoners of the Republican stripe. Outside Chester, Pennsylvania, the former president registered a mock protest of those valuables that could not be sent by water — Nelly's pets, for example. "On the one hand, I am called upon to remember the parrot," he confessed to Lear, "on the other, to remember the dog. For my own part, I should not pine much if both were forgot."

"As I ride on matters occur to me . . . " The house must be turned over to Adams in good order, spic and span and with the rent fully paid up. Could Lear obtain half a dozen of the best white silk stockings? New carpeting for the blue parlor at Mount Vernon? A thermometer registering the rise and fall of temperatures over a twenty-four-hour span? Never one to dwell on the past, Washington enthusiastically anticipated his new life at Mount Vernon, where he arrived at four o'clock on the short afternoon of March 15. Before the week was out, however, a familiar voice called him back to a garden in Philadelphia and remembered confidences, spoken and implied. Eliza Powel had purchased the president's French rolltop desk at a public auction and now disclosed the existence of some ancient love letters from its former owner to his present lady. Eliza slyly reassured her friend that he had nothing to fear from these documents, found quite by accident in a drawer. They would be well guarded until such time as they could be returned to their original recipient.

Washington rose to the bait with deadpan humor, insisting, "I had no love letters to lose." Even if the correspondence were to fall into prying hands, he could sleep undisturbed. For anything he may have written to Martha was bound "to be more fraught with expressions of friendship, than of enamored love." Indeed, to give such missives the warmth of true romance, said Washington, it would be necessary to commit them to the flames.

"At home all day alone" ran the first entry in Washington's Mount Vernon diary. The former president might well reflect on something he had written under similar circumstances after the Revolution, when he told his friend Nathanael Greene that he had had but few differences with those around him before conceding, "I bore much for the sake of the peace and the public good." In the years since, he had borne much more to maintain the independence won through the barrel of a gun, not least of all from the men sworn to assist him in establishing America's first republican government.

PART THREE

Farmer Washington

1797–1799

❖ 14 ❖

AT THE BOTTOM
OF THE HILL

"I am once more seated under my own vine and fig
tree, and hope to spend the remainder of my
days . . . making political pursuits yield to the more
rational amusement of cultivating the earth."

George Washington,
April 7, 1797

BEING NATURALLY PARTIAL to hedgerows and roof repairs over diplomats and congresses, Washington slipped easily into the rhythms of
country life. "Grandpapa is very well, and has already turned farmer
again," Nelly Custis wrote to a friend less than a week after taking up
residence on the banks of the Potomac. While awaiting shipment of her
English harpsichord, the young woman waxed eloquent over the grandeur
of the river outside her window and the superiority of rural callings to
urban frippery. "Since I left Philadelphia everything has appeared to be
a dream," she confessed. "I can hardly realize my being here and that
Grandpapa is no longer in office — if it is a dream I hope never to awaken
from it."

The trancelike state was soon broken. Within a month Nelly ventured
north as far as the Federal City, where she attracted unwanted attention
by dancing with Charles Carroll of the famous Maryland family. "I wish
the world would not be so extremely busy and impertinent," she blurted.
"E. P. Custis desires not its notice, and would thank those meddling
reporters never to mention her name." Her grandfather sympathized with
her objections. Writing before the war, he had protested by "the great
searcher of human hearts . . . that I have no wish . . . beyond the humble
and happy lot of living and dying a private citizen on my own farm."

Now he was home to stay, although there was some doubt about the
staying power of Mansion House, which seemed to its owner "exceedingly

out of repairs." The floor under Washington's handsome green dining room was especially precarious, so weakened that even a moderate-size dinner party might tumble into the basement below. Meanwhile, not every member of the household found the transition from cosmopolitan Philadelphia as painless as Nelly. Hercules, the family cook, ran off, driving Mrs. Washington to seek Eliza Powel's help in finding a replacement — unsuccessfully, as it turned out. "Sixteen dollars is the most we have ever given to a servant," explained Martha, the sole exception being house stewards, who were assigned three times the responsibilities of a common cook.

The disappearance of Hercules was "a most inconvenient thing," said Washington, as it compelled him to break his resolution "never to become the master of another slave by purchase." When Lawrence Lewis, Washington's future son-in-law, lost a servant in similar circumstances, it prompted an angry outburst from the former president. There would be many more "elopements," he predicted, so long as persons were held in bondage against their wishes and the dictates of nature. "I wish from my soul that the legislature of this state could see the policy of a gradual abolition of slavery," he wrote to Lewis in August 1797. "It would prevent much future mischief."

Washington's more immediate problems included the dislocation and inconvenience familiar to any homeowner embarked upon ambitious repairs. There were curtains to hang and carpets to lay down, plaster to repair and foundations to strengthen. "I am already surrounded by joiners, masons, painters, etc., etc.," he disclosed to a friend. "I have scarcely a room to put a friend into or to set in myself, without the music of hammers, or the odoriferous smell of paint." Fortunately he was able to rely on a new manager, an honest and industrious Scotsman named James Anderson. For his neglected grounds Farmer Washington sought a skilled gardener, but he was in no position to drive a hard bargain and he knew it: "I would prefer a single man to a married one, but shall not object to the latter if he has no children, or not more than one, or at most two."

The death of his sister Betty, revealed early in April, did nothing to slow Washington's building program. With the peculiarly stilted voice he reserved for such occasions, her brother advised his nephew to accept uncomplainingly "the debt of nature." In the next sentence Washington returned to the joys of repair and adornment, asking young George Lewis to recommend a carpenter, black or white, capable of making "a rich finished panel door, sash, and wainscot." The pleasures of activity outweighed those of contemplation; renewing his estate provided an outlet for Washington's creative energies. As always, the proprietor was happiest outside mired in agricultural details: protecting his six hundred sheep against the poisonous rose laurel; showing off his octagonal barn, where grain was threshed by trampling horses; admiring the Nova Scotia spruces and Spanish chestnuts that gave the bowling green both symmetry and variety.

An elderly soldier stopped Washington's adopted grandson in the woods one morning to inquire how to find his former commanding officer. That was easy, replied Custis. The visitor should look for "an old gentleman riding alone in plain drab clothes, a broad-brimmed white hat, a hickory switch in his hand, and carrying an umbrella with a long staff, which is attached to his saddle . . . that person, sir, is General Washington." A somewhat less picturesque account of Washington's daily routine was supplied in a letter the former president wrote late in May 1797 to Secretary of War James McHenry. After thanking him for the latest gossip from the capital, Washington made no apology for failing to respond in kind. McHenry was posted at the political epicenter, with no shortage of topical tidbits to relate, "while I have nothing to say that could either inform or amuse a Secretary of War in Philadelphia."

Washington's days began at sunrise. "If my hirelings are not in their places at that time I send them messages expressive of my sorrow for their indisposition." He breakfasted at seven — "about the time I presume you are taking leave of Mrs. McHenry." At midmorning he left on horseback for a five-hour inspection of his fields, crops, and workmen. Rubbernecking tourists predominated around his dinner table, Washington observed ruefully, "and how different this, from having a few social friends at a cheerful board." One day the future king Louis-Phillipe appeared on Washington's doorstep, at twenty-four not so much older than Lafayette's son, another orphan of the storm that had carried Louis's father to the guillotine. The Orleans pretender joined a throng making its way to the lofty dining room with its dimity curtains, East Indian floor mats, and oil paintings of the Hudson River and Great Falls of the Potomac. At the time of his death, Washington's "New Room" held twenty-one canvases, part of a burgeoning art collection that featured engravings by John Trumbull and a sketch of the Bastille presented in happier times by George W. Fayette's father.

Washington's table was as crowded as his dining room walls. At the end of July he informed Tobias Lear that "unless someone pops in unexpectedly, Mrs. Washington and myself will do what I believe has not been within the last twenty years by us, that is, to sit down to dinner by ourselves." On those rare instances when company did not demand his presence, after-dinner conversation or reading aloud was replaced by paperwork in his study. Later there was tea in the "Prussian blue" parlor, a plate of walnuts, and a firm, frequently broken, resolve to answer the latest correspondence. "But when the lights are brought I feel tired," said Washington, "and disinclined to engage in this work, conceiving that the next night will do as well: the next comes and with it the same causes for postponement . . . and so on."

With his house cluttered by workmen, Washington had little time for serious reading. Perhaps it would be different when he found himself alone on long summer nights, by which point "I may be looking in Doomsday book." Notwithstanding such gloomy patches, the former president remained in good spirits and robust health. Rumors of a serious fever were denied by Mrs. Washington. "On a hot day in May," she reported to Eliza Powel, "he threw off his flannels; and a sudden change of weather at night gave him a cold, which disordered but never confined him."

After a peripatetic lifetime on the road, Washington did not expect to venture more than twenty miles from his riverside hermitage, yet even this narrow radius allowed him to monitor progress in the Federal City. By the summer of 1797, the President's House and one wing of the 350-foot-long Capitol were ready for roofing; an "elegant" bridge spanned the Potomac. Accelerating efforts to extend the river's navigable length promised handsome returns for the port of Alexandria, much changed during Washington's eight-year absence. He watched with unconcealed pride as streets were built over the former riverbed and fine houses rose on a Common recently enclosed.

Returning from one such excursion, Washington halted his horse at the scene of an accident and rushed to aid a female passenger who lay unconscious on the roadside. Just then a second Good Samaritan approached from the opposite direction. This was John Bernard, a famous English comedian about to conquer the former colonies. Bernard described what followed as the hale, well-made man, still vigorous although evidently advanced in years, strained to free a carriage buried under half a ton of luggage. Upon regaining consciousness, the injured woman began spewing invective at her spouse, a New Englander heading home to collect an inheritance. After turning down the Yankee's invitation to join him for a drink in town, the old man in his blue coat and buckskin breeches offered to dust off Bernard's suit.

"Mr. Bernard, I believe," said Washington with a sudden glint of recognition. "I had the pleasure of seeing you perform last winter in Philadelphia." Would the distinguished thespian care to accompany him to Mount Vernon, not a mile distant, where both men might rest from their strenuous exertions under the merciless Virginia sun?

"Mount Vernon!" exclaimed Bernard. "Have I the honor of addressing General Washington?"

Washington extended his hand. "An odd sort of introduction, Mr. Bernard, but I am pleased to find you can play so active a part in private, and without a prompter."

Talk of mutual friends at Annapolis and Bernard's impressions of America made their short ride even shorter. Through it all, the English visitor reflected on how most country gentlemen, seeing a carriage upset near their gates, would have sent for their servants to render assistance. His favorable impression grew to a conviction during the next few hours of intimate exposure to the most famous man in the world. "In conversation his face had not much variety of expression," Bernard observed. "A look of thoughtfulness was given by the compression of the mouth and the indentation of the brow (suggesting a habitual conflict with and mastery over passion) . . . Nor had his voice, so far as I could discover in our quiet talk, much change, or richness of intonation, but he always spoke with earnestness, and his eyes . . . burned with a steady fire which no one could mistake for mere affability."

To each topic introduced by his guest, Washington responded with common sense and a rare thoughtfulness. "He spoke like a man who had felt as much as he had reflected and reflected more than he had spoken; like one who had looked upon society rather in the mass than in detail," Bernard noted. When he mentioned the differences separating New Englanders from their southern countrymen, Washington took the side of the Yankees. "I esteem those people greatly," he remarked. "They are the stamina of the Union and its greatest benefactors." Told that his observations flattered Great Britain, Washington's face lit up. "Yes, yes, Mr. Bernard, but I consider your country the cradle of free principles, not their armchair. Liberty in England is a sort of idol; people are bred up in their belief and love of it, but see little of its doings. They walk about freely, but it is between high walls; and the error of its government was in supposing that after a portion of their subjects had crossed the sea to live upon a common, they would permit their friends at home to build up those walls about them."

At this point Washington was interrupted by a black servant carrying a jug of water. Bernard could not repress a smile or Washington an explanation. "This may seem a contradiction," he acknowledged, "but . . . it is neither a crime nor an absurdity. When we profess, as our fundamental principle, that liberty is the inalienable right of every man, we do not include madmen or idiots; liberty in their hands would become a scourge. Till the mind of the slave has been educated to perceive what are the obligations of a state of freedom, the gift would insure its abuse. We might as well be asked to pull down our old warehouses before trade had increased to demand enlarged new ones. Both houses and slaves were bequeathed to us by Europeans, and time alone can change them; an event, sir, which, you may believe me, no man desires more heartily than I do. Not only do I pray for it on the score of human dignity, but I can clearly foresee that nothing but the rooting out of slavery can perpetuate the existence of our union, by consolidating it in a common bond of principle."

Washington's sincerity was transparent. So was his pleasure in Bernard's complimentary references to Philadelphia's intellectual luminaries, particularly as they came from an Englishman, whose fellows were ordinarily so astringent on the subject of American arts and letters. Indeed, said a resentful Washington, the Abbé Raynal had gone so far as to inquire whether America had produced a single great poet, statesman, or philosopher. Yet it took no great insight to perceive the unique circumstances fashioning a scientific rather than literary or imaginative bent among Washington's countrymen. "And in this respect, America has surely furnished her quota. Franklin, Rittenhouse, and Rush are no mean names," he insisted, to which he might easily have added those of the politicians Jefferson and Adams and the theologian Jonathan Edwards.

Washington had nothing but praise for Bernard's royal patron, the Prince of Wales, to whom the republican hero looked for England's emancipation. "She is at present bent double, and has to walk with crutches," he said of King George's realm, "but her offspring may teach her the secret of regaining strength, erectness, and independence." Bernard, not surprisingly, went away charmed by the venerable sage, who had not entirely lost his taste for strangers, least of all those whose company allowed him to expound upon the principles on which he had based his life.

❦ 2 ❧

John Adams's presidential honeymoon was of short duration. It ended abruptly on May 15, 1797, when the man Bache's *Aurora* demeaned with a wink as "President by three votes" appeared before Congress to arraign French insolence toward the United States and its designated representative, Charles Cotesworth Pinckney. Even worse was the Directory's fawning treatment of the departing Monroe, the latest in a string of provocations calculated, in Federalist eyes, to drive a wedge between the American people and their government. Adams took the occasion to propose an expanded program of naval construction and coastal fortifications. Yet even as he brandished the sword, the new president held out an olive branch by sending two additional negotiators to buttress the unfortunate Pinckney in a final attempt at peaceful resolution of the differences between Philadelphia and Paris.

Adams looked out upon a world at war, in which the bloody rivalry of England and France posed greater perils than ever for the lightly defended American republic. In rejecting Pinckney, the Directory had denied the very legitimacy of Adams's (not to mention Washington's) government. At the same time, both France and England were emboldened to carry their mutual hostilities to third parties, with the result that American ships and crews were nowhere safe from maritime predators. Philip Freneau blamed Yankee greed:

> Americans! why half neglect
> The culture of your soil
> From foreign traffic why expect
> Sure payment of your toil?

More assertive Americans — Washington among them — might be united in wishing a plague upon both European combatants, but they were sufficiently nationalistic to oppose any threatening power, whatever past bonds or future blandishments argued for conciliation.

Adams's statesmanlike address to Congress proved characteristic of his administration: too submissive for Federalist ultras, too warlike for Francophile Republicans, too moderate for extremists on all sides who would make the middle of the road a perilously lonely place to travel during the final years of the eighteenth century. Jefferson, who had already turned down the president's invitation to go to Paris himself, regarded the speech as openly hostile to France. In the vice president's estimation, French animosity was the certain, if unpalatable, fruit of Jay's Treaty.

Washington dissented from this view. He greeted Adams's initiative as the first clap of thunder in a summer squall: if nothing else, it would at least clear an unhealthy atmosphere. "Things cannot, ought not, to remain any longer in their present disagreeable state," he wrote. The scandalous idea, so prevalent in France, that the government and people of the United States were fundamentally at odds held lethal consequences for a regime founded on the public interest. "It remains to be seen whether our country will stand upon independent ground," the former president told Thomas Pinckney on May 27, "or be directed in its political concerns by any other nation. A little time will show who are . . . true Americans." Until then, Washington regretted the inclination of many Republicans in the House to make excuses for "our great and magnanimous Allies."

Washington was in no mood for appeasement, as he made clear in a letter to Pinckney's brother Charles. "I look with regret on many transactions which do not comport with my ideas," he confessed. Yet he could not believe, should the ultimate crisis come, that a majority of his countrymen would fail to act an honorable part. Washington strongly endorsed President Adams's course. As for himself, he told his English admirer, the earl of Buchan, that he hoped to view the present storm by the "calm light of mild philosophy." Within days of proclaiming this detached stance, he was thanking an English parliamentarian for sending him a copy of his recently published pamphlet "View of the Causes and Consequences of the Present War with France." To characterize the conduct of another government might be "stepping beyond the lines of prudence," said Washington. Still, his sympathy with the British was as obvious as his contempt for those he held responsible for the bloodiest war of modern times.

All this undercut Washington's assertion to Oliver Wolcott, his former treasury secretary who had stayed on to advise (and eventually betray) Adams, that "having turned aside from the broad walks of political into the narrow paths of private life," he would leave to others the debate and implementation of official policies. Among the heaviest burdens Washington had carried throughout his years in office was the recognition that every action he took established a precedent to guide or limit those who would follow. Now, as the nation's first ex-president, he shed some of his habitual caution. Less than a month after Adams's inauguration, his predecessor invited Secretary of War James McHenry to send him regularly "such matters as are interesting and not contrary to the rules of your official duty to disclose."

Washington justified his request as an alternative to unreliable popular gazettes. In fact, as the former president's world contracted, he came increasingly to rely on official sources of information. Over the years, much has been made of Hamilton's backstage manipulation of Adams's Cabinet — originally Washington's Cabinet — and of the direct pipeline that ran from Hamilton's law office in New York to the inner sanctum of Federalist rule. Far less has been said about the two-way correspondence between Philadelphia and Mount Vernon or the craft with which a former president might cloak his requests for the latest intelligence. Certainly Washington's claim to be interested exclusively in the sale of flour, the repair of houses, and the construction of a permanent home for his military and civilian archives fell short of truth.

For example, after Pickering sent him a long, inflammatory account of Pinckney's abusive treatment at the hands of the Directory, Washington told McHenry that he would not puzzle his brain trying to fathom such unaccountable behavior — thus leaving it to Adams's military chief to fill in the blanks. Or again, on learning of a special session of Congress called for mid-May, the retired statesman pumped Wolcott about the "various conjectures" then being made about Adams's possible motives. Some went so far as to suggest that a trade embargo with France was in the offing, Washington mused. Unfortunately, "persons at a distance" from the unfolding drama, with no information but what they could glean from partisan editors, could hardly make sense of the confusing dialogue between Philadelphia and Paris.

Washington made no secret of his pleasure when Adams chose the outspoken Federalist John Marshall, who had won a general's epaulets by helping to quell demonstrations in support of France at the time of the Whiskey Rebellion, to lend his legal brilliance and nationalist fervor to the Pinckney mission. (Less welcome was the appointment of Elbridge Gerry, an erratic New England Republican who would prove all too susceptible to the wiles of Talleyrand. Adams clung to his friend anyway, believing him as stubbornly resistant to party loyalties as the president himself.) En route to the capital, Marshall paid a visit to Mount Vernon, where the mutual admirers talked animatedly about a new threshing machine and the stalled negotiations. Afterward Washington composed for C. C. Pinckney's eyes a strongly worded testimonial to his fellow Virginian's "sensible and discreet" character.

Long before Marshall sailed out of Delaware Bay in the third week of July, Washington had shocking new evidence of the connection between foreign intrigue and domestic treachery. To Mount Vernon and Philadelphia came copies of a letter implicating William Blount, the former governor of the Southwest Territory, in a conspiracy to evict Spain forcibly from her North American possessions. The degree to which Washington was surprised can only be guessed at. He had long known Blount as a thieving speculator who had enriched his purse and advanced his career by proclaiming to his Indian-hating Tennessee neighbors a roguish brand of manifest destiny. This was more than enough to gain him admission to the Senate, from whose rarefied precincts he hatched plans to forestall France's possible takeover of the Spanish Mississippi Valley by seizing it for himself.

The revelations could not have come at a worse time. Spanish authorities, realizing the bad bargain they had entered into with Thomas Pinckney, were looking for the slightest pretext to abrogate the Treaty of San Lorenzo. Adding to the delicacy of the situation, for a time it appeared as if Washington's friend Robert Liston was implicated in the plot. Actually, Liston had revealed Blount's conspiracy to Whitehall, where it was rejected out of hand. But Washington had no way of knowing this in the summer of 1797. All he knew was that a duly elected member of the United States Senate was engaged in treason for profit, rousing Indian emotions by blaming the former president for their alleged mistreatment at the hands of the United States. On July 8 Blount's embarrassed colleagues in the Senate expelled him from their councils. Undaunted, the swaggering Tennessean went home and was promptly elected to the state senate, where he remained a power until death cut short his career in 1800.

With Blount discredited, Washington turned his attention to an old adversary, James Monroe. The returning diplomat planned to vindicate himself, in the fashion of Edmund Randolph, by drafting a long and tedious appeal to the American people, but first he demanded from Timothy Pickering a public justification for his sacking. Washington professed indifference, noting sarcastically that although Monroe had passed through Alexandria late in August, he failed to honor Mount Vernon with a visit. Monroe's literary blast to come caused no sleepless nights along the Potomac. Said Washington, "If what he has promised the public does him no more credit than what he has given to it in his last exhibition, his friends must be apprehensive of a recoil."

A far greater wound was caused by the publication of a year-old letter from Jefferson to an Italian friend in which the current vice president used scathing language to revile "men who were Samsons in the field and Solomons in the council, but who have had their heads shorn by the harlot England." Amid a hurricane of recrimination Jefferson held his tongue, neither accepting nor denying responsibility for the explosive passage. His private explanation — that he was referring not to Washington personally but to the Society of the Cincinnati — fooled no one. As the aggrieved party, Washington maintained a discreet silence of his own, at least until a second bizarre exchange of letters gave fresh impetus to his suspicions.

It all began late in September 1797, when one John Langhorne of Albemarle County sent the former president some effusive condolences upon the recent attacks in the press. Washington assured his unknown correspondent that he felt "perfectly tranquil," notwithstanding the envenomed darts of his enemies. There the matter rested until another son of Albemarle, the Republican congressman John Nicholas, weighed in with unsubstantiated allegations that "Langhorne" was none other than Jefferson, hoping to draw the former president into a politically embarrassing slip of the pen. Early in December, Nicholas shifted ground, this time fingering as the culprit Peter Carr, Jefferson's lifelong friend and neighbor. He kept the pot boiling well into the new year by reporting a conversation in which Monroe's original appointment to Paris was characterized by "that man" Jefferson as a deliberate attempt by the executive to undermine Senate Republicans who looked to Monroe for leadership.

Nicholas would probably never have gained Washington's trust, even in the vulnerability of old age, but for his friendship with the former president's nephew Bushrod and the fact that his present accusations reinforced earlier reports from the tattler Henry Lee. Washington's anguished reply said as much: "Nothing short of the evidence you have adduced, corroborative of intimations which I had received long before through another channel, could have shaken my belief in the sincerity of a friendship, which I had conceived was possessed for me by the person to whom you allude." By this time eager to believe the worst of his former secretary of state, Washington with grim humor denied that Monroe's selection was part of a plot by the administration to cripple the Republican minority, for as president he had "designated several others, not of the Senate, as victims to this office *before* the sacrifice of Mr. Monroe was . . . in contemplation."

Autumn cast its spell along the Potomac, lavishly painting the woods around Mount Vernon in orange and gold. One October day, Washington's black body servant, Christopher, was bitten by a mad dog, and his concerned master sent the youth to a physician in Lebanon, Pennsylvania, experienced in such cases. Here was a metaphor for the rabid strain infecting the American body politic. Nelly Custis doubtless reflected household opinion when she wrote to a friend that fall, "Although I am no politician . . . yet I cannot avoid expressing my opinion of the French — were I drowning and a *straw* only in sight, I would as soon think of trusting to that *slender support* . . . as place the smallest dependence on the stability of the *French republican* government — neither would I trust the life of a *cat* in the hands of a set of people who hardly know religion, humanity or justice, even *by name*."

❦ 3 ❧

Washington could not escape the loneliness and isolation that often act as depressing portals to old age. "Our circle of friends of course is contracted," wrote Martha in the summer of 1797, "without any disposition on our part to enter into *new friendships*, though we have an abundance of acquaintances and a vast variety of visitors." Before leaving office Washington, in a twinge of sentimentality, had urged his former secretary David Humphreys to come home from Portugal and serve "as a companion in my latter days, in whom I could confide." But Humphreys had failed to take the hint, choosing instead to marry the daughter of an English banker.

At a time in life when many men dandled grandchildren on their knees, Washington, defrauded of children by nature, turned to Nelly Custis's two married sisters, who lived in the Federal City. Martha, called Patsy, resided with her husband, Thomas Peters, in a house on K Street. Peters, a speculator, prospered by constructing offices and living quarters for the prospective army of federal workers. (Asked whether there would be sufficient housing for the new government, Washington joked that "they can camp out — the Representatives in the first line, the Senate in the second, the President with all his suite in the middle.") A visitor to the Peters household was charmed to see the former president holding out a roll of peach cheese for the sixteen-month-old daughter of Patsy's sister Eliza. She was married to Thomas Law, a British native considerably older than his lively bride. Having been reared in the Indian colonial service, Law brought to his second marriage a healthy portion of imperial arrogance, along with three sons born to an Indian woman whose name was never mentioned. From the doomed developers James Greenleaf and Robert Morris, Law purchased five hundred building lots in the raw village. In the process, he exhausted his resources and began the steep descent into bankruptcy and divorce.*

All this was far in the future in the summer of 1797 when Washington visited the neighborhood called Twenty Buildings, where the stump of the future Capitol was flanked by a handful of boardinghouses, a tailor shop, shoemaker, print shop, grocery, and oyster house. Like other old men who proverbially plant trees because they do not expect to live to see them blossom, the former president looked at the muddy construction site and imagined greatness. Back at Mount Vernon, he asked his widowed nephew Lawrence Lewis to take over some of the burden of entertaining guests from his aunt and uncle, a couple "in the decline of life and regular in our habits." Washington begged off attending the wedding of his brother Samuel's boy Lawrence Augustine, whose names recalled the former president's long-dead father and half brother. "Wedding assemblies are better calculated for those who are *coming into* than to those who are *going out* of life," Washington told his nephew.

It is never safe to assume affluence in the aristocracy, and Washington's already precarious financial situation was not improved by retirement. After subtracting his presidential expense account of $25,000, the squire found himself in straitened circumstances. He had been forced to part with several thousand acres in western Pennsylvania, he said, "just to clear me out of Philadelphia and to lay in a few necessaries for my family." Six months later, the $22,000 this promised was still withheld. Henry

---

*In later years, Law revisited India while his wife busied herself with youthful admirers in military uniform. When his divorce became final in 1810, the ruined real estate developer celebrated by showering friends with gifts of imported English china.

Lee tried to palm off nearly worthless bonds in exchange for a piece of the Great Dismal Swamp, causing Washington to send dunning letters to Lee and others delinquent in their payments. The former president sought assurances that his franking privilege would continue for letters coming to as well as leaving Mount Vernon. Still needing cash, Washington instructed his agent in Philadelphia to dispose of the table ornaments left behind at 190 Market Street. The proposed sale was delayed by a recurrence of yellow fever, which was just as well, for Washington hoped to interest the members of Congress in his tableware, and he knew from bitter experience how fleet-footed was a congressman with a whiff of danger in his nostrils.

Even the elements seemed to conspire against Farmer Washington's solvency. Excessive rains destroyed his hay crop and battered his corn and wheat. This did not prevent his building a new distillery on Dogue Run, capable of manufacturing up to 12,000 gallons of whiskey a year, or from purchasing several lots in the Federal City. Thinking to build accommodations for the future officers of government, Washington designed a three-story double house of brick containing sixteen bedrooms, ideally situated for congressmen deliberating in the Capitol not more than a hundred yards away. The amateur architect, accustomed to the cheap labor of Mount Vernon's slave force, was shocked to receive an estimate of $11,250, exclusive of painting, glazing, and ironwork; these he must provide himself at additional expense.

When his spendthrift nephew Samuel applied for a loan beyond Washington's resources, the retired officeholder bristled. Scrounging up even $1,000 would be difficult, but "because I have heard that you are industrious and sober" he would make the sacrifice. Then, after a few hoary admonitions on the evils of borrowing, Washington let his nephew have the money without interest, to be paid back at his convenience. Tobias Lear likewise discovered his august employer's bark to be much worse than his bite, receiving an identical sum to assist in establishing his new household at nearby Walnut Tree Farm. Then there was Robert Lewis, who expressed admiration for a tract of several hundred acres belonging to his uncle. A few days later, Washington made him an outright gift of the property.

Washington's bank account in Alexandria was all but empty when a windfall dropped into his lap. An eager speculator named James Welch offered to take 23,000 acres of the former president's western holdings off his hands, and a long-term lease with option to buy was soon prepared. Under its terms, Welch agreed to pay $5,000 in 1798 and another $8,000 the following year, more than enough to ease Washington's chronic need for money. Even before the deal, however, he found $300 to help George

Washington Lafayette fly to his father, who had been released from a Prussian jail at Olmutz in September. Ironically, it was Napoleon Bonaparte, fast building a dictatorship on the rubble of French liberalism, who freed the broken symbol of Gallic liberty. Acting on nothing stronger than rumors and his own wishes to be reunited with the parent from whom he had been separated for four long years, Fayette hastily packed his bags and set off in the company of his tutor, Monsieur Frestal. Washington feared that by prematurely setting foot upon a continent far from pacified, the boy's life might be in danger, but he kept his worries to himself. In an emotional letter to Lafayette, he praised the youth and apologized for "the delicate and responsible situation in which I stood as an officer" — a condition preventing Washington as president from doing more to gain his friend's freedom.

His sorrow over young Fayette's departure was deepened by George Washington Parke Custis's continuing travails in the scholarly cloisters of Princeton. How dissimilar the pair must have seemed to their namesake at Mount Vernon, who asked the departing Fayette to visit the campus long enough to gratify Custis's latest plea for funds. Wearily Washington supplied the college president with a candid assessment of the boy's shortcomings: "From his infancy I have discovered an almost inconquerable disposition to indolence in everything that did not tend to his amusements." Young Wash's aversion to sustained labor had persisted in the face of repeated appeals to family expectation and personal pride. With diminishing hopes that it would do any good, Washington fired off fresh rounds of grandfatherly counsel. His missive of January 7, 1798, is worth quoting in full, in part for the light it sheds on his own rigorous use of time.

"System in all things should be aimed at," Washington told his grandson before a holiday visit to Mount Vernon, "for in execution it renders everything more easy. If now and then, of a morning before breakfast, you are inclined . . . to go out with a gun, I shall not object to it, provided you return by the hour we usually set down to that meal. From breakfast until about an hour before dinner (allowed for dressing, and preparing for it, that you may appear decent), I shall expect you will confine yourself to your studies and diligently attend to them, endeavoring to make yourself master of whatever is recommended to, or required of you.

"While the afternoons are short, and but little interval between rising from dinner and assembling for tea, you may employ that time in walking or any other recreation. After tea, if the studies you are engaged in require it, you will no doubt perceive the propriety and advantage of returning to them until the hour of rest. Rise early, that by habit it may become familiar, agreeable, healthy and profitable. It may for a while be irksome to do this; but that will wear off, and the practice will produce a rich harvest forever thereafter, whether in public or private walks of life.

"Make it an invariable rule to be in place (unless extraordinary circumstances prevent it) at the usual breakfasting, dining, and tea hours. It is not only disagreeable, but it is also very inconvenient, for servants to be running here and there and they know not where to summon you to them, when their duties and attendance on the company who are seated render it improper.

"Saturday may be appropriated to riding, to your gun, and other proper amusements.

"Time disposed of in this manner makes ample provision for exercise and every useful or necessary recreation; at the same time that the hours allotted for study, *if really applied to it* instead of running up and down stairs and wasted in conversation with anyone who will talk with you, will enable you to make considerable progress in whatever line is marked out for you . . . that you may do it is my sincere wish."

Washington might have saved his breath. The holiday ended disastrously in the youth's being bundled off to the Hope Park estate of his stepfather, David Stuart. The hero who had bested British generals and stared down congressional opponents now conceded defeat. He had tried to keep Custis in his room for part of every day, he told Stuart, but he could not instill a love of learning through a locked door. Briefly, Washington considered sending the boy to Harvard, but Martha's suffering at the prospect of her favorite grandchild's being posted to distant Massachusetts ruled out the idea. William and Mary was eliminated for reasons better communicated orally than by letter "unless he could be placed in the Bishop's family." In the end Annapolis was chosen, "from the nature of its composition and strictness of its police."

The winter of 1797–98 was a harsh one along the Potomac. During the third week of November, Nelly Custis reported her grandfather's estate sheeted in ice. The glassy river, so majestic in the spring, was now sluggish and desolate, the Maryland shore "so bleak and sublimely horrifying" that Nelly was quite prepared to bury herself in the dark beauty of *Ossian's Poems*. A visit from Robert and Henrietta Liston raised everyone's spirits, Mrs. Liston writing afterward that she had found the former president remarkably changed, "like a man relieved from a heavy burden. He has thrown off that prudence which formerly guarded his every word." Confirmation of this came in a letter written on December 17 from Martha to Eliza Powel. Martha looked forward to a springtime visit from Mrs. Powel, for by then everything would be ablaze with new life "except the withering proprietors of the mansion." After conveying sympathy for the plight of Philadelphians stricken with the yellow fever and saying a prayer for Robert Morris and his family, on the verge of public and humiliating financial ruin, Mrs. Washington added a few words (actually dictated by her husband).

What followed was an astonishing, if rambling, dialogue with death: "Despairing of hearing what may be said of him, if he should really go off in an apoplectic or any other fit (for he thinks all fits that issue in death are worse than a love fit or fit of laughter, and many others which he could name), that he is glad to hear *beforehand* what will be said of him on that occasion . . . and besides, as he has entered into an agreement with Mr. Morris and several other gentlemen, not to quit the theater of *this* world before the year 1800, it may be *relied upon* that no breach of contract shall be laid to him on that account unless dire necessity should bring it about . . . At present there seems to be no danger of his giving them the slip as neither his health nor spirits were ever . . . greater . . . notwithstanding, he adds, he is descending, and has almost reached the bottom of the hill — or in other words, the shades below."

For sixty-plus years Washington's invariable reaction to human mortality had been a dutiful and not entirely convincing fatalism. Now, as he drew closer to the end, he adopted an irreverent attitude toward the grinning skull that rode with him around his farms and shared the quiet hours before dawn spent scribbling in his study. Determined to cheat time, he not only promised to stay on to see at least a little of the nineteenth century, he even jauntily offered to sign his name to it. No man's word was more reliable. Of course, his cosigner Mr. Morris had made no less sacred contracts of his own, and he was headed for a debtor's cell in Philadelphia's Prune Street Prison.

{ 4 }

Far from the red clay fields of Virginia a very different tune was playing, a bugle summoning Americans to war. Washington listened with a thirsty ear for the latest developments from Europe, and what little he heard stirred the embers of military ambition. Dissatisfied with his narrowed sphere of action, he was torn between agricultural pleasures and the gratifications of ego that had propelled him through forty-five years of public service and sacrifice. Observant family members, stealing sidelong glances at the distracted warrior, noticed his lips moving wordlessly and his hand raised in silent affirmation before imaginary audiences. To them he appeared fixated on scenes that could hardly be influenced, much less controlled, from a Virginia estate.

Feelings too strong to be disguised prompted anxious inquiries of sitting

Cabinet officers and members of the American negotiating team who arrived in Paris early in October. It had not been a happy experience for John Marshall and his colleagues, forced to look on helplessly as the serpentine Talleyrand — still angry over Washington's refusal to receive him as an émigré in Philadelphia — dangled hints of a diplomatic settlement like French cuisine before starving men. Peace had a price, and a steep one at that. Through a trio of intriguers immortalized as X, Y, and Z in the correspondence that touched off a firekeg of national indignation in the spring of 1798, France's foreign minister conditioned his meeting the Yankee representatives upon a substantial loan for the Directory and a $240,000 bribe to line his own capacious pockets.

Talleyrand's mercenary ploy was a well-kept secret in the first week of December, when Washington sent Marshall a peppery account of domestic politics and the treacherous partisanship of Adams's congressional foes. The former president found it "laughable" to observe members of the Republican opposition who had detected executive encroachment in his every act now applauding the Directory's latest moves toward iron-fisted dictatorship, writing: "But so it always has been, and I assume ever will be with men who are governed more by passion and party views than by the dictates of justice, temperance, and sound policies." Washington could hardly credit reports of an impending land war on the North American continent, yet in France's present intoxicated state, "nothing is too absurd or unjust to be encountered."

By the start of 1798, he had a new and inviting target. "Mr. Monroe . . . appears in voluminous work," he wrote to Oliver Wolcott that January. "What is said of it?" A week later Washington repeated the query to James McHenry as part of a long list to be answered by the secretary of war unless "you have not leisure, or if any of them are embarrassing." Pickering's turn came on February 6, when Washington thanked him for sending a copy of Monroe's 507-page suicide note, for that is very nearly what the cashiered diplomat had produced in attempting to vindicate his conduct and damn the executive responsible for his ill-fated mission. With the book actually in his hands, Washington shed his earlier pose of lofty disinterest and spent several unhappy days in March blackening the margins of Monroe's sulfurous pages with factual rebuttals and scathing asides.

His appetite for the latest political intelligence was barely whetted when, on March 1, Washington asked Alexander White, a trusted friend and a commissioner of the Federal City, to devote "an hour or two . . . now and then" to filling him in on the shocking altercation between Representative Roger Griswold, a Connecticut Federalist, and his Republican nemesis from Vermont, Matthew Lyons. Verbal sparring between the two had turned nasty and ultimately violent when Lyons spat in his adversary's face on the floor of the House. Efforts to expel "the spitting animal" (Abigail Adams's words) failed on a party line vote, causing Griswold to take the law — and a heavy cane — into his own hands. Lyons reciprocated by seizing a nearby pair of iron tongs to defend himself. By the time order was restored, both the House's reputation and republican dignity were in tatters.

Washington's reaction was predictable. Misrepresentation and party feuds had grown to frightening dimensions, the president concluded. "Where and when they will terminate or whether they can end at any point short of confusion and anarchy is *now* in my opinion more problematical than ever." Plunging him even deeper into gloom was France's continued trifling with American diplomats. "Are our commissioners guillotined?" Washington asked McHenry early in March, resorting to black humor to veil his alarm at the ominous silence from Paris. In such an atmosphere the wildest stories flourished; rumors were circulating through Alexandria that certain members of Congress had been caught red-handed in a treasonable correspondence with the Directory. "The period is big with events," said Washington, "but what it will produce is beyond the reach of human ken. On this, as upon all other occasions, I hope the best." But his supplications to Providence, which had "not led us so far in the path of Independence of one nation to throw us into the arms of another," sounded less than wholly convincing.

As international tensions escalated, the old man's anger spilled over to purely domestic concerns. Washington sharply upbraided his grandson for implying a romance between Nelly Custis and Charles Carroll, then got into a heated wrangle with James Anderson, his reliable if overly sensitive manager, who threatened to quit in protest of the squire's smothering supervision. "Strange and singular indeed would it be if the proprietor of an estate . . . should have nothing to say in, or control over, his own expenditures," asserted Washington. Could Anderson be more specific in his criticism? How, exactly, had he been thwarted in his plans? Had his employer withheld the means to implement suitable improvements? Had he interfered in any way with the crops, the carpenters, ditchers, millers, or coopers who answered to the Scotsman? "If I cannot remark upon my own business, passing every day under my eyes, without hurting your feelings," said Washington, "I must discontinue my rides or become a cipher on my own estate."

Having spent his anger on paper, he proposed a fair division of labor and profit. Let Anderson confine his efforts to Mount Vernon's mill, distillery, and fishing operations, sufficient in themselves to demand the full-time services of a conscientious manager. It was a generous offer, duly accepted after a decent interval in which to salve Anderson's pride. If only the national political scene could be so rationally governed. The prospects were not bright: on March 19, President Adams formally notified Congress of the failure of the French negotiations. Worse, he reported new directives from Paris shutting off French ports to Yankee vessels and authorizing the seizure of any neutral ship containing British cargo. Adams used the occasion to renew his earlier call for strengthened defenses, and the Republicans drew back in horror at what they saw as a certain precursor to war. Jefferson, for one, thought the message "insane." Six weeks went by, allowing opposition forces to regroup and point a finger of blame at Adams's bellicosity for the failure of the talks.

"The Demo's seem to be lifting up their heads again," Washington wrote to McHenry early in May. From the standpoint of what a later generation would label the Blame America First crowd, official dispatches detailing French perfidy were downgraded into "harmless chitchat and trifles . . . So much for a little consultation among them," Washington harrumphed. But his successor did not make things any easier for the advocates of preparedness. Displaying his genius for making enemies out of prospective friends, Adams had noisily boycotted a celebration of Washington's sixty-sixth birthday on the grounds that no private citizen deserved such an observance — especially when the current chief magistrate's anniversary went unnoticed. Jefferson, watching from the sidelines, hugely enjoyed the divisions thus widened between "Adamites" and "the Washingtonians."

The vice president's delight was fleeting, however, for when Congress demanded the complete record of Franco-American discussions, Adams was only too willing to oblige. On April 3 he supplied lawmakers with more than enough evidence to document Talleyrand's studied insults and outrageous solicitation of bribes. War fever swept the nation, and Adams was cheered lustily wherever he appeared. The first lady noticed that tradesmen raised their hats as she passed. "In short, we are wonderfully popular except with Bache and Company, who in his paper calls the President old, querulous, bald, blind, crippled, toothless Adams. Thus in scripture was the prophet mocked, and though no bears may devour the wretch, the wrath of an insulted people will by and by break upon him."

In the ensuing uproar, the administration won passage of twenty separate measures aimed at increasing national security or at least raising the price France must pay if it wished to make good on its warlike threats. During the first week of May, Congress established a Department of the Navy. Three frigates carrying thirty-eight guns each were approved, along with a dozen sloops of war and an infant armaments industry.

Following Washington's advice, the largest of the new federal armories was located at Harper's Ferry, Virginia. When an army of 10,000 regulars was authorized, Alexander Hamilton was dazzled by visions of martial glory and convinced of an overwhelming public demand for Washington's return should an open rupture with France lead to fighting on American soil. He proposed that his former chief undertake a tour of doubtful areas in Virginia and North Carolina "under some pretense of health, etc. This would call forth addresses, public dinners, etc., which would give you an opportunity of expressing sentiments in answering toasts, etc., which would throw the weight of your character into the scale of government and revive an enthusiasm for your person that may be turned into the right channel."

Washington questioned the usefulness of what would be, in effect, a campaign swing. He told Hamilton that his health had never been better, thus giving the lie to the ostensible reason for his journey. More important, he doubted whether any tour would dissuade enemies of the administration, for whom Washington himself was part of the problem. He questioned the likelihood of French aggression against the United States proper, "although I think them capable of *anything bad*." Whatever happened, he would put his faith in the general population, whose spirit of resistance would surely cower French hotspurs and discredit their Republican sympathizers. Nevertheless, Washington did not rule out a military comeback, "for if a crisis should arrive when a sense of duty, or a call from my country, should become so imperious as to leave me no choice, I should prepare for the relinquishment and go with as much reluctance from my present peaceful abode as I should do to the tombs of my ancestors."

To borrow a later maxim, Barkis was willing. More than willing, it would seem, as the long-retired soldier pressed Hamilton for the names of his likely military subordinates "and whether you would be disposed to take an active part if arms are to be resorted to." That same month, in another flashback to the virile days of his military past, Washington resumed a conversation with Sally Fairfax, interrupted for a quarter century by war and politics. All the intervening changes could not erase from his mind "the recollection of those happy moments, the happiest in my life, which I have enjoyed with you," he wrote. Talk of war alternated in his letter with a nostalgic longing for colonial Virginia. Washington claimed to be exhausted by his past toils. Yet even when seated once more under the vine and fig tree that served as his favorite agricultural metaphor, he fretted that "those whom we have been accustomed to call our good friends and allies are endeavoring, if not to make us afraid, yet to despoil us of our property."

He often cast his eyes upon the ruins of Belvoir, said Washington, and never without pangs of regret that its former inhabitants, "with whom we lived in such harmony and friendship," were no longer in residence. Might not Sally, now a fading widow, consider passing her remaining days in the neighborhood of her youth? Hardly the first old man to recapture his youth on paper, Washington must have known that his offer of hospitality was unlikely to be accepted. Martha in a separate letter called the mournful roll of departed friends and neighbors, so many that not a single familiar family remained in Alexandria; "our visitors on the Maryland shore are gone, and going likewise." As for her own offspring, Martha assumed that Jack Custis's death in 1781 was long since known to Sally. "He left four fine children, three daughters and a son, a fine promising youth now. The two eldest of the girls are married and have children; the second, Patty, married before her eldest sister; she has two fine children, both girls. The eldest, Elizabeth, married Mr. Law, a man of fortune from the East Indies and brother to the Bishop of Carlisle. She has a daughter. Martha married Mr. Thomas Peter, son of Robert Peters of Georgetown, who is also very wealthy. Both live in the Federal City. The youngest daughter, Eleanor, is yet single and lives with me, having done so from an infant, as has my grandson, George Washington — now turned of seventeen — except when at college, to three of which he has been, viz. Philadelphia, New Jersey and Annapolis."

⟨ 5 ⟩

For Washington there could be no holiday from the eyes of the world. Early in June, Thomas Law encamped at Mount Vernon, bringing with him a forty-year-old Polish nobleman turned revolutionary named Julian Ursyn Niemcewicz. As a refugee from his country's failed uprising against the Russian bear in 1794, Niemcewicz revered the founder of American liberties, but even the émigré was pleasantly surprised by the charm of a household whose owner could not live without beauty, beginning with the stunning river vista that stretched for almost five miles from a broad piazza where family members gathered for conversation to the music of robins and blue titmice. Inside, Niemcewicz saw portraits of various Washingtons scattered throughout the house and "very neatly and prettily furnished" apartments set aside for Madame Washington, her extravagantly gifted granddaughter, and guests. At two in the afternoon Washington himself appeared on a gray mount. After dinner the Pole wandered through the gardens, where Law showed off some poppies and explained the finer points of opium production. It being the Sabbath, there was no music to fill the evening, "not even a game of chess," before bedtime at the sober hour of nine.

Over the next two weeks, the patriot from Warsaw peeled away Washington's storied reserve. From agriculture and natural history, the former president's conversation moved easily to politics, domestic and foreign. Washington contrasted the French declarations of universal freedom and happiness with the merciless conquest of peaceful Holland, Italy, and Switzerland. He submitted gamely to the foreigner's questions about America's Revolution and displayed his geographical (and business) acumen by rattling off every river, creek, and other means of water transport in a two-thousand-mile arc from Portsmouth, Maine, to the mouth of the Mississippi River. For her part, the lady of the house exhibited a cherished collection of medals struck during the Revolution and presented the Pole with a china cup containing her monogram and the names of the American states. One day Niemcewicz, accompanied by James Anderson and part of Mount Vernon's slave population, went fishing in the Potomac. They harvested a rich crop of mottled garfish and white-whiskered catfish, so named for the distinctive cry they gave out when disturbed.

Returning to Mansion House, Niemcewicz found the dining room table set with elegant Sèvres porcelain for twenty. "The general, in high spirits, was gracious and full of attention to everybody," among them a young couple, their three children, and a corpulent grande dame who stormed one platter after another as her husband offered laughing encouragement: "Betsy, a little more, a little more." Later that evening, after the rest of the company had departed, Washington read aloud from a letter postmarked Paris and written by an old friend whose words sparked the first real show of wrath since Niemcewicz's arrival ten days earlier.

"Whether we consider the injuries and plunder which our commerce is suffering, or the affront to our national independence and dignity in the rejection of our envoys, or . . . the oppression, ruin and final destruction of all free people through this military government, everywhere we recognize the need to arm ourselves with a strength and zeal equal to the dangers with which we are threatened." According to Washington, the time for patience had passed. "Submission is vile," he thundered. "Yea, rather than allowing herself to be insulted to this degree, rather than having her freedom and independence trodden underfoot, America — every American — I — though old, will pour out the last drop of blood which is yet in my veins."

Gathering force as he went, Washington denounced the critics at home who thought Adams's administration unnecessarily warlike. From the first hour of his retirement to the present moment, he had neither contacted his successor nor received any communication from him. Yet were he in Adams's place, said Washington, he would take similar precautions (even though he might be "less vehement in expression"). Four days after delivering this assessment, Washington broke his self-imposed silence to invite Adams to Mount Vernon should he come south to see the future capital city for himself. There was nothing accidental about the timing of his note or the carefully worded praise directed to the embattled Adams. As grateful as the New Englander was for Washington's gesture, he was just as keen to detect his predecessor's unhappiness over his forced inactivity.

In his reply, dated June 22, Adams disparaged his own martial qualifications, going so far as to express a wish that he might constitutionally swap places with the hero of the Revolution. Adams also dropped tantalizing hints of military adventures to come. To lead the force recently authorized by Congress, the president must choose between experienced generals, many of them well advanced in years, and a younger, untested set of officers. Personnel aside, one thing was certain. "If the French come here we must learn to march with a quick step and to attack, for in that way only they are said to be vulnerable. I must tax you some times for advice," Adams concluded. "We must have your name, if you in any case will permit us to use it. There will be more efficacy in it than in many an army."

Although Adams stopped short of formally proposing Washington's return to active command, the inference was unmistakable. Only death, it seemed, would release the old soldier from the obligations that went with his symbolic standing and the inner conflicts caused by unquenchable ambition. Even now, part of Washington longed for the unrelenting grind of mobilizing an essentially defenseless country. The threat of a French invasion left him no other course. But he would not be rushed into anything, nor was he about to surrender a commander's right to surround himself with trusted subordinates. On July 4, Washington did an extraordinary thing, pulling rank in separate letters composed for the attention of his War Department confidant, James McHenry, and President Adams.

"I see, as you do, that clouds are gathering and that a storm may ensue," Washington wrote to McHenry. From "a variety of hints," the squire guessed that his retirement might soon be interrupted by an official request to enter "the boundless field of responsibility and trouble." How, he asked, would it look if he charged back into the fray less than a year after the publication of his definitive farewell? On what evidence was it claimed that his countrymen wished to entrust him with their defenses or that any American force taking the field would be organized along lines conducive to victory and creditable to its commanding officer? Given the Gallic predilection for "Generals of juvenile years," Washington questioned the wisdom of placing so aged a warrior as himself in charge of the American war effort.

But his chief preoccupation was knowing who among his colleagues would give America's military much of its strategic character. No commander in chief could be any better than his general staff. Drawing upon his vast experience, Washington emphasized the need for energetic men in the vital posts of inspector general, quartermaster general, and adjutant general and as commanders of Artillery and Engineers. "Viewing them in this light, it will readily be seen how essential it is that they should be agreeable to him," said Washington, hastening to add that he knew precisely where to recruit such an official family if it came to that.

Unfortunately, Washington did not feel at liberty to go into such details with Adams. Before leaving for Alexandria's celebration of the Fourth, Washington wrote to the president in Philadelphia, dancing gracefully around an invitation that was as yet only implied. Much as the former president preferred "the smooth paths of retirement [to] the thorny ways of public life," he readily contrasted the current foe and modes of warfare with the bygone days of 1775. Answering Adams's question about personnel, he held out little hope of finding among "the *old set* of generals" men of sufficient energy and political soundness to repulse the French invaders. Washington's solution was a meritocratic revolution in the ranks, relying on the most experienced and intelligent officers without respect to seniority. Yet with no list to refresh his memory, the former president held back from naming names while asserting in uncompromising terms the prerogative of any commander to select his most trusted coadjutors.

On July 5 he wrote a second letter to McHenry, still less guarded than the first. Again he stressed the critical importance of recruiting the right general staff. "If I am looked to as commander in chief," Washington stated bluntly, "I must be allowed to choose such as will be agreeable to me." He set forth these conditions unaware that the impulsive Adams had already sent his name to the Senate on July 2 or that the upper chamber had twenty-four hours later unanimously designated him lieutenant general and commander in chief of all armies to be raised within the United States. Before McHenry could formally tender the position, the new commander revealed his strategic thinking in a letter to Timothy Pickering dated July 11. Washington anticipated that a French invasion, should it come at all, would be aimed squarely at the South, whose huge Negro population, combined with its Republican sympathies and proximity to Louisiana, made it most vulnerable to insurrectionary fevers. This alone argued persuasively for giving second rank in the army to a prominent Southerner such as Charles Cotesworth Pinckney.

Washington's enthusiasm for Pinckney did not in the least diminish his confidence in Pickering's candidate for the number two position, Alexander Hamilton. Indeed, said Washington, Hamilton's service "ought to be secured at *almost* any price" notwithstanding John Adams's antipathy to the scheming New Yorker. That same day McHenry arrived from Philadelphia, bearing not only a letter from the president but one from Hamilton, urging Washington's acceptance. "War is on again, General," said McHenry, "this time with France. I bring you the will of the nation." In the response Washington drafted for McHenry to carry back with him, he catalogued the Directory's attempts to extort money from American diplomats and sow the seeds of dissension among his countrymen.

"Believe me, Sir, no one can more cordially approve of the wise and prudent measures of your administration," he told Adams. "They ought to inspire universal confidence." Fully satisfied that the president had drained the cup of reconciliation and exhausted every peaceful avenue, Washington was equally convinced that "we can with pure hearts appeal to heaven for the justice of our cause." He attached two conditions only to his service — that he not be called into the field until such time as circumstances demanded, and that he not receive any salary, settling for only such expenses as directly incurred while in uniform.

Washington no doubt meant all that he said. But he did not say all that was on his mind. In a letter to Hamilton on July 14 marked "private and confidential," the former president made explicit a new and overriding qualification. He would lead the American army if, and only if, "the principal officers in the line and of the staff shall be such as I can place confidence in." Thus the stage was set for an unnecessary, if historic, test of wills between the aging hero and his civilian superior. Washington unwittingly prepared to fight two wars, one on paper against a mythical French expeditionary force, and the other, far more immediate, against the political bumbler who had appointed him.

❧ 15 ❧

POTOMAC TWILIGHT

"I little thought when I retired to the shades of private life . . . that any event would happen *in my day* that could bring me again on the public theater; but so it is; and the remnant of a life which required ease and tranquility will end more than probably in toil and responsibility."

George Washington,
August 12, 1798

WASHINGTON'S WAR GOT OFF to a bad start, its early weeks marked by confusion, crossed signals, and the clash of egos. Before adjourning in mid-July, Congress belatedly repealed the 1778 treaties binding the United States to King Louis's France and authorized a tripling of the regular army, to more than 14,000 soldiers and officers. But the lawmakers shrank from any formal declaration of hostilities, with the result that Washington found himself waging a quasi-war, backed by a phantom force and with an uncertain mandate. President Adams did not improve matters by decamping for Quincy, where he remained for four critical months, little more than a spectator to events, while he nursed his dangerously ill wife.

Adams left behind a series of harshly worded measures aimed at countering possible domestic subversion. The first extended from five to fourteen years the necessary period for any foreign-born resident to attain U.S. citizenship. Late in June, Congress adopted the Alien Act, empowering the president to expel any alien viewed as a threat to public safety. War-whooping congressmen marked the Glorious Fourth by passing the Sedition Act, whose terms included fines of up to $2,000 and jail terms of as much as two years for any American convicted of publishing writings deemed "false, scandalous and malicious" or likely to undermine the government of the United States, its chief executive, or Congress.

Washington and others in the Federalist camp worried that a fragile republic might be torn asunder by 30,000 French émigrés who took their orders from the Directory in Paris and an even larger number of disaffected Irishmen and English republicans. While Americans today reflexively condemn this overreaction to a largely imagined danger, anyone who lived through the fever dream of the 1950s and the Communist scare fueled by Joseph McCarthy can attest to the ease with which the old ghosts can again be summoned to point their fingers. At least the United States in 1798, barely a decade into its constitutional experiment and essentially friendless in a hostile world, had the excuse of political immaturity to explain its paranoia.

No legislation could suppress sectional rivalries or forestall an unseemly scramble for position by armchair warriors. Congress had provided for three major generals to support the commander in chief. Knox, Hamilton, and Pinckney were the obvious contenders, each well positioned to satisfy the requirements of his region. But who would take precedence? Should their revolutionary rank carry over into this new and potentially very different kind of conflict? Washington thought not. For both strategic and political reasons, he wanted the South Carolinian placed first among equals. After conferring with McHenry, however, Washington reversed himself and put Hamilton's name at the top of the chain of command, a critically important step given his own refusal to take the field except in opposition to a full-scale French invasion. Thus Washington's strong right arm, so to speak, would crack the whip and give the orders that the old soldier was reluctant to issue himself. Hedging his bets, Hamilton's friend told the New Yorker that "after all it rests with the President to use his pleasure."

That might be so, but it fell to Washington, not Adams, to inform the sensitive Knox that he was to rank third. This news was not well received, to put it mildly. Under mounting strain from speculative debts that threatened to land him in jail, the placid Yankee snapped, accusing Washington of betrayal. After twenty years of apparently false intimacy, Knox did not like one bit the thought of being thrown over for a mere brevet colonel. Hurt feelings aside, he disparaged Hamilton's claim to popular preference and dashed cold water on Pinckney's willingness to accept second place. He pointedly questioned whether New England, which must in his opinion supply the bulk of America's troops, would suffer exclusion from the general staff. (That it was also John Adams's back yard and political base hardly needed repeating.)

Washington experienced other setbacks, hardly less embarrassing. He offered his Richmond intimate Edward Carrington the post of quartermaster general in the provisional army, not realizing that Congress had thus far refused to establish the position. More worrisome, the furloughed soldier seemed tentative in his reading of French intentions. To Carrington he observed that the South was a likely target of attack, yet he continued to hope that an aroused public opinion would ward off land action and confine any hostilities to a watery battlefield. (In fact, the infant U.S. Navy acquitted itself honorably throughout the quasi-war, thanks to three forty-four-gun frigates whose construction costs had tripled even as their completion dates were pushed back from eighteen months to four years. Other vessels flying the Stars and Stripes managed to sink one French frigate, seize more than a hundred enemy privateers, and recapture seventy ships of Yankee origin.) An invasion of the American continent appeared remote as long as Britain clamped a naval blockade around the French ports. Still, the prospect of a sudden peace between King George's island and its continental adversary left Washington feeling ambivalent, "for if peace takes place in Europe, the Directory must find employment for the troops, or the troops will find employment for the Directory."

"I am assailed from all quarters, and by all descriptions of people, for commissions, introductions, recommendations, etc.," Washington complained to McHenry at the end of July 1798. The freshly commissioned officer asked if he might have a secretary, and within a month Tobias Lear resigned from the presidency of the Potomac Company and returned to Mount Vernon's welcoming embrace. Lear found enough paperwork for ten secretaries. To begin with, Washington required a suitable mount of between four and eight years of age, "a *perfect* white, a dapple gray, a deep bay, a chestnut, a black, in the order they are mentioned." The animal must be proportioned to its 210-pound rider. "Being long legged . . . would be no recommendation," said Washington, "as it adds nothing to strength, but a good deal to the inconvenience in mounting."

When a battery of "graybeards," as fervent as they were venerable, formed themselves into a company to defend Alexandria, Washington ordered a stand of colors at his own expense, telling McHenry to procure banners "handsome, but not more expensive than becomes Republicans (not Bachite Republicans)." Everything, it seemed, was in short supply, from the latest artillery to stationery and copying paper for the commanding general.

Everything, that is, but political counsel. Washington himself warned McHenry against neglecting Federalist Maryland in the appointments process. On August 2 the commander in chief criticized the pace of national preparedness, insisting that "more energetic" measures were called for if the Directory was to be dissuaded from aggression. Fearing a loss of the country's initial enthusiasm sparked by the XYZ Affair, he did not have far to look for a convenient scapegoat, a well-organized if shadowy "French Party" crying out for disarmament. Initially, said Washington, the Directory's domestic supporters had fallen silent, "like a man stunned by a severe blow," but only until new orders could be given, new assaults prepared for the Bachite press.

On August 9 the general wrote a long, defensive reply to Knox's petulant letter, blaming Congress and, by implication, the president for rushing to judgment without allowing time for "harmonious consultation" among those charged with the nation's defense. In their haste to get out of Philadelphia for recess, the legislators had thrust upon Washington an unsought command first learned of through a newspaper. If Knox's feelings were hurt, then what of his own emotions, "brought as I was, without the least intimation, before the public, after it had been officially announced to the world . . . that my soul panted for rest and that the first wish of my heart was to spend the remnant of a life worn down with care in ease and retirement." Washington reminded his friend that any dissension over rank would be sweet music to French ears and appealed to Knox's patriotism. "I hope to God that at no time, much less the present, when everything sacred and dear is threatened, that local distinctions and little jealousies will be done away with."

Washington's distress extended well beyond the pretensions of a single vainglorious general. The United States hung in the balance, yet no less a patriot than Henry Knox chose to sulk rather than serve. Coming just a year after Washington's Farewell Address, with its majestic admonition against sectional loyalties, Knox's behavior was an unhappy parable of the internal diversions that posed a greater danger than any foreign army to the survival of republican institutions. As such, it was enough to make the former president question his whole life's work.

Compounding his gloom, he shared Hamilton's low opinion of McHenry's qualifications for office. On August 10 he rebuked the secretary for keeping him as ignorant of army recruitment and munitions "as if I had just dropped from the clouds." The unfortunate McHenry was caught in a crossfire when Washington's southern volley was matched by a fusillade from the New England camp of Adams's favorite artilleryman. Late in August, the president declared unhesitatingly that Knox was entitled to rank immediately behind Washington. "No other arrangement will give satisfaction," Adams told McHenry, adding in a foreboding tone, "There has been too much intrigue in this business, both with General Washington and me." Should Washington accept his ranking of

Knox, Pinckney, and Hamilton in that order, then the commander in chief might be called at once into active service. Anything less would cause delays and bad feelings.

Before McHenry could reveal this latest roadblock to his master at Mount Vernon, Washington took to his bed with a high fever. On the night of August 18 he was seized with a malarial attack, whose debilitating effects he tried for three days to fight off through sheer willpower. By the time he at last summoned Dr. Craik to administer quinine, the former president was perilously weakened. Bed rest and "the bark" halted his decline, but it was more than a month before he regained his customary vigor or the twenty pounds burned away by tropical fever. With exquisitely bad timing, George Washington Parke Custis chose this moment to abandon his desultory scholarship at Annapolis after just four months. An exasperated guardian invited the boy's stepfather to probe Custis's mind: "He appears to me to be moped or stupid, says nothing and is always in some hole or corner excluded from company."

During the first week of September the company included John Marshall, who was lionized by the citizens of Alexandria for his defiant part in the aborted French negotiation. Not yet well enough to raise his glass at the public dinner accorded Marshall, Washington successfully pressed the Federalist's man of the hour to run for Richmond's House seat in the coming elections. The former president's pen was incessantly active as he instructed the civilian McHenry on the importance of turning the contents of powder magazines frequently, lest none be fit for use in an emergency, and proclaimed the superiority of southern horses for cavalry operations. "I hope they are rigid and pointed to good men," said Washington of the new military recruitment rules, "for it is much better to have a few good soldiers than a multitude of vagrants and indifferent ones."

Holding to these same exacting standards, an angry commanding general demanded justification for McHenry's raising Tennessee's John Sevier to the status of brigadier. The man had never been celebrated for anything, Washington professed, "except the murder of Indians." On September 10 the convalescing patient sent $200 to aid the poor of Philadelphia as their city was again invaded by yellow fever. The disease carried off his bitterest enemy, Benjamin Franklin Bache, but the voice of the *Aurora* was not to be stilled; the editor's widow was soon succeeded by William Duane, according to the historian Paul Johnson, "a malcontent Irishman who had been expelled from British India for sedition." Duane compared Washington's fall from grace to that of Adam and Eve. He carried on Bache's anti-Federalist crusade with no discernible loss of fervor.

McHenry's back-channel reports of Adams's intransigence filled Washington with "disquietude and embarrassment." Yet he could do nothing without exposing his prominent sources or risking a permanent rupture with the prickly chief executive. Brooding on his predicament and the unaccountable delays in organizing the nation's defense, Washington finally decided to challenge his successor directly. "With all due respect which is due to your public station, and with the regard I entertain for your private character," the general wrote on September 25, using an exaggerated courtesy to soften the coming blow. He faulted Adams for neglecting to consult with him prior to his original appointment. Had the president done so, many misunderstandings might have been avoided, starting with the commanding general's conception of his role. According to Washington, he had made clear to McHenry that the sine qua non of his service was the right to choose his military family. Washington *needed* Hamilton, Pinckney, and Knox, in descending order, in order to unite the country for whatever tests lay ahead. "But you have been pleased to order the last to be first and the first to be last," the general wrote, bristling. Nearly as bad, of four brigadiers in the provisional army, "one whom I never heard of as a military character has been nominated and appointed; and another is so well known to all those who have served with him in the Revolution as . . . to have given the greatest disgust." The situation was no better with respect to adjutant generals.

Washington insisted that he had no desire to accumulate power at the expense of his civilian superiors. His concern was more practical. At heart he dreaded losing, not only American independence, but, like a gift that might be snatched away, "that reputation which the partiality of the world has been pleased to bestow on me." Even now he felt insecure in his hold upon public opinion, fearful that all his past services might be forgotten in the backwash of a failed defense. Beyond this, the coming battle bore little resemblance to the revolutionary campaigns, when "worrying the enemy until we could be better provided with arms" had been a strategy born of desperation. This time the United States must be prepared to move with boldness and celerity to forestall any French foothold south of the Mason-Dixon Line, a region whose disloyal Republicans and disaffected slaves could spell disaster for the federal cause. Implicit in this was Washington's belief that the lumpish Henry Knox, to cite only the most obvious of yesterday's heroes, had none of the impetuosity demanded by the present crisis. The general did not say this; he did not have to.

He did make a strong case for his favorite, Hamilton: "By some he is considered an ambitious man, and therefore a dangerous one. That he is ambitious I shall readily grant, but it is of that laudable kind which prompts a man to excel in whatever he takes in hand. He is enterprising, quick in his perceptions, and his judgment intuitively great." The loss of such a paragon, said Washington, would be "irreparable." Can anyone doubt that in drawing this sketch of the venturesome New Yorker, Washington was describing himself as a young soldier, hell-bent on fame, status, and the gratitude of posterity?

Washington could not conclude his letter, already lengthy, without a gentle rebuke of the president, who had squandered a season without any noticeable progress toward filling the ranks of an army that at the moment existed on paper only. A cresting wave of martial enthusiasm, likely to bear a flood of good men into enlistment offices, had given way to vacillation and second thoughts. Soon there might be nothing but raw recruits and cowardly militia to stand between the French invaders and defenseless America. "I have addressed you, Sir, with openness and candor," wrote Washington. With equal frankness he now hoped that Adams might yet reverse his ranking of Hamilton and Knox and accede to his commander in chief in the selection of adjutant generals.

Unwilling to let the matter rest there, Washington sent a copy of his letter to McHenry, enjoining his Cabinet ally to keep its contents secret "unless the result should make it necessary for me to proceed to the final step." Until then, "even the *rumor* of a misunderstanding between the President and me, while the breach can be repaired, would be attended with unpleasant consequences." On the other hand, should Adams persist in his stubborn course, said his predecessor, "the Public must decide which of us is right and which wrong." One can well imagine how Washington in the presidential chair would react to a truculent general who promised to bring down the temple if thwarted in the selection of his subordinates. In at least one respect, however, he was painfully accurate in his perceptions: the slightest leak of his insubordination or wire pulling with McHenry and others in Adams's Cabinet would cripple the war effort and likely destroy the administration. It was a dangerous game played for stakes as high as any in a career full of risk taking.

On October 1, in a letter to McHenry marked "(Private and quite confidential)," Washington prepared the ground for his resignation. Simultaneously he asked the secretary of war to supply him with a copy of Oliver Wolcott's recent correspondence with Adams, in which the treasury secretary had added his voice to the Cabinet chorus demanding Hamilton's elevation to what was, in practical effect, field command of the nation's armed forces. A week later, the post at last brought Washington's screed of September 25 to a president still deeply worried for his wife's survival. Adams's response was surrender on all fronts. He signed the three commissions on the same day, leaving it to his commanding general to determine the order of preference. As for potential adjutant generals, Adams invited his predecessor to submit the names of candidates to McHenry. Should controversies arise, Adams promised to confirm Washington's judgment, reserving to himself this modest fig leaf as a way of formally asserting the president's exclusive authority under the Constitution "to determine the rank of officers." The old soldier, it appeared, had won a total victory.

In his brief reply to Adams, Washington was blandly magnanimous, voicing "sincere concern" for the first lady's health and skirting the adjutantcy question by pronouncing Adams's latest selection "acceptable." He could not know how costly his triumph would prove. For Wolcott's intervention, coupled with Washington's unyielding stance and the continuing pressures exerted by Hamilton's partisans, had caused the scales to fall away from Adams's eyes. Not the sort to be under the thumb of any man, even one so illustrious as George Washington, late in October Adams dismissed McHenry's fears about sluggish recruitment, saying, "Regiments are costly articles everywhere and more so in this country than in any other under the sun." Mindful of American's traditional resentment of standing armies, Adams feared popular disaffection if a large force were organized with no obvious enemy to fight. Yet that was exactly what his advisers were urging upon him. "At present there is no more prospect of seeing a French army here than there is in heaven," declared Adams with a certainty that could only send shudders through the warmongers in his own party.

Washington, meanwhile, shared his triumph with the secretary of war, at the same time requesting that McHenry burn his letter and say nothing of the president's capitulation or the events leading up to it. Otherwise, the general remarked piously, Adams might conclude that state secrets were being spilled and conspiracies hatched behind his back. Indeed, it would not take long for the suspicious New Englander to conclude "that intrigues are carrying on in which I am an actor, than which nothing is more foreign from my heart."

❦ 3 ❧

"This morning arrived in town the Chief who unites all hearts," enthused the *American Daily Advertiser* for November 10, 1798. Washington had returned to Philadelphia for the first time in twenty months to discuss with Hamilton and Pinckney the recruitment and supply of a provisional army. (The president, remaining by his wife's side until she was out of danger, did not appear until November 25.) Scant warning of Washington's plans did nothing to diminish the city's joyous welcome. Nearly the whole of McPherson's Blues stood at attention on Market Street for the general's review, and an enthusiastic throng gathered outside Mrs. White's boardinghouse on Eighth Street, which would be Washington's headquarters for the next five weeks. It was a busy place, as the former president greeted admirers and renewed acquaintances with his old secretary, Major William Jackson, now a prosperous businessman in the Quaker city, dined at the Bingham mansion on Third Street, and enjoyed both breakfast and tea with Eliza Powel. Washington's most melancholy meal was taken with the Robert Morris family in the so-called Debtors Apartment of the Prune Street Jail, into which the Financier of the Revolution had been tossed for not paying taxes and interest on his speculative empire.

One day Washington broke bread with Robert and Henrietta Liston. "I have scarcely seen a change of situation produce a greater or more agreeable one in manners than in him," said Mrs. Liston afterward. Her estimate of a "kind, affable, cheerful and happy" former president might be attributed in part to the prospect of new teeth, Washington's having ordered a replacement set from John Greenwood after his old dentures turned black. Greenwood told Washington to soak them in water, not port wine. If the teeth blackened anyway, he should scrub them with chalk. Alternatively he could place them in broth or "pot liquor" but never tea or acid. Holes in the dentures could be filled easily enough by hot wax applied with a nail.

Washington maintained his amiability in spite of, or perhaps because of, the cumbersome business of forging a 50,000-man army from a congressional resolution. At planning meetings that took up most of each day, Sundays not excepted, the vigorous strategist pondered which western outposts to fortify, how to avoid a plague of profiteering contractors, and the proper number of musicians to assign to each corps of artillery. By decreasing the number of officers, he hoped to save money and increase mobility through the elimination of long baggage trains. Finding qualified officers for twelve new regiments was no easier than finding money to pay the army during the year or more that would be required to whip it into fighting shape. In mustering such a force, Washington advised steering clear of "great cities," for "the collection of troops there may lead to disorders and expose more than elsewhere the morals and principles of the soldiery." He also proposed that federal authorities take upon themselves the responsibility for supplying rations, not least because of the enlisted man's propensity to spend too little on provisions and too much on ardent spirits.

With an old man's vanity, Washington spent an inordinate amount of time on military dress. His own uniform, for example: it should consist of a blue coat with yellow buttons and gold epaulettes of three stars on each shoulder, buff-colored linings in the cape and cuffs; the winter outfit to feature a buff-colored vest and breeches, a coat without lapels, and embroidery on cape, cuffs, and pockets. A white plume in his hat would serve as a crowning mark of distinction, with various colored feathers assigned to major generals, brigadiers, the quartermaster's staff, and so on, down to the black cockade and small white eagle in the center to be worn by every soldier under his command. It was easier to order such a magnificent costume, as events would prove, than to secure it. Washington's long-delayed uniform was to prove emblematic of the frustrations he felt in giving commands that led to — nothing.

While Washington prepared for war, other men bargained for peace. Soon after his arrival in the capital, Washington coldly received Dr. George Logan, a Quaker and self-appointed Republican emissary to France who, since returning from Europe, had tried unsuccessfully to persuade Timothy Pickering of the Directory's change of heart. Evidently a hard man to put off, Logan endured Washington's indifference bordering on rudeness as the former president spoke exclusively to the amateur diplomat's companion, the Reverend Blackwell. When Blackwell rose to leave, Washington accompanied him to the door. But Logan stood his ground, to his host's astonishment and chagrin. "As I wished to get quit of him," said Washington in a memorandum dictated soon after, he had remained on his feet "and showed the utmost inattention to what he was saying."

No matter; the unwanted visitor prattled on, justifying his unorthodox diplomacy made possible by credentials from Vice President Jefferson. When Washington objected to such free-lancing, it left Logan "a little confused," but not for long. The Quaker doctor claimed to have discovered in the Directory a warm desire for improved relations. In that case, said Washington, Logan was much more fortunate than America's accredited diplomats, who had not been so much as received by the ruling circle in Paris. If the Directory was truly interested in bettering relations, it could demonstrate its sincerity by repealing the obnoxious measures violating American commerce and rights and by making restitutions for past damages.

When Logan replied that France entertained fears of ingrained American hostility, the former president flared up. Had not the United States sent Marshall, Pinckney, and Gerry to demonstrate its desire for improved relations? What further proof was required of his country's pacific intentions? For how much longer could a self-respecting people submit to Talleyrand's humiliations? Did the arrogant men of the Directory regard Americans "as worms . . . not even allowed to turn when tread upon?"

The mood was only slightly warmer on November 26, when Washington returned to his former quarters at 190 Market Street. It was apparently at this meeting that President Adams pressed the military claims of Aaron Burr. Washington readily conceded Burr's bravery but questioned his reputation for intrigue. Adams was nonplussed; speaking of Hamilton in later years, he acidly recalled how Washington had compelled him to promote over the heads of senior officers "the most restless, impatient, artful, indefatigable, and unprincipled intriguer in the United States, if not in the world, to be second in command to himself, and now dreaded an intriguer in a poor brigadier!"

The two men laid aside their differences for the moment. On December 8, Washington, Hamilton, and Pinckney arrayed themselves behind the president for his annual address in Congress Hall. Adams gave a deliberately temperate performance, his very moderation making for uneasiness among Federalist fire eaters while impressing the skeptical Jefferson. Although the president vowed not to send another minister to Paris "without more determinate assurances that he would be received," he was careful to leave the door to renewed negotiations ajar. Washington, as mystified as anyone about Adams's true intentions and eager to get home, rode out of Philadelphia early on the morning of December 14. Disappointing news awaited him at the other end of his journey. Richard Parkinson, a British agronomist and prospective renter of Washington's River Farm, was unimpressed with the general's yellowish soil, his wheat crop, his sheep, and seemingly everything else he saw except Mount Vernon's mule population.

Parkinson's host repaid his uncomplimentary remarks with a flattering estimate of America's rising cities. As recounted by the Briton, Washington forecast great things for Baltimore and New York. Philadelphia's best days were behind it, he said, as the present capital was fated to yield both commercial and political supremacy to its upstart rival on the banks of the Potomac.

{ 4 }

While Washington was off in Philadelphia organizing for a war that might never come, his granddaughter at Mount Vernon raised the white flag after a long romantic besiegement. Cupid's arrow had found Nelly Custis although, true to form, that irreverent young woman approached the altar with a grin on her face. Her unlikely suitor was Lawrence Lewis, a son of Washington's late sister Betty and a widower nearly twice the age of his intended bride. Describing "the Beau" in a letter early in 1798, Nelly said that "his face is fat, fair and rather pallid, his eyes light blue, full and very unmeaning; he keeps them generally cast downwards, as if afraid of trusting them to gaze at the objects around, or rather, in *affectation* of extreme diffidence."

Hardly the lovesick comments of a girl swept off her feet. But then Lawrence Lewis, troubled by inflamed eyes and boasting none of his uncle's legendary work ethic, seemed an unlikely Romeo. Since coming to live at Mount Vernon the previous year, he had contributed little to relieving the elder Washingtons of their social obligations. When the war tocsin sounded in the fall of 1798, Lewis accepted a captaincy in the Light Dragoons. His fellow drifter, George Washington Parke Custis, himself on the rebound from an unhappy love affair, was to be made a cornet in the same troop. Forced to abandon her intention to live "as a *prim starched spinster*," Nelly's prospects for happiness were clouded only by the thought of leaving "my beloved grandparents who have been every-thing to me . . . and this dear spot, which has been my constant *home.*"

The wedding was set for February 22, the former president's sixty-seventh birthday. Washington, hoping to wear his smart new uniform at the ceremony, urged his tailor in Philadelphia to redouble work thus far delayed by a shortage of gold thread. On second thought, Washington wrote to James McHenry, he leaned to the view that embroidering the cape, cuffs, and pockets of his coat while leaving the waistcoat free of ornamentation might result in "a disjointed and awkward appearance." Unable to decide, Washington left it to the secretary's discretion. "As I also do whether the coat shall have slash cuffs (with blue flaps passing through them) and slash pockets or both to be in the usual manner."

Against a backdrop of wedding preparations, Washington was increas-ingly anxious over threats posed to another union, that of the American states. Since the adoption of the Alien and Sedition Acts the previous summer, a handful of Republican editors and printers had been con-demned to prison. Inevitably political repression bred the historically ominous doctrine of nullification as first Kentucky and then Virginia repudiated the wartime measures and reiterated their pinched view of the Union as a mere compact of states. Enter Thomas Jefferson. As secretary of state, he had succored the opposition press and secretly written a bill of impeachment against his colleague Hamilton. Now, as vice president, fearing that Congress might soon declare a president for life, Jefferson moved aggressively if furtively to contest the legality of the Alien and Sedition Acts.

"If no other state in the union thinks as we do," he wrote at the height of the crisis, "Virginia, the ancient, the great, the powerful, the rich and the republican state of Virginia, still remains free and independent." As Jefferson put fighting words into the mouths of Kentucky legislators, so his friend Madison penned a less sweeping protest for the Old Dominion, denouncing Federalist tyranny and calling on Virginia's sisters to join a crusade to preserve endangered liberties. In his private correspondence Jefferson went a step further, even contemplating secession as a last resort. Still he confessed, drolly enough, that since Virginia must have somebody with which to quarrel, "I had rather keep our New England associates for that purpose than to see our bickerings transferred to others."

Few of his countrymen shared Jefferson's merriment. Seven northern states stepped forward to refute the vice president's claim that individual states had equal rights with the United States Supreme Court in judging the constitutionality of federal legislation. That Jefferson's doctrines enjoyed far from unanimous support in his own back yard was demonstrated when John Marshall put aside his personal qualms over the Alien and Sedition Acts and rallied a substantial minority of legislators against the Virginia Resolution of December 24, 1798. Although pleased with Marshall's leadership, Washington cast about for still more potent champions to enter the fray, finally settling on the unlikely figure of Patrick Henry. The acclaimed orator, ravaged by cancer, had resisted earlier appeals to run for Congress. But after Washington reached out to him as "a rallying point for the timid and an attraction of the wavering," the Virginia Demosthenes came out of retirement to stand for his state's House of Delegates.

In a plain wooden courthouse Henry addressed the people of Charlotte County, mocking Virginia's Assembly for "planting thorns upon my pillow" and daring anyone in his audience to lift a hand against the Father of His Country. When a drunken listener shouted his willingness to do precisely that, the old man's voice filled the room with silver-toned contempt. "You dare not do it," Henry shot back. "In such a parricidal attempt, the steel would drop from your nerveless arm!" Henry won the argument and the election.

Yet Washington could not rest. Politics was just one factor depressing his thoughts as death stole his contemporaries and debt consumed much of his agricultural bounty. Mount Vernon's latest wheat and corn crops were so poor that the squire was forced to purchase six hundred barrels of Indian corn from his kinsman William Augustine Washington, bartering Potomac fish for Virginia maize. Future harvests looked no better, thanks to the latest attack of the Hessian fly on Mount Vernon's winter wheat. To make matters worse, heavy new taxes levied to pay for the provisional army drained his bank account just as Washington was embarking on his housing project on Capitol Hill. In offering for sale three descendants of the celebrated Royal Gift, he explained that "ready money would be very convenient to me, as my buildings in the City call for it."

He pressed his nephew Robert Lewis to collect land rents earlier than usual. At length Washington was compelled to do what he had never done before — obtain a bank loan in Alexandria. When the former president's nephew Samuel renewed his plea for financial assistance, his helpless uncle replied that he could do nothing until he received a long-delayed payment for his lands in western Pennsylvania. On learning that Samuel might be forced to part with his Negro slaves, Washington relented, sending $1,000 he could ill afford and insisting "that sum will take nearly every farthing I have in the bank."

Nor could Washington expect to replenish his account with income from land sales. His deal with James Welch involving thousands of acres on the Great Kanawha River hadn't produced a single dollar, and the former president's suspicions were aroused. It would be "uncandid," he said, "not to inform you that I have heard too much of your character lately" to place stock in Welch's excuses for failing to keep his word. "To contract new debts is not the way to pay old ones," he concluded with a flourish. Yet that is exactly what Washington himself was doing with his houses in the Federal City. Moreover, even now he was sending out feelers to a landowner in Loudon County who might sell 400 acres of prime real estate.

As if to reflect the old man's spirits, it rained on the morning of February 22. Afterward a strong northwest wind sent the temperature plummeting. The Reverend Thomas Davis, Episcopal rector of Fairfax Parish, came to dinner in the afternoon, part of a large and doubtless convivial assemblage that included Stuarts, Carters, Lewises, and Calverts. After the meal, Washington changed into his revolutionary outfit of continental blue coat and buff-colored breeches. Any passing annoyance over the failure of his elegant new uniform to arrive in time for Nelly's wedding was surpassed by mingled pride and sorrow over a much greater loss. At dusk, just after candles were lit to hold off the advancing darkness, Nelly and Lawrence Lewis were married in the great hall, at the foot of the staircase whose banister the bride had liked to ride as a child.

Then Washington had given his wife's granddaughter a box on the cheek. Now he rewarded her with a kiss and more. Heeding Nelly's hints and reluctant to consign his favorite grandchild to the wilds of Frederick County, Washington provided the newlyweds with a large tract where William Thornton designed the house called Woodlawn. This at least promised to keep Nelly within sight of her old home. Still Mansion House must have seemed a lonelier place after February 22. Within twenty-four hours, most of the wedding guests were on their way. Outside Washington's window the mercury fell to twelve degrees, and a freshening northwest wind served as a portent of change.

❦ 5 ❧

Alexander Hamilton was spoiling for a fight. Not satisfied to raise paper regiments, the pugnacious inspector general directed James Wilkinson, a western soldier of flexible principles and endless schemes, to prepare an armada of seventy-five riverboats. In the event of open hostilities with France, he was to move against Louisiana and Florida and prevent their possible cession by Spain to the Directory. "Little Mars" ("a second Bonaparty," said Abigail Adams) craved battle wherever it could be had or instigated. Early in February 1799, Hamilton proposed a feint in the direction of seditious Virginia, an action that he claimed would "give time for the fever of the moment to subside, for reason to resume its reins, and, by dividing its enemies, enable the government to triumph."

John Adams had other plans. To be sure, he showed no hesitation in ordering 500 militiamen to crush a revolt by taxpayers in Pennsylvania, incensed over the high cost of arming for a war few desired. Through this gesture Adams protected his political flank as well as his government's sources of revenue. Secretly, however, he spent the winter of 1798–99 mulling alternatives to combat. Lord Horatio Nelson's sweeping victory over a French fleet at the Battle of the Nile gave Adams some breathing room by forestalling the likelihood that Americans would awake anytime soon to see a forest of French masts menacing their harbors. Meanwhile, Adams picked up unmistakable signals that Talleyrand might be looking for a way out of the diplomatic impasse created by his greed and arrogance toward the upstart Yankees.

Elbridge Gerry, the wayward member of Marshall's delegation sent to settle Franco-American differences, had remained in the French capital long after his colleagues' indignant departure. Gerry's later seriocomic flight across the English Channel to escape his supposed friends inspired a wave of ridicule in which Washington joined heartily. According to him, Gerry's mind was insufficiently "enlarged" not to be led astray by vanity and self-importance. Yet Adams, to the horror of many in his party, welcomed the black sheep back into the flock on his return. Worse, he vouched for Gerry's credibility at a time when some Federalist lawmakers hoped to indict the thoroughly discredited envoy for treason. In part, this may have been because Gerry was telling him what he wanted to hear, namely, that Talleyrand was rethinking his assumption of most Americans as French sympathizers.

It was at this same juncture that a French diplomat passed on to William Vans Murray, the U.S. minister to Holland and a confidant of the president's son John Quincy, encouraging reports of George Logan's Parisian activities. Murray learned of a dinner at which leading members of the French government outdid even the Quaker ambassador in drinking to peace. On February 1, Washington got into the act by sending the president a conciliatory letter from Joel Barlow, a poet turned Republican polemicist who had close ties to the Directory. Washington took pains to dispel any appearance of being in league with the controversial expatriate, rather seeking Adams's guidance on how best to respond to Barlow should the president seize the moment "to bring on negotiation upon open, fair and honorable grounds." Adams's reply was not encouraging; Barlow, it turned out, was persona non grata with the sensitive executive. "Tom Paine himself is not a more worthless fellow," he told his predecessor.

Yet even as he denounced meddling amateurs in the business of diplomacy, Adams was preparing the boldest stroke of his presidency. On February 18 he stunned members of both parties by launching his own peace offensive, designating Murray to reopen talks with Talleyrand on the assumption that an American representative would at last be received with due courtesy. Not that Adams entertained any illusions about the difficult mission ahead. The day after releasing his bombshell, he wrote to Washington that his greatest fear was "the babyish and womanly blubbering" for peace at the risk of appeasement. But this may have been another ruse, intended to reassure the old soldier whose dramatic emergence from retirement had suddenly been rendered anticlimactic. The trenchant Abigail Adams had it right as usual when she said that her husband's eleventh-hour initiative had electrified the public: "The whole community were like a flock of frightened pigeons; nobody had their story ready; some called it a hasty measure; others condemned it as an inconsistent one; some swore, some cursed."

And some did what they could privately to scuttle the new mission before it ever got off the ground. Among these shadowy plotters was "a very intelligent gentleman (immediately from Philadelphia)" who called on Washington at Mount Vernon days after he learned of Murray's appointment from Pickering. Contrary to what Adams implied in his message, Washington understood "that there had been no *direct* overture" from the Directory. Based on his sources, it appeared as if "Mr. Talleyrand was playing the same loose and roundabout game he had attempted the year before with our envoys." Clearly Washington would have much preferred an open and unambiguous invitation from the men in Paris as evidence of their sincerity. But he would hold his fire all the same, "not being acquainted with all the information and the motives which induced the measure."

He was similarly noncommittal in a letter to Adams, limiting himself to good wishes for the president's health and a long life in which to enjoy the blessings that must inevitably flow to Americans "if we should be so happy as to pass this critical period in an honorable and dignified manner, without being involved in the horrors and calamities of war." For both Washington and his country, Adams's courageous move marked a turning point. Letters addressed to Hamilton and McHenry continued to flow from the study at Mount Vernon regarding an army that would never take the field. Many bore evidence of Washington's chronic dissatisfaction over the pace and professionalism with which officials at all levels were preparing the nation's defenses. "Astonishment and discontent" were widely felt among the government's warmest friends, he wrote late in March, when prospective officers were still peppering him with applications, many accompanied by plaintive inquiries about the long delays in recruiting.

"What could I say?" Washington asked McHenry. "Am I not kept in as much ignorance as they are themselves? Am I advised of any new appointments? any changes which have taken place? any of the views or designs of government relative to the army?" Washington stiffly protested that his honor was at stake. "For I shall frankly declare that I do not, nor ever shall, consider myself in the light of a mercenary officer. Nothing short of a high sense of the Amor Patrie could have placed me in my present situation," causing him to neglect his farms, his family, and the friends whose estates he had agreed to administer. "My greatest anxiety is to leave all these concerns in such a clear and distinct form as that no reproach may attach itself to me when I have taken my departure for the land of spirits."

Like a traveler who knows where he is headed but is in no hurry to get there, Washington hoped to turn his attention to private affairs without neglecting public obligations. He took heart from the French setbacks inflicted by a European military coalition and from the turmoil that by July had swept away the offending Directory in favor of young General Bonaparte and his Consulate. The former president proudly hung Edward Savage's engraving of the dramatic encounter between the U.S. frigate *Constellation* and France's *L'Insurgent*, which had ended in a rout of the enemy vessel. True to his word, he rejected McHenry's offer of two months' pay, despite the precarious state of his finances and the continuing heavy drain of hospitality extended to Mount Vernon's visitors. "I am resolved to draw nothing from the public but reimbursement of *actual* expenditures," Washington told the secretary of war. Any other course would embolden critics to say that the former president "was enjoying retirement on very easy and lucrative terms."

Gradually, almost imperceptibly, Washington began to disengage himself from Hamilton, whose audacity looked more and more like rashness and whose thrusting ambition threatened Federalist hopes in the elections of 1800. The former president made no comment when Adams's party insisted on adding a pair of Federalist warhorses to Murray's mission. He was equally silent about (and presumably ignorant of) Hamilton's putative adventuring against Spanish colonies throughout the Americas. Just two days before his death, Washington complimented his protégé's intention to establish a military academy at West Point — as well he might, given his long-standing advocacy of the idea — while begging off any formal endorsement of Hamilton's plan "as it has already been submitted to the Secretary of War, through whom it would naturally be laid before Congress." He had not always been so respectful of administrative niceties nor so reluctant to share his expert opinion with the nation's civilian leaders.

Washington never lost his distrust of French intentions or his doubts over the likelihood of a permanent peace with domineering France. As late as April 10, 1799, he voiced skepticism over "that faithless nation, whose injustice and ambition know no bounds." But he did not despair, and he seemed grateful enough to leave the hard decisions to others. Like the accomplished performer he was, Washington knew when to quit the stage, especially if the next act involved farce. And what of Adams? The cantankerous New Englander split his party irretrievably as Pickering, Wolcott, and, finally, McHenry each made his way into Hamilton's camp, to which they had already pledged secret allegiance. But just as Washington had braved a political hailstorm to avert a disastrous war with England, so his successor now fell on his sword or, more appropriate to this farm-loving Yankee, beat it into a plowshare.

Peace with France cost Adams the presidency; history has been more generous than his contemporaries. For in saving face on both sides of the Atlantic, he at last stepped out from the long shadow cast by his predecessor. Asked late in life what he would have inscribed on his tombstone, he replied, "Here lies John Adams, who took upon himself the responsibility of peace with France in the year 1800."

It was a fitting epitaph.

{ 6 }

Fifty years after a callow youth with family connections earned his first wages by helping to survey the future site of Alexandria, his elderly counterpart ventured out on a blustery April day in 1799 to trace the exact boundaries of a 1,200-acre parcel he owned some four miles north of the port. Washington suspected the residents of helping themselves to valuable timber and wished to put an end to the practice. Later in the month, he issued a seigneurial warning to hunters making sport of his deer. Never having killed any of the gentle creatures himself, "I should have hoped that upon the principle of doing as one would be done by, they would not have been injured by my neighbors."

On April 25, Washington returned to Alexandria to support the Federalist slate of candidates for the U.S. Congress and Virginia's House of Delegates. It was with "infinite pleasure" that he learned of John Marshall's victory at the polls, lamenting only that the margins by which Marshall and Henry Lee prevailed were not more decisive. Although Federalism appeared on the ascendant, the former president warned his nephew Bushrod, now a justice of the Supreme Court, against letting down his guard. Certainly there would be no relaxation on the part of "the Republicans, as they have very erroneously called themselves." A few weeks later Washington broke his self-imposed rule against "intermeddling in any public matter which did not immediately concern me" to admonish the commissioners of the Federal City against straying from their original plan, as engraved for prospective land buyers. To mark off private lots where none existed on the plan was deceptive to foreigners and others who were unable to form a firsthand estimate of the city to be.

All that summer letters flew between Washington and his versatile friend, the architect and doctor William Thornton, who besides supervising the construction of the houses on Capitol Hill was also treating Tobias Lear for an undisclosed ailment. Work on the houses proceeded smartly, if expensively. The former president was a frequent visitor to the city that bore his name. One resident of Alexandria, standing near the stern of his vessel at the wharf, chanced to see Washington returning from Georgetown. He was seated alone in his carriage, accompanied only by a servant on horseback. As a mark of tribute, the shipowner hoisted his banner to the mizzenmast. The elderly statesman noticed the gesture and responded with one of his own, removing his hat and holding it in his hand until the ship reached the other side of the river.

The organizers of a ball in Alexandria invited the Washingtons to grace the event with their presence. "Alas! our dancing days are no more," replied the prospective guest. But he remained accessible and surprisingly tolerant with bores and timewasters. On May 10 he dined with James Welch, who had yet to make good on his promises regarding the vast Kanawha lands. Washington granted the feckless spectator an extension on his payment until November. A few days later the squire greeted John Searson (called Season in Washington's diary), an Irish-born poet who had invited himself to Mount Vernon in hopes of versifying the beauties of the place. That same week the former president attended an Alexandria horse race with a purse of £55. Chief Justice Oliver Ellsworth, selected to join William Vans Murray and Patrick Henry on the latest peace mission to France, dropped by for a visit and stayed to partake of a dinner where no fewer than fifteen guests sampled Washington's hospitality. "All the strangers went away after breakfast" is a typical diary entry for this period.

Henry, it turned out, was too ill to go to Paris. In May he swallowed a dose of liquid mercury designed to kill or cure. His death obliterated any earlier disagreements between this spellbinding champion of states' rights and the nation's foremost advocate of a strong central government. Nor had Washington ever forgotten the Virginian's steadfast support at the time of the Conway Cabal. His regret at Henry's passing was genuine. Closer to home, Washington braced himself for the passing of his brother Charles, who lingered on until September. When at last the expected bulletin arrived at Mount Vernon, Charles's brother made no attempt to conceal the "awful and affecting emotions" that washed over him. "I was the *first* and am now the *last* of my father's children by the second marriage," he wrote to a friend. "When I shall be called upon to follow them is known only to the giver of life. When the summons comes, I shall endeavor to obey it with a good grace."

Washington marked the Fourth of July by dining with the residents of Alexandria. The next few days brought the rumbling sounds of distant thunder and a mostly unfulfilled promise of rain. Farmer Washington retreated to his study and scratched out a twenty-eight-page will, whose opening lines held an unmistakable political statement: "I, GEORGE WASHINGTON, of Mount Vernon, a citizen of the United States, and lately President of the same." Not "a citizen of Virginia," not as a Southerner or a Tidewater aristocrat, but as an American, Washington chose to round out his life with the creed to which he had devoted himself for forty years.

The will contained another significant philosophical assertion. For years Washington had struggled to reconcile his ownership of human beings with his country's professed love of liberty. He had hoped that Virginia's legislature would take the decision out of his hands by providing for gradual emancipation. The chances of such action were faint and growing fainter as long as the lawmakers in Richmond, their hackles raised, talked of defying federal authority. It was thus left to Washington himself to fashion the most humane yet practical solution possible. To free his slaves during the life of his widow would cause pain and resentment among the dower Negroes who had come to him through his marriage and whom he could not legally manumit.

Instead, he would release all three hundred plus from bondage on Martha's death, making certain that as long as aged or sick slaves lived, they would be fed and clothed by his heirs. Washington took an even more radical step in challenging his state's legal ban on educating Negroes, directing that all those under the age of twenty-five should be taught to read and write and "brought up to some useful occupation . . . And I do hereby expressly forbid the sale or transportation out of the said Commonwealth of any slave I may die possessed of, under any pretense whatever." As if to reinforce his determination, Washington added a clause ordering his executors to carry out his wishes "religiously . . . without evasion, neglect or delay."

In recognition of his services during the Revolution, Washington offered his dipsomaniac body servant William Lee the choice of immediate or deferred freedom plus an annuity of $30 a year. Public bequests included $1,000 to educate Alexandria's poor and orphans. His continuing interest in a university in the District of Columbia, designed "to do away [with] local attachments and state prejudices . . . from our national councils," prompted Washington to earmark fifty shares of Potomac Company stock for this purpose. He confirmed an earlier gift of James River Company stock to Liberty Hall Academy — today's Washington and Lee University.

For the rest, despite being financially strapped, Washington canceled debts owed him by a clutch of relations. He gave Tobias Lear lifetime use of the farm he now occupied rent-free. Lots in Fredericksburg and Richmond were deeded to nephews by blood or marriage. Dr. Franklin's gold-headed cane with the cap of liberty was reserved for the dying Charles Washington. "I add nothing to it," said his brother, "because of the ample provision I have made for his issue." Lawrence and Robert Washington, friends of his youth, received additional canes and spyglasses used to track British movements during the late war. Dr. Craik was down for the "Tambour secretary" and revolving chair in the study. From the same room Washington's telescope and shaving and dressing tables were tagged for David Stuart. And there was more: a Bible in three volumes for the Reverend (more recently Lord) Bryan Fairfax. A pair of "finely wrought steel pistols, taken from the enemy in the Revolutionary War," for Lafayette. Five mourning rings for as many female relatives and friends, "not for the intrinsic value of them but as mementos of my esteem and regard." A similar number of swords for his nephews, "accompanied with an injuncture not to unsheath them for the purpose of shedding blood, except it be for self-defense or in defense of their country and its rights; and in the latter case, to keep them unsheathed, and prefer falling with them in their hands to the relinquishment thereof."

Perhaps most painful was the division of Mount Vernon made necessary by Washington's childless state. Following Martha's death, Mansion House was to go to Bushrod Washington, whose father, Jack, had been Washington's favorite brother. Bushrod would also receive the general's papers and library, becoming in effect his literary executor and custodian of his historical reputation. George Fayette and Lawrence Augustine Washington, the sons of the doomed George Augustine and Fanny Bassett, were to get 2,000 acres in grateful remembrance of the young manager who had supervised the estate while its owner was preoccupied with public responsibilities. A similar parcel along Dogue Creek, together with Washington's mill and distillery, were set aside for Nelly and Lawrence Lewis. As George Washington Parke Custis was already well provided for in his father's will, Washington left the youth a lot in the Federal City and his Four Mile Run tract (the future site of Robert E. Lee's Arlington House and the national military cemetery, where, in another bit of posthumous irony, Charles L'Enfant would have his final resting place). What remained was to be sold, with the proceeds apportioned twenty-three ways among Washington's blood relations.

Prudent to the last, the former president cautioned his executors not to sell in a weak market. Hopeful as ever, he predicted a sharp rise in the value of his western lands. Washington directed that a new brick burial vault be constructed, larger than the current tomb and not far from his Potomac wharf. This, too, was only appropriate for a man who liked nothing better than building things. He designated as executors "my dearly beloved wife Martha" and four nephews and instructed them to refer possible disputes to three impartial men, "known for their probity and good understanding," whose decision was to be as binding "as if it had been given in the Supreme Court of the United States." Washington's tribute to the court was a final endorsement of the political system that was in many ways his greatest monument and most enduring legacy. Here was one Virginian who would go to his grave denying the legitimacy of the Virginia Resolves.

❮ 7 ❯

John Adams's Federalist critics could hardly decide which was worse — the unpredictable policies the president pursued in Philadelphia or his all too frequent absences from the capital during periods of crisis. Adams's predecessor was not alone in wishing that someone would go to the executive and convince him that his long vacations in Massachusetts only played into the hands of his enemies. In fact, said Washington, it had been suggested that he be the messenger but he had declined, believing that Adams would receive the news better if it came from one "more in the habits of social intercourse and friendship."

But if Washington would not argue with the president, neither would he attempt to replace him. Connecticut's governor, Jonathan Trumbull, after first trying to enlist the support of Adams's Cabinet for his scheme, invited Washington to come out of retirement and save the Federalists' chestnuts in 1800. For his pains Trumbull got a courteous but firm refusal. It would be a matter of "sore regret" to Washington if "well meant but mistaken" friends looked to Mount Vernon for Adams's successor. Such a course would violate his wish to remain "undisturbed . . . unless called upon to defend my country (which every citizen is bound to do)." Moreover, given his rapidly fading powers, it would be "criminal" for him to accept a draft when there were others far better equipped to fill the executive's shoes.

In the highly polarized climate of the times, Washington doubted his electability. As for the opposition, "Let that party set up a broomstick and call it a true son of Liberty . . . and it will command their votes in toto!" To believe that he, type and symbol of Federalist orthodoxy, would receive so much as a single vote from "the Anti-Federal side" was to engage in self-deception. Neither did he desire at his stage of life to make himself "a mark for the shafts of envenomed malice . . . when I should be charged not only with irresolution but with concealed ambition, which wants only an occasion to blaze out . . . in short, with dotage and imbecility." Principles, not men, should form the objects of political contention.

Washington developed this theme in a second exchange with Trumbull a month later. "It is too interesting not to be again repeated," he wrote, "that if principles instead of men are not the steady pursuit of the Federalists, their course will soon be at an end. If *these* are pursued, they *will not divide* at the next election of a President; if they do divide on so *important* a point, it would be dangerous to trust them on any other." Washington stated with poignant finality that he was too old to withstand the buffetings of a campaign. "A mind that has been constantly on the stretch since the year 1753, with but short intervals and little relaxation, requires rest and composure." On this point he was immovable; only a physical violation of his country's territory could draw him out of the Potomac twilight.

Yet he retained an interest in public matters long after his need to dominate them had waned. When William Duane's *Aurora* charged corruption by the U.S. consul at Santo Domingo, it prompted a wicked retort from Washington to James McHenry: "And pray, good sir, what part of the $800,000 have come to your share . . . I hope you did not disgrace yourself by the acceptance of a paltry bribe, $100,000 perhaps." Duane, targeted under the Sedition Act, got no sympathy from the former president. That same month he attended his final meeting of the financially troubled Potomac Company at Georgetown's Union Tavern. Income was off and construction at a standstill pending a fresh infusion of capital from the state of Maryland.

Another kind of frustration filled the pages of Washington's diary, as overcast skies taunted parched fields that badly needed moisture. On August 17 he reported his meadows "bare as the pavements," his oats destroyed, and his corn crop imperiled. Three days later, rain came at last to the soil, but after thirty-six hours it gave way to another dry spell and fitful showers "not more than enough to lay the dust." Washington's unfamiliarity with banking procedures made him apologize to a loan officer in Alexandria for the late renewal of a sixty-day note. It seemed that the former president collected his mail only every other day now. Even so, he had no intention of saddling the banker with the cost of stamps, "and therefore pray to be charged with their cost and to be told where and in what manner I can be provided with others."

A sudden family crisis arose in the first week of September when Martha took to her bed with a persistent fever. On Sunday, the first, a concerned husband sent for Dr. Craik, but Mrs. Washington proved uncooperative, refusing medicine until a midnight attack brought Craik back to the house a week later. Martha remained "uneasy and restless" well into the autumn; not until the end of October could Washington describe his wife as feeling "tolerably well." Turning his attention from the sickroom, he instructed William Thornton in the art of painting houses to resemble stone. Late in September he dined with William Richardson Davie, Patrick Henry's replacement on the long-delayed peace mission to France. Several weeks later Washington learned of the commissioners' imminent departure. "I shall take it for granted that the measure has been duly considered in all its relations," he wrote Timothy Pickering, "and that a favorable result is expected."

Writing to William Vans Murray, Washington sounded genuinely relieved, asserting that it was time for mankind to enjoy the fruits of peace. He seemed more equivocal in other correspondence, telling Hamilton, for example, that he saw nothing in the present aspect of European affairs to give cause for optimism. Through Murray the former president tried to dissuade Lafayette from visiting the United States at this critical juncture. Such a mission could have but one outcome, said Washington, a result "embarrassing to himself, embarrassing to his friends, and possibly embarrassing to the government." McHenry revealed a split within the Adams administration, where Pickering and Wolcott were increasingly regarded as Hamilton's agents. This alone ensured that both men's days were numbered. The news left Washington speechless, but only for a moment. Finding his voice, he confessed to viewing the nation's political affairs "with an anxious and painful eye. They appear . . . to be moving by hasty strides to some awful crisis." He caught himself just short of an indiscretion. As "a passenger only," it was not his role to judge the ability of the current pilot to steer the ship of state into safe harbor.

In the third week of November, politics gave way to Nelly's pregnancy and the imminent birth of her first child. The young wife retained her sense of humor, confessing that "the once rattlepated, lazy Eleanor P. Custis, who was generally styled a thoughtless giddy mortal, extremely fond of going to balls," had been transformed almost overnight into "a sedate matron attending to domestic duties and providing for a young stripling who could call her Mother." The Edward Carringtons arrived on the eve of Nelly's delivery, Betsey Carrington recalling later how the former president greeted her husband like a long-lost brother: "He took each of us by the hand and with a warmth of expression not to be described pressed mine and told me that I had conferred a favor never to be forgotten in bringing his old friend to see him." Washington entertained his guests "most facetiously" until the women of the house appeared.

On the morning of November 27, attended by the faithful Dr. Craik, Nelly gave birth to a daughter, named Frances Parke Lewis. "You will have heard that Nelly Lewis has a girl born," reported a beaming grandfather, in the same letter fretting over the expense of maintaining a large slave population to serve two old people. Should he and Martha survive another year, "some change which may benefit myself and does not render their condition worse" would be unavoidable. To one visitor he pointed out the old family vault, gradually undermined by spreading roots, whose replacement was high on Washington's list, for "I may require it before the rest." Yet he was not melancholy, only realistic. About one cherished project he was utterly confident. Early in December he prophesied to

William Thornton that the Federal City, having passed through "a fiery trial," would survive and prosper.

Two days later he skipped a meeting of the Potomac Company to immerse himself in a crop rotation plan governing the operations of Mount Vernon through the year 1803. "More good is derived from looking into the minutiae on a farm," Washington told James Anderson, who hardly needed reminding of his employer's penchant for detail, "than strikes people at first view." As if to prove his point, Washington supplied his manager with an exhaustive catalogue of agricultural instructions, including what crops to plant in which fields, how much manure to apply to his potatoes, the advantages of Potomac mud as fertilizer, the importance of clean stables, and the susceptibility of common fence rails to firewood thieves. Farmer Washington concluded with a passage that may have summed up his entire career, saying that "whenever I order a thing to be done, it must be done . . . having been accustomed all my life to more regularity and punctuality, [I] *know* that system and method is required to accomplish all reasonable requests."

Washington informed Anderson that he planned to visit his western holdings as soon as the winter snows evaporated. The next day, half a dozen dinner guests joined the Washingtons. Before turning in for the night, the former president noticed a large ring around the moon.

❈ 8 ❈

Thursday, December 12, dawned overcast. At ten that morning Washington left for his usual inspection tour. Soon snow began falling, mixed with hail and settling into a cold, steady rain by the time he returned at midafternoon. The storm kept a servant from taking the mail to the post office. Yet Washington, his hair matted with snow, refused to change before dinner, insisting to Lear that his greatcoat had kept him dry, and that evening the squire appeared his usual self. The next day brought an escalation of the wintry conditions that would shortly isolate Mount Vernon from the outside world. In his final diary entry, the former president noted, "Morning snowing and about 3 inches deep. Wind at northeast and mercury at 30. Continuous snowing till 1 o'clock and about 4 it became perfectly clear." Although the storm and a developing sore throat kept him indoors most of the day, Washington took advantage of the late afternoon break to venture outside and mark some trees for removal from an exposed spot between the house and the river.

That evening his throat seemed noticeably worse, and it was in a hoarse voice that he read aloud from newspaper passages that caught his fancy or sparked indignation. After Martha retired to visit Nelly, still confined following her delivery, Lear shared the latest intelligence about Virginia's election contest for governor and United States senator. Washington snorted disapprovingly at the mention of James Monroe, and Lear, no Federalist, tut-tutted his employer's partisan reaction "as I always did on such occasions." When at length Washington got up to leave, Lear urged him to doctor his throat. "You know I never take anything for a cold," replied Washington. "Let it go as it came."

Several hours later, sometime after two in the morning, a feverish Washington woke his wife, who saw at a glance that he was having trouble breathing. He could barely speak, yet he refused to let Martha get out of bed long enough to summon a servant, fearing that she might herself contract a chill and suffer a relapse of her recent illness. So the couple huddled in their bed for a few terrifying hours until dawn brought a domestic to light a fire and call for assistance. The sun was barely visible above the Maryland shore of the Potomac when Lear hurried into the room at Mrs. Washington's behest. There he found his friend, nearly unintelligible, struggling to force air into his lungs. His condition was later classified as "an inflammatory affection of the upper part of the wind pipe called in technical language cynanche trachealis." According to another leading practitioner of the period, this translated into "an inflammation of the glottis, larynx or upper part of the trachea . . . known by a peculiar croaking sound of the voice" and accompanied by an obstruction of air leading to suffocation. In short, George Washington was dying of a lethally sore throat.

The patient responded in character, taking charge of his treatment by sending for an overseer, George Rawlins, to open his veins and bleed him even before Dr. Craik could arrive. While waiting for Rawlins, Washington tried to swallow a mix of molasses, vinegar, and butter and nearly choked to death in the process. Rawlins duly appeared shortly after dawn. Understandably nervous about his role in the unfolding drama, the overseer had to be steadied by the sick man. "Don't be afraid," Washington assured him as he held out his arm. The cut was made and the blood flowed, but not to Washington's satisfaction. "The orifice is not large enough," he said, ordering the gash to be lengthened. Standing by her husband's bed, Martha begged him to halt the procedure, but he refused. "More, more," he told Rawlins with difficulty.

After half a pint had been drained off to no effect, the bleeding was stopped. Washington remained unable to swallow, and when Lear gently swabbed his throat with ammonium carbonate, the patient muttered, " 'Tis very sore." A piece of flannel soaked in the liquid was placed around his neck and his feet were bathed in warm water. About this time Washington, restless, managed to get out of bed and into his clothes. He sat in a chair beside the fireplace for the next two hours. At nine o'clock Mrs. Washington sent for Dr. Gustavus Richard Brown, a nearby physician of the Edinburgh school and highly regarded by James Craik, who had encouraged the Washingtons to call for Brown in an emergency.

Lear's note made no effort to hide the gravity of the situation or the family's mounting alarm.

"General Washington is very ill with Quinsy," it began, citing yet another popular name for the vague throat ailment with the deadly results. "Dr. Craik is sent for from Alexandria but has not yet come down. Mrs. Washington's anxiety is great, and she requests me to write you desiring you will come over without delay, as it is impossible for the General to continue long without relief. I expect Dr. Craik every moment, but cannot wait for his coming before the messenger goes for you." As for the patient, "he grows worse, can swallow nothing, and can scarcely breathe."

At eleven the rotund Craik appeared in the second-floor bedroom and at once concluded that Washington's condition was mortal. In the few hours before Brown joined the battle, he tried several remedies born of desperation. A blister of Spanish fly was placed on Washington's throat to no avail; the patient's latest attempt to gargle with vinegar and sage tea produced a little phlegm and horrible choking sounds. Not wishing to bear the terrible responsibility alone, Craik called for Dr. Elisha Cullen Dick, a prominent Alexandria Mason who on an earlier visit to Mount Vernon had extracted a servant's tooth and left the man dangerously bleeding.

On that occasion the loss of blood had been accidental. Now, as Washington lay sprawled on his bed, suffering in silence, the doctors twice drained blood from his body and twice put calomel into his system. Only the latter had any effect, causing Washington's bowels to move "without any perceptible advantage; the respiration becoming still more difficult and distressing." The room reeked of blood and stench and sweat. Dick's arrival at three was a signal to open Washington's veins a fourth time. Still more blood was siphoned off until the flow slowed and thickened. The general's personal servant, Christopher, after standing most of the day, took a seat at his master's urging. Vapors of vinegar were held up to Washington's nose. Ten grams of calomel and half as large a dose of emetick tartar were poured down his constricted throat, with no result but a second copious discharge from the bowels.

Washington's doctors were able to empty their patient's system of everything but the true source of his complaint. But it would be too easy to blame them for something they could hardly comprehend, let alone prevent. In an age when antibiotics were unknown, the outcome was never in doubt, least of all by the perspiring man restlessly tossing throughout the afternoon. Around four-thirty, Washington asked Martha to go to his study and retrieve two wills from the desk. When she brought them to her husband, he handed one over to be burned and directed that the second be preserved in her closet. Lear resumed his place at the bedside, holding his friend's hand. Outside it was twilight of a short winter afternoon. Inside Washington seemed already to be wearing his death mask, calling on depleted reserves of strength to stage a final performance, keenly aware that every word and gesture would be preserved as a vital part of his legend for posterity.

To the end he remained awesomely organized. "I find I am going," he told Lear, instructing the secretary to arrange his papers and have Rawlins finish recording the letters already begun. Might there be anything else he was neglecting, Washington inquired, for he had but a short time to live. Lear answered in the negative, expressing the hope that his friend might yet recover. At this the old man smiled, repeating the imminence of death and adding "that as it was the debt that all must pay, he looked to the event with perfect resignation." But even as he spoke, Washington's distress was apparent. Lear stretched out beside the large figure on the bed, turning him as gently as possible. Several times Washington apologized for the trouble he was causing. Lear, fighting tears, said that he only hoped to alleviate the patient's anguish.

"Well," answered Washington, "it is a debt we must pay to each other, and I hope when you want aid of this kind you will find it."

Late in the afternoon Washington roused himself to inquire when Lawrence Lewis and George Washington Parke Custis might return from their visit to New Kent. Lear informed him that the pair was not expected back for five or six days. At sunset Dr. Craik reappeared. Washington offered what consolation he could: "Doctor, I die hard, but I am not afraid to go. I believed from my first attack that I should not survive it." And then, as if to absolve the doctors for their ineffectuality, the patient added in an almost businesslike tone, "My breath cannot last long." But Washington underestimated his strength, as so often he had undervalued his military and political talents. As Craik looked on wordlessly, his professional colleagues returned. Could the sick man sit up? they inquired. Washington held out his hand and with Lear's help was elevated.

As the life force ebbed, so did the patient's tolerance for hopeless ministrations. The hero who had won his reputation in war begged to be allowed to die in peace. "I feel myself going," he told Craik and his associates. "I thank you for your attentions, but I pray you to take no more trouble about me. Let me go off quietly; I cannot last long."

Brown and Dick withdrew from the room, leaving Craik silhouetted in the yellow glow of the fireplace. Washington resumed a prone position, his silence broken by occasional requests for the time. Around eight o'clock, in a last, desperate ploy to clear the patient's system, the doctors applied blisters to his extremities and poultices of wheat bran to his throat. Lear took a moment to write a note summoning the Laws and Peterses, knowing that they could not reach the house in time to exchange a final word with Martha's husband. Had Lear put off this urgent courtesy out of a reluctance to share the tragedy with outsiders? He continued hovering by the general's side, the room silent but for the ticking of a clock and the sharp, increasingly labored sounds of Washington's respiration. Martha occupied a chair near the foot of the bed. The servant Christopher stood nearby, gazing quietly at the contorted face of his master. Two other servants were in the doorway.

It was now ten o'clock, twenty-four hours after Washington had dismissed Lear's medical advice with the jaunty phrase "Let it go as it came." Several times the dying man tried to speak; nothing coherent came out of his mouth. At length, summoning all his strength, he turned to Lear with a final set of instructions. "I am just going," he whispered, self-conscious to the last. "Have me decently buried, and do not let my body be put into the vault in less than three days after I am dead."

Lear nodded, for it was his turn not to be able to speak. Washington gave him a penetrating look. "Do you understand me?"

"Yes," said Lear.

" 'Tis well." Washington was accustomed to having his orders carried out, even on his deathbed.

A few minutes later the patient took his own fading pulse. The look on his face changed perceptibly. Lear called out to Dr. Craik. At ten-twenty the shallow breathing ceased. Washington's hand fell from his wrist; Lear reached out and pressed it to his own chest.

Martha broke the silence. "Is he gone?" she asked, in a voice that betrayed little emotion. Lear, dumb with grief, raised his hand in silent affirmation. The widow took in the news. " 'Tis well," she said, sighing to no one in particular. "All is now over. I shall soon follow him. I have no more trials to pass through."

Around midnight the body was taken downstairs and laid out in the green dining room before the magnificent Italian mantel that Washington had protested was too grand for one of his republican tastes but had installed anyway. That night, moonlight poured through the Palladian window, bathing the dead man's features. The stars came out and the ring was gone from the white disk overhead.

"OUR WASHINGTON"

"Our Washington is no more. The Hero, the Sage, and the Patriot of America — the man on whom in times of danger every eye was turned, and all hopes were placed — lives now only in his own great actions and in the hearts of an affectionate and afflicted people."

John Marshall,
December 19, 1799

NOT EVERYONE WAS WILLING to consign "our Washington" to the family vault at Mount Vernon. Among the first to reach the house of death was Washington's friend William Thornton. The eclectic West Indies native, equally versed in architecture, medicine, astronomy, and finance, had secretly designed the Capitol as a final resting place for America's first president. On learning from Tobias Lear and Thomas Law that his eminent friend was locked in mortal combat with "the Croup," Thornton hurried to Mount Vernon in hopes of performing an emergency tracheotomy.

He arrived too late, or so it seemed to everyone but Dr. Thornton. Never at a loss for ideas, he proposed to resurrect Washington "in the following manner. First to thaw him in cold water, then to lay him in blankets, and by degrees and by friction to give him warmth, and to put into activity the minute blood vessels, at the same time to open a passage to the lungs by the trachea, and to inflate them with air, to produce an artificial respiration, and to transfuse blood into him from a lamb."

Friends of the late president intervened to permit him a peaceful departure. On Wednesday, December 18, a little procession moved south from Mansion House to the old tomb a few hundred feet away. A schooner anchored in the Potomac fired minute guns, answered by the booming sounds of eleven artillery pieces brought down from Alexandria and a dirge played by a Masonic band. Local militia preceded the dead man's horse with its empty saddle, followed by a handful of relations and friends. Martha remained inside the house as the Reverend Mr. Davis, who had earlier officiated at Nelly's wedding, now read a brief service of farewell over the shrouded figure in its mahogany coffin lined with lead. Afterward, the company returned to the green dining room for refreshments. What the mourners did not eat was distributed among Washington's slaves.

Tobias Lear left the grim hospitality to Thomas Law and retired to his room, as he put it, "to give a loose to those feelings which I had been able to keep under control, while I found it necessary for me to give personal attention to the preparations for interring the body of my deceased friend. What those feelings were is not to be told, if it were even possible to describe!" Washington would have appreciated both Lear's self-command and his final surrender to grief away from prying eyes. The president's widow was no less staunch, agreeing to have her husband's remains moved to a vault beneath the Capitol rotunda after stipulating that she be allowed to lie beside him, a condition John Marshall presented for Congress's approval in secret session.

Four years later, Marshall would attempt in five ponderous volumes what Thornton had only theorized with his blankets and his lamb's blood — to restore Washington to life. By most accounts he failed. According to the waspish John Adams, Marshall's work was not a biography at all but "a Mausoleum, one hundred feet square at the base and two hundred feet high." Artists fared no better than writers, for Washington proved an elusive quarry. Even during his lifetime family members had complained that his portraits barely did him justice. Gilbert Stuart insisted that conveying Washington's personality on canvas was the most difficult thing in the world. (He deliberately painted the great man's eyes too blue, on the assumption that they would fade to the correct shade within a century.) Notwithstanding such liberties, Stuart's Washington, as coldly irresistible as a glacier, became an instant icon, inspiring Mark Twain's well-worn jibe that should Washington ever return from the grave and fail to resemble Stuart's wintry likeness, he would no doubt be denounced as an impostor.

Sooner or later everyone who writes about the first president must contend with Stuart and the bloodless image stamped on our currency and car sales. In an age suspicious of heroics and squeamish about duty, it is not hard to discern why Washington falls victim to his well-advertised virtues. For surely the greatest disservice done by Parson Weems and his adulatory ilk has been to rob Washington's life of conflict, tension, and the slowly gathering forces of character. Taking the opposite tack from William Thornton, early idolaters embalmed Washington before his time, in the process ensuring a savage counterthrust by modern debunkers. Latter-day Marshalls seeking to humanize Washington have often wound up unintentionally trivializing him, telling us more than we need to know about his expense accounts, his fondness for Madeira, and his shadowy love affair with Sally Fairfax.

As a result, nearly two centuries after his death George Washington is out of fashion, too remote in time and temperament, too encased in marbled veneration, to engage our emotions. Even among contemporaries his physical and moral courage, his endless capacity for self-sacrifice, and his patience in adversity may have sparked more awe than affection. This, too, he would have understood, for he grasped the limitations of his fellows even as he refused to see them through the tinted glass of ideology. When Emerson declared, "Every hero at last becomes a bore," he was thinking of America's first president. Modern scholars delight in finding flaws in the marble, arraigning Washington for his treatment of Native Americans, for example, or denouncing his part in an economic system that wrung luxury for a privileged few from the sweat of slave labor.

Moreover, Washington does not conveniently fit the mold of executive greatness as defined by twentieth-century standards. He was no Roo- seveltian swashbuckler, wielding the personal pronoun like a deadly weapon while placing his personal stamp upon every program of his age. He did not martyr himself for a great cause, like Lincoln, or thrill the multitudes with Wilsonian eloquence; indeed, by all contemporary evi- dence he was something less than a Great Communicator. Even Marshall called Washington "more solid than brilliant." For him silence, backed by deeds and buttressed by character, was the most eloquent language of all.

Then, too, there is the curious fact that what Washington did as pres- ident was hardly more important than what he *did not do*. He did not take sides in the continental wars that swept Europe as a result of France's revolutionary experiment, buying precious time for the United States to evolve a sense of nationhood. He did not organize a king's party, nor regard himself as a democratically chosen monarch (the *Aurora's* assertions to the contrary), nor designate his vice president to serve as a kind of prime minister, nor turn the secretary of the treasury into an American chancellor of the exchequer, all of which he might easily have done. Most important of all, by voluntarily relinquishing office at the end of two terms, Washington forced a world more accustomed to Caesars than Cincinnatus to revise its definition of greatness.

"George Washington was one of the few in the whole history of the world who was not carried away by power," said Robert Frost without a hint of poetic license. Poignant confirmation of this came from none other than Napoleon Bonaparte, who, on his deathbed at St. Helena, far removed from military pomp and glory, sighed, "They wanted me to be another Washington."

Washington's death prompted a wide range of emotions from the sorrowful and the envious. Alexander Hamilton told Martha that no man alive had equal cause to deplore the loss of his old friend, for "I have been much indebted to the kindness of the General, and he was an Aegis very essential to me." President Adams put on his black and struggled to make sense of the contradictory sensations that he had always felt about the towering Virginian whose entry into a room exacerbated the graceless Yankee's inferiority complex. Thomas Paine, angry as ever over his perceived abandonment, left a bitter quatrain to guide sculptors in freezing the late president's marble visage:

Take from the mine the coldest, hardest stone,
It needs no fashion, it is Washington;
But if you chisel, let your strokes be rude,
And on his breast engrave *Ingratitude!*

Lord Byron saw things in a different light when he asked:
Can tyrants but by tyrants conquered be,
And freedom find no champion and no child,
Such as Columbia saw arise, when she
Spring forth a Pallas, arm'd and undefiled?

Fisher Ames, that rock-ribbed Federalist from Dedham, Massachusetts, delivered the most perceptive eulogy. Others might quote Henry Lee's tribute to the hero, "First in war, first in peace, and first in the hearts of countrymen," but Ames mined gold in the fewest words. Of George Washington, said Ames, "he changed mankind's ideas of political greatness." *George Washington a better politician than soldier?* The idea seems preposterous to Americans for whom the first president has traditionally appeared the most apolitical of Founders, a bronze equestrian shunning partisan attachments or ideological abstractions. Certainly no leader showed greater reluctance on assuming office.

"My movements to the chair of government will be accompanied by feelings not unlike those of a culprit who is going to the place of his execution," Washington had confessed to Henry Knox in the first days of April 1789, "so unwilling am I, in the evening of a life nearly consumed in public cares, to quit a peaceful abode for an ocean of difficulties, without the competency of political skill, abilities and inclination which is necessary to manage the helm."

Until now, historians taking Washington at his modest word have caricatured him as a bit player shunted to the wings by more dynamic actors like Hamilton and Jefferson — a front for one, a foil for the other, a stouthearted, thin-skinned figurehead. Perhaps the only thing more offensive than deification of the historical Washington is patronization. We have Jefferson himself to thank for much of this. Writing fifteen years after Washington's death brought an end to their painful estrangement, the Sage of Monticello, a master of the backhanded compliment, declared of his former patron:

"His mind was great and powerful, without being of the very first order; his penetration strong, though not so acute as that of a Newton, Bacon, or Locke . . . It was slow in operation, being little aided by invention or imagination, but sure in conclusion . . . His heart was not warm in his affections, but he exactly calculated every man's value, and gave him a solid esteem proportioned to it . . . He has often declared to me that he considered our new Constitution as an experiment on the practicality of republican government, and with what dose of liberty man could be trusted for his own good; that he was determined the experiment should have a fair trial, and would lose his last drop of blood in support of it."

And then, as if to contradict what he had just written, Jefferson added, "I do believe that General Washington had not a firm confidence in the durability of our government. He was naturally distrustful of men and inclined to gloomy apprehensions."

So much for Jeffersonian eulogy, with its implication that Washington had learned more from battles than from books. In truth, Washington's whole life up to his first inauguration had been a veritable Montessori school in the management of men and events. Fifteen years as a Virginia burgess, plus eight more as a citizen-soldier in thrall to a balky Congress and his own lively conscience, had supplied abundant political training. As subtle and deceptive as the constitutional system, which strained popular opinion through institutional filters, George Washington was a gentlemanly paradox: proud and modest, simple and canny, aristocratic by nature and republican by choice. Because he credited rigid self-discipline in realizing his personal destiny, he embraced an energetic government as the only means of protecting the American union against its centrifugal tendencies. Because he balanced executive vigor with personal restraint, he fostered a government strong enough to lead and wise enough to listen.

Like Franklin Roosevelt one and a half centuries later, Washington was a patrician idolized by the man in the street and opposed by entrenched forces to whom his — and Hamilton's — economic policies promised social upheaval. The realization that he had nowhere to go but down made his entry into the presidency all the more poignant. "I fear I must bid adieu to happiness," he blurted out to his confidant David Humphreys not long before his inauguration, "for I see nothing but clouds and darkness before me: and I call God to witness that the day which shall carry me again into public life will be a more distressing one than any I have ever yet known."

For eight years he strained to control mighty currents without himself being swept away. Republics are notoriously ungrateful, and it was the old soldier's fate to have his reputation shredded by the very forces of liberty he had set in motion. The presidency cost Washington his friendship with Thomas Jefferson as it alienated him from others, in Virginia and elsewhere, whose devotion to the cause of revolutionary France temporarily blinded them to the long-term interests of the United States. Far more than either Hamilton or Jefferson, Washington was the real visionary, for he saw beyond the immediate provocations of Old World powers to a day when a mature and united America might defy any aggressor on earth.

In the end, Washington's gloomy prophecy to David Humphreys was largely realized. The president's brief, bittersweet retirement completed a decade-long conversion to Federalist thinking. Yet it was also during these final years, otherwise marked by loss and disillusionment, that Washington waged his greatest battle to vindicate republican government at a time when divine right held most of mankind in the grip of dead tradition. Having practically invented the American presidency, Washington left it with a sigh of relief and turned his fading energies to subduing the earth instead of recalcitrant political rivals. Today, as Napoleon anticipated in his windswept exile, the first president remains that rarest of historical figures, of whom it can be said that in conceding his humanity, we only confirm his greatness.

NOTES AND
SELECT BIBLIOGRAPHY

INDEX

NOTES

Biography of all literary undertakings may be the most daunting, for who among us possesses the omniscience (or humility) to authoritatively interpret the character and motivations of another human being? This is especially true of one so distanced in time, culture, and outlook as America's first president. Of all American lives, George Washington's may be the single most intimidating to write in this antiheroic age. Library shelves groan beneath the accumulated weight of Washingtoniana, from nineteenth-century tributes to a dull, if spotless, pillar of virtue to the shallow debunkers of the 1920s and the massive sets written by Douglas Southall Freeman and James Thomas Flexner in our own time.

Four decades after the death of its author, Freeman's work remains as gravely majestic as Washington himself and for that very reason a bit over our heads. Beginning in the mid-1960s, a decidedly more approachable Washington emerged in the four volumes of James Thomas Flexner, whose colorful prose and searching eye for detail testified to his training as an art historian. Both Freeman and Flexner, for all their differences in tone and temperament, share a trait common to virtually every author who has attempted to scale Mount Washington in that their portrayals reveal as much about the age in which they were written — in Freeman's case, the heroic, confident liberalism of the postwar period, and the rebellious 1960s whose irreverent challenge to authority formed the backdrop for Flexner's work — as they do about their subject.

No less than Jefferson and far more than Lincoln, George Washington has served each generation as both totem and target, a blank canvas on which to project shifting attitudes toward patriarchal authority and the age-old conflict between liberty and equality. He thus requires periodic reinterpretation amid the changing light and shadows of republican government. This fact, as well as the desire to produce the first comprehensive one-volume account of Washington's presidency, will explain and, I hope, justify my entry into a field crowded with distinguished predecessors.

In one respect, at least, my timing proved fortunate, for my research coincided with the bicentennial observances of not only the American presidency but the executive establishment, Congress, the federal judiciary, Washington, D.C., and the Bill of Rights (not to mention France's own revolution). As a result, I have profited from the numerous books, monographs, popular articles, and special interest journals that these anniversaries have inspired.

Just as any Washington biographer must stand on the broad shoulders of

Freeman, Flexner, and their lesser colleagues, so anyone who writes about the first president in this era must begin by acknowledging a debt to Donald Jackson, Dorothy Twohig, and the Mount Vernon Ladies Association for making possible a definitive new edition of Washington's diaries. Published between 1976 and 1979, the Jackson-Twohig collaboration easily supersedes an earlier edition bearing the stamp of John C. Fitzpatrick. Throughout the present volume, I have drawn on the richly annotated Jackson-Twohig text for all cited material in the diaries; for example, Washington's 1791 southern tour and his conduct during the Whiskey Rebellion that nearly tore his government asunder three years later.

My account of Washington's stormy second term is similarly informed by Miss Twohig's skillfully edited *Journal of the Proceedings of the President, 1793–97*, published by the University of Virginia and the Mount Vernon Ladies Association of the Union. The same scholarly team (with the substitution of W. W. Abbot for Mr. Jackson) is even now producing what promises to be the ultimate in Washington documentation, an exhaustively inclusive collection of correspondence to as well as from the soldier-patriot-president. Until the Washington Papers Project is completed sometime in the next century, anyone writing about Washington must of necessity rely on an earlier, thirty-nine-volume set of his writings, edited by John C. Fitzpatrick and published between 1931 and 1944. This is the source for the vast majority of my quotations from Washington's correspondence.

On a personal level, I am grateful to John P. Riley, Barbara McMillan, and Christine Meadows at Mount Vernon's Library who make it such a pleasure to excavate the past; their archival holdings include numerous Washington family letters quoted in the text. Thanks also to the Mount Vernon Ladies Association itself, for preserving intact an estate that provides a surer portrait of Washington than any painted from life. When my research took me to Philadelphia, where so much of the drama of Washington's presidency was played out, I was fortunate indeed to make the acquaintance of David Dutcher, the chief historian at Independence National Historical Park and a man whose knowledge of the eighteenth century is matched only by his enthusiasm for the period inhabited by Washington, Jefferson, Adams, Hamilton, and the rest of the giants who invented America. The same holds true for his National Park Service colleagues who kindly allowed me to use their extensive library.

Also in Philadelphia, I had the pleasant experience of doing research at the Pennsylvania Historical Society, where I was tipped off to the Baker Collection, a treasure trove of Washingtoniana out of which William S. Baker fashioned several books in the nineteenth century. I have found Baker's *Washington After the Revolution* particularly useful for its reconstruction of the first president's calendar. Closer to home, I was aided by the friendly staff and voluminous holdings of the University of Iowa Library in Iowa City.

Four separate editors — Michael Janeway, Henry Ferris, John Sterling, and

Richard Todd — have left their mark on this project since its inception in 1988. To each I owe a debt of gratitude. Dick Todd did most to shape the final text, and it would be impossible to find a more sensitive or discerning reader. I have been equally fortunate to work with Luise Erdmann, a superb manuscript editor, whose painstaking attention to details of style and composition would no doubt have pleased Washington himself. Judy Kaeser did a masterly job typing and retyping a long manuscript. Rafe Sagalyn proved once again to be the perfect agent; his faith in "Great Washington" helped sustain me through four years of hard labor, compounded by the vicissitudes of modern publishing.

Most important, I want to thank the friends and colleagues whose names grace the dedication page. Ever since John Fawcett offered me a dream job in the summer of 1987, his support and encouragement have been mirrored by the Hoover Library family. The same holds true for my Chicago family: Steve, Fern, Ross, Keith, and Isabelle.

From the outset this was intended as a work for the general reader. Consequently, I have tried to keep chapter notes as brief as possible, supplying general sources for each thematic area and more specific ones where necessary.

SELECT BIBLIOGRAPHY

Abbot, W. W. *The Papers of George Washington*, Presidential Series, vol. 2. Charlottesville, Va., 1987.

Adams, Henry. *History of the United States During the Administration of Thomas Jefferson*. New York, 1986.

Aikman, Lonnelle. *Rider with Destiny, George Washington*. McLean, Va., 1983.

Alden, John P. *George Washington*. Baton Rouge, 1984.

Alexander, Holmes M. *To Covet Honor*. Belmont, 1977.

Allen, W. B. *George Washington: A Collection*. Indianapolis, 1988.

Ambler, Charles H. *George Washington and the West*. Chapel Hill, N.C., 1936.

Ammon, Harry. *The Genêt Mission*. New York, 1973.

———. *James Monroe, The Quest for National Identity*. New York, 1971.

Baker, Leonard. *John Marshall, A Life in Law*. New York, 1974.

Baker, William S. *Character Portraits of Washington as Delivered by Historians, Orators and Divines*. Philadelphia, 1887.

———. *Early Sketches of George Washington*. Philadelphia, 1883.

———. *Washington After the Revolution*. Philadelphia, 1890.

Baldridge, Letitia, intro. *George Washington's Rules of Civility*. Mount Vernon, Va., 1989.

Baldwin, Leland. *Whiskey Rebels: Story of a Frontier Uprising*. Pittsburgh, 1935.

Banning, Lance. *The Jeffersonian Persuasion: Evolution of a Party Ideology*. Ithaca, N.Y., 1980.

Bathe, Greville. *Citizen Genêt, Diplomat and Inventor*. Philadelphia, 1946.

Bellamy, Francis R. *The Private Life of George Washington*. New York, 1951.

Bemis, Samuel F. *Jay's Treaty*. New York, 1923.

———. *John Quincy Adams and the Foundations of American Foreign Policy*. New York, 1949.

———. *Pinckney's Treaty*. New York, 1926.

Binkley, Wilfred E. *American Political Parties*. New York, 1943.

Binning, A. C. *The Rise of American Economic Life*. New York, 1943.

Boorstin, Daniel J. "The Mythologizing of George Washington." In *George Washington, A Profile*, ed. James Morton Smith. New York, 1969.

Bourne, Miriam Anne. *First Family: George Washington and His Intimate Relations*. New York, 1982.

Bowling, Kenneth, ed. *Washington History*, vol. 3, no. 1, Spring/Summer 1991. The Historical Society of Washington, D.C.

Bowling, Kenneth, and Helen E. Veit. *The Diary of William Maclay*, March 4, 1789–March 3, 1791. Baltimore, 1988.

Bowman, Albert Hall. *The Struggle for Neutrality: Franco-American Diplomacy During the Federalist Era*. Knoxville, Tenn., 1974.

Boyd, Julien P., ed. *The Papers of Thomas Jefferson*, vols. 17–24. Princeton, 1950–91.

Brant, Irving. *James Madison, Father of the Constitution, 1787–1800*. Indianapolis, 1950.

Bray, Hammond. *Banks and Politics in Early America*. Princeton, 1957.

Brissot de Warville, J. P. *Travels in the United States of America*. Cambridge, Mass., 1964.

Brodie, Fawn. *Thomas Jefferson, An Intimate History*. New York, 1974.

Brown, Stuart Gerry. *The First Republicans*. New York, 1943.

Buell, Richard. *Securing the Revolution: Ideology in American Politics, 1789–1815*. Ithaca, N.Y., 1972.

Carroll, John Alexander, and Mary Well Ashworth. *George Washington: First in Peace*. New York, 1957.

Caughey, John W. *McGillivray of the Creeks*. Norman, Okla., 1938.

Childs, Francis S. *French Refugee Life in the United States, 1790–1800*. New York, 1940.

Chinard, Gilbert. *George Washington as the French Knew Him*. Princeton, 1940.

———. *Honest John Adams*. Boston, 1933.

Christman, Margaret C. S. *The First Federal Congress, 1789–91*. Washington, D.C., 1989.

Clarfield, Gerard. *Timothy Pickering and the American Republic*. Pittsburgh, 1980.

Conway, Moncure D. *George Washington of Mount Vernon*. Brooklyn, 1889.

———. *Omitted Chapters of History Disclosed in the Life and Letters of Edmund Randolph*. New York, 1888.

Corbin, John. *The Unknown Washington*. New York, 1930.

Corner, G. W., ed. *The Autobiography of Benjamin Rush*. Westport, Conn., 1970.

Cresson, W. P. *James Monroe.* Chapel Hill, N.C., 1946.

Cunliffe, Marcus. *George Washington, Man and Monument.* London, 1959.

———. *In Search of America.* Westport, Conn., 1991.

———. *The Presidency.* Boston, 1968.

Cunningham, Noble E. *The Jeffersonian Republicans: The Formation of Party Origins, 1789–1801.* Chapel Hill, N.C., 1957.

Custis, George Washington Parke. *Recollections and Private Memories of Washington.* New York, 1860.

Davis, Burke. *George Washington and the American Revolution.* New York, 1975.

Decatur, Stephen. *Private Affairs of George Washington, from the Records and Accounts of Tobias Lear.* Boston, 1933.

De Chastellux, Marquis. *Travels in North America in the Years 1780, 1781, 1782.* Chapel Hill, N.C., 1963.

De Conde, Alexander. *Entangling Alliances: Politics and Diplomacy Under George Washington.* Durham, N.C., 1958.

de Forest, Elizabeth Kellam. *The Gardens and Grounds of Mount Vernon.* Mount Vernon, Va., 1982.

Destler, Chester M. *Joshua Coit, American Federalist, 1758–98.* Middletown, Conn., 1962.

Eisen, Gustavus. *Portraits of Washington.* New York, 1932.

Ernst, Robert. *Rufus King, American Federalist.* Chapel Hill, N.C., 1968.

Fauchet, Joseph. *A Sketch of the Present State of Our Political Relations with the United States.* Philadelphia, 1797.

Ferling, John E. *The First of Men: A Life of George Washington.* Knoxville, Tenn., 1988.

Fitzpatrick, John C. *George Washington, Colonial Traveler, 1732–75.* Indianapolis, 1927.

———. *George Washington Himself.* Indianapolis, 1933.

———. *The Last Will and Testament of George Washington.* Mount Vernon, Va., 1960.

———. *The Writings of George Washington,* 39 vols. Washington, D.C., 1931–44.

Flexner, James Thomas. *George Washington: Anguish and Farewell.* Boston, 1972.

———. *George Washington: The Forge of Experience.* Boston, 1965.

———. *George Washington and the New Nation.* Boston, 1970.

———. *George Washington in the American Revolution.* Boston, 1968.

———. *The Young Hamilton.* Boston, 1978.

Foner, Philip S. *Democratic-Republican Societies, 1790–1800.* Westport, Conn., 1976.

Ford, Paul L. *The True George Washington.* Philadelphia, 1896.

———. *Washington and the Theatre.* New York, 1899.

Ford, Worthington C. *George Washington as an Employer and Importer of Labor.* Brooklyn, 1889.

Freeman, Douglas Southall. *George Washington*, vols. 1–6. New York, 1948–54.

Frothingham, Thomas G. *Washington: Commander in Chief*. Boston, 1930.

Garvan, Beatrice B. *Federal Philadelphia 1785–1825, The Athens of the Western World*. Philadelphia, 1987.

Gibbs, George, ed. *Memoirs of the Administration of Washington and Adams, from the Papers of Oliver Wolcott*. New York, 1846.

Griswold, Rufus W. *The Republican Court, or American Society in the Days of Washington*. New York, 1854.

Haraszti, Zoltan. *John Adams and the Prophets of Progress*. Cambridge, Mass., 1952.

Hart, Albert Bushnell, ed. *Honor to George Washington*, vols. 1–4, 9. Washington, D.C., 1932.

Hart, James. *The American Presidency in Action, 1789*. New York, 1948.

Haworth, Paul L. *George Washington, Country Gentleman*. Indianapolis, 1933.

Hazen, Charles D. *Contemporary American Opinion of the French Revolution*. Baltimore, 1897.

Helderman, Leonard. *George Washington: Patron of Learning*. New York, 1932.

Henderson, Archibald. *Washington's Southern Tour of 1791*. Boston, 1923.

Hendrickson, Robert A. *The Rise and Fall of Alexander Hamilton*. New York, 1981.

Hughes, Rupert. *George Washington*, vols. 1–3. New York, 1926–30.

Humphreys, David. *The Life of George Washington, with General Washington's "Remarks,"* ed. Rosemary Zagari. Athens, Ga., 1991.

Humphreys, Frank L. *Life and Times of David Humphreys*. New York, 1917.

Irving, Washington. *Life of George Washington*, ed. Jess Stein, introduction by Richard B. Morris. Tarrytown, N.Y., 1975.

Jackson, Donald, and Dorothy Twohig. *Diaries of George Washington*, vols. 1–6. Charlottesville, Va., 1976–79.

Jenkins, Charles F. *Washington Visits Germantown*. Germantown, Pa., 1932.

Johnson, Gerald W., and Charles Cecil Wall. *Mount Vernon, The Story of a Shrine*. New York, 1953.

Kamminiski, John P., and Jill Adair McLaughan. *A Great and Good Man, George Washington in the Eyes of His Countrymen*. Madison, Wis., 1989.

Ketchum, Richard M. *Presidents Above Parties: The First American Presidency, 1789–1829*. Chapel Hill, N.C., 1984.

——— . *The World of George Washington*. New York, 1974.

Kinnaird, Clark. *George Washington: The Pictorial Biography*. New York, 1967.

Klapthor, Margaret Brown, and Howard Alexander Morrison. *George Washington: A Figure upon the Stage*. Washington, D.C., 1982.

Knollenberg, Bernhard. *George Washington: The Virginia Period, 1732–75*. Durham, N.C., 1964.

Knopf, Richard C. *Anthony Wayne*. Pittsburgh, 1960.

Kohn, Richard H. *Eagle and Sword: The Federalists and the Creation of the Military Establishment in America, 1783–1802.* New York, 1975.

Krout, John Allen, and Dixon Ryan Fox. *The Completion of Independence, 1790–1840.* New York, 1944.

Lear, Tobias. *Letters and Recollections of Washington . . . with a Diary of Washington's Last Days.* New York, 1906.

Leary, Lewis. *That Rascal Freneau.* New Brunswick, N.J., 1941.

Levin, Phyllis Lee. *Abigail Adams.* New York, 1987.

Link, Eugene. *Democratic-Republican Societies, 1790–1800.* New York, 1942.

Lodge, Henry Cabot. *George Washington.* Boston, 1889.

Longmore, Paul K. *The Invention of George Washington.* Berkeley, Calif., 1988.

Lossing, Benson J. *Mary and Martha, the Mother and Wife of Washington.* New York, 1886.

Malone, Dumas. *Jefferson and the Ordeal of Liberty.* Boston, 1962.

———. *Jefferson and the Rights of Man.* Boston, 1951.

Mapp, Alf J., Jr. *Thomas Jefferson: A Strange Case of Mistaken Identity.* Lanham, Md., 1987.

Marling, Karal Ann. *George Washington Slept Here.* Cambridge, Mass., 1988.

Mazyck, Walter H. *George Washington and the Negro.* Washington, D.C., 1932.

McDonald, Forrest. *Alexander Hamilton.* New York, 1979.

———. *The Presidency of George Washington.* Lawrence, Kans., 1974.

McGuire, E. C. *The Religious Opinions and Character of Washington.* New York, 1836.

Miller, John C. *Alexander Hamilton and the Growth of the New Nation.* New York, 1959.

———. *Crisis in Freedom: The Alien and Sedition Acts.* Boston, 1951.

———. *The Federalist Era.* New York, 1952.

Mines, John F. *A Tour Around New York.* New York, 1893.

Minnigerode, Meade. *Jefferson, Friend of France, 1793.* New York, 1928.

Mitchell, Broadus. *Alexander Hamilton, The National Adventure, 1788–1804.* New York, 1962.

Mitchell, Stewart, ed. *New Letters of Abigail Adams.* Boston, 1947.

Mitnick, Barbara. *The Changing Image of George Washington.* New York, 1989.

Monaghan, Frank. *French Travelers in the United States, 1765–1932.* New York, 1933.

———. *John Jay: Defender of Liberty.* New York, 1935.

———, and Marvin Lowenthal. *This Was New York.* New York, 1943.

Moore, Charles. *The Family Life of George Washington.* Boston, 1926.

Morgan, Edmund S. *The Genius of George Washington.* New York, 1980.

———. *The Meaning of Independence.* New York, 1976.

Morison, Samuel Eliot. *The Oxford History of the American People.* New York, 1965.

Morris, Richard B. *Encyclopedia of American History.* New York, 1961.

Nagel, Paul S. *Descent from Glory, Four Generations of the John Adams Family.* New York, 1983.

Nettels, Curtis P. *The Emergence of a National Economy, 1775–1815.* New York, 1962.

————. *George Washington and American Independence.* Boston, 1951.

Nevins, Allen, ed. *American Social History as Recorded by British Travelers.* New York, 1948.

Niemcewicz, Julian U. *Under Their Own Vine and Fig Tree: Travels Through America, 1797–99, 1805,* trans. and ed. Metchie J. E. Budka. Elizabeth, N.J., 1965.

Niles, Blair. *Martha's Husband: An Informal Portrait of George Washington.* New York, 1951.

Nordham, George W. *George Washington and Money.* Washington, D.C., 1982.

————. *George Washington's Women.* Philadelphia, 1971.

Padover, Saul K. *Writings of Thomas Jefferson.* Norwalk, Conn., 1967.

————. *The Washington Papers.* New York, 1955.

Paltsis, Victor Hugo. *Washington's Farewell Address.* New York, 1935.

Perkins, Bradford. *The First Rapprochement, England and the United States 1795–1805.* Philadelphia, 1955.

Perret, Geoffrey. *A Country Made by War.* New York, 1989.

Peterson, Merrill D. *Thomas Jefferson and the New Nation.* New York, 1970.

Pomerantz, Sidney I. *New York: An American City 1783–1803.* New York, 1938.

Powell, J. H. *Bring Out Your Dead.* Philadelphia, 1949.

Prucha, Francis P. *American Indian Policy in the Formative Years.* Cambridge, Mass., 1962.

————. *The Sword of the Republic: The United States Army on the Frontier, 1783–1846.* Bloomington, Ind., 1977.

Prussing, Eugene E. *The Estate of George Washington, Deceased.* Boston, 1927.

Rakove, Jacob N. *The Beginnings of National Politics.* New York, 1979.

Reardon, John J. *Edmund Randolph.* New York, 1974.

Ritter, Halstad L. *Washington as a Businessman.* New York, 1931.

Rutland, Robert A. *James Madison, The Founding Father.* New York, 1987.

Schachner, Nathan. *Alexander Hamilton.* New York, 1949.

————. *The Founding Fathers.* New York, 1954.

————. *Thomas Jefferson.* New York, 1951.

Schwartz, Barry. *George Washington: The Making of an American Symbol.* New York, 1987.

Sears, Louis Martin. *George Washington and the French Revolution.* Detroit, 1960.

Shaw, Peter. *The Character of John Adams.* Chapel Hill, N.C., 1976.

Slaughter, Thomas P. *The Whiskey Rebellion: Frontier Epilogue to the American Revolution.* New York, 1986.

Smith, James Morton, ed. *George Washington, A Profile.* New York, 1969.

Smith, Page. *John Adams.* New York, 1962.

————. *The Shaping of America.* New York, 1980.

Smith, Thomas E. V. *New York in the Year of Washington's Inauguration.* New York, 1899.

Spaulding, Oliver L. *The United Sates Army in War and Peace.* New York, 1937.

Stephenson, G. W., and W. H. Dunn. *George Washington.* New York, 1940.

Stewart, Donald H. *The Opposition Press of the Federalist Period.* Albany, 1969.

Swiggert, Howard. *The Extraordinary Mr. Morris.* Garden City, N.Y., 1952.

————. *The Great Man: George Washington as a Human Being.* New York, 1953.

Sword, Wiley. *President Washington's Indian War: The Struggle for the Old Northwest, 1790–95.* Norman, Okla., 1985.

Tagg, James D. *Benjamin Franklin Bache and the Philadelphia* Aurora. Philadelphia, 1991.

Tebbel, John. *George Washington's America.* New York, 1954.

Thane, Elswyth. *Mount Vernon Family.* New York, 1968.

————. *Potomac Squire.* New York, 1963.

————. *Washington's Lady.* New York, 1954.

Thomas, Charles M. *American Neutrality in 1793, A Study in Cabinet Government.* New York, 1931.

Tindall, George Brown. *America, A Narrative History.* New York, 1984.

Twohig, Dorothy, ed. *The Papers of George Washington: The Journal of the Proceedings of the President, 1793–97.* Charlottesville, Va., 1981.

Van Every, Dale. *Ark of Empire: The American Frontier, 1784–1803.* New York, 1963.

Wall, Charles Cecil. *George Washington: Citizen Soldier.* Charlottesville, Va., 1980.

Walter, John F. *Annals of Philadelphia.* Philadelphia, 1907.

Weigley, Russell F., ed. *Philadelphia, A 300 Year History.* New York, 1982.

Wharton, Anne Hollingsworth. *Martha Washington.* New York, 1897.

Whitaker, Arthur P. *The Mississippi Question, 1796–1803.* New York, 1934.

White, Leonard. *The Federalists.* New York, 1948.

Whitney, Janet. *Abigail Adams.* Boston, 1947.

Wildes, Henry T. *Anthony Wayne.* New York, 1941.

Wills, Garry. *Cincinnatus: George Washington and the Enlightenment.* Garden City, N.Y., 1984.

Withey, Lynne. *Dearest Friend: A Life of Abigail Adams.* New York, 1981.

Wright, Esmond. *Washington and the American Revolution.* New York, 1962.

Young, Eleanor. *Forgotten Patriot: Robert Morris.* New York, 1950.

Zahniser, Marvin. *Charles Cotesworth Pinckney.* Chapel Hill, N.C., 1967.

PROLOGUE: THE MAN IN THE MACOMB HOUSE

1: Abigail Adams's description of plague-ravaged New York and her fears for the country's future should Washington die appear in *New Letters of Abigail Adams,* ed. Stewart Mitchell, pp. 46–50. The Washington Influenza was first reported in the *Boston Gazette*, Nov. 30, 1789. The Macomb House, its decoration and daily routine, are described in Washington's Diary for Feb. 1, 1790, as well as in Decatur's *Private Affairs of George Washington, from the Records and Accounts of Tobias Lear*. Since Lear was both confidant and bookkeeper, Decatur's volume is among the most intimate ever written about the first president. Dorothy Twohig told me early in my research that I would find it invaluable, and she was right.

Mrs. Washington's response to her husband's illness is conveyed in a June 12, 1790, letter to Mercy Otis Warren preserved at Mount Vernon (as is virtually all of the Washington family correspondence cited here). One should also see Thane's *Washington's Lady*, and Bourne's *First Family*. Decatur describes Washington's household staff; both Lear and Humphreys reappear in Thane's *Potomac Squire*, pp. 258–62. Washington's self-deprecatory remarks to Humphreys can be found in the recently published biography of the first president written by Humphreys and covering his life through the early days of the Washington administration.

William Loughton Smith's taunting remarks about slavery and the grand constitutional bargain of 1787 are in Christman, *First Federal Congress*, p. 157.

2: For information on Dr. Jones, see Corner, *Autobiography of Benjamin Rush*. Here and throughout the text I have relied on the personal information supplied by Ford in *The True George Washington*, which ushered in a new era of realistic portraiture when published in 1896. Nearly a century later, it remains fresh and revealing. On p. 204, for example, one will find the Addison quote that so embodies Washington's fatalism. Washington's appearance eluded most of his contemporaries. Gilbert Stuart, for one, claimed that he was "like no one but himself." Brissot de Warville, on a visit to the United States in 1791, put the president's elusiveness in another light. "He has no characteristic traits in his figure, and this has rendered it always so difficult to describe him." At the same time, noted de Warville, "his modesty must be very astonishing, especially to a Frenchman."

For the crisis in Washington's illness, see Bowling and Veit, *Diary of William Maclay*, p. 269. Jefferson was told by two of the president's three physicians that Washington was "in the act of death." John Fenno's extravagant relief found voice in the *Gazette of the United States* for June 5, 1790.

CHAPTER 1: "SUMMONED BY MY COUNTRY"

1: On June 6, Jefferson reported to William Short that Washington was "perfectly re-established" and looking better than before his illness. Still, the president did not resume his diary entries until June 24. For a balanced portrait of Mary Ball Washington, see Ford's *True George Washington*, pp. 17–21. The anecdote about Mrs. Washington and the revolutionary messenger is from Conway, *George Washington of Mount Vernon*, p. 41. That Washington never fully resolved his ambivalent emotions toward his mother is demonstrated in the irritable comments he made at the time of her death in 1789. "She had a great deal of money from me at times," he complained to his sister; Bourne, p. 122.

For Lord Fairfax's prescient forecast of young Washington's future, see Stephenson and Dunn, *George Washington*, 1:33–34. A sensitive account of the Washington–Sally Fairfax affair is Samuel Eliot Morison's "Young Man Washington," in *By Land and by Sea*. The revolutionary hero's editing of his youthful correspondence is described in "An Uncommon Awareness of Self: The Papers of George Washington," by W. W. Abbot, in the National Archives' publication *Prologue*, Spring 1989, p. 15.

2: For an alternative to the Parson Weems school of hagiography, see Bernhard Knollenberg's unsentimental *George Washington: The Virginia Period, 1732–1775*. Washington's encounter with Payne is told by Corbin, *Unknown Washington*, pp. 43–46. In recounting Washington's evolution from planter to patriot, I have found no better source than Nettels's *George Washington and American Independence*. Nettels is especially good at explaining the economic web of British mercantilism. See also Richard Ketchum's excellent *World of George Washington*, pp. 66–73, and "George Washington's Generalship," in Cunliffe's *In Search of America*. "His overriding service to America lay in his steadfastness," wrote Cunliffe. "He was a fixed point in a shifting universe" (p. 50).

For Martha's role in the Revolution, one should examine Ford's chapter "George Washington and the Fair Sex," *True George Washington*, along with Niles, *Martha's Husband*. Among the indignities that accompanied Washington's sudden celebrity were slurs on his sexual faithfulness, a 1776 pamphlet published in London suggesting that the American commander in chief was rowed across the Hudson every night to visit his Jersey mistress, and another British publication, the misnamed *Gentleman's Magazine*, printing forged letters describing a liaison with "pretty little Kate, the washerwoman's daughter." See Dixon Wecter, "President Washington and Parson Weems," pp. 20–21, in Smith, *George Washington*. A provocative essay on Interest and Honor as the wellsprings of Washington's character is found in Edmund Morgan's *Meaning of Independence*, pp. 29–55.

3: A good source for Washington's humor is "The Amiable Washington," by Peter R. Henriques, *Northern Virginia Heritage*, February 1979. Washington made no effort to conceal his distaste for the scheming Thomas Conway, telling one congressman that he despised "the arts of dissimulation . . . My feelings will not permit me to make professions of friendship to the man I deem my enemy." An even greater rival was Charles Lee, whose hatred of the man he mocked as "our Great Gargantua, or Lama Babak" is gauged in Ford, *True George Washington*, pp. 248–55.

4: Martha's anguished comments about "my pretty little Dear Boy" are in her letter to Fanny Basset Washington, Feb. 25, 1780. For evidence that Washington did indeed wear glasses before the famous Newburgh affair in 1783, Mount Vernon's manuscript collection contains the notice of an auction of a Washington letter dated June 18, 1781, requesting his correspondent to "make him a pair of pincers." Thane, *Potomac Squire*, pp. 268–69, is the source for the story of Washington and his tippling gardener. Regarding Washington's unwillingness to assume the presidency, Humphreys in his putative biography quotes the old soldier on pp. 47–48: "My life has been a very busy one, I have had but little leisure to read of late years, and even if I had been favored with more leisure, my memory is so bad I can get little advantage from reading."

5: For an opposition perspective on the early days of Washington's administration, see Bowling and Veit's *Diary of William Maclay*. In the Dec. 15, 1991, *Washington Post*, "1789: The Congress That Could" points out that Madison himself arrived in New York with somewhat equivocal feelings about the legal, as opposed to political, need for a Bill of Rights. Decatur, p. 175, publishes a bill for laudanum, presumably purchased to alleviate the president's aching teeth. Additional details are available in Bernard Wolf Weinberger, "George Washington and His Dental Disturbances," *Trained Nurse and Hospital Review*, February 1946.

The famous levees are described in several sources, including Maclay's dyspeptic diary and Rufus Griswold's *Republican Court*. These highly stylized functions represented a compromise for a busy executive who did not wish "to be run down by a crowd of visitants" nor to shut himself up like some eastern potentate. They apparently were something of a trial for Washington himself, whether or not we choose to believe Jefferson's gossipy retelling of a tale originally passed on by Tobias Lear. It seems that at an early levee the pompous David Humphreys threw open the door to the audience chamber and announced sententiously, "The President of the United States." To this an irate Washington is said to have responded, "Well, you have taken me in once, but, by God, you shall never take me in a second time" (Griswold, p. 150).

As for the president's wardrobe on these formal occasions, which, next to the stiffness of his bows, came in for the most severe republican criticism, Washington generally dressed simply, having figuratively outgrown the ruffled shirts ordered in his youth from a London tailor in Fish Street. "Do not conceive that fine clothes make fine men," he had admonished his nephew Bushrod, "any more than fine feathers make fine birds." While he favored suits of native broadcloth, fashion and comfort sometimes overrode his patriotism by forcing him into superfine velvet of Dutch or British weave. A Parisian watch bought in emulation of Jefferson hung from a pocket of his fitted waistcoat. Except on rare occasions, such as reviews of the aristocratic Order of the Cincinnati, the president avoided military garb. Then he donned his blue and buff uniform as a Virginia colonel of volunteers.

A letter from Nelly Custis to Elizabeth B. Gordon on Feb. 23, 1823, recalls the sad spectacle of Washington cut off from Nelly's young friends by the same Olympian bearing that caused Abigail Adams to label him "awful as a God."

CHAPTER 2: WASHINGTONOPOLIS, D.C.

1: Domestic details concerning the executive mansion are found in Ford's chapter "Social Life" in *True George Washington*, as well as in Decatur, *Private Affairs of George Washington*, Griswold, *Republican Court*, and Bourne, *First Family*. Abigail Adams described Martha Washington's Friday night receptions in a letter to her sister, Feb. 6, 1791. Also see "Washington's Days as Host in New York," *New York Times*, Apr. 26, 1989. Two hundred years earlier, William Maclay reported on a typical meal at the Washingtons': "It was the most solemn dinner ever I sat at. Not a health drank; scarce a word said until the cloth was taken away . . . The ladies sat a good while, and the bottles passed about; but there was a dead silence almost." At length Mrs. Washington and the other women withdrew, after which the president made a feeble jest about a New England clergyman who lost his hat and wig while crossing the Bronx River. "He now and then said a sentence or two on some common subject," Maclay allowed, "and what he said was not amiss." John Jay tried to inject some levity into the proceedings with a risqué reference to the duchess of Devonshire's heroic campaigning on behalf of Mr. Fox. Soon after, the president rose from the table and went upstairs for coffee. Seeing his opportunity to escape, Maclay grabbed his hat and disappeared into the night; *Diary of William Maclay*, pp. 136–37.

2: A good account of the furious debate swirling over assumption and the nation's permanent capital is in Smith's *Shaping of America*, pp. 147–67; Christman, *First Federal Congress*, has a similarly lively tale to tell, pp. 170–88, as does McDonald, *Presidency of George Washington*, pp. 48–60. For an overview of the diverse society Washington was called upon to lead, see Schachner, *Founding Fathers*, ch. 2; Brissot de Warville, *Travels in the United States*; Tebbel, *George Washington's America*; Krout and Fox, *Completion of Independence*; Esmond Wright's *Fabric of Freedom*, 1763–1800; and Merrill Jensen's *New Nation*.

3: For background on New York during Washington's presidency, see Monaghan and Lowenthal, *This Was New York*; Sidney Pomerantz, *New York*; Smith, *New York in the Year of Washington's Inauguration*; and Mines, *A Tour Around New York*. John Adams was scandalized over the high cost of maintaining his official station, telling his wife in July 1789 that their rent in New York would consume $2,700 a year, with $1,500 more to keep a carriage. "Secretaries, servants, wood, more to charities which are demanded as rights, and the million dittos present such a prospect as is enough to disgust anyone. Yet not one word must we say" (White, *Federalists*, p. 294n). John Page's disparaging remark about New York's inferiority to Philadelphia is quoted in "Washington in New York in 1789," an undated article in the Baker Collection at the Pennsylvania Historical Society. See also "Back to the Presidency's Beginnings," *Washington Post*, Apr. 27, 1989. An excellent picture of Washington's republican bête noire is Robert C. Aberts, "The Cantankerous Mr. Maclay," *American Heritage*, October 1974.

Also see Richard A. Baker, "The Senate of the United States: Supreme Executive Council of the Nation, 1787–1800," *Prologue*, Winter 1989, pp. 299–314. The proposed Georgia Indian treaty was not the only rebuff experienced by Washington. His proclamation of a national Thanksgiving holiday prompted complaints from a South Carolina representative that it was none of Congress's business. Nor could the people decide whether "to return thanks for a Constitution until they have experienced that it promotes their safety and happiness." Washington went ahead with his observances of the day, taking part in a sparsely attended church service and making a gift to buy beer and other provisions for prisoners confined for debt.

The tribute to Washington's constancy amid the depravity of Manhattan is in Griswold, *Republican Court*, p. 207. Mrs. Adams's lament over the scarcity of reliable, sober servants is in Christman, *First Federal Congress*, p. 148.

4: The intense battle over where to place a capital is well covered in Smith, *Shaping of America*, and in Christman, *First Federal Congress*, pp. 181–90. See both the Editorial Note in *Papers of Thomas Jefferson*, 18:163–83, as well as the harshly critical polemic by Junius Americanus, July 12, 1790, in the same publication, pp. 183–92. William Smith's notion of calling the new capital Washingtonopolis is recounted in Pamela Scott, "L'Enfant's Washington Described," *Washington History*, Spring–Summer 1991. Freneau's sarcastic ditty is reproduced by Griswold, *Republican Court*, p. 237. That Jefferson, for one, would much prefer either Philadelphia or Baltimore was made plain in his correspondence. About this time he wrote of New Yorkers and their dour climate, "Spring and fall they never have: as far as I can learn, they have ten months of winter, two of summer with some winter days interspersed."

The anger felt by New Yorkers toward what they saw as a presidential betrayal spilled into the *New York Journal*, July 12, 1790. A possible conflict of interest involving the president, the Potomac Navigation Company, and his proposed site along the Eastern Branch is argued by Ferling in his excellent one-volume biography *First of Men*, pp. 396–98. Other scholars of the period, Julian Boyd among them, have contended that a desire to win over George Mason played a significant role in Washington's final determination of the new district's boundaries.

CHAPTER 3: CAUNOTAUCARIUS AND HIS CABINET

1: Washington's diary entry for July 1 contains John Adams's belligerent counsel toward Great Britain as well as the president's suspicions of Spain's attempt to bribe Alexander McGillivray before his arrival in New York. For McGillivray's visit and the ensuing negotiations, see Gary L. Roberts's superb rendering of Hoboi-Hili-Miko, "the Good Child King," in "The Chief of State and the Chief," *American Heritage,* October 1975.

John Adams comes to life in Morgan's *Meaning of Independence,* Shaw's *Character of John Adams,* and especially Smith's illuminating two-volume biography *John Adams.* Adams's scathing review of Washington's intellectual shortcomings is in Haraszti's *John Adams and the Prophets of Progress,* p. 3. Jefferson's wry assessment of Adams at the peace table is in Morgan, p. 18.

2: See "A Slave's Memory of Mr. Jefferson," *American Heritage,* October 1959, for Monticello's skylit dining room and elaborate hospitality. Charles B. Van Pelt, "His Head and His Heart," *American Heritage,* August 1971, describes Jefferson's infatuation with Maria Cosway. Mapp covers the same territory with sensitivity and insight in *Thomas Jefferson.* See also Brodie's controversial *Thomas Jefferson.* Jefferson's initially ambiguous reaction to the new Constitution is documented in Malone's *Jefferson and the Rights of Man,* pp. 158–69. An excellent account of the first State Department is David S. Patterson, "The Department of State: The Formative Years, 1775–1800," *Prologue,* Winter 1989, pp. 315–30; also Peterson, *Thomas Jefferson and the New Nation,* pp. 395–96. Malone, *Rights of Man,* pp. 256–58, describes the new secretary's earliest days in New York. Edmund Randolph's description of his "mongrel" department is in Conway's *Omitted Chapters of History,* p. 135.

3: Miller's *Alexander Hamilton and the Growth of the New Nation* is my chief source for young Hamilton. For a more overtly partisan narrative, see Hendrickson's *Rise and Fall of Alexander Hamilton,* a provocative work marred by some gratuitous swipes at Jefferson. James Thomas Flexner's "The American World Was Not Made for Me," *American Heritage,* December 1977, captures both his subjects' combativeness and the poignancy of a man without a country. Hamilton's theory of executive power is outlined in White's *Federalists,* pp. 89–92. "It is one thing to be subordinate to the laws," explained Hamilton with breathtaking consistency, "and another to be dependent on the legislative body."

4: Henry Knox, who deserves a full-scale modern biography, is sketched in Christman, *First Federal Congress,* pp. 145–46, and also in Bowling and Veit, *Diary of William Maclay.* Curiously, the usually astringent Maclay had something of a soft spot for the huge New Englander, "a Bachanalian Figure" who he thought showed more natural dignity and ease than either Hamilton or Jefferson. Theodore J. Crackel, "The Common Defence: The Department of War, 1789–94," *Prologue*, Winter 1989, pp. 331–44, is a good rendering of Knox's service at the woefully undermanned War Department. McGillivray's arrival in New York and Washington's greeting are described by Arthur Orrmont in *Diplomat in Warpaint: Chief Alexander McGillivray of the Creeks* (New York, 1967). Another source for the ensuing negotiations is Caughey, *McGillivray of the Creeks*. Georgia Senator James Jackson's tirade against the Treaty of New York is in Roberts, "The Chief of State and the Chief," p. 88.

5: The story of John Trumbull's portrait and the president's practical joke is in Roberts, "The Chief of State and the Chief," p. 87. For Washington's departure from New York, see the *Gazette of the United States*, Sept. 1, 1790, the *New York Journal*, Aug. 31, 1790, Decatur, p. 150. According to Lear's expense accounts, the president spent $41,268.47 while residing in New York, with an average weekly cost of $143 for the executive table alone. This did not include another $800 for his wardrobe.

CHAPTER 4: TOWN AND COUNTRY

1: Numerous books are devoted to Washington and Mount Vernon. Among the best are Haworth's *George Washington*, and Thane's *Potomac Squire*. An excellent contemporary description of Washington's country seat is in *Osborne's Portsmouth* (New Hampshire) *Spy*, May 4, 1791, which notes that while "venerable and convenient" and "much embellished," Mount Vernon was "yet not perfectly satisfactory to the chaste taste of the present possessor." See also Marshall B. Davidson, *The American Heritage History of Notable American Houses* (New York, 1971), and the Mount Vernon issue of *Antiques, The Magazine*, February 1989, pp. 463–72. Thomas Lee Shippen's tribute to the Washingtons' hospitality is in Baker, *Washington After the Revolution*, p. 197. Fanny Basset Washington, in a letter to her father on Sept. 21, 1790, detected signs of the president's most recent illnesses "which I fear will never wear off." For Martha's daily routine, see the introduction to *The Mount Vernon Cookbook*, published in 1987 by the Mount Vernon Ladies Association.

2: "The War Crisis of 1790," pp. 35–107, in Boyd, *Papers of Thomas Jefferson*, vol. 17, gives a comprehensive view of those tense weeks when the United States hovered on the brink of a new European conflict. Boyd, the editor of the Jefferson papers, pursued his research further in *No. 7: Alexander Hamilton's Secret Attempts to Control American Foreign Policy* (Princeton, 1964).

3: Aikman's *Rider with Destiny*, pp. 67–71, describes Washington's real estate ventures in the fall of 1791. For an overview of the controversy surrounding the placement of the capital, see "Fixing the Seat of Government on the Potomac" in vol. 17 of the Jefferson papers, pp. 452–60. Maclay's angry complaint about Washington's interference is in Bowling and Veit, *Diary*, p. 368.

4: The background on Philadelphia's exalted status is in Beatrice B. Garvan's *Federal Philadelphia, 1785–1825*. The new presidential residence is described in Washington's correspondence and in Decatur, *Private Affairs of George Washington*, pp. 159–62. Abigail Adams's unhappiness over yet another move and a house uninhabited for four years fills her letters of the period, especially that of Dec. 12, 1790; see also Christman, *First Federal Congress*, p. 150. Griswold, *Republican Court*, p. 252, reprints the lament of James Monroe. Decatur, p. 183, is the source for Congressman Smith's scathing comments about Philadelphians. Christman, pp. 196–97, recounts some of the difficulties experienced by lawmakers in reaching the new capital (four members of the Massachusetts delegation, for example, were injured when the wagon in which they were riding overturned). South Carolina's always quotable William L. Smith concluded, "What a serious business it is to move the seat of government . . . The Quakers wish us at the Devil. I need not tell you where I wish them."

5: An excellent account of America's nascent economy and of Hamilton's vision for the future is in Miller, *Federalist Era*, pp. 55–69. See also Krout and Fox, pp. 66–71. Specifics of the excise debate, including James Jackson's denunciation of elitist Philadelphians, are in Christman, *First Federal Congress*, pp. 204–7. On Jan. 27, 1791, the House approved Hamilton's plans, leading a despondent Representative John Steele of North Carolina to write, "Thus you see, my Friend, that assuming, funding and excising have taken root in America. How these foreign plants will flourish in free soils, time must determine." See also Nettels, pp. 116–17. The debate over foreign commerce and Washington's continuing hostility toward British predators is in "Commerce and Diplomatic Relations with Great Britain," *Papers of Thomas Jefferson*, 18:220–83.

6: Leary's *That Rascal Freneau* remains the best biography of the great republican editor. Additional details can be found in *A Literary History of the United States*, ed. Spiller et al. (New York, 1953), p. 171; also "American Newspapers and Editorial Opinion, 1789–93," Appendix VI-2; Freeman, *George Washington*, vol. 6; and Banning, *Jeffersonian Persuasion*, pp. 167–72. Jefferson's letter of Feb. 28, 1791, to Freneau makes clear the less than demanding nature of his proffered position and adds, "Should anything better turn up within my department that might suit you, I shall be very happy . . . to bestow it."

CHAPTER 5: TO SEE AND BE SEEN

1: The best primary source for Washington's journey is two hundred years old, the traveler's own diary, with its tart observations on the country and its people, expertly annotated for modern readers in vol. 6 of Jackson and Twohig, *Diaries of George Washington*. Nearly as good is Henderson's *Washington's Southern Tour of 1791*, which incorporates extensive newspaper reporting of the trip and a judicious amount of local tradition about the presidential visit. Details of the new coach ("said to be the handsomest altogether that has been made in the country") are in Lear's Mar. 16, 1791, letter to Humphreys in the Mount Vernon Archives. In a second missive, dated Apr. 12, 1791, Lear justifies the journey on political grounds, informing Humphreys of the "extremely disagreeable" debate over the Bank and excise. Washington hoped to conquer the South as he had won New England during his triumphal progress in 1789.

2: See "Washington's Breakfast" in Adelaide Hechtlinger, *The Seasonal Hearth: The Woman at Home in Early America* (Woodstock, N.Y., 1986), p. 221.

3: Jefferson's journey as well as his growing disagreements with the vice president are in Schachner's *Thomas Jefferson*, pp. 433–38. White, *Federalists*, pp. 224–25, describes the tug-of-war between Jefferson and Hamilton over the Treasury Department vacancy. John Dos Passos, "Lafayette's Two Revolutions," *American Heritage*, December 1956, is an eloquent portrayal of the French aristocrat-turned-revolutionary.

4: John Fenno's adulatory lyric on Washington's safe return appeared in the *Gazette of the United States*, July 9, 1791.

CHAPTER 6: ROUGH WATERS

1: Jefferson's report on Washington's latest illness and on the economic sickness caused by excessive speculation is in his July 24, 1791, letter to Edmund Pendleton. For Madison's reaction, see Brant, *James Madison*, pp. 341–42. Benjamin Rush's wry description of scriptomania is to be found in his Commonplace Book for Aug. 10–17, reproduced in Corner, *Autobiography of Benjamin Rush*, pp. 202–6. Also see Alexander, *To Covet Honor*, pp. 242–44.

2: George Augustine Washington's letter to his uncle of Aug. 1, 1791, preserved at Mount Vernon, contains depressing news of drought and George Augustine's continuing decline in health. The latter is amplified in James Craik to George Washington, Aug. 31, 1791.

Washington's advice to his unfortunate niece Harriot is contained in a long letter dated Oct. 30, 1791. After first reminding the girl that "it is better to offer no excuse than a bad one, if at any time you should fall into error," Washington urged that "instead of associating with those from whom you can derive nothing that is good . . . become the intimate companion of and aid to your cousin in the domestic concerns of the family . . . It is by a steady and rigid attention to the rules of propriety that such confidence is obtained, and nothing would give me more pleasure than to hear that you had acquired it."

Washington's Aug. 10 meeting with Ternant is described in the Frenchman's Aug. 13, 1791, letter to Montmorin in Paris, quoted in Chinard's *George Washington as the French Knew Him*, pp. 91–92. The controversy over Philadelphia's plans to build a grand executive mansion is covered at length in Washington's correspondence for the period.

3: For measurements of economic growth under the Washington administration, see Nettels, *Emergence of a National Economy*, pp. 121–23.

4: For the origins of the newspaper war, see Appendix VI-2 in Freeman, *George Washington*, vol. 6; also Stewart, *Opposition Press*, pp. 7–10; Miller, *Alexander Hamilton*, p. 343. I cannot praise too highly the definitive concluding volume of Freeman's opus, *George Washington: First in Peace*, by John A. Carroll and Mary W. Ashworth. Besides being beautifully written and deeply researched, the Carroll-Ashworth collaboration is a rich primary source for the nation's press. Madison's sustained campaign during the winter of 1791–92 is in Brant, *James Madison*, pp. 346–48. See as well Rutland, *James Madison*, pp. 105–9. Swiggert, *Extraordinary Mr. Morris*, pp. 224–26, describes the controversial envoy's appointment to Paris. Among the senators who opposed his nomination were Aaron Burr, whose claim that Morris was unfitted for the post after having earlier offended British ministers was no more far-fetched than James Monroe's criticism of Morris's indiscretions. Perhaps most typical, and damning, of the complaints was that lodged by stern old Roger Sherman of Connecticut. In his censorious eyes, Morris was "irreligious and a profane man."

5: For SUM, see Miller, *Alexander Hamilton*, pp. 308–33. Mitchell, *Alexander Hamilton*, pp. 138–52, examines the *Report on Manufactures* and its implications for the American economy and political system. See also Krout and Fox, *Completion of Independence*, pp. 68–70, and Nettels, *Emergence of a National Economy*, pp. 123–26. Jefferson's heated confrontation with the president over the *Report* and his own plans to leave office is recounted in the diary-like "Anas," in Padover, *Writings of Thomas Jefferson*, pp. 122–27. Hendrickson, *Rise and Fall of Alexander Hamilton*, pp. 315–28, has a provocative account of the Hamilton–Maria Reynolds affair.

6: Two good, recent accounts of Wayne's disastrous engagement and the administration's policies of which it was part are Prucha, *Sword of the Republic*, and Sword, *President Washington's Indian War*. See also Dale Van Every, "President Washington's Calculated Risk," *American Heritage*, June 1958, and Sears, *George Washington and the French Revolution*, pp. 70–117. Griswold, *Republican Court*, p. 480, tells the traditional version of Washington's reaction to St. Clair's forest humiliation. St. Clair resigned his commission on Apr. 7, 1792. War Department mismanagement is described in White, *Federalists*, pp. 148–

49. Washington's "Opinion of the General Officers," dated Mar. 9, 1792, is in the Fitzpatrick edition of his papers, 31:509–15.

7: For the long, frustrating, ultimately failed campaign to keep L'Enfant on the job, see "Fixing the Seat of Government," in Boyd, *Papers of Thomas Jefferson*, 20:3–72; also Elizabeth S. Kite, ed., *L'Enfant and Washington, 1791–92* (Baltimore, 1929). For Lear's reaction to the controversy, see his letter to David Humphreys, Apr. 8, 1792, preserved at Mount Vernon.

CHAPTER 7: THE CURSE OF DUTY

1: The Hamilton-Duer connection is described in Irving Brant, *The Fourth President*, pp. 258–59. Jefferson's "Anas" for Mar. 12 and Apr. 9, 1792, conveys his emerging doubts about the president's policies. Malone, *Rights of Man*, pp. 400–5, has the secretary's latest strictures against Gouverneur Morris. Abigail Adams's fears for the future are in her Apr. 20, 1792, letter to Mary Cranch. William Thornton's uncharitable yet irresistible portrait of the president, in an Apr. 2, 1792, letter to Sir James Bland Burges, is reproduced in Baker, *Washington After the Revolution*, pp. 235–36.

2: For the Madison-Washington meeting and its sequel, see Brant, *James Madison*, pp. 355–56. Betty Washington Lewis's financial problems are described in a letter to her brother dated Sept. 25, 1792. It seemed that the last time Harriot stayed with her aunt she had been unable to appear in public for lack of a suitable wardrobe. Such want was nothing new to the president's sister, already supporting three grandchildren. Indeed, according to Betty Lewis, her son Fielding's children "would go naked if it was not for the assistance I give him." The complete text of Jefferson's extraordinary letter of May 23, 1792, can be found in Boyd, *Papers of Thomas Jefferson*, 23:535–40.

3: For Washington as a scientific farmer, see Ford's chapter "Farmer and Proprietor," *True George Washington;* see also Haworth, *George Washington*, and Hart, *Honor to George Washington*, vol. 9. The latest Washington-Jefferson confrontation is described in Jefferson's "Anas," July 10. Of Howell Lewis, Lear had this to say: "Mr. Lewis possesses excellent dispositions but unfortunately he has been too much in the habits of a young Virginian; but I think a few years residence with the President will correct them." Obviously Washington had, in Lear's estimation, escaped the snares common to his native state (Bourne, *First Family*, p. 158.)

Hamilton's letter to the president asking him to run for a second term is quoted at length in Baker, *Washington After the Revolution*, p. 241. The secretary's successful defense of his conduct and policies is in Flexner, *George Washington and the New Nation*, pp. 364–70.

4: Standard sources for the newspaper war of 1792 are Leary, *That Rascal Freneau*, and Stewart, *Opposition Press*. See also Miller, *Alexander Hamilton*, pp. 343–52; Appendix VI-2, in Freeman, *George Washington*, vol. 6; Hendrickson, *Rise and Fall of Alexander Hamilton*, pp. 346–48. Randolph's flattering letter imploring Washington to drop his retirement plans is in Baker, *Washington After the Revolution*, p. 242.

5: The best general sources are Slaughter, *Whiskey Rebellion*, and Kohn, *Eagle and Sword*. Jefferson's brief, unmemorable reply to Washington's Sept. 15 proclamation may have read that way because the master of Monticello had already kept an express messenger waiting for twenty minutes. A more revealing measure of his feelings came in a Sept. 30 conversation with George Mason, whose sentiments against Hamilton he quoted with relish. According to Jefferson, Mason held the secretary of the treasury responsible for more harm to America than all of Great Britain's fleets and armies.

6: Jefferson's Oct. 1 meeting with the president is described in the "Anas" for that date. Washington's religious views are debunked by Paul F. Boller, *George Washington and Religion* (Dallas, 1963). For a very different perspective, see Nelly Custis's correspondence with Jared Sparks, an early Washington biographer, as summarized in Hart, *Honor to George Washington*, vol. 9. Nelly recalled that her grandfather never missed Sunday services in Philadelphia or New York unless indisposed. The president stood during the devotional parts of the service "as was then the custom." See also Baker, *Washington After the Revolution*, p. 297.

There are several firsthand descriptions of Washington saying grace at meals as well as a story, perhaps apocryphal, that testifies to his humor and his devotion. Overlooking the presence at his table of a minister, Washington unthinkingly slighted his guest by pronouncing a blessing of his own. Mrs. Washington upbraided her husband, leading to this punning response: "My dear, I wish all men to know that I am not a graceless man." For details of Washington's treatment of his workers, paid and unpaid, see Ford's chapter "Washington as Employer and Master," *True George Washington*, and Flexner, *George Washington: Anguish and Farewell*, pp. 112–25.

7: The vice president's unhappy experiences during the 1792 campaign are captured in Smith, *John Adams*, 2:826–33. Eliza Powel's Nov. 17, 1792, letter to her friend pleading for him to accept a second term can be read at Mount Vernon. David Humphreys's congratulations of Mar. 24, 1793, are reproduced in Humphreys, *Life and Times of David Humphreys*, 2:169–73. See Jefferson's "Anas" for Dec. 13 for the slightly mystifying encounter in which the president broadly hinted at his own plans to leave office halfway through his second term.

CHAPTER 8: A HIGHLY FAVORED AGE

1: Dunlap's *American Daily Advertiser*, Jan. 10, 1793, and Jacob Hiltzheimer's diary both describe Jean Pierre Blanchard's daring ascent and brief airborne journey; they are quoted in Baker, *Washington After the Revolution*, p. 248. The mocking ode "O Federal Town" is reproduced in Stewart, *Opposition Press*, p. 77. Jefferson's "Anas" for Feb. 7 sets out his version of the meeting with Washington. For Giles's attack on the treasury secretary, see Mitchell, *Alexander Hamilton*, pp. 247–66. Typical of the journalistic criticism being aimed at Washington in the last weeks before his second administration is this shaft fashioned by Freneau personally and appearing in the Jan. 30, 1793, *National Gazette:* "It appears . . . that a new order of citizens has been created . . . consisting only of the officers of the federal government. The privileges of this order . . . consist in sharing exclusively in the profits of the $25,000 allowed for the President's table and in the honor of gazing upon him once a week at his levees." For Washington's second inaugural as viewed by the press (and Edward Thornton), see Baker, *Washington After the Revolution*, pp. 251–53.

2: General sources for this period include Sears, *George Washington and the French Revolution;* De Conde, *Entangling Alliances;* Thomas, *American Neutrality in 1793*; and Minnigerode, *Jefferson*. Also useful are Garry Wills, "Liberté, Fraternité, Animosité," *American Heritage*, July–August 1989, and "Let Them Eat Hot Dogs," *New Republic*, July 31, 1989, in which Henry Fairlie comments upon revolutions on both sides of the Atlantic. See Jefferson's "Anas" for Feb. 25 and Mar. 30 for the Cabinet's debate over whether to receive Genêt, May 6 for the larger issue of U.S. neutrality.

3: An excellent source is Hazen, *Contemporary American Opinion of the French Revolution;* also see Foner, *Democratic-Republican Societies*, as well as De Conde, *Entangling Alliances*, Garvan, *Federal Philadelphia*, and Childs, *French Refugee Life*. The story of Talleyrand and the aborted émigré colony of Asylum is in Young, *Robert Morris*, pp. 189–90. Griswold, *Republican Court*, p. 332, tells of the mismatch involving France's future king and William Bingham's daughter. Jefferson's stormy encounter with the president over Freneau's latest attacks is in the "Anas," May 23.

4: For background on Genêt, see Bathe, *Citizen Genêt*; Ammon, *Genêt Mission;* and Minnigerode, *Jefferson*. Freneau's public letter rebuking Washington's neutrality is in the *National Gazette*, May 15, 1793. For Genêt's uproarious reception, see Peterson, *Thomas Jefferson and the New Nation*, pp. 487–88. Genet's June 19, 1793, letter to Mangourit, reproduced in Chinard, *George Washington as the French Knew Him*, p. 104, suggests both the diplomat's cockiness and his misreading of American opinion.

5: Link, *Democratic-Republican Societies*, provides details on the rapidly growing democratic movement, as does Foner, *Democratic-Republican Societies*. Cabinet discussions over the *Little Sarah* are reported in detail in Jefferson's "Anas" for July 5–15. For another view of the same events, see Miller, *Alexander Hamilton*, pp. 372–78.

6: Jefferson's "Anas" for Aug. 1–3 vividly depicts the breakdown of civility within the Cabinet and the loss of presidential composure that may have led Jefferson, a generation later, to characterize Washington's personality as "naturally irritable." For the Jay-King-Hamilton affair, see Monaghan, *John Jay*, pp. 351–60. Angered by Washington's seeming ingratitude for their blatantly political attacks on the French envoy, the chief justice and senator from New York dashed off a heated protest, leading Washington in turn to compose a defense of his conduct. When passions cooled, Washington burned both documents as Jay looked on.

CHAPTER 9: PHILADELPHIA FEVERS

1: For Polly Lear's death, see Ray Brighton, *Checkered Career of Tobias Lear* (Portsmouth, N.H., 1985), pp. 114–15, and Martha Washington to Fanny Basset Washington, Aug. 4, 1793. Polly's special status in the Washington household is verified by Decatur, *Private Affairs of George Washington*, p. 129. The standard account of the epidemic is Powell, *Bring Out Your Dead*. Modern sources include Weigley, *Philadelphia*. Benjamin Rush claimed success in ninety-nine out of one hundred cases, blaming his rare failures on "the pride, ignorance and prejudice of my medical brethren." Jefferson's scathing comment on Hamilton's alleged cowardice is in Malone, *Jefferson and the Rights of Man* (New York, 1962), p. 141. Clarfield, *Timothy Pickering and the American Republic*, pp. 146–47, tells the sad tale of Pickering's son, who fell victim to the fever and his father's faith in Rush's heroic remedies. For Hamilton's difficulties in escaping quarantined Philadelphia, see Alexander, *To Covet Honor*, pp. 280–82. Oliver Wolcott's harsh strictures on human nature are in Gibbs, *History of the Washington and Adams Administrations* (New York, 1857), 1:109. Freneau's fate is described by Leary, *That Rascal Freneau*, pp. 240–46, and *A Literary History of the United States*, p. 174, ed. Spiller et al.

2: A contemporary account of the ceremony on Jenkins Hill is in the *Alexandria Gazette*, Sept. 21, 1793, reproduced in Baker, *Washington After the Revolution*, p. 264. For information on Blodgett's Hotel, see Aikman, *Rider with Destiny*, pp. 109–10. Randolph's part in the debate over where to convene Congress is in Reardon, *Edmund Randolph*, pp. 240–42.

3: "The Heirs of Madame Guillotine," *U.S. News and World Report*, July 1989, recounts the strange twists by which a device promoted as a humane way to kill graduated into a bloody symbol of revolutionary terror. Jefferson's "Anas" for November 1793 provides abundant detail of stormy Cabinet debates over Genêt and the British Provision Order. See also Malone, *Jefferson and the Ordeal of Liberty*, pp. 147–60.

4: Many details in this section are drawn from the popular press of the period, above all *Dunlap's American Daily Advertiser*. Other general sources include Garvan, *Federal Philadelphia;* Weigley, *Philadelphia;* Griswold, *Republican Court;* Decatur, *Private Affairs of George Washington;* and Marshall B. Davidson, "The Athens of America," *American Heritage*, February 1961. The New Theatre is well described in Destler, *Joshua Coit*, pp. 57–60. Additional details about the cultural side of Federal Philadelphia are in Leary, *That Rascal Freneau*, pp. 195–96, and Christman, *First Federal Congress*, p. 199. The dazzling Mrs. Bingham appears on p. 177 of Weigley and pp. 200–1 of Christman. The Trumbull-Giles controversy is in Griswold, p. 363.

5: George Washington's use of time is attested to by Crèvecoeur in Chinard, *George Washington as the French Knew Him*, pp. 119–20. Henry Wansey's breakfast encounter is preserved in Nevins, *American Social History as Recorded by English Travelers*, pp. 44–46. Martha's daily routine is in Conway, *George Washington of Mount Vernon*, pp. 1-xxxii. The first lady's disapproval of anything like coddling the young is displayed in Bourne, *First Family*, p. 143. For young Tub, see Thane, *Mount Vernon Family*, p. 108, and Martha Washington to Fanny Basset Washington, Sept. 28, 1794. Martha's criticism of Nelly is in her June 8, 1789, letter to Fanny Basset Washington. Another good source is Donald Jackson, "George Washington's Beautiful Nelly," *American Heritage*, February 1977.

6: Washington's birthday celebrations and the partisan reactions they inspired are recounted by Peter Van Gaasbeek to John Addison, Feb. 23, 1794, Van Gaasbeek Papers, Senate House Museum, Kingston, N.Y. For Congress's debate over military preparedness, see Smith, *Shaping of America*, pp. 216–18, and Flexner, *George Washington: Anguish and Farewell*, pp. 132–35. Hamilton's angling for a diplomatic appointment is in Alexander, *To Covet Honor*, pp. 287–88. Jay's chilly letter to his wife on the prospects for war is in Baker, *Washington After the Revolution*, p. 275.

CHAPTER 10: "DASH TO THE MOUNTAINS, JERSEY BLUE"

1: Washington's discomfiture over slavery was longstanding. As early as 1783 Lafayette had invited his revolutionary comrade to join with him in "purchasing a small estate, where we may try the experiment to free the Negroes, and use them only as tenants." In his response, Washington praised his friend's benevolence while putting off concrete action until the two men could discuss it face to face. Needless to say, nothing came of the scheme. Monaghan, *John Jay*, is the standard biography of the first chief justice. Bemis's *Jay's Treaty* holds a similar position among students of the controversial treaty with Britain. See Flexner, *George Washington: Anguish and Farewell*, pp. 139–43, for insights into Jay's aristocratic station. The story of Monroe's appointment is told by Ammon, *James Monroe*, pp. 112–17.

2: Martha's concerns are vividly etched in her June 30, 1794, letter to her niece Fanny, preserved at Mount Vernon. Nor had things improved much two weeks later, when the first lady reported to the same correspondent that the president's back injury was likely to bother him as long as he lived. For the Morris-Greenleaf-Nicholson speculations (which in time devoured the firm of Tobias Lear and Company), see Bob Arnehill, "Tracking the Speculators," *Washington History*, Spring–Summer 1991, pp. 113–25. John Quincy Adams's observations of Washington and his Native American guests are quoted in Baker, *Washington After the Revolution*, pp. 279–80.

3: Long the standard account of the Whiskey Rebellion, Baldwin's *Whiskey Rebels* has more recently been supplemented — perhaps even supplanted — by Slaughter's *Whiskey Rebellion*. Slaughter is noticeably more sympathetic to the Washington administration and does an excellent job of linking the unrest of 1792 to the 1794 explosion and its sequel, the resignation of Edmund Randolph. See Smith, *Shaping of America*, pp. 227–42, for the simultaneous uprisings in western Pennsylvania and Wayne's successful campaign in the West. Also Richard H. Kohn, "The Washington Administration's Decision to Crush the Whiskey Rebellion," *Journal of American History*, 59 (1972), pp. 567–84, and Bernard A. Weisberger, "Seeking a Real Tax Revolt," *American Heritage*, May–June 1991. Nelly Custis's Sept. 8, 1794, letter to Elizabeth B. Gibson describes the charms of Germantown, a subject also covered in *Washington Visits Germantown* (Germantown, Pa.: Germantown Historical Society, 1932).

4: General accounts for the period include Kohn, *Eagle and Sword*, Wildes, *Anthony Wayne*, and Sword, *President Washington's Indian War*. See Elroy M. Avery, "The Battle of Fallen Timbers," *American Heritage*, August 1958; Spaulding, *United States Army in War and Peace*, pp. 168–75; Mitchell, *Alexander Hamilton*, pp. 308–25.

5: Jackson and Twohig, *Diaries of George Washington*, 6:178–97, provide the best source for the president's expedition into the heart of disaffected Pennsylvania. Washington's enthusiastic reception in Carlisle is reported in Baker, *Washington After the Revolution*, pp. 285–86. Howell's anthem of solidarity is in Carroll and Ashworth, *George Washington*, p. 208n.

6: On Nov. 30, 1794, Jonathan Trumbull, Jr., wrote to his father about a recent meeting with the president: "I found him in fine health and mighty good spirits — highly pleased with the cheerful temper and alacrity of the militia troops — and anticipating the happy issue of this unfortunate affair — unfortunate I say as I fear it may prove in its temporary influence on Mr. Jay's negotiation." Independence National Historical Park Archives. For Jefferson's acerbic response to Washington's speech, see Malone, *Jefferson and the Ordeal of Liberty*, pp. 188–90. Details of the ensuing seriocomic debate are in Baldwin, *Whiskey Rebels*, pp. 261–62. Flexner, *George Washington: Anguish and Farewell*, pp. 182–92, examines Washington's general attitude toward the Democratic societies. The appearance of MacPherson's Jersey Blues was described in Dunlap and Claypoole's *American Daily Advertiser*, Dec. 11, 1794.

CHAPTER 11: DOWN FROM OLYMPUS

1: The *Aurora*'s attacks on Jay's Treaty, part of the editor's escalating campaign to discredit Washington and his administration, are recounted by Tagg, *Benjamin Franklin Bache*, pp. 239–44. Hamilton's lament about the cost of government service is in Griswold, *Republican Court*, p. 352.

2: General sources include Perkins, *First Rapprochement*, Bemis, *Jay's Treaty*, and Monaghan, *John Jay*. Miller, in *Federalist Era*, pp. 164–68, convincingly disputes the traditional view that Hamilton undermined Jay's bargaining position by informing Hammond in advance that the United States had no interest in joining a league of armed neutrals, spearheaded by the Scandinavian countries. He argues that both Hamilton and Jay recognized the negative effect upon the negotiations of empty threats. Miller, *Alexander Hamilton*, pp. 422–23, examines the former secretary's strategy regarding the controversial Article 12.

3: For Bache's spirited campaign to inflame public opinion against the treaty, see Tagg, *Benjamin Franklin Bache*, pp. 247–50. Writing of Jay at the height of the debate, Jefferson claimed "that while all hands were below deck mending sails, splicing ropes, and every one at his own business, and the captain in his cabin attending to the logbook and chart, a rogue of a pilot has run them into an enemy's port" (Monaghan, *John Jay*, p. 394). Popular reaction to the treaty is in Schachner, *Founding Fathers*, pp. 365–69, and Smith, *Shaping of America*, pp. 223–25. For the tumultuous New York rallies of July 1794, see Mitchell, *Alexander Hamilton*, pp. 341–43. Hamilton's newspaper campaign moved one angry Republican editor to fume:

> Sure George the Third will find employ
> For one so wise and wary,
> He'll call Camillus home with joy
> And make him secretary.

The conflicting signals coming out of Washington's Cabinet are in Carroll and Ashworth, *George Washington*, pp. 276–78.

4: Reardon, *Edmund Randolph*, is the only modern biography of this neglected founder. Still useful is Moncure D. Conway's *Omitted Chapters of History Disclosed in the Life and Papers of Edmund Randolph* (New York, 1888).

5: Excellent modern accounts of the Washington-Randolph break are Mary K. Bonstell Tachau, "George Washington and the Reputation of Edmund Randolph," *Journal of American History* 73 (1986); Irving Brant, "Edmund Randolph, Not Guilty!," *William and Mary Quarterly*, April 1950; and "Was Edmund Randolph in Default?" Appendix VII-1 in Carroll and Ashworth, *George Washington*. For Pickering, see Clarfield, *Timothy Pickering and the American Republic*, and White, *Federalists*, pp. 194–97. Gibbs, *Memoirs of the Administration of Washington and Adams*, conveys both Wolcott's urbanity and his High Federalist contempt for democracy.

6: Tachau's careful reading of the incriminating dispatches in both French and English translations makes a strong case for Randolph's naiveté, not his treachery. The disgraced secretary's frantic attempts to reach Fauchet are in Reardon, *Edmund Randolph*, pp. 312–15. See also Edmund Randolph, *A Vindication of Mr. Randolph's Resignation* (Philadelphia, 1795). Again, one is indebted to Tachau for pointing out Randolph's error in relying on the badly translated versions of Fauchet's dispatches handed him by his accusers, thereby surrendering the fight before it was even fairly begun. Griswold, *Republican Court*, p. 305, reports Washington's profane comment on Randolph's veracity.

CHAPTER 12: "THE GOOD CITIZEN"

1: McHenry's limitations are expounded at length in the Washington-Hamilton correspondence for the period; see White, *Federalists*, pp. 154–55. Oliver Wolcott said of his new Cabinet colleague that he was "a man of honor . . . entirely trustworthy" and politically compatible, "but he is not skilled in the details of executive business and he is at the head of a difficult and unpopular department." The Rutledge fracas is in Ernst, *Rufus King*, p. 211. Angry press reaction to Washington's increasingly open Federalism is in Link, *Democratic-Republican Societies*, pp. 193–95, as well as Stewart, *Opposition Press*, and Leary, *That Rascal Freneau*.

Adet's scathing comments on the president are in Chinard, *George Washington as the French Knew Him*, pp. 106–8. Freneau is quoted on Washington's aspiration to kingship in Carroll and Ashworth, *George Washington*, p. 321n. For the *Aurora*'s criticism of "Saint Washington" and his financial embarrassments, see Tagg, *Benjamin Franklin Bache*, p. 278.

2: The complete text of Washington's address is in Fitzpatrick's edition of his papers, 34:386–93.

3: Madison, writing to Jefferson on Feb. 29, 1796, noted that the House rejected, 50–38, a motion to adjourn for half an hour to pay its respects to the president on his birthday — a good measure of just how divided Washington's government had become. For descriptions of the birthday celebrations as carried in Claypoole's *American Daily Advertiser* for Feb. 23, 1796, and Isaac Weld, Jr.'s *Travels Through the States of North America during the Years 1795, 1796, and 1797*, see Baker, *Washington After the Revolution*, p. 320. The vice president's letter to his wife of March 5 recounting his latest meeting with Washington is in Baker, *Washington After the Revolution*, p. 321. The standard source for the Treaty of San Lorenzo is Bemis, *Pinckney's Treaty;* for the shameful treatment of Gallatin, see Smith, *Shaping of America*, p. 237.

4: John Adams's satisfaction is evident in his letter to his wife, dated Mar. 25, 1796, and quoted in Baker, *Washington After the Revolution*, p. 322. Yet he was far from certain, even now, that the old president would finally step aside. As late as midsummer, the vice president was writing that while friends assumed Washington meant what he said about retiring — "Pickering has given out publicly that he will" and "Mrs. Washington takes it for granted that he will" — still, he could always change his mind "and thus furnish an apology for accepting after all the talk," July 17, 1796, in vol. 3, *Diary of John Adams, 1782–1804*, ed. Lyman Butterfield (Cambridge, Mass., 1961).

For the Cabinet discussions over the House's demand for papers relating to Jay's mission, see Carroll and Ashworth, *George Washington*, pp. 353–55. Flexner, an art historian with a rare gift for literary composition, employed both talents in describing the Washington–Gilbert Stuart relationship in *George Washington: Anguish and Farewell*, pp. 309–17. The joke about Washington's temper is in Bellamy, *Private Life of George Washington*, pp. 53–54. For the House's climactic debate over funding the treaty, see Brant, *James Madison*, pp. 438–39, and Miller, *Alexander Hamilton*, pp. 432–33.

5: The standard source is Paltsis, *Washington's Farewell Address*. For Hamilton's role in editing the great document, see Mitchell, *Alexander Hamilton*, pp. 388–95. Thomas Twining's visit is recounted in Robert C. Alberts, "Protégé of Cornwallis, Guest of Washington," *American Heritage*, August 1973. Henrietta Liston's quotable descriptions of Washington and his court form the heart of "A Diplomat's Wife in Philadelphia: Letters of Henrietta Liston, 1796–1800," ed. Bradford Perkins, *William and Mary Quarterly*, 3rd ser., XI (1954): 592–632. Washington's interest in books is detailed in Longmore, *Invention of George Washington*, pp. 213–26. For his fascination with Cato, see Samuel Eliot Morison's "Young Man Washington," in Smith, *George Washington, A Profile*.

The end of Monroe's mission is described by De Conde, *Entangling Alliances*, pp. 380–88. The fateful July 4 toast is recounted by Cresson, *James Monroe*, pp. 155. See also Zahniser, *Charles Cotesworth Pinckney*. The leak of Cabinet information dating from Washington's original Neutrality Proclamation appeared in the June 9, 1796, *Aurora*. For Jefferson's response, see Malone, *Jefferson and the Ordeal of Liberty*, pp. 269–72. The retired secretary of state did not stint in his personal criticism of Washington, writing about this time that "his mind has been so long used to unlimited applause that it could not brook contradiction, or even advice offered unasked." Continuing, Jefferson said that the best course for "the republican interest" was "to soothe him by flattering where they could approve his measures, and to be silent where they disapprove." It was a telling comment.

CHAPTER 13: AN HONORABLE DISCHARGE

1: For Latrobe's comments on Mount Vernon, see Paul F. Norton and E. M. Halliday, "Latrobe's America," *American Heritage*, August 1962, and Thane, *Potomac Squire*, pp. 356–58.

2: Monroe's majestic patronization of Washington is quoted in Alexander, *To Covet Honor*, p. 316. The politically intrusive counsel of Delacroix to Adet is outlined in De Conde, *Entangling Alliances*, p. 457. See also Zahniser, *Charles Cotesworth Pinckney*.

3: See Paltsis, *Washington's Farewell Address*, and Carroll and Ashworth, *George Washington*. An unlikely source of praise for the president's valedictory was the London *Times*, which on Nov. 11, 1706, opined, "The authority of this Revolutionist may be set up against the wild and wicked Revolutionists of Europe, if not as Altar against Altar at least as Altar against Sacrilege." Washington's emphasis on duty and interest as twin pillars of human nature and political service lay at the core of his thinking. See Morgan's *Genius of George Washington*, and his essay on Washington in *Meaning of Independence*.

4: James McHenry and Bart Dandridge both reported to the president that his address had met with universal approval. A more realistic reading of the public's mood is in Carroll and Ashworth, *George Washington*, p. 410n. La Rochefoucauld's observations are quoted in Chinard, *George Washington as the French Knew Him*, pp. 111–13. For Hamilton's bungling efforts to replace Adams in the campaign of 1796, see Miller, *Federalist Era*, pp. 198–202. Malone, *Jefferson and the Ordeal of Liberty*, pp. 279–83, describes the campaign of abuse aimed at both major contenders. Abigail Adams's well-founded suspicions of Hamilton are in Smith, *John Adams*, 2:907–9. Rather condescendingly, the vice president regretted what he called "the sting at the retiring hero . . . Science in some of its branches he may not have been possessed [of] in any eminent degree, but talents of a very superior kind are his. I wish I had as good." The amusing tale of the French mistresses is in Alexander, *To Covet Honor*, p. 319. For Adet's campaign activities, see De Conde, *Entangling Alliances*, pp. 440–43, 471–78. Mrs. Liston's account of the president's annual address is in the *William and Mary Quarterly*, 3rd ser., XI (1954): 606. For Paine's diatribe see Thomas Paine, *Letter to George Washington* (Philadelphia, 1796).

5: French designs on the American West are explored in De Conde, *Entangling Alliances*, pp. 449–55. Oliver Wolcott, not surprisingly, had no difficulty telling which of Europe's warring powers posed the greatest danger should it get a foothold on American territory. The French, he said, would be "like ants and weasels in our barns and granaries." For the sad story of young Custis the scholar, see Bourne, *First Family*, pp. 177–78, Thane, *Potomac Squire*, pp. 359–60, and Washington's correspondence for the period.

6: A general source for the period is Custis's *Recollections of Washington*. Washington's crowded social schedule during his final weeks in office is in Baker, *Washington After the Revolution*, pp. 338–42. Henrietta Liston's wonderful description of the final Birthday Ball is in the *William and Mary Quarterly*, 3rd ser., XI (1954): 608. For the March 3 dinner, see Baker, *Washington After the Revolution*, p. 343. The inauguration was covered at length by Claypoole's *American Daily Advertiser*, reproduced in Baker, *Washington After the Revolution*, pp. 344–45. Nelly Custis's emotional state is in Moore, *Family Life of George Washington*, p. 143. See also Carroll and Ashworth, *George Washington*, pp. 436–39, and *The Literary Museum*, February 1797, pp. 109–10, for Philadelphia's lavish good-byes. Lear's help in the executive move is detailed by Bourne, *First Family*, p. 173. For the Eliza Powell–Washington exchange of letters see Carroll and Ashworth, *George Washington*, pp. 449–50.

CHAPTER 14: AT THE BOTTOM OF THE HILL

1: Nelly's report of life along the Potomac is in her Mar. 18, 1797, letter to Elizabeth Bordley. For her resentment of the press, see Donald Jackson's "George Washington's Beautiful Nelly," *American Heritage*, February 1977, p. 83; see also Thane, *Mount Vernon Family*, p. 85. Martha's letters to Eliza Powel of May 1 and July 14, 1797, detail her domestic problems. See also Bourne, *First Family*, pp. 195–96. As for her husband's growing repugnance to slavery, Washington had come a long way since 1766, when he shipped a disobedient Negro off to the West Indies with the following instructions: "With this letter comes a Negro (Tom) which I beg the favor of you to sell in any of the islands you may go to, for whatever he will fetch, and bring me in return for him one hhd (*sic*) of best molasses, one ditto of best rum, one barrel of limes, if good and cheap, one pot of tamarinds, containing about 10 pounds, two small ditto of mixed sweetmeats, about 5 pounds each. And the residue, much or little, in good old spirits. That this fellow is both a rogue and a runaway . . . I shall not pretend to deny. But that he is exceedingly healthy, strong, and good at the hoe, the whole neighborhood can testify . . . which gives me reason to hope he may with your good management sell well, if kept clean and trimmed up a little when offered for sale" (Ford, *George Washington as an Employer*, p. 145).

The former president's daily routine is in Nelly's letter to Elizabeth Bordley, Feb. 23, 1823. Custis's word picture of Washington making his daily rounds is quoted in Haworth, *George Washington*, p. 309. For Washington's interest in art, see Wendy Wick Reaves, "The Prints," *Antiques, The Magazine*, February 1989, pp. 501–10. Martha denied her husband had been seriously ill in her July 14, 1797, letter to Eliza Powel, the same missive in which she refuted the rumor that Nelly had recently been injured in a carriage accident. For John Bernard's remarkable encounter with Washington, see chapters 5 and 7 of his *Retrospections of America, 1797–1811* (New York, 1887).

2: Adams's address and the reaction it provoked are in Smith, *John Adams*, 2:956–57. See also Clarfield, *Timothy Pickering and American Diplomacy, 1795–1800*, pp. 95–105, as well as Leary, *That Rascal Freneau*, p. 280, and Stewart, *Opposition Press*, p. 285. The Blount controversy is in Miller, *Federalist Era*, pp. 186–92. Malone seems excessively generous in his treatment of the notorious Mazzei letter, saying of Jefferson's choice of words, "Though often stilted, he was rarely vulgar." He contrasts Jefferson's language favorably with the more violent tone adopted by Bache and Paine, while conceding that as far as the vice president was concerned, "there appears to be no record that he expressed any regret over their excesses . . . Not until he himself became president did he become thoroughly aware of the dangers that lie in the abuse of freedom of the press" (Malone, *Jefferson and the Ordeal of Liberty*, pp. 303–11). Nelly's Federalist loyalties are displayed extravagantly in her Nov. 23, 1797, letter to Elizabeth Bordley.

3: For the Washingtons' contracting circle of friends, see Martha's letter to David Humphreys, June 26, 1797. For a good picture of the Law and Peters' households, see Niemcewicz, *Under Their Own Vine and Fig Tree*, pp. 84–87. Washington's financial difficulties during this period occupy much of his correspondence; see also Thane, *Potomac Squire*, pp. 370–71. Young Fayette's departure is in Ford, *True George Washington*, p. 235.

4: Washington's detachment is described in Custis, *Recollections*, p. 171. For a good account of the XYZ Affair, see Leonard Baker, *John Marshall*, pp. 230–53. Monroe's efforts at vindication are in Ammon, *Genêt Mission*, pp. 165–69. Abigail Adams had a characteristically tart comment to make regarding Washington's birthday observance in a Feb. 15, 1798, letter to her sister: "The

President of the United States to attend the celebration of the birthday in his public character of a private citizen! For in no other light can General Washington be now considered, however good, however great his character, which no person more respects than his successor . . . That the Virginians should celebrate the day is natural and proper if they please, and so may any others who choose. But the propriety of doing it in the capital, in the *Metropolis* of America as these proud Philadelphians have publicly named it, and inviting the Head of the Nation to come and do it too, in my view is ludicrous beyond compare." For a similarly brisk characterization of Bache, see Smith, *John Adams*, 2:961–62. At the same time that Washington wrote his oft-quoted letter to Sally Fairfax, Martha sent along a communication of her own, dated May 17, 1798, and preserved at Mount Vernon. Additional information about Patty and Eliza is in Thane, *Mount Vernon Family*, pp. 48–51.

5: Niemcewicz, *Vine and Fig Tree*, pp. 95–108, is a richly detailed account of the Polish visitor's extended visit to Washington's Mount Vernon. Events leading up to Washington's military appointment and his subsequent misunderstanding with President Adams are exhaustively covered in Washington's correspondence for the period. See also Carroll and Ashworth, *George Washington*, pp. 518–20, and Flexner, *George Washington: Anguish and Farewell*, pp. 394–400.

CHAPTER 15: POTOMAC TWILIGHT

1: The best work on the Alien and Sedition Acts is Miller, *Crisis in Freedom*. Interestingly, even Hamilton took a dim view of the legislation. "Let us not be cruel or violent," he wrote to his Federalist disciple Oliver Wolcott before reminding him, "Let us not establish a tyranny. Energy is a very different thing from violence." Washington's courtship of Knox and his humiliation of Adams is in Schachner, *Founding Fathers*, pp. 471–74. See also Thane, *Potomac Squire*, pp. 393–94.

2: Adams's dilemma is in Smith, *John Adams*, 2:980–83; see also, Carroll and Ashworth, *George Washington*, pp. 532–34. Still furious at being passed over, Knox told a friend that "the miserable animals who were the cause of it are known to me, and ere long they will be compelled to hide their heads in their original obscurity" (Mitchell, *Alexander Hamilton*, p. 431).

3: Freeman, *Washington's Diary*, 6:323–26, describes his Philadelphia journey. "Memorandum of an Interview," dated Nov. 13, 1798 (37:18–20), of the Fitzpatrick edition of Washington's papers tells of the stormy meeting with George Logan. Adams's Dec. 8 address is in Smith, *John Adams*, 2:990–91. Indicative of the primitive state of the nation's military organization is this account of a visit to Secretary McHenry's office by a former French officer: "It was about eleven o'clock in the morning when I called. There was no sentinel at the door; all the rooms, the walls of which were covered with maps, were open, and in the midst of the solitude I found two clerks each sitting at his own table, engaged in writing. At last I met a servant, or rather *the* servant, for there was but one in the house, and asked for the secretary. He replied that his master was absent for the moment, having gone to the barber's to be shaved. Mr. McHenry's name figured in the State Budget for $2,000, a salary quite sufficient in a country where the secretary of war goes in the morning to his neighbor, the barber, to get shaved" (White, *Federalists*, p. 147).

For Parkinson's disappointing visit to Mount Vernon, see Carroll and Ashworth, *George Washington*, pp. 557–58.

4: Nelly's description of her unlikely beau is in her Mar. 20, 1791, letter to Elizabeth Bordley. More details are conveyed in a second note to the same correspondent, dated Feb. 3, 1799. See also Thane, *Mount Vernon Family*, pp. 87–88, Bourne, *First Family*, pp. 191–92. For Jefferson's response to the Alien and Sedition Acts, see Mapp, *Thomas Jefferson*, pp. 374–83; also Schachner, *Founding Fathers*, pp. 485–91. For Henry's final days, see Robert Douthat Meade, *Patrick Henry, Practical Revolutionary* (Philadelphia, 1969), pp. 447–50. Nelly's wedding is in Thane, *Mount Vernon Family*, pp. 90–91. Her reported fondness for sliding down banisters is recorded in Conway, *George Washington of Mount Vernon*, pp. 1-xxxxii.

5: Hamilton's relationship with Wilkinson is described in Mitchell, *Alexander Hamilton*, pp. 440–52. For Gerry's return and Adams's politically courageous course, see Page, *John Adams*, 2:998–1003. The diplomatic pipeline opened through the president's son is described by Bemis, *John Quincy Adams*, pp. 98–102. In later years John Adams himself said that Talleyrand's letter was the decisive factor in his peace initiative while crediting his son's reports, as well as correspondence from Americans in France (Joel Barlow among them), for creating the right mood for action.

6: Washington's Capitol Hill building project is described in his correspondence of the period as well as in Aikman, *Rider with Destiny*, pp. 119–20. The image of the former president crossing the Potomac is from a Mar. 29, 1856, letter from Henry Lunt to his grandchildren, preserved at Mount Vernon. The Washingtons' decision to skip the Alexandria ball is in Ford, *True George Washington*, p. 188. Washington's will and related schedule of property is printed in full in the Fitzpatrick edition of his papers, 37:275–303. See also Prussing, *Estate of George Washington*.

7: Freeman, *Washington's Diary*, vol. 6, Sept. 1–6, 1799, tells of Martha's illness. For Nelly's lying in and the visit to Mount Vernon by the Carringtons, see Thane, *Potomac Squire*, pp. 403–4. More information about Mrs. Lewis and Woodlawn is in Minnie Kendell Lowther's *Mount Vernon* (Chicago, 1933), pp. 133–38.

8: My account of Washington's death is based on Tobias Lear, *Letters and Recollections*, pp. 129–41, as well as the signed statement of Dr. James Craik and Dr. Elisha C. Dick, which first appeared in the *Alexandria Gazette*, Dec. 21, 1799, and Appendix VII-2 of Carroll and Ashworth, *George Washington*. See also Walter A. Wells, "Last Illness and Death of Washington," *Virginia Medical Monthly*, 53 (1926–27). While it has been popular to suggest that Washington's doctors killed him by excessive bleeding, it might more fairly be said, given the limitations of medical knowledge and procedure, that Washington was correct in regarding his sickness as fatal from the first. For details on Brown and Dick, see Carroll and Ashworth, *George Washington*, pp. 621n–22n.

EPILOGUE: "OUR WASHINGTON"

William Thornton's extraordinary plan to restore his friend to life is in an undated document entitled "Sleep" and preserved among the Thornton papers at Mount Vernon. For the funeral, see Brighton, *The Checkered Career of Tobias Lear*, pp. 165–68. John Marshall's tribute is quoted at length in David Ramsay, *The Life of George Washington*, pp. 319–20. For Stuart's artistic license, see Dixon Wecter's "George Washington and Parson Weems," in *George Washington: A Portrait*, ed. James Morton Smith. The same article contains Emerson's dismissive quote. Napoleon's deathbed comparison is in *A Literary History of the United States*, ed. Spiller et al., p. 200.

Paine's bitter directions to any sculptor portraying Washington are in Link, *Democratic-Republican Societies*, p. 196. Fisher Ames's eulogy before the Massachusetts legislature early in 1800 said of Washington: "Mankind perceived some change in their ideas of greatness . . . The splendor of power, and even the name of Conqueror, had grown dim in their eyes . . . They knew and they felt that the world's wealth, and its empire too, would be a bribe far beneath his acceptance" (quoted by Robert C. Winthrop, Feb. 21, 1885, Baker Collection, Pennsylvania Historial Society). For Jefferson's posthumous portrait of his onetime mentor and later adversary, see his letter of Jan. 2, 1814, to Walter James, "Anas," pp. 343–46. After Washington's death, Lear "withdrew" potentially controversial documents from the president's archive. So he confided to Hamilton, raising the possibility that the secretary, desperate for cash, had deliberately destroyed politically embarrassing letters exchanged between Washington and Jefferson. Giving credence to this theory, advanced by Brighton in *Checkered Career of Tobias Lear*, is the fact that both Lear and the Mount Vernon overseer Albin Rawlins were subsequently compensated — Lear being named consul to Santo Domingo by President Jefferson, and Rawlins, who had shared Lear's privileged access to Washington's correspondence, becoming the manager of Lear's Walnut Tree Farm. Hounded by political enemies — including some pressing him for an accounting of the missing letters — and depressed, Lear shot himself in October 1816. He was fifty-five years old.

Washington's pre-inaugural lament about the end of happiness is in David Humphreys's "Life," p. 51. See also Edwin M. Yoder, Jr., "He Broke the Mold," *Washington Post*, Apr. 30, 1989.

Abolitionism, GW on, 29–30
Adams, Abigail: illness of, xiii; on
possibility of Washington's
death, xvi–xvii; on GW's
personality, xix; on Martha
Washington's levees, 28; Greenwich residence of, 38; on servants' drinking, 39; on misplaced criticism of John Adams,
47; on McGillivray and Indian
companions, 55; and move
to Philadelphia, 72; on dinner
with GW, 81–82; North-South
split forecast by, 131; John
Adams nurses, 149, 326, 334; on
abuse of GW, 153; on Anne
Bingham, 191–92; on Hamilton,
284, 340; on spitting representative, 318; on John Adams's peace
initiative, 341
Adams, Charles (son of John and
Abigail), xiii
Adams, Henry, on Pennsylvania,
33
Adams, John, 24, 46–47, 149–50;
influenza escaped by, xiii; and
GW during Revolution, 12; on
Boston vs. New York, 31–32;
Greenwich residence of, 38; Maclay on, 38; and Nootka Sound
crisis, 45, 68; as GW companion,
46; as VP and president of Senate, 46; and Hamilton, 46, 50,
284, 325, 336, 446; on GW's
success, 47; *Discourses on Davila*
by, 99; in Senate's reply to GW
address, 117; and Fenno, 118; as
successor to GW, 134; attempts

to replace as vice president, 149;
reelection of, 152; on vice presidency, 152; on attacks against
GW, 158; on celebration for
French Revolution, 160; on publishing of foreign policy negotiations, 187; and embargo bill,
202; university-importation
scheme of, 228; on GW retirement, 258, 260; at welcoming of
Lafayette's son, 263; quoted on
inauguration, 273; in 1796 campaign, 284–85, 288; GW's furnishings to, 292; as American
luminary, 306; on Marshall's biography of GW, 357; feelings of
toward GW, 359
PRESIDENCY OF: inauguration,
294–95; response to French hostilities, 306–7, 319–21, 332,
333; and Wolcott, 308; and XYZ
Affair, 317, 329; GW's support
for, 322–23; and GW's resuming
command, 323–25; in Quasi-
War with France, 326, 340, 343
(*see also* Quasi-War with
France); absences from capital,
326, 348; and Alien and Sedition
Acts, 326–27, 337–38; annual
address to Congress, 336; taxpayers' revolt crushed, 340;
GW's view of, 350
Adams, John Quincy, 292–93; as
GW companion, 46; John Adams
to on France, 149; at meeting
with Chickasaws, 210; social and
intellectual assimilation attempted by, 229; ambassadorship

Adams, John Quincy (*cont.*)
  to France suggested for, 271; and
  Murray, 341
Adams, Samuel, 12; John Adams at-
  tacked by, 150; and Adet's attack
  on GW, 252
Addison, Joseph, xix
Adet, Pierre, 248, 252, 257, 270,
  276, 281, 283, 285–86, 289
Agriculture: at Mount Vernon, 65–
  66, 138, 285, 336, 349; GW's
  comments on, 137–38
Alexander I (czar of Russia), 67
Algiers, U.S. captives in, 80, 82,
  131, 180, 258
Alien and Sedition Acts, 326–27,
  337–38; Duane targeted under
  Sedition Act, 349
Allen, John, 94
Allen, Richard, 181–82
Ambuscade, L' (French frigate),
  164, 174–75
American Daily Advertiser, 278
Ames, Fisher, 27, 55, 198, 265,
  284, 359
Anderson, James, 302, 318, 322,
  351
Anti-Federalists, 34
Arkwright, Richard, 76
Arnold, Benedict, 125, 243–44, 249
Articles of Confederation, 21
Assumption of state debt, 22–23;
  GW on, 30, 34–35, 42–43, 139;
  and Morris, 32; critics of, 33;
  and private speculation, 35; Ma-
  clay vs. proponents of, 35, 37;
  deal concluded on, 41–42; Vir-
  ginia protest against, 76; and
  Hamilton against state sover-
  eignty, 77
Aurora, 132, 204–5, 230, 235,
  253, 259, 262, 270, 285, 288,
  289, 295, 306, 358; under
  Duane, 330, 349

Bache, Benjamin Franklin, 132,
  133, 188, 231, 235, 236, 271,
  289, 319; and *Aurora,* 132, 204–
  5, 230, 235, 253, 259, 262, 270,
  289, 295, 306; death of, 330
Bank of the United States: Hamil-
  ton's proposal for, 78, 81, 82–
  83; instant success of, 107, 115;
  speculation over, 109–10; Fed-
  eral City loan rejected by, 286
Barbados, GW visits, 6
Barlow, Joel, 341
Bartram, William, 32
Bassett, Burwell, 152
Bassett, Fanny (niece of GW and
  Martha). *See* Washington, Fanny
  Bassett
Bassett, Nancy (sister of Martha
  Washington), 14
Battle of Fallen Timbers, 218–19
Battle of Monmouth Courthouse,
  16
Beckley, John, 252, 253
Beckwith, George, 45, 53, 55, 68,
  69, 81, 82
Bernard, John, 304–6
Bill of Rights, 22, 48
Bingham, Anne, 191–92, 236, 242,
  263–64
Bingham, William, 162–63, 177,
  191, 267; GW dines at mansion
  of, 334
Bipartisanship, GW's abandonment
  of, 252
Black Friday, 109
Blackwell, Reverend, 335
Blame America First, as compari-
  son with U.S.-French hostilities,
  319
Blanchard, Jean Pierre, 154
Blodgett, Samuel, 183
Blount, William, 309–10
Boston (British frigate), 174–75
Boston Massacre, 11

Boston Tea Party, 11
Boyd, Julian, 80
Braddock, Edward, 7, 123
Bradford, David, 212, 214, 216, 219–20, 223
Bradford, William (attorney general), 203, 213, 242, 251
Brant, Joseph, 137, 292
Brehan, Madame de, xiv
Brissot-Warville, Jean Pierre, 39
Britain. *See* Great Britain
Brown, Gustavus Richard, 353, 355
Brown, John (Kentucky senator), 170
"Brutus" (author), 118
Buchan, Earl of, 161, 308
Bunker Hill, 13
Burke, Edmund, 67, 99
Burr, Aaron, 98; and Hamilton-Reynolds affair, 122–23; and John Adams, 150; vice presidential votes for, 152; and Jay approval, 205; as ambassadorial candidate, 206; and Jay's Treaty, 235; and selection of generals against French, 336
Butler, Pierce, 96
Butler, Richard, 124

Camillus (pen name), 238
Capital city of U.S. *See* Washington, D.C.
Carmichael, William, 179
Carr, Peter, 310
Carrington, Betsey, 350
Carrington, Edward, 92, 96, 251, 265, 328, 350
Carroll, Charles, 301, 318
Cary, Robert, and Company, 10
Casa Yrujo, Marquis de (Carlos Martinez), 270
Catherine the Great, and Genêt, 164

Caunotaucarius (Indian name for GW), 55–56
Census, U.S., first, 116, 130
Charisma, of GW, 12
Charleston, South Carolina: GW's visit to, 95–98; Citizen Genêt in, 165
Chestnut, John, 102
"Child of Mount Vernon." *See* Custis, George Washington Parke
Childs, Francis, 84
China trade, 29, 80
Chisholm v. *Georgia,* 205
Christopher (GW servant), 311, 353, 355
Church, Angelica, 53, 201, 230
Claypoole, David, 278
Clinton, George, 29, 52, 57–58, 98, 149, 150, 152, 169, 234, 246
Cobb, David, 152
Coit, Joshua, 190, 192
Coles, Isaac, 104
Congress: arguments within, xvii; GW addresses to, 73, 74, 115–16, 147–48, 187, 255–56, 287–88; and St. Clair defeat, 124; reapportionment plan for vetoed, 130; and attempt to put Jefferson in line for presidency, 130; problem of convening during yellow fever epidemic, 184–85; Madison attempts to un-cloister, 190–91; House refuses recognition of GW's birthday, 257; Adams addresses, 306–7, 336
Constitution, U.S.: and Hamilton on implied powers, 78; and National Bank proposal, 82; GW as responsible for enacting, 85; and Madison's views on sovereignty, 118; and convening of Congress outside seat of government, 184; Eleventh Amendment to, 205; GW as defender of, 225, 226;

Constitution, U.S. (*cont.*)
and issue of disclosure of confidential treaty records, 261–62;
GW's view of (Jefferson), 360
Continental Association, 12
Controversies. *See* Issues and controversies in Washington presidency
Conway, Thomas, 17, 249
Conway Cabal, 249, 345
Cook, Joseph, 79
Cornplanter, Chief, 74, 292
Cornwallis, Lord Charles, 18, 102, 103, 267, 268
Cosway, Maria, 48
Coxe, Tench, 98
Craik, James, 10, 110, 149, 330, 346, 349, 350, 352, 353, 354, 355
Crèvecoeur, J. Hector St. John, 31
Cromwell, Oliver, GW compared to, 153, 262
Custis, Daniel Parke (first husband of Martha Washington), xviii
Custis, Eleanor (Nelly) (adopted granddaughter of GW), 18, 196–97, 227, 274; with GW at theater, xvi; on GW at home, 25; with Jefferson's daughter, 116; minor illnesses of, 195; and Germantown house, 213; at Adams inauguration, 295; on life at Mount Vernon, 301; on French, 311; on condition of GW's lands, 315; romance of implied, 318; in Martha Washington letter, 321; marriage of, 337, 339–40; in GW's will, 347; birth of daughter to, 350, 352
Custis, Elizabeth Parke (granddaughter of Martha Washington), 197, 312, 321
Custis, George Washington Parke (adopted grandson of GW), xix,

18, 92, 196, 290–92, 303, 314, 318, 321, 330, 337, 347, 354
Custis, Jack (son of Martha Washington), xviii, 18, 196, 321
Custis, Martha (Patsy) (daughter of Martha Washington), xviii, 13
Custis, Martha (Patsy) (granddaughter of Martha Washington), 312, 321

Dallas, Alexander, 171, 176
Dandridge, Bartholomew, 139, 168–69, 194, 195, 221, 295, 296
Dandridge, William, 14, 218
Danton, 159, 165
Davie, William Richardon, 349
Davis, Thomas (Reverend), 339, 357
Declaration of Independence, Farewell Address compared to, 279
Delacroix, Charles, 276
Democratic Society of Pennsylvania, 170
Democratic Societies, 172, 212, 214, 217–18, 223, 224, 255
Dick, Elisha Cullen, 353, 355
Dinwiddie, Robert, 7, 215
Discourses on Davila (Adams), 99
Dismal Swamp, 9, 274, 313
Dispatch #10, 243–49
Dobson's Encyclopedia, 76
Dorchester, Lord, 68, 198
Duane, William, 330, 349
Dueling, GW's contempt for, 9
Duer, William, 125, 130–31
Dunmore, Lord, 11

East Indies trade, 29
Economics: foreign trade, 29, 80; independence sought by GW, 65; Hamilton's program, 75, 76 (*see also* Hamilton, Alexander ECONOMIC PROGRAM OF); indus-

trial revolution and industrial es-
pionage, 76–77; Hamilton's
National Bank plan, 77–78, 81,
82–83, 108–10; GW's optimistic
assessment on (1791), 115–16;
attainments and limitations, 120;
Hamilton's vision of corporate
state (SUM), 120, 121. *See also*
Taxes
Edwards, Jonathan, 306
Eisenhower, Dwight D., and Wash-
ington's cabinet, 83
Elie, Eleonor François, the comte de
Moustier, xiv
Ellicott, Andrew, 127, 128, 155
Ellsworth, Oliver, 201, 260, 345
Embargo on foreign trade, Con-
gress enacts, 200–201
Emerson, Ralph Waldo, on heroes,
358
"Emetic for Aristocrats, An," 227
England. *See* Great Britain
"Entangling alliances," 283n
Everleigh, Nicholas, 98
Eyre, Emmanual, 194

Faction, Washington's opposition
to, xi, 134; in Farewell Address,
266, 280, 281, 282; in 1783 cir-
cular, 279; and GW's role, 279;
and present-day politics, 282
Fagan, John, 88–89
Fairfax, Anne, 5
Fairfax, Lord Bryan, 347
Fairfax, George William, 6, 13, 14,
66
Fairfax, Sally, xviii, 6, 13, 66, 228,
320–21, 358
Fairfax, Lord Thomas, 4, 5, 66
Fairfax Resolves, 12, 66
Fallen Timbers, Battle of, 218–19
Farewell Address of Washington,
278–83; first draft edited by

Hamilton, 266–67, 276–77; and
national university proposal,
277–78; review of, 278; publication of, 278; authorship of, 279;
and love of country, 280; importance of, 283; reactions to, 283–
84
Fauchet, Jean Antoine, 199, 202,
234; and Dispatch #10, 241–42,
243–49
Federal City. *See* Washington, D.C.
Federal Hall, New York, 37, 91
Federalist(s): and response to British seizure of U.S. ships, 200;
GW as, 279; GW counsel for,
348; and GW presidency, 361
Federalist, The: Number 72, 76;
and Madison's doctrines, 118;
Jay as contributor to, 204
Federalist program, 34
Fenner, Arthur, 251
Fenno, John, xx, 84, 99, 106, 117–
18, 129, 141
Findlay, William, 221
First Continental Congress, 12
"First in war, first in peace, and first
in the hearts of countrymen,"
359
Flexner, James Thomas, 119
Foreign relations under Washing-
ton: with Spain, 23, 67–69, 179,
253–54, 258, 261 (*see also*
Spain); and Jefferson as Secretary
of State, 24; and France-Spain-
England contest over Mississippi
Valley, 44–46; and Nootka
Sound affair, 67–69; and naviga-
tion rights, 80–81; with Great
Britain, 80–81, 179–80, 198,
205–6, 229–30, 231–39, 287
(*see also* Great Britain); with
France, 113, 159–68, 170–77,
243–49, 287, 289–90 (*see also*

Foreign relations (*cont.*)
France); and recognition of nations not governments, 161; GW
on presidential preeminence in,
259; and disclosure of confidential records, 261–62; and Farewell Address, 282–83
Fort Necessity, 7
Fox hunting, and GW, 66
France: as Revolutionary War ally,
17, 18; GW's view of, 23, 57,
343; and Jefferson, 24, 36, 50; in
contest for Mississippi, 44; and
Nootka Sound affair, 69; and
navigation rights conflict, 80–81;
help for in Hispaniola, 113;
Hamilton and ambassador of,
118; and Hamilton vs. Jefferson,
118, 173; Morris as representative in, 119, 160, 162, 199; Monroe as representative in, 206–7,
230, 270; and trans-Appalachian
region, 211; rumors of fleet from,
266; U.S. shipping assaulted by,
270, 271; Treaty of 1778 abrogated by, 270; deteriorating relations with, 275–76, 289–90;
policy of toward neutral vessels,
285; GW on relations with, 287;
and U.S. policy toward Britain,
290; Nelly Custis on, 311
REVOLUTION IN, 99, 154–55,
185–86; GW on, 85–86, 111,
112, 163, 176, 308, 322; Jefferson on, 99, 154, 155; John
Adams on, 149; war against royalist neighbors, 159; U.S. neutrality proclaimed, 159–62, 169,
175, 176, 186, 187; and Citizen
Genêt, 160–61, 164–68, 170–
77, 188 (*see also* Genêt, Edmond
Charles); Hamilton sees as dissolving treaty, 161; and émigrés
in U.S., 162–63, 191, 327; Lee's

plan to join, 163; and GW's shel-
tering of Lafayette's son, 254; GW
presented with colors of, 257
AND ADAMS ADMINISTRA
TION: hostilities and provoca-
tions, 306–7, 319–21, 332, 333;
XYZ Affair, 317, 329; Quasi-
War with, 326–27, 340, 343 (*see
also* Quasi-War with France)
Franklin, Benjamin, 24; Jones as
surgeon of, xvii; harmonica of, 3;
and Philadelphia, 33; and Genêt,
164; GW cites as luminary, 306
Franks, David, 193, 213
Fraunces, Samuel, 27
Frederick the Great (king of Prussia), and Lafayette, 267
Freeman, Douglas Southall, 118
Freneau, Philip, 83–84, 117, 118,
141, 144; on site for capital, 42;
and Jefferson-Madison tour, 98;
Fenno attack on, 129; GW attacked by, 132, 133, 152; GW
criticizes, 139; and Hamilton in
Revolution, 142; Federalists attacked by, 157–58; GW's outburst against, 163; on neutrality
policy, 165; Genêt supported by,
170, 181; GW satirized by, 174;
on GW and Genêt, 176; and yellow fever epidemic, 181, 182; re-
signs from State Department,
185; and Whiskey Rebellion,
212; GW attacked by, 252–53;
and attacks on U.S. shipping, 307
Frestal, Felix, 254, 314
Frost, Robert, on GW and power,
359

Gallatin, Albert, 114, 216, 220,
260
Gates, Horatio, 17
Gazette of the United States, xxi,
117, 118; quoted, 130; and

Hamilton, 141; on American vs. French Revolution, 162

Genêt, Edmond Charles ("Citizen"), 155, 160–61, 164–68, 170–77, 180; Freneau's support for, 170, 181; and Jay, 176, 188, 205; Louisiana expedition slowed, 179; controversy over sharing of information about, 186; GW message condemns, 188; and Jacobins on Morris, 194; and Whiskey Rebellion, 212

George II (king of England), on GW's remark about bullets, 7

George III (king of England), in *Annals of Agriculture,* 67; and Freneau, 84

George IV, GW lauds as future king, 306

Georgia, 33; and Creeks, 24, 45, 55, 56, 250 (*see also* Indians CREEKS IN GEORGIA); GW visits, 100

Germain, James, 207

Gerry, Elbridge, 309, 335–36, 340

Gettysburg Address, Farewell Address compared to, 279

Giles, William Branch, 157, 193, 225

Godoy, Manuel de, 258, 261

Grand Columbian Federal City. *See* Washington, D.C.

Grasse, Comte de, 18

Great Britain: peace treaty violations by, 24, 44, 69, 81, 136, 173, 188, 198, 216; in contest for Mississippi Valley, 44; and Northwest Indians, 44, 68, 69, 198, 216, 218–19; and Hamilton, 45, 68, 69, 81, 136, 187, 245; and Creek Indians, 55; GW's view of, 57; as encircling U.S., 67; and Nootka Sound affair, 67–69; in navigation rights

controversy, 80–81; and U.S. response to French revolution, 160, 165, 166, 168; blockade and seizure by, 179–80, 186, 188, 198, 236, 251; embargo on trade with threatened, 202; Jay mission to, 205–6, 207, 216, 229–30; and trans-Appalachian region, 211; Jay's Treaty with, 231–39 (*see also* Jay's Treaty); and Fauchet's Dispatch #10, 242, 248; Northwest forts evacuated by, 287; negotiation with over Canada boundary, 287; GW's view of, 305, 306

Greene, Catherine, 101

Greene, Nathanael, 52, 103, 297

Greenleaf, James, 209, 312

Greenleaf, Thomas, 42

Greenwood, John, 76

Grenville, Lord, 187, 204, 229, 233, 248, 276

Griswold, Roger, 317–18

Gustavus III (king of Sweden), 132

Hall, John, 64

Hallet, Stephen, 156, 168

Hamilton, Alexander, 50–53, 140–41, 206; and Madison, xiii, 33, 40, 142; and assumption of state debt, 22–23, 33, 52, 77 (*see also* Assumption of state debt); anti-Federalists fear, 34; and deal on assumption and location of capital, 40–41, 42; and England-Spain rivalry, 45, 53; and Nootka Sound affair, 68; western expansion opposed by, 68, 69; and Morris as ambassador to Britain, 69; and navigation rights conflict, 80–81; and comptroller position, 98; Fenno's support for, 117, 118; at height of power,

Hamilton, Alexander (*cont.*)
118, 119–20; in affair with
Maria Reynolds, 122–23, 137;
and Duer, 130–31; and monarchy, 135; and Hammond, 136,
173, 187, 245; aliases of, 141; and
resistance to law, 145–46; in Polly
Lear's funeral, 178; as yellow fever
victim, 180, 181; and Pendleton,
183; vs. British seizure of U.S.
ships, 199; as candidate to be
emissary to London, 201–2; and
Whiskey Rebellion, 217, 222–23;
resignation of, 230; as lawyer, 230,
234; and Jay's Treaty, 236, 237,
238, 264; and Wolcott, 242; on
McHenry, 251; and Lafayette's
son, 254; and House request for
confidential papers, 259, 261;
and Madison on GW, 262; for
Pinckney as president, 284
AND WASHINGTON, 206, 217;
accompanying GW, 3, 46; for
GW second term, 140; and Jefferson allegations, 140; GW to
on controversies, 143–44; and
Hamilton resignation, 230; Hamilton bullying overlooked, 241;
GW seen as dependent on, 252;
and GW's Farewell Address,
266–67, 276–77, 277–78, 280;
as natural partners, 280; GW
seeks advice from on Adet, 285;
on GW's debating in press, 286;
and GW on leading against
French, 325; GW on as general,
332; GW disengages from, 343;
Hamilton's debt to GW, 359; historians on, 360
VS. JEFFERSON, 50, 51, 81,
121–22, 144; and Britain vs.
France as ally, 118, 173; and
GW's concerns, 122, 133, 142–
44, 146–47, 157; threats and accusations, 137; and Freneau,
141–42, 144; Jefferson's campaign, 157; Hamilton mocked
during epidemic, 180; Jefferson
bill of impeachment against, 337
ECONOMIC PROGRAM OF, 75,
76; excise taxes, 77, 103, 104,
116, 145–46, 164, 210, 211;
National Bank, 77–78, 81, 82–
83, 107; and Bank speculation,
109–10; corporate state (SUM),
120, 121, 130; and *Report on
Manufactures,* 120, 122, 144;
westerners' detestation of, 210
AND FRENCH REVOLUTION: as
dissolving U.S.-France treaty,
160–61; on Genêt's war-debt deal,
166, 167; and *Petite Democrate*
escape, 171; and neutrality-proclamation enforcement, 175; and
British blockade measures, 186
AND JOHN ADAMS: Adams's
opinion of, 46, 50, 325, 336;
Hamilton on Adams, 284; and
Adams Cabinet, 308; and preparations for war with France, 320,
340; as possible general against
French, 325, 327, 330, 331, 342
Hamilton, Betsey, 53, 180, 181,
195, 230
Hammond, George, 116–17, 118;
and Thornton, 131; and Hamilton, 136, 173, 187, 245; and
Genêt, 165; and northwestern
forts, 186; and Binghams, 192;
bullying tactics of, 199; departure of and Jay's Treaty, 239,
245; and Dispatch #10, 242,
248; and Randolph, 246; removal of, 268
Hancock, John, 150
Hand, Edward, 106, 125
Harmar, Josiah, 69, 71, 74, 77, 85,
123, 145, 219

Harvard College: GW recommends, 231; and GW's grandson, 315

Hayes, Moses, 164

Hemmings, Sally, 284

Henry, Patrick: on GW, 12; GW to on drawbacks of command, 13; as Virginian, 40, 92; vs. Hamilton economic program, 76; as candidate for Spanish ambassadorship, 216; and constitutional ratification, 240; as candidate for secretary of state, 251; and presidential race, 284; vs. nullification doctrine, 338; on peace mission to France, 345

Hercules (family cook), 302

Hiltzheimer, Jacob, 113

Hoban, James, 168, 183

Horse(s): GW's expertise with, 66; Prescott (GW's saddle horse), 89, 93, 209; treatment of on GW's southern journey, 93; GW sells, 292; GW's requirement for, 328

Howard, Carlos, 45, 55

Howard, John Edgar, 251

Howard, Mrs. John Edgar, 89

Howell, Richard, 222

Humphreys, David, xvi, 6; on GW's personality, 20; GW to on life's ambition, 21; on negotiations with Creeks, 55; as envoy to Spain, 68; GW letters to, 84, 106, 128, 156, 159, 269, 361; Lear to on GW's southern trip, 88; on GW's reelection, 152; on mission to Algiers, 180; GW urges to be companion, 311

Hunting (fox), and GW, 66

Hyde, John, 58–59

Indians: and four-power conflict over Mississippi, 44–45; GW's approach to, 73–74, 116, 229, 277; Jefferson on tactics against, 75; GW's assurance to Chickasaws, 79; New York State negotiations with threatened, 91; Catawbas' claims, 102; commercial relations urged, 187–88; Chickasaw delegation met, 210; and trans-Appalachian region, 211; GW seeks protection for, 256; and GW's replacing "God" with "Great Spirit Above," 286; and GW on Sevier, 330; GW criticized for treatment of, 358

CREEKS IN GEORGIA, 24, 45, 55, 56; and GW's alliance with McGillivray, 45, 55–57, 100; GW on Georgians' attitude toward, 104; unrest among, 143, 167; gifts to, 187; and Chickasaw delegation, 210; GW seeks protection for, 255–56; and Georgia's sale of reserved acreage, 259

WAR AGAINST IN NORTHWEST: 57, 68–69, 71–72, 73, 74–75; defeat of Harmar, 74, 85; defeat of St. Clair, 123–25; rightness of questioned by U.S. citizens, 125; Wayne chosen to lead, 125–26; peace attempts, 137, 156, 173, 198; Wayne's expedition, 198; Wayne's victory (Battle of Fallen Timbers), 218–19; GW sees peace, 255

CHEROKEES: Spanish intrigues with, 143; GW's protest over murder of, 156–57; compensation for, 187; GW's recommendation to, 277

Industrial revolution, 76

Influenza, U.S. political leaders attacked by (1790), xiii

Intolerable Acts, 11

Inventions, GW's consideration of, 193

Iredell, James, 293
Issues and controversies during
    Washington presidency: in Con-
    gress, xvii; Bill of Rights, 22; as-
    sumption of state debts, 22–23,
    30, 41–42, 42–43 (*see also* As-
    sumption of state debt); uniform
    currency, 36; Maclay's anti-Fed-
    eralist posture on, 37; location of
    capital, 40, 41, 42–43 (*see also*
    Location of capital); westward
    expansion, 68; excise taxes, 77,
    145–46 (*see also* Taxes); Hamil-
    ton's plan for National Bank, 78,
    81, 82–83; free trade and naviga-
    tion, 80–81; development plan in
    Hamilton's *Report on Manufac-
    tures,* 120–22; neutrality toward
    French revolutionary govern-
    ment, 160–62, 169, 175, 176,
    186, 187; response to British sei-
    zure of U.S. ships, 179–80, 186,
    188, 199, 200, 202; Jay's Treaty,
    231–39 (*see also* Jay's Treaty);
    disclosure of confidential papers
    to Congress, 259, 260–62
Izard, Ralph, 96

Jackson, Andrew, 288
Jackson, James, 56
Jackson, William, xvii, 22, 35, 73,
    89, 93, 110, 334
Jay, John, 24, 204–5; GW in com-
    pany of, 29; as successor to GW,
    134; and strategy toward excise
    tax resistance, 145; Clinton in
    race against, 149; on foreign pol-
    icy and courts, 173; as secretary
    of state candidate, 175; and
    Genêt, 176, 188, 205; and Ham-
    ilton as emissary, 201; as emis-
    sary to Britain, 202, 204, 205–6,
    207, 229–30, 231, 233, 237;
    GW letter to, 223; ridicule of

("An Emetic for Aristocrats"),
    227; as New York governor, 234;
    and controversy over Treaty, 264,
    265
Jay's Treaty, 231–33; French reac-
    tion to, 234, 276, 286; debate
    over, 234–35; passage of, 235;
    public reaction against, 235–37,
    239; GW's position on, 236,
    237–38; proponents of, 238–39;
    and Wolcott, 243; GW's ratifica-
    tion of, 245; and Dispatch #10,
    248; in GW's address to Con-
    gress, 255; House appropriations
    needed for, 257; House debate
    on, 259–62, 264–65; and
    Franco-American alliance, 266;
    and Jefferson on French animos-
    ity, 307
Jefferson, Maria (daughter of
    Thomas Jefferson), 116
Jefferson, Martha (daughter of
    Thomas Jefferson), xxi
Jefferson, Thomas, 47–50; mi-
    graine attacks of, xiii, 172; on
    GW's humor, 20; on American
    prospects, 24; on road system,
    30; and New York City, 36; as
    Virginian, 40; and Hamilton on
    assumption plan, 41; and En-
    gland-Spain rivalry, 45; on politi-
    cal parties, 47; on John Adams,
    47, 99; on rebellion, 48; weights
    and measures system developed
    by, 49, 122; and Angelica
    Church, 53; and Nootka Sound
    affair, 68; and creation of capital
    city, 70; and National Bank pro-
    posal, 78, 81, 82, 83, 108; and
    Algernine pirates, 82; on consti-
    tutional powers, 82; New En-
    gland tour of, 98; on peace in
    Europe, 117; and comptroller
    position, 98; retirement intended

(1792), 121, 136; and development of Washington, D.C., 127, 128; on European monarchies, 132; as successor to GW, 134; personal indebtedness of, 136; vs. GW/Federalist viewpoint, 139; as Republican, 142; and resistance to excise tax, 146; vice presidential votes for, 152; decision to remain in office, 157; on Randolph, 173, 240; and yellow fever epidemic, 178, 180, 185; on fortifying of harbors, 187; and publication of negotiations with Britain, 187; and Anne Bingham, 192; and Trumbull, 193; zoological discussions by, 211; as candidate for Spanish ambassadorship, 216; and leak on Cabinet deliberations, 271; and "entangling alliances," 283n; in 1796 campaign, 284, 288; on presidency, 288; as vice president-elect, 294–95; as American luminary, 306; on Adams's policy toward France, 307; on Adams's reaction to French, 319; and "Adamites" vs. "Washingtonians," 319; and Logan's self-appointed mission to France, 335; and Adams's address to Congress, 336; on Alien and Sedition Acts, 337–38

AS SECRETARY OF STATE, 24, 48–49, 69, 80; Portuguese consul presented by, 73; and Algiers problems, 80, 131; and Freneau, 83–84; and runaway slaves in Florida, 101; and British ambassador, 118–19; and France, 131, 155; resignation, 173; and Genêt, 188; retirement welcomed, 188

VS. HAMILTON, 50, 51, 81, 121–22, 144; and Britain vs.

France as ally, 118, 173; and GW's concerns, 122, 133, 142–44, 146–47, 157; threats and accusations, 137; and Freneau, 141–42, 144; Jefferson's campaign to drive from office, 157; Hamilton mocked during epidemic, 180; Jefferson bill of impeachment, 337

AND WASHINGTON: and GW's illness, xxi; accompanying GW, 3, 46; GW remarks to, 21; on GW's Cabinet system, 53; and GW's view of French, 57; and GW's southern journey, 91; on GW's illness, 108; on GW's running for second term, 135–36; GW to on dissensions, 142–43, 144; and Freneau, 163; Jefferson's view of GW, 163, 271, 272; criticism of GW, 215–16; and GW on Whiskey Rebellion, 225–26; Jefferson's guile overlooked, 241; as GW adversary, 253; on GW vs. Republicanism, 265; GW presidency criticized, 310; historians on, 360; on GW's qualities, 360; friendship lost, 361

AND FRENCH REVOLUTION, 99, 160; quoted, 154; and war debt payments, 155; and Citizen Genêt, 166, 170–72, 175; and neutrality-proclamation enforcement, 175

Jenkins Hill, 105, 182
Johnson, Paul, 330
Johnson, Samuel, and Latrobe, 273
Johnson, Thomas, 194
John Street Theater, 38
Jones, Absolom, 181–82
Jones, John, xvii, xix, xx
Jones, Willie, 93–94
Jordan, Mrs. (hostess to GW on southern trip), 104

Journalists (press): Fenno vs. Freneau, 117–18 (*see also* Fenno, John; Freneau, Philip); GW's feeling toward, 119, 147; and Whiskey Rebellion, 211; GW sees as ignoring Indians' cause, 229; and Jay's Treaty debate, 233; and GW on popular discontent, 266; critique of in Farewell Address draft, 266. *See also* Bache, Benjamin Franklin
Journal of Major George Washington, The, 7

King, Rufus, 41, 109–10, 175, 176; and Genêt, 188; as candidate for secretary of state, 251; Hamilton letter to, 264
Knox, Henry, xi, 54–55; as GW companion, 46; at Creek treaty signing, 56; and Harmar campaign, 57, 71, 74; and help for French in Hispaniola, 113; and St. Clair defeat, 124; and *Petite Democrate* escape, 171; Hamilton on, 173; and Freneau attack, 174; in Polly Lear's funeral, 178; on Philadelphia during epidemic, 181; reports from to GW in Baltimore, 182; resignation of, 194; Maine investments of, 217; GW letters to, 250, 359; GW condolences to, 293; as possible general against France, 327, 329–30, 331
Knox, Lucy, 54, 72, 195

Lafayette, George Washington Motier de (son of Marquis de Lafayette), 254–55, 262, 263, 274, 313–14
Lafayette, Madame de, 156, 162
Lafayette, Marquis de, xv, 20, 99; GW letters to, 57, 85–86, 111,

112; French Revolution imprisonment of, 156, 162, 164–65, 201; GW seeks release of, 267; GW presented sketch by, 303; released from jail, 314; GW dissuades from visiting, 350
Landsdowne, Lord, 192, 263
Langhorne, John, 310
Latrobe, Benjamin, 273–75
Laurens, John, 17
Lavien, Rachel, 50
Law, Thomas, 197, 312, 321, 356, 357
League of neutrals, and Jay negotiations, 205, 233
Lear, Benjamin Lincoln, 168, 178, 183
Lear, Polly, 168, 178
Lear, Tobias, xv–xvi; and departure from New York, 57; and Philadelphia house, 58–60; with GW on walks, 73; letter-writing task for, 79; on GW's southern trip, 88; and GW's adopted grandson, 92; GW letters to, 94, 101; and inquiries over Philadelphia as capital, 114; on GW's swearing, 123, 124; and L'Enfant, 128; business career pursued by, 139, 168; and newspaper war, 142; on GW's slaves, 148–49; as schoolmaster to Martha's grandson, 196; on Nelly's maturity, 197; as information source, 203; and selling of GW's lands, 203; Fanny Washington wife of, 262; Twining letter of introduction from, 267; with GW at Mount Vernon, 274, 351, 352; Farewell Address delivered to printer by, 278; packing done by, 295–96; with GW in retirement, 303; GW loan to, 313; as GW secretary, 328; illness of, 344; in GW's will,

346; and GW's final illness, 352, 353, 354, 355, 356; and GW's funeral, 357

Lee, Charles, 16, 215, 251, 261, 286

Lee, Henry (Light-Horse Harry): GW letters to, 21, 152, 160, 172–73, 203; GW considers for command against Indians, 126; GW portrait for, 135; plans to fight in French Revolution, 163; and Whiskey Rebellion, 214, 222; report from on Jefferson's criticisms, 216; and remark on GW's temper, 263n; GW property sold to, 274; and Nicholas, 311; in land deal, 312–13; election victory of, 344; GW tribute by, 359

Lee, Robert E., house of, 347

Lee, William, 27, 346

Leeds, Duke of, 44

Legion of the United States, 125, 167

L'Enfant, Pierre Charles, 37, 90–91, 105, 115, 120, 126–28, 156, 347

Lenox, David, 211, 212

Lewis, Betty Washington (sister of GW), xvii, 21, 91, 135, 197, 302

Lewis, Frances Parke (son of Nelly Custis), 350

Lewis, George (nephew of GW), 222, 302

Lewis, Howell (nephew of GW), 139, 168

Lewis, Lawrence (son of Betty Lewis and husband of Nelly Custis), 302, 312, 337, 339, 347, 354

Lewis, Robert (nephew of GW), 21, 110, 313, 339

L'Hoste, Julian, 27

Liberty Hall Academy, 346

Lightning rods, GW's use of, 138

Lincoln, Abraham, and GW's reservation scheme, 73

Lincoln, Benjamin, 97, 125, 156

Liquor. *See* Whiskey

Liston, Henrietta, 268; on GW's attributes, 268–69, 272, 275; and 1796 election, 284, 286; on GW's speech to Congress, 287; on GW birthday party, 293; on GW's farewell, 294; on GW after retirement, 315, 334

Liston, Robert, 268, 309, 315, 334

Little Sarah (captured British merchantman), 166, 168, 171, 205

Little Turtle, 74, 218–19

Livingston, Edward, 259, 260

Livingstone, Robert, 98, 206, 231

Location of capital, 40; and Morris, 32; Philadelphia as candidate, 32–33, 40; New York as candidate, 36, 40, 41–43; Hamilton-Morris attempted deal on, 40–41; Hamilton-Jefferson-Madison deal on, 41; Potomac site chosen, 41; GW on question of, 42–43. *See also* Washington, D.C.

Logan, George, 335, 341

Louis XVI (king of France), 23, 49, 154–55

Louis Philippe (duke of Orleans, later king of the French), 163, 177, 303

Love, GW's advice on, 197–98, 227

Lund Washington Letters, 289, 294

Luzerne, Marquis de la, 23, 42

Lyons, Matthew, 317–18

McCarthyism, and Alien and Sedition Acts, 327

McGillivray, Alexander, 45, 50, 55–56, 100, 142–43, 167

McHenry, James, 201, 251; as information source, 303, 308, 317,

McHenry, James (*cont.*)
331; GW letters to, 318, 319, 323, 324, 328, 332, 333, 337, 342, 349; and support for GW as general, 325; and procurement of banners, 328; Hamilton and GW on, 329; and selection of adjutant general, 333; GW offered pay by, 343; in Hamilton's camp, 343
Maclay, William, xx, 25, 28, 33, 35, 37–38, 79–80; on New York, 38, 39; on assumption-capital deal, 42; on Knox, 54; on capital city boundaries, 71; on undertaking war, 74; federal power opposed by, 75; and National Bank, 78, 81; and GW's charming side, 113
Macomb, Alexander, xiv
Macomb House (39 Broadway), xiv; Washington's occupancy of, xiv–xv, 27
MacPherson, William, 226
Madison, Dolley Todd, 206
Madison, James: influenza attack on, xiii; as convention note taker, xvii; on GW's humor, 20; and Bill of Rights, 22; vs. Hamilton, xiii, 33, 40, 142, 202; Maclay on, 37–38; and New York, 40; as Virginian, 40; in deal on capital and debt assumption, 41; and National Bank proposal, 78, 81, 82; and Freneau, 84; and Jefferson, 98, 99, 142; on National Bank, 108–9; and GW's annual message and replies, 117; and Republican opposition, 118; and development of Washington, D.C., 127, 128; and supply request to Hamilton, 130; and GW's second-term decision, 133–34; as Republican, 142; on

neutrality proclamation, 161–62; as secretary of state candidate, 175; reports to on yellow fever toll, 184; and Britain's seizure of U.S. ships, 198, 199; and selection of Jay as emissary, 202; as candidate for Paris ambassadorship, 206; and Monroe, 206; and GW on Whiskey Rebellion, 225; on GW's sixty-fourth birthday, 257; on GW and Hamilton, 262; and Jay's Treaty debate, 264, 265; and GW Farewell Address, 266; and nullification of wartime measures, 338
Mansion House Farm, 64, 66, 110. *See also* Mount Vernon
Marie Antoinette, 186; Jay's wife mistaken for, 204
Marriage, GW's advice on, 197–98, 228
Marshall, John, 205; and Jay's Treaty, 264; in mission to Paris, 309, 317, 330, 335–36; vs. Virginia Resolution, 338; electoral victory of, 344; quoted on GW's death, 356; and Martha Washington's tomb request, 357; on GW's character, 358
Martin, Alexander, 103
Martinez, Carlos (Marquis de Casa Yrujo), 270
Mason, George, 11, 12, 40, 66, 140
Media. *See* Journalists
Mercantilism, 10
Michaud, André, 170
Middle States, 31–32
Mifflin, Thomas, 171, 175, 213, 217, 219, 222
Mississippi River: and Spain, 23, 44, 45, 179, 204, 211, 250, 258; contention for, 44–45
Monarchy as implicit in Washing-

ton presidency: and GW's entertainments, 25; and Abigail Adams on "Royal George," 28; and "silversmith to the President," 79; and form of address, 95; Freneau on, 132, 152; and Hamilton, 135; intent of imputed to GW, 174; Jefferson on proponents of, 175; GW accused of imitating, 252–53; and Bache's attack on GW, 262; GW resists, 358

Monroe, Elizabeth, 206

Monroe, James, 72; Jefferson defended by, 142; on neutrality proclamation, 161; in attempt to open Congress to public, 190–91; and response to British transgressions, 200; and Hamilton, 201; and Jay approval, 205; as ambassador to France, 206–7, 230, 270, 276, 281, 306; and GW, 270–71; vindicating letter by, 310, 317; GW sees as sacrificed, 311

Morgan, Daniel, 125

Morgan, Edmund S., 15

Morris, Gouverneur, 38; GW's furnishings located by, xv; as ambassador to Britain, 44, 45–46, 53; and Hamilton, 69; GW letters to, 75, 107, 112, 147, 256, 259; and navigation rights, 81; as representative to France, 119, 160, 162, 199; Jefferson on, 131; GW message to, 136–37; on Citizen Genêt, 165; on GW's importance, 176–77; Jacobins demand removal of, 194; sent to Britain, 201; on Hamilton as emissary, 201; replacement for, 204, 206, 207; communication to intercepted, 275

Morris, Robert, 16, 32; and siting of capital, 40–41; house of taken over by GW, 58, 59; in land fraud, 209; Federal City lots bought by, 253; financial ruin of, 253, 316; at GW farewell, 294; Law buys lots from, 312; in contract about dying, 316; in debtors' prison, 334

Morris, Mrs. Robert, 191, 195

Moultrie, William, 125

Mount Vernon, 63–67, 188–89; GW's acquiring of, 6; GW's touch in, 64–65; agricultural economy of, 65–66; and boundaries of new capital, 71; crop failures at, 104, 110, 338–39, 349; GW to after southern journey, 104–5; GW's fears for, 134; GW's desire to retire to, 134, 137; and agricultural experimentation, 138, 285; GW visits to, 146, 208–10, 237, 239, 270; management problems at, 167, 168; deer park at, 169; manager found for, 180; GW's rental plan for, 188, 258; and GW's anticipation of embargo, 201; GW with Liston at, 268; library at, 269; GW's retirement at, 273, 278, 293, 296, 301–6, 321–22, 349; Latrobe's view of, 273–74; Mansion House in disrepair, 301–2; and manager (Anderson), 318–19; agronomists' criticism of, 336; in GW's will, 347; instructions for, 351

Mount Vernon (merchant ship), 270

Moustier, comte de (Eleonor François Elie), xiv

Muhlenberg, Frederick, 35, 226, 265

Murray, William Vans, 341, 345, 350

Napoleon Bonaparte, 270, 342; on military victory, 186; Lafayette freed by, 314; on GW and power, 359, 361
National Bank, Hamilton's proposal for, 78, 81, 82–83. *See also* Bank of the United States
National Gazette, 117, 139, 153, 158, 185
National military academy plan, 187, 287, 343
National university, Washington's proposal for, 228–29; and Latrobe's visit, 275; and Farewell Address, 277–78; and Washington, D.C., plans, 285; in final address to Congress, 287
Nelson, Lord Horatio, 340
Nelson, Thomas, 21–22
Neutrality proclamation (1793), 160–61, 169, 175, 186, 187; Jay's draft of, 205
Neville, John, 209, 211–12
Neville, Presley, 209
Newburgh Conspiracy, 18–19, 215
New England, 31; GW on, 305
New York City, 36–37, 38–39; Macomb House in, xiv-xv; as candidate for permanent capital location, 36, 40, 41–43; Maclay on, 38, 39; GW's departure from, 57–58
Nicholas, John, 310–11
Niemcewicz, Julian Ursyn, 321–22
Noailles, viscount de, 162
Nootka Sound, 44; feather dress from, 191
Nootka Sound affair, 44, 67–69, 205
North Carolina, 33
Northwest Territory, 29; British

forts remaining in, 24, 69, 81, 136, 173, 188, 198, 216; Indian Wars in, 68–69, 71–72, 73, 74–75, 85, 123–26; secessionist talk in, 74; attempts to settle with Indians in, 137; GW sees peace in, 255; British forts evacuated in, 287
Nullification doctrine, 337–38

Oconee Strip, 55–56
Oney (Martha Washington's slave), 149
Otto, Louis-Guillaume, 25

Page, John, 36
Paine, Thomas, 98–99, 270, 288; on GW, 359
Palyrat, Ignatius, 73
Parkinson, Richard, 336
Parks, Andrew, 262–63
"Patriarch" of liberty, Lafayette sees GW as, xv
Patriotism, GW sees as insufficient, 16
Payne, Lucy (sister of Dolley Madison), 79
Peale, Charles Willson, 191, 295
Pearce, William, 180, 189, 201, 208, 234, 270, 273
Pendleton, Edmund, 108, 183, 229
Penn, William, 32
Pennsylvania: Henry Adams on, 33; center of Whiskey Rebellion in, 210, 217–18. *See also* Philadelphia
Pennsylvania Democratic Society, 174, 224. *See also* Democratic Societies
Perret, Geoffrey, 54
Peter Porcupine's Gazette, 296
Peters, Richard, 194
Peters, Thomas, 312, 321

Petite Democrate, Le (converted French warship), 168, 171

Philadelphia, 32–33; as candidate for new Federal City location, 32–33, 40; as nation's capital, 41; GW's arrival in, 72; desire to remain nation's capital, 105, 113–14; hostility toward GW in, 131; and Noailles, 162; yellow fever epidemic in, 178–79, 180–82, 184–85, 186, 189–90, 313, 330; entertainment and attractions of, 190–92; GW's return to after retirement, 333–34

Philip, Hypolite, 191

Phyfe, Duncan, 76

Pickering, Edward, 180–81

Pickering, Timothy, 242; as Indian representative, 74; at Sandusky conference, 156; and end of yellow fever, 185; and Jay's Treaty advice, 239; and Randolph affair, 242, 243, 244, 246, 249; and Conway cabal, 249; becomes secretary of state, 251; and disclosure issue, 261; and Monroe, 271, 310, 317; GW discussions with, 275; information from, 308; GW letter to, 324–25; and Logan on French change of heart, 335; and Hamilton, 343; seen as Hamilton agent, 350

Pinckney, Charles, 96, 97

Pinckney, Charles Cotesworth: secretary of state post turned down, 251; as emissary to France, 271, 276, 290, 306–7, 308, 335–36; and sexual innuendo about Adams, 285; GW letter to, 307; GW testimonial to, 309; as possible general against French, 324–25, 327, 330, 331; with Adams at Congress Hall, 336

Pinckney, Thomas: as envoy to Britain, 155, 201; and French ambassadorship, 204; as envoy to Spain (Treaty of San Lorenzo), 216, 223, 253–54, 258, 271, 301; GW letter to, 258; as Hamilton presidential choice, 284; GW to on U.S. independence, 307

Piomingo, 210

Pitt, William, 67

Pitt, William, the Younger, 179, 188

Potomac Navigation Company: GW's connection with, 31, 71; GW examines locks of, 208; GW offers stock in, 228; Lear president of, 328; final meeting of, 349; GW skips meeting of, 351

Potomac River, 40

Powel, Eliza, 113, 132, 150–51, 184–85; birthday verses from, 128–29; and GW's ambition, 151, 230; on GW's reserve, 152; and Nelly Custis's neck brace, 196; Henrietta Liston compared to, 268; GW horses sold to, 292; and GW letters to Martha, 296; help from in finding servant, 302; Martha to on GW, 304, 315–16; GW meets in Philadelphia, 334

Powel, Samuel, 113–14, 184–85

Prescott (GW's saddle horse), 89, 93, 209

Presidential campaign (1796), 284–85, 286

Press. *See* Journalists

Putnam, Rufus, 156

Quasi-War with France, 326–27; selection of generals for, 324–25, 327–30, 331–33; and Alien and Sedition Acts, 326–27, 337–38; organizing army for, 334–35; Hamilton's plan for, 340, 343; peace initiatives, 340–42, 343; peace commission, 349

Quebec Act, 11
Quesnay, Monsieur de, 191

Randolph, Beverly, 76, 156
Randolph, Edmund, 240–42; as attorney general, 49, 240–41; and Bank of the United States, 82; and GW's first veto, 130; and second term for GW, 143; and western dissidents, 145; and neutrality proclamation, 161, 175; and *Petite Democrate* escape, 171; Jefferson on, 173, 240; as secretary of state candidate, 176; GW asks to rent temporary quarters, 184; on convening of Congress, 185; and Hamilton, 202; and Monroe's assignment to Paris, 206–7; and Whiskey Rebellion, 213; Jefferson remark to, 216; Supreme Court seat sought by, 230; and Jay's Treaty, 234, 236, 239; and Fauchet's Dispatch #10, 243–49; and accusation of GW overdrawn salary, 253; and leak on Cabinet deliberations, 271; and British behavior, 290; Monroe's vindication to be fashioned after, 310
Rappahannock River, tale of GW throwing dollar across, 60
Rawlins, George, 352, 354
Raynal, Abbé, 306
Redick, David, 221
Reflections on the Revolution in France (Burke), 67
Report on Manufactures (Hamilton), 120, 122, 144
Report on the Public Credit (Hamilton), 52
Repository for Natural Curiosities, 191
Republican Party (original): beginnings of, 99; and Jefferson letter

to GW, 136; Jefferson as leader of, 142; and response to British seizure of U.S. ships, 200; GW on, 348
Revolutionary War, 13–18; and revolutionary conditions, 10, 11–13; and GW's charisma, 12; GW assumes command, 13; Franco-American alliance, 17; Battle of Yorktown, 18; and postwar government, 19–21; Hamilton's record in, 142; and Cornwallis's mistake, 268
Reynolds, James, 122–23
Reynolds, Maria, 122–23, 137
Rights of Man (Paine), 98–99
Roads, in time of GW, 30
Roberdeau, Isaac, 127
Rochambeau, comte de, 18, 57
Rochefoucauld Liancourt, duc de La, 163, 192, 284
Rodgers, John, 58
Roosevelt, Franklin, GW compared to, 360–61
Roosevelt, Theodore, and Hamilton, 51
Ross, James, 209, 213
"Royal George" (Abigail Adams epithet), 28
Royal Gift (jackass presented by Spanish king), 23, 101, 209, 339
Royalty as Washington's goal or attribute. *See* Monarchy as implicit in Washington presidency
Rush, Benjamin, 109, 179, 180, 185, 306
Rutledge, John, 12, 251–52

St. Clair, Arthur, 29, 71, 74, 75, 79, 116, 123, 145, 219, 259
St. Mercy, Moreau de, 191
Savage, Edward, 342
Savannah, Georgia, GW visits, 100

Scriptomania, 109–10
Seabury, Samuel, 76
Seagrove, James, 101
Searson, John, 345
Second Continental Congress, 13
Sedition Act, 326–27, 337–38, 349
Seneca, 6
Sevier, John, 330
Shay's Rebellion, 48, 214–15
Shenandoah Valley, 33
Shippen, Thomas Lee, 64
Shubrick, Mrs. Richard, 97
Slater, Samuel, 76, 77
Slavery: and GW on abolitionists, 29–30; and Southern life, 33; in New York City, 39; and GW's disposal of lands, 204; GW's view on, 209, 302, 305–6; and Jay's Treaty, 232, 235; and GW's will, 345–46
Slaves: of GW, 27; payment for runaway slaves in peace treaty with British, 81; East Florida as haven for, 101; GW's treatment of, 148–49; GW on overseers' views of, 234; GW to end dependence on, 258
Smith, Claudia, 97
Smith, Jeremiah, 72
Smith, William Loughton, xvii
Society of the Cincinnati, 310
Society for Useful Manufactures (SUM), 120, 130
South Carolina, 33
Spain: and Mississippi, 23, 44, 45, 179, 204, 211, 250, 258; and Nootka Sound affair, 44, 67–69; and Creek Indians, 45, 143, 166–67, 168, 258; GW's view of, 57; and Northwest Indians, 74; and Louisiana threat from Genêt, 179; and trans-Appalachian region, 211; Pinckney mission to, 253–54; Treaty of San Lorenzo with, 258, 261; and plot to seize Southwest Territory, 309–10
Speculation, over Bank of United States, 108–10
Stagg, John, 218
Stamp Act Congress, 10
State debt assumption. *See* Assumption of state debt
Stephens, Edward, 180
Steuben, Baron von, 125
Stuart, David, xxi, 71, 115, 194, 258, 289, 315, 346
Stuart, Gilbert, 192, 263–64, 275, 357
Supreme Court: GW's choices for, 34; and Genêt affair, 172, 173
Symbolism, and GW presidency, 22, 279

Talleyrand-Périgord, Charles Maurice de, 162, 206, 317, 319, 336, 340, 341
Tate, James, 208
Taxes: excise taxes by Hamilton, 77, 103, 104, 116, 145–46, 164, 210, 211; Hamilton vs. Washington on burden of, 140; on transport of public journals, 188
Telfair, Edward, 101
Ternant, Jean Baptiste de, 113, 163
Thacher, George, 199
Theater: GW's first visit to, 6; GW sees satire in, 38–39; politics as, 87; GW attends in Philadelphia, 190, 257, 292; and Bernard's meeting with GW, 304
Thornton, Edward, 131–32, 158, 176
Thornton, William, 156, 168, 340, 344, 350–51, 356
Tiber Creek, 182
Ticonderoga, Fort, 14

Tilghman, Tench, 16
Toasts, at GW Annapolis dinner,
    89–90
Treaty of Greeneville, 219
Treaty of London, 246
Treaty of New York, 56, 57, 100,
    143, 259
Treaty of Paris, 44
Treaty of San Lorenzo, 258, 271,
    284, 309
Trumbull, John, 42, 56, 57, 184,
    192–93, 242, 293, 303
Trumbull, Jonathan, 348
Turkey Foot (Ottawa chief), 218
Twain, Mark, on GW's portrait,
    357
Twining, Thomas, 267–68
Tyron, William, 94

Uniform, GW design for, 335, 337
United States under Washington:
    GW on difficulties of, 24; Jeffer-
    son on prospects of, 24; as sur-
    rounded by foes, 24, 67; GW's
    optimism toward, 29; trade flour-
    ishes, 29; geography of, 30–31;
    geographic divisions of, 31–34;
    population of (1790 census), 76;
    economic attainment and limita-
    tions, 120; GW's optimism over,
    259, 293–94; scientific instead of
    literary bent in, 306
University, national. *See* National
    university, Washington's proposal
    for

Valley Forge, 14, 17, 54, 148
Van Gaasbeck, Peter, 200
Vaughan, Samuel, 65
Virginia, 33; GW on agriculture of,
    137–38
Virginia Plan, 240

Virginia Resolution or Resolves,
    338, 347
Volney, C. F., 30

Wansey, Henry, 193, 194
Washington, Augustine (father of
    GW), 4, 5
Washington, Betty (sister of GW,
    later Betty Lewis), xvii, 21, 91,
    135, 197, 302
Washington, Bushrod (nephew of
    GW), xx, 34, 197, 274, 311,
    347, 344
Washington, Charles (brother of
    GW), 345, 346
Washington, Fanny Bassett (wife of
    George Augustine Washington),
    18, 137, 152, 156, 193, 195,
    208, 262, 347
Washington, George: and Sally
    Fairfax, xviii, 6–7, 320–21;
    childlessness of, xix, 13, 20, 311;
    early life of, 3–4; education of,
    4; travels of, 4; as surveyor, 4–5;
    as country gentleman, 5–7; and
    Mount Vernon, 6, 63–67, 188–
    89 (*see also* Mount Vernon); as
    colonial military leader, 7–8, 9,
    10; electoral efforts of, 8; mar-
    riage of, 9–10, 13 (*see also*
    Washington, Martha); as "Caun-
    otaucarius," 55–56; portraits of,
    56–57, 135, 263–64, 357; six-
    tieth birthday of, 128–29; sixty-
    first birthday of, 158; museum
    contributions by, 191; sixty-sec-
    ond birthday of, 199–200; sixty-
    third birthday of, 231; sixty-
    fourth birthday of, 257; sixty-
    fifth birthday of, 293; sixty-sixth
    birthday of, 319; sixty-seventh
    birthday of, 337, 339; will of,
    345–47, 354; final illness and
    death of, 351–55, 356; funeral

of, 356–57; biographies of, 357–58; reputation of, 358

HEALTH PROBLEMS OF, xiii–xiv; influenza, xiii, xiv, xvii, xix, xx–xxi, 3; teeth, xiii–xiv, xx, 23–24, 231, 334; thigh tumor, xvi; deafness, 73, 75; carbuncles, 108; wrenched back, 208; growth on face, 208; malarial attack, 330; final illness, 351–55

PERSONAL CHARACTERISTICS OF, xx; gravitas, xix; appearance, xix, 131; need for control, 4; reserve, 4, 10, 87–88, 132, 153; Humphreys on, 6; physical strength, 6; from self-help maxims, 6, 7; as speaker, 8; insecurities, 8; dueling contemned, 9; recklessness, 9; humor, 15–16, 20, 275; integrity, 16; sense of deprivation over family, 20; modest ambition, 21; handshake, 55; and tobacco, 56; thrift, 60; dining habits, 66; swearing, 123; religion, 148; and livening effect of wine, 194; and music, 196; in Stuart portraits, 263–64; Twining's impression of, 268; Henrietta Liston on, 268–69, 272; reading, 269; Latrobe on, 275; Bernard on, 305; rigorous use of time, 314

DOMESTIC LIFE AS PRESIDENT: in Macomb House, xiv–xv; entertaining, 21, 28–29; servants, 27, 104–5, 208, 295, 302; Philadelphia household, 58–60; daily routine, 193–94; rules for household management, 207–8

VIEWS AND PERSONAL VALUES OF: Humphrey as reporter of, xvi; desire for glory and love from countrymen, 7, 14; on patriotism, 16; on soldiers' motivation, 16; on French pre-Revolution spirit, 23; on variation in men's opinions, 29; on living conditions in South, 34; on persons deserving to be served Madeira, 193; on love and marriage, 197–98, 227–28; practical idealism, 215; on public opinion, 256, 265–66; on mineral wealth of country, 274; in counsel to grandson, 291; on wedding assemblies, 312; in admonition to grandson, 314–15; on America's rising cities, 336; on regularity and punctuality, 351; on Constitution, 360

POLITICAL BELIEFS OF: in strong central government, 15, 19–20, 83, 226; in civilian-rule supremacy, 15, 222; on assumption of state debts, 30; in interest and honor or duty, 54, 279–80, 282; on westward expansion, 69; in order and personal accountability, 111–12; in Congress-president separation, 131; vs. Jefferson's viewpoint, 139; and presidential endorsement, 146; and veto power, 184; and self-government, 214–15; in constructive isolation, 229

AS LANDOWNER AND SPECULATOR, 5, 9–10, 138, 203–4; sale to Morris and Greenleaf, 209; and Whiskey Rebellion, 210–11; land put up for sale, 258, 312, 313, 339; lots in Federal City purchased, 313; rights enforced on Alexandria plot, 344; and GW's will provisions, 347

IN REVOLUTION: and GW's charisma, 12; assumes command, 13; brashness, 14; GW's de-

IN REVOLUTION (*cont.*)
meanor, 15; veneration toward,
15; reaction to adversity, 16, 17,
18; and free Negroes, 16–17;
number of battles fought/won,
16–17; and Gates, 17; at Yorktown, 18; at Newburgh protest,
18–19; and postwar government,
19–21

AS PRESIDENT, 78–79, 297; inauguration, 21; and site for capital, 22 (*see also* Location of
capital); symbolic function in,
22, 279; GW's misgivings, 24;
popularity, 25; Tuesday afternoon levees, 25; celebrity, 25–
26, 38; and religious pluralism,
31; government appointments,
34; and relations with Congress,
37; and Cabinet, 53; departure
from New York, 57–58; and creation of capital city, 70–71, 90–
91, 105, 126–28, 182–83, 285
(*see also* Washington, D.C.); in
Philadelphia, 72–73; addresses
to Congress, 73, 74, 80, 115–16,
147–48, 187, 255–56, 287–88;
and role of advisers, 83; on journey through South, 85, 88–98,
100–104, 106, 107; theatricality
in, 87–88, 159; Hamilton's economic programs endorsed, 110,
120–21; thoughts of retirement,
121, 129; and Jefferson-Hamil-
ton conflict, 122, 133, 139, 140,
142–44, 146–47, 157; first veto,
130; hostile views of and attacks
on, 131–33, 139, 153, 172–73,
252, 253, 262, 269–70, 271–72,
288–89; and second-term decision, 133–136, 143, 150–52; reelection, 152; thought of
retirement after two years, 152;
second inauguration, 158–59; at

July 4 celebration, 169; Morris
on need for, 176–77; disarming
tactics of, 184; military defense
program, 187, 188; Martha's
feelings toward, 195; and executive powers, 206; and Hamilton,
206, 217, 230, 252, 280 (*see
also* Hamilton, Alexander AND
WASHINGTON); and appreciation
of trans-Appalachian West, 211;
Randolph/Dispatch #10 affair as
low point of, 245; and bipartisanship, 252; overdrawing on
salary, 253; and Jefferson, 253,
310, 360, 361 (*see also* Jefferson,
Thomas AND WASHINGTON);
refusal to surrender confidential
papers, 260–62; intention to retire, 266, 269; as psychologist
over politician, 279; and orderly
transfer of power, 280; final days,
292–96; as precedent-setting,
308; virtues of, 358–59, 360,
361

RETIREMENT YEARS OF: life at
Mount Vernon, 301–6, 321–22,
339, 349, 338–39; and Federal
City, 304, 312, 313, 339, 344;
and U.S.-French conflict, 307–9,
317, 322; information gathering,
308, 317–18; loneliness, 311;
and Martha's granddaughters,
311–12; financial troubles, 313–
14, 339; Henrietta Liston on
change in, 315, 334; thoughts on
death, 316; distracted behavior,
316; and Hamilton scheme for
campaign trip, 320; and letter to
Sally Fairfax, 320; and Hamilton,
343; local activities, 344–45;
and 1800 election, 348–49

RECALL TO COMMAND: con-
templation of, 323–24; named
commander-in-chief, 324, 329;

and selection of generals, 324–25, 327–30, 331–33; organizing and outfitting army, 334–35; and peace initiative, 342–43

QUOTED: denying lust for power, 3; on U.S. government, 44; on agricultural affairs, 63; on Whiskey Rebellion, 203; on maxims followed, 250; on retirement, 301; on return to public life, 326

Washington, George Augustine (nephew of GW), 105, 110, 134, 137, 139, 143, 152; GW's farewell to, 155–56; death of, 156; funeral of, 159; sons of, 347

Washington, George Fayette, 347

Washington, George Steptoe (nephew of GW), 79, 138

Washington, Harriot (niece of GW), 112, 135, 197, 262–63

Washington, John Augustine (brother of GW), 13

Washington, John Augustine (nephew of GW), 347

Washington, Lawrence (half-brother of GW), 5, 6, 66, 222

Washington, Lawrence Augustine (nephew of GW), 79, 138, 312, 347

Washington, Lund (cousin of GW), 17, 110; Lund Washington Letters, 289, 294

Washington, Martha, 194–95; and Tobias Lear, xv–xvi; and GW's illness, xvii–xviii; marriage of to Custis, xviii; marriage of to GW, xviii, 13, 296, 346; and GW's personal characteristics, xx; smallpox inoculation for, 9; religious feelings of, 13; during Revolutionary War, 13–14; and life in New York, 27–28; household administration by, 64, 137; and GW's southern trip, 88, 90; and

Maria Jefferson, 116; and yellow fever epidemic, 182, 185; on lifting of performance ban, 190; and children of family, 195–97; and GW on marriage, 197–98; and GW's wrenched back, 208; and Stuart remark about GW's temper, 263n; during Latrobe's visit, 274; and Adams's election victory, 288; on retirement from presidency, 293, 296; letter written by with GW's view on death, 315–16; letter written by to Sally Fairfax, 321; and GW's will, 347; illness of, 349; and GW's final illness, 352, 355

Washington, Mary Ball (mother of GW), xvii, xx, 4, 5, 14

Washington, Robert, 346

Washington, Samuel (brother of GW), 79, 112

Washington, Samuel (nephew of GW), 313, 339

Washington, William Augustine (nephew of GW), 110, 338–39

Washington, D.C. (Federal City): site selection for, 22, 41, 42–43 (*see also* Location of capital); GW's plans for, 70–71; GW appeals to residents near, 90, 105; naming and development of, 115; and L'Enfant, 90–91, 105, 115, 126–28; and Ellicott, 155; and Thornton vs. Hallett, 156, 168; celebration in, 182–83; financial difficulties of, 253, 286; slow progress on, 267; GW's interests in, 285; GW monitors progress of, 304; GW property in, 313, 339; GW's concern over, 344

Washington and Lee University, 346

Watermelon Army, 221

Wayne, "Mad" Anthony, 125–26, 130, 167, 198, 199, 210, 218–19

Webster, Noah, 238
Weedon, George, 125
Weems, Parson, 357
Welch, James, 313, 339, 345
West Point (national military academy), 187, 287, 343
Whiskey (liquor): Hamilton's excise tax on, 77, 145–46, 210, 211; GW on evils of, 189
Whiskey Rebellion, 211–13; and GW as landowner, 210–11; GW's response to, 213–14, 217–18, 219–20; and GW on self-government, 214–15; and GW's worldview, 215; rebels' stance in, 216; spread of, 217; military expedition against, 218, 220–24; and Battle of Fallen Timbers, 219; collapse of, 220, 221, 223; GW's speech on, 223–26, 255; Thanksgiving service for defeat of, 231; GW second thoughts on, 244; and Randolph, 244, 245, 246, 247; GW pardons participants in, 294
White (Episcopal bishop), 294
White, Alexander, 317
Whiting, Anthony, 105, 110, 137, 148, 167, 168
Wignall, Thomas, 190
Wilkinson, James, 125, 340

Willing, Thomas, 191
Wilson, James, 213
Wine: GW on persons eligible to be served Madeira, 193; effect of on GW, 194
Wolcott, Oliver, 242; on government relocation, 57; and comptroller position, 98; on French Revolution, 155; on Democratic Societies, 170; as secretary of state possibility, 175; on yellow fever epidemic, 181; replaces Hamilton, 230; and Randolph, 243, 244, 246, 248; and House request for documents, 259; and Adams, 308; information from, 308–9; GW letter to, 317; and Hamilton for commander, 332, 333; in Hamilton's camp, 343; seen as Hamilton agent, 350
Wollstonecraft, Mary, 192

XYZ Affair, 317, 329

Yeates, Jasper, 213
Yellow fever epidemic in Philadelphia, 178–79, 180–82, 184–85, 186, 189–90, 313, 330
Young, Arthur, 67, 138, 188
"Young Wash." *See* Custis, George Washington Parke